Government and Politics in Britain

John Kingdom

Government
and
Politics
in
Britain
An Introduction

Third Edition

polity

To the memory of my father, John Henry Kingdom

First edition published 1991
Reprinted 1991, 1992, 1994, 1995, 1996, 1997

Second edition published 1999
Reprinted 2000, 2002

This edition published 2003 by Polity Press in association with Blackwell Publishing Ltd, a Blackwell Publishing Company.

Editorial office:
Polity Press
65 Bridge Street
Cambridge CB2 1UR, UK

Marketing and production:
Blackwell Publishing Ltd
108 Cowley Road
Oxford OX4 1JF, UK

ISBN 0–7456–2593–2
ISBN 0–7456–2594–0 (pbk) ⊢

A catalogue record for this book is available from the British Library.

Typeset in 10 on 12 pt Sabon
by Kolam Information Services Pvt. Ltd, Pondicherry, India
Printed and bound in Great Britain by TJ International, Padstow, Cornwall.

For further information on Polity, visit our website: http://www.polity.co.uk

Contents

Preface

The chapters of this book represent an exceptionally wide-ranging introduction to British politics. The expectation is that it will be studied over some time (one or two years) and the chapters generally reflect a sense of cumulative development so that, for example, chapter 4 is written on the assumption that chapters 1, 2 and 3 have been mastered. However, it is also the case that each has a clearly discernible focus and assumes no detailed prior knowledge of the topic. Hence the chapters can (under the direction of the teacher/tutor) be studied in a different order without major conceptual difficulty. Each chapter concludes with a summary of main points, a list of key terms and concepts, questions for discussion (which may be treated as essay topics to be completed under various conditions chosen by the teacher/tutor, or used for group discussion) and a guide to further reading.

The summaries and key terms and concepts

The summary of main points is intended to highlight the essential thrust of the discussion in the chapter, providing a means of quick recapitulation and revision aid. The lists of key terms and concepts are intended as a form of self-testing upon completion of each chapter. One should feel able to give concise definitions of all these before proceeding. Usually they are explained fully in the chapter.

The Glossary and Chronology

The Glossary can be used variously as an aid to revision, in essay writing and to provide speedy clarification of a meaning during the course of reading. The definitions offered are necessarily brief and greater clarification should be sought in that part of the text where it is dealt with most fully (as indicated in the index). New terms appear in **bold** type when they are first discussed.

The Chronology will enable you to see at a glance the sequence of the major events in British politics and their relationship to world events. It is often surprising to discover what happened when.

Further reading

The study of politics at an introductory level is essentially concerned with reading and thinking. We are not able to study our subject in a laboratory and we cannot manipulate the real world to conduct experiments. There is of course a real world of political activity, and it is profoundly dangerous to forget this fact, but the amount any individual can find out by direct observation is minuscule and, in the early stages of study, we must rely on accounts from various sources, including the mass media, historians, and academics from the range of disciplines discussed in chapter 1.

The further reading suggested at the end of each chapter cannot pretend to be comprehensive and students should feel free to explore the literature of the disciplines according to their particular interests. The recommended sources are chosen for various reasons: sometimes the work is a classic, sometimes it is controversial, and sometimes unusual. Generally the suggestions are made because they are regarded as of an intrinsically high quality as well as being stimulating.

Material for light relief is not included as a joke. Much literature and drama, light and serious, addresses the big questions of life and politics. It is important to remember that politics is not something outside normal social experience, unable to explain everyday problems; on the contrary, it lies at the very root of our social condition.

Journal articles are not included in the reading because there are so many, though of course references can be found throughout the text. However, for students new to the subject two journals will be of special value: *Politics Review* and *Talking Politics*. Other accessible journals are *Parliamentary Affairs* and *Political Quarterly*. There is also some excellent political reporting and analysis in the quality press.

Since the first edition of this book was published, the growth of the internet has given students another source of information. A number of websites are mentioned at the end of most chapters; by using a search engine and following hypertext links you will find countless others. Although government websites provide much useful information, remember that they are also purveying the 'official' line.

Discussion

Mere width of reading and acquisition of information does not constitute good study practice; it must be accompanied by thought and a search for understanding. It is better to study a limited number of sources thoroughly, so that they are understood, than to try to cover a wider range in order to commit things to memory 'parrot fashion'. The subject requires thought as much as factual knowledge, and we develop this through argument and discussion with others. This was the essence of the method employed by Plato in the Grove of Academos (hence 'academic') in Ancient Greece, and in spite of the breathtaking advances in modern information technology, it cannot be bettered. Talking seriously about politics is more than an academic enterprise, it is part of the process of being a citizen; it is itself an element of the good life (the prohibition of such talk is a sign of oppression). It can also lead to self-revelation: we can better understand the way we are by recognizing the forces which govern our environment. For example, many people (often working class, women, or members of ethnic minorities) blame themselves for various forms of 'failure' in their lives rather than entertain the possibility that they have been subject to greater political forces. However, this possibility of gaining understanding of one's life can be dangerous; it is sometimes better for the powerful if those without power *do* blame themselves for their conditions. You will see throughout this book that much in politics is about power, and the tension between the powerful and the powerless.

Assignments and questions for discussion

The assignments and questions included at the end of each chapter are integral to the study. The assignments ask you to use a wider range of skills than are required for essay writing. They are to encourage you to see in the media a further rich source for understanding the contemporary world. The 'essay-type' questions may be discussed in groups, made the subject of an address by one member to the others or used as the basis of an essay. They are posed in order to address your mind to certain issues of fundamental importance in the chapter. Even so, the more you study the more you will realize that they have many variants and teachers and tutors will provide a never-ending supply!

Topics for debate

These are intended to be controversial and should be used to stimulate sustained argument. The process of taking part in academic argument and debate can (under the stimulus of the adrenalin coursing through our veins as a result of anger, indignation or frustration over the impertinence or stupidity of others) stimulate thought in a way that lone contemplation may not. Of course discussion and debate are empty and sterile if one does not read and think by way of preparation. If people attend your debates without having done this you are entitled to shred their egos with your knowledge and wit.

Acknowledgements

This third edition is able to benefit from the helpful comments of those who assisted in previous editions. Professors John Dearlove, John Greenwood, Howard Elcock and Andrew Gamble read drafts of the first or second editions and the depth of their scholarship has materially enhanced the book. The same can be said of Peter Holmes, who looked at the text from the perspective of a school teacher. I must also acknowledge Professor Bob Haigh's seminal influence on the book. Numerous colleagues have read particular chapters and Richard Allan MP made helpful comments on the chapters on Parliament. Rebecca Humphries prepared some of the diagrams. In addition there are the teachers and lecturers who took part in a survey organized by Polity and whose comments were both encouraging and influential. I am also grateful to all those students, teachers and lecturers who have emailed, written and talked to me with kind and helpful observations about the book.

At Polity, Professor David Held's enthusiasm remains unflagging and inspirational. Ali Wyke as production manager suffered the headache of the design and layout of so complex a book and finally came up with a cover that everyone liked. In addition, the usual suspects were rounded up. Sue Leigh has remained at the heart of the operation, delivering unwelcome reminders of impending deadlines with unfailing patience and charm, as well as providing horticultural inspiration. Sue has become an outhouse desk editor, and anyone who has visited her idyllic cottage will understand why. Trish Stableford, the proof-reader's proof-reader, is tough on solecism and the causes of solecism, and can spot one at a hundred yards. Still wearing the hairshirt we gave her for Christmas 1999, she would only take on the job if we promised to credit, in future editions, any reader who spots a solecism to beat the 'business magnets' lurking in the second edition! The one suspect who cannot escape is my wife Ann who, as an experienced copy-editor and indexer, now learning to work without sleep, has again brought consummate knowledge and expertise to all she has done. This includes research assistance, copy-editing, drawing diagrams, seeking permissions, and compiling the excellent index, which so enhances the value of a book of this kind.

However, unlike some of those populating the pages of this book, I alone take responsibility for all inconsistencies, solecisms and errors of judgement.

I am grateful to the following for permission to reproduce material previously published elsewhere. Basil Blackwell and Polity for figure 17.4 from John Scott, 'The British upper class', in D. Coates, G. Johnston and R. Bush (eds), *A Socialist Anatomy of Britain*, 1985, p. 45; Charter88 for the photograph on p. 364; *The Economist* for the extract on p. 525; the European Parliament for the photographs on pp. 126, 129, 130 and 518 and the diagrams on pp. 125 and 141; Noel Ford for the cartoons on pp. 258 and 304; Friends of the Earth, for the photographs on pp. 2 and 585; the *Independent* for the extracts on pp. 84, 383, 456 and 697; the Mary Evans Picture Library for the pictures on pp. 62, 192, 241, 283, 369, 421, 460, 502, 631 and 645; Express Newspapers for the cartoon on p. 316; Paul Fitzgerald for the cartoon on p. 98; Simon Meyrick-Jones for the cartoon on p. 163; The Controller of Her Majesty's Stationery Office for the diagram on p. 614; The *New Statesman* for the extract on p. 560; Peter Oborne for the extract on p. 343; Oxford University Press and the Hansard Society for the extracts on pp. 146 and 171; Terence Parks (Larry) for the cartoons on pp. 238 and 250; the Political Studies Association for the extract on p. 309; the Public Records Office, Kew, for the cabinet minutes on p. 433; Punch Ltd for the cartoons on pages 13, 34, 220, 290, 423, 475, 568, 639 and 689; Random House Group for the extract on p. 114; Albert Rusling for the cartoon on p. 619; Harley Schwadron for the cartoon on p. 473; the Scottish Parliament for the photograph on pp. 152; *The Socialist* for the photographs on pp. 76, 217 and 673; Helen Stone and the End Child Poverty coalition for the photograph on pp. 532; Bill Tidy for the cartoon on p. 667; Time Warner Books Ltd for the extract from *Stark*, by Ben Elton on p. 57; Times Newspapers Ltd for the photographs on pp. 49, 95, 108, 167, 211, 357, 377, 451, 549, 579 and 615 and the extracts on pp. 200, 627 and 660 © Times Newspapers Ltd. I am also grateful for the assistance I received in obtaining illustrations from Ellie James of News International Syndication; Claire Kober of the End Child Poverty coalition; Calliste Lelliott of Friends of the Earth; James Mackenzie at the Scottish Parliament press office; Jane Newton at the Centre for the Study of Cartoons and Caricature; Alexandra Runswick at Charter88; Ken Smith of *The Socialist*, and the staff of the Punch Library and the library of the European Parliament UK Office. Every effort has been made by the publishers to trace the copyright holders. If any have been inadvertently overlooked, appropriate arrangements will be made at the earliest opportunity.

1

Introduction: Studying Politics

No one is unaffected by politics. Speaking very broadly, it is about the way people organize their lives together in a community. The important collective decisions shaping the very quality of life – concerning wealth, health, education, morality – are all essentially political in their nature. Studying and talking about politics are a necessary part of the good life which we seek. To be denied the right to do this is one of the first symptoms of oppression. This chapter aims to ponder the essential nature of the subject and the terms and concepts associated with its study. These include power, authority, legitimacy, the state, and society. Finally we address the actual study of politics.

What is Politics?

Encountering politics

Human social life is not a tranquil experience. People seem able to argue and disagree over most things – education, nuclear weapons, the National Health Service, race, gender, the European Union, genetic engineering, the north–south divide, the future of Northern Ireland, and so on *ad infinitum*. Differences are voiced in arguments in pubs and clubs and MPs are elected to continue the arguments in Parliament. Even religious leaders enter the fray; the Church of England's 1985 report, *Faith in the City*, was a damning indictment of inner-city decay and neglect.

Not only do people argue, they resort to violence. Today we see demonstrations, race riots, attacks on the police, attacks by the police and bitter strikes. We see blood and death as people fight for their rights, the rights of others or even the rights of animals. Some are prepared to die. In 1913 Emily Wilding

Ben Bradshaw MP and Charles Secrett of Friends of the Earth demonstrating in support of the Road Traffic Reduction (National Targets) Bill, January 1998

Photo: Jennifer Bates/Friends of the Earth

Davison fatally flung herself under the hooves of the King's horse in the Derby and other women threatened to starve themselves to death in Britain's prisons because they wanted the right to vote. In February 1995 animal rights campaigner Jill Phipps was martyred beneath the wheels of a lorry carrying veal calves for export. People, and even the government, will also kill for their beliefs, as planted bombs and shoot-to-kill policies testify. Throughout all, the unblinking eye of the mass media watches, reports and incites.

These widely-disparate patterns of behaviour, involving matters great and small, serious and trivial, originating at home or abroad, involving ordinary people and the high and the mighty, which may be enacted within the great state institutions of Westminster, Whitehall and the Inns of Court, or in streets and factories, share little in common except for one thing: along with countless other such examples they would be recognized as *events in politics*. It is clear that if we are to study this subject seriously it is necessary to make some order of a world of bewildering complexity; to try to distil the essence of the activity known as *politics*. This is by no means easy; scholars continue to dispute the definition of politics.

I hope I will not destroy faith in the omniscience of professors entirely if I now confess that I do not really know what my subject is.

F. F. Ridley, 'The importance of constitutions', *Parliamentary Affairs* (1966: 312)

Politics arises from certain basic facts of human existence: that people generally choose (indeed find it necessary for survival) to live together and that they differ in myriad ways in their opinions as to how the community should be organized and the nature of the decisions it makes. The source of conflict may either be the simple fact that individuals are self-interested and greedy, never able to feel content with their lot, or that they hold differing views on big moral questions. Disputes are inevitable because the world's resources are finite (no one can have all he or she wants) and the range of opinion on moral questions is limitless.

However, when we come to address directly the fundamental question 'What is politics?' we find it impossible to give a simple answer. Politics can be seen variously as concerned with the art of *compromise*, the exercise of *authority*, the acquisition of *power* and as a form of devious *deception*. It is not the case that any one of these categories of definition is correct and the others wrong, but rather that politics is a many-sided concept, only to be understood if viewed from various angles.

Politics as compromise: the 'art of the possible'

Politics as 'the art of the possible' is a well-known but enigmatic definition (authorship of which is attributed variously) and retains its relevance because it encapsulates a particular view of politics as a process of participating and finding agreement which has been attractive to western minds since the time of the famous Ancient Greek philosopher Aristotle (384–322 BC). Amongst modern thinkers it is most eloquently expressed by Bernard Crick:

> Politics is not just a necessary evil; it is a realistic good. Political activity is a type of moral activity; it is a free activity, and it is inventive, flexible, enjoyable, and human. (Crick 1964: 141)

However, if such a view were rigidly adhered to, there would be little material for political scientists to study in the real world of violence, murder, duplicity and self-interest. Yet this definition remains important for several reasons.

- ◆ It defines the pure essence of politics.
- ◆ It stands as an ethical ideal.
- ◆ It provides a measure against which real-world systems may be judged.

The view of politics as a compromising and conciliatory activity might suggest that it is opposed to the idea of sovereignty and rule by a central authority. This is wrong because differences cannot be reconciled without some overarching authority, even if this is no more than the idea of *agreement* (or contract) reached between the parties. This leads to a second definition.

Politics as authority

David Easton, an influential American political scientist, argued that politics was concerned with the 'authoritative allocation of values' (1953: 129). Authority is the right of some person or institution (king or government) to make decisions affecting the community. A woman with a gun, or a man with a large wallet, may be able to get their own way but will not have authority if those obeying do so with a sense of grievance. Such rule is unstable; those subjected may be expected to revolt when they glimpse their chance. Authority is derived from legitimacy.

Legitimacy When a government enjoys **legitimacy** people will obey because they believe it right to be ruled in this way. This is a key to the success of any political system, and explains why military dictatorships taking power by force are soon seeking the appearance of democratic civilian rule.

The strongest is never strong enough to be always the master, unless he transforms strength into right, and obedience into duty.

Jean Jacques Rousseau (French philosopher and writer), *The Social Contract* (1762: ch. 3)

Forms of authority The great sociologist Max Weber (1864–1920) distinguished three kinds of authority: *rational legal* (bestowed by normative rules, such as constitutions and election); *traditional* (conferred by history, habit and custom – like a hereditary monarchy); and *charismatic* (where the personal qualities of the leader inspire the confidence, and even adulation, of the masses).

Of course, to say that a government enjoys legitimacy does not necessarily imply that it is a *good* government; legitimacy merely resides in popular consciousness. Hence political regimes will devote considerable time and energy not to making policies for the people's education, welfare, and so on, but to the shaping of attitudes – the process of **legitimation**. We shall see that a great deal of British political life serves this end. For example, when Elizabeth II was crowned by the Archbishop of Canterbury the British people witnessed a tradition whereby the monarchs of old sought to present their earthly power as a manifestation of the will of God.

While it is clear that the exercise of authority is part of politics, this presents a rather legalistic and simplistic picture. Governments cannot always expect to possess legitimacy; in a complex society there will be elements opposed to the government of the day, questioning and challenging it and even seeking to destroy it. Governments can aim to maintain themselves by deception of the masses and by force. This leads to an analysis of one of the most central concepts in politics – power.

Politics as power

American political scientist Harold Lasswell (1936) gave the discipline a memorable catch-phrase in the title of his book *Politics: Who Gets What, When, How?* Here the essence of politics is **power**, and those who get most of what is going are the powerful. Power can be defined as the ability to achieve some desired effect, regardless of the opposition. Authority is one form of power, but a glance at the world today quickly reveals that many regimes are based on cruder forms such as wealth, gender, physical might and violence.

> I put for a general inclination of all mankind,* a perpetual and restless desire for power after power, that ceaseth only in death.
>
> Thomas Hobbes (English philosopher), *Leviathan* (1651: ch. 11)

Concentration on pure power takes us beyond the trappings of government into shadowy corners behind the throne. The authority of the government is often nothing more than an empty legal (*de jure*) title; the real (*de facto*) power to get what is wanted, when it is wanted, lies elsewhere. Although some are content to study only the trappings of the state, it should be a central task of political analysis to track down the real source of power, to find the constitutional Mr Big, though the trail can often resemble the Yellow Brick Road to the elusive end of the rainbow.

We will discover later in this book that the most important approaches to the study of politics centre around hypotheses about where real power lies. Does it lie with the people, *some* of the people, a particular race, the male sex, the armed forces, the talented, the wealthy, the aristocracy, Parliament, the Cabinet, the prime minister, the civil service, the mass media, the professional classes, the managers of industry, the controllers of capital, and so on? Alternatively, does it lie outside the state territory altogether with superpowers like the USA, international groupings like NATO, or mighty transnational corporations with budgets dwarfing those of many nations? We shall find that power – like wealth – is unevenly distributed; some people have much while others have little.

Politics as deception

A popular use of the term 'political' denotes devious, shifty behaviour generally aimed at securing personal advantage – usually position or office. Many of Shakespeare's plays dwell on the intrigue in politics so that Enoch Powell could say in a 1950s BBC series: 'The stage used to be called the Court, now they call it a Cabinet, but all the characters are in Shakespeare...Only the costumes

---

*The terminology in this and other quotations is not intended to exclude women; it is merely an example of sexist language and is itself a manifestation of male power (see chapters 2 and 7).

> Get thee glass eyes;
> And, like a scurvy politician, seem
> To see the things thou dost not.
>
> King Lear in Shakespeare's *King Lear*

date.' Such activity can take place at the micro level (within government organizations), as well as the macro level (between rulers and the ruled).

Deception in micro-politics It was probably in this sense that the word 'politics' first appeared in English, as a term of disapproval applied to the activities of those engaged in faction, intrigue and opposition to established governments. People who are 'politicking' are usually understood to be plotting against rivals. The term is often applied to the behaviour of individuals in large organizations, where those engaged in politics (from planning to oust the chairman to gaining a larger desk) are unlikely to be contributing to the organization's collective goal. Much activity of this kind takes place within the corridors and tearooms of the Palace of Westminster, and in the clubs and bedsits around about. Indeed the British Cabinet itself was originally a secretive group of ministers scheming together as a *cabal*.

> One has to be a bit of a lowbrow, a bit of a murderer, to be a politician, ready and willing to see people sacrificed, slaughtered for the sake of an idea.
>
> Henry Miller (1891–1980; American writer), *Writers at Work*

This view is often linked with the ideas of the Italian Renaissance thinker Niccolò Machiavelli; to be labelled 'Machiavellian' is usually taken as insulting. However, Machiavelli's essential point was that intrigue and plotting were justified by the greater purposes of government (see chapter 2). In other words, he believed the old adage that the ends justify the means: 'when the act accuses, the end excuses'. This leads to deception at the level of macro-politics.

Deception in macro-politics This is by far the more important in the outcomes of politics and was captured by the great nineteenth-century prime minister Benjamin Disraeli in the aphorism that politics was 'the art of governing mankind through deceiving them'. Legitimation itself can be seen as

> I have lots of enemies.... Hurd has always been against me, told the lady [Margaret Thatcher] not to make me Minister for Trade – which she very splendidly repeated to me on the evening of my appointment. Arsehole. He's looking more and more like Aldridge Prior.
>
> Alan Clark on ministerial rivalries, *Diaries* (1 Feb. 1991)

> The erosion of public confidence in the holders of public office is a serious matter. In so far as a culture of moral vagueness, a culture of sleaze has developed, we seek to put an end to it.
>
> The Nolan Committee on Standards in Public Life, quoted in the *Guardian*
> (12 May 1995)

a form of deception. The perceptive English political essayist Walter Bagehot (1826–77) placed particular stress on deception of the masses as a key to successful government (see p. 63). Today, as the term 'spin doctor' enters common parlance, one is presented with a great mist of deceptive activity (including official secrecy) and the attempt to shine a searchlight through it is one of the principal duties of the political scientist.

As we conclude this discussion on the nature of politics, it should be apparent that all our definitions are inextricably interwoven. There is no doubt that society harbours many conflicting interests which must be reconciled, often by the exercise of authority, and the process is clouded by evidence of great inequality of power and much devious behaviour.

> Politics is the art of preventing people from taking part in affairs which properly concern them.
>
> Paul Valéry (1871–1945; French writer), *Tel quel*

What do political scientists study?

Individuals and groups disagree over ends and means in most walks of life. There are countless institutions that can resolve such conflict, including religious groups, trade unions, clubs, schools, universities, business firms, families, and so on. Does this mean that these are political institutions? Some academics do in fact study the politics of small communities, usually taking a psychological perspective, but the particular focus of attention for the political scientist is the state – a very special, unique, and profoundly important social formation.

The state

A state is a community formed for the purpose of government. The Ancient Greeks talked of the **city-state** (sometimes termed the **polity**, from the Greek *polis*) and today we speak of the **nation-state**, a relatively recent formation. Philosophers dispute the nature of the state (see chapter 2), the German Hegel giving it a particularly metaphysical significance as the highest expression of ethics; only through allegiance to, and service in, the state could individuals fully realize themselves. Generally the state is taken to be a community with the following characteristics (Lasswell and Kaplan 1950: 181).

- ◆ A clearly defined territory.
- ◆ A legitimate government.

- Sovereignty within its territory.
- An existence recognized by other states in international law.
- A 'persona', in which name it is able to make treaties and have obligations and rights independent of any actual person. Thus we speak of the state doing this and that: prosecuting people (state prosecution), providing welfare (welfare state), being sinned against (crimes against the state), keeping secrets (state secrets), educating citizens (state education), and so on.
- Perpetual succession – rulers may change but the state continues to exist, with no alteration to its commitments and responsibilities.
- Universality – all those living within the jurisdiction of the state (there are some exceptions for diplomats) are subject to its rules. Unlike other associations (say, sports clubs or a church), members do not have the right to opt out of state jurisdiction (unless they emigrate, though in this case they would soon come under some other state).
- The right to use force and coercion against members. Weber saw this as the most singular characteristic of the state, distinguishing it from all other organizations. If other agencies, say bouncers outside a disco, teachers, or even parents, use force, they may find themselves subject to the law, but the state can legally imprison, harass, and sometimes kill. From this it becomes starkly obvious that operating the state apparatus confers great and threatening power.

Today some argue that a process of globalization (see chapter 4) through economics and technology and the horror of modern weaponry make the concept of the nation-state dangerously outmoded. With the increasing role of international associations and transnational groupings, the borders of modern states are becoming softened (Giddens 1998: 130). Moreover, human rights and security concerns lead states or groups of states to demand rights of inspection over others.

The state and society The notion of the state may be differentiated from that of society; the former is constructed and based upon law, while the latter arises naturally from the free association of people (sometimes termed **civil society**). In the state, individual members stand as **citizens** with legally prescribed rights and obligations, but no such conditions attach to them as members of society, where they are constrained more by economic and ethical norms. The same distinction was made by the German sociologist Ferdinand Tönnies (1855–1936), who spoke of *Gesellschaft* (a community formed by artificial, human contract) and *Gemeinschaft* (a community arising from bonds of affection or kinship). The national community is both state *and* society, a fact that is a source of friction. While all citizens are legally equal, as members of society they can be decidedly unequal. When the legal equality of citizenship is markedly at variance with the real level of societal equality, there will be the potential for political tension.

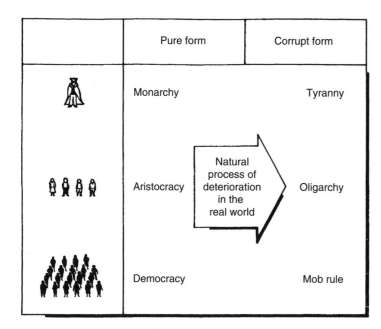

Figure 1.1 Forms of government.

Government

The idea of **government** lies at the heart of political science. Indeed no society has ever been found that did not have some kind of government (Mair 1970). It can take various forms: it may be *constitutional* (limited by laws, see pp. 68–73), *absolutist* (unlimited by laws), *primitive* (a chieftain's rule over a tribe), or *pluralist* (consisting of several institutions sharing the role). Following Aristotle, it is customary to group forms of government in terms of the number of rulers, thus distinguishing **monarchy** (rule by one person), **aristocracy** (rule by an enlightened few) and **democracy** (rule by all the people – the *demos*). However, each of these may be said to tend in practice towards a corrupt variant: **tyranny, oligarchy** and **mob rule** (figure 1.1).

> Politics and the fate of mankind are shaped by men without ideals and without greatness. Men who have greatness within them don't go in for politics.
>
> Albert Camus (1913–60; French philosopher and writer), *Notebooks, 1935–42*

Government and self-interest The fatal deterioration of the forms of government is usually attributed to the corrupting influences of power, which may lead those holding it to act in their own interests rather than that of the community. The historian Lord Acton (1834–1902) observed memorably:

> Power tends to corrupt, and absolute power corrupts absolutely. Great men are almost always bad men.

The selfish tendency of human beings is a hard truth that forms the starting point for much political thought. The key issue is reconciling the common good with the need for government. Scottish philosopher David Hume (1711–76) believed that 'every man ought to be supposed a knave and to have no end other than private interest', arguing that it was crucial for a state to devise a form of government that would inhibit the corrupting tendencies.

> A republican and free government would be an obvious absurdity, if the particular checks and controuls [sic], provided by the constitution, had really no influence, and made it not in the interest, even of bad men, to act for the public good. (Hume 1882 edn: 6–7)

The Philosophical Radicals of the nineteenth century (see chapter 2) took the individual pursuit of self-interest as the key to understanding human behaviour. This idea was very influential in shaping many of our modern institutions.

Government and politics Government will necessarily entail politics, even in primitive societies where institutions have taken only the most rudimentary form. In developed societies, politics is often seen as being about the formal working of the **machinery of government** – taking control of it, influencing its decisions, reforming it, changing those in office, and so on. However, it is important to remember that politics does not belong exclusively to the world of institutions. From the boardrooms of industry to the clubs, pubs and launderettes – politics is found wherever people gather and express their anger, hopes and anxieties, and assess their potential to influence events.

The state and the government

The state and the government are conceptually distinct. In the UK, the position of the Queen, who plays no effective part in government yet is head of state, underlines the distinction. For practical purposes the British government is usually regarded as the collection of around a hundred secretaries of state, ministers, junior ministers and their various assistants drawn from Parliament. In contrast, the state can be seen to comprise a much wider set of institutions (the civil service, the Bank of England, local authorities, health authorities, various quasi-autonomous bodies, nationalized industries, the judiciary, the military and the police). Some would go further and include the mass media, the institutions of the capitalist economy and trade unions (Middlemass 1979).

The political and the non-political

It will be apparent that if politics is about reconciling diverse interests it must have many manifestations; indeed no area of life can be seen as intrinsically non-political. Some people find this thought peculiarly disturbing and it is common to hear calls to 'take education (or health, or the siting of power stations, and so on) out of politics'. If something is to be taken out of politics, where is it to go? We have seen that politics is a process whereby differences and conflicts are resolved through conciliation, the exercise of authority and power. However, politics is by no means the only way of resolving such differences; there are three particularly important alternatives.

- ◆ The *economic market place* allows the forces of supply and demand to set prices and determine who gets what.
- ◆ Through *rational decision-making* experts weigh up the pros and cons of a case to arrive at the 'best' solution.
- ◆ *Violence* enables the unsatisfied, dispossessed or greedy to attempt to take what they want by physical force.

All these are present in Britain today, though each has limitations.

The market The eighteenth- and nineteenth-century classical economists believed the **market** to be a wondrous mechanism for bringing buyers and sellers together at a mutually acceptable price resulting in the optimum allocation of resources within society. However, this raises difficult ethical problems. In the first place it is undemocratic, favouring the economically strong against the weak because it does not *redistribute* resources; it gives only unto him or her that already hath (that is, can afford the price). Thus, rather than taking matters out of politics, it creates a new basis for dissatisfaction and conflict. Secondly, not all allocations can be determined by the laws of supply and demand. Matters such as the level of sex and violence on television, the decision whether to send troops to Iraq, the degree of religious toleration to be allowed within society, or the age of consent for homosexuals lie in a territory of value-judgement and morality where the market is quite silent. When governments try to bring the market into areas such as education and health care many people are deeply disturbed. Indeed, because the human capacity to disagree over value-judgements is potentially limitless, there are infinitely more areas of dispute to be settled by politics than by the market.

> Market sovereignty is not a complement to liberal democracy: it is an alternative to it.
>
> Eric Hobsbawm in the *New Statesman* (5 March 2001)

Rational decision-making The idea of making communal decisions on the basis of rational criteria seems very attractive; it is the argument for the use of experts (town planners, architects and the like). Organizational theorist Herbert Simon (1947) believed that state decision-makers should arm themselves with all the available information, calculate the outcomes of all possible courses of action, and choose the best policy for the community. However, in practice certain intractable problems beset such processes.

◆ The principle is essentially elitist and paternalistic, based on the notion that certain people know what is best for the masses.
◆ It is difficult to decide who the experts should be; obviously election cannot be the answer.
◆ In reality, experts can never be sure that they have all the information necessary to make the 'right' decisions.
◆ Experts may be tempted to place their own personal interests before those of the community.
◆ Experts frequently disagree with each other.

Rational decision-making also carries with it connotations of a threatening 'Big Brother' style of bureaucratic rule as depicted in George Orwell's novel *1984*. Both fascist and totalitarian communist governments can be accused of trying to govern by putting experts in charge, while the call to replace politics with managerialism is ever-present in Britain.

Violence In the real world there can be little doubt that making and enacting collective decisions for communities is often accomplished by various forms of physical force and **state violence**. Two world wars, the Nazi extermination of the Jews, the treatment of blacks in South Africa, the silencing of dissidents in Eastern Europe, the brutality of the Tiananmen Square massacre or the ethnic cleansing in former Yugoslavia can leave no one in any doubt of this harsh reality. Historically Britain has been a very violent nation and the Suez invasion, Northern Ireland and the Falklands war have revealed modern politicians still willing to seek violent solutions to political problems. After the Falklands war, Mrs Thatcher employed the language of force on the home front, speaking of the 'enemy within'. This turned out to be the miners, who were to find themselves embroiled in a physical confrontation with the police and security services.

As an alternative to participating in conventional political processes, guerrilla warfare is increasingly chosen by groups wishing to gain their ends or make their voices heard. Today nobody is immune; several thousand civilians have been killed over Northern Ireland, hijacks and atrocities such as the Lockerbie air disaster can occur anywhere, and in 1989 the Ayatollah Khomeini set a chilling precedent with his *fatwa* on author Salman Rushdie because his book *The Satanic Verses* gave religious offence. Most dramatically of all, the events of 11 September 2001 sent reverberations throughout the political system, challenging norms and testing conventions. It was said that things could never be the same again. However, like the market and the rational decision-making model, violence is not very effective at resolving problems. Violence breeds more violence and, when the fighting has ceased, the parties must sit round the conference table to seek a durable solution. This has been the case in both the Northern Ireland and Arab–Israeli conflicts, despite the high price paid in blood.

War is nothing more than the continuation of politics by other means.

Karl von Clausewitz (1780–1831; German military expert), *Vom Kriege*

"Maurice has always been politically active."

Reproduced by permission of *Punch*

Is there really a world beyond politics?

It will become apparent throughout this book that when reformers believe they are taking an issue out of the sordid world of politics by handing it over to the market or the experts they delude themselves. Similarly, the idea that violence is not part of politics is unrealistic. Hence, in defining what is political we must be guided not by the nature of the issue but by the way people react to it. If we accept that politics is about reconciling diverse interests then it follows that anything can become political. The world that some believe to exist outside politics is a fantasy land, as inaccessible as that discovered by Alice when she went through the looking-glass.

> Man is by nature a political animal.
>
> Aristotle (Ancient Greek philosopher), *Politics*

Political Science

A master science?

Throughout the history of western civilization there runs a great tradition of **political thought** with a pantheon of giant figures who have applied their minds to profound questions relating to politics (chapter 2). The subject is also the stuff of much great drama, literature and art. Aristotle described politics as the 'Master Science' and it is not difficult to see what he meant. All we do in our lives, in society, the sciences and arts, will be influenced by politics; it is through politics that the totality of social existence is orchestrated.

> Every intellectual attitude is latently political.
>
> Thomas Mann (1875–1955; German writer), quoted in the *Observer* (11 Aug. 1974)

Politics is not a science... but an art.

Otto von Bismarck (1815–98; Prusso-German statesman), speech, Reichstag (15 March 1884)

Political scientists do not wear white coats, peer through microscopes or fill up test tubes. Is **political science** really a science? Can it produce the systematic, ordered, predictive propositions associated with a subject such as physics? This is not a new question. The work of Aristotle, which involved him in a famous classification of the constitutions of the many Greek city-states, was just as systematic and 'scientific' as his work in the natural sciences. However, the advent of Galileo and Newton in physics led to developments that seemed to transport the physical sciences into new realms of precision, uniformity and prediction.

Yet some social scientists have tried to build a body of **political theory** – laws of society and politics resembling those of the physical sciences. Karl Marx (1818–83) was one of these (see chapter 2). Under the influence of *logical-positivism* (a school of philosophy holding that only statements capable of being disproved can be meaningful), the post-war era saw renewed efforts by political scientists to steer the discipline towards rigorous theoretical propositions by the use of careful techniques and methods of empirical observation. In this effort to ape the objective observational methods of the 'hard' sciences they sought to ally the discipline more closely with anthropology and psychology. This movement was termed **behaviouralism** and one of its results was a pre-occupation with the observable, or more particularly, the quantifiable. The problem with this was that many of the studies (from attitude surveys to voting statistics) were often tedious and sometimes essentially trite. They did not address the really big questions of politics, such as: What is power? Where does it really lie? Why do states go to war? Why do people die of starvation amidst abundance?

Others, including Max Weber, were sceptical of the idea that people and organizations could be studied in this way. Human beings reason and interpret the world, and the proposition that they are best treated as unthinking molecules in a test tube is dubious, if not ludicrous. He argued that the study of human affairs should take account of reason, motives and emotions in order to afford a deeper level of understanding, which he termed *verstehen*.

Today few would deny Weber's argument. Ironically, as the hard sciences push further into the unknown they encounter less rather than more precision and are obliged to construct 'uncertainty principles', 'fuzzy logic' and 'chaos theories' reflecting the vagaries that have long confronted the social scientist. Yet behaviouralism has left a beneficial legacy in that political scientists can no longer allow their minds to dwell for too long in the stratosphere of abstraction and metaphysics, like medieval scholastics who disputed how many angels could balance on the point of a needle. Hence, the modern discipline of political science combines many approaches and includes a number of interrelated subdisciplines with various focuses and methodologies.

◆ *Political theory* examines theories of political institutions, including the law, the state, systems of representation, forms of government, and so on.

- *Political philosophy* searches for highly generalized answers to major questions such as the meaning of freedom, justice, equality and rights. Ultimately **political philosophy** addresses the biggest questions of all: what is the nature of the 'good life' and what must the state do to promote this?
- *Political ideology* is concerned with ideas about the way the state should be organized (see chapter 2).
- *Political economy* examines the state in the economic system. It leads us to the power of economic forces and the working of the global economy.
- *Political sociology* looks more towards the social world for an understanding of politics. It is concerned with how political attitudes are formed and how they are influenced by those with power. It also studies social stratification, including class formation and elites.
- *Political institutions* lead students to the formal machinery of the state, a key site of much political activity.
- *Policy studies* focus on the policy-making process of government and are centrally concerned with the analysis of power.
- *Comparative government* searches for generalizations about politics derived from widespread examination of groups of countries. Conceptually straightforward, it can be immensely daunting in practical terms.
- *International relations* studies the ways in which states relate to each other in war and in peace.

The interdisciplinary perspective

Not only does political science comprise the subdisciplines outlined above, it is itself multidisciplinary; magpie-like, it draws upon a wide range of other disciplines. The social sciences study one single, complex reality and the different disciplines are artificial territories staked out to facilitate microscopic study of particular aspects. However, this can hinder understanding if we adopt a blinkered view.

Hence, while this book is rooted in the territory of political science, it is open to other perspectives. It is, for example, an inescapable fact that many of the forces acting upon the political system are *economic* in origin, whether originating from the stock exchange or the plight of the homeless. To understand the British constitution we require a *legal* perspective, although this must be seasoned with an understanding of the balance of power, which breathes life into the formal constitution. The discipline of *sociology*, concerned with education, culture, class, racism and gender – all of which fuel much political activity – must also have a central place. Underlying all is the *historical* dimension. It is almost impossible to comprehend the present without understanding patterns of development. We do not take an historical perspective by way of neat chronological introduction; we do so because the politics of today is only an ephemeral bloom on the tree of the past.

There is also an important *geographical* dimension to politics. At home there are issues of territorial management and in the world there is a global economy populated by more and less developed countries as well as giant corporations, many of them richer than states. Beyond the world economy is a political order reflecting the balance of military power, political alliances and a global ecological system innocent of national boundaries, underscoring the interdependence of states in the modern world. Only by rejecting the narrow disciplinary approach can the study of politics aspire to the title the 'master science'.

The governance perspective

The existence of inter-state groupings, particularly the development of the European Union (EU), has led some scholars to focus on the concept of multi-level **governance** (Smith 1997). In the case of the UK, bodies such as NATO, the World Bank and the EU imply a level of governance above the state. In addition there are transnational corporations, which are themselves virtual institutions of governance, and international non-government organizations (NGOs) pursuing social goals such as the relief of child poverty, peace or environmental protection.

Below the Westminster government there are new provincial assemblies, regional institutions (and pressure for elected regional assemblies) in England, a complex structure of elected and non-elected local authorities, composed of yet more tiers, public–private partnerships and a network of private organizations and groups with varying degrees of power over the lives of citizens. Hence, it no longer makes sense (if it ever did) to study state governments in isolation as if they are in complete command of their destinies.

Chapter 4 introduces the complex nature of the globalized world of governance and further chapters variously anatomize the EU itself, the new territorial politics resulting from devolution and regionalism, the world of quangos and private–public partnerships, pressure group politics and the multi-tiered system of local government. All these are linked in the complex network of governance.

In this world, state boundaries become blurred and hierarchical relationships slacken or disappear entirely, to be replaced by more subtle processes of negotiation, bargaining, exchange and compromise. Thus the EU does not necessarily command state governments and state governments do not necessarily command local governments. Regional and local authorities, or even private companies, can bypass nation-states to treat directly with international bodies.

Governance, as used in this context, becomes more than a synonym for the act of governing (Pierre and Stoker 2000). It aims to characterize the processes of contemporary politics in a more realistic way. Approaches taking the formal institutions of government as the fount of all power (examining what is sometimes termed the 'Westminster model') appear outmoded and misleading.

Peering behind the facade

The political scientist must be attentive to the real world before all else and, like Machiavelli, seek to peel away the facade in search of a deeper reality for, as observed above, much in politics is about deception. Writers in the orthodox liberal-democratic tradition betray a tendency to describe what they see as a beautiful stately home. Like overawed paying visitors, they are content to admire the ornate outer facade and the fine draperies and furniture inside but remain too timid to push beyond the red ropes into the living quarters. A central concern of this book is to encourage the habit of enquiry, of looking beneath the surface or, where we are not permitted (and we are talking about one of the most secretive systems in the world), to remain conscious of the limitations of conventional pictures and to be open to those theories about what *might* be there.

Orthodox writing on British politics purports to take an objective position, without a commitment to any political ideology. The cogs and cams of the system are detailed in much the same way as the internal combustion engine might be. The implication of this approach is that the state itself is an apolitical machine, not favouring any particular interest within society, which a government takes over like the driver of a car. This belief is a central plank in the theory of British liberal democracy. However, the idea of the neutral state, easily controlled by anyone in the driving seat, may be contested. To Marxists and others it serves the interests of capital and wealth. Hence, writers implying it to be impartial are actually making a political (anti-left) statement. Rather than peeling away the facade they are contributing to the process of concealment.

Key points

- A common definition of politics is the resolution by compromise and conciliation of the inevitable conflicts in any community.
- Politics necessarily entails the concept of authority, an accepted or legitimate form of power.
- It is possible to speak of politics in the context of any organization but political scientists mainly study the state.
- The state is a community with a territory within which it enjoys legal sovereignty.
- The government of the day may be in control of the state, but is conceptually distinct from it.
- The decisions made through politics can be made by other means but the idea that politics can be removed from life is an illusion.
- The study of politics should be concerned with looking behind the formal facade of government to understand where power lies; to understand who gets what, when and how.

Review your understanding of the following terms and concepts

aristocracy	*Gemeinschaft*	oligarchy
art of the possible	*Gesellschaft*	*polis*
authoritative allocation of	governance	political philosophy
values	government	political science
authority	legitimacy	polity
behaviouralism	legitimation	power
citizen	machinery of government	rational decision-making
city-state	market	society
civil society	mob rule	state
democracy	monarchy	state violence
demos	nation-state	tyranny

Questions for discussion

1   What is politics?
2   'Politics is the art of the possible.' Discuss.
3   Distinguish between power and authority.
4   Distinguish between the concepts of 'state' and 'society'.
5   'Violence is the abrogation of politics.' Discuss.
6   'Power tends to corrupt, great men are almost always bad men.' Discuss.
7   'Education should be taken out of politics.' Why do people say this? How realistic is their suggestion?
8   'Politics is the means whereby the powerful get what they want.' Discuss.
9   To what extent can the study of politics be described as a science?
10 Can the study of politics validly claim to be the 'master science'?

Topic for debate

This house believes with Camus that 'men who have greatness within them don't go in for politics'.

Further reading

Cornford, F. M. (ed. and translator) (1941) *The Republic of Plato*.
Accessible edition of the great masterwork, raising many of the questions and conundrums of the study of politics today.

Crick, B. (2000) *In Defence of Politics*, (5th edn).
Classic essay on the idea of politics as a peaceful and highly desirable process of conciliation.

Duverger, M. (1966) *The Idea of Politics.*
Classic text by French scholar. Analyses political conflict from its roots in primitive societies to modern times.

Heywood, A. (1994) *Political Ideas and Concepts.*
Perceptive and thought-provoking.

Lasswell, H. (1936) *Politics: Who Gets What, When, How?*
Seminal statement of the power view of politics.

Leftwich, A. (1984) *What is Politics? The Activity and its Study.*
Accessible introduction.

Mackenzie, W. J. M. (1969) *Politics and Social Science.*
Breathtaking 'Cook's Tour' of a wide range of approaches to the study of politics.

Miller, J. B. D. (1962) *The Nature of Politics.*
Stresses the ubiquity of politics; it will always be found in some form or other.

Wallas, G. (1948) *Human Nature in Politics.*
Criticizes the idea that people act rationally in politics.

For light relief

Jean Anouilh, *Antigone.*
Highlights conflicts between personal morality and the hypocrisy of a corrupt society, the main character preferring death to compromise.

Anthony Arblaster, *Viva la Libertà! Politics in Opera.*
Uncovers the political dimension and the ideals of freedom in a vast range of operas, from 'The Marriage of Figaro' to 'Nixon in China'.

Bertolt Brecht, *The Caucasian Chalk Circle.*
Who owns what? What is the moral authority for ownership? Brecht's play makes brilliant use of analogy to explore these questions.

Jermy Paxman, *A Political Animal.*
Does power corrupt? A forensic examination of people in power in Britain by one of their scourges.

William Shakespeare, *Macbeth.*
Intrigue of politics and the corrupting effects of high-vaulting ambition.

L. Niel Smith, *The Venus Belt.*
A sci-fi story about two parallel universes, one with and one without a government.

Anthony Trollope, *The Pallisers.*
The world of the nineteenth-century political establishment, with its intrigue, romance and arrogant power.

Part I

Politics in Context

A central tenet of this book is that politics does not take place in a vacuum; it is enacted against a larger world canvas as well as being inextricably interwoven into the domestic social and economic fabric. Hence Part I of the book aims to set the scene by establishing the context of British politics. Much political debate and action is derived from beliefs about how we should live, what is fair and what is unfair, and chapter 2 explores the world of ideas and ideology. Chapter 3 considers the legal environment in which politics takes place; the constitution laying down the rules of political engagement and giving people the political rights they need to participate. Increasingly our lives are touched by events taking place thousands of miles away in a compelling contemporary development termed globalization. This is examined in chapter 4 on the world economy and world political order. Chapter 5 centres on that sector of the world into which Britain is becoming ever more closely integrated – the European Union. The final two chapters in Part I return to the domestic stage, examining the increasingly important problems of territorial management and the complex of social organizations and attitudes that form the political culture. The substance of all these chapters remains a backcloth to the rest of the book.

2

The World of Ideas: Political Ideology

Ideologies are theories about how people should live together in society. As such they provide a central motive force in politics, associated not only with party politics but also with great revolutions and wars. At the heart of such thinking lie fundamental concepts such as justice, freedom, equality, community, rationality, sovereignty, the character of human nature, human happiness and fulfilment: the good life as sought from the time of the Ancient Greeks. People do not easily agree on such big questions, and centuries of debate have generated a body of profound thought, perhaps more important to human survival than any other. Ideas cannot be studied *in vacuo* like butterflies under glass: they are the products of particular times and bound in political struggle and conflict. Hence this chapter aims to introduce not only the ideologies but also the great thinkers and events with which they are associated.

Does ideology matter?

The extent to which ideas influence events can be disputed; sometimes events influence the ideas. Only rarely do thinkers have the joy of seeing their words directly translated into action. Yet ideas permeate the cultural air shaping our attitudes on what is right and what is wrong. When 'men of action' renounce the abstract world of thinkers they delude themselves. When despots hear voices they are often receiving echoes of some cloistered academic ringing down through the ages.

Although **ideologies** are often associated with political parties, even to the extent of bestowing names on them, there is no consistent one-to-one identification. Members of communist parties can espouse conservative values, conservative parties can support liberalism, and so on in a complex square dance of changing partners. Indeed, ideologies are not the exclusive property of parties; they inspire political movements and pressure groups fired with ambitions to change the way we live.

A common basis for distinguishing ideologies is in terms of a left–right dichotomy. The distinction originated in the seating arrangements of the French Estates General in 1789, when the nobility (opposing change) sat on the king's right and those favouring change on his left. Never used with academic precision, modern usage tends to parallel the distinction between **collectivism** (members of society work together) and **individualism** (people live competitively, each acting self-interestedly). A more realistic conceptualization is in terms of a continuum, with an infinite range of intermediate positions, although it is generally believed that most members of the British public are nearer the centre than either extreme. Even this model is simplistic; in addition to substantive policy outcomes there are ideological questions related to means. It is possible to take a tough (*authoritarian, secretive, centralist*) or tender (*libertarian, open, decentralized*) attitude towards government, and these preferences may not coincide with the left–right divide (Eysenck 1951). Fascists, with extreme right-wing views, have taken tough attitudes, but so have communists. This addition creates a two-dimensional matrix (figure 2.1).

Moreover, in the real world ideology cannot be divorced from sectional self-interest. Indeed, Karl Marx saw ideology as a prevalent body of ideas

> [Those] who believe themselves to be quite exempt from any intellectual influences are usually the slaves of some defunct economist.
>
> John Maynard Keynes. *The General Theory of Employment, Interest, and Money* (1936)

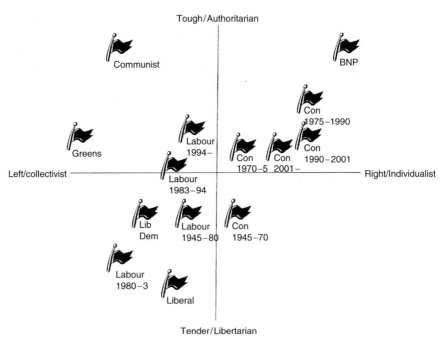

Figure 2.1 A notional two-dimensional distribution of British political parties in the post-war era.

Note: BNP = British National Party.

shaping mass political consciousness and largely controlled by the dominant class to consolidate its power and privileges. Accordingly, in considering ideologies we shall pay some attention to the way they serve particular interests.

Ideas, like commodities, can travel. Hence political ideas in Britain have evolved from two sources: the response to domestic society and the response to wider developments within the western world.

Ideology and the Western Tradition

The modern western ideological tradition emerged through a dramatic break with the intellectual habits of past ages. Some momentous events stand as milestones along the evolutionary road, influencing and influenced by the new ways of thinking.

The Renaissance This intellectual rebirth in the arts and literature of the fifteenth and sixteenth centuries was associated with such great figures as Leonardo da Vinci, Michelangelo and Erasmus. Centring on Italy, it entailed a rediscovery of classical learning (buried away in the monasteries during the Dark Ages when free thought was stifled by religious dogma) and a challenge to medieval doctrine and authority. A key political thinker of the period was Niccolò Machiavelli (1469–1527), perhaps the first theorist of the modern nation-state, which rejected religion and superstition as a basis for government.

The Reformation The stranglehold of the medieval church under the Pope was further challenged by Martin Luther. In a reform movement sweeping Europe in the sixteenth century he asserted the right of individuals to defy authority and worship in their own way. The ground was being prepared for the idea of individual political rights.

The Enlightenment The seismic intellectual shift that raised the curtain on the modern era was the **Enlightenment**. Seventeenth-century Europe saw spectacular advances in scientific thinking which spread to other areas, including politics and religion. The consequences were to be revolutionary. Although the French Enlightenment (which between 1751 and 1772 saw publication of the famous *Encyclopédie*) is the most feted, the movement enveloped Europe as an intellectual forest fire. At its heart was **rationalism** – a new confidence in human reason – and a conviction that people had both a right and the ability to improve the way they lived. Metaphysical thinking and superstition were challenged, as were traditional forms of authority, including the church, aristocracy and monarchy. The very term 'ideology' was coined by French philosopher Destutt de Tracy as the science of human ideas.

> The liberation of man from his self-caused state of minority.
>
> Immanuel Kant, German philosopher, in *What is Enlightenment?* (1784)

The western tradition These great events, altering the fundamental nature of western civilization, were inextricably bound with a ripening of ideas that together constituted the 'western tradition'. Two ideologies of change were to achieve supremacy in the west – liberalism and socialism – which in turn promoted a powerful reaction under the name of conservatism. Even later came further challenges in the form of feminism and environmentalism.

Liberalism

Liberalism, as the word implies, cherishes freedom. However, this is not as simple as might at first appear. We must ask what we mean by freedom, and from whom or what we are to be free. Contrasting answers to these questions result in various strands within a broad liberal tradition. It is hardly possible to overestimate the significance of liberalism in modern western history. Early thinking opposed autocratic regimes based on royal power, aristocratic privilege, religion and the divine right of kings. It spawned the major revolutions that transformed the world from the ancient to the modern.

Human nature Early liberal thinkers stressed the essential individuality in human nature. People are seen as separate entities, driven by egotistical desires. However, later liberals modified this view.

The form of government For classical liberals, the state is not virtuous in itself, as it was for the Ancient Greeks. It is a necessary evil, enabling individuals to pursue their private ends. Good government is minimal government. Hence, in a **liberal democracy** government is limited in scope and power.

The pattern of development: *liberté, egalité, fraternité*

Two key figures in the emergence of this tradition were Thomas Hobbes and John Locke, who wrote against the background of the English civil war. Their method of reasoning was to imagine life in a **state of nature** (without society or government) and logically deduce what the role of the good state should be.

Thomas Hobbes Hobbes (1588–1679) is probably England's greatest political thinker. Writing in the spirit of the Enlightenment, he sought to harness the methods of science to the study of politics. In analysing society he saw the individual as the basic atom, driven by a fundamental instinct of self-preservation. In a state of nature this egoism would prove fatal; it would lead to an unrelenting war of all against all. Therefore they must place themselves under an all-powerful hereditary sovereign (hereditary to prevent fighting over the succession) – a *Leviathan* (the title of his greatest work, published in 1651). This is hardly a liberal conclusion; indeed, it can be seen as a defence of monarchy in the civil war. However, although government is absolute it is not arbitrary; the people enter into a compact with each other to create a sovereign for their common good.

Solitary, poore, nasty, brutish and short.

Hobbes's description of life in a state of nature, Leviathan (1651)

John Locke Another English philosopher has a clearer claim as the founder of modern liberalism. In the second of his *Two Treatises of Government* (1690), John Locke (1632–1704) took a less bleak view of human nature. In a state of nature people would cooperate rather than fight; government should be minimal in order to maximize the freedom and rights to life that nature bestows, allowing people to live in civil society. The state cannot *create* rights; it merely protects those present in nature. Once government exists there is an ever-present threat that it will break its part of the contract and operate in its own interests. Constitutional provisions are needed to prevent this. Hence, Locke approved of the 1689 settlement limiting royal authority (see pp. 71–2) and advocated key principles that lie at the heart of the liberal constitution including:

◆ a minimal state;
◆ representative government;
◆ majority rule;
◆ separation of powers;
◆ constitutional monarchy.

> Necessity is the plea for every infringement of human freedom. It is the argument of tyrants; it is the creed of slaves.
>
> William Pitt (1759–1806; prime minister), House of Commons speech (18 Nov. 1783)

Montesquieu Abhorring the absolutist reign of Louis XVI, French scholar Baron de Montesquieu (1689–1755) became an admirer of what he saw as freedom and toleration following the 1689 settlement. In his *L'Esprit des Lois* (1748) he developed Locke's ideas, stressing the separation of powers and distinguishing more clearly between the executive, legislative and judicial organs of government. Liberty is best protected when the constitution renders tyranny impossible.

Jean Jacques Rousseau More than any other thinker Rousseau (1712–78) is identified with the French Revolution. He was concerned with individual freedom, the role of the state, the basis for political obedience, the nature of sovereignty and the idea of contract. Like Hobbes and Locke, he imagined a state of nature but placed a quite different construction on liberty. Submission to a Leviathan 'is to suppose a people of madmen' (1913: 7), while a 'natural' freedom to pursue selfish ends was bondage to the appetites. For Rousseau, people in nature are not selfish egoists but 'noble savages' with compassion for one another. Civilization corrupts this with private property generating greed, vanity, inequality, privilege and envy. The liberal contract is really a trick; the poor are offered protection but what is protected is the wealth of the rich. True freedom in society can only be realized through a communal life where all are equal.

Man was born free, yet everywhere is in chains.

Jean Jacques Rousseau, *The Social Contract* (1762: ch. 1)

Rousseau pioneered a new conception of popular sovereignty – a social contract whereby people do not forfeit freedom in return for state protection; rather they forfeit rights unconditionally to the community. Because all do so equally, each recovers all they lose. Natural freedom is exchanged for social freedom. Individual wills are unified into a *volonté generale* (**General Will**), something greater than a sum of 'petty self-interest' and the only legitimate sovereign force. It is difficult to underestimate Rousseau's influence, which spread to the arts, literature and education. In replacing the atomized theories with an organic view of the state, he inspired much moral philosophy, his ideas leading to the New Liberalism (see p. 32) that was to lay the foundations of the modern social democratic state.

Tom Paine An Englishman who emigrated to America, Paine (1737–1809) has a legendary fame as a champion of the oppressed. A passionate exponent of Enlightenment thinking, he held much in common with Locke, arguing in his pamphlet *Common Sense* (published in 1776 on the eve of the American War of Independence) that government was a necessary evil. The only grounds for obedience were that it was fulfilling its obligations. However, unlike Locke he was a radical. His *Rights of Man* (1791) used **natural rights** reasoning to defend the French Revolution.

> A share in two revolutions is living to some purpose.
>
> Epitaph of Tom Paine

James Madison The American constitution, drafted after independence, re-flected much of Paine's sentiment. One of the founding fathers, James Madison (1751–1836), developed liberal thinking into a more coherent theory and political strategy. Like many liberals he feared advancing democracy as a 'tyranny of the majority'. In *The Federalist* (1788) he argued for strong repub-lican government of enlightened rulers regularly called to account through elections. He saw virtue in the large state which increased the possibility of finding good rulers and produced pluralism (see chapter 17), which would prevent domination by any single interest.

That this nation, under God, shall have a new birth of freedom, and that the government of the people, by the people, for the people, shall not perish from the earth.

Abraham Lincoln (US president), Gettysburgh Address (19 Nov. 1863)

The liberal revolutions

Post-Enlightenment thinking gave new meaning to the idea of revolution (Gamble 1981: 22). For the Ancient Greeks (particularly the Stoics) it had meant a cyclical process of decay and renewal beyond human control: mon-archy, tyranny, aristocracy, oligarchy, democracy and 'mobocracy'. Christian-ity had strengthened the attitude; life was to be endured, a better existence would come beyond the grave. However, the new thinking asserted that the wheel could be turned and made to stop in a new position. Major revolutions, in the new meaning of the term, were to usher in the modern age of politics.

The English civil wars and the Glorious Revolution In the 1640s a conflict began in England within the landowning classes, one section (the Whigs) rebelling against royal authority and the other supporting it. The Royalists were initially defeated, Charles I beheaded and a republic proclaimed. Although within little over a decade the monarchy was restored, things were fundamentally different; there had indeed been a 'Glorious Revolution'. In the 1689 constitutional settlement the traditional belief that kings enjoyed absolute power by divine right was destroyed.

The American revolution Using the Whigs' language of rights and freedom, the American colonists cast off the British imperialist yoke in the American Declaration of Independence of 1776.

> Men are endowed by their creator with certain inalienable rights; that among them are life, liberty and the pursuit of happiness...whenever any form of government becomes destructive of these ends, it is the right of the people to alter or abolish it. (Part of the American Declaration of Independence)

The French Revolution In the history of modern politics the great revolution in France, beginning in 1789, stands as an indelible landmark. The supreme manifestation of Enlightenment ideals, it influenced all modern ideologies.

It was the best of times, it was the worst of times, it was the age of wisdom, it was the age of foolishness, it was the epoch of belief, it was the epoch of incredulity, it was the season of light, it was the season of darkness.

Opening lines of Charles Dickens's novel on the French Revolution, *A Tale of Two Cities*

Initially the revolutionaries held the sentiments of the English and American revolutionaries: opposing royal absolutism and ancient privilege. The 1789 *Declaration of Rights* established people as citizens rather than subjects. In 1791 a new Constitution enfranchised a large section of the male population and a democratic spirit began to permeate the cultural air. Political clubs blossomed (the largest being the Jacobins) and popular debate was extended through newspapers and pamphleteering. The momentum was to carry things beyond the middle classes. Government fell under the radical wing of the Jacobins, the Republic replaced the monarchy and the country became more democratic than any previous state. Laws provided for the radical redistribution of property and a bloody Reign of Terror saw thousands of high-born heads roll from the guillotine.

> O liberté! Que de crimes on commet en ton nom. (Oh liberty! What crimes are committed in thy name!)
>
> Madame Marie Jeanne Philipon Roland de la Platière (French revolutionary) at her execution in view of the Statue of Liberty (8 Nov. 1793)

However, opposition forces began to regain the initiative. The Jacobins and revolutionary statesman Robespierre were overthrown in 1794 and the nation subjected to a military dictatorship under Napoleon. Yet the old order could never return. The new *Code Napoléon* accepted that sovereignty rested with the people. In Europe it was recognized that a road had been opened that others could follow.

Economic liberalism

A different strand in the liberal tradition came from the new discipline of political economy. Here the justification for limited government lay not in natural rights but in the quest for economic prosperity.

Adam Smith and laissez-faire A leading figure in the Scottish Enlightenment, Adam Smith (1723–90) argued in *An Inquiry into the Nature and Causes of the Wealth of Nations* (1776) that in a free market, where individuals pursued self-interest, every transaction made both parties better off; otherwise it would not take place. A 'hidden hand' would guide the economy towards the best possible result. This *laissez-faire* principle extended to international dealings, where free trade became a liberal rallying cry. Though it might appear cruel it was still right. Other classical economists, David Ricardo (1772–1823) and Thomas Malthus (1776–1834), saw poverty, famine and death as automatically preventing overpopulation. This approach was supported by Social Darwinists, such as Herbert Spencer (1820–1903). Reasoning from the principle of the survival of the fittest, they saw the competitive economy as a way of improving the species, while government intervention would weaken it. This idea appealed to the rising bourgeoisie, who could add to growing wealth a conviction of their own superiority.

> Respectable professors of the dismal science.
>
> Thomas Carlyle (Scottish essayist and historian) on the classical economists in 1850

> It is not from the benevolence of the butcher, the brewer or the baker that we expect our dinner, but from their regard to their own interest.
>
> Adam Smith, *An Inquiry into the Nature and Causes of the Wealth of Nations* (1776)

Jeremy Bentham and the Utilitarians A further strand of liberalism, with much in common with free-market reasoning, was led by Jeremy Bentham (1748–1832). The moral guide for life, law and government was to be not natural rights but **utilitarianism**: promoting 'the greatest happiness for the greatest number'. Although individuals can generally best judge their own happiness and should be free to do so, the legal and political systems should set patterns of reward and punishment so that the self-interested behaviour of individuals and governments produces the maximum public benefit or *utility*. Together with the philosopher James Mill (1773–1836), Bentham founded the Philosophical Radical movement, which advocated a wide range of constitutional reforms, including frequent elections, a wide franchise, secret ballots, competition between candidates, a free press, freedom of speech, freedom of association and a separation of powers.

Nonsense on stilts.

Jeremy Bentham's view of natural rights

However, utilitarianism contained paradoxical implications. Dispensing with natural rights undermined the liberal argument for minimum state interference, clearing the intellectual path for paternalistic state action (Gamble 1981: 81). Indeed, Bentham supported intervention in areas such as education, wage levels, guaranteed employment and sickness benefits. The reasoning was to be taken much further by J. S. Mill.

J. S. Mill With the good fortune, or otherwise, to be the son of James, John Stuart Mill (1806–73) was subjected by his father and Bentham to an intense utilitarian education. After a period of acute depression he resolved to change his life and in doing so changed utilitarianism. Influenced by French thinker Alexis de Tocqueville (1805–59), he questioned Bentham's narrowly materialistic approach, arguing that the freedom that liberals had seen mainly in terms of the economy should extend to other walks of life. This interpretation had radical implications for wider emancipation and a generally more permissive society. Mill's most influential work, *On Liberty* (1859), gave a moral view of freedom.

> The only freedom worthy of the name is that of pursuing our own good in our own way, so long as we do not attempt to deprive others of theirs.
>
> J. S. Mill, *On Liberty* (1859)

Mill's arguments for democracy go beyond preventing corruption or maximizing utility. Like the Ancient Greeks he saw political participation as a good in itself, necessary for dignity. However, in his *Considerations on Representative Government* (1861) he echoed de Tocqueville's fear of the 'tyranny of the majority'. Hence, while favouring representative democracy he recommended plural voting, the 'wiser' having more (up to six) votes than others (with property the measure of wisdom!). Equality should be withheld until the populace was fully trained in civic virtue. Mill's more sophisticated thinking on individualism, freedom and the role of the state was to prove hugely influential.

The industrial revolution Economic liberalism spawned its own revolution, less bloody than previous ones but no less profound in its political effects. First occurring in Britain, between 1760 and 1860, as the new scientific thinking was applied to production, it was to create a new kind of civilization – an industrial one. Driving the new order was a thrusting entrepreneurial class, who used the freedoms gained in 1689 and the thinking of the classical economists to create the *laissez-faire* economy. Their escalating wealth was to rival that of the landed class and they were to transform economic strength into political power, with far-reaching consequences. It was this, rather than the astonishing application of technology, that justified the term 'industrial *revolution*'.

New Liberalism

Persistent poverty, inequality and unemployment mocked the free market's claim to promote the common good. Some liberals began to feel that freedom in modern society was more complex than their classical forebears had believed. In this they were influenced by the German philosopher Hegel, one of the intellectual giants of the modern age.

Georg Hegel Hegel (1770–1831) shared Rousseau's view that the state was not an infringement of freedom but its highest expression. Rejecting the idea of a pre-social state of nature he believed human nature to be a product of social interaction. Rights could only have meaning in a social context and in *The Philosophy of Right* (1821) he asserted that true freedom lay not in a life lived away from the state but in its service. Such an idea could be seen as dangerous; it could lead to a crushing of the individual in totalitarianism. However, in late-nineteenth-century England a group of thinkers leavened this extreme collectivism with a radical form of individualism. They formed the school of English Idealists, under their most notable member, T. H. Green.

T. H. Green An Oxford classicist, Thomas Hill Green (1836–82) believed in the goodness of human instinct. The state was not the all-consuming ideal of Hegel but its essential purpose was to secure the 'common good', something greater than the sum of individual happiness sought by utilitarians. Other New Liberals continued the argument. L. T. Hobhouse argued that, whereas classical liberalism had sought to liberate individuals from the state, New Liberalism used the state to liberate individuals from social and economic restrictions. J. A. Hobson viewed society as a living organism, each part promoting the well-being of the whole. In these terms, *laissez-faire* was a disease requiring treatment.

John Maynard Keynes A radical economic thinker, Keynes (1883–1946) refuted the classical economists' view that the market would necessarily allocate resources in the best way. The state could not stand aside; it should take on the job of managing the market, increasing demand through public borrowing and expenditure to maintain full employment. This is the essence of **Keynesianism** (see p. 512).

Essentially New Liberalism saw freedom not as a product of nature but as a creation *of* the state. Its influence was seen in the Liberal governments of 1905–15, which helped lay the foundations of the welfare state. Indeed, for critics it was socialism rather than liberalism. However, in principle, the individual is given only the *means* to pursue fulfilment; self-help remains central (Simhony 1991).

Defining freedom

While most ideologies claim to cherish freedom, they vary in how they define it and can come to sharply conflicting policy conclusions.

◆ **Negative:** Classical liberal thinkers saw freedom as the absence of restriction. This negative concept of freedom is achieved by non-action on the part of the state. It leaves people alone and does not limit their right to do as they please.

◆ **Positive:** New liberal thinkers argued that the freedom offered by the absence of state interference was bogus. Poverty, ignorance, illness, unemployment, bullying by the rich and so on left the mass of people quite *unfree*. They advocated positive state action, through social policies, to release people from their social fetters. In his great report of 1942, which laid the foundations of the post-war welfare state, William Beveridge used the language of New Liberalism when he spoke of the state *freeing* people from what he termed the evil giants of ignorance, disease, squalor, poverty and idleness.

Neoliberalism

Amidst the transformation within liberalism there remained critics who clung to the earlier classical formulation. Isaiah Berlin (1970) saw in the new idea of freedom the foundation of oppression, but perhaps the most tenacious critic was Friedrich von Hayek.

Friedrich von Hayek During his long lifetime Hayek (1899–1992) witnessed both fascism and Stalinism and most of his work was preoccupied with the threat posed by the state. He perpetuated a body of neoclassical economic thought originated by Carl Menger (1840–1921), known as the Austrian School, which admitted only a limited role for the state in offsetting hardship. A fellow member, Ludwig Von Mises (1881–1973), stressed the impossibility of state planning. Hayek's mission was to show modern capitalism to be an essential element of the free society. The market resolves social problems, producing a 'spontaneous order', the outcome of human action but not of human design. Hayek's work is frequently coupled with that of US economist Milton Friedman (b. 1912) and the Chicago School, which again associated the market with freedom and democracy and, in opposition to Keynesianism, advocated an economic policy known as monetarism (see p. 514).

The system of private property is the most important guarantee of freedom, not only for those who own property but scarcely less for those who do not.

Friedrich von Hayek, *The Road to Serfdom* (1944)

There's no such thing as a free lunch.

Attributed to neoliberal economist Milton Friedman

From the 1980s **neoliberalism** seized the heart of the British polity in a new consensus. First it became associated with those thinkers and politicians, including Enoch Powell and Margaret Thatcher, who labelled themselves Conservative. They formed the '**New Right**' and the term **Thatcherism** entered the ideological lexicon. However, after an initially sceptical response, the Labour Party was to reinvent itself as New Labour and don much of the new garb (see p. 302).

Whose interest?

Early liberalism used rationalism and the value of freedom to undermine the claims of monarchy, aristocracy and religion, clearing the way for lasting democratic and egalitarian reforms. However, the principle that governments keep out of private affairs was very much in the interests of those becoming economically powerful through capitalism. The liberal claim that all people were of equal worth sounded a hollow ring in an economic system that created poverty as well as riches (Arblaster 1984: 84–91). While New Liberalism acknowledged the harsh effects of capitalism, it sought to save rather than replace it. However, alternative views of the nature of freedom and society spawned two more western ideologies: socialism and conservatism.

Reproduced by permission of *Punch*

Socialism

Socialism stands as the antithesis of liberalism, repudiating its central precepts of individualism, the free market and private property. However, the two share a common core of western assumptions and values: faith in science, belief in industrialization and confidence in the possibility of rationalist improvement.

Human nature Socialists typically view people optimistically, not as isolated individuals but as part of a larger society, with a sense of moral responsibility towards one another. Human nature cannot be found in some imaginary state of nature; it is a product of society. The individualism of liberal thought encourages people's worst characteristics. In contrast, the collectivism of socialism fosters values such as altruism and fraternity.

The form of government A major misconception about socialism is that it entails a dominant state. On the contrary, some early socialists were libertarians and associated with **anarchy**. However, such thinking was undermined by industrialization, and socialism was forced to advocate either a particular form of government within the liberal tradition or an alternative to it. Both models featured in subsequent developments.

The pattern of development: in search of Utopia

Initially seen as cranks and eccentrics, the early socialists set the climate for new thinking. Central to this was the value of a sense of community, as opposed to competitive individualism. Many of these ideas evolved in France, an important pioneer being the aristocrat Claude Saint-Simon (1760–1825), whose ideas were spread by his secretary, the philosopher and sociologist Auguste Comte (1798–1857). He envisioned a centrally planned industrialized economy administered for the common good, though, with liberal instincts, he had no wish to abolish private property. François Fourier (1772–1837) saw in large-scale industrialization not progress but impoverishment. Like Rousseau, he valued a simple unsophisticated life, arguing for industry based on small craftsmen and farmers living in cooperatives (*phalanstères*) of fewer than 2,000. Though rejecting *phalanstères* as rustic fantasies, Pierre-Joseph Proudhon (1809–65) felt industrialization led only to exploitation, inequality and oppression.

Not all capitalists applauded the harsh logic of individualism. Self-made English industrialist Robert Owen (1771–1858) thought the workplace could be a socialist community. His New Lanark Mills were run paternalistically, providing workers' families with housing, health care and education. The experiment aroused considerable interest at home and in the USA.

> Property is theft.
>
> Proudhon's memorable indictment of capitalism in *Qu'est-ce que la Propriété?* (1840)

Marx and Marxism

The rural peasantry and the disorganized urban poor of the early nineteenth century could hardly transform society. Hence a key circumstance in the development of socialism was industrialization and the new class structure. This inspired a strand of thought intended to revolutionize the modern world. It came from liberalism's most trenchant critic, the German polymath Karl Marx (1818–83). Influenced variously – by the Enlightenment, the French Revolution, English liberalism, classical economics, Hegel, Darwin and the earlier socialists, as well as European literature and classical philosophy – Marx identified the most compelling question of the modern era: how can a just community exist in the context of modern industrial society? (Gamble 1981: 114). No modern thinker has a greater claim to have placed his stamp on the intellectual climate of the twentieth century and on the course of world events.

Marx aimed to portray political development rather like natural history: a process obeying scientific laws. His theory was one of **historical materialism**: the key lay in the way work, a necessity imposed by nature, was organized. This 'mode of production' shaped laws, arts, politics, state institutions and the dominant ideology. This simple though little appreciated fact of survival unlocked a Pandora's box. In the new industrial society the vital tools, factories and land necessary for survival were not owned by those who did the work, but by relatively few private individuals – the **bourgeoisie** or capitalists.

Although liberalism made citizens legally free, in reality they were bound to the capitalists who purchased their labour, just like any other commodity (the commodification of labour). While labour was purchased in one market, the workers' products were sold in another, so that prices were unrelated to wages. Employers would seek to widen the gap between the two by keeping wages down and retaining a surplus for themselves. Although Locke had asserted that each had a right to the product of their labour, that of the modern worker was being expropriated (stolen). This exploitative relationship was inescapable under **capitalism**, for without it no one would invest in capital.

Moreover, domination went beyond the workplace to penetrate the state itself. Marx disputed the claim that the liberal state had broken free from class domination. Capitalism is not possible unless the state operates in the bourgeois interest, ensuring the conditions for maximizing profit (maintaining

> Capital is reckless of the health or length of life of the labourer, unless under compulsion from society. To the outcry as to the physical and mental degradation, the premature death, the torture of overwork, it answers: Ought these to trouble us since they increase our profits?
>
> Karl Marx, *Capital* (1867: ch. 10)

order, protecting property, limiting trade union activity and fostering an ideology of inequality). The bourgeoisie becomes, in effect, a ruling class.

Marx's socialism Because the system of government was a function of the mode of production, it was here that the fundamental change had to be made. Marx's socialism followed a broadly Fourierist vision of a workers' state. However, this was but a transitory stage leading to an even greater transformation: a society without a wages system, with no division between manual and intellectual labour, and no private property or classes. Far from being totalitarian, this was to be a **communist** society in which the state would wither away.

How could such change come about? Here lies the secret of Marx's extraordinary appeal to oppressed peoples the world over. He believed revolution was not only necessary but, owing to the tensions and contradictions within capitalism, inevitable. Such an idea deeply unnerved those living behind the bastions of privilege, making Marx a hated figure within the liberal establishment. The French Revolution had demonstrated what a united people could achieve and Marx saw the new working class as a Frankenstein's monster which would destroy its capitalist creators. He identified a two-stage process: a bourgeois revolution with the liberal overthrow of the aristocratic order and a proletarian revolution with the workers' overthrow of the bourgeoisie. In Britain, the first had already taken place; the second was predestined.

The possibility of this dramatic challenge preoccupied a growing socialist movement and parties formed to prepare for the revolution. However, differing interpretations and circumstances led to tension between those favouring violent action (**voluntarism**) and the moderates prepared to wait for the inevitable collapse of capitalism (**determinism**).

Revolutionary socialism In Russia, the revolutionary leader Lenin (1870–1924) began in a determinist position. However, the backward development of Russian capitalism led him towards voluntarism. He developed a theory of the party as an intellectual vanguard force to spearhead the revolution. The Tsarist regime was weakened by its inability to manage the world war, the government was divided and the country in chaos. In the great revolutions of 1917 the Tsar was overthrown and in July 1918 the first Soviet Constitution was proclaimed. Whether or not this model was applicable to the special conditions of Russia, its subsequent export led to the inflexible and ruthless imposition of a theory that abandoned Marx's vision. In Russia itself the subsequent reign of Stalinist terror was a mockery of the liberty the revolution had promised.

Reformist socialism In the light of Italian conditions, Antonio Gramsci (1891–1937) advocated more subtle means of reform. He argued that the predicted crisis of capitalism could be averted by the ruling class because they exercised continuing dominance (**hegemony**) by holding influential positions throughout the state and shaping the prevailing common sense of society to legitimize their role. Hence the task of the revolutionary was to infiltrate these establishment bastions, ultimately to unleash the social forces below.

A committee for managing the affairs of the bourgeoisie.

Karl Marx's view of democratic government under capitalism

A leading revisionist, the German Eduard Bernstein (1850–1932), believed socialism could be pursued through liberal constitutional structures. This was an attractive idea in those West European nations where such systems were relatively well established. Moreover, the goals were also more moderate – **social democracy** with welfare policies rather than communism. Such an approach was advanced in Britain by the Fabian Society, a group of intellectuals influential at the turn of the century and instrumental in the formation of the Labour Party (see chapter 10).

The anarchistic tradition

Although mainstream socialism after Marx took either the radical or parliamentary forms, other strains continued the ideology's more anarchic tendencies, envisaging socialism through workers' associations rather than the state. A movement began in France in the 1890s known as Syndicalism, while in England guild socialism in the early twentieth century sought to incorporate into workers' associations the fraternal spirit of the ancient guilds.

> The majestic egalitarianism of the law, which forbids rich and poor alike to sleep under bridges, to beg in the streets, and to steal bread.
>
> Anatole France (1844–1924; French writer), *The Red Lily*

Others have argued for market socialism whereby a free market functions without capitalism. Production is by private cooperatives operating competitively but without profit accumulation. The theory aroused interest in the 1930s though it had many critics. With the collapse of Soviet-style socialism and the failure of nationalization, some form of market socialism could still have a future.

Whose interest?

Socialist doctrines make a sectional appeal and were particularly attractive to the rising labour movements. The principal objection from liberals concerned the threat to freedom; they have associated socialism with large bureaucracies, high taxation and totalitarianism. Others saw the ideology as a class-based threat to the natural order of society. These were conservatives, who also opposed liberalism on the same grounds.

Conservatism

Conservatism provides a rationale for resisting change; it is a doctrine of reaction. Indeed, the first political use of the term came with English aristocratic resistance to the Enlightenment and French Revolution. Later conservatives have resisted variously republicanism, industrialism, liberalism, utilitarianism and socialism. Although reform may sometimes be necessary, it should not arise from abstract principles that will inevitably distort and oversimplify (Oakeshott 1962). There is also a certain pragmatism: if a thing works it is accepted, with little theory of *why* it works.

> If it ain't broke don't fix it.
>
> An Americanism

Human nature Conservatives aim to see people as they actually are. Hence they reject individualistic theories; real people are always part of society, surrounded by cultural accretions – language, customs, literature and so on. Human reason is limited, wisdom is not the product of rational thought but of feelings, instincts and prejudices evolved over the generations.

The sense of realism leads to a recognition of the Christian idea of original sin; people are not perfect and cannot be made so. Life and politics are about making the best of a bad job.

Conservatives know there are books to read, pictures to look at, music to listen to – and grouse to shoot.

Harold Macmillan (1894–1986; Conservative leader), quoted by Nigel Nicolson in Thames
TV programme *The Day Before Yesterday* (1970)

The form of government Conservatism does not lay down a blueprint; constitutions are not designed, they evolve. Each nation will have its own uniquely fitted system of government and countries should not import alien practices. The particular features British conservatives see as *their* tradition tend to include social hierarchy, the monarchy, the House of Lords, the patriarchal family, property, and a natural ruling class. Inequality is natural and socially necessary; it cannot be eradicated. Consequently poverty is nothing to be ashamed of.

I believe it to be of the utmost importance that a territorial aristocracy should be maintained. I believe that in no country is it more important than in this, with its ancient constitution, ancient habits and mixed form of government.

Sir Robert Peel (Conservative prime minister), House of Commons speech (4 May 1846)

The pattern of development: the retreat from rationalism

Its anti-rationalism suggests conservativism will produce fewer thinkers than most ideologies. On the other hand, the argument that it is a natural cast of mind allows it to claim a long tradition, exponents not realizing they were talking conservative prose. Thus, 'conservative' thinking can be traced from the Ancient Greeks, including Plato (Auerback 1959: 26), through a range of thinkers who have challenged rationalism in one way or another. However, modern conservatism arose largely as a response to the French Revolution, an event striking fear into English aristocratic hearts.

Classical conservatism Ironically, the father of modern 'Conservatism' was a Whig. An opponent of the Enlightenment, Irish-born writer and politician Edmund Burke (1729–97) outlined the rationale for resisting change in his *Reflections on the Recent Revolution in France* (1790). Generally he argued for a presumption in favour of the status quo; virtue should be assumed in existing institutions. Burke was not against revolution as such, but this should be to reassert the natural order rather than destroy it. Hence he welcomed the outcome of the Glorious Revolution of 1688, which he believed restored the ancient rights of the aristocracy against encroaching royal authority. Similarly he supported the colonists in the American War of Independence, who were demanding traditional English liberties. However, the French affair was a different matter. Here, an ancient order was being challenged, an affront to God, its creator. He saw the enterprise as doomed, predicting the rise of a military dictatorship (he was of course partly right in this). However, Burke's conservatism was augmented with other strains.

> Society is a partnership not only between those who are living, but between those who are living, those who are dead and those who are yet to be born.
>
> Edmund Burke, *Reflections on the Revolution in France* (1790)

Romantic conservatism Industrialization destroyed old patterns of life. For many it created gross ugliness, disfiguring the landscape with factories and urban squalor and undermining the social fabric by replacing the harmonious feudal order with exploitative relationships. A romantic reaction in the form of a body of artistic work expressing nostalgia for the more simple way of life arose in Germany and England. Numerous figures were involved, including Coleridge, Carlyle, Wordsworth and Sir Walter Scott. Unlike classical conservatives, the romantics were not necessarily opposed to rationalism; indeed Wordsworth wrote enthusiastically of the French Revolution. There was even a romantic strain within the New Right from those such as Enoch Powell, Roger Scruton and Maurice Cowling, advocating traditional conservative values from monarchy to foxhunting (Scruton 1980: 34).

> Bliss was it in that dawn to be alive.
>
> William Wordsworth on the French Revolution, in *The Prelude* (xi: 108)

One-nation conservatism With property as the basis of power, the aristocracy was seen by early conservatives as the only group that could be trusted to govern, its interest being identical with the common good. There is no case for limiting government; state intervention was recognized as a necessity of the industrial age well before the reforms of the Liberal and Labour parties. This paternalism continued the feudal doctrine of *noblesse oblige*. Perhaps the most important representative of this strain was Benjamin Disraeli (1804–81), astute Tory Party leader who, in 1854, expressed the sentiment in a novel *Sybil, or: the Two Nations*. The 'two nations' of rich and poor must be united if the whole is to be maintained (see chapter 10). However, conservatives have taken a Janus-like stance over the one-nation principle, some looking more fondly towards the liberal free market.

Liberal conservatism Opposition to capitalism had, for both principled and political reasons, certain limitations: too much social reform would resemble a rationalist blueprint and paternalism could weaken the nation's moral fabric. Moreover, state interference could threaten property, the traditional basis of aristocratic power. As a Whig, Burke had himself favoured free trade because it weakened monarchy (Hampsher-Monk 1987: 20), and believed that industrialization, as a natural development, should not be hindered. Furthermore, in the early stages of industrialization the aristocracy had shared some interests with the bourgeoisie as the railways scored the surface of their land and the mines burrowed beneath. This version of conservatism was to come to the fore in the 1980s (chapter 10). Indeed, the term 'liberal conservatism' has been used to describe the ideology of New Labour (Driver and Martell 1988).

Fascism Further to the right-wing extreme is **fascism**. Developing in the 1920s, the term was chosen by Italian leader Benito Mussolini for the movement that carried him to power. The legend was a bundle of rods, a *fasces*, symbolizing the spirit of community, beneath an axe-head representing the state's authority. A fascist movement began in Britain in the 1930s under Oswald Mosley, but the horrors of the second world war left this ideology indelibly tarnished and most modern-day conservatives would deny any association with it. However, its values of **nationalism**, inequality, anti-liberalism and anti-socialism are essentially conservative. Other aspects, such as racism and militarism, may also be seen as logical derivatives from nationalism in its more extreme form. There can be no denying that Enoch Powell's inflammatory speeches in the 1970s evoked racist sentiments, while the Falklands war revealed a joy in militarism. Such sentiments were not, however, confined to one party.

Whose interest?

The conservative position is seductive; it can be said that we are all conservative at heart (Cecil 1912: 9), and many speak nostalgically of a 'golden age' of, say, football or theatre or popular music. Moreover, the world is littered with examples of failed rationalist reforms, including the socialist 'utopias' of Eastern Europe. In the arts much is made of wisdom built up over centuries. The great Kirov Ballet, for example, prides itself on a tradition of over two hundred years and the result is unrivalled artistry. Yet there is a fundamental paradox. In

Power has only one duty – to secure the social welfare of the people.

Benjamin Disraeli, *Sybil, or: the Two Nations* (1854: book IV, ch. XIV)

A democracy of the dead.

G. K. Chesterton (1874–1936; British writer) on conservatism, in *Orthodoxy* arguing for tradition and prejudice over rationalism, conservatism uses reason to attack reason; it is an ideology not to be ideological (Vincent 1992: 82). Moreover, there is much evidence (cannibalism, witch-burning, female circumcision, racism, religious fundamentalism) to show that tradition can sometimes be dangerous. In many walks of life we do not slight reason; most would prefer a trained physician to the ministrations of a witch doctor. In practice, many conservative thinkers allow some place for rationalism but stress its limitations. However, in the world of politics, conservatism must by definition serve the interests of the 'haves' rather than the 'have nots'.

A Changing Climate

Liberalism, socialism and conservatism espouse contrasting views of human nature, society and the good life. Enough ink and blood have been spilled to leave little doubt of these differences. However, they have shared certain things in common, unstated assumptions forming the bedrock of their views of society – a universe of male supremacy, industrialism and economic growth.

Male supremacy Conservatism must necessarily accept male dominance through its veneration of tradition. In contrast, the precepts of liberalism and socialism do not logically imply sexual inequality yet they too are guilty. Even the great rallying cry of the defining event of the modern era, the French Revolution, called not only for *liberté* and *égalité* but also for *fraternité*. There were to be no *sisters* of the revolution. Were they to remain at home to bake the fabled cake? Similarly socialism in Britain, whether through the Labour Party or the trade unions, has been largely a male preserve.

Industrialism and growth Classical liberalism provided the intellectual bedrock for the industrial revolution itself. Even though romantic conservatives and utopian socialists inveighed against industrialism, mainstream thinkers have accepted its material largesse. The landed classes were to benefit from industrialism and British socialists were influenced more by the Fabians than Karl Marx, their goal to secure for workers a fairer share of the economic cake, not to incinerate it.

It is difficult to overestimate the impact of the western ideological tradition (Gamble 1981: 17). However, it is increasingly revealed as ill equipped to address the most compelling questions of contemporary life. A new uncertainty gives rise to philosophical searching in various directions, some of which are described as postmodern – a vaguely defined concept denoting a stage, or epoch, beyond that ushered in by the Enlightenment (Harvey 1989). This expresses a scepticism towards rationalism, and is more open to a wider range of voices in social enquiry, art and political empowerment. From the dissatisfaction have emerged two ideologies assuming growing importance. Feminism and environmentalism are not entirely subsumed within **post-**

modernism but they resonate with its mood, compelling politicians to modify their agendas. Students of contemporary politics cannot ignore them.

Feminism

> You cannot entrust the interests of one class entirely to another class, and you cannot entrust the interests of one sex entirely to another sex.
>
> David Lloyd George (1863–1945; Liberal statesman), speech (1911)

Political thinkers refer variously to man, his rights, his liberation, his equality, his nobility and so on *ad infinitum*. This is no accident; for many the intention is deliberately to exclude women on the grounds that the territory of politics is beyond bounds. Even Rousseau, champion of freedom and equality, made this exclusion. Sometimes the sexist language merely reflects convention but such usage shrouds deeper forces at the level of the subconscious. In the same way that Gramsci saw patterns of class hegemony woven into a 'common sense' of life, so male domination is built into common consciousness through language, family life, personal relationships and work patterns. Hence, many people, including some political scientists (Randall 1982: 1–5), regard it as 'natural' that women are not political. The body of ideological thought termed **feminism** arose as a reaction to this anomaly. Feminism seeks sexual justice. While not presenting an alternative to liberalism or socialism, it meets the requirements of an ideology in its own right, being concerned with human nature and the social arrangements whereby people can live.

People call me a feminist whenever I express sentiments that differentiate me from a doormat or a prostitute.

Attributed to Rebecca West (1892–1983; British novelist)

Human nature Here the key issue concerns the idea of gender difference. This is of central importance because difference implies distinct male and female roles. However, we must ask how far differences are natural or the result of conditioning. All strains of feminism agree that the degree of natural difference is far *less* than has been assumed.

The form of government Feminists broadly attack male dominance in the state territory, calling for more women in government, where their presence will feminize the political agenda.

The pattern of development: *liberté, egalité* and sisterhood

It is difficult to plot the development of feminism since history has largely been written by men. A key early figure is Christina de Pizan, who wrote *The City of the Ladies* in 1405. There was also the exotic Aphra Behn (1640–89), who spied for the court of Charles II and was a prolific author of plays and novels ridiculing prevailing patterns of sexual inequality. However, its real birth lies, like other major ideologies, in the Enlightenment. In *A Vindication of the Rights of Man* (1790) Mary Wollstonecraft (1759–97), the greatest of the early feminists, countered Burke's attack on the French Revolution (in which women were active). Two years later she applied the same reasoning to argue for equality for her own sex in *A Vindication of the Rights of Woman*, a major feminist landmark. In America, women were active in another great cause, the fight against slavery. However, after the civil war, when political rights were extended to black men, but not women (black or white), they mobilized as a specifically feminist force. Indeed, the USA has always provided a major spearhead of the movement.

Added impetus came from industrialization, which brought poor women into the new workplaces, while giving their bourgeois sisters issues to ponder and the leisure to do so. The movement saw them active in charitable work, education, propaganda and a sustained fight for the franchise (chapter 9). However, with the franchise secured the movement fell dormant, submerged by economic depression, the second world war and subsequent reconstruction.

The 1960s saw a renaissance as an international civil rights movement sought emancipation for various oppressed groups. Changing attitudes towards sex, marriage, divorce and the family, the availability of the contraceptive pill and easier access to abortion altered women's perceptions. In 1961, Simone de Beauvoir's influential 1949 classic, *The Second Sex*, appeared in paperback, while in 1970 Germaine Greer's *The Female Eunuch* sent tremors through university campuses and suburbia. The movement has continued to grow, with new journals, books and plays, and the rediscovery of earlier writers, such as Virginia Woolf. Specialist publishers, such as Virago (1977) and The Women's Press (1978), emerged and universities mounted courses in Women's Studies.

Forms of feminism

As with most ideologies, there is no single version of feminism and approaches range from moderate to extreme. Much present-day analysis is structured around liberal, socialist and radical forms. We also consider the possibility of a conservative variant.

Liberal feminism One could logically expect classical liberalism to be hospitable to feminism. The idea of natural freedoms should surely include women. Similarly, the utilitarian principle of maximum happiness should endorse sex equality. Moreover, rationalism should be suspicious of ancient patriarchal customs. Yet this has not proved so. The resounding call for emancipation from oppression largely addressed a male world. Indeed, it was a Liberal government that held out against the suffragettes (pp. 243–4). Where women were concerned, liberals fell into the very conservativism they castigated. Mary

Wollstonecraft was a lone swallow and J. S. Mill, as a male thinker deeply concerned with women's rights, was a rare bird indeed.

To Wollstonecraft sexual imbalance was a social creation and women's oppression was harmful to society at large. Unique in questioning male presumptions, J. S. Mill noted how the liberal distinction between state and civil society confined women to the latter. In *The Subjection of Women* (1869), he saw their position as a relic of slavery grounded ultimately in force. Such conclusions were deeply disturbing to a male establishment and, compared with Mill's other writings, were to languish in obscurity (Held 1987: 80). However, his prescriptions, including reform of the marriage laws, equal educational opportunities and female enfranchisement, were limited to freeing women to help themselves (Pateman 1983).

Today liberal feminists continue to be distinguished by a moderate agenda framed in terms of equal legal, social and political rights. The goal is *freedom* to pursue their own advancement for the benefit of all society. Although called to share domestic duties, men are not seen as the enemy and the heterosexual family remains the norm.

Socialist feminism The basic premise of early socialist feminism was that women's plight was rooted in class oppression. Some saw sexual equality as integral to a broader socialist vision entailing alternative lifestyles. Fourier borders on eroticism in advocating free love, bisexuality and lesbianism. Owen believed patriarchal marriage sustained the competitive economy lying at the heart of much misery. Marx himself was rather unsympathetic but his collaborator, Friedrich Engels (1820–95), argued in *The Origin of the Family, Private Property and the State* (1884) that women's oppression was rooted in capitalism, their role the maintenance and reproduction of labour without payment.

The demands of socialist feminists today include free and widespread birth control, abortion on demand, state payment for domestic work, state child care and full equality in the workplace (Jaggar 1983: 132). Heterosexual families are not necessarily seen as the norm, though where they exist, they should be restructured to share the domestic burden. Activism takes place largely within established parties of the left.

Radical feminism Partly a breakaway from the socialists, the radical variant sees Marxism as 'sex blind'. The most fundamental basis for discrimination in society is sex; more significant than race or class. The problem lies in the nature of men, with their tendency towards aggression, violence, rape and so on. Yet the natural differences between the sexes are seen as minimal; conditioning is the key. This leads to calls for androgyny, both sexes playing identical roles, not only in rearing children but in work and even (with medical intervention) nurturing foetuses. Where radicals do concede difference they argue for female superiority, women's life-giving qualities making them more peaceable, caring and intuitive.

> The *divine right* of husbands ... may, it is hoped in this enlightened age, be contested without danger.
>
> Mary Wollstonecraft, *A Vindication of the Rights of Woman* (1792: ch. 3)

The movement has attracted overtly sexual lesbians but in addition a form of *political* lesbianism has emerged advocating separatism (living in sisterhood communities), sperm banks (to facilitate birth without direct male participation) and lesbian marriages. It is difficult to discern in radical feminism an underlying theory (Jaggar 1983: 84). Drawing more from postmodernism, it embraces aspects of eastern philosophy and mysticism, seeing rationalism itself as a male characteristic. Action can take direct forms outside mainstream politics and peaked in the 1960s, when passions inflamed brassieres as well as debate. This is the arm of the movement that gains its notoriety and 'women's lib' moniker.

Conservative feminism? It is unusual to speak of conservative feminism; indeed, the term may be an oxymoron. The subjugation of women is historic reality sanctified by ancient custom, the very thing conservatives venerate. Moreover, conservativism often takes religious forms, revering sacred texts and, the world over, these tend to be anti-feminist (Hawley 1984). Muslim fundamentalism confines women to the home (Mahl 1995) while, in the USA, the Christian Right, with 1.6 million active supporters, campaigns for the restoration of 'family values' and pursues strenuous anti-abortion crusades (Dutt 1995). The Anglican Church long opposed women priests, a stance still maintained by the Catholic Church. Moreover, anti-feminism is often a hall-mark of the far right. Nazism stressed women's role in rearing children, outlawed birth control and denounced women in politics. Similar calls come from the self-proclaimed Moral Majority in the USA and bodies such as the Salisbury Group in Britain.

Yet despite all, groups bearing names such as 'conservative pro-family femi-nism' see traditional roles, such as male-supporting and child-rearing, as valid feminist goals. This can be seen as radicalism in a different guise, according the family role greater value. Such thinking is not entirely foreign to mainstream feminists when they advocate a wage for parenting and housework.

Neo-feminism Another wave can be characterized as neo-feminist. Feminist writer Nikki van der Gaag (1995) notes a younger generation recognizing a need to work with rather than against men. Helen Wilkenson (1995) from the think-tank Demos discerns an historic shift in the relations between the sexes, an 'unravelling of not only 200 years of industrial society, but millennia of traditions and beliefs'. In bringing about a more fully egalitarian society, reform can be seen to be in men's interest as much as that of women. The idea that women are naturally more caring and compassionate makes them eminently suitable for the public sphere, promising a more ethical and compas-sionate society (Elshtain 1981).

Whose interest?

Superficially, feminism could be said to promote an unashamedly sectional interest; women calling for a better deal for women. The entry of over a hundred women into Parliament after the 1997 and 2001 general elections helped to soften policy on certain fronts, although in other areas, such as benefits to single mothers, there was disappointment (see p. 190). However, not all women share the same interests and the movement is fragmented into various groups. British examples include the National Women's Network, Change, Womankind, Women against Fundamentalism and the Women's Environmental Network. Some organize around specific issues, such as reproductive rights, lesbian rights, welfare, violence, sexist advertising, children and professional career development. Liberal feminists are accused by radicals of accepting patriarchal values. The free market, for example, glorifies competitiveness, seen as a male characteristic. Socialists find both liberals and radicals blind to the economic basis of patriarchy. Moderates fear that radicals will alienate public sympathy, while neo-feminists reject the attack on men. Further divisions reflect class, race, nationality and sexuality (Dutt 1995).

Yet feminism has successfully permeated civil society and the state, its global nature underlined in the high-profile UN World Women's Conferences. Although having further to go, the ideology is woven into the fabric of contemporary politics, with many seeing greater equality as in the interest of society in general.

Environmentalism

Today the view is forming that the western ideological tradition is dangerously myopic. Under a broadly liberal banner, the post-war era has seen staggering industrial growth, raising material standards beyond imagination. Yet its costs are becoming increasingly apparent, not only to scientists but to ordinary people in their daily lives. In towns, polluted air causes chronic bronchial conditions, in the countryside rivers and lakes turn brown and lifeless. In supermarkets, shoppers worry about contaminated meat, pesticides and whether the hygienic packaging is wasting limited resources. At the macro level there are problems of overfishing, deforestation, nuclear leakages and the 'greenhouse effect'. There seems no escape; those opting out of the rat race for a place in the sun expose their bodies to ultraviolet radiation seeping through the depleted ozone layer. Modern science and rationalist ideologies may have brought humanity to a 'multifaceted global crisis' (Spretnack and Capra 1986: xv) that prompts new ideological thinking – **environmentalism**. This has a scientific basis in ecology, the study of the relationship of living organisms to their environment, a discipline founded in the late nineteenth century by German zoologist Ernst Haeckel. Its essential view is holistic: a single species cannot be understood without reference to its interactions with other species.

Paradoxically, although many environmentalists betray socialist leanings, the approach follows a conservative logic in questioning progress. Rationalist meddling is arrogant and dangerous; life has a logic beyond our understanding. Environmentalism also reflects the conservative conviction that we inhabit the planet for but a limited time, with a responsibility to future generations.

Human nature Unlike most ideologies, environmentalism downgrades human nature, shifting it from centre stage of the ecosphere much as, in the sixteenth century, Copernicus displaced the earth from the centre of the universe. There are two distinctive perspectives, the **anthropocentric** and the **eco-centric**.

- ◆ *The anthropocentric perspective.* Human life remains the principal criterion of value; nature must be respected because it serves us. The depletion of fish stocks, for example, is bad because species may die out and humans will suffer the consequences.
- ◆ *The ecocentric perspective.* Value is judged in terms of the ecosystem as a whole; this is the more controversial position (sometimes termed 'deep ecology'). A popular version is the Gaia theory of James Lovelock (1979), which sees the earth as a single organism, worthy of surviving with or without the human species.

The form of government While moderates believe that environmental goals can be met through existing forms of government, radicals see the nation-state as outmoded and call for a return to small communities.

The pattern of development: industrialism in question

> The emergence of intelligence, I am convinced, tends to unbalance the ecology... It is not until a creature begins to manage its environment that nature is thrown into disorder.
>
> Clifford D. Simak, US journalist, *Shakespeare's Planet*

Environmentalists see in ancient pre-industrial societies a greater ecological awareness than is found in modern society. However, modern environmentalism is tied in with science and industrialization. In 1661, diarist John Evelyn's tract *Fumifugium: the Inconveniencie of the Aer and Smoak of London Dissipated* argued for more trees to purify the city air. In the nineteenth century, the great public health movement, spearheaded by arch-Benthamite Edwin Chadwick, did more to eradicate diseases such as typhoid and cholera than would an army of physicians. The threat of resource depletion was also recognized. Malthus's grim late-eighteenth-century warning that population would outstrip food supply coloured much thinking, as did Darwin's theory of evolution, which underlined the close integration of the human species with nature. Romantic conservativism, with its belief that industrialism despoiled nature, was also influential. For some, including Haeckel himself, nature acquired a spiritual significance, a pantheistic substitute for the God Darwin had eliminated.

Contemporary environmentalism took off in the 1960s. In 1962 Rachel Carson published her influential *Silent Spring*; silent because the birds no longer sang, their reproductive cycles disrupted by pesticides. Other catastrophes followed. In the 1970s the Cuyahoga River became so polluted that it caught fire, while Lake Erie was pronounced dead. In 1968 Paul Ehrlich's *The Population Bomb* heightened the sense of alarm by reviving the Malthusian nightmare of overpopulation. Yet these appeared as local issues, within the scope of national governments to solve (Goodin 1992: 3). The problem moved onto an entirely new plane as global warming revealed that actions by single countries (curbing emissions, cleaning up rivers) could not meet the challenge. Traditional ideologies, premised upon a world of competitive nation-states, began to look more like the problem than the solution.

More heterogeneous than most, the movement takes four broad manifestations: individuals pursuing green lifestyles, propagandists working through traditional institutions (political parties, media, churches), green pressure groups and green parties (Parkin 1988: 168). The pressure groups, notably Friends of the Earth and Greenpeace, formed at the end of the 1960s. Many take a high-profile, headline-catching stance. In its daring oceanic encounters, *The Rainbow Warrior*, literally the Greenpeace flagship, featured dramatically on television screens around the world. Political parties followed, with fully fledged agendas embracing foreign policy, the economy, education, and so on. In 1983 Die Grünen (the Greens) seized the public imagination with a

No-fly zone: eco-warriors Matt, Denise and Muppet Pete wait to be evicted from their 'Cakehole' protest camp near Manchester Airport, May 1997

Photo: Times Newspapers Ltd

breakthrough into the West German Bundestag, the psychedelic garb of their 27 members contrasting symbolically with the serried ranks of establishment grey. Greens have also penetrated the European Parliament, forming a separate group in their own right. Posing challenges quite beyond the contemplation of traditional politicians, the movement takes two broad forms: one anthropocentric and moderate, the other ecocentric and radical.

Forms of environmentalism

Moderate environmentalism Here action is through the usual political channels. The ecological lifestyle can be achieved by national governments pursuing regulatory policies (Porritt and Winner 1988: 151). This approach accommodates other ideologies.

- ◆ *Neoliberal.* Eco-capitalists keep faith with the free market; if green products are demanded, competition will ensure their supply (Elkington and Burke 1989: 239). In this 'New Age Capitalism' firms will, without governmental direction, use alternative energy sources, cleaner technology and biodegradable materials and practise recycling. In Britain, local authorities have developed various policies for recycling waste and protecting the environment as a matter of routine, while shoppers increasingly demand green products. Although the car remains supreme, exhaust standards are growing more stringent. The mainstream parties continue to green their manifestos. For liberals growth is not sacrificed but becomes *sustainable*.
- ◆ *Socialist.* Alternatively, eco-socialists continue to see capitalism as a serious problem, calling for state power to take on multinational corporations with regulative regimes and a range of social policies to combat the suffering stemming from environmental abuse (Ryle 1988: 46). In 1992, the government banned the use of two pesticides increasingly found in drinking water and, by 1998, road traffic reduction appeared to be a serious policy goal.

The moderate approach has proved the more effective so far. However, for many the idea that the crisis can be ultimately met within existing political frameworks is naive delusion.

Radical environmentalism Traditional politics is about compromise. However, the issue environmentalists address is not about 'who gets what' and there can be no halfway solutions (Goodin 1992: 12). The crisis demands seismic shifts in lifestyles, economies and systems of government.

- ◆ *Lifestyle.* Generally life must be less materialistic, with greater emphasis on spiritual values (often of a Buddhist character). Many contemporary shibboleths (the supremacy of the car, children, foreign holidays) are

> Other parties have literally copied parts of our programme. But they don't implement them. They only do it cosmetically.
>
> Petra Kelly (Die Grünen MP, whose sudden death was shrouded in mystery), interview in *Living Marxism* (4 Feb. 1989)

challenged. People would live more frugally and populations would be stabilized through immigration control, abortion and sterilization.

◆ *Economics*. A 'New Economics' questions both liberalism and social-ism. The talisman of growth is unnatural: the goal is a steady-state economy. Gross national product (GNP) should be replaced with an *adjusted* measure (AGNP), reflecting pollution, waste, health and other quality-of-life indicators. Energy would come mainly from renewable sources (sun, sea, wind), with consumption drastically cut. The global economy must be shut down; the liberal orthodoxy of free trade re-placed by autarky (national self-sufficiency).

◆ *Government*. The centralized nation-state undermines the ecological community and is no longer viable (Goldsmith 1972: 52). Seeking popu-larity through rising material standards, employment creation and so on, governments have worked hand in glove with large corporations, legit-imating their activities and restricting information on pollution and harmful effects upon food. Radical environmentalists see people living rather like the Ancient Greeks in small communities in sustainable 'bio-regions'. Within deep ecology there are strongly anarchic undertones.

The global challenge

Like feminism, environmentalism has permeated western consciousness. How-ever, environmental problems are global and the real solutions must come at the supranational level, often at the expense of national sovereignty. As Vidal (1996) asserts: 'The changes now taking place in society are, I believe, as profound as in the Enlightenment'. In the USA, the Carter administration published a *Global 2000 Report* and the Club of Rome produced *The Limits to Growth* (Meadows et al. 1972). The role of the European Union (EU) (chapter 5) becomes increasingly significant. Although the Rome Treaty was silent on environmental policy, by 1971 environmentalist lobbying had placed it on the agenda. The Paris Summit adopted an environmental policy and established an Environmental Protection Service. Since then goals have been outlined in Environmental Action Programmes (EAPs). The Single European Act (SEA) of 1987 (see p. 121) introduced the environment as one of its Titles (VII) and 1990 saw the creation of the European Environmental Agency to conduct research and publish reports on environmental issues. The Maastricht Treaty enlarged the environmental provisions, promising financial assistance to states where disproportionate costs were imposed by EU requirements. At the

United Nations Rio Earth Summit in 1992, John Major enthused on matters ecological and *Agenda 21* was accepted for implementation at national and local levels. In November 1998 the British government published its first 'quality of life barometer', going beyond economic data to include housing, road transport, waste disposal, life expectancy, pollution and number of wild birds.

Whose interest?

Although
containing only
4.6% of the
world's
population the
US is respon-
sible for 21.9%
of carbon
dioxide
emissions.

World Resources,
1996–7

Although claiming to serve humanity as a whole, environmentalism is some-times characterized as the self-indulgence of a middle-class intelligentsia. Lowe and Goyder (1983: 25) note how peaks of activity follow expansionary phases of the business cycle (the 1890s, late 1920s, late 1950s and the 1970s), when affluence affords a leisured class the luxury of self-criticism. Moreover, the ideology challenges many western values, provoking both scorn and wrath from many interests within society and generating various criticisms.

◆ *Scientific contradiction.* When environmentalism attacks Enlightenment ideals of progress, science is used to attack science. Consequently, some scientists are hostile, doubting the doomsday scenarios.
◆ *Authoritarianism.* Despite an anarchic tone, the scale of reform required, and the potential for conflict, would call for a strong central authority. Some critics speak of 'eco-fascism'. Indeed, the Third Reich promoted wind technology, nature reserves, reforestation programmes and organic farming (Vincent 1992: 213–14), and Hitler himself was a vegetarian.
◆ *Inadequacy.* Although a green mantra exhorts us to 'think globally, act locally', this can hardly achieve the response demanded. Environ-mentalism lacks an adequate theory of overarching authority: a world government to match the scale of the crisis it forewarns of (Goodin 1992: 5).
◆ *Utopianism.* Some see the proposals, particularly of the deep ecologists, as utopian (or 'ectopian') dreams unrealizable in the real world.

Many see their interests threatened rather than served. Parties will not gain votes by offering, say, to outlaw the motor car. Having discovered Benidorm, who will forsake the Mediterranean sun for the Blackpool pleasure beach of their grandparents? Globalization adds a further dimension. Multinational corporations masterminding global expansion, and sometimes funding polit-icians and parties, will not sit back while economies are radically recast. At their head is the oil industry, now stronger economically than any country outside the G8. This awesome power was underlined at the UN's Kyoto Climate Summit in 1997, where progress was held back by US obstructionism. Attending in force was the self-styled Global Climate Coalition, representing oil and car interests and claiming that action on climate change would cause economic crisis. As a result, the agreed target for reducing greenhouse gas emissions fell far short of the EU's proposals and nowhere near the level recommended by many scientists.

Bill Clinton's successor in 2001, the Republican George W. Bush, was bank-rolled by US energy companies (the coal industry alone contributing $4 million in 1999/2000; *Guardian*, 16 March 2001). In the election campaign he trumped his Democratic opponent, the greenish Al Gore, by promising manda-tory reductions for carbon emissions. However, once installed in the White House he angered the EU, Japan and UN General Secretary Kofi Annan by backtracking.

In Eastern Europe environmentalists initially played a significant role in the overthrow of communism, the movement often becoming a focus for anti-Soviet sentiments. However, as western values gained ascendancy environmen-talists became marginalized (Tickle and Welsh 1998). Similarly, by 1998, the UK's New Labour government was showing signs of reneging on its traffic reduction promises, while supporting genetically modified foodstuffs.

Hence, environmentalism appears designed to offend more interests than it serves. However, environmentalists see their opponents as confusing short-term self-interest with the more important long-term interest of all. While we enjoy our cars and foreign holidays, we are storing up appalling catastrophe for future generations.

On the eve of the 2002 Earth Summit, the WWF Living Planet Report concluded that the earth's natural resources were being destroyed at such a rate that by 2050 two extra planets would be needed.

A Third Way?

For some critics, the traditional ideologies are unable to meet the challenge of the modern age, while environmentalism and feminism do not in themselves offer comprehensive solutions. The problems of the twenty-first century are multifaceted, with increasing cultural and economic globalization, the domin-ance of free markets and corporate wealth, a state of permanent technological revolution in communications and production, omnipresent ecological threats, the collapse of communism, and growing levels of inequality and international terrorism in an unstable multi-polar world.

The response has been to search for a new position that can draw upon both traditional and newer ideologies while rejecting their fundamentalist versions. Termed 'the **third way**', its charting has been to a considerable extent the work of British scholar Anthony Giddens (1998), who gave his ideas wider audience in the BBC Reith Lectures in 2000. The idea that there is a viable position between right and left is seductive and by no means new. New Liberalism had tempered individualism with collectivism and the fledgling Labour Party sought a moderate position between Marxism and capitalism. In the early post-war decades the social democracies took a stance between unbridled capitalism and Soviet communism.

Broadly a revision of social democracy, the third way recognizes the necessity and power of markets but aims to modify them with strategies for promoting equality and social inclusion. While classical social democracy was concerned to mitigate suffering resulting from capitalism, the third way sees welfare policies as a means of investing in human resources to benefit an entrepreneurial culture. Hence, for example, 'unemployment benefits...should carry an obligation to look actively for work' (Giddens 1998: 65). At the same time businesses must accept social responsibilities. Neo-Keynesian economist Will Hutton (1996) suggests that British shareholders are too demanding of quick returns so that companies cannot take a long-term view of development and growth. He argues for 'stakeholder capitalism' in which businesses look beyond their shareholders: to communities, the environment, their employees and customers. When investors unload their shares for short-term profit, government should levy a high capital gains tax. However, globalization limits the opportunity for political control over social and economic life in any detail (see chapter 4). The operations of transnational corporations, global finance, terrorism, international crime and ecological threats lie beyond the arm of national governments. Hence, the third way also calls for a cosmopolitan orientation, promoting a sense of world citizenship, and for global governance to regulate this global society.

Attempts to adopt third-way nostrums were apparent in the USA under President Clinton but less so under George W. Bush. They were part of the New Labour agenda and were in evidence throughout Europe, albeit to a more limited extent.

Whose interest?

On the face of it, the ideal version of the third way, as enunciated by writers such as Giddens, seeks synergy through a harmony of many interests. Indeed, one criticism is that it tries to 'take the politics out of politics'. However, as with all ideologies, the ideals become distorted in government policies. Thus, for example, Tony Blair's commitment to social justice appears to mean equality of *opportunity*, while Giddens's vision also emphasizes equality of *outcome*, a requirement calling for redistributive measures to protect society's inevitable 'losers' (Giddens 1998: 101–2; 1999). Again, by fostering an entrepreneurial culture, with mistrust of the public sector, weakened trade unions, 'welfare to

---

A radically meritocratic society would create deep inequalities of outcome, which would threaten social cohesion... A top tennis player or opera singer earns vastly more than one who isn't quite so good.

Anthony Giddens, *The Third Way* (1998: 101)

work' policies, a low-income-tax regime and so on, New Labour is seen by critics to be favouring the interests of capital beneath a cloak of third-way rhetoric.

An End of Ideology?

Some writers envisage an age when ideological debate will cease. Marx's vision of a communist future in which the state would wither away did this. More recently, Daniel Bell's *End of Ideology* (1960) captured the post-war spirit when western political parties converged around a Keynesian social democratic consensus. With the collapse of East European communism and the neoliberal ascendancy in the West, US academic Francis Fukuyama's (1992) *End of History* proclaimed a final triumph of liberalism. In the idea of the 'third way', critics again saw an implication that there was only 'one way' – in other words, yet another attempt to find an end of ideology.

Yet such theories prove fanciful. States did not wither under communism and the emergence of the New Right exposed the frailty of the western post-war consensus. The neoliberal triumph itself soon looked insecure. In Russia and Eastern Europe, people generally used to full employment soon learned that the gods of capitalism demand sacrificial offerings in the form of losers as well as winners, and some communist leaders found themselves back in favour. Moreover, the attack of 11 September 2001 came as a stark reminder that, with many millions inhabiting a globalizing but culturally diverse world, the western tradition did not enjoy an ideological monopoly.

Today we inhabit a world of increasing inequality, where the 26 most developed countries, with under 15 per cent of the world's population, live in comfort while another 3,000 million live in abject poverty, suffering disease and even starvation (see pp. 96–8). The unending quest for economic growth threatens ecological as well as social disaster. This is hardly a stable world with no room for ideological debate.

Key points

- Ideologies are theories about how people should live together in society.
- Although ideologies are often reflected in political parties, there is no consistent one-to-one identification.
- The western ideological tradition emerged from a dramatic break with the intellectual habits of past ages – the Enlightenment.
- Liberalism cherishes freedom from oppression. It spawned major revolutions which opened the modern era.
- Economic liberalism influenced the new discipline of political economy where the justification for limited government lay not in natural freedom but the quest for economic prosperity.

- New Liberalism perceived freedom as liberation from social and economic restrictions.
- Neoliberalism rose in the late 1970s and saw the free market as the *sine qua non* of the free society.
- Socialists reject the view of people as isolated individuals; they are part of a greater whole.
- Karl Marx, the key figure in socialism, believed socialist revolution was necessary to change society.
- Conservatism provides a rationale for resisting rationalist change.
- Feminism seeks sexual justice and an end to male domination.
- Environmentalism judges value in terms of the ecosystem as a whole.
- The third way represents the most recent attempt to reconcile conflicting traditions in a moderate consensus within capitalist society.
- Despite theories proclaiming an end to ideological politics, the potential for disagreement over the best way to organize life is probably limitless and fuels political action at all levels.

Review your understanding of the following terms and concepts

anarchy	hegemony	postmodernism
anthropocentric	'hidden hand'	pragmatism
capitalism	historical materialism	rationalism
collectivism	ideology	Reformation
communism	individualism	reformist socialism
conservatism	Leviathan	Renaissance
ecocentric	liberal democracy	revolutionary socialism
Enlightenment	liberalism	social democracy
environmentalism	Marxism	socialism
fascism	nationalism	state of nature
feminism	natural rights	third way
General Will	neoliberalism	utilitarianism

Assignment

Study the extract from Ben Elton's *Stark* and answer the following questions.

		Mark (%)
1	Which ideologies are brought to mind by the extract? Are they in harmony or conflict?	15
2	Why does Sly know so little about the waste disposal company?	15
3	How do you think the world had changed since the Pastel's honeymoon?	30
4	How can politics successfully address these problems?	40

As Sly entered the restaurant in Los Angeles some of his money was floating off the coast of Britain. Of course Sly was aware that a few of his bucks had found a temporary home as a majority holding in a Belgian waste disposal group, his brokers always consulted him before making a share purchase. But what did that tell Sly? nothing about reality. Certainly Sly knew about the company's collateral, its profit and loss curve, its disposable assets, its history on industrial relations and the chances of an injection of public funds should it hit the skids. But that was all he knew. He saw his investment purely and simply as a device by which to make money. What the company actually did was a matter of supreme indifference to him.

He did not know about Captain Robertson; he did not know about the great toilet irony; he did not know about the Pastel family on holiday...

Captain Robertson was a sad and bitter man. All his life he had wanted to be a master of a ship. And what sort of ship did he end up being master of? a sludger. Scarcely a dashing or romantic command.

'What do you do for a living mate?'

'I lug shit up the Thames and dump it in the North Sea.' Captain Robertson would occasionally try to cheer himself up. 'It's a rotten job but then people have to do toilet,' he would say to himself as yet another great steaming slick slid out of the bowels of his barge and began its slow journey back to Britain....

The Pastels had had a lovely day wandering around in the freezing rain and the whole family were getting peckish.

'Now then, kids,' said Mr Pastel, 'I'll tell you what we're going to have for our tea...Mussels, that's what, just like your mother and I had on our honeymoon.'

So they did, they had mussels and the whole family got the utter and total shits, because the mussels weren't just like on the honeymoon, since then the world had changed and the mussels with it.

Mussels and oysters feed by filtering tiny particles out of the sea water. These days that includes chemical wastes, agricultural poison and heavy metals. Also an awful lot of bacteria and viruses from human excreta, which cooking and cleaning does not always remove (cooking and cleaning the mussels that is, very few people cook and clean their excreta). Poor Mummy Pastel ended up with acute viral gastroenteritis and died, but we've all got to go sometime.

Sly didn't know Mrs Pastel, she didn't know him, but they were bound together in life and death by money.

Extract from Ben Elton, *Stark*, London, Sphere Books, 1989.

Questions for discussion

1 How important are ideologies to political parties today?
2 Outline the key stages in the evolution of the modern western ideological tradition.
3 Explain the principle of classical liberalism.
4 Contrast the view of freedom implicit in New Liberalism with that of the earlier liberals.
5 Outline Marx's critique of liberalism.
6 Contrast revolutionary socialism and reformist socialism.
7 'Conservatism presents a rationalist case against rationalism.' Discuss.

8   'Feminism does not present an alternative to liberalism or socialism; rather, it draws upon them, noting how they have fallen short of their ideals.' Discuss.
9   How far can a moderate form of environmentalism meet the ecological challenge facing today's world?
10   How valid is the claim that the 'third way' can end ideological debate?

Further reading

Barker, R. (1994) *Politics, Peoples and Government.*
Shows how the main lines of ideological debate have shifted during the twentieth century.

Crick, B. (1987) *Socialism.*
Leading figure of the intellectual left charts growth of various variants of socialism.

Gamble, A. (1981) *An Introduction to Modern Social and Political Thought.*
Places ideas in their historical contexts.

Giddens, A. (1998) *The Third Way: The Renewal of Social Democracy.*
Presented not as an 'end to politics' but as a strategy to renew the left.

Goodin, R. (1992) *Green Political Theory.*
Philosophical discussion of the green political programme, developing the 'green theory of value'.

Gray, J. (1995) *Enlightenment's Wake: Politics and Culture at the Close of the Modern Age.*
Stimulating set of essays examining major ideologies in a contemporary context.

Greer, G. (1970) *The Female Eunuch.*
An important and challenging book, which set the tone of much British debate.

Hayek, F. von (1976) *The Road to Serfdom* (first published 1944).
Classic and profound critique of the concept of the social state. The starting point of much of the New Right thought of the 1970s and 1980s.

Held, D. (1987) *Models of Democracy.*
The nature, application and importance of democracy from classical Athens to modern times.

Hobbes, T. (1985) *Leviathan,* Penguin Classics version edited by C. B. Macpherson (first published 1651).
One of the greatest works in the English language. Editor's introduction makes the ideas crystal clear.

Hutton, W. (1996) *The State We're In.*
Trenchant critique of the neoliberal 1980s and definitive statement of the concept of stakeholder capitalism.

Jaggar, A. (1983) *Feminist Politics and Human Nature.*
Influence of feminist thinking on political philosophy and political thought.

Oakeshott, M. (1962) *Rationalism in Politics and Other Essays.*
Classic by a modern-day conservative.

Scruton, R. (1980) *The Meaning of Conservatism.*
Essays by controversial contemporary thinker.

Smith, A. (1982) *The Wealth of Nations*, Penguin edition (first published 1776).
Classic statement of *laissez-faire* theory.

White, S. (ed.) (2001) *New Labour: The Progressive Future?*
Examines the dilemmas of social democracy in the contemporary world. Critique of the third way.

For light relief

Bertolt Brecht, *The Good Woman of Seczwan*.
Brilliant Marxist satire. The 'good person' is made bad when she tries to run a shop under the constraints of capitalism.

Deborah Cartmell, I. Q. Hunter, Heidi Kaye and Imelda Whelehan (eds) (1997) *Sisterhoods*.
Examines female relationships as portrayed in the (patriarchal) media, particularly Hollywood.

Terry Christiansen, *Rebel Politics: American political movies from* Birth of a Nation *to* Platoon.
Studies over 200 films. Notes that Hollywood films are suffused with conservative values.

Margaret Cook, *Lords of Creation: the Demented World of Men in Power*.
Critique of male politicians by the ex-wife of one of them.

Charles Dickens, *A Tale of Two Cities*.
Novel on the French Revolution by one of England's greatest writers.

Ben Elton, *Gridlock*.
A surreal vision illustrating corporate power.

J. B. Priestley, *An Inspector Calls*.
Makes the case for collectivism against individualism with ingenious theatricality.

R. Tressell, *The Ragged Trousered Philanthropists*.
Working-class protagonists ruminate on life. They are 'philanthropists' because it is their willingness to be poor that allows the rich to stay rich.

3

The Constitution: the Unwritten and the Unknowable

In this chapter we discuss the British constitution as a set of rules and prescriptions establishing the legal framework in which governments operate. This is not a simple matter; what is and is not part of the constitution is not always clear, and the opinions of experts can vary. Moreover, the constitution does not stand above politics; its content, the way it changes, and the criticisms people make of it are themselves manifestations of the political process. The chapter falls into four main sections. The first is concerned with the concept of a constitution, examining the importance of its study, identifying its sources and understanding its evolution. The second and third sections focus on two key constitutional principles – the limitation of government and the protection of individual rights. The final section addresses the important constitutional reform debate.

Seeking the Constitution

Defining the constitution

All kinds of organizations (from sports clubs and hamster societies to trade unions and political parties) have **constitutions**. They usually do two things: define the powers of those holding office and guarantee the rights of ordinary members. At the level of the state the principle remains the same. Hood Phillips describes a constitution as

> the system of laws, customs and conventions which define the composition and powers of organs of the state, and regulate the relations of the various state organs to one another and to the private citizen. (Hood Phillips 1987: 5)

However, another meaning of the term portrays the state constitution as a *description* of everything that takes place on a regularized basis in the process of government. This is a *behavioural* definition; found by discovery rather than laid down by prescription, it was the way in which the political essayist Walter Bagehot (1867) approached the study in his famous work *The English Constitution*.

For the most part, this chapter adopts the first definition – the constitution as a set of rules regularizing behaviour in the process of government. However, this focus does not mean that the distinction between the prescriptive and descriptive aspects of political life is ignored. Indeed, it is particularly import-ant to observe the dissonance between the two, for the belief that they coincide (that the prescriptive rules *describe* actual behaviour) has given the study of constitutions a bad name. Two games of cricket, although played according to the same rules, will be quite different and, although for the English politics might lack the nuances of the revered game, its reality reflects a myriad factors of personality and environment upon which the constitution can only remain silent.

Why study the constitution?

The inevitable discrepancy between prescribed and actual behaviour can render the study of formal constitutions a limited approach. This has led to another tradition of writing on British politics (following the 'behavioural revolution') which ignores the constitution altogether (Bellamy and Castiglione 1996: 413). However, this has as many dangers as an excessive constitutionalism; there are three good reasons for studying the rules of the game.

The constitution bestows authority Chapter 1 showed that politics is about power. In prescribing a framework the constitution bestows legitimacy on certain players. Thus, for example, the prime minister can send people to war and generals can have them shot if they refuse to fight, the police can arrest citizens and judges can send them to prison.

The constitution represents a political prize It is itself *part of* the political process. Many of those engaged in historic struggles have seen constitutional change as their ultimate goal. Thus, for example, after humbling King John, the barons insisted that the new order be enshrined in the Magna Carta at Runny-mede in 1215. The Glorious Revolution of 1688 led to the Act of Settlement in 1701, and the rising nineteenth-century bourgeoisie, the working class and the suffragettes all sought the constitutional goal of the right to vote. Many of today's most heated political debates – over Parliament, the monarchy, local government, secrecy, civil liberties, the electoral system, devolution, EU mem-bership, police powers and so on – are essentially constitutional. In fact, the particular features of the British constitution make it more a part of the political process than most (Prosser 1996: 473).

Magna Charta, and the Charter of the Forests signed by King John.

Source: Mary Evans Picture Library

The constitution shapes political consciousness Finally, even if the political analyst wishes to dismiss the constitution as a facade masking the reality of power, it remains important because of what people believe it to be. Thus, for example, even if people did not really possess effective freedom of speech (perhaps because of libel laws or access to the media), it interests political scientists that they *believed* themselves to have it; their consciousness shapes the political culture (see chapter 8).

Britain's elusive constitution

An American citizen can spend an edifying half-hour perusing the constitution on the bus or as a bedside companion. In contrast, the British constitution – the 'Great Ghost' – is notorious for its mysteriously unwritten manifestation. This is not strictly true because most of it certainly can be found in written form. However, the provisions are *uncodified*; they have not been drawn together in a single document grandly entitled 'The Constitution'. This is just as well, for if all the material was bound together, the British counterpart of the American patriot would be faced with something approaching the seven labours of Hercules.

The constitution takes this form because, unlike many other polities, including great ones such as France, Russia and the USA, Britain has never experienced a popular revolution in which a new class of rulers has wanted to erase all trace of the *ancien régime* and make a fresh start. There has been no defining moment comparable to the great Philadelphia convention of 1787, which established the US constitution, or the debates that led to West Germany's Basic Law in 1949.

Efficient and dignified elements

In looking at constitutions all may not be as it seems. In 1785 Paley noted how in 'the actual exercise of royal authority in England we see these formidable prerogatives dwindled into mere ceremonies', and in the nineteenth century Bentham and the great constitutional authority Dicey both charged the eighteenth-century constitutional chronicler Blackstone with being beguiled by what were no more than *fictions*. The passage of time has much to do with this; Bagehot likened the constitution to an elderly gentleman wearing the fashions of his youth, the outward finery belying the changes taking place beneath.

However, unlike the reforming radicals, Bagehot did not want to consign the outmoded garb to the shelves of the political curiosity shop. He discerned a special significance in empty 'ceremonies', arguing that all well-established constitutions required both **dignified** and **efficient elements**. The latter regulated those getting on with the job of ruling, defining what actually happens in the process of government. The dignified constitution fulfilled a vital function in generating authority. Bagehot believed it useless to expect the masses to understand the arcane mysteries of government but they could be kept happy if given pageantry at which to gawp and wonder. Modern political scientists agree with Bagehot that a political system must incorporate some mechanism for securing legitimacy.

The notion of dignified elements in a constitution means that we cannot ignore things that on the surface seem irrelevant to policy-making; they may be important in shaping mass attitudes. We must also be alert to the possibility that various state institutions may no longer play the part formally assigned to them. Indeed, we see throughout this book that imperceptible shifts from its efficient to its dignified pages leave the constitution in a state of permanent flux. Since 1970 Britain has seen a period of dramatic constitutional change, greater than that of any time since the eighteenth century (King 2001: 53).

> The lower orders, the middle orders, are still, when tried by what is the standard of the educated..., narrow-minded, unintelligent, incurious.
>
> Walter Bagehot, *The English Constitution* (1963 edn: 63)

Sources of the constitution

The constitution has traditionally been seen to flow from five sources: royal prerogative, statutes, common law, convention and authoritative opinion (figure 3.1). However, more recent developments have seen it affected by factors external to the domestic polity: the European Union (EU) and the European Convention on Human Rights (ECHR).

The royal prerogative This is a set of privileges enjoyed exclusively by monarchs since medieval times. *Personal* prerogatives are held by the monarch in

Figure 3.1
The British
constitution flows
from a number of
sources.

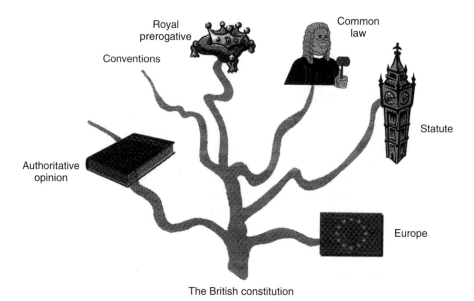

The British constitution

person and *political* prerogatives as head of state. The latter are the more
important to the efficient constitution and include the rights to declare war or
make peace, pardon criminals, dissolve Parliament and appoint ministers.
These, like the Crown Jewels, have been carefully preserved. However, with
the gradual erosion of the powers of the monarchy, today the **royal prerogative**
is in effect exercised by the Cabinet and prime minister.

Statutes These are no more than ordinary laws passed by Parliament. It is a
rather unnerving fact that a **statute** changing the constitution is not required to
undergo any special procedures, as is usually the case under written constitutions. Thus the monumentally important extensions of the franchise were all
made by politically motivated governments with little elevated thought of
democratic or constitutional principle. Similarly, in 1986 the government was
able to erase from the political map part of the local government system (see
chapter 19) to do little more than settle a political score. Again, the devolution
reforms of 1998 flowed from no more than the normal legislative process,
although referendums were held.

Common law This is based on precedent, from an accumulation of court
decisions in specific legal cases throughout history (see p. 646). **Common law**
is particularly useful for resolving ambiguities in other constitutional sources.
The two great virtues claimed for the common-law element are that it reflects
past wisdom and is independent of politics. On the other hand, it can be very
untidy, leaving judges to wrestle with a bewildering mass of precedents.
Recent governments have sought to rationalize much common law into new
statutes.

> Common law has developed many civil liberties. Examples from hundreds of important cases include the *Case of Proclamations* in 1610 (the king could not create new offences by proclamation), *Anderson v. Gorrie* in 1895 (the immunity of judges) and *Bradlaugh v. Gossett* in 1884 (the supremacy of Parliament over its internal affairs). As recently as 1999, in *DPP v. Jones*, the House of Lords, in reversing a conviction by the Salisbury magistrates under recent public order legislation, decided that a peaceful assembly on the verge of the A344 at Stonehenge did not constitute trespass.

Conventions These are regularly observed practices, having no legal basis and not enforceable in the courts. All states must evolve **constitutional conventions** to breathe life into their constitutions if they are to be flexible enough to survive. (The conventional elements of the constitution are the most easily changed.) However, in no other country have conventions been as important as in Britain, where they regulate the key processes of government. Democracy itself is based on conventions limiting the prerogative powers of the Crown and enabling them to be exercised by elected leaders. The Cabinet, the epicentre of government, is known only through convention.

In addition, there are many lesser conventions. For example, MPs never tell lies to the House of Commons or, to be more precise, no MP ever accuses another of having done so. In 1987, Labour MP Tam Dalyell broke with this, accusing Margaret Thatcher of lying over the Westland scandal. Consequently, he was 'named' by the Speaker; that is, barred from the chamber. There can be disagreement as to whether or not a convention actually exists. Thus, for example, John Major argued that there was a convention that prime ministers did not appear before parliamentary select committees.

> **Excuse my parliamentary language**
>
> MPs are not supposed to accuse fellow members of lying or of being drunk, or to use unparliamentary language, but according to ex-MP Matthew Parris (1996) some insults have managed to slip past the Speaker's ear, including the following:
>
> - 'devoid of any truth'
> - 'cooking the figures'
> - 'shameless lack of candour'
> - 'the attention span of a gerbil'
> - 'the hamster from Bolsover'
> - 'a sex-starved boa constrictor' (of Margaret Thatcher)
> - 'shut up, you old windbag'

Although conventions are the most obviously 'unwritten' part of the constitution, they are probably the most *written about* because there is more need for guidance where the formal law is silent. This leads to the next source.

Authoritative opinion It is considered appropriate that learned works of great authority and wisdom be regarded as legitimate constitutional sources, though there may be difficulty in defining precisely what is meant by authority.

Statutes override all other domestic constitutional sources. Some, such as the 1689 Bill of Rights (defining the relationship between Crown and Parliament and ratifying the 1688 Glorious Revolution) and the 1701 Act of Settlement (determining the succession), are extremely venerable. More recently, there have been the Parliament Acts of 1911 and 1949 (determining the relationship between the two Houses of Parliament) and the 1963 Peerage Act (enabling peers to renounce their titles). In addition to statutes, and having much the same character and force, are certain revered historical documents, the most notable of which is the Magna Carta.

Great age is taken as important because it may be presumed that ancient texts distilled the wisdom otherwise lost. Examples of such treasures include, among others, Fitzherbert's *Abridgement* of 1516, Hawkins's *Pleas of the Crown* (1716) and Foster's *Crown Cases* (1762). Of course not all authorities agree; indeed it is in their nature to be disputatious. The very belief that one can discover the constitution from the authorities of the past is itself open to question and was challenged by the Philosophical Radicals. An oft-quoted authority is Walter Bagehot, perhaps the one who first 'discovered' the constitution. Peter Hennessy (1994), one of his modern counterparts, argues that, before Bagehot wrote, there was no constitution that could be recognized or apprehended as a living and working thing.

The European factor The EU is also a source of the modern constitution, the scale of which was perhaps not fully recognized when Britain entered the EEC in 1973. It affects the powers of all domestic institutions since the EU comprises supranational institutions with law-making powers. If a legal dispute containing a European element reaches the House of Lords (the final Court of Appeal), there must be an application to the European Court of Justice (ECJ, the EU court) for a ruling. Lower courts may also seek ECJ guidance. Moreover, the courts assume that in all UK legislation it was Parliament's intention to be consistent with EU law (unless an expressed statement to the contrary is made). Hence, in *Pickstone* v. *Freemans PLC* (1987), regulations amending the Equal Pay Act were interpreted in a manner different from their literal meaning, to comply with EU law. A further constitutional strand comes from the ECHR, incorporated into British law in the 1998 Human Rights Act (see pp. 73–9).

Change and development

All constitutions are political but Britain's is particularly so because it may be changed as part of the normal process of politics. This is potentially threatening because, following the game metaphor, it is impossible to play if the rules are not fixed. On the other hand, a constitution cannot work if it is entirely inflexible and, even in the USA where its veneration rouses religious fervour (there have been only twenty-six formal **constitutional amendments**), small changes occur continually through judicial decisions and the establishment of

---

Amending a written constitution

Amendments to the US constitution must be first proposed and then ratified. Proposals may be made by two-thirds majorities in both houses of Congress voting separately, or by a national convention called by Congress at the request of two-thirds of the state legislatures. Ratification requires a vote of three-quarters of the state legislatures or state conventions in three-quarters of the states. However, written constitutions need not be inflexible. Since 1809 Sweden's has been amended over 200 times – like the workshop hammer, with several new heads and shafts, one wonders whether it is any longer the same thing.

---

conventions. However, written constitutions are usually given a propensity to resist change; they are **entrenched** through deliberately cumbersome processes of amendment. Does this mean the British constitution is unstable and but a flimsy defence of citizens' rights? There is some truth in this, though it contains both conservative and flexible elements.

Art or Nature: are constitutions machines or organisms? There are two broad theoretical views on constitutional change: the mechanistic and the organic. The former sees constitutions as machines designed to give people the kind of government they desire. The English philosophers Thomas Hobbes and John Locke belong within this tradition, though it was the Philosophical Radicals who really addressed the issue of *rational* constitutional reform. The essence of their position was that, if a constitution was to serve the needs of a people at any particular time, they should deduce it from first principles. The principle was utilitarianism (see pp. 30–1). For this school of thought statute law is the obvious constitutional source.

While the mechanical contrivance of political inventors has died away...the goodly tree of British freedom selecting from the kindly soil and assimilating its fit nutriment still increases its stately bulk...Outliving the storms and vicissitudes of centuries, deeply rooted in the habits and affections of the people, it spreads far and wide its hospitable shade.

W. E. Hearn, *The Government of England* (1868)

In contrast, the **organic** view argues that a constitution grows and develops naturally like a living organism; for thinkers of this school it is a thing of untouchable beauty. Frequent references liken the British constitution to a great tree. Blackstone's view of the constitution, with its veneration of the past, would belong in this category and the cover of Sir Ivor Jennings's *The British Constitution* (1966) is actually adorned with a picture of a spreading oak.

The organic idea has a distinguished pedigree, extending from the Ancient Greeks. Hegel and T. H. Green also conceived the state in organic terms, while Edmund Burke suggested that the constitution should be treated with awe as a repository of the collective wisdom of the ages. He argued for

> a presumption in favour of any settled scheme of government against any untried project, that a nation has long existed and flourished under it. (Burke 1782: 146)

This distinction is related to the question of the moral justification for constitutions, leading into an important area of philosophical debate centring on a distinction drawn between positive law and natural law.

Positive law is laid down by human agency, say a government or a monarch, or through the accumulation of customs. Prominent among the positivists was the Philosophical Radical John Austin (1790–1859), who saw law as nothing more than the commands of the sovereign. Bentham was himself influenced by Austin. Some find this approach (legal positivism) unsatisfactory because it lacks a deeper justification.

Natural law is supposedly derived from something more fundamental than the dictates of any earthly sovereign. This idea can be traced back to the Ancient Greek philosophers, particularly the Stoics, whose ideas were adopted by the Romans when seeking a legal system that could extend over their empire independently of the customary laws of different lands. Natural law can be said to derive from an expression of the will of God, though some philosophers, including Hugo Grotius (1583–1645) and Immanuel Kant (1724–1804), argued that this is virtually a special kind of positive law with God as the sovereign. Others argue that it is derived from the idea of certain 'natural rights'. However, this introduces the problem of what these rights actually are. For Locke they included security of life, limb and property, and the US constitution begins by speaking grandiloquently of certain 'inalienable rights'.

Development and change in the British constitution have shown both organic and mechanistic characteristics. Common law and conventions have evolved gradually, while statute law has facilitated some great leaps, such as the extensions of the franchise. The two contrasting views are marked by more than a dispassionate search for the truth; they have been used to support political positions. For Burke's followers (the landowners) the organic and mystical view provided a basis for resisting the forces threatening to erode their privileges, while for the rising industrial bourgeoisie, attempting to shape the constitution in their own interests, the radical mechanistic view was irresistible.

Limiting Government

The essence of **constitutional government** is **limited government**. This is held to be necessary because there can never be any guarantee that rulers will not exercise power in their own self-interest. Most political thinkers have agreed that power corrupts. This limitation can be secured by other institutions, the law, or popular control, and is sought through three fundamental principles: the **separation of powers**, the **rule of law** and **parliamentary sovereignty**. The first was regarded by the French jurist Montesquieu, in his *L'Esprit des Lois* (1748), as the key to British liberty. The last two were seen by Dicey as the twin pillars of the constitution (1959: xvii), a view that has continued to colour much constitutional writing (Harden and Lewis 1986: 4).

The separation of powers

The idea of dispersing or separating power between various institutions so that they will curtail each other's actions is based on the theory that there are distinct functions of government, each of which can be entrusted to a different institution. Montesquieu followed Locke in arguing that the best safeguard of freedom was to ensure that those making the laws (the **legislature**) should not also be those with the power of carrying them out (the **executive**). Similarly, those enforcing the laws (the **judiciary**) should be independent. The founding fathers of the American constitution were deeply impressed by the doctrine and today the executive (president), legislature (Congress) and judiciary are not only separate but have extensive power over each other; the constitution imposes 'checks and balances'. It is not unusual for the president to be thwarted in his policy ambitions by both Congress and the Supreme Court; indeed, at times the system seems in danger of grinding to a complete standstill as vetoes are exercised like power-assisted brakes. George W. Bush found himself with a Republican House and a Democrat Senate. In December 2001 this divided Congress killed off his recovery package in the wake of the 11 September terrorist attack. Further separation is inherent in the US constitution through its federal structure, apportioning jurisdiction between the federal government and the states.

> The accommodation of all powers ... in the same hands ... may justly be pronounced the very definition of tyranny.
>
> James Madison (1751–1836; one of America's 'founding fathers'), in *The Federalist* (1788)

In February 1989, John Tower, the Defence Secretary nominee of President George Bush senior, was vetoed by the Senate Armed Services Committee because of his reputation as a hard-drinking womanizer with too cosy a relationship with defence contractors.

In fact Montesquieu was wrong about the British constitution. Bagehot was to stress that its 'efficient secret' was not a separation but a *fusion* of powers (figure 3.2) through the Cabinet – heading both the executive and the legislature. Furthermore, the Lord Chancellor is head of the judiciary, and a member of the Cabinet (in the happy position of receiving two salaries) and of the legislature, when he sits on the 'Woolsack' as the Speaker of the House of Lords. The appointment of Derry Irvine in 1997 threw the anomalies of the

Figure 3.2 A fusion rather than a separation of powers.

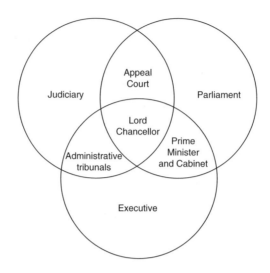

position into stark relief. As head of the chambers in which Tony Blair had worked as a fledgling barrister, Lord Irvine was closer to the prime minister than any previous incumbent. And not only was he chairing cabinet committees, he openly engaged in party fundraising when, in February 2001, he called upon members of a Labour lawyers' association to donate £200 each to the party. This increasingly political role heightened debate on the office itself. To critics it had become untenable and it was argued that judicial appointments should be passed to an independent commission, the Lord Chief Justice should head the judiciary and the Lord Chancellor's role as a judge should come to an end (Woodhouse 2001b).

To increase the fusion, the House of Lords, as well as being part of the legislature, is the final Court of Appeal. The judiciary also makes laws through the doctrine of *precedent* (see p. 646). Moreover, the growth of a myriad administrative tribunals means that the executive acts widely in a judicial capacity and, through the practice of *delegated legislation*, is able to make laws (see p. 395). Consequently there is little scope for applying checks and balances. The executive is virtually unimpeded by Parliament because of party discipline (see pp. 388–91) and the courts have no authority to veto legislation in the manner of the US Supreme Court.

However, Britain is seeing an increased level of judicial constraint. Although a judicial decision disliked by the government can be reversed by a new statute, the courts may consider the legality of executive action through the **judicial review** process. This was used increasingly from the 1980s (see p. 648) (Klug et al. 1996: 548; Woodhouse 2001a: 223–5). As home secretaries increasingly tried to influence sentencing policy, the principle of the separation of powers was adduced by Lord Chief Justice Peter Taylor in defence of judicial independence. The 1998 Human Rights Act promises further developments and increases both judges' power and the need for judicial independence. Existing legislation, new legislation, administrative practice and common law in breach of the ECHR may all now be challenged in British courts.

The rule of law

This principle holds that the law is above the whims of any individual ruler. Lying at the heart of the idea of constitutional government, it can be traced back to the Ancient Greeks. It has been brought to bear throughout history wherever people have sought to resist arbitrary rule or despotism; in the Middle Ages the notion that the monarch was subject to God and the law provided a fundamental rationale for challenging royal absolutism. Dicey (1959) expressed the rule of law in terms of three precepts.

- No person can be punished except for a distinct breach of the law.
- No person, of whatever rank, is above the ordinary law.
- The general provisions of the constitution are the result of decisions made by an independent judiciary in deciding particular cases, rather than of declarations by rulers.

However, these break down in practice.

- Innocent people may be detained on the basis of police suspicion that they *might* commit a crime.
- There are various categories subject to different laws. For example: judges, MPs and diplomats are accorded extra privileges; the police have special powers and members of the armed forces are subject to martial law.

In Britain, the practical meaning of the rule of law has varied throughout history (Harden and Lewis 1986: 8) but today it largely holds that the government will operate within the law. This is not to say that it, or its agents, such as the secret services, do not sail close to the wind. In July 1993, the House of Lords in its appeal capacity ruled Home Secretary Kenneth Baker in contempt of court over the deportation of an asylum seeker in 1991 in defiance of a court order. The government had claimed that the law had no power by injunction or contempt proceedings against a minister acting in an official capacity, but the Court asserted that such a proposition would reverse the result of the Civil War! However, the rule of law is logically incompatible with the second of Dicey's great 'pillars' – the doctrine of the sovereignty of Parliament.

Parliamentary sovereignty

This doctrine enshrines the outcome of the prolonged constitutional struggle culminating in the Glorious Revolution of 1688, when the Bill of Rights (1689) set out the supremacy that Parliament had gained over the king through a succession of common-law decisions dating from the fourteenth century. However, not until the nineteenth century, following the great Reform Acts that changed the political system out of all recognition, was the principle formally enunciated by Dicey as the one fundamental (or entrenched) element in the British constitution. Parliamentary sovereignty entailed

> ...the right to make or unmake any law whatever; and...that no person or body is recognised by the law of England as having a right to override or set aside the legislation of Parliament. (Dicey 1959: 39–40)

From this follow two principles: that the courts have no power to veto legislation and that no Parliament is bound by existing laws. As Bill Walker MP told the Commons in February 1993: 'If we get something wrong, as we often do, we can rectify it the following year' (quoted in Klug et al. 1996: 537).

At the time Dicey wrote, the generally accepted doctrine of **sovereignty** was that of Austin, that every state must contain some body with ultimate power. This carried no particular moral justification, but Dicey distinguished between two forms of sovereignty – *legal* and *political* – asserting the moral supremacy of the latter. Thus the sovereignty of Parliament was derived not from its inheritance of the absolute powers of the monarch, nor from God, but from the people.

Today, membership of the EU poses questions for the doctrine. British courts must give effect to laws emanating from Brussels and, in any conflict, these take precedence over those of Westminster. Although such conflict has generally been over technical matters, fundamental questions were raised in 1988 when the British government passed an Act to prevent foreigners from registering ships as British (permitted under the 1894 Merchant Shipping Act) in order to use British fishing quotas. In *R* v. *Secretary of State for Transport ex parte Factortame* (1990) this was challenged by Spanish fishermen as contrary to Community law. A decision of the European Court of Justice effectively suspended part of a British statute.

Incorporation of the ECHR through the 1998 Human Rights Act also limits parliamentary sovereignty. While the courts are not empowered to strike down legislation, they are able to declare a specific Act to be in breach of the Convention and refer it back to Parliament. Parliament's Human Rights Committee scrutinizes new bills and the ministers introducing them are required to produce human rights statements; any breaches must be debated. Should these occur, a special fast-track procedure is available to amend the legislation. Judgements of the European Court of Human Rights must also be considered. Thus, in 2000 the court considered that UK legislation prohibiting consensual non-violent sexual acts between more than two men in private infringed their rights and should be amended.

Further restrictions on sovereignty are associated with devolution, which has given the UK a more federal character (see chapter 6). The Westminster and provincial bodies must now accept judicial ruling in any conflict over their respective powers.

However, we shall see in chapter 13 that the greatest challenge to parliamentary sovereignty comes not from judges, power-hungry Eurocrats or a dissident Celtic fringe but from the political dominance of the British executive.

Protecting Individual Rights

In addition to regulating government a constitution also guarantees **civil rights** – freedoms and protections for citizens. The two functions are not really distinct; the quantity and quality of personal freedom offered is linked with the nature and degree of the state's authority. Many written constitutions include positive guarantees of fundamental freedoms. In 1787, the framers of the US constitution neglected this and ten amendments were passed subsequently as the Bill of Rights. This guaranteed freedom of worship, speech, assembly, and to petition for redress of grievances; freedom from deprivation of life, liberty or property by unlawful means; freedom from cruel or unusual punishments; and security from unreasonable search of persons or houses and private papers and effects.

However, in Britain laws protecting basic freedoms were for long nothing more than the ordinary laws of the land. Granted only *negatively*, rights were not conferred by the constitution, they were merely not withheld. People could do anything not expressly prohibited; the freedoms were *residual* and governments were free to impose any restrictions they wished.

Of course, under certain circumstances people may be quite happy to relinquish freedom. Hobbes argued that we should all submit to the *Leviathan* in order to be safe from each other (see p. 26), and in his *Essay on Liberty*, J. S. Mill argued that one person's freedom should be permitted only in so far as it did not harm others. Much modern legislation (e.g. libel laws limiting freedom of expression) reflects this principle. However, in Britain there was nothing to prevent governments enacting harsh laws, and this led to calls from libertarian groups and leading lawyers such as lords Scarman and Lestor for an entrenched US-style **Bill of Rights**. This came a step closer with the 1998 Human Rights Act, although the ECHR was incorporated in modified form.

Although it could be said that the Act did not make any new rights available, it made them much easier to claim at all levels of the judicial system. Before this, aggrieved citizens could petition the European Court of Human Rights at Strasbourg, a journey that had proved too long and costly for many (though the

---

The Glorious Revolution

The Bill of Rights following the Glorious Revolution is not like those of France or the USA. Conferring various privileges upon MPs, it is concerned with the rights of Parliament in relation to the monarch, rather than those of citizens in relation to the state.

Court had found British governments of left and right in violation of the Convention more often than any other signatory state; Klug et al. 1996: 538).

Fundamental rights

The significance of the new Human Rights Act in a state that has resisted such a move for centuries cannot be underestimated (Klug 2000). There are a variety of rights with importance to politics in the ECHR. The right to a fair trial (Article 6) would mean that the use of public interest immunity certificates (as in the Matrix Churchill case) would be outlawed. The right to privacy (Article 8) was a new right for UK citizens and would rule against Section 28 of the Local Government Act prohibiting the promotion of homosexuality in schools. On the other hand, a right to privacy could also threaten press freedom. In a political culture renowned for secrecy, the right to freedom of information (Article 10) promised great significance. One surprising possibility might be a challenge to the thirty-year rule for non-disclosure of public records. However, in the case of David Shayler, an ex-MI5 officer prosecuted under the Official Secrets Act, the courts rejected his application to use a defence of public interest in September 2001 on the grounds that the need to protect national security overrode the Human Rights Act.

Perhaps the most significant rights bearing on politics concern freedom of the *person*, of *speech*, and of *association* and *assembly*.

Freedom of the person The right to go about one's business has long been regarded as a central pillar of the temple of liberty. In the eighteenth-century case of *Leach* v. *Money and Others* (1765) it was held that a general warrant for the arrest of unnamed persons was illegal and void. In *Liversidge* v. *Anderson and Another* (1942) it was held that 'every imprisonment is *prima facie* unlawful, and that it is for a person directing imprisonment to justify his act'. People who have been wrongfully imprisoned have a range of remedies available in civil and common law, on grounds such as malicious prosecution, false imprisonment, assault and battery. In addition there is the classic guarantee of individual liberty in Britain – the writ of habeas corpus – enabling anyone confined to demand to be brought before the court for a just trial. This has served a variety of purposes, including removing apprentices from cruel masters, freeing slaves and establishing that a husband has no right to detain his wife against her will. To these may now be added freedom of life and personal liberty in Articles 2 and 5 of the ECHR. In Scotland, applicants detained under the 1999 Mental Health Act claimed that their rights had been infringed under Article 5 but the courts decided that the safety of the community came first (*The Times*, 21 June 2000).

However, the executive has the authority to limit freedom of the person by taking on unrestrained powers of arrest on the basis of great national emergency. The 1939 Emergency Powers (Defence) Act allowed the home secretary to detain anyone whom he 'has reasonable cause to believe' may be of 'hostile origin or association'. All ministers must show is that they acted in good faith. Under emergencies, even habeas corpus can be suspended, as was the case, for example, in the fight against the Chartists (see p. 242). The policy of internment in Northern Ireland, the operation of the 'sus' law against young blacks and the detention of asylum-seekers have all represented further serious infringements of freedom of the person. In a matter of a few days before Easter 1996, the Home Secretary, fearful of IRA activity, was able to give the police new stop-and-search powers under the Prevention of Terrorism Act. The police also have powers of arrest and the use of force at airports under the 1989 Prevention of Terrorism (Temporary Provisions) Act. In addition, there are stop-and-search powers under such legislation as the 1984 Police and Criminal Evidence Act, the 1991 Emergency Provisions Act and the 1994 Criminal Justice and Public Order Act. Moreover, the protection of the Human Rights Act began to look flimsy when, in November 2001, Home Secretary Blunkett placed an order before Parliament to ignore Article 5 of the ECHR, which bans detention without trial.

Freedom of speech It is clear that in a democracy the freedom to express political opinion is fundamental; throughout the world the absence of such a right is held to be one of the most visible symptoms of oppression. Various cases have given this freedom to those such as political speakers, publishers, newspaper editors and pamphleteers. Freedom of expression is guaranteed in Article 10 of the ECHR. Yet in Britain the freedom has been restricted in various ways. Individuals are protected from verbal and written assault through the laws of slander and libel, while in the wake of the 11 September attack, Home Secretary Blunkett proposed enacting legislation that would have made incitement to religious hatred a criminal offence. There are also laws on obscenity, though the impossibility of deciding what exactly is obscene often produces ludicrous scenarios, as in the *Lady Chatterley's Lover* trial.

The most serious restrictions on freedom of speech tend to come from the agencies of the state. The repressive apparatus, though often lying dormant, carries a formidable potential, which is thrown into starkest relief in the reporting of politics by the media and the vexed question of government secrecy (see pp. 472–80). The 1986 Public Order Act could well fall foul of the Human Rights Act, as could ancient laws on indecency, criminal libel, blasphemy and sedition. Article 8 of the ECHR upholds a right to privacy for individuals and in December 2000 film stars Catherine Zeta-Jones and Michael Douglas succeeded in a High Court challenge against intrusive journalism by *Hello* magazine.

Freedom of association and assembly Politics is essentially about collective action through associations such as parties, trade unions and pressure groups. However, the constitution has placed considerable restrictions on this. There have been, for example, the crimes of conspiracy and public nuisance, and the common-law offences of riot, rout and unlawful assembly, later codified in the 1936 Public Order Act. Further restrictions were enacted in the 1986 Public

Legitimate
violence:
policing an NUS
demo against
student loans,
November 1988

Photo: *The Socialist*

Order Act, the 1994 Criminal Justice and Public Order Act and the 1998 Crime and Disorder Act. The police hold extensive powers in the event of a breach of the peace, or even the suspicion that such a breach might occur. Under normal circumstances the authorities claim to exercise their discretion in a liberal manner, but within this velvet glove is the clenched fist of state repression (see chapter 21). People can be bound over to keep the peace, road blocks can stop movement (as in the miners' strike of 1984/5) and powers to disperse crowds can curtail rights of assembly, including events such as rock festivals. In 1988, workers at the Government Communications Headquarters at Cheltenham lost their right to trade union membership (restored nine years later). Indeed, trade unions have been particular victims, with Combinations Acts and various common-law decisions in the nineteenth century restricting their growth. Not until the 1875 Conspiracy and Protection of Property Act were strikes effectively legalized and the 1906 Trade Disputes Act reversed the anti-union Taff Vale Judgment.

However, freedom of assembly becomes a positive right under Article 11 of the ECHR, with widespread implications for police and local authority powers to ban marches and demonstrations under the Public Order Acts. It would also question the imposition of bail conditions that prevent people awaiting trial from attending meetings and demonstrations.

Towards a rights culture?

> A citizen's person or property may not be interfered with – unless it may. A person is not liable for what he speaks or writes – unless he is. No liability attaches to one who takes part in a public meeting – unless it does.
>
> O. Hood Phillips, *Constitutional and Administrative Law* (1987: 39–40)

In Britain, individual rights have been so hedged with qualifications, ambiguities and what has been praised as the 'glorious uncertainty of the law' that it was difficult to know what one may actually do without impediment. In 1995, the UN Human Rights Committee, following its fourth periodic review, concluded that Britain failed to secure basic civil and political rights and provided inadequate remedy where rights were violated (Klug et al. 1996: 537). The government's defence was that the report failed to appreciate the subtle glories of the system (Weir and Boyle 1997).

Britain has not developed a rights culture. As part of the pattern of deference, strong government and public order have been elevated over individual liberties and the rights of minorities (Weir and Boyle 1997: 129). Such views are buoyed by much tabloid journalism. Attitude surveys penetrating beyond the drawing rooms of Hampstead and Islington reveal greater interest in *social* rights (education, health care) than *civil and political* ones. In one poll, fewer than a third of respondents supported the principle of a defendant's right to silence (Weir and Boyle 1997: 32–3). A MORI poll for the *News of the World* (24 Sept. 2001) after the 11 September attack showed 85 per cent of the population in favour of tougher measures on all fronts. Moreover, popular xenophobia produces resistance to 'foreign' notions of rights. This may be stimulated by tabloid jingoism and a revolt against 'meddling judges'.

Hence, the incorporation of the ECHR in the Human Rights Act (in effect, a Bill of Rights) offers the possibility of a cultural sea change. Will it lead to the establishment of a 'rights' culture in Britain? This remains open to question. Some outcomes will undoubtedly prove unpopular with government and people. For example, in 1999 the European Court of Human Rights ruled that the length of time Thompson and Venables (the youths who had murdered the toddler Jamie Bulger) could be detained at Her Majesty's pleasure should not be determined by the home secretary. Following this, in October 2000, Lord Chief Justice Lord Woolf recommended their early release, resulting in tabloid outrage and fears that it could lead to the release of 'Moors Murderer' Myra Hindley.

Although New Labour ushered in the Human Rights Act, its strongly centralized style, tabloid sensitivity and neoliberal agenda left reason for apprehension. Even 'old Labour' had been ambivalent in government. Although ratifying the ECHR in 1951 and granting citizens the right to petition Strasbourg, it had not incorporated the Convention and fought shy of a domestic Bill of Rights. It could be argued that it was the influence of John Smith rather than Blair that set the 1998 reforms in train and New Labour's 'tough on crime' mantra had seen it supporting many Conservative measures that violated the ECHR. Thus, in 1996 it had supported a Police Bill allowing state bugging and burgling without prior judicial approval, which reversed common-law principles respected since the eighteenth century. Moreover, the espousal of US 'communitarian' thinking emphasized *duties* of citizenship at the expense of *rights* and carried strongly authoritarian overtones (Klug 1997). This was exemplified by, for example, curfews on the young and Blair's advice to employers during the 1998 World Cup to sack football hooligans.

The 11 September terrorist attack demonstrated how easily freedoms could be removed. Within days Parliament was debating a draconian list of anti-terrorism measures, including: the power to monitor emails, the admission as court evidence of transcripts of phone conversations bugged by MI5, rules compelling banks to release customers' details, the power to seize the assets of suspected terrorists, a fast-track extradition system, and the scrapping of certain appeal rights of people refused entry into Britain. Longer-term plans included proposals for identity cards, euphemistically named 'entitlement cards'.

Continuing debate on this topic centres on the delicate executive–judicial balance. New Labour, buoyed by massive majorities in 1997 and 2001, did not appear keen to bow to a bewigged superior authority in areas such as sentencing policy.

> It is elected representatives who are held to account by the electorate, and it is they who should be the prime protectors of our rights rather than having to rely on the judicial system.
>
> Home Secretary David Blunkett (*Guardian*, 24 Sept. 2001)

Hence, despite the enormous potential for cultural change from incorporation of the ECHR, the full impact cannot be known until the dust settles in that uncertain constitutional territory between what is written and what actually happens. Far from emancipating citizens it may prove an exercise in gesture politics. Reform organizations such as Charter88 call for a Human Rights Commission to promote public understanding, provide advice to Parliament and public authorities and assist individuals. Without this there is a danger that the impact of the ECHR will be largely limited to arcane judicial debate. However, the government has shown no enthusiasm for such a Commission. For reformers, only constitutional earth movements will produce the soil for a rights culture. At the heart of this is a written constitution.

A Written Constitution?

Despite the praises sung to the mysterious virtues of the British constitution, its unwritten manifestation is not universally acclaimed. Some argue that the twin guarantees of limited government and individual rights would be far safer if placed beyond the hand of the government of the day through entrenchment. A written constitution would mean the end of parliamentary supremacy because certain laws would be so fundamental that they could no longer be changed by normal legislative means and parliaments would be bound by any constitutional amendments made under their predecessors. Moreover, new laws would be subject to judicial scrutiny to ensure their constitutionality. In addition, the executive could be made subject to effective checks by Parliament.

Various other provisions could be made, covering any aspect of government – fixing the powers of local government to reduce meddling by the centre, setting out rules for the cabinet system, fixing the lengths of parliaments and limiting the use of political patronage. A genuine Freedom of Information Act could guarantee people's right to know and a home-grown Bill of Rights could meet UK needs more fittingly than did incorporation of the ECHR. Reformers argue that such change would release British people from the grip of their monarchical past. No longer subjects claiming privileges from the powerful, they would become citizens legally entitled to demand rights.

However, there is a case for the unwritten constitution that has served Britain for centuries. In the first place, any attempt to codify all the relevant material into a document of manageable size would rob it of its infinite subtlety. Moreover, the great virtue of flexibility would be sacrificed: no longer could changes take place imperceptibly to accommodate social developments. With the loss of parliamentary sovereignty would go the sovereignty of the people; non-elected organs of the state (Lords, monarchy, judiciary) would be able to thwart the wishes of an elected government. Judges and lawyers would become overpowerful, their fingers stained by the acrid alchemy of politics as they thwart the designs of elected politicians. Moreover, throughout the world evidence suggests that written constitutions do not work with anything like the precision implied by the legalists; serious abuses of freedom take

CHARTER88

We have been brought up in Britain to believe that we are free: that our Parliament is the mother of democracy; that our liberty is the envy of the world; that our system of justice is always fair; that the guardians of our safety, the police and security services, are subject to democratic, legal control; that our civil service is impartial; that our cities and communities maintain a proud identity; that our press is brave and honest.

Today such beliefs are increasingly implausible. The gap between reality and the received ideas of Britain's "unwritten constitution" has widened to a degree that many find hard to endure. Yet this year we are invited to celebrate the third centenary of the "Glorious Revolution" of 1688, which established what was to become the United Kingdom's sovereign formula. In the name of freedom, our political, human and social rights are being curtailed while the powers of the executive have increased, are increasing and ought to be diminished.

A process is underway which endangers many of the freedoms we have had.

The time has come to demand political, civil and human rights in the United Kingdom. The first step is to establish them in constitutional form, so that they are no longer subject to the arbitrary diktat of Westminster and Whitehall.

We call, therefore, for a new constitutional settlement which would:

Enshrine, by means of a Bill of Rights, such civil liberties as the right to peaceful assembly, to freedom of association, to freedom from discrimination, to freedom from detention without trial, to trial by jury, to privacy and to freedom of expression.

Subject executive powers and prerogatives, by whomsoever exercised, to the rule of law.

Establish freedom of information and open government.

Create a fair electoral system of proportional representation.

Reform the upper house to establish a democratic, non-hereditary second chamber.

Place the executive under the power of a democratically renewed parliament and all agencies of the state under the rule of law.

Ensure the independence of a reformed judiciary.

Provide legal remedies for all abuses of power by the state and the officials of central and local government.

Guarantee an equitable distribution of power between local, regional and national government.

Draw up a written constitution, anchored in the idea of universal citizenship, that incorporates these reforms.

place in countries that boast model bills of rights. Finally, it can be argued that the entire exercise would be futile because the reality of politics is shaped by the economic power structure, which would be little affected by any redrawing of the constitutional architecture. Thus, for example, the so-called Nolan rules, designed to place constitutional reins on public appointments, did little to remove the charge of cronyism under New Labour (see p. 588).

The political debate: limited government or social rights?

Constitutional reform is never out of the realm of the political. In December 1988, Charter88 was established to call for a range of constitutional reforms. Although bringing together figures from many points along the political spectrum, amongst the major parties only the Liberal Democrats give wholehearted support for a written constitution; both Labour and Conservatives have been more vociferous in opposition than in government. Moreover, the motives of left and right can be quite different.

The call from the right: limited government The right is haunted by the spectre of 'big government', which is seen as directly opposed to the minimal government desired by capitalist interests and inherent in the nineteenth-century liberal constitution. Extensions to the role of the state are portrayed as the first steps along the dark road to totalitarianism. The rights that the liberal constitution protects are civil and political, rather than social.

During the 1960s and 1970s, when Labour began to look like a party of government, the right became preoccupied with the idea of a written constitution to curb the power of a government that was an 'elective dictatorship'. The advent of the Thatcher government in 1979 produced the opportunity to put ideas into practice, but fears for the liberty of the 'man in the street' seemed to evaporate. The state was certainly rolled back in some respects, but its repressive arm was extended to suppress any rising social unrest resulting from neoliberal economic policies (Ewing and Gearty 1990). Indeed, a free-market society requires a particularly strong state and this was maintained by subsequent New Labour governments.

The call from the left: a positive state The interest in liberties is by no means a prerogative of the right. The restoration of ancient medieval rights has been an historic rallying cry for radicals challenging the established order. The left extends the concept of rights beyond the political and civil to include social rights. Here the call is for more, rather than less, state action. At the same time, bodies such as Liberty, a pressure group established in 1934 (Peele 1986: 146), are concerned about excessive police powers, penal sentencing policy, the militaristic use of the police in industrial disputes, government secrecy and electronic state surveillance of political activists. Hence, the case from the left for a written constitution is not to limit government but to use the state to create social rights while protecting individuals against its coercive power.

Unwritten and Unknowable?

The fact that the constitution is unwritten means that it can never be entirely known; it must forever be subject to interpretation and dispute. Moreover, there is more to a constitution than what is written in the lawyers' books. The real constitution is the living constitution – what is actually happening in the process of government. In this sense it is forever in flux (see King 2001).

Hence, the constitution is only part of the political landscape, the full extent of which we shall explore in the following chapters. This will sometimes take us into parts of the constitution that have passed from the efficient into the dignified realm and sometimes into areas of which the constitution remains formally silent. Underlying all is the distribution of power within society, which overrides all else and determines how the polity actually works. Yet the constitution remains central to political life, a crucial element in legitimation and an obscure object of desire for all actors, whether they be reformers or conservatives.

Key points

- The term constitution refers either to all that happens in the process of government, or the set of rules prescribing and limiting the powers of rulers and safeguarding the rights of citizens.
- The British constitution is not codified as a single document. Although unwritten, many documents are involved and much is written about it.
- The constitution is said to flow from five sources: the royal prerogative, statute, common law, convention and authoritative opinion, to which may now be added the EU.
- The role of conventions is far greater in the British constitution than in that of any other country.
- A constitution does not stand above the process of politics; the latter involves interpreting the constitution and seeking to change it.
- Reformers from right, left and centre call for a written constitution, for both political and rational reasons.
- In reality the British constitution can be seen as extremely fragile, requiring government willingness to impose self-restraint if it is to furnish the range of freedoms expected in a true democracy.
- The incorporation of the ECHR gives Britain an important element of a written constitution, a Bill of Rights.

Review your understanding of the following terms and concepts

authoritative opinion
Bill of Rights
civil rights
common law
constitution
constitutional amendment
constitutional convention
constitutional government
dignified and efficient
  elements

ECHR
entrenchment
executive
judicial review
judiciary
legislature
limited government
natural law
organic system
parliamentary sovereignty

positive law
royal prerogative
rule of law
separation of powers
sovereignty
statute law

Assignment

Study the extract from the *Independent* on p. 84 and answer the following questions.

		Mark (%)
1	Why does Geoffrey Robertson QC regard the Human Rights Bill as the most important piece of legislation in his time?	5
2	Critically evaluate the view that there are situations where the right to privacy should be denied to politicians.	15
3	How far do you accept the distinction Geoffrey Robertson draws between 'toes sucked on a public beach' and 'toes sucked in a private bedroom'?	20
4	What does the extract tell us about the role of lawyers in protecting rights?	30
5	How far is the optimistic view about the way legal reforms may be secured justified?	30

Questions for discussion

1 Identify the sources of the British constitution and evaluate their relative importance.
2 Why does Britain have an unwritten constitution?
3 Discuss the meaning and value of constitutional government.
4 Outline the advantages of a written constitution.
5 'The British constitution is itself more dignified than real.' Discuss.
6 Discuss the principal ways in which you think the introduction of a written constitution would change British politics.

The pinstriped revolutionary

The wizard of Oz is a true 90s radical who wants the establishment to have a heart. **Banny Poostchi** reports

He is the man who cut his legal teeth on the infamous *Oz* trial, when, in the summer of 1971, three long haired participants of the permissive society appeared in the Old Bailey facing the threat of life imprisonment. The charge: conspiracy to corrupt public morals. There was the time when he protected *Gay News* from the wrath of Mary Whitehouse.

Today Robertson has not lost any of his zeal for reform. His new mission? Incorporating the European Convention on Human Rights into UK law.

"The Human Rights Bill is the most important piece of legislation in my time."

He believes that the Bill will provide an enormously valuable bedrock set of principles which go all the way back to the Sermon on the Mount and to the life and canons of Christ.

Of all the principles in the Human Rights Bill, it is perhaps the individual's right to privacy for which Robertson has campaigned most vociferously. But does 'privacy' mean that the private life of politicians remains private? Was the exposure of Robin Cook's affair in the public interest? 'Of course. It was a situation where the private life could not be disentangled from the public.'

What if famous people – even Duchesses – were in a semi-private space such as the pool in Fergie's villa in the South of France?

"Hard cases. Toes sucked on a public beach falls on one side. Toes sucked in a private bedroom – a camera secretly put in the wall – invades privacy."

He is the first to concede that the practical application of a privacy law may prove to be extremely complicated: "This is one of the interesting things that you struggle with as a lawyer. You talk in general terms and then when you come to individual cases you see grey areas. Only when these hard cases are taken to trial and tested by the courts can a sensible line gradually emerge."

While legal reform is one way of civilising society, the winds of change can also blow from another quarter. Robertson credits the Sixties flower children, the members of the alternative society for changing the mind-set of the Old Establishment, making legal reforms possible.

Independent, 25 Feb. 1998

7   Contrast the arguments from the left and the right in British politics for a written constitution.
8   'So-called individual or human rights are no more and no less than political claims made by individuals on those in authority.' Discuss.
9   Assess the constitutional implications of Britain's membership of the EU.
10 'Incorporation of the ECHR does not solve Britain's problem of protecting individual rights.' Discuss.

Topic for debate

This house believes that the incorporation of the ECHR gives new and dangerous powers to the judiciary.

Further reading

Bagehot, W. (1963) *The English Constitution.*
First published in 1867, a classic and immensely readable account of politics during the fleeting period of genuine parliamentary government before the 1867 Reform Act.

Bogdanor, V. (1996) *Politics and the Constitution: Essays on British Government.*
Collection of essays aiming to show how the struggle over the constitution is essentially political.

Chrimes, S. B. (1967) *English Constitutional History.*
This slim volume is concise yet erudite on the subject.

Dicey, A. V. (1959) *An Introduction to the Study of the Law and the Constitution,* 10th edn.
Classic account (first published in 1885) of the theory of liberal democracy, though author's heart is perhaps more with liberalism than democracy.

Evans, M. (1995) *Charter88: A Successful Challenge to the British Tradition?*
Examines the rise of the 'New Constitutionalism'. Analyses how the movement influenced the Labour Party.

Ewing, K. D. and Gearty, C. A. (1990) *Freedom under Thatcher: Civil Liberties in Modern Britain.*
Essay by leading authorities on civil liberties. Argues that Thatcher government eroded freedoms by pushing back the frontiers of the common law, the traditional guardian of the people.

Hailsham, Lord (1978) *The Dilemma of Democracy.*
The views of Lord Hailsham, a prominent and rumbustious Conservative politician and lawyer (and Lord Chancellor), must be read with due caution. His 'dilemma' is perhaps felt more acutely when the electorate is misguided enough to elect a Labour government.

Harden, I. and Lewis, N. (1986) *The Noble Lie.*
Adopting a US-style approach (critical legal studies), explores gulf between orthodox constitutional theory (deriving largely from Dicey) and the reality of political power today.

Hennessy, P. (1995) *The Hidden Wiring: Unearthing the British Constitution.*
'Health check' on the British constitution assesses its response to changing circumstances.

Holme, R. and Elliot, M. (eds) (1988) *1688–1988: Time for a New Constitution.*
Critical and reformist essays marking tercentenary of the Glorious Revolution.

King, A. (2001) *Does the United Kingdom Still Have a Constitution?*
Text of the Hamlyn Lectures. A critical microscope placed on the modern constitution in a stimulating and accessible yet erudite essay. Makes an illuminating comparison with the Netherlands.

Klug, F. (2000) *Values for a Godless Age: The Story of the United Kingdom's New Bill of Rights*. Written as a layperson's guide to the Human Rights Act, it is authoritative and stimulating.

For light relief

William Golding, *Lord of the Flies*.
Allegory exploring mayhem when constitutional rule breaks down and deep-seated savagery takes over.

George Orwell, *Animal Farm*.
Modern fable satirizing Russian revolution and, by extension, all revolutions. New tyranny replaces old.

William Shakespeare, *Coriolanus*.
One of the most political of Shakespeare's plays. Deals with the relationship between governors and the governed – Coriolanus and the common people.

On the net

http://www.charter88.org.uk
Charter88's website contains a wealth of information on constitutional reform and links to other relevant sites.

http://www.parliament.uk
Follow the links from Parliament's home page to locate debate on the Human Rights Act and even the Act itself.

4

The Global Context: This Sceptred Isle

This chapter stresses that British politics cannot be seen as a self-contained process; the ship of state is tossed on a stormy sea of world affairs. The idea promoted in much politicians' rhetoric, and some traditional textbooks, that the government charts its own course with political compass and sextant is illusory. The globe is encircled with electronic communications networks, trading and financial flows, production patterns, labour movements, military operations, media output and cultural exchanges. Giant corporations, intergovernmental organizations and multinational pressure groups inhabit a political space bearing little relation to traditional state boundaries. At the same time, many of the problems confronting states, including terrorism, international crime, environmental degradation, over-fishing and disease, can no longer be solved within any one state. This is all part of what is termed 'globalization' – a defining feature of the age. For students of governance and politics the questions it poses concern the extent to which states retain the ability to control their own destinies and serve their citizens. The chapter addresses Britain's early entry onto the global stage, the post-war reconstruction of world capitalism, the contemporary global economy, the phenomenon of globalized violence, the absence of global governance and Britain's three spheres of world influence. We conclude by evaluating the real extent of globalization and examine some problems Britain has experienced in coming to terms with the modern world.

Much traditional writing on British politics assumes a high degree of state autonomy and government control. If the economy does well it is to our credit, and if it fails we look for culprits at home (from trade unions and scroungers to the civil service and management). Explanations looking only inwards are termed **endogenous** and are essentially short-sighted. The endogenous tendency arises from various factors, including a degree of arrogance, a 'Rule Britannia' conviction that we control world events, the egotistical rhetoric of politicians and intellectual laziness. In reality, few countries have been more closely enmeshed in the economy and politics of the world than Britain; any study ignoring this is incomplete. When we do direct our attention at *external* forces we are adopting an **exogenous** perspective.

Much is written on the subject of **globalization**, a phenomenon defining the age in which we live. Essentially it is the intensification of worldwide social relations that links distant localities in such a way that what happens locally is shaped by events occurring many miles away, and vice versa (Giddens 1990: 64). At its heart are changes to the relationship between time and space. Giddens speaks of time–space distanciation to stress how physical space is overcome in modern interactions. Distances travelled to conduct business or transport commodities are defined in terms of journey time. From the horse to supersonic travel, from the penny post to email, technology compresses space, so that today we speak of a 'global village'. There are enormous political implications in this process of globalization.

> And what should they know of England who only England know.
>
> Rudyard Kipling (1865–1936; British writer), 'The English Flag'

Britain Entering the Global Stage

Many writers have dwelt with pride on the idea of Britain's insularity (physical and metaphorical) and a conviction, implicit or explicit, of political superiority. A much-vaunted factor is the country's geographical setting, shielding it from physical and cultural invasion or other forms of contamination. As it was for Shakespeare's John of Gaunt, it has been

> [a] fortress built by Nature for herself
> Against infection and the hand of war.
> (*Richard II*, Act 2, Scene 1)

The last invasion took place in 1066, and the defeat of the Spanish Armada in 1588 encapsulated in a legendary way this island advantage. Yet despite its protective 'moat', Britain's world position has for long shaped its politics. Central to developments has been the emergence and rapacious growth of a capitalist **world economy**. Nothing preoccupied the political elite or influenced political affairs as much as this. Indeed, Britain played an early role in its formation and has continued as a key actor.

The era of colonialism and mercantilism

The great 'age of discovery' beginning in the fifteenth century opened up a New World and a new world economy. Developing from the mid-sixteenth century and traversing the Atlantic, it was to be shared by Portugal, Spain, Holland, France and Britain. This sea-borne trading network was based on **imperialism**, its emphasis on protecting colonies and trading with them. The **colonial** period was characterized by competitive struggle for territory, raw materials and people. As a sea-going nation, with enough farmland for self-sufficiency and safe from land attack, Britain was uniquely fitted to survive. While rivals warred on land, Britain could develop a strategy of oceanic domination of a world trade in commodities and slaves. In this the state willingly assumed a **mercantilist** role, protecting the commercial endeavours of its traders and settlers; trade wars were fought and Navigation Acts passed granting monopolies. Ultimately, with the gaining of India and Canada and the defeat of France in the Napoleonic wars, Britain emerged as the supreme world power. This dominance was to be increased through industrialization, although the role of the state would change.

> The British Empire is one of the greatest enslavers of human beings in the world.
>
> Paul Robeson (black American singer; victim of colour prejudice), quoted in *News Review* (3 Oct. 1946)

The era of free trade

Beginning in the eighteenth century, the **industrial revolution** was further good fortune for the English elite. The first country to industrialize, its domination could be increased through superior productivity, feeding on raw materials from the colonies and disgorging manufactured goods to the world. **Free trade**, rather than mercantilism, became the rallying cry of the new bourgeoisie. Following Adam Smith's principle of **comparative advantage** (that each country should specialize in what it could do best), Britain abandoned protection and threw open its doors to all-comers, urging others to do likewise. The country produced a third of the world's manufactured goods and half its iron, steel, coal and cotton goods. The cost of this policy was to expose British agriculture (through the relaxing and ultimate repeal of the Corn Laws in 1846) to destructive competition, with an ensuing loss of national self-sufficiency (Deane 1963: 188). The industrial bourgeoisie were fully prepared to put at risk the future of the whole of society; it was perhaps the most decisive event in modern British history (Gamble 1990: 52).

The state was brought under the control of the newly enriched bourgeoisie through far-reaching constitutional reforms, and policy acquired an international outlook. Britain pledged itself to a world policing role to secure the vital trade routes. The pound, fixed to the gold standard, became the universal currency, with a financial, trading and communications network centred on London. Britain's economic empire was to extend even beyond the bounds of its political one. Yet there were risks involved; the dependency on food, raw materials and markets around the world contained the seeds of decline.

Signs of decline

After so exhilarating a start in the industrial race some relative decline was inevitable, as the new markets were penetrated by rivals. However, Britain's eclipse by Germany and the USA was accomplished not by following the free-trade doctrines of Adam Smith, which were seen as a pseudo-theory designed to perpetuate British domination, but by erecting tariff barriers.

In response, a tariff reform movement led by Joseph Chamberlain grew up, but was killed in 1905 with the election of a Liberal government. Britain remained the world policeman, the system continued to centre on sterling and British capitalists continued to invest vast sums abroad. The burden was to take its toll; intense European competition culminating in two world wars left Britain gravely disabled and obliged to look to the USA for succour (pp. 107–8).

Reconstructing World Capitalism

The Bretton Woods era

A defining moment in post-war reconstruction was the July 1944 conference at Bretton Woods, New Hampshire, where forty-four capitalist nations agreed a grand plan for rebuilding the world economy. Britain played a central role, a key figure being economist John Maynard Keynes. The conference sought a new order based on cooperation, cohesion and free trade. However, central to the arrangement was the domination (hegemony) of one nation, which alone had emerged from the war in a strengthened state. The world capitalist economy would centre on the US dollar – to which other currencies would be tied (and through the dollar to gold) at fixed **exchange rates**. There would be an International Monetary Fund (IMF), largely administered by the USA, and a World Bank to make loans to weak countries. The regime was cemented by a General Agreement on Tariffs and Trade (GATT) drawn up in 1947. Intended to be temporary, this became central, negotiations to remove tariffs taking place in 'rounds'. Following the conclusion of the Uruguay Round, GATT was succeeded in 1995 by the even more powerful World Trade Organization (WTO; see p. 95).

The post-war boom

The outcome was an astonishing new era of plenty for the capitalist states – a '**long boom**' of some twenty-five years. 'Economic miracles' were wrought in West Germany, Japan and France. The boom was fired by a third 'technological revolution', advanced automation and electronics raising productivity to new pinnacles. In western states, political conflict could be replaced by consensus, the parties benignly sharing assumptions about the genius of the mixed economy, Keynesian economics and the welfare state (see pp. 287–91). Yet it was not to be a boom without end; it was sustained by features that could not be counted upon to last. From the mid-1970s began what Eric Hobsbawm (1995: 403) has called the crisis decades, 'during which the world lost its bearings and slid into instability and crisis'.

The crisis decades

In the mid-1970s, ominous clouds began to gather over the capitalist horizons as the annual growth in world trade fell from 8.5 to around 5 per cent. The reasons were tied to the very globalizing tendencies that had fuelled the boom. The increasingly tight integration of the world economy meant that slumps were less likely to be confined to particular states; once a recession set in, all could crash together.

Of particular importance was a serious decline in the US economy. The financial burden of world leadership and anti-communist militarism (see pp. 99–100) had begun to tell, and Western Europe and Japan had also caught up, even beginning to penetrate internal US markets. In 1971, the US balance of trade slid into deficit for the first time in the century, forcing the dollar's devaluation and signalling the end of currency stability. Within the European Community (see p. 138) a regional solution was sought, with agreement in 1971 to fix exchange rates and float together against the dollar, although Britain remained aloof. In 1978, revision of the IMF's Articles of Agreement marked the formal end of the Bretton Woods Agreement.

The collapse of the Bretton Woods system saw governments trying to sustain home demand by increasing money supply and allowing exchange rates to float downwards. However, this fuelled inflation. Further pressure came from price rises as companies tried to maintain profits. On top of these problems was the oil crisis following the 1973 Yom Kippur war; nothing illustrated the reality of global interdependence more vividly than the quadrupling of prices by the Organisation of Petroleum Exporting Countries (OPEC), which sent inflationary shock waves throughout the developed economies. Industrial stagnation, high inflation and unemployment stood side by side. Unconstrained by territorial boundaries or loyalties, multinational companies moved to more profitable climes, increasingly restricting governments' abilities to regulate their national economies.

With Keynesianism discredited and inflation undermining export potential and sucking in imports (a trend that was to continue; see table 4.1), Britain's Labour government looked exhausted. In 1975 it turned humiliatingly to the IMF for a loan. The conditions imposed included renouncing Keynesianism in favour of monetarism (see pp. 513–14), an approach embraced with enthusiasm by the Thatcher government that replaced Labour in 1979.

Table 4.1 UK trade with the world (£ billion)

	1984	1986	1988	1990	1992	1994	1996	1998	2000
Exports	70.6	73.0	80.7	102.3	107.8	135.1	167.2	164.0	187.6
Imports	76.0	82.6	102.3	121.0	120.9	146.3	180.9	185.9	218.0

Source: Data from *United Kingdom Balance of Payments* (2001 edn).

Perpetual crisis

A second oil crisis in 1979, following the Iranian revolution, saw a further doubling of prices, opening a new era for the world economy, one promising perpetual crisis. Neoliberalism moved into the ascendant in all westernized economies. Unemployment rose, unions were weakened, tax became more regressive and welfare states were cut back (Armstrong et al. 1991: 310–11). Even Sweden, the model social democracy, followed the trajectory. Indeed, it was to honour free-market gurus Friedrich von Hayek and Milton Friedman with Nobel Prizes for economics in 1974 and 1976, respectively.

Among the more developed states, Germany, Japan and the USA proved best fitted to survive, though the protectionist fight between them was to dominate the world economy, transforming the USA from the world's largest creditor nation to its largest net debtor (Cohen 1995: 521). At the same time, the newly industrializing countries (NICs) of the East began aggressively entering the global arena, China and much of South-East and East Asia becoming the most dynamic economic region in the world, but adding to the potential for destabilization. In the less-developed world, oil-rich countries also sought to industrialize and the markets of the weaker capitalist countries (particularly Britain's) were increasingly penetrated by imports.

A new world order

Another factor was the collapse of communism (see p. 100). Despite the problems within capitalism, there was triumphalism from the right as the former Soviet states began to embrace free-market ideals. The term 'New World Order' was coined to denote 'capitalism's complete and definitive global sway' (Panitch and Miliband 1992: 1–3), while US economist Francis Fukuyama (1992) saw in the triumph the 'end of history'. There were important implications for the West. No longer needing to prove capitalism's superiority, the spur driving governments to care for the disadvantaged was blunted. At the same time, socialist parties were to have their claims of an alternative to capitalism seriously discredited.

Yet if capitalism had not collapsed in the post-1970s period, for Hobsbawm it had become uncontrollable (1995: 408). This alarming conclusion was demonstrated to Britain in September 1992 when, on 'Black Wednesday', speculation against the pound destroyed the government's economic strategy, forcing the country out of the European Monetary System (see p. 138). It was illustrated on a larger scale in June 1997 as shock waves from the financial crisis in the Asia–Pacific region reverberated around the world.

> A soundly functioning American economy is so important to the world that what is good monetary policy for us is good monetary policy for the world.
>
> President of the New York Federal Reserve Bank, quoted in *Financial Times* (27 Aug. 1998)

New world disorder

Although the world economy showed a capacity to recover, the opening years of the new millennium saw it on a downward trend, largely as a result of three factors: the end of the hi-tech bubble resulting from a bizarre over-inflation of the prices of the new dot-com shares, ever-climbing oil prices and interest rate rises. Yet all was to be overshadowed by the realization that not only was global capitalism uncontrollable in its own terms, it was vulnerable to destabilization by seismic events in world politics.

The attack on New York's World Trade Center and Washington's Pentagon on 11 September 2001 sent shock waves around the world: the Dow Jones index of blue-chip US stocks suffered its biggest decline since the depression of the 1930s, job losses in the distressed airline industry shot up to around 120,000 and insurance companies were sent reeling by a bill estimated to be over £15 billion. Consumer confidence plummeted and Federal Reserve chairman Alan Greenspan called for a $100-billion package to rescue the US economy. In its biannual report on the world economic outlook the IMF predicted that the global economy was unlikely to reach its forecast 2.6% growth for 2001, declaring that it stood on the brink of recession (i.e. growth below 2.5 per cent).

Around the developed world, leaders made concerted efforts to restore shattered markets, their hopes balanced on the complex psychology of millions of US citizens, forming views from what they read in newspapers, saw on television or learned through rumours. If they continued to spend and hold their shares, things would be expected to recover. If they did not, demand would collapse, companies would sack employees, business confidence would fall and the downward spiral of recession would send ripples around the world. The mayor of New York urged citizens to resume normal economic activities. In the second world war the British had been asked to 'dig for victory'; in the so-called 'war against terrorism' Americans were called upon to 'shop for victory'.

The Global Economy Today

Economic globalization today is no mere academic construct, it is a defining feature of contemporary experience, shaping political and social life. The contents of our fridges, the cars we drive, the television programmes and films we watch and the machines on which we play computer games – all provide daily reminders of the astonishing reach of **advanced capitalism**. Although not a new phenomenon, the exponential rate of technological development, the growing mobility of capital and cheaper communications and transportation have taken the process to quite a new plane (Strange 1992). One key measure is the scale of direct foreign investment made by capitalists in countries other than their own. This tripled during the 1980s to stand at an estimated minimum of US$1.5 trillion by 1990 (Magdoff 1992: 44); during the 1990s, from Britain alone, net outward foreign direct investment increased from £21 million to £127 million, £71 million of which was in the USA.

The *dramatis personae*

States are not alone on this global stage. Other key players are huge private companies – the **transnational corporations** (TNCs). Manifest in multiple locations around the globe, their reach is magnified by their influence over many thousands of smaller companies. Owing allegiance to no particular country, they are able to command political decision-makers everywhere. They can fund political parties, threaten regimes and determine what people think through their media conglomerates. The TNCs are owned and controlled by an international capitalist elite which, in its quest for profits, works to maintain a global economic environment beyond the regulation of any state (Brett 1985: 80–102). By the 1990s, a mere 500 corporations controlled some 70 per cent of all world trade (*Ecologist* 1992), with just ten controlling 'virtually every aspect of the worldwide food chain' (Vidal 1997). While some behave responsibly, creating jobs, providing training and bringing in skills, others seek out low-wage economies with passive, non-unionized workforces and repressive and sexist regimes, such as South Korea and the Philippines.

> Capitalism is to the market what cancer is to our bodies. We get cancer when a genetic defect causes a cell to forget that it is part of our body.
>
> David Korten (US economist), speech to the 1999 AGM of the
> World Development Movement

Matching the global reach of the TNCs are the financial and banking institutions monitoring developments in Tokyo, London and New York through advanced computerized networks. In the City of London is the august Bank of England and the futuristic glass and metal stock exchange; currencies, stocks and shares, and 'futures' can speed around the globe at the click of a mouse button. A few streets away overlooking the Thames is the London International Financial Futures and Options Exchange (LIFFE), opened in 1982. Here the

New Labour, New Friends: traders in the Liffe short sterling futures pit react to Gordon Brown's first budget

Photo: Times Newspapers Ltd

action can be manic as the 'open outcry traders', young men clad in psychedelic blazers (and professing 'balls of steel'), compete for enormous bonuses in a frenzy of shouting and waving, gambling on what future prices and exchange rates around the world will be (Baird 1998).

In addition, there are international economic organizations working to maintain an environment in which TNCs and world financiers can thrive. At the very heart of the global economy has been GATT, replaced in 1995 by the WTO, with an even wider mandate to facilitate trade negotiations, administer agreements, monitor trade policies, give technical assistance to developing countries and liaise with other international organizations. Unlike other international bodies it has teeth; it is able to adjudicate in trade disputes and authorize sanctions against countries stepping out of line. Although each of its over 140 members has a vote, in practice the rich (G8) economies dominate. Indeed, many states cannot even afford to support full-time staff at the Geneva headquarters.

Another key association is the Organisation for Economic Cooperation and Development (OECD), founded in 1961 by the world's twenty-nine richest countries as an exclusive club to promote their economic interests. In February 1998 it pushed for a Multinational Agreement on Investment (MAI), giving TNCs the right to sue a government for any loss of profits resulting from national policies. This threatened workplace and environmental legislation, as well as UN treaties on climate change. Although negotiations collapsed under fierce opposition from pressure groups, the French government and the

The WTO and MAI in fact represent the birth of a world government by, of and for transnational companies.

Phil McLeish, in *Red Pepper* (April 1998)

European Parliament, its spirit was to resurface in the General Agreement on Trade in Services (GATS).

A child of the WTO, the GATS extended the GATT regime into *services* such as water supply, health and tourism, forcing a country's obligations to free trade to take precedence over domestic regulatory laws. Thus, for example, international tour operators moving into a country cannot be compelled to hire or train local people, while local competitors cannot be encouraged with subsidies or tax relief (Suresh 2001: 11). In the name of lifting trade restrictions, health and safety requirements can be forced down to the lowest common denominator. Hence the labelling of GM foods was opposed by Canada and the USA as a barrier to trade.

However, the TNCs and economic institutions do not entirely monopolize the global arena. By the mid-1980s there were some 365 **intergovernmental organizations** as well as almost 5,000 international non-governmental organizations (NGOs), the most rapid growth having taken place since the early 1970s (Held 1989: 196). Charities and pressure groups such as Save the Children, the Red Cross and Oxfam organize internationally to combat the social effects of the profit-hungry states and companies because the global economy does not distribute its benefits equally.

Uneven development: global imbalance

The spread of markets far outpaces the ability of societies and their political systems to adjust to them.

Kofi Annan, UN Secretary General, quoted in Woodroffe (1999)

Liberal optimism that globalization would spread the fruits of material progress have even proved ill-founded as the economic landscape continues to exhibit uneven development. Technological advances have made it possible for affluent states, working closely with the TNCs, to maintain a lead. Increased international trade in industrial products, and the growth of the 'knowledge economy', left them richer at the opening of the new millennium than they were in the early 1970s.

The uneven world is characterized in various ways, often reflecting the particular vantage point of the observer. There are also political motives in the choice of terms. No western politician or businessman would refer to the 'exploited world' for example, and generally the term 'developing' is preferred to 'underdeveloped'. The distinction between the 'rich north' and the 'poor south' is more often used by those critical of the inequality. Much use has also been made of the terms 'first', 'second' and 'third world'. Wallerstein (1979) delineated three zones: a core, a semi-periphery and a periphery.

> While the poor get poorer, the rich get richer. Here in Britain the richest *ten* people have more wealth than *15 entire countries* in Africa, with over *100 million people*.
>
> Barry Coates (Director, World Development Movement) letter to supporters (Dec 1998)

◆ *The core zone* comprises the G8 countries (formerly the G7, before Russia was admitted to this rich nations club).

◆ *The semi-peripheral zone* was formed by ex-colonial settlements (Latin America, the white Commonwealth and South Africa), where a dominant bourgeois class established through white settlement facilitated capital accumulation and economic development. The oil-rich countries of the third world began to enter this zone with ambitious development programmes, as did the Asian 'Tiger' economies.

◆ *The peripheral zone* comprises a wide range of countries in Africa, Asia and South America, with poorly developed, narrowly based economies.

> **The Group of Eight (G8)**
> USA
> Britain
> France
> Germany
> Italy
> Canada
> Japan
> Russia

In fact all the terms used are rather vague, with countries ranged along a complex spectrum of economic power and dependency. However, what is certain is the reality of inequality. It is common today to distinguish between 'more economically developed countries' (MEDCs) and 'less economically developed countries' (LEDCs).

◆ *MEDCs*. Here, broadly based economies and high levels of consumption of the world's resources allow generally high material standards of living. Together the MEDCs consume 80 per cent of the world's energy but have 25 per cent of its population. The most voracious consumers are in the USA, the average citizen consuming 35 times more than the average Indian. From within the MEDCs the levers controlling the world economy are operated and the TNCs reach out profit-hungry tentacles to encircle the globe.

◆ *LEDCs*. These are characterized by low wages, child labour, female exploitation, low levels of consumption, poverty, disease, starvation and low life expectancy. Economically dependent on the core states (for markets, imports and loans), they are rarely in any position to control the prices of their exports and find it almost impossible to accumulate sufficient capital for self-sustaining growth. High research and technology costs mean that even indigenous extractive industries are controlled from outside. The LEDCs are forced to produce more 'primary commodities' such as coffee, foodstuffs and metal ores but, when this results in a glut, prices fall, leaving them even poorer.

The position of the LEDCs was worsened by the willingness of western banks to make huge loans to stave off world recession, creating crippling debts. In 1995, severely indebted low-income countries paid $1 billion more into the IMF than they received. Under pressure from international groups and the United Nations, the World Bank mellowed somewhat during the 1990s. At a joint World Bank–IMF meeting in September 1995, for the first time all creditors, commercial banks, multinational institutions and governments agreed to relieve the most heavily indebted poor countries. However, the IMF set stringent conditions, keeping countries under the western yoke for decades to come (Brazier 1997: 5–7). A report from the WTO (1998) revealed 986 million

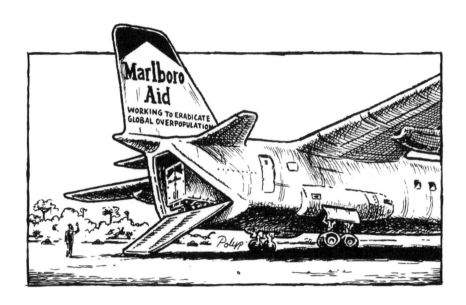

people to be living on less than $1 a day. Without radical change this figure was predicted to reach 1117 million by 2008.

Globalization also creates uneven distribution within the core states. An international division of labour drives down workers' wages, weakens unions and, by transferring production to low-wage economies, leaves behind rust belts and unemployment. Ironically, it also creates pressure to raise salaries and perquisites at the higher managerial levels (Hoogvelt 1997: 146) as, for example, when executives in privatized water authorities in Britain demand parity with their US counterparts. Gordon and Townsend's (2001) analysis of poverty in EU and ex-communist states in the post-Reagan/Thatcher era found widespread and deepening inequality, with prosperity for the few at the cost of degradation for the many in terms of life expectancy, income and social security provision.

According to the World Development Movement, in 1998 girls making Barbie and Action Man dolls in Asia received less per week than the price of one doll

Clearly the global economy, far from being a neutral machine operating like clockwork is a dangerous environment, where wealth exists alongside poverty, secularism comes up against primitive religious beliefs and politics intrudes into economics to form a volatile mixture threatening violence and unrest.

Globalized Violence

Violence has from the earliest times been central to globalization. Britain's economic empire was founded upon organized violence; not only were the colonies themselves captured by force, European rivals fought fierce battles over them. Britain established military bases throughout the world to defend its empire and trade routes.

Militarism is advanced by another feature of globalization, industrialization, which consolidated the imperialism of the western powers in the nineteenth century. Railways as well as guns, and telecommunications as well as tanks, could be instruments of war in the hands of the developed nations. Today, countries and terrorist organizations have the capability to unleash awesome destructive power across vast distances at the touch of a button.

The global arms bazaar

Militarism also stimulates the global economy; the arms trade ships the merchandise of death and destruction from the developed world, sometimes into the hands of dictators and megalomaniacs. The quest for profit can make light of arms embargoes, the arms-for-Iraq scandal revealing the extent of official involvement. Britain has always been a major arms producer, hosting glitzy arms fairs where manufacturers show off their wares, often in the delicate hands of super-models, and with enticing displays, rather like an ideal-homes exhibition. Although New Labour promised an 'ethical foreign policy', an Oxfam report (1998) alleged business to be very much as usual, with a secret trade worth some £660 million to over a hundred countries, many with citizens in abject poverty. Refuting claims that few British companies were involved, the report listed 120, all encouraged with taxpayers' money in the form of export credit guarantees.

The world at war

Nothing could better symbolize the reality of military globalization than the twentieth century, an age of violent conflict that could be accurately termed *world* war. In the 1914–18 conflict the imperial possessions were quickly drawn in and hostilities spread to Africa and the Middle East. The concept of the battlefield was extended to engulf continents and civil populations. The second world war, with unprecedented levels of destruction and suffering, became even more global in its reach, with only Latin America and southern Africa escaping. Its close, far from ending global conflict, opened a new era of tension – the **cold war** between East and West.

War in a cold climate

Although the term was coined in America, the cold war grew from early British warnings of the Soviet threat. A divide entailing tense psychology, it was directly related to the world economy, being a clash of economic ideologies. In this bizarre confrontation the capitalist and communist blocs both acted as if at war (manufacturing weapons, and conducting espionage and economic and political subversion), while generally avoiding actual combat.

From Stettin in the Baltic to Trieste in the Adriatic an **Iron Curtain** has descended upon the Continent.

Winston Churchill, public speech, Fulton, Missouri (March 1946)

For capitalist interests, the cold war had the advantage of keeping populations permanently hostile to left-wing policies. 'Reds under the beds' scares were fanned by the media, the hysteria reaching epic proportions in the USA with the medieval-style witch-hunts of McCarthyism, when famous figures were pilloried for left-wing sympathies and sometimes hounded from the country. In Britain, the climate helped the Conservatives maintain their badge as the party of patriotism. When Labour adopted an anti-nuclear stance it proved electorally suicidal.

> Our scientific power has outrun our spiritual power. We have guided missiles and misguided men.
>
> Martin Luther King (US civil rights campaigner; assassinated 1968), *Strength to Love* (1963)

The chill was also felt in the supposedly **non-aligned world**, with the USA bolstering up a motley collection of oppressive anti-socialist regimes (including the Taliban in Afghanistan) in accordance with an intellectually dubious 'domino theory'. An anti-communist war was fought in Korea, the democratically elected socialist government of Chile was illegally brought down by an American-backed insurrection, and the fatal involvement in Vietnam dragged on inconclusively to ignominious withdrawal (mitigated only by a spate of *Rambo*-style movies to feed the fantasies of American hawks).

British governments of all shades maintained full commitment to the cold war spirit. It was a Labour prime minister (Attlee) who agreed to an independent nuclear deterrent despite the US 'nuclear umbrella'. (With imagery appropriate enough for a 'cold' war, Bevan declared that, without the atom bomb, a foreign secretary would go 'naked' into the world conference chambers.)

> Militarism ... is one of the chief bulwarks of capitalism, and the day that militarism is undermined, capitalism will fail.
>
> Helen Keller (1880–1968; blind and deaf US writer and lecturer), *The Story of My Life* (1947)

The thaw Throughout the period the degree of frost in the cold war fluctuated, with attempts at *détente* interspersed with aggression. An entrenched feature was arms manufacture (Thompson 1980), insistently demanding resources and exerting a heavy economic toll on both blocs. In the 1980s, the unthinkable began to happen with the accession of Mikhail Gorbachev in the USSR. His programme of reform (*perestroika* and *glasnost*) set off reverberations throughout the eastern bloc and a permanent thaw set in as one by one hard-line Stalinist regimes were popularly rejected. Meetings between Gorbachev and US president Reagan even led to reductions in nuclear arsenals. On 9 November 1989, with profound symbolism, the Berlin Wall dividing the city between east and west began to crumble, physically dismantled by the ordinary people who had lived in its shadow. This unexpected end to the cold war appeared to mean victory for the West, though the communist regimes had fallen before economic forces, not marching boots.

From cold war to hot peace

Yet there was a paradox: although few could mourn the passing of a tense era, the new world order brought new uncertainties. Disillusion and discontent with the free market in former communist countries saw them respond variously: in some, old leaders returned to favour; in others, communism was replaced not by liberalism but by rampant nationalism, territorial conflict, civil war, religious fundamentalism and the fascist-like horrors of ethnic cleansing. Moreover, the Russian bear remained a mighty military force, while the dragon of China promised to become a new superpower. Bipolarity gave way to **multipolarity**, with potential flashpoints that could be ignited by religious fanatics and unbalanced dictators. Many leaders of developing states were keen to acquire weapons and world economic growth had done little to remove provocative disparities of wealth. This multipolar world was to resemble that of the nineteenth century, but it differed in that one country possessed vastly superior firepower over the rest. Critics feared bullying by the USA on the grounds that 'might is right'.

Military globalization

Not only did militarism drive the pattern of globalization, it has itself become part of the phenomenon with an expanding network of military ties embracing the globe as a single geostrategic space. The Western European Union (WEU), a joint defence association of Britain, France and the Benelux states, emerged from the Brussels Treaty of 1948, but before the ink was dry it was superseded as Western Europe allied with the USA to form the North Atlantic Treaty Organization (NATO) in 1949, after the Russian blockade of Berlin. In mirror image, the communist bloc allied under the banner of the Warsaw Pact. The USA was to be the biggest contributor to the NATO budget and, with its vast armoury, offered the protection of a 'nuclear umbrella'.

The end of the cold war cast doubts over NATO's future but a defining moment was reached in the 1991 Gulf war. This showed that 'mid-intensity conflicts' could flare up at any time and provided a rationale for continuing strategic alliances (Klare 1992); a November 1991 summit erected a 'business as usual' sign. Some eastern bloc countries even expressed an interest in joining, although fear of antagonizing Russia made the West chary. Closer relations were forged after the failed Soviet coup of August 1991 through the establishment of a North Atlantic Cooperation Council (NACC), offering former Warsaw Pact members and the European states of the former Soviet Union

non-military participation in NATO. In addition, fears of instability in Eastern
Europe saw a revival of the WEU (relaunched in Rome in 1984 in response to
the US 'Star Wars' programme). The 1993 Maastricht Treaty made it central to
the common foreign and security policy pillar of the European Union (see
chapter 5).

The day the world changed: global terror

However, in 2001 the idea of military alliance was taken to new levels by the
terrorist attack on the USA, which united the Americans with Western Europe,
Eastern Europe and much of the Islamic world. (For Russia, one of the incentives was the possibility of joining NATO.) Yet this was a fragile union and
Tony Blair, seeing himself as one of its main architects, worked assiduously to
hold things together with frantic shuttle diplomacy.

On the morning of 11 September three hijacked US airliners swooped from
the sky into the twin towers of New York's World Trade Center and the heart of
the US defence establishment, the Pentagon in Washington (the fourth crashed
before reaching its target). More potent symbols of western supremacy could
hardly have been chosen. Some saw this as the day the USA, previously
considered impregnable, entered the real world. For others it was variously
the ripening of a harvest sown by years of violent US foreign policy or a result
of global fragmentation into rich and poor worlds.

The attack was masterminded by Osama bin Laden, operating his worldwide
al-Qaeda terrorist network from the unsignposted caves of Afghanistan. The
chilling demonstration revealed an unsuspected inability of highly developed
states to protect either the vast achievements of their culture or the lives of their
citizens. The year 2001 was to see more deaths from terrorism than any before.

When President Bush declared a 'war on terrorism' he was illustrating how,
in the global world, threats can come not only from nations but from groups, be
they eco-warriors, oppressed minorities, freedom fighters, anti-capitalists or
religious fundamentalists. A suicidal pilot or a woman passing through customs
with a suitcase of anthrax could be as menacing as a guided missile. Instability
is increased by an underground global economy of laundered money, drugs
trading and government corruption. Ironically, in combating this new kind of
menace developed states were forced to question the traditional articles of faith
of world trade: banking secrecy, free passage between states, support for
corrupt regimes and tax havens.

Globalized Governance: the Missing Dimension?

The mixtures of the modern world are marked 'highly inflammable'. Although
driven by economics, globalization is clearly highly political and a form of
world politics has evolved in arenas formed around issue areas, policy sectors
and geographical regions. States, intergovernmental associations, bureaucra-

cies, TNCs and international voluntary organizations are locked in a complex process of negotiation, bargaining, brinkmanship, and sometimes violence. This is clearly a world of politics, but it is not a world of government. There is no overarching authority to exercise control. Can states still exercise control?

An end of sovereignty?

Our world is ruled by sovereign governments. Or is it? Although the legal and political sovereignty of states is technically unimpaired by globalization, we have seen that in economic terms their powers are seriously weakened. More than ever before, governments sit, Canute-like, at the mercy of the global economic tides. Yet it does not end there. Beyond the march of capitalism are many other global dimensions that defy the power of governments (Camilleri and Falk 1992; Horsman and Marshall 1994). Environmental problems such as marine pollution and acid rain are often beyond the scope of any single state to solve. The communications revolution has made possible the formation of virtual communities bearing no relation to formal state boundaries. Much the same music, films and theatre can be seen the world over and media conglomerates beam TV and radio signals around the globe. Terrorism and violence can see acts in one country planned in another (sometimes Britain) and financed globally (considerable IRA funds have been raised in the USA), sometimes through networks of crime, drugs dealing and money laundering. At the same time, military alliances remove strategic autonomy from governments. Thatcher declared any idea of refusing to allow the US Libyan attack to be launched from British soil as 'unthinkable'.

> I am not an Athenian or a Greek, but a citizen of the world.
>
> Socrates (470–399 BC; Greek philosopher), in Plutarch, *Of Banishment*

Virtual governance: global power

While state authority is weakened, other institutions emerge to fill a governance vacuum. So great is the might of the TNCs, they have from the mid-1970s transformed international relations (Hobsbawm 1995: 403). Virtually units of governance, with massive global advertising making their logos more widely recognized than most national flags, governments must negotiate with them much as they conduct diplomacy with other states. They are indeed richer than many states: of the world's hundred largest economies, fifty-one are companies rather than countries. The goal of enticing them to locate is now as important as traditional foreign policy, and factors such as union freedoms, wages legislation and welfare policies must often be sacrificed to this end. The option of single-country socialism is foreclosed by competitive tax cuts and the power of financial markets (Dunleavy 1993: 144).

The economic organizations offer further units of virtual governance. Conflict between the duty of states to protect citizens and the demands of the free trade lobby make the WTO an important political cockpit. Thousands of meetings take place each year with hordes of corporate lobbyists dominating its numerous technical committees. Trade ministers assemble every two years at high-profile WTO 'Ministerials'. Another setting is the annual World Economic Forum in Davos, Switzerland, where some 1,000 top companies rub shoulders with political leaders and representatives of the World Bank, the IMF and the WTO to discuss policies affecting the lives of countless millions. In addition, there are EU summits two or three times a year. Not surprisingly, NGOs pursuing political goals such as child welfare, food aid, environmentalism, human rights and anti-capitalism often bypass state governments to set their sights on the TNCs and economic organizations.

Indeed, it is possible to argue that the close of the imperial era was not to mark the end of subjugation or exploitation. Resident representatives of the World Bank, GATS and IMF are able to act rather like colonial governors of old, dictating to governments, ordering them to deflate, reduce taxes and cut public services in order to compete globally. Critics speak of **neocolonialism**, and to some it is 'the American conquest of most of the world' (Pilger 1998: 62).

However, global governance by the economically powerful does not mean global government or democracy. The system is one of potential anarchy, containing enormous potential for catastrophe, and justifying the call for political authority to maintain social stability – a world polity with a world government (Gray 1998; Monbiot 2002). However, in an atmosphere of military alliances and ideological arm-wrestling, the idea of a world government has been little more than a philosopher's pipe-dream. Despite seeing their independence eroded, states have jealously sought to protect an illusion of **autonomy**, though there has been one serious step along the road to overarching world authority, the United Nations Organization.

> These eight men have set themselves up as de facto world government.
>
> Barry Coates, World Development Movement Director, on the G8 countries (*WDM in Action*, summer 2002)

Uniting the nations

The precursor of the United Nations (UN) was the League of Nations, established after the first world war through the 1919 Treaty of Versailles. Here was a forum where diplomats could upstage the generals. However, the enterprise collapsed into the tragedy of the second world war and the UN was a second attempt to pick up the pieces. In 1941, Britain and the USA had signed an Atlantic Charter and the following year twenty-nine other countries signed an agreement (the Declaration of United Nations) to work together to defeat Germany, Japan and Italy. At the Yalta conference in February 1945, it was agreed to set up the UN as a permanent organization for world peace. Membership continued to grow, reaching 185 by the mid-1990s. With headquarters in New York it comprises the following institutions.

- ◆ *The Security Council.* This consists of the five permanent founder members (Britain, France, the USA, Russia and China) and ten others serving two-year terms. Members can veto decisions, which has often inhibited action.

- *The General Assembly.* This main forum contains delegations from all member states. Each has one vote regardless of size, giving a prominence to weak countries not always welcomed by the strong. It meets regularly and may be summoned in emergencies (e.g. the Suez Crisis, the Cuban Missile Crisis, the Gulf war, 11 September).
- *The Secretariat.* The assembly is serviced by a 4,000-strong bureaucracy drawn from all states and headed by a Secretary General, whose role includes monitoring world events and negotiating with disputants.
- *The International Court of Justice.* Located at The Hague and presided over by judges (serving limited terms) from member countries, the Court upholds international law.
- *Specialized organizations.* The UN fulfils a large range of social and cultural functions through an extensive network of specialized and largely autonomous agencies such as UNICEF (children), WHO (health) and UNESCO (education).

The UN is an **international association**, not world government; it neither passes laws nor imposes taxes. Member states retain full sovereignty and can withhold contributions (the USA has been a major offender). During the 1980s it came close to bankruptcy and in 1992 Secretary General Boutros Boutros-Ghali talked of organizational paralysis. By 1995, member states owed $2.6 billion.

Although it sends peacekeeping forces to trouble-spots, the UN's essential purpose is dialogue, the value of its resolutions lying mainly in influencing opinion. Generally countries are loath to accept restrictions: Israel has ignored UN resolutions in its conflict with Palestine, as has Iraq over the inspection of its weapons, while in the Falklands war Britain resorted to gunboat diplomacy, despite UN efforts. If powerful countries refuse to be bound, then the principle that 'might is right' must continue to set the tone for international relations. Left as a monopolistic superpower, the USA has used the UN as a cover for tough military action, as in the Gulf war.

Moreover, in a strange paradox, globalization and the end of the cold war have coincided with a revival of chauvinistic nationalism and terrorism. Increasingly UN forces have found themselves in dangerous intra-state, ethnic, tribal and religious conflicts (as in Bosnia and Rwanda), but with confusion over their

---

The Falklands war

In early 1982 Argentina invaded the Falklands (or Malvinas), seeking to repossess the islands, one of the few tiny jewels remaining in the British imperial crown. As Britain's task force set sail, the UN Secretary General and the US Secretary of State shuttled between London and Buenos Aires, desperately seeking a diplomatic solution. However, the controversial sinking of the Argentinian warship the *General Belgrano* put paid to such hopes. British troops landed on the islands and, amidst orgasms of jingoism in the English press, quickly secured an Argentinian surrender. Telling people to 'Rejoice!', Thatcher proclaimed: 'We have ceased to be a nation in retreat' (Barnett 1982: 149–53) and a hitherto little-known rock in the South Atlantic remained, in the face of UN resolutions, forever England.

role leaving them largely ineffective. A UN convention for the suppression of terrorism adopted by the General Assembly in 1999 was ratified by only four countries, one of which was the UK.

With no resources of its own and no power of independent action, perhaps the best that could be said for the UN was that it survived throughout the second half of the twentieth century (Hobsbawm 1995: 430). In the next century it was to be faced with the challenge of reforming its structure, culture and decision-making processes to cope with the post-cold-war world (Rau 1996). The case for its policing role was made more insistent by the events of 11 September 2001 and the USA began to adopt a less disdainful attitude towards it.

Britain and the World: Three Spheres of Influence

There are other groupings and relationships in the world beyond military alliances and encompassing regions rather than the entire globe. Britain, historically an outward-looking state, has seen its world position in terms of three spheres in the post-war era. In the first place there was the empire, through which tentacles reached from Westminster to encircle the world; secondly there was a so-called 'special relationship' with the USA, and thirdly there was mainland Europe, through which much British dynastic history has been enacted.

Retreating from empire: the British Commonwealth

Disastrously weakened by the second world war, Britain still retained a high imperial commitment. Imposing unrealistic burdens on the 'mother country' and detested by most of the colonies, this could not be sustained. A process of retreat was painfully negotiated, virtually completed in 1967 when troops withdrew from east of Suez. The most spectacular of the remaining outposts, Hong Kong, was handed back to China in a sombre ceremony in June 1997.

I have not become the King's First Minister in order to preside over the liquidation of the British Empire.

Winston Churchill, speech at Lord Mayor's Banquet (10 Nov. 1942)

The bitter pill of vanishing splendour was sugared by the idea of the British Commonwealth, an echo of empire. Initially consisting of the 'white' dominions of Canada, Australia, South Africa and New Zealand, these were joined from 1945 by the 'New Commonwealth' countries in Asia, Africa and the West Indies. No longer an imperial layer of governance, the Commonwealth today is a loose family of nations with no formal rules, treaty or constitution. Although many are republics, they unite under the Crown rather than the British government. Member states remain sovereign, with the right to leave (as did South Africa, Pakistan and the Republic of Ireland). Indeed, the collapse of many Westminster-style constitutions, bequeathed upon independence, demonstrated that the imposed rule had done little to inculcate English political culture.

However, the legacy of empire inhibits equality of partnership, the UK disdaining Commonwealth support when making important foreign policy decisions (Suez, the Falklands, supporting the USA). Strong differences of opinion surfaced during the 1980s over sanctions against the white South African regime, British opposition threatening to shatter the association. Even the Queen was reported to be alarmed by Thatcher's hard line. Issues have included suspicions of racism, heightened from 1962 with a series of Immigration Acts eroding rights of settlement in Britain (see chapter 7). In 1996, the House of Commons Foreign Affairs Committee called for a more positive approach to the Commonwealth and emphasized its business advantages.

The Commonwealth embraces a wider cultural, political and economic range than most other groupings, giving it potential as a force for cooperation and understanding (Ramphal 1997). With a membership of around fifty countries – four with advanced economies – economic development, democratization and the alleviation of poverty are among its central concerns. Its stand against apartheid finally bore fruit: South Africa's first democratic elections in 1994 made Nelson Mandela an heroic president and the country rejoined the Commonwealth, offering renewed impetus. The four-year suspension of Nigeria in 1996 and the one-year suspension of Zimbabwe in 2002 again showed the association as a potential force for democracy and human rights.

> It seems that the British Government sees black people as expendable.
>
> Bishop Desmond Tutu (black South African civil rights campaigner), speech (1986)

Special relations

One alliance that was to prove central to Britain's relationship with the outside world was not based on treaties. Unlike its relationships with any other country, that with the USA was termed, at least by the British, 'special'. To the political elite it was as important as the relationships with the Commonwealth and the rest of Western Europe. Although America had spurned British rule in 1776 and a festering legacy of hostility towards the British establishment lingered, cultural links remained. The language that took root in that polyglot society was English and white Anglo-Saxon Protestants (WASPs) formed an elite class. There was also hard necessity. Whether or not the Americans were special relations, they were certainly rich ones. Winston Churchill had worked adroitly to secure US aid and participation in the war and their support was just as necessary in the aftermath.

It was no small irony that in working to defeat one rival Britain was obliged to succumb to the hegemony of the other. British economic interests and a continued world role for its political class were seen to lie in two conditions: maintaining the international trading network for British capital and securing liberal ideology against communism. Hence the cold war was a key circumstance in maintaining the special relationship. The USA was the only state with the resources to restore political and economic order to the world, and Britain worked assiduously to involve it through the Bretton Woods agreement.

Yet securing US aid was not easy. Initially Americans were loath to support a continuing British empire, seen as a serious trade threat. In addition, with

> You see, Mr President, I have nothing to conceal from you.
>
> Winston Churchill to Franklin Roosevelt, when found dictating a letter stark naked in his White House bedroom in 1941, quoted in *The Economist* (7 Feb. 1998)

Labour's 1945 election victory they had no desire to finance socialism. However, Foreign Office courtship continued ardently until the British view of the Soviet threat prevailed (Gamble 1990: 108). From July 1948 funds to refurbish West European capitalism as a buttress against communism flowed through the generous Marshall Aid programme, marking 'the *peacetime* assumption of superpower responsibilities by the United States and their *de facto* relinquishment by Britain' (Hennessy 1992: 286).

Britain generally supported the USA in its foreign policy and military adventurism, as well as shouldering the burden of a costly world military presence. In return, the USA enabled Britain to retain some semblance of world leadership, not pressing it to dismantle the empire and preserving an international role for sterling. The view of Britain's elite was that, while the USA was rich, the British had the know-how and experience for world leadership. This was self-delusion. When asked whether Whitehall had ever changed Washington's mind on any issues of substance, Robert Cecil, First Secretary at the British Embassy at Washington during the immediate post-war years, could recall no such occasion (Hennessy 1992: 365).

Waxing and waning during the post-war era (Louis and Bull 1986), the relationship seemed stronger when there was ideological convergence between leaders. Macmillan courted the Americans adroitly after the Suez crisis but the relationship weakened again under Wilson. Thatcher and Reagan were simpatico, both personally and in terms of economic philosophy, but relations between Major and Clinton became strained (not least because Major's

> Give us the tools and we will finish the job.
>
> Winston Churchill, as US Lend–Lease legislation was going through Congress, broadcast (9 Feb. 1941)

> Great Britain has lost an Empire and has not yet found a role.
>
> Dean Acheson (US Secretary of State), speech at Military Academy, West Point (5 Dec. 1962)

Dinner with friends: the Blairs and Clintons at a restaurant at Butler's Wharf on the Thames, May 1997

Photo: News Group Newspapers

government tried to assist Clinton's presidential opponents by unearthing information on his Oxford student days).

Increased European integration and US economic crisis weakened the special relationship and, by the late 1990s, the USA was showing more interest in an economically strong Germany. However, Labour's return to office in May 1997 was greeted warmly by Clinton, who even played a part in Blair's peace efforts in Northern Ireland. The similarities between the two were obvious: young, personable, telegenic leaders of the centre-left repackaging the neoliberal policies of their predecessors in 'third way' rhetoric. Indeed, the New Labour elite had benefited from many Kennedy scholarships and Harvard secondments (Pilger 1998: 95).

The extent of Britain's commitment to the relationship was emphasized by support for the controversial August 1998 bombing of a pharmaceutical plant in Sudan and a huge missile attack on Iraq in December 1998, the eve of Ramadan. In the eyes of critics the action, in the midst of an impeachment process against Clinton over the Monica Lewinsky sex-in-the-Oval-Office scandal, was a cynical diversionary tactic.

When the Republican George W. Bush entered the White House in 2001, there was expectation that the relationship would again cool. Bush did not endear himself to the British left, refusing to honour the Kyoto protocol on environmental protection and reneging on the nuclear non-proliferation treaty by reviving Reagan's 'Star Wars' nuclear shield. However, Blair courted the new president with a loyalty swelling to astonishing proportions after the 11 September terrorist attacks, becoming, in the eyes of some, a roving ambassador for the USA. Yet any idea that he could influence US policy was a delusion. As the US train moved to war, Britain was merely a passenger with no place on the footplate. In 2002, as the USA contemplated a highly dangerous first strike against Iraq, only Britain stood by its side.

In May 2002, President of the European Commission Romano Prodi scolded the British government for cherishing the special relationship at the expense of European integration. Similarly, economist Will Hutton (2002) saw the special relationship, far from preserving Britain's world role, as giving the USA a wide-ranging domination over Britain extending beyond the military and political to embrace finance, academic life, culture, film, music, television, fashion. The British even watch films in which acts of British heroes (such as the breaking of the Enigma code in the second world war) are portrayed as the work of Americans. Like Prodi, Hutton regarded Britain's values and destiny as lying across the Channel rather than the Atlantic.

Britain and mainland Europe

The third sphere is where much British history since (and even before) 1066 has been played out. Dynastic intrigues, strategic alliances, imperial struggles and two world wars testify to a European heritage. Yet separated by its defensive moat, Britain's position has remained ambiguous. The post-war drive towards

European integration has heightened this. While domination by the global economy and the USA is largely accepted, the idea of sacrificing any sovereignty to the European Union is viewed by 'Eurosceptics' as a constitutional catastrophe. This increasingly important issue calls for more detailed consideration and is the subject of the next chapter.

Globalization in Question

Three aspects of the ineluctable process of globalization can be questioned: will it make the world a better place, what is its real extent and what is Britain's place within it?

A global Utopia?

Liberal optimism sees globalization leading to a harmonious and affluent world society as information, knowledge, services and material goods circulate freely. However, many critics take a less optimistic view, seeing governments competing more fiercely in the quest to attract capital, militarism continuing to place the world on a knife edge, and greater mutual awareness between societies creating suspicion and tension as ideological, ethnic and religious differences emerge (Bull 1977: 208). Moreover, billions of the world's population living at subsistence level or below have little to lose from violent rebellion.

Globalization does not automatically cherish human rights; dictatorships can offer a stable environment for investment. Shell's search for profit led to environmental degradation in Nigeria and world opinion associated it with the execution in November 1995 of Ken Saro-Wiwa and eight Ogoni environmental activists. Moreover, the spread of the western rationalist tradition can evoke violent responses within traditional societies, prompting religious fundamentalism and bellicose nationalism. Such discontent can be intensified when the process is seen as a form of colonialism by the USA, a country hated in many parts of the world.

There are also critics from within the developed world. Throughout the 1990s a global anti-capitalist coalition grew up comprising socialists, human rights campaigners, environmentalists and others. Direct action at EU, G8 and WTO summits has become increasing violent as militaristic police forces confront demonstrators with riot shields, weapons and tear gas and the summit meetings retreat to ever-more inaccessible locations to evade the protesters. The absence of a world authority allows the global economy to become a form of anarchy.

Sovereignty preserved?

Some argue that globalization is less advanced, and state sovereignty less diminished, than is supposed. It is a process rather than an end-state (Hoogvelt

1997: 131). Many international companies still trade with only a limited number of states and maintain a base in a single country. Footloose capital is more a feature of Anglo-American business culture; in Germany or Japan 'there would be a massive political price to pay were a major part of manufacturing to be shipped abroad' (Hirst and Thompson 1996: 198). Another key development of the post-1970s era has been the formation of regional trading blocs (e.g. the North American Free Trade Association, the Asia–Pacific Economic Cooperation and the EU), with members placing a relatively small proportion of their trade in a truly global marketplace.

Why then does the thesis hold such sway? Part of the answer may lie in its usefulness to politicians. The right and the modernizing left can use it to justify limited social programmes, weakened trade unions and falling wage levels. Thus New Labour came to power in 1997 promising no income tax rises. When faced with the closure of the Fujitsu plant in his Sedgefield constituency, Tony Blair was quick to blame global forces, offering no more than sympathy to the jobless. On the other hand, the left can use globalization to stress the weakness of conventional politics and argue for more radical action against capital. In contrast, those doubting the real extent of globalization are able to see a continuing role for modern governments in shaping social and economic policies. A position somewhere between the extremes leads to a conclusion that governments and states remain powerful actors, but they now share the arena with an array of other organizations (Held et al. 1999: 50).

Still a 'Sceptred Isle'? Decline and fall

When Britain's position is considered in a world setting the most striking feature since the late nineteenth century is that, while remaining amongst the wealthy core, it has experienced a relative economic and political decline. The search for an explanation from both left and right has attached blame variously to most political, social and economic institutions, but the historical links with the world order are frequently ignored. However, the remarkable overseas expansion of the state and its location at the very epicentre of the developing world economy, while serving capitalist interests, were to bequeath damaging obsessions with free trade and world leadership.

A free trade *idée fixe* The commitment to free trade meant that as world conditions changed, Britain's markets were penetrated and many home industries destroyed. At the same time, its global orientation saw capital exploring the world for profitable investments, putting the number of British-based multinationals second only to that of the USA. For the domestic economy this meant persistent under-investment (generally about half that of rivals such as the USA, Japan and West Germany) and restricted productivity (Gamble 1990: 17). This was accelerated by the complete removal of exchange controls by the Conservative government in 1979.

Folie de grandeur Although imperialism and free trade made Britain open to the world, this was a world to be dominated and led rather than joined on equal terms. Consequently it has not been easy for the political class to come to terms with reality. A rejection of the European embrace in the 1950s (see chapter 5) reflected the belief that the UK could retain great power status in its own right, with heavy overseas defence commitments. It preferred to cultivate connections with the USA, to preserve a world leadership role, and with the Commonwealth, from which could be heard the echoes of an imperial past. The result was a persistent desire to punch beyond the country's weight, placing heavy burdens on the domestic economy. The delusion of grandeur was exposed in the humiliating Suez crisis, a defining moment of the new era.

The Suez crisis

In July 1956, Colonel Nasser of Egypt, generally suspected of anti-westernism, nationalized the Suez Canal Company. An ill-fated military action ensued with the intention of toppling him. It was based on the bogus pretext of separating the warring factions in the Arab–Israeli conflict, the Israelis advancing upon the canal with RAF cover. The disclosure of the true facts produced world outrage, Prime Minister Eden's position became untenable and he soon resigned on the grounds of ill health. The greatest humiliation was the USA's chilly response. Not only did the 'special relation' openly disapprove, it refused to intervene to halt a run on sterling until an ignominious withdrawal was effected. The acutely divided British elite was confronted with the harsh reality of its diminished world authority.

However, this *folie de grandeur* could serve the political class, gilding the Establishment with status in the eyes of citizens. Thus, when the Falklands war allowed the decrepit lion again to yawn its arthritic jaws, the Conservative government, amidst triumphalism and jingoism, was able to surmount previous unpopularity. Similarly, in standing shoulder to shoulder with George Bush in September 2001 against the Taliban in Afghanistan, Blair demonstrated that Britain had not lost the ambition to punch beyond its weight. A government chronically unable to fully fund many services at home was suddenly willing to shoulder a massive burden. The other price tag on the action was chillingly announced by Metropolitan Police Commissioner John Stevens, who warned that Britain was the most vulnerable terrorist target after the USA.

The essential message of this chapter is that the globalization process is a reality that no country can escape or master; territorial boundaries and government authority continue to dissolve before a battery of economic, social and technological forces (Held and McGrew 1993: 262). Despite xenophobic characteristics in its culture, the British polity has been conditioned by this world context to a greater extent than most. Today, perhaps the most significant of these groupings is the European Union. There are strong arguments for seeing this as the key to Britain's global future. It is the subject of the next chapter.

Key points

- British politics cannot be seen as an autonomous activity; today a process of globalization locks states into world economic and political systems that influence internal politics.
- The modern world economy can be conceptualized in terms of three zones: a developed and wealthy core, an underdeveloped periphery, and a fluid middle section.
- The relationship between zones is seen by some as a form of neocolonialism based on money rather than guns. Others see it as a process of helping poor nations through trade.
- This system consists not only of states, but of rich transnational corporations that span the globe and can blackmail and destroy regimes. They are generally controlled from the core states.
- Britain, as the first country to industrialize, played a crucial role in developing the world economy, remaining a firm advocate of the concept of free trade.
- Although we can speak of world politics, there is no such thing as a world authority; states are generally loath to give up legal sovereignty.
- Underlying Britain's relative decline in the world has been an obsession with retaining a world leadership role.

Review your understanding of the following terms and concepts

advanced capitalism
autonomy
Bretton Woods system
cold war
colonialism
comparative advantage
détente
exchange rate
exogenous and endogenous
    explanations

free trade
imperialism
industrial revolution
international associations
Iron Curtain
long boom
mercantilism
multinational corporations
multipolarity
nationalism

neocolonialism
New World Order
non-aligned world
special relationship
transnational corporations
world policeman role

Assignment

Study the extract below and answer the following questions:

		Mark (%)
1	'It's the economy stupid!' Discuss.	20
2	What kinds of policies can be expected by countries from the IMF 'assuming economic control . . . until the conditions for safe global investment have been restored'?	20
3	Why is 'the current system . . . working to the great advantage of the US economy'?	20
4	Discuss the economic, political and moral implications of the US drive towards the disbanding of regulations and government controls around the world.	40

Without US co-operation there is no chance of global financial regulation beyond . . . global information systems and more transparency in accounting procedures and book keeping, for governments, banks and corporations, plus more secure, and expeditious, bankruptcy laws. And more money for the IMF, so that, as lender of last resort (or financial rapid deployment force), it can intervene or lead pre-emptive strikes in countries in danger of financial turmoil – in exchange for assuming economic control in those countries until the conditions for safe global investment have been restored. Why has the USA so adamantly opposed financial regulation, and why will it do so in the foreseeable future? Simple: the current system, at least in the short term, is working to the great advantage of the US economy and US firms, particularly those financial firms which are channelling a growing proportion of global investments. As for government officials, their mantra remains, 'It's the economy stupid!'. With its tremendous comparative advantage in technology, networking, information and management, the US economy is thriving. There is evidence that the US government . . . spearheaded the effort to expand global capitalism by opening up emerging markets, demanding the disbanding of regulations and government controls around the world.

Extract from Manuel Castells, 'Information technology and global capitalism', in W. Hutton and A. Giddens (eds), *On The Edge: Living with Global Capitalism*, London, Vintage, 2002, pp. 52–74.
Reprinted by permission of the Random House Group Ltd.

Questions for discussion

Because this chapter is concerned with the link between the international environment and internal politics, some of these questions may be easier to answer when further chapters have been studied.

1   Discuss the value of taking an exogenous perspective in the study of British politics.
2   What is meant by the term 'globalization'? To what extent can it be overstated.
3   'Britain has been open to the world, yet at the same time politically insular.' Discuss.
4   Explain the meaning of the term 'neocolonialism' in the context of the modern world economy.
5   How far is it true today that Britain has a 'special relationship' with the USA?
6   What were the implications of the 11 September crisis for internal British politics?
7   'Britain's relative post-war decline was largely attributable to its leaders' delusions of grandeur.' Discuss.
8   Examine the implications of the end of the cold war for British politics.
9   'The unwillingness of states to sacrifice national sovereignty means that the United Nations is doomed to fail.' Discuss.
10 'The Commonwealth is a mere shadow of the British Empire with no relevance to the modern world.' Discuss.

Topic for debate

This house believes that the idea of national autonomy in today's world politics is a complete illusion.

Further reading

Bauman, Z. (2000) *Community: Seeking Security in an Insecure World.*
Argues that globalization reduces security and freedom.

Callaghan, J. (1997) *Great Power Complex.*
Ideas of supremacy within Britain's elites led to costly attempts to maintain a world role in the post-war era.

Camilleri, J. A. and Falk, J. (1992) *The End of Sovereignty?*
Examines the theory and practice of state sovereignty against the backdrop of rapid economic, political and technological changes in the modern world.

Chomsky, N. (1997) *World Orders, Old and New.*
Devastating critique of the 'new world order', as ingenious 'historical engineering' whereby old pretexts for cold war have been replaced by new.

Deane, P. (1963) *The First Industrial Revolution.*
Detailed account of the industrial revolution in Britain. Critical of the minimal role played by the government, which is blamed for the later eclipse by rivals.

George, S. (1991) *The Debt Boomerang*.
Critique of World Bank and IMF policies, which accelerate deforestation, mass migration, the drugs trade, third world debt and global instability.

Gray, J. (1998) *False Dawn: The Utopia of the Global Free Market*.
Critique of unregulated global capitalism by leading thinker who discarded earlier free-market advocacy.

Hennessy, P. (1992) *Never Again, Britain 1945–1951*.
Rich account of British politics in a crucial stage of reappraising its world position.

Hirst, P. and Thompson, G. (1996) *Globalization in Question*.
Argues against the more extreme versions of the globalization thesis.

Hobsbawm, E. (1995) *Age of Extremes*.
Marxist perspective on the evolving world economy.

Hutton, W. (2002) *The World We're In*.
Sequel to *The State We're In*, argues challengingly that Britain has more in common with Europe than the USA and should place less importance on the 'special relationship'.

Pilger, J. (2002) *The New Rulers of the World*.
An exposé of the secrets that lie behind corporate and state power by a radical journalist committed to getting behind the propaganda.

Stiglitz, J. (2002) *Globalization and its Discontents*.
Stinging critique of the IMF by Nobel Prize winner and one-time chief economist at the World Bank.

Wallerstein, I. (1979) *The Capitalist World Economy*.
Outlines the zones of the capitalist world economy.

For light relief

Tom Clancy, *Debt of Honour*.
Thriller set within the international economy. Political intrigue and military threat in the context of trade conflict between the USA and Japan.

Ben Elton, *Stark*.
Surreal novel about global capitalist power.

Arthur Miller, *The Crucible*.
A modern classic play about the hysteria surrounding a witch hunt, satirizing McCarthyism.

A. Sampson, *The Seven Sisters*.
Penetrating account of the oil crisis.

On the net

www.fco.gov.uk
www.dfid.gov.uk
The Foreign Office and the Department for International Development sites include a wide range of information on foreign policy and current international issues, together with links to related organizations.

www.newint.org
The New Internationalist site deals with issues of world poverty and inequality, and the relationship between rich and poor nations. Also includes a comprehensive guide to relevant organizations and resources.

www.wdm.org.uk
The World Development Movement is just one of many organizations campaigning for justice for the world's poor.

www.un.org
For a truly international flavour, try the United Nations site.

5

Britain in Europe: Awkward Partners?

This chapter considers an aspect of Britain's international setting that is assuming increasing importance and has deepening implications for domestic politics. The first section examines the origins of the European Union and the protracted process that finally brought Britain into what was then the European Community. Next we chart developments through the Single European Act and the Maastricht, Amsterdam and Nice treaties to the present. A third section details the anatomy of the EU, explaining the nature and role of the institutions, their internal workings, the relationships between them in the policy-making process and the debates associated with their powers. After this we identify some key domestic debates over British membership and conclude with a consideration of the future.

We are part of the community of Europe and we must do our duty as such.

Lord Salisbury (1830–1903; Conservative leader), speech (11 April 1888)

Despite the empire, the special relationship with the USA and a long history of European rivalry and warfare, Britain remains an offshore island of Western Europe, sharing much of its history and culture. The geographical logic has exerted an inexorable pressure towards integration, which became more compelling during the post-war era. The 1948 Brussels Treaty aimed to promote collective defence and in 1949 a Council of Europe was established to facilitate cooperation, producing the European Convention on Human Rights (see p. 72). However, of all Britain's relationships none has generated more internal political heat than that with what is now termed the European Union (EU).

It will be seen throughout this book that membership of the EU sends ripples to all corners of the political system. No other association to which Britain belongs promises to penetrate so deeply into the state and the lives of its citizens. While other associations are intergovernmental, the EU is **supragovernmental**: its legislation is distinct from, and constitutionally superior to, that of member states. This has led to profound concern over a feared loss of British sovereignty, dividing the political Establishment and continuing to colour debate on domestic issues.

The Entry Process

The UK has long performed a kind of stately square dance with Europe; advancing, pausing before the promised embrace, only to turn aside to another partner, the USA or the Commonwealth.

The origins of the integrationist movement lay in the need to repair the devastation wrought by the second world war. Yet there was a deeper purpose: to prevent further war in Western Europe. Hence, although the early moves were ostensibly concerned with economic integration, the real agenda was political. During the second world war Winston Churchill had enthused over the idea of a United States of Europe, envisaging the Great Powers accepting government through a joint council backed by a court and an army. However, the moves to establish a Council of Europe revealed a fundamental difference between Britain and its continental neighbours. Again, when in June 1948 sixteen West European countries established the Organisation for European Economic Cooperation (OEEC) to coordinate post-war recovery and administer the US aid programme, hopes that it might develop into a permanent supranational institution were dashed by British and Scandinavian opposition. Yet a **federalist** movement gathered pace under the inspiration of French economist and international administrator Jean Monnet. Even as war raged, he was warning that a post-war reconstruction reflecting nationalistic pride and protectionism would never guarantee peace.

> We must build a kind of United States of Europe.
>
> Winston Churchill, speech in Zurich (19 Sept. 1946)

The first major event came in 1951 with the establishment of the European Coal and Steel Community (ECSC). Monnet's reasoning was that if key areas of production were integrated war would be impossible. Yet as Italy, France, West Germany and the Benelux countries joined the dance, the UK again chose to remain a wallflower. Wishing to drive things further, Monnet resigned the ECSC presidency in November 1954 to help found an Action Committee for a United States of Europe, which led to the establishment of a European Atomic Energy Community (Euratom) and the European Economic Community (EEC).

> The political unity of tomorrow will depend on making the economic union effective in everyday activities.
>
> Jean Monnet (1888–1979), *Memoirs*

Based on the ECSC model, the EEC was headed by a Council of Ministers in which decisions were based on the votes of ministerial leaders from the member states. It was served by a European Commission, a bureaucracy containing civil servants and headed by commissioners appointed by state governments. In addition there was an assembly with members nominated by governments from national parliaments, leaving each with two jobs (dual mandate). The nature and powers of these institutions and the relationships between them were to generate considerable tension and influence their evolution.

However, there was to be no British signature on the 1957 Treaty of Rome establishing the EEC. This decision to stay out was momentous. Why did a state that had captained a huge empire, pioneered the development of the world economy, been a devoted worshipper at the altar of free trade, taken a prominent role within NATO, with a seat on the UN Security Council and a credible claim to have 'won the war' relinquish all claim to a leadership role in this major arena? The reasons lie in its past success. Despite the ravages of war Britain believed in its world leadership destiny. The political class looked beyond Europe for status on the world stage: to the special relationship with US brawn and to the Commonwealth, with its echoes of empire. Britain flexed its diplomatic biceps by becoming a nuclear power.

In 1959, Britain, with Norway, Denmark, Sweden, Switzerland, Austria and Portugal, formed an alternative grouping – the European Free Trade Association (EFTA), a trading bloc without political overtones. However, this was no rival to the EEC; Britain's relative economic decline during the long boom, and the particular success of West Germany and France, suggested that the decision had been misguided. The cold US response to the Suez crisis revealed that the 'special relationship' did not give Britain political omnipotence and in 1961 Prime Minister Harold Macmillan finally announced that the UK would apply for EC membership.

Although the USA welcomed the decision, Macmillan moved with characteristic languor. His vision was of economic union, with little place for the political dimension cemented into the foundations of the Treaty. Moreover, there was opposition within the EEC, French President General de Gaulle, suspicious that Britain would prove a Trojan horse for US influence, vetoing the application. He did the same with a second overture from the Labour government and only after his resignation in 1969 did the UK receive a sympathetic hearing. Hence, in 1973, Edward Heath, clearer in his European intentions than his predecessors, took the historic step. Yet British scepticism died hard. Labour had opposed the entry terms and, returning to office in 1974, held a promised referendum on continued membership with renegotiated terms. A 'Yes' vote duly came, with a 65 per cent turnout and a two-thirds majority, on 5 June 1975. However, the debate was by no means over. British statesmen had studiously avoided an explicit statement on the loss of national sovereignty (Young 1998) and the gradual realization of this was to fuel the efforts of the **Eurosceptics** and prevent a whole-hearted commitment to the European project.

The Integration Process

The career of the Community has been fitful, with periods of stagnation (*immobilisme*) and dynamism. Although many aspects of the Rome Treaty remained paper promises, the initial decade was dynamic. It was, however, followed by four years of stagnation, beginning with de Gaulle's first veto of UK membership. His retirement permitted further progress; the goal of advancing political union was affirmed at the 1969 Hague Summit and plans were made to coordinate foreign policy. In 1970 the Werner Plan argued for the harmonization of economic, fiscal and budgetary policy and 1979 saw the launch of the European Monetary System (EMS) and democratic elections for the European Parliament.

However, 1979 also heralded a further phase of tension when a new head of government, as nationalistic as de Gaulle, entered the stage and the UK was to underline its role as the 'awkward partner' (George 1990). Britain did not enter the EMS and, echoing her 'No such thing as society' sentiment on the domestic front, Margaret Thatcher was to declare:

> There is no such thing as a separate community interest; the community interest is compounded of the national interests of the ten member states. (Quoted in Urwin 1989: 369)

She began with an acrimonious campaign to reduce the size of the UK contribution to the Community budget. The goal was not unreasonable; Labour also favoured negotiations. However, the tactics entailed denigrating the Common Agricultural Policy (CAP), regarded by the six original members as their greatest achievement, and Thatcher's style of diplomacy did little to enhance the UK's Euro-credentials.

The Single European Act

In 1986 Portugal and Spain joined the Community, preparations for this reinvigorating the integrationist spirit. In June 1985 the European Commission, under the presidency of avowed integrationist Jacques Delors, produced a white paper, *Completing the Internal Market*. The following year saw the Single European Act, with its commitment to cooperation in foreign policy, strengthened social cohesion mechanisms and a programme for a genuine internal market, free of persisting non-tariff trade barriers, by 1992. The target year became a symbol of progress. Although it had signed the treaty, the UK government became alarmed at the idea of a social dimension concerned with workers' rights, social dialogue, collective bargaining and worker participation, and Thatcher was to pour a douche of cold water on the idea in a key speech at Bruges. Yet she did little to dampen the enthusiasm of other member states for a quickened pace of integration; an Intergovernmental Conference in December 1990 on Economic and Monetary and Political Union at Rome foreshadowed a major advance.

A centralised European government would be a nightmare. We have not rolled back the frontiers of the state at home only to see them reimposed at a European level.

Margaret Thatcher, speech in Bruges (Sept. 1988)

The Maastricht Treaty

The previously little-known Dutch town of Maastricht achieved celebrity in February 1992 as the site for the signing of the Treaty on European Union. Its 61,351 words went further than any other Community agreement in promoting integration. The event assumed additional significance because of its momentous historical conjuncture, including the end of the cold war, German reunification and the collapse of the Soviet empire. The term 'Union' signified that the EC became part of a wider framework, which was to include a foreign and security policy and justice and home affairs. (In discussions the UK government initially chose ostentatiously to eschew the term Union.) Yet it did not satisfy all. For true federalists the image would have been of a tree with three branches extending from a common trunk. What emerged was a temple built upon three pillars, combined but essentially separate (figure 5.1).

In the common foreign and defence policy the existing joint defence association, the Western European Union (WEU), was to become central, with the international situation monitored by a Political Committee. The justice and home affairs pillar would see cooperation in various areas previously left within national competence. Significantly, the second and third pillars were to remain outside the competence of the EC legislative and judicial institutions;

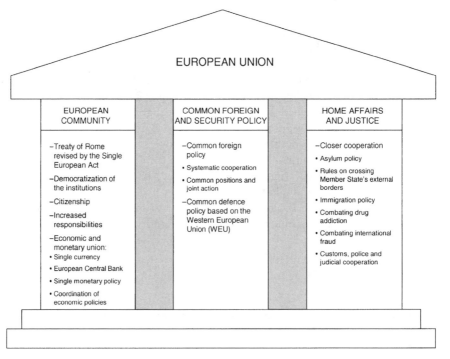

Figure 5.1
The three pillars of the European Union.

Source: European Parliament.

> **What's in a name?**
>
> Like the association itself the name has evolved. Initially the European Economic Community (often the 'Common Market'), the Single European Act rebaptized it the European Community, signifying concerns wider than trade. After the Maastricht Treaty the term 'European Union' gained wide currency and, although not strictly correct, is widely used in place of EC.

they were based upon cooperation rather than supragovernmentalism. This limitation was one of the proclaimed successes of the UK government in the negotiations. Amongst the treaty's most important features were the following.

- ◆ *EC citizenship.* Of both symbolic and practical significance, the concept of EC citizenship had received little publicity. It allowed all nationals certain rights: to reside and move freely throughout the Community, and vote and stand in municipal and European Parliament elections.
- ◆ *Policy competence.* The policy remit was extended to cover aspects of education, culture, public health, industry and consumer protection.
- ◆ *The institutions.* Decision-making procedures were made more supranational and the powers of the Parliament and the Court increased (see below).
- ◆ *Subsidiarity.* An inelegant neologism became much used and abused in the debate. Essentially it established a principle of devolution: EU institutions should act only if the objectives could not be better met at a lower level. For the UK government **subsidiarity** meant leaving power at Westminster, yet the term could also mean devolving power to regional and local governments, an interpretation largely at variance with trends in Britain since 1979.
- ◆ *Social policy.* A set of revised objectives to promote employment and improve working conditions became known as the Social Chapter. It was opposed by the UK, which was allowed by the other members effectively to opt out (see p. 140).
- ◆ *Economic integration.* The treaty placed considerable emphasis on the open market economy, the convergence of economic indicators and monetary union, including the establishment of a single currency (from which the UK, along with the Danes, also negotiated an opt-out; see p. 138). Economic policy would be determined by qualified majority voting (see p. 125) so that no single country could veto developments.

Once signed, the Treaty required ratifying by national assemblies and, in some cases, the courts. The process was not entirely smooth. There were stormy scenes in the House of Commons and the behaviour of his Eurosceptics forced

John Major to announce a confidence motion for 23 July 1993. The gamble paid off with a majority of 40 and the UK finally ratified the treaty in August 1993.

'Son of Maastricht' The next major advance also took place in Holland. Sometimes billed as 'son of Maastricht', the 1997 Amsterdam Treaty proved a disappointingly puny child. For many the overriding priority was to avoid shaking monetary union, the project at the heart of the push for political union. Reforms to voting procedures and the powers of the European Parliament were relatively modest.

The Nice Treaty

After the failure at Amsterdam, the Nice summit of December 2000 was called to approve a new governing treaty laying down a framework to accommodate twelve further members from ex-communist Eastern Europe who were knocking on the door. The meeting proved chaotic and fractious and, breaking all records for length, extended the usual two-day schedule to five. It ended in the early dawn of the final day at 3.25, when weary leaders finally buried their differences over voting power and agreed changes to the EU decision-making process. Majority voting was extended to over 30 new areas. The Blair government trumpeted its success in retaining the veto in social security, taxation and immigration policy, areas that had never really been seriously threatened. The French presidency's attempt to turn the planned European rapid reaction force into a rival to NATO was also defeated. The Nice Treaty was, like its Amsterdam predecessor, a compromise securing little more than the bare minimum, and the process was thrown into further disarray when the people of Ireland, in a referendum, voted not to ratify it.

An Anatomy of the EU

The institutional architecture of the EU (figure 5.2) is more than a theme park of modernistic buildings and offices in Brussels, Strasbourg and Luxembourg; it is the physical embodiment of the values of supranationalism. Certain key institutions dominate the landscape, their powers and relationships providing the mainspring of the system.

The Council of Ministers

Meeting in Brussels and consisting of national ministers, the Council was created as the political head of the Union; from here come the decisions that increasingly shape the lives of people and organizations in member states. Although the Council is a powerful law-making body, its meetings are shrouded in secrecy. Decisions emerge as:

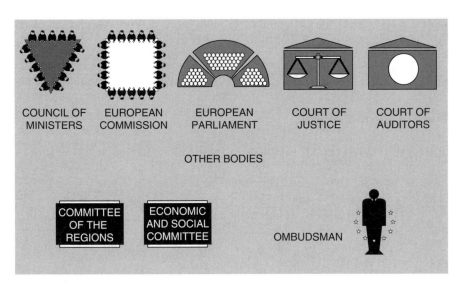

Figure 5.2
Institutions of the
European Union.

Source: European Parliament.

- ◆ *regulations* – having immediate force of law;
- ◆ *directives* – binding, but in practice leaving member states with leeway in implementation;
- ◆ *recommendations and resolutions* – not compelling.

The Council is led by the country holding the EU presidency, held for six-monthly terms (semesters) in rotation. With extensive coordination responsibilities, the office can be pivotal and states usually try to make their mark during their stewardship. The composition of the Council changes with the policy under consideration. The General Council comprises foreign ministers but a range of other 'councils' bring together ministers for particular policy areas: trade, finance, agriculture and so on. The Council is served by a bureaucracy of some 2,000 headed by a Secretary General. It is also aided by a Committee of Permanent Representatives (COREPER), comprising national ambassadors and their deputies. The system is held together by a dense web of official committees, subcommittees and working parties, some permanent and some ad hoc.

The Council tends to be a forum where ministers fight their corners. To mitigate this, the Rome Treaty made provision for a system of **qualified majority voting** (QMV) so that decisions did not require unanimity. However, tensions resulted in the French boycotting the community and, to resolve this deadlock, the 1966 'Luxembourg compromise' permits a state to veto any proposal judged to threaten its vital national interest. Although not often used, it was a severe restriction.

The Single European Act and the Maastricht and Amsterdam treaties extended QMV, particularly over issues relating to the single market. Each minister's vote is weighted to reflect population size, acceptance of a policy requiring 62 votes cast by no fewer than 10 members. Alternatively, 26 votes

Weighted voting

Votes per country
France 10
Germany 10
Italy 10
UK 10
Spain 8
Belgium 5
Greece 5
Portugal 5
Netherlands 5
Austria 4
Sweden 4
Denmark 3
Finland 3
Ireland 3
Luxembourg 2

against a measure (a 'blocking minority') will block it. Voting is characterized by complex bargaining, with national interests to the fore. Moreover, unanimity is still required in a significant number of areas and on all issues it is generally considered desirable.

The European Council

In December 2000 French President Jacques Chirac arrived at the enormous Acropolis Centre at Nice with tears in his eyes. This was not due to federalist emotion, or even the promised confrontation with British Prime Minister Tony Blair over the European rapid reaction force. The air outside was thick with tear gas thrown by his riot police at the massed ranks of protesters, including students, trade unionists and left-wing activists, protesting variously about the failure of governments to address social divisions within the EU, economic globalization and the EU record on human rights.

This was the violent backdrop to a meeting of the European Council and it demonstrated a growing recognition that here was the key centre of EU power. Yet it was never planned to be like this. The framers of the Rome Treaty did not create such a body; it has been a product of an irresistible political evolution in which heads of state and foreign ministers have, from the early 1970s, come to play a dominant role through regular 'summit meetings'. Formalized at the Paris summit of December 1974 and recognized in both the Single European

The Leopold Complex at Brussels

Photo: Airprint

Act and the Maastricht Treaty, it is here that major community issues are thrashed out. The 1969 Hague summit gave the community its 'own resources', the 1985 Milan summit will for ever be associated with the Single European Act, the 1989 Madrid summit with the Social Charter and the 1991 Maastricht summit with the Treaty on European Union.

These high-profile meetings, taking place two or three times a year in the country holding the presidency, are ornamented by lavish ceremonial and wining and dining for the political glitterati in the palaces and embassies of Europe's capitals. Two days in Amsterdam in June 1997 reportedly cost £10 million. Providing a major focus for media attention, the run-up usually sees protracted negotiations, febrile rumour-mongering and speculation. The presidency can offer a head of state a chance to shine and Tony Blair was fortunate in coming to it in his first year as prime minister. However, he also had the embarrassment of presiding over the launch of the single currency while his own country remained outside.

Although this development illustrates the increasing importance of the EU, it also testifies to the persistence of nationalism. Thus it was at the Fontainebleau summit of 1984 that Margaret Thatcher fought successfully for a budget rebate, while Major claimed 'game, set and match' for Britain at Maastricht and Blair repeated the 'Britain first' mantra and consulted Thatcher before his first Eurosummit. The priorities he outlined there showed little of the Delors vision and could have come straight from her handbag.

The European Commission

In the demonology of Eurosceptics, the Brussels-based Commission is redolent of a Kafkaesque superstate. It is effectively the EU civil service and the institution most removed from democratic influence. Indeed, it is more than a civil service. Not only does it implement Council policy, it has sole responsibility for initiating legislation, it drafts the budget and it conducts negotiations with non-member states.

At its head sit twenty commissioners nominated by member states: two from Britain, France, Germany, Italy and Spain and one from each of the smaller countries. Each is responsible for one or more policy portfolios and is expected to develop a supranational perspective, a requirement sometimes putting them at odds with their own governments. However, they can take comfort from their remuneration, receiving salaries over 70 per cent greater than that of the British prime minister, as well as other generous allowances. Britain's commissioners, generally prominent ex-politicians, traditionally come from each of the two main parties. The incumbents in 2001 were Neil Kinnock, who had resigned the Labour leadership in 1992 after his party's second general election defeat, and Chris Patton, a prominent Conservative MP before rejection by the electorate in 1992, who had been governor of Hong Kong until 1997.

Not fit to run a fish and chip shop.

Said to be Norman Tebbit's comment on Neil Kinnock when the latter was about to be appointed as a commissioner

The president The Commission is led by its president, a high-profile figure in world politics. The position has been seen as the motor of integration and Jacques Delors, coming to office in January 1985 and reappointed four years later, was a particularly forceful advocate. Reviled by Eurosceptics, he was often pilloried in the British tabloids. Appointment must be with the common accord of member states and the Maastricht Treaty also made it subject to approval in the European Parliament. At the June 1994 Corfu summit, in a nationalistic move to appease his Eurosceptics, John Major vetoed the appointment of Jean Luc Dehane (a federalist and the preferred choice of France and Germany). The result was the appointment of Jacques Santer of Luxembourg, who was forced to resign in 1999 after becoming embroiled in a major corruption scandal. His successor, the mild-mannered, bicycling, Bologna University Professor Romano Prodi, contrasted with his more charismatic predecessors. Described by political opponents as 'the Mortadella' (a rather bland sausage for which his city was famous), he was one of Italy's most successful post-war prime ministers. The particular talent he brought to the presidency was one much needed in the evolving EU: an ability to find consensus and compromise. Yet despite his reputation, he soon revealed himself to be a firm integrationist and was to criticize Britain's special relationship with the USA.

A democratic deficit? The Commission is largely free from the constraints of national interest that bedevil the Council of Ministers and the European Council. It can also take a broader and longer-term world perspective than national politicians. However, its role occasions fierce argument in Britain. It is seen by Eurosceptics as driving the Euro-train at breakneck speed towards federalism with no democratic accountability to the hundreds of millions whose lives are affected, although the nationalistic tendencies of the superior institutions have been a restraining force. Conscious of its vulnerability, the Commission has generally shown itself anxious to gain legitimacy by working in harmony with the European Parliament and welcoming consultation with interest groups at various levels (see chapter 17). Even so, its relationship with the Parliament reached a point of crisis in 1999 over a serious corruption scandal (see p. 131).

> ...neither seek nor take instruction from any government or any body...
>
> Part of the solemn undertaking given by commissioners upon taking office

The European Parliament

Some citizens of continental Europe can expect to be disturbed in the night by fleets of lorries trundling between imposing buildings in Brussels, Luxembourg and Strasbourg. Their cargo consists of many tons of documents, reproduced in all official EU languages on paper of various hues. The reason for this nomadic behaviour is nationalistic wrangling, which has prevented the establishment of a single seat for the EU's assembly. The single-chamber European Parliament (EP) holds plenary sessions one week every month in the splendid Palais de l'Europe at Strasbourg. Although these are the headline-catching occasions, detailed work is done in between, through a committee network working close

Table 5.1 Representatives at the European Parliament, 1999

Country	MEPs	Country	MEPs	Country	MEPs
Austria	21	Germany	99	Netherlands	31
Belgium	25	Greece	25	Portugal	25
Denmark	16	Ireland	15	Spain	64
Finland	16	Italy	87	Sweden	22
France	87	Luxembourg	6	UK	87

Despite its three locations and multilingual operation, the EP running costs are a modest 1.5 euro for each EU citizen.

to the heart of EU power at Brussels. Servicing these operations is the work of the secretariat located in yet a third venue, at Luxembourg.

The 626 Members of the European Parliament (**MEPs**) are elected for five-year terms, the number of representatives from each country reflecting population (table 5.1). Although they do not confront each other in the semicircular chamber like a government and opposition, they do form political groupings, which cut across national boundaries (figure 5.3 and table 5.2).

Members themselves are torn by conflicting loyalties: to EP group, national interest and national party. The Euroscepticism of British Conservatives creates major problems within the EPP grouping. Although often terming themselves parties, the groupings are not like those of national politics. They do not have mass organizations or fight elections with clear manifestos and, with no executive to support, have little need for continuous party discipline. Indeed, a show of

Inside the Palais de l'Europe at Strasbourg

Photo: European Parliament

The European Parliament buildings at Strasbourg (left) and Brussels (right)
Photos: European Parliament

cross-group solidarity can actually be preferred, since this can strengthen the EP hand in negotiating with Council and Commission.

Political complexion Unlike most national parliaments, the EP does not fall under the domination of a single party or coalition. However, it does show an ideological complexion (figure 5.3). The first two elections produced centre-right leanings based around the EPP. In 1989 the balance shifted to the

Table 5.2 Party allegiances of UK MEPs after the 1999 European Parliament election

Party	No. of MEPs	European grouping
Conservative	36	European People's Party and European Democrats (PPE–DE)
UUP	1	Party of European Socialists (PSE)
Labour	29	
SDLP	1	
Liberal Democrat	10	Liberal, Democratic and Reformist Party (ELDR)
UK Independence Party	3	Europe of Democracies and Diversities (EDD)
Green Party	2	Greens/European Free Alliance
SNP	2	(Verts–ALE)
Plaid Cymru	2	
UUP	1	Not attached

Source: Data from European Parliament.

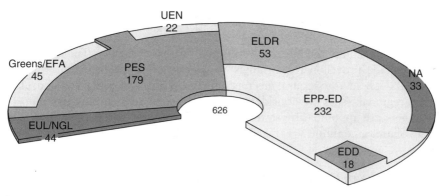

Figure 5.3
Political groupings
in the European
Parliament after the
1999 election.

Source: Data from European Parliament.

Note: EDD = Europe of Democracies and Diversities; ELDR = European Liberal, Democratic and Reform Party; EPP–ED = European People's Party (Christian Democrats) and European Democrats; EUL/NGL = European United Left/Nordic Green Left; Green/EFA = Greens/European Free Alliance; PES = Party of European Socialists; UEN = Union for Europe of the Nations; NA = non-attached.

centre-left, with increased Green representation which, although large enough to form a separate group, allied with the Socialists. The 1994 elections saw an almost Europe-wide swing back to the right except in Britain, where the first-past-the-post voting system (except in Northern Ireland) greatly inflated Labour's representation. Proportional representation was introduced (by the Labour government) for the 1999 EP elections (see chapter 9).

Power A major debate concerns EP powers which, despite increasing involve-ment in legislative procedures (see below), have remained very limited. For-mally it may reject the budget and dismiss the Commission *en bloc*, but these have been seen as draconian measures, too dangerous to use, although some have argued that the 'nuclear button' should be pressed. Events reached fever pitch in January 1999 in a tense stand-off amidst parliamentary accusations of Commission fraud and mismanagement. A report by a 'Committee of the Wise' detailed a catalogue of fraud, mismanagement and nepotism reaching to the highest level and the outcome was the most dramatic bloodbath in EU history. Outraged MEPs gave the commissioners an ultimatum: 'go with honour or be forced out without honour'. The ensuing mass resignations included that of the President himself.

The Economic and Social Committee (ECOSOC)

Another body with a quasi-democratic function is the Brussels-based ECOSOC, which considers industrial policy. Members are nominated by state govern-ments for renewable four-year terms and are broadly representative of three interests: employers, workers and miscellaneous social and professional groups. As a consultative forum it lacks executive powers, though its presence repre-sents a nod in the direction of corporatism (see pp. 543–4), a style of govern-ment more prevalent in continental Europe than in Britain.

The Committee of the Regions (COR)

Some see a vision of the future in terms of a Europe of regions. The Maastricht Treaty made provision for an advisory committee to articulate the regional voice and it held its inaugural meeting at Brussels in March 1995. It is consulted when regional issues are considered and can also issue own-initiative reports. Members are appointed by states and most have clear party affiliations. The COR shares a common organizational structure with ECOSOC.

The European Court of Justice (ECJ)

The ECJ is the EU's own special court, its existence testifying to its uniqueness amongst international associations. Sitting at Luxembourg, it comprises judges from each member state, one of whom is elected as president. As an international court, a court of appeal, a court of review and a court of referral, it aims to ensure that Community law is applied uniformly across member states. It also plays a creative role by establishing precedents and has ruled on the relative power of institutions and their relationship with member states. It has even clarified Council policy in various substantive areas.

The Court hears actions brought variously by EU institutions, member states and natural or legal persons. The Commission is its best customer, having brought the greatest number of actions and been taken to the Court more than any other body. The procedures would be unrecognizable to anyone versed in the ways of UK courts. Advocates General present the cases before the judges and deliver reasoned opinions as to what the verdict might be; these carry considerable weight and are frequently followed. Decisions, which are made by majority, are binding upon member states. The Court also has a responsibility to consider the constitutionality of any laws passed by a domestic legislature, a power not possessed by the British courts. However, it works slowly, is expensive and many of its decisions may be seen as fudged compromises.

A political role? The role of the Court is not only practical, it is deeply symbolic of the EU's supranational character. Some allege that it has a political agenda, generally advancing a federalist vision through its interpretations and precedents (Burley and Mattli 1993). The 1990 *Factortame* case (see p. 72) brought home its ability to limit the legal sovereignty of Parliament.

The legislative process

The formal process of making EU policy is one of the key areas of debate. In this the EP and Council negotiate and bargain, the former being the weaker partner. The process entails rounds of formal meetings, much informal discussion, deal-making and covert lobbying where interests extend beyond governments to a myriad of pressure groups operating in the Brussels hothouse.

Initially the Council reigned supreme but the EP has fought continuously for a greater formal involvement in the evolution of the following procedures.

Consultation From the outset a number of articles in the original EEC treaty have required that draft legislation from the Commission be submitted for an EP opinion before going to the Council of Ministers, but with no compulsion upon the Council to act, the consultation procedure offers little power to the EP.

Cooperation A significant extension of EP power came in the 1986 Single European Act with a cooperation procedure between EP and Council for particular areas, including measures facilitating the internal market. In essence, a further stage was added to the consultation process, giving the EP another bite at the legislative cherry. Upon receiving the EP opinion the Council must consider it and reach a 'common position', returning it to the EP for a second reading. Although not formally increasing EP power, the procedure compels both Commission and Council to consider its views and encourages inter-institutional bargaining. It also helps to publicize an issue and mobilize political forces, including public opinion.

Co-decision The Maastricht Treaty introduced the co-decision procedure (figure 5.4) to increase EP power in a limited number of areas such as research, culture, health and consumer affairs. The Amsterdam Treaty enlarged its scope by transferring to it most items formerly subject to the cooperation procedure, making the EP the 'big winner' of that summit (Duff 1997: 143). Areas covered include the free movement of workers, establishing the internal market, technological research and development, the environment, consumer protection, education, culture and health. If, after two readings, the EP remains unhappy with the Council's common position and rejects it by an overall majority, it can request it to set up a conciliation committee drawn from both institutions and the Commission. Here tough negotiations can take place. Where both parties are able to reach agreement, the legislation is promulgated in their joint names, thereby making the EP a coequal legislator. The procedure was simplified by the Amsterdam Treaty, allowing the EP to reject a proposal if the conciliation process fails. There is evidence that the co-decision procedure has made ministers more willing to compromise.

Assent Some enhancement of EP rights to genuine joint decision-making came in the Single European Act with a procedure whereby EP assent, by absolute majority, is required for certain Council or Commission decisions. It is used where new states are admitted to the EU and in association agreements with other countries. The Maastricht Treaty extended its scope to include such areas as citizenship, the structural fund, the creation of a uniform electoral system and international agreements. The EP would like the scope of the assent procedure to be increased further.

Figure 5.4
The co-decision
procedure.

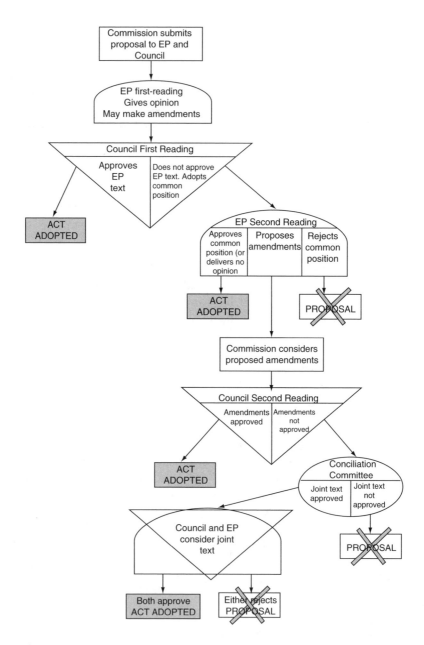

Legislative initiation Since Maastricht the EP has been able to set the legislative process in motion by submitting an 'own initiative' report to the Commission. This then forms the basis of a proposal to the Council.

Redress of grievance The Maastricht Treaty also gave the EP power to investigate citizens' complaints of maladministration in the implementation of Community law and appoint an ombudsman to assist in this.

A democratic deficit? As EU integration and the growth in its power continue, so fears of a European superstate increase. Although the EP is the EU's most democratic institution it made a bad start. Direct elections were not introduced until 1979 owing to the fear, particularly on the part of the French, of an erosion of national sovereignty. During this period the other institutions were able to gain a head start in the power struggle. However, the Commission can often make common cause with the EP since both tend towards a supranationalist perspective. The Commission also gains some legitimacy from its association with the elected body and has encouraged the gradual increase in EP power vis-à-vis the Council. However, the fact remains that the only elected EU institution has little power to penetrate a web of secrecy concealing the dealings and settlements between national governments within the Council and the powerful interests lobbying them. Although the Amsterdam summit moved things forward, a greater role for the EP, together with reforms of the institution itself, are still high on the agenda.

The Budget

Like any international association the EU needs money and much can be learned about its dynamics and balance of power from a study of the budget (which finances the EC rather than all three EU pillars). The EC Treaty calls for a balanced budget (Article 199); revenue must equal expenditure. However, the simplicity of this equation does not mean the process is uncontroversial. Major political tensions arise over the redistribution of wealth from richer to poorer areas, the balance of power between institutions and the inextinguishable disputation between federalists and internationalists.

Scale

Although the budget has grown steadily with EU enlargement and the acquisition of new functions, it remains small by domestic standards, representing only some 1.2 per cent of the total GNP of member states. However, this can give a misleading impression: further expense is borne by member states, whose national bureaucracies share the task of policy implementation.

Revenue

Unlike national governments, which raise money by taxing citizens, international associations such as NATO or the UN are usually financed by members' contributions. They can never be entirely confident of funds; some states are too poor to pay, others may withhold payment in protest. For such reasons the ECSC founding fathers instigated direct funding from levies imposed on production. However, when the EEC was created, wrangling resulted in finance by government contributions related to national wealth. This source proved limited and, as crises threatened, the Commission called for the Community to raise its own resources. The consequent loss of national control would be offset by allowing the EP to share the budgetary role with the Council. However, de Gaulle objected and it was not until his resignation in 1969 that the reform could materialize (at the Hague summit). The 'own resources' were to be customs duties, agricultural tariffs, sugar levies and, most importantly, a proportion of the VAT collected by member states. This last item was to constitute the lion's share (figure 5.5).

Yet revenue remained inadequate and the 1988 Brussels summit accepted a Commission proposal that it be fixed as a proportion of total Community GNP, thereby linking it to the fortunes of state economies. Once annual Community expenditure was agreed, the total revenue from the existing own resources would be calculated and the difference made up by a payment from each member state in proportion to its GNP. This became increasingly important; starting at 10 per cent of total revenue in 1988, it had reached 43 per cent by 2002. However, with the character of a national contribution, it presents problems for Community autonomy. Moreover, future developments are expected to require yet further sources of revenue and the nature of these will influence the degree of supranationalism the EU can achieve.

Expenditure

Generally the funds required by international associations are for running costs; they are not burdened with responsibility for substantive policies or redistributing income in the manner of states. However, with the Common Agricultural Policy, overseas aid and regional grants, the EU *does* pursue government-style objectives, making its budget not only far larger than those of other intergovernmental associations but different in character. Expenditure decisions must create winners and losers, thereby producing high-octane fuel

Figure 5.5 The EC budget, 2002: income (left); expenditure (right).

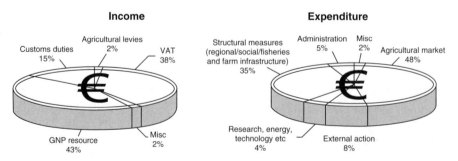

Source: Data from European Commission website (http://europa.eu.int/comm/budget).

for political machination. Rich countries resist redistribution of wealth, poorer regions lobby for social and economic development grants, those with large agricultural constituencies favour price guarantees, and so on.

The budgetary process has provided a key site for trials of strength between the Council and the EP. More than an institutional power struggle, it encompasses the federalist/internationalist debate. In this the EP shares the federal aspirations of the Commission, which promoted major budgetary reforms in 1988, increasing its influence.

A budgetary cycle (Article 203 of the EC Treaty) follows a number of stages in the EU financial year (1 January to 31 December). In addition there is an auditing process, a detailed examination of the Commission's accounts made by the Court of Auditors. The EP, with advice from the Council, decides on the basis of the Court's report whether to grant the Commission a 'discharge'. This is no mere technicality; fraud, alleged and uncovered, constitutes a major problem. In early 1998 misgiving over the 1996 budget led to discharge being deferred for a year. In November 1998 the Court revealed alleged fraud and misspending of £3 billion, some 5 per cent of the total EU budget, precipitating a major crisis in the EP's relationship with the Commission (see pp. 131–2).

Europe as a Domestic Issue

It will be seen throughout this book that UK government and politics are increasingly touched by EU membership. As an issue in political debate, it has precipitated considerable political fury, even forcing a break with tradition in the use of a referendum. In the 1980s and 1990s, it contributed to the fall of the UK's most dominant post-war prime minister, blighted the political life of her successor and saw the Conservative Party in disarray in the 1997 general election. At its most fundamental, the question relates to the degree to which the integration project should go: the federalism versus internationalism debate centres on economic and monetary union and social policy. At the outer extremities sceptical voices continue to question membership itself. At heart this debate revolves around the principle of national sovereignty.

Economic and monetary union

Monetary union is the linking of currencies to minimize exchange-rate fluctuations. It is highly conducive to free trade, a key feature of the neoliberal agenda (Grahl and Teague 1990: 97–140). In the days of empire sterling was a world currency and in the post-war years Britain remained enthusiastic about the Bretton Woods Agreement and preserving a sterling area. Yet paradoxically, it had been decidedly cool towards European **economic and monetary union** (EMU), dropping out of the system known as the Snake in the Tunnel in 1972 after only one year and remaining out of the **Exchange Rate Mechanism (ERM)** until October 1990, only to fall out again on 'Black Wednesday' (16 September 1992) following widespread currency speculation (see p. 516). Despite further turmoil in the foreign exchange markets causing many currencies to slump in value during 1993, a continuing commitment to EMU was revealed and enthusiasts argued that events had demonstrated the case for a single currency in which destructive speculation was impossible.

A single European currency The Maastricht Treaty included an historic agreement to take monetary union beyond the ERM with a **single currency** for all EU states. This would centre upon three institutions:

◆ a European System of Central Banks (ESCB) responsible for implementing domestic monetary and exchange rate policy and managing foreign reserves;
◆ a European Central Bank (ECB) under a council comprising the governors of the national central banks, with an exclusive right to issue bank notes;
◆ a European Investment Bank (EIB) to grant loans to underdeveloped regions.

The process would come in three stages, though Britain secured an 'opt-out' from the final one.

After some initial doubts, what emerged was a multi-track development with some states moving ahead of others. In May 1998, eleven countries formally adopted the single currency based on the new unit: the euro. From January 1999 it was used for cheque and credit transactions, the new notes and coinage entering circulation in January 2002 and rapidly replacing national issues. As far as Britain was concerned, Labour Chancellor Gordon Brown maintained a cautious 'wait and see' approach, insisting that his 'five economic tests' should be met before Britain would consider entering the eurozone (see p. 519).

Against the instincts of his party's Europhiles, William Hague chose 'Save the pound' as the Conservatives' main rallying cry in the 2001 general election, although it did little to save either his party or his own political life (see p. 305). In contrast, after Labour's second victory Tony Blair began to sound a more enthusiastic note; the expectation was that the question would be put to the British people during that parliament.

Plus ça change?

As long ago as the eighth century, Offa, the ambitious king of Mercia (i.e. England), attempted to take the country into the single European currency created by the emperor Charlemagne. This was the largest currency zone that had existed until the creation of Euroland.

In the meantime, debate continues (see pp. 518–20) and British public opinion remains lukewarm. Enthusiasts see the sceptics as in the emotional grip of the past, clinging to a nineteenth-century view of Britain's world role. It can be argued that a currency is like language: to hang on to a dead one for sentimental or nostalgic reasons inhibits communication and development. Some agree with the Conservatives' most prominent Europhile, Kenneth Clarke, that within a generation no country will have its own currency, each having adopted that of a trading bloc. Fearing that Britain was once again sacrificing a 'seat at the top table' and risking being sidelined in the global economy, one senior mandarin was to lament: 'we'll be shut outside with our noses pressed to the glass' (*The Economist,* 1 May 1998).

The social dimension

The single currency is not the only EU issue bearing upon national economies. Another concerns social policy. As presently constituted, the EU cannot have a social policy in the sense that a country does. Not responsible for schools, health care, social services and so on, its role is limited to protecting workers within a largely capitalist system – a role with clearly economic implications. This is not new; the Rome Treaty included provisions for the free movement of workers through equivalence in social security entitlement, educational exchange facilities, working conditions, labour law, vocational training, health and safety at work, rights of association and collective bargaining and equal pay for men and women. It also established a European Social Fund to promote worker mobility and created a framework for a Community vocational training policy. At the same time, the Euratom Treaty established basic standards for the protection of workers and public against radiation.

However, this aspect became more central as economies boomed and social costs, including pollution, health and safety-at-work problems and uneven economic development became apparent. There was also the essentially polit-ical problem of maintaining the legitimacy of a predominantly capitalist system which did not distribute the fruits of enterprise evenly. World slump from the mid-1970s heightened awareness by not only precipitating unemployment but stimulating a resurgence of New Right thinking which threatened workers' security and conditions. Hence, the 1980s saw renewed attempts to rekindle the social dimension. A key figure was Jacques Delors. Formerly a socialist finance minister in France, his opening speech to the European Parliament as President of the Commission presented a European vision going beyond a gigantic market-place. His programme for the completion of the single market by 1992 included a range of social objectives to mitigate disruption caused by economic restructuring.

After considerable debate, a Charter of the Fundamental Social Rights of Workers was adopted by the European Council in 1989. There was only one dissenting voice, that of the UK. The mood was to carry through beyond the Thatcher era to Maastricht, where Major negotiated a special opt-out of the

Let them have
the Social
Chapter, we'll
have the jobs.

John Major after
the Maastricht
summit

Social Chapter. Although, to the satisfaction of the unions, the Labour govern-ment signed up at the Amsterdam summit, government spin-doctors stressed that there was no need for its early implementation.

Debating the Social Chapter: the case against The UK position owed much to its domestic neoliberal agenda. Crucial to the vision was a deregulated labour market with lower wages, making British products more competitive and raising profits. There was also an argument based on the subsidiarity principle, social policies falling within that area of administration best left to national governments. Perhaps the darkest fear of the right came from the belief that a social dimension equates with socialism.

What Next?

The future shape of the EU promises to be one of the most important factors influencing British politics. Will it become more democratic? Will it become more federalist in character? A key issue will concern its size.

Enlargement

The EU has been subject to a continuous process of enlargement (figure 5.6) and there remains a queue of would-be members, including those EFTA states remaining outside, former communist states and a Mediterranean group. They are attracted by the prospect of access to EU markets, grant aid and a chance to participate in decision-making over trade issues. However, this has various implications. The fourth enlargement (in 1995) brought in Austria, Finland and Sweden, increasing membership from twelve to fifteen, extending the periods between which each state holds the presidency from six to seven-and-a-half years and increasing the number of votes in Council from seventy-six to eighty-seven. Norway was invited in but, for a second time, fearful of the Spanish invading their fishing waters, voted 'No' in a referendum.

Enlargement enhances the political project of reducing the potential for war. In this respect the collapse of the Soviet empire created an historic opportunity. Yet with more members the process of deepening integration becomes more difficult. Voting procedures designed for a community of six, particularly the veto principle, become increasingly inappropriate. In addition, wealth redistri-bution poses heavy demands on the richer countries. Finally, human rights issues emerge as states with dubious reputations knock on the door.

One of the ostensible purposes of the Nice summit was to prepare for a dramatic influx of twelve additional members from Eastern Europe. New Council voting weightings were accepted, provision made for an enlarged Commission, and agreement reached to increase the Parliament from 626 to 740. The change in voting weightings favoured the larger countries, placing Germany in a pivotal position. The smaller countries' losses also meant a

Figure 5.6
The process of EU enlargement.

Source: European Parliament.

decline in the power of the Commission, traditionally their champion. There were grounds for seeing the summit as a further move towards *l'Europe des patries*, or even *l'Europe des grandes patries*. However, serious decisions were deferred and no firm date set for the accession of the first of the new entrants (although 2004 was mentioned). Other key issues, including the division of powers between the Union, member states and the regions, and ways of bringing national parliaments into the EU decision-making process, were left to a follow-up conference in 2004.

Variable geometry

There are grounds for anticipating that future integration will take place according to a principle of '**variable geometry**', permitting states to proceed at various speeds. Indeed, this is built into the very architecture of the Union. The Maastricht Treaty, in its schedule for achieving a single currency, established that no member would be forced along and no state could hold the others back. Critics worried that this could create a 'hard core' to the detriment of the others.

Democracy

Enthusiasts and sceptics alike agree that the EU cannot progress without further democratization. The events of 1999 (see pp. 131–2) may prove a defining moment. The EP came of age, ending the life of the unelected Commission in the name of democratic accountability. For many MEPs, this was a new dawn presaging expanded powers to regulate and supervise the Commission, though such an ambition could be bitterly contested by the Council of Ministers.

National sovereignty and European integration

It is clear from chapter 4 that national sovereignty in the contemporary world is not as simple as much political rhetoric implies. Despite its dominance in international discourse, the centralized nation-state is by no means the only way in which people can live or have lived. A recent creation of modern Europe, it can be argued that, as traditionally understood, it is becoming an ethical and practical anachronism.

The ethical question Nationalism is a questionable virtue. The value of patriotism has all too often deteriorated into racism and fascism and it was to avert the latter that the movement for European union arose. Today we witness an alarming paradox noted by Hobsbawm (1990) of increasing global interdependence coinciding with a revival of nationalism, often associated with religious fundamentalism and ethnic conflict. The sovereign right of nations to do what they like in their own territories is also questionable. Do governments have a right to violate human rights, persecute minorities or hold political prisoners? Can one state legitimately claim a sovereign right to generate acid rain to fall on another? The maldistribution of world resources is in part perpetuated by nationalistic competition.

The practical question We saw in chapter 4 that the reality of national sovereignty today is questionable under a continuing process of globalization. The globalizing economy undermines national systems of control and advanced weaponry decreases rather than increases sovereignty because confrontation promises mutual destruction and gives power to non-state actors, be they terrorists or freedom fighters.

Beyond the state The response to globalization comes in the growth of new political formations to recapture much of the role of nation-states. Security alliances limit the right to wage war. Regional economic groups combat the superpowers and transnationals. The fight against terrorism and crime sees police and security forces amalgamating and systems of international law become increasingly important in the lives of citizens, organizations and states. Associations such as the UN agencies unite governments and also work in partnership with international charities and business associations. The logic of European integration lies within such developments. It can be seen as the retrieval of autonomy rather than its sacrifice (Grahl and Teague 1990: 15).

The story so far

With membership having grown from six to fifteen states, and promising to increase to twenty-one or more by 2010, the EU has come a long way since 1951. Its major achievements include a complex institutional structure, a common body of law, a wide range of policies and practices, and a spirit of cooperation that has replaced the hostility of the early twentieth century. Progress has, however, been fitful, with spurts of activity punctuated by periods of *immobilisme*. The rapid development of the 1960s was followed by a dormant period that ended in the mid-1980s with a renewed push towards integration. The 1990s, with a more pessimistic economic climate and growing popular disenchantment, saw another deceleration so that, in contrast to the Maastricht Treaty of 1992, the 1997 Amsterdam Treaty aimed to consolidate rather than address pressing issues of further reform.

This uneven progress is in large measure the result of a range of unresolved debates, many made more acute as a result of developments in Eastern Europe. There are fundamental questions about what the EU is and what it is to achieve. Is it to be merely an economic free-trading bloc or does it pursue the grander aim of political union? There is also the question of 'deepening' or 'widening': whether to concentrate upon further integrating existing members, or to spread membership to more nations. A further issue is supranationalism versus intergovernmentalism. Despite the EU's essentially supranational design, governments remain reluctant to cede control to its institutions. Hence, the major treaty reform at Maastricht saw the temple structure emerge as the most acceptable model.

The reluctance to countenance radical institutional reform has been most pronounced in security policy. When required to move from a common policy position to action, members failed to present a coherent front in both the Gulf war and in former Yugoslavia. The defence issue is further clouded by the continuing presence of NATO.

There is also the issue of what ordinary people feel – the question of legitimacy. European integration has been largely a product of elite initiatives and agreements, with little reference to national electorates. In the 1990s, however, demands for harmonization, and the Maastricht Treaty ratification process, revealed popular suspicion and discontent, indicating that people could no longer be taken for granted. While much EU activity has been devoted to constructing institutional structures for the equivalent of a state, little effort has been made to create a new nation with a common culture and sense of European identity.

These broad areas of debate take place within countries rather than between them. Moreover, they resonate differently within each. It is probable that no country is as internally riven with misunderstanding and indecision as the UK, where interest groups and parties are split, sometimes to near destruction. Yet despite the unresolved debates the EU has become a permanent feature of the political landscape, with countries enmeshed together in a host of economic interdependencies and cooperative practices. What remains at issue is not its survival, but its nature and purposes. It promises to occupy a central position in the politics of the twenty-first century.

Key points

- Of all Britain's relationships none has generated more internal political heat than that with the EU, the key feature being concern over a feared loss of sovereignty.
- The EU's origins lie in the attempt to repair the devastation wrought by the second world war. Yet there was a deeper purpose: to prevent further war in Western Europe.
- The EU differs from all other international associations in that it creates a supra-national authority and is partly funded by its own resources rather than member states' contributions.
- The career of the EU has itself been fitful, with periods of stagnation (*immobilisme*) and dynamism.
- Edward Heath took Britain into the Community in 1973.
- Key developments include the June 1985 White Paper, *Completing the Internal Market*, the 1986 Single European Act and the 1992 Treaty on European Union (Maastricht).
- The relationships between the various EU institutions and their relative power are important areas of debate, the balance gradually shifting towards the Parliament.
- The future shape of the EU promises to be one of the most important factors influencing British politics into the new millennium. Key areas of development are the single currency, social policy, democracy and enlargement.

Review your understanding of the following terms and concepts

Amsterdam Treaty	EFTA	intergovernmental
assent procedure	euro	organization
Brussels Treaty	European Central	Maastricht Treaty
co-decision procedure	Bank	MEP
Committee of the Regions	European Commission	qualified majority voting
conciliation committee	European Council	single currency
consultation procedure	European Court of Justice	Single European Act
cooperation procedure	European Parliament	Social Chapter
Council of Europe	European Union	sovereignty
Council of Ministers	Eurosceptic	subsidiarity
economic and monetary	exchange rate mechanism	supragovernmental
union (EMU)	(ERM)	Treaty on European Union
EEC	federalism	variable geometry

Assignment

Study the extract from *Parliamentary Affairs* on page 146 and answer the questions that follow. You may find it easier to return to this assignment when you have studied further chapters.

		Mark (%)
1	'The EU has become something of a "moderniser's" talisman.' Discuss.	10
2	If the issue of Europe has 'never offered a core election-winning strategy', can it be said to have offered an *election-losing* strategy for the Conservatives?	25
3	To what extent does British political culture look across the Atlantic rather than the English Channel?	25
4	Discuss the advantages and disadvantages of a referendum on joining the single currency.	40

Questions for discussion

1 Why did Britain stay out of the early moves towards European integration?
2 Evaluate the importance of the Single European Act and the Maastricht Treaty in the process of integration.
3 How real is the threat of a loss of national sovereignty through EU membership?
4 Is it fair to characterize Britain as the 'awkward partner' in Western Europe?
5 Outline the various processes whereby the Council, the Commission and the European Parliament work together in policy-making.
6 Assess the importance of the European Council in the working of the EU.
7 Examine the case for a single currency within the EU.
8 In what senses can the EU be said to suffer from a democratic deficit?
9 Why is it considered important that the EU is financed from its own resources?
10 Discuss the implications of substantial enlargement of the EU.

Topic for debate

This house believes that the idea of 'batting for Britain' undermines the EU's fundamental rationale.

Further reading

Butler, M. (1986) *Europe: More than a Continent.*
An inside view by a UK permanent representative.

Labour and Europe

TONY BLAIR is aware that the issue of Europe has never offered a core election-winning strategy for either Labour or the Conservatives (for example Labour in 1983 and the Conservatives in 1997). Europe has also been an elite project of high politics and has always proved difficult (and dangerous) to translate into an electoral issue. Greatly in his favour, however, is the fact that by 1997 the battle had been won inside the Labour Party. A rump of Old Labour MPs and peers remained hostile on economic and/or political grounds...[but] the great majority of the parliamentary party was pro-euro and pro-European, especially the large intake of young Labour MPs; indeed, the EU has become something of a 'moderniser's' talisman.

Yet in spite of these factors, New Labour's response has been guarded, and in some ways little seems to have changed for Britain in its uneasy relations with Europe since John Major's defeat in 1997. After a brief flurry of Europhilia by the Blair government, enacting the Social Chapter into British law, pushing the agenda of closer defence co-operation and partially supporting the proposed EU immigration changes, things cooled noticeably. Fearing a backlash amongst the newly converted 'middle England' voters, the government failed to reverse Major's wait and see 'Opt Out' on the single currency.... The Prime Minister argued that the government remained in favour 'in principle' of Britain joining if the economic conditions were favourable (i.e. convergence between the UK and European economic cycles and specific benefits for the British economy). Before the 1997 election, he had promised a national referendum on joining the Single Currency in the event of the Treasury's 'five economic tests' being met. Since then this endlessly repeated mantra has avoided any recommendation on entering the euro – for triggering a referendum could awaken a mass populist British Euroscepticism.

Extract from David Baker, 'Britain and Europe: the argument continues',
Parliamentary Affairs, 54(2), 2001, pp. 276–88.
Reproduced by permission of Oxford University Press and the Hansard Society.

George, S. (1994) *An Awkward Partner: Britain in the European Community*, 2nd edn.
Examines and explains the tortuous nature of British relations with Europe.

Giddings, P. and Drewry, G. (1996) *Westminster and Europe: The Impact of the European Union on the Westminster Parliament*.
Considers the problems experienced by Parliament in exercising influence over EC legislation.

Jones, R. A. (2001) *The Politics and Economics of the European Union*, 2nd edn.
Concise, accessible and jargon-free introduction to the EU institutions and associated debates.

Lodge, J. (ed.) (1993) *The European Community and the Challenge of the Future*.
Collection of essays on various aspects by specialists.

Mazey, S. and Richardson, J. (1993) *Lobbying in the European Community.*
Sheds light on the less institutional aspect of Community politics.

Nugent, N. (1994) *The Government and Politics of the European Union,* 3rd edn.
Looks at institutions, decision-making processes and policies.

Urwin, D. (1997) *A Political History of Western Europe since 1945.*
Addresses the major political and economic developments, including the consequences of the end of the cold war and progress towards integration post-Maastricht.

Young, H. (1998) *This Blessed Plot: Britain and Europe from Churchill to Blair.*
Excellent guide to the high and low politics of Britain's position in Western Europe.

For light relief

Edwina Currie, *The Ambassador.*
The EU 100 years on is the most powerful state in the free world. Genetic engineering is widespread and the US Ambassador is sent over to investigate.

Jean Monnet, *Memoirs.*
Taste of the cocktail of passion and calculation in early integrationist moves. Also insight on British emotional reservations.

On the net

http://www.fco.gov.uk/europe/index.html
For UK policy on the EU.

http://europa.eu.int/index.htm
The EU home page will lead you to a wealth of information on the EU and its institutions; available in any EU language at the touch of a button.

6

A Disunited Kingdom: Territorial Politics

The constitution has for long been seen as unitary, binding England, Wales, Scotland and Northern Ireland into a single state under the Westminster Parliament as the United Kingdom. Yet although formally established in 1800 with the parliamentary union of Great Britain and Ireland, this kingdom has become something of a constitutional curate's egg – united only 'in parts'. By 1997 a centrifugal process of gathering momentum was creating a constitution with clearly federal features. Recognition of these territorial movements is essential to an understanding of the dynamics of contemporary British politics. This chapter begins by examining Scotland and Wales where, after chaffing against the English bit, their peoples voted in 1997 for devolution. Next we turn to the regions of England which, while undeveloped in political terms, have their own identities. Finally we examine the territorial struggle which, with extreme violence and bitter enmities, has placed UK politics in the world headlines: the vexed question of Northern Ireland.

Political scientists once tended to see the British electorate as essentially homogeneous, divided mainly by class but, as chapter 7 will reveal, there are greater complexities in the social fabric. Moreover, the post-war era saw the reopening of another historic schism, reminding politicians in London that the kingdom, though united, comprised four nations. Elections began to reveal a nation dividing, with territories pursuing different agendas, sometimes through different political parties. Paradoxically this mood of **separatism** appeared to heighten under a highly centralizing government from 1979.

Beyond the ballot box was an economic fissure (figure 6.1). The 1980s and 1990s saw massive deindustrialization in the north as heavy industry and textiles declined, while the collapse of mining devastated the communities

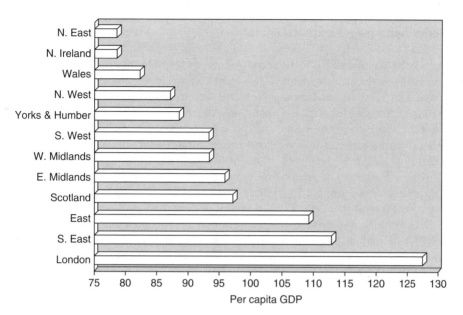

Figure 6.1
Regional disparities in per capita GDP within the UK, taking the UK average as an index value of 100.

Source: Data from *Social Trends* (2002: table 5.27).

around the pits. A European Commission report of November 1996 found a growing regional divide; post-war economic modernization had closed the gaps between Western Europe's richer and poorer states, but wide differences in living standards remained at regional level and these were greatest in the UK. A study of the 459 district councils in England, Wales and Scotland published in 1996 by the economic forecasting organization, the Henley Centre, found per capita income in the south-east to be 20 per cent higher than in the rest of Britain. Those in this favoured garden of England were also likely to be better qualified, to live longer and to do so in larger homes (Wagstyl 1996). The growing divide was compounded by an historical sense of cultural subjugation at the Celtic fringes. These strains on the integrity of the UK were to result in tectonic constitutional shifts in 1998.

Unity and Devolution

Unity was seen by the English political class as essential for security. They needed to capitalize on the insular position provided by nature and remove both the possibility of challenge from within and the establishment of bases for challenge from overseas. The Wars of the Roses and the subsequent Tudor and Stuart dynasties saw the central authority of the Crown established. Scotland and Wales, under English domination, followed a unified pattern of development into the agricultural and industrial revolutions and the age of empire.

Scots, wha hae: Scotland

Unlike the Welsh and Irish, the Scots were never forcibly subdued, unity coming politically with the succession of James VI of Scotland to the English throne in 1603. The 1707 Act of Union established a common parliament but protected certain Scottish institutions, including the legal system, the Presbyterian Church, the education system and local government (Kellas 1975: 2). In modern times much public administration came under the Scottish Office at Edinburgh and a Secretary of State for Scotland sat in the Cabinet. At Westminster a Scottish Grand Committee examined Scottish issues, but since its composition was supposed to reflect party balance, Scotland's mainly Labour MPs were joined by a leavening of English Conservatives.

A nationalist movement was represented by the Scottish National Party (SNP) founded in 1928, a Scottish Labour Party founded in 1976, and a Scottish press (broadsheet and tabloid). The early 1970s saw a resurgence of nationalist feeling with the discovery of North Sea oil. Seen by the government as a UK asset, many Scots believed the revenues belonged to Scotland. In 1974 the SNP won eleven seats in Parliament with 30 per cent of the Scottish vote. The Labour government held a referendum on **devolution** in 1979 but, when voters shuffled to the polls amidst snow and hail, the hurdle of 40 per cent of the eligible electorate saying 'Yes' proved too high. Under Heath the Conservatives had supported devolution but Thatcher returned to hard-line unionism, which Major maintained. Yet ironically, it was Thatcher's poll tax, visited upon Scotland one year earlier than England, that hardened support for a break from Westminster.

Within two months of taking office in 1997 the Labour government had published white papers on devolution to a Scottish parliament and a Welsh assembly (Senedd). Arousing unprecedented interest, *Scotland's Parliament* sold 500 copies within two hours of going on sale at one Glasgow bookshop (Webster and Bowditch 1997). This foreshadowed the biggest change in the link to the rest of Britain for nearly 300 years.

'Yes, Yes' The referendum combined two questions: one on a parliament and one on tax-varying powers. On 11 September 1997 (the 700th anniversary of William Wallace's victory over the English at the Battle of Stirling Bridge) the Scots voted decisively 'Yes, Yes'.

The Parliament The Scottish Parliament in Edinburgh has primary legislative powers in all areas previously administered by the Scottish Office and a right to vary the basic level of income tax by up to 3p. Matters reserved for Westminster include foreign policy, defence, central economic affairs, social security matters and the constitution (in theory preventing Scotland voting for independence, though a referendum could hardly be prevented if the Parliament voted for it). The Scottish Executive (the equivalent of the Cabinet) is headed by a First Minister.

The West Lothian question

A devolution conundrum was first raised by MP Tam Dalyell when representing that constituency: should Scottish MPs at Westminster be permitted to debate policy for England, while English MPs are excluded from the Scottish Parliament? Again, should Scotland maintain its existing over-representation at Westminster? This was a sobering question for Labour, since without its tartan contingent its Westminster ranks would be depleted. Although there were no proposals to modify the role of Scottish MPs at Westminster, the Scotland Act promised to end their over-representation. The next boundary review (to be finalized by 2006) recommended bringing constituency sizes into line with those in England, reducing the number from 72 to 59. Subsequently, the boundaries for the Scottish Parliament's additional members would be addressed, the aim being to produce a 50:50 ratio with constituency MSPs (see chapter 9).

The 'new politics' of coalition In its willingness to adopt partial proportional representation (PR) in the form of the additional member (d'Hondt) system (see p. 271) to elect the 129 Members of the Scottish Parliament (MSPs), Labour sacrificed its historic advantage in Scotland. Under first-past-the-post, it would have gained a comfortable overall majority, with the Liberal Democrats as the main opposition and the Conservatives entirely wiped out. Labour claimed high motives for its decision, but the system would make it very unlikely that the SNP would ever gain power on its own, should the political sands shift that way. The Liberal Democrats were naturally happy with a system that promised them a taste of power; following the 1999 election (table 6.1), they found themselves in a coalition with Labour.

Labour leader Donald Dewar, who became First Minister with Liberal Democrat leader Jim Wallace as his deputy, welcomed this as the 'new politics' promised by devolution. Yet whether or not fighting between parties was reduced under the 'new politics', there was tension within them. For Labour, this was intensified following Dewar's death. He was succeeded by Henry McCleish, a hitherto little-known Westminster MP, whose rival, Jack McConnell, was wounded by his relationship with a lobbying company. However, McConnell was to have the last laugh, replacing McCleish when the latter was

Table 6.1 Scottish Parliament election results, 1999 (no. of MSPs)

Party	Constituency	List	Total
Labour	53	3	56
SNP	7	28	35
Conservative	0	18	18
Liberal Democrat	12	5	17
Scottish Socialist	0	1	1
Green	0	1	1
Independent Labour	1	0	1
Total	73	56	129

The chamber of the
Scottish Parliament

Photo: Scottish Parliament

forced to resign in November 2001 over a scandal concerning the irregular
renting out of his constituency office as a Westminster MP.

Life was changed for the SNP. From being a small but effective guerrilla band
at Westminster, its members were required to become a serious opposition.
However, the party's *raison d'être* was constitutional rather than day-to-day
policy and it began to appear ineffectual (Bradbury and Mitchell 2001: 261).

Under the coalition, the Scottish Parliament began to find its voice and the
Liberal Democrats gained a compromise over the abolition of student fees. In
January 2001 they again cheered and punched air as Scottish Labour conceded
free universal personal care for the elderly, despite Westminster disapproval.
However, a promise to remove the notorious Clause 28 was watered down after
a vigorous press campaign supported by the Catholic Church.

Land of my Fathers: Wales

Wales was yoked to England in 1282 following its conquest by Edward I. The
Tudors consolidated this subjugation, banning the Welsh language in administration. Industrialization assisted the colonizing impact with massive English
immigration into the South Wales coalfields and steel industries, leaving mid-
and north Wales custodians of the remnants of a national culture. The principality was brought under the English legal, health and education systems, the

domination underlined when the 1870 Education Act banned the Welsh language for teaching in the newly emerging state schools.

The Plaid Cymru party was founded in 1925 to preserve the Welsh cultural heritage but discontents led to more overtly political ambitions and a call for self-government. Campaigning led the Labour government to hold a referendum in 1979 but, with deep English penetration, many non-Welsh speakers feared second-class citizenship in an independent Wales; devolution was decisively rejected. Some distinctiveness was provided for the principality through a Welsh Secretary in the Cabinet, a Welsh Office (a Whitehall outpost at Cardiff), a Welsh Grand Committee of Welsh MPs and a Select Committee on Welsh Affairs at Westminster. However, Conservative MPs were always heavily outnumbered (disappearing completely in 1997) and a quangocracy (see chapter 18) of Conservative placemen and a succession of (English) Conservative Welsh Secretaries prompted a renewed desire for independence. Other factors added to disenchantment. With 43 per cent of the population working in the public sector, Thatcher's privatization drive hit Wales disproportionately. On the other hand, the Welsh Development Agency, despite serious scandals, was remarkably successful in attracting inward investment from EU countries and the global economy, suggesting possibilities of an independent existence within a wider context (Jones 1997).

Upon returning to office in 1997, Labour's white paper promised *A Voice for Wales*. A referendum on Thursday 18 September 1997 provided one of the most nerve-wracking electoral outcomes of modern politics. In the small hours of Friday morning Wales's 'No' voters might have felt they could retire contentedly to bed with the might of Cardiff, the principality's capital, declaring against the assembly. However, in the final minutes came the voice of Carmarthenshire in south-west Wales, shifting the mathematical sands to a timid 'Yes'. Yet despite the slender margin, the swing from 1979 of 30 per cent was greater than in Scotland and the government acted as if the result were unequivocal.

The Senedd Comprising sixty members elected by the additional member system, the Senedd assumed the responsibilities of the Secretary of State for Wales but with certain areas (foreign affairs, defence, social security and macro-economic policy) reserved for Westminster. It is led by an Executive Committee comprising the leaders of a range of subject committees and chaired by a First Secretary, elected by the Senedd. The committees were given prominence, with a policy-deliberation role as well as the more traditional one of scrutinizing the executive. With no ability to vary tax or pass primary legislation, the Senedd's powers fell well below those of the Scottish Parliament. However, it inherited the decision-making functions of the Welsh Office, together with a large budget (£7 billion in 1997), and was expected to derive some influence through implementing Westminster legislation. Ministers even suggested that, had it existed during the Thatcher administration, it might have been able to opt out of the poll tax.

As the main architect of Welsh devolution, the decision of Welsh Secretary Ron Davies to follow the Scots with PR (against the wishes of the Welsh Labour

Table 6.2 Senedd election results, 1999

Party	Constituency	List	Total
Labour	27	1	28
Plaid Cymru	9	8	17
Conservative	1	8	9
Liberal Democrat	3	3	6
Total	40	20	60

Party) was partly to appease the Liberal Democrats and Plaid Cymru. Some of the gloss was wiped off the new venture in October 1998, when he resigned after an 'error of judgement' on Clapham Common. Following prime ministerial intervention, the succession passed to Alun Michael, but seeing him as 'Blair's poodle', many favoured the more assertive Rhodri Morgan. The acrimony led many voters to abstain or switch parties, with the result that, in a province where it had appeared invincible, Labour failed to secure an overall majority (table 6.2). Elected as first minister, Michael rebuffed a Liberal Democrat coalition offer, choosing to establish a minority administration (Jones 2000). Presiding over an all-Labour Executive Committee with an even gender balance, he managed to win most Senedd votes by striking judicious deals with Plaid Cymru or the Liberal Democrats. Yet his triumph, always of doubtful legitimacy, was to be short-lived. Ignoring local opinion, he appeared to critics like a Welsh Secretary from London. Finally, a no-confidence vote forced his resignation in February 2000, allowing Rhodri Morgan to take the place he held to be rightfully his.

Marriage of convenience: coalition politics The vote-by-vote process needed by the minority administration made long-term planning impossible and Morgan opted for formal coalition. Failing in his overtures to Plaid Cymru, he turned to the Liberal Democrats, who received two 'cabinet' seats. Many Labour members were unhappy about this marriage of convenience. There were even some misgivings within the Liberal Democrat camp. Marginalized for the time being, Plaid Cymru and the Conservatives looked forward to new opportunities when fault lines in the coalition might begin to show.

Although in principle opposing any dilution of the union, the Conservatives had come round to a pragmatic acceptance under William Hague, but Welsh political elites remained unenthusiastic. Plaid Cymru wanted complete independence in the context of Europe, while the Liberal Democrats argued for tax-varying powers (McAllister 1998: 164–5). Concern was expressed by the EU at the slow progress in implementing its aid programme and there was little sign of the much-vaunted 'bonfire of the quangos' that had been prophesied. Ordinary people could see little change in their day-to-day lives. Early conflicts with Westminster arose over various issues, including performance-related pay for teachers, the establishment of a GM-free Wales and local government reform.

By 2002 the Senedd was still seeking its role. Whether it could find this without powers comparable with its Scottish counterpart remained to be seen.

English regionalism: the forgotten dimension

For the English, the conflict of citizenship within a multinational state goes largely unfelt; indeed 'English' and 'British' are often taken as synonymous. Hence, the regional dimension has hung as a withered limb of the body politic. While Whitehall has practised administrative decentralization and governments have created many ad hoc regional bodies to provide services such as gas, water and health care, calls for regional government (for example, from the 1969 Redcliffe-Maud Commission on local government and the minority report of the 1973 Kilbrandon Commission on the Constitution) have long been resisted.

Labour had appeared favourably disposed towards reform for some time and its 1992 manifesto contained a commitment to create Regional Development Agencies (RDAs), which would later form the basis for elected regional assemblies. The 1997 manifesto retained this commitment, while recognizing regional variations: 'Only where clear popular consent is established will arrangements be made for elected regional assemblies'. The subsequent white paper, *Building Partnerships for Prosperity*, and a Regional Development Agencies Act empowered the Secretary of State for the Environment, Transport and the Regions to create RDAs and designate voluntary regional chambers comprising representatives of local authorities and other interests, to which the RDAs would be accountable. Local people would be given the opportunity to make the chambers directly elected some time after a further general election.

An additional impetus for **regionalism** comes from the European stage (Elcock 1997). The EU often works at a regional level in its social and economic programmes and the Maastricht Treaty made provision for an advisory Committee of the Regions. The Association of County Councils argues that regional groupings of local authorities increase their effectiveness in preparing EU funding bids. Many authorities have indeed combined regionally or subregionally, even forging continental partnerships. Some have formed regional consortia with industry and labour organizations, the northern region making the earliest advances (Elcock 1997: 427). However, without genuine regional government, England could be at a disadvantage in the EU. Prior to devolution, Wales and Scotland had already established Brussels offices for lobbying purposes, while the EU had bases in Belfast, Cardiff and Edinburgh. In an enlarged EU the pressure may be expected to increase (Martin and Pearce 1994).

A white paper, *Your Region, Your Choice* (Department for Transport, Local Government and the Regions, 2002), was eventually published in May 2002, setting out the proposed responsibilities for regional elected assemblies, to which the existing RDAs would be accountable. Some commentators fear a further erosion of local government (Jones and Stewart 1995), although advocates claimed that it was the centre that would be relinquishing power. Any

Regional assemblies		
Strategic responsibilities		**Executive functions**
economic development	transport	Responsibility for RDAs
skills and employment	housing and regeneration	Finance
land use and regional	health improvement	Oversight of regional
planning	sport, culture and	bodies (e.g. Learning and
environmental protection,	tourism	Skills Councils)
biodiversity and waste		

necessary restructuring of local government to create a unitary structure (see chapter 19) would only occur after a regional referendum.

The assemblies envisaged would be small, streamlined bodies of twenty-five to thirty-five members, elected by the additional member system, and with a leader and cabinet of up to six. Largely funded by a central government grant, they would be able to raise additional revenue through the council tax. Campaigners were optimistic that the first would be up and running within four or five years.

However, public support was uneven. A poll commissioned by the BBC in March 2002 showed that, while 63 per cent were in favour overall, the main support was confined to the West Midlands, the North East, North West and Yorkshire and Humberside. Moreover, almost half believed that the assemblies would be 'a talking shop for politicians and a waste of money'. Another dampener comes from regional business communities, with no enthusiasm to see economic strategy in the hands of elected laymen.

Ireland: a Terrible Beauty

With its grim chronology of violence, Ireland has mocked claims to unity. The problem of Northern Ireland has seemed an incomprehensible religious conflict, explained in terms of the 'hot-headedness' of the red-headed men, disdainfully contrasted with the secular rationality of the English, who have long avoided religious war. This is wrong; the problem is a cocktail of racism, apartheid, imperialism, class domination, violent resistance and brooding memories of ancestral cruelty and injustice – it is a political issue. Perhaps more than any other, the Irish problem has roots deeply embedded in a long and vicious history.

The seeds of discontent

Although uncomfortably close to England, Ireland remained stubbornly separated by the Irish Sea, hindering English domination. Conquest was finally completed by the Tudors, though the Irish, like the aborigines of the New

World, resented subjugation on their own soil. In the English civil wars they saw their chance by favouring the Royalist cause but in the aftermath incurred terrible English wrath in the form of reconquest first by Cromwell and later by the Protestant William of Orange (in the famous Battle of the Boyne in 1690). Relegated to the status of second-class citizens in their own country, Irish Catholics were barred from state office and the professions, denied landowner-ship rights and lived in a squalor unparalleled in Europe. Land in the south was confiscated by the English, who remained comfortably at home as absentee landlords, extracting crippling rents. In the north, where resistance was fiercer, domination required settler colonization. A Scottish Presbyterian landowning class emerged around Belfast, ruling the natives and dependent upon English mainland support. Rebellions were put down with extreme severity, the troops given full licence to torture, maim and kill. The Catholics rose in 1798 only to be cut down in the battle of Vinegar Hill. The Act of Union of 1800, in which the Irish parliament was swallowed up by Westminster, was adorned with manacles rather than wedding rings.

The industrial revolution reinforced the division. In the north the Protestants shared in English prosperity while subjugating the Catholics. In contrast, the south was excluded from the process of industrialization; it was more useful as a granary to feed workers on the mainland, even when the Irish were themselves starving. The suffering was compounded in 1845 and 1846 when a serious potato blight in Ireland removed the means of sustenance for some four million people. England did little to help, around a million people died and over two million crossed the Atlantic, taking with them a cargo of festering resentment.

Thus you have a starving population, an absentee aristocracy, and an alien Church, and in addition the weakest executive in the world. That is the Irish Question.

Benjamin Disraeli (Conservative leader), Commons speech (16 Feb. 1844)

The Home Rule Bills For most Irish people, the concept of a United Kingdom was farcical, a fact realized in his later years by the great Liberal politician W. E. Gladstone, who determined with some fervour to right the wrong (Bentley 1984: 245). His first Home Rule Bill of 1886 was defeated in the Commons and his second fell in the House of Lords in 1893. Events surrounding a third bill were dramatic, revealing naked class hatred. Although the Liberals had become convinced home-rulers there were other matters to occupy them when they returned to government in 1906, including bitter battles with the suffragettes and the House of Lords. Losing their overall majority in 1910, they became dependent upon support from Irish MPs, and to win this Prime Minister Asquith pledged himself to another Home Rule Bill. Although this passed through the Commons in 1912, the Conservatives regarded Irish MPs as infer-ior in status and not entitled to vote on constitutional issues (Cross 1963: 123–4). It became apparent that they considered themselves, and the class they represented, to be above the constitution. In 1906 Balfour had declared:

'The great Unionist party should still control, whether in power or whether in opposition, the destinies of this great Empire' (Blake 1985: 190).

In the Lords the Conservatives defeated the bill, thereby delaying it until 1914. This allowed the Protestants of the north to arm as the Ulster Volunteers under the fanatical leadership of Edward Carson, while Conservatives on the mainland contemplated a *coup d'état*. Conservative leader Bonar Law (himself of Ulster descent) told a crowd outside Blenheim Palace:

> There are things stronger than parliamentary majorities...I can imagine no length of resistance to which Ulster can go in which I should not be prepared to support them. (Cross 1963: 177)

No left-wing orator would have dared utter such sentiments; the Conservative Party began to resemble a guerrilla band (Bentley 1984: 365).

I have passed with a nod of the head,
Or polite meaningless words.
All changed, changed utterly:
A terrible beauty is born.

W. B. Yeats (1865–1939; Irish poet), 'Easter 1916'

The Easter Rising However, an impending holocaust was eclipsed in June 1914 by the assassination of Archduke Franz Ferdinand of Austria-Hungary. The bill was passed but placed in cold storage for the duration of the first world war. Yet Irish activists, mistrusting the English, sought German help and, on Easter Sunday 1916, declared a republic. This was put down harshly, the English toasting their triumph with the blood of martyrs through executions and imprisonments. Roger Casement, a British Consul in Germany who had enlisted enemy assistance, was hanged for high treason and his standing undermined by the circulation of diaries revealing his homosexuality.

In the post-war general election Sinn Féin (the republican party) gained an overwhelming victory in Ireland and those elected refused to enter Westminster, establishing an independent Irish parliament at Dublin, the Dáil. Renewing the republic of Easter 1916, they appointed a president, Eamon de Valera, and government. At the same time an Irish Republican Army (IRA) formed under Michael Collins, to which the British responded in 1920 with measures that Asquith said 'would disgrace the blackest annals of the lowest despotism in Europe' (Taylor 1965: 155). The infamous Black and Tans, chosen for their penchant for violence, were recruited to assist the Royal Ulster Constabulary (RUC) in a reign of terror.

Partition After much tortuous negotiation, Prime Minister Lloyd George and the Irish politicians signed a compromise treaty based on **partition** on 6 December 1921, giving birth to the Irish Free State (Eire). The twenty-six counties of the south received dominion status on the Canadian model and six of the nine counties of Ulster remained as a UK province with an elected bicameral assembly (at Stormont) and an executive exercising certain devolved powers. The fact that Ulster had far more autonomy than Wales or Scotland reflected hopes that it would eventually decide to reunite under Dublin. The arrangement was to leave the Ulster Catholics as second-class citizens, living in ghettos in the poorest housing, doing the most unpleasant jobs and receiving the worst education. Between 1920 and 1922 'ethnic cleansing' took place on an epic scale; Catholic relief agencies estimate that some 23,000 Catholics were driven out of Belfast alone (Hennessy 1997: 11). Constituency boundaries were gerrymandered to ensure Protestant dominance. For the south, the 'solution' had come not as a result of statesmanship but through violence and bloodshed, leaving a fermenting sense of grievance; 1949 saw Eire's departure from the Commonwealth.

Belfast from the 1960s: the killing streets

Although the settlement contained the germs of further violence, the Irish question ceased to be a scourge of British politicians as republicanism gave way to a less confrontational nationalism. However, economic decline was to fan the embers of discontent in the north; heavy dependence on industries in irrevocable decline (shipbuilding and textiles) produced unemployment higher than in the rest of the UK. Prime Minister Terence O'Neil attempted to attract new industries and sought closer involvement with the south. A new generation of Catholics grew into political awareness, inspired by the international civil rights movements of the 1960s. Protestants became alarmed and a reaction set in, partly under the demagogic influence of the Reverend Ian Paisley. The B-Specials, an auxiliary unit of the RUC, attacked civil-rights demonstrators, leading to a retaliatory rejuvenation of the IRA, which had effectively disarmed.

Again the politics of Northern Ireland was to open as a running sore on the British body politic. The divisions were not only reflected in ideological battles, they were overlain with the machinery of violence and death. The participants are religious groupings with constitutional aspirations and sometimes para-military connections, rather than conventional parties. With marches and violence their politics have often been of the street rather than the debating chamber.

The two leading Protestant/unionist parties were the Official Unionists and Paisley's more working-class and fundamentalist Democratic Unionist Party (DUP). The Protestants also mobilized through organizations such as the Orange Order and the Apprentice Boys of Derry, engaging in political symbolism through provocative parades and marches. Protestant paramilitary organizations included the Ulster Volunteers, splintering into the Ulster Defence Association and the Ulster Freedom Force. In addition, the RUC was Protestant dominated and itself used unusual and extremely violent methods. The Catholic/nationalist cause was represented by the Social Democratic and

Labour Party (SDLP), favouring constitutional methods, and Sinn Féin (the political wing of the IRA). The IRA splintered, from the 1970s, into the more extreme Irish National Liberation Army (INLA) and Provisional IRA, and latterly the Real IRA.

In this ferment non-sectarian politics had little place and the mainland parties did not seek a serious presence. However, the Ulster Unionists had historic links with the Conservatives, generally supporting them at Westminster. In 1970 a non-sectarian Alliance Party formed, with links with the Social Democrats, though its broad position was to maintain the mainland connection. A new player entered the game in 1969 when, following a request from the RUC, backed by militant civil rights leader Bernadette Devlin (Hattersley 1996: 77), the British government took the fateful decision to send in the army to restore the peace. From initially welcoming the move, Catholics were to develop a feeling of menacing harassment and the pattern of violence began an unremitting escalation (figure 6.2).

Developments were to see the powers of state repression increase, hardening Catholic and world sympathy for the IRA. Internment without trial was introduced in August 1971 and on 20 January 1972 British troops fired on civil rights demonstrators, leaving thirteen dead. Television brought the violence into living rooms on the mainland, entering the inventory of grim anniversaries as 'Bloody Sunday'. In March 1972 the Heath government assumed *direct rule* over the province. The gerrymandered constituencies had meant that Stormont remained under an indelible Protestant majority offering no voice to the Catholics. It was suspended and a Northern Ireland Office created under a

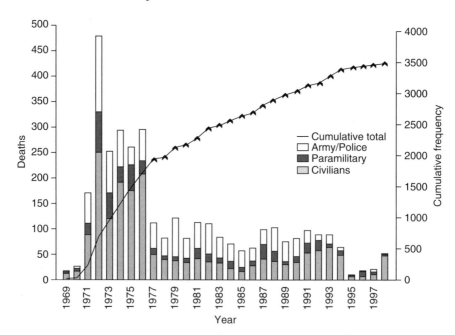

Figure 6.2
Violence in Northern Ireland: deaths associated with the civil disturbances, 1969–98.

Source: Data from the CAIN project website (http://cain.ulst.ac.uk).

Secretary of State, a poisoned chalice for any British politician. In 1974 the Prevention of Terrorism Act was rushed through Parliament (following devastating bombs in pubs in Guildford and Birmingham), outlawing the IRA and further extending police powers. Special (Diplock) courts were created in Ulster which dispensed with juries to avoid their intimidation. Harsh treatment of prisoners was to be condemned by the European Court of Human Rights.

Evidence that the RUC had adopted a 'shoot-to-kill' policy in 1982 occasioned the notorious Stalker affair, in which a British police officer heading an inquiry into the matter was impeded in his investigations, subjected to character assassination and suspended from duty in May 1986, just days before he was to travel to Belfast to interview RUC chief Sir John Hermon. In 1984, an IRA bomb exploded in the Brighton hotel housing Conservative Party leaders (including Margaret Thatcher) attending their annual conference. As the violence escalated, the feared British SAS became involved, shooting eight IRA men and a civilian at Loughall, County Tyrone, in 1987 and, on 6 March 1988, to an echo of excited public celebrity, gunning down three alleged would-be bombers in Gibraltar. No bomb was ever found and the European Court of Human Rights ruled that unreasonable force had been used. The judgement was seen by Downing Street as 'defying common sense' (*The Times*, 28 Sept. 1995).

Seeking a political solution

Paradoxically, although wanting to end the bloodshed British governments refused to talk; Sinn Féin remained a pariah party. Ministers empowered themselves to exclude named individuals from the mainland, including Sinn Féin leader Gerry Adams. In 1988 access to the British media was denied to Sinn Féin (though broadcasters made a mockery of this by using actors to speak their words).

Clearly any return to the Stormont model, with gerrymandered constituencies and no voice for the Catholic minority, could not work. Moreover, the shifting demographic sands had seen, during the 1980s and 1990s, a steady rise in the nationalist vote, reflecting an increase in the Catholic population. UK governments recognized the need to break the stranglehold with some form of **consociationalism** (see O'Leary 1989) and a **power-sharing executive** permitting Catholic involvement.

I can only say that it would turn my stomach.

Prime Minister John Major, House of Commons (1 Nov. 1993), in response to suggestion by left-wing MP Dennis Skinner that the government talk with Gerry Adams and the Provisional IRA

The Sunningdale Agreement In 1973 the Heath government tried to establish an assembly elected by PR and a Council of Ireland to facilitate liaison between Belfast, London and Dublin. However, the 1974 general election saw eleven of the twelve Ulster seats won by Unionists hostile to the policy, a unionist general strike paralysed the province and the agreement collapsed. The next Labour government encountered continuing Unionist intransigence and an attempt by the Thatcher government to establish a PR-based assembly was abandoned in 1985.

The Anglo-Irish Agreement An alternative political solution was seen in a forum that would permit the Republic some involvement in Ulster's affairs. This was attempted in the Anglo-Irish Agreement, signed in November 1985 by Thatcher and Irish Premier Dr Garret Fitzgerald. To Unionists, this was the thin end of a republican wedge. Paradoxically, Sinn Féin opposed the Agreement on the grounds that it condoned partition.

The Downing Street Declaration With the departure of Thatcher the Anglo-Irish Agreement was suspended and fresh talks initiated. These proceeded uneasily, but in 1993 John Major and Irish prime minister Albert Reynolds signed an historic Downing Street Declaration, asserting the right of the peoples of north and south to unite should they ever so wish, and denying any British government strategic interest in Northern Ireland. Most controversially, it offered a place at the negotiating table to Sinn Féin on the condition that it renounce violence. An IRA ceasefire was declared on 31 August 1994 and Protestant paramilitaries responded with a similar renunciation. A changing climate was apparent when it was revealed that secret talks had been taking place between the British government and the IRA.

In February 1995 a Framework Document outlined a consociational democracy (Lijphart 1996). This entailed an assembly elected by PR exercising devolved powers, **cross-border bodies** to consider joint issues such as tourism, and the involvement of all parties in both north and south, including Sinn Féin. Popular support would be ascertained through a referendum.

Unionists remained suspicious, and a series of disastrous by-elections left Major's government increasingly dependent upon their support in Westminster. He began holding up progress by demanding that the IRA hand in its weapons – a gesture of surrender. A stalemate developed that continued until 7.01 p.m. on 18 February 1996, when the seventeen-month ceasefire came to an end as a bomb in Docklands rocked east London. A widespread pattern of IRA bombs and bomb scares in the run-up to the 1997 general election left Major with no peace memorial.

There is doubt whether the Government will ever accept that the IRA ceasefire is permanent and that Sinn Féin has renounced violence.

Northern Ireland Secretary Sir John Mayhew, on the eve of the 1994 Conservative Party conference
(*Guardian*, 11 Oct. 1994)

"It's a card from Gerry Adams. While he deeply regrets the shooting of Colonel Mustard in the Library, the responsibility lies with the British Government."

The Good Friday Agreement Tony Blair's first official journey as prime minister was to Ulster, where he declared that 'the settlement train would leave with or without Sinn Féin', who were invited into renewed talks, subject to a ceasefire (*Financial Times*, 26 June 1997). He pledged to put new proposals to the people in a referendum. There would be negotiations on decommissioning weapons and a Parades Commission to regulate marches. In the summer of 1997, a number of parades by Protestant Orangemen through Catholic areas were abandoned and Northern Ireland Secretary Mo Mowlam persuaded the IRA to instigate a second ceasefire. Although Ian Paisley denounced them as a 'total surrender', all-party talks began. Mo Mowlam, the first woman to play such a central role, proved exceptionally tenacious, even entering the Maze Prison to talk with convicted terrorists.

Another key factor was US President Clinton. From its initial nationalist sympathies, the USA began to assume the role of an honest broker. Senator George Mitchell, who chaired the peace talks, was a Catholic with Irish grandparents, but he trod carefully through the minefield. In November 1995, Clinton himself visited Belfast and Dublin. After tortuous negotiations, often extending into the small hours, a potentially ground-breaking sixty-seven-page agreement emerged on Good Friday, 10 April 1998. The proposals, to be put to referendums in north and south, included the following:

The violence behind the violence

A Catholic teenager frustrated at not being able to go to a Chinese restaurant at the end of his own street in a Protestant area finally cracked and went for a takeaway. He was stabbed in the eye with a screwdriver.

One of thousands of sectarian incidents in Northern Ireland remaining unreported amid the greater atrocities; reported in the Guardian (11 April 1998)

---

1 a Northern Ireland Assembly of 108 elected by PR, with legislative powers and a power-sharing executive;

2 a North–South Ministerial Council to consider issues such as cross-border cooperation;

3 the Irish government to renounce constitutional claims to Northern Ireland and Westminster to replace the Government of Ireland Act;

4 a Council of the Isles comprising members from the north and south of Ireland and the Scottish and Welsh assemblies.

There were also to be releases of prisoners coupled with a decommissioning of arms.

The referendums Tensions mounted in the days before voting, the situation aggravated by the release of terrorists on both sides. However, Blair made the vote a highly personalized affair and John Major, Paddy Ashdown and William Hague weighed in to signal cross-party support. At a pop concert featuring Irish band U2 from the south and Ash, a group with Protestant backgrounds, from the north, Unionist leader David Trimble (with his teenage daughter) and SDLP leader John Hume symbolically shook hands.

The referendums showed resounding support for the Agreement. With the 81 per cent turnout in the north exceeding expectations, 677,000 voted 'Yes' and 275,000 'No'. In constituency terms, seventeen were for and only one against. However, the greatest support was from Catholics, a *Sunday Times*/Coopers and Lybrand exit poll revealing 96 per cent of them voting 'Yes' compared with 55 per cent of Protestants. In the Republic, a turnout of 56 per cent showed 94 per cent support for relinquishing claims to the north.

The Assembly The next vote was the election to the Assembly. This took place in June 1998, by single transferable vote (STV; see p. 268) in eighteen constituencies. However, the referendum had not succeeded in quelling opposition; Ian Paisley's DUP and the UK Unionists stood only in order to secure enough seats to wreck the Assembly. In the event, some 75 per cent of voters supported a party favouring the Agreement. Fringe parties, including the Women's Coalition, which had campaigned for peace, made some gains (table 6.3). Trimble's Ulster Unionists won a majority and the Unionist dissidents failed to win enough seats to prevent his election by the assembly as First Minister. His deputy was the Catholic Seamus Mallon.

The power-sharing principle ruled out single-party governance. Elected by the Assembly rather than chosen by Trimble, the executive was a coalition of the four main parties: three seats each for the UUP and SDLP and two each for Sinn Féin and the DUP. This was a system intended to surmount the almost insurmountable: to forge a consensus amongst politicians more hostile towards each other than would be expected in any system where normal politics prevailed.

Yet fears that the peace process might unravel were ever-present. The Protestant Orangemen appeared intent upon defying a Parades Commission ban on

Table 6.3 Seats in the Northern Ireland Assembly, June 1998

Party	Seats	Party	Seats
Unionist		*Nationalist*	
Ulster Unionist	28	SDLP	24
DUP	20	Sinn Féin	18
UK Unionist	5	*Other*	
Independent Unionist	3	Alliance	6
Popular Unionist	2	Women's Coalition	2

their march through the Catholic Garvaghy Road. Banner-waving and clad in their bowler hats and regalia, they faced the RUC in military-style riot gear across trenches and barbed wire. The pendulum of violence would swing both ways and in August 1998 twenty-nine people were killed and many more injured by a bomb planted in Omagh by the self-styled Real IRA.

Delayed by continuing disagreement over decommissioning, devolution from Westminster eventually came on 1 December 1999 and the new executive began operation. Yet the following years saw the spirit of the Agreement and the referendum outcomes mocked by atrocities that shocked the world. Negotiations with the body set up to supervise decommissioning under the Canadian General John de Chastelain were protracted and tortuous. In the 2001 UK general election the battle lines appeared to harden as extremists on both sides made gains at Westminster.

As his position within the party weakened, in July 2001 Trimble resorted to desperate measures to bring the decommissioning issue to a head by resigning as first minister. With the peace process on a knife edge, the British and Irish governments set out a package of measures aiming to deliver the Good Friday Agreement. This identified four outstanding issues:

1   reforming the police in line with recommendations made in the 1999 Patton report (see p. 166);
2   normalizing security arrangements;
3   stabilizing the newly created institutions;
4   decommissioning weapons.

But if illustration of the lingering hatred were needed it came in September 2001 with the vision of girls on their way to the Catholic Holy Cross primary school (in the heart of nationalist North Belfast) running a 300-metre gauntlet of loyalist spittle and cries of 'animals', 'scum', 'Fenian bastards' (*Guardian*, 4 Sept. 2001).

Acting under heavy pressure from its political wing and the USA, the IRA finally announced a scheme agreed with the decommissioning body to put weapons 'completely and verifiably beyond use'. Trimble welcomed 'the day

> The leadership of the Ulster Volunteer Force and Red Hand Commandos – in their own time and their own space – will give whatever answer to the question of whether they will or will not reciprocate.
>
> David Ervine of the Progressive Unionists in response to the IRA's 2001 decommissioning offer

we were told would never happen', and the UK government responded swiftly on 'normalization', scaling back on military bases. Yet there was a mountain still to climb. When Trimble stood for re-election as first minister, all thirty-eight nationalists supported him, but the required majorities in both blocs was embarrassingly prevented by the desertion of two of his own party. The impasse was only overcome by the non-aligned Alliance Party redesignating some members as Unionists.

Optimism could not be high, and was lowered further on 6 October 2002, when twenty police officers raided the Sinn Féin offices at Stormont and homes in north and west Belfast. The object was to seize electronic files in response to suspicions of IRA spying within the Northern Ireland Office. The result was some arrests and, at midnight on 14 October, the Assembly was suspended for the fourth time since devolution.

Policing the troubles

Unionist hostility had been fired by the 1999 Patton report on the RUC, which had called for an equal balance of Catholic and Protestant recruits and the renouncing of the force's very name. Some attempt to sugar the pill was made later that year in collectively honouring the force with the George Cross. The symbolic break with the past came on 3 November 2000 when the RUC became the Police Service of Northern Ireland (PSNI – selected in preference to Northern Ireland Police Service for fear of its abbreviation to Nips) and the first recruits, selected on a 50:50 basis, began intensive training. The Police Authority was replaced by a Policing Board, ten members being drawn from the UUP, DUP and the SDLP (Sinn Féin refused to take seats) and the remaining nine, including the chairman, appointed on a non-political basis. PSNI Chief Constable Sir Ronnie Flannagan spoke of the 'poignancy in this weekend'. The RUC had existed since the partition of 1921 and had lost over 300 members to terrorist attacks during the years of violence, with thousands more injured. Yet against this it was argued that its tactics since the early 1960s had shown astonishing levels of violence and brutality, occasioning thousands of complaints.

However, as the bombing continued, Flannagan observed that there were still 'people who just want to wreck everything'. It was hardly propitious that the new force's first investigation was into an unseemly brawl in Stormont's Great Hall between leading politicians, which marred David Trimble's re-election as first minister.

Orange Order
march, July 1998

Photo: Times Newspapers Ltd

A time to forget

> But if the focus remains on the past, the past will become the future, and that is something no one can desire.
>
> *Report of the International Body* (the Mitchell Commission) (22 Jan. 1996: para. 16)

Optimists hoped that the time had come to forget the troubled past. Yet there was much to forget: deaths of hunger strikers, 'Bloody Sunday', 3,500 lost lives and 40,000 wounded over the previous thirty years. One in four of those voting in the 1998 referendum could claim to have known someone who had been killed. The ancestral voices speak from even greater distance, regularly re-kindled by ceremonies and marches to mark bitter anniversaries such as the Battle of the Boyne, the Siege of Londonderry and the Easter Rising.

Territorial Politics in the UK

In the days of empire, world dominance forged a British identity and helped unify the kingdom, but with decolonization this cement began to crumble. Hence, an era that has witnessed the end of empire also sees a questioning of the bond between the four nations of the UK and the state is confronted with increasingly demanding problems of **territorial management**. The Labour government (with Liberal Democrat approval) saw the solution in devolution, which aims to preserve the union by releasing a safety valve upon a pent-up nationalistic fervour. The new settlements were intended to offer a new stability and opportunities for 'new politics' reflecting constructive harmony rather than the adversarial style of Westminster. In contrast, the Conservatives saw devolution as the thin end of a wedge that would ultimately fracture the union.

New politics – dull politics?

The new assemblies elected by PR certainly gave more opportunities to minority parties (including the Conservatives, whose numbers had been decimated in the provinces) and coalition administrations became the norm. In addition, positive discrimination in candidate selection (except by the Conservatives) brought in more women (table 6.4). Greater use of committees offered new opportunities for assembly members to be constructively involved in shaping policy. There was even hope that the new system would spread to Westminster.

Yet new politics posed new questions. In the first place was the possibility that constructive harmony would exorcise all passion from politics. Rhodri Morgan (2000) himself argued that committee work lacked the sense of theatre that aroused public interest. Moreover, there remained doubts whether assembly members or voters, conditioned by adversarial politics and first-past-the-post (see p. 239), were ready for consensual politics. Coalitions did not end party fighting and often increased tensions *within* parties. PR also gave more representation to the political extremes including, in the case of Northern Ireland, those with no desire to see the system work. Here coalition was not optional, it was built into the power-sharing architecture. While the Liberal Democrats and

Table 6.4 Gender balance in the Scottish Parliament and Welsh Assembly, 1999

Party	Scottish Parliament		Welsh Senedd	
	Men	**Women**	**Men**	**Women**
Labour	28	28	13	15
Conservative	15	3	9	0
Liberal Democrat	14	3	3	3
SNP	19	16		
Plaid Cymru			11	6
Scottish Socialist	1	0		
Green	1	0		
Independent Labour	1	0		
Total	79	50	36	24

Labour may sometimes have been uncomfortable in bed together, the four-partner Stormont executive placed a constitutional duvet over a ménage of the most bitter enemies. Here debates over questions such as health or education could melt into insignificance beside the passionate issue of the constitution itself.

Westminster may also lack the appetite for an entirely new kind of politics in the provinces; New Labour was a centralizing government and devolution was introduced to bind the union, not to weaken it. The relationship between London and the capitals remained uncertain, with potential for turf wars. Secretaries of State for Wales and Scotland remained and the provincial officials continued to be members of the home civil service. The Alun Michael/Rhodri Morgan fiasco showed the Welsh the iron hand of Westminster, while north of the border the parliament soon found itself at loggerheads with Scottish Secretary Helen Liddle (Nicholson 2001). There would be even greater cause for tension should a Conservative government at Westminster be confronted by Labour first ministers in the provinces.

Federal drift

Federal leanings

It is frequently suggested that the UK is acquiring a federalist character but, constitutionally, devolution does not of itself mean federalism. The former is, by definition, created by the act of a superior body, devolving some of its own powers and responsibilities to a subordinate one; these could be revoked at any time. In a federal system, the centre and regions stand constitutionally equal, with the distribution of powers and responsibilities set out in a written constitution.

Despite its aspiration, the New Labour settlements may not represent points of constitutional stability, for in all cases further ambitions remain. For nationalists in Northern Ireland the goal remains a united republic, while many Unionists still crave the *status quo ante*. For the SNP the long-term objective is full independence; Scottish founder of the Adam Smith Institute, Madsen Pirie, anticipated this within a decade of devolution (Groom 1997). In Wales, where devolution offered the most limited gains, there was the more modest aspiration to the same powers as the Scottish parliament.

Enthusiasm for the union may even wilt in England. During the 2002 World Cup many supporters rediscovered the red cross of St George, which was painted on faces, waved in foreign stadiums and flown over English pubs. In addition, there were the calls for devolution to the English regions. Uneven development had seen economic prosperity and political power concentrated in the south-east, leaving much of the country with demands for self-determination much like those of Wales and Scotland.

The centrifugal drift of power is enhanced by EU membership, which may undermine the role of the central state while emphasizing the region. The presence of small EU states, including the Irish Republic, makes a separate

Scotland and Wales look viable. Paradoxically, if the new assemblies are successful, the case for autonomy is strengthened. Moreover, the Good Friday Agreement, in conceding the right of Belfast to secede from the UK, weakens the case for denying the same rights to Wales and Scotland.

Chapter 4 revealed the limitations of nation-state autonomy in a globalized economy; this chapter has exposed the challenge from within. Multinational states look increasingly like ill-adapted dinosaurs, vulnerable to legitimacy crises and rising nationalism. In the UK citizens begin to wonder how united the kingdom is and how united it should remain.

Key points

- The UK is a multinational state vulnerable to legitimacy crises and requiring territorial management.
- The English political class saw unity of the British Isles as essential for security, accomplishing this by conquest of the Celtic fringe.
- In modern times the distinctiveness of Wales and Scotland was preserved through administrative outposts of Whitehall and Grand Committees at Westminster.
- Increasing disenchantment eventually led to a Welsh Senedd and a Scottish Parliament and calls for English regional devolution.
- The EU's regional perspective adds momentum to the movement.
- English conquest over Ireland was problematic and three attempts to grant home rule proved unsuccessful.
- The compromise of partition established the Irish Free State (Eire) while Ulster remained as a UK province.
- In Ulster the Catholics were treated as second-class citizens.
- The Irish question flared up again in the 1960s as Catholic demands for civil rights met Protestant resistance and led to direct rule from Westminster.
- The violence was to continue for three decades.
- A protracted peace process, culminating in the Good Friday Agreement, led to a new Assembly exercising devolved powers in 1998.
- The life of the Northern Ireland Assembly has been fitful and has not seen an end to the culture of violence.

Review your understanding of the following terms and concepts

Anglo-Irish Agreement	nationalism	SDLP
consociationalism	Orange Order	Senedd
cross-border body	partition	separatism
devolution	Plaid Cymru	Sinn Féin
DUP	power-sharing executive	SNP
federalism	regional assemblies	territorial management
home rule	regionalism	Ulster unionism
IRA	RUC	West Lothian question

Assignment

Study the extract from *Parliamentary Affairs* and answer the following questions.

		Mark (%)
1	Contrast the likelihood of success for the Scottish, Welsh and Northern Ireland assemblies.	25
2	Discuss the extent to which the UK is ready for 'New politics'.	25
3	'The early operation of devolution in Scotland and Wales suggests the emergence of the normal politics of decentralised political systems rather than new politics.' Discuss.	25
4	'Paradoxically, if the new assemblies are successful, the case for autonomy is strengthened.' Discuss.	25

Devolution: new politics for old?

DEVOLUTION represents a large constitutional upheaval for the territories of the UK.... In Scotland and Wales, it was suggested that a semi-proportional electoral system would usher in a 'new politics', by which was generally meant a more co-operative style of inter-party relations than at Westminster. In Northern Ireland it was hoped that an elaborate system of consociational checks and balances, including the use of the STV voting system, would coerce a form of 'new politics' in which parties had to co-operate for practical government to go ahead at all....

The reality of devolution has been somewhat less remarkable than those hopes. Evidence of 'new politics' is limited. Instead the early operation of devolution in Scotland and Wales suggests the emergence of the normal politics of decentralised political systems rather than new politics. Coalition government has been considered a necessity in Scotland from the start and latterly also in Wales, but there have been strong tensions between political parties both within and outside coalition arrangements. In Northern Ireland, the Assembly has had an unprecedented political composition and previously unthinkable steps have been taken towards power sharing but the continued inter-party animosities threaten the very agreement that established devolution in the first place.

Extract from Jonathan Bradbury and James Mitchell, 'Devolution: new politics for old?' *Parliamentary Affairs*, 54(2), 2001, pp. 257–75. Reproduced by permission of Oxford University Press and the Hansard Society.

Questions for discussion

1 Why did England need to unite the countries of the British Isles?
2 Explain why Wales and Scotland rejected devolution in 1979 but voted 'Yes' in 1997.
3 Why has the Conservative Party opposed devolution?
4 Discuss whether Scottish devolution will lead to further moves towards independence.
5 How important is the historical perspective in understanding the post-war conflict in Northern Ireland?
6 'Without the power to vary tax rates the Welsh Assembly can be no more than a talking shop.' Discuss.
7 Identify the factors inhibiting the establishment of a power-sharing executive in Northern Ireland?
8 Examine the case for political devolution to the English regions.
9 Why do you think referendums were used to decide the devolution issues? Was their use justified?
10 What should be the role and significance of cross-border bodies in the constitutional and political position of Northern Ireland?

Topic for debate

This house believes that the United Kingdom cannot remain intact in the contemporary world.

Further reading

Aughey, A. (2001) *Nationalism, Devolution and the Challenge to the United Kingdom State.*
Examines the threatened concept of 'Britishness' and finds it alive if not entirely well.

Crick, B. (ed.) (1991) *National Identities: The Constitution of the United Kingdom.*
Essays considering the government of the UK and relations with Ireland in the light of national and regional senses of identity.

Kearney, H. (1990) *The British Isles: A History of Four Nations.*
Emphasizes how an understanding of the present is hindered if we fail to emphasize that a historical perspective must encompass more than just *English* history.

Keating, M. and Loughlin, J. (1997) *The Political Economy of the Regions.*
International examination of regionalism, with chapters on the EU, Wales, Scotland and the English regions.

MacDonald, M. (1986) *Children of Wrath: Political Violence in Northern Ireland.*
Argues that the colonization of Ireland created a problem that could not be resolved.

McGarry, J. and O'Leary, B (1997) *Explaining Northern Ireland: Broken Images.*
Excellent analysis of the political complexities of the contemporary Irish situation.

Marr, A. (1992) *The Battle for Scotland*.
Explains the 'Scottish question'.

Trench, A. (ed.) (2001) *The State of the Nation: The Second Year of Devolution in the United Kingdom*.
Second in a series of yearbooks on the progress of UK devolution.

For light relief

The Crying Game.
Award-winning video/film set amidst the contemporary violence over Northern Ireland.

Michael Collins.
Video/film about the Irish civil war.

Braveheart.
Video/film saga of thirteenth-century Scottish revolt against English tyranny.

Michael Shea, *The State of the Nation*.
Set in a Scotland in deep economic crisis after four years of independence. Sinister TNC moves in to take advantage.

On the net

http://www.local-regions.odpm.gov.uk
http://nio.gov.uk
The Office of the Deputy Prime Minister is a good starting point for material relating to regionalism, and the NI Office for Irish issues.

http://www.plaidcymru.org
http://www.snp.org.uk
Visit the Celtic fringe through its websites.

7

The Social Context:
Our Divided Society

In this chapter we examine the social context in which British politics is enacted. A political system does not stand above society as an autonomous machine; it is as much part of society as our weather system is part of the planet's ecosphere. It has long been proclaimed that British society is benignly cohesive but we shall argue that this unity has been a veneer concealing the cracks beneath. The chapter includes four principal focuses. The first examines a key feature of the political culture, the attitudes of people towards the political system. Do they trust figures in authority to act in the general interest? Are they willing to obey the law and respect the institutions of the state? The following three sections expose great divides arising from class, gender and race.

Political Culture

What is political culture?

Political culture is a rather vague concept referring essentially to the set of attitudes citizens hold towards society and the political system. It reflects a myriad factors including some already encountered in previous chapters: history, geography, the constitution, the institutions and the range of informal practices associated with government. The study of political culture reminds us that maintaining a political regime depends upon thoughts as well as actions. For this reason much political activity at all levels is symbolic, aiming to make people happy with the system – to *legitimate* it. It will become apparent throughout this book that the legitimating function has been performed very well in Britain.

British political culture

A classic investigation of British political culture was carried out in the early 1960s by the American political scientists Almond and Verba (1963), who enthused that in Britain they had found a veritable jewel of a polity; nothing less than the ideal conditions for liberal democracy – a '**civic culture**' entailing respect for government and an unwillingness to resort to disruptive protest. There were three important ingredients in this civic mix: continuity, deference and consensus.

Continuity We saw in chapter 3 that Britain has never made a dramatic revolutionary break with the past. The evolutionary pattern of change has preserved many ancient symbols and ceremonies. A brief republican period was seen as an aberration and was soon ended with the Restoration. However, critics see this conservative strain as holding back the process of social and political change. One symptom of this is the preservation of deferential attitudes belonging to a distant monarchical past.

Deference The best political culture for a capitalist state is a deferential one, where the masses willingly accept inequality and show little desire for change or to participate in government. Indeed, the essence of **deference** is that ordinary people believe that running the state should be left to those who 'know best'. It was noted by Walter Bagehot in 1867, when he argued that the masses were unable to understand the reality of government but were beguiled by a 'theatrical show' of monarchy and other *dignified* elements of the constitution.

Although the virtues of deference are questionable (for Aristotle, not to be involved in politics degraded one to the level of a beast), texts in the orthodox liberal-democratic tradition have generally admired it. This passivity was demonstrated in the depressions of the 1920s and 1930s (the General Strike of 1926 failed to mobilize mass support). The feeling that things must be accepted has been seen as a very British characteristic, helping to explain why the Labour Party has been at its least electable whenever it has offered a radical programme. Gramsci argued that those wishing to dominate society encourage such a view in order to maintain their hegemony (see p. 37).

A crisis of deference? By the late 1960s orthodox writers began to fear that this 'civic society' was turning sour. Surveys suggested a greater willingness to protest through unofficial strikes and demonstrations (Marsh 1978). When a miners' strike appeared to precipitate the downfall of Heath's government in 1974, the liberal-democratic apologists began a Cassandra-like lament that the country was becoming 'ungovernable'. To some extent Margaret Thatcher's call for a return to 'Victorian values' in the 1980s, and John Major's 'back to basics' the following decade, could be seen as nostalgic attempts to restore the age of deference.

By the opening of the twenty-first century British political culture was certainly different. Aggressive political journalism, declining respect for teachers, Christian priests and the police, 'laddish' behaviour, and a growing drug culture, showed a society that had moved some way from the order and respect for hierarchy that characterized the early post-war decades. Moreover, increasing voter apathy and a greater willingness to resort to various forms of direct action, sometimes leading to violence, suggested disdain for politics and institutions.

However, the obituary for deference can be exaggerated. In 1980 Almond and Verba had 'revisited' the British political culture in a study that confirmed that, although there was cynicism, and even support for unlawful violence against the state, these were confined to a small, unpopular minority (Kavanagh 1980). Labour leaders were actually condemning the actions of their non-deferential left-wing elements with as much ferocity as the Conservatives. From the early 1980s the rulers sought to persuade the masses that redundancies, cultural impoverishment and increasingly large differences in wealth were necessary for their own good. Thatcher denigrated the welfare state with reference to 'feather-bedding' and 'scrounging'.

Like the General Strike, the recessions of the 1980s and 1990s were weathered with considerable patience and stoicism; in the acclaimed 1997 film *The Full Monty*, the men cast aside by the economic system became not revolutionaries but strippers. In 1998, as French students took to the streets, their British counterparts were enduring reduced grants, student loans and tuition fees with largely token resistance. There was talk of Britain becoming a more **meritocratic** society in which the talented and thrusting would rise to the top. Yet curiously, such a society is not necessarily non-deferential. On the contrary, the 'success ideology' has been seen as a basis for quiescence by the working class and other disadvantaged groups in the face of social inequalities. Victims have only themselves to blame and revolution is unjustified.

Although newspapers increasingly report the behaviour of the high and mighty in non-deferential terms, the message remains broadly sympathetic to powerful capitalist interests (see chapter 8). The Queen may have been mocked but it was a public-school-educated prime minister that media tycoon Rupert Murdoch helped into Downing Street in 1997. Despite the public's increased resort to direct action (see p. 548) over issues such as animal rights and the environment in the 1990s, the Labour Party itself swung massively to the right. When it finally regained office in 1997, it did so with the voices of its left-wing members muted, a tough law-and-order line and promises of 'no favours' for the unions. The crowds lining the route of the Queen Mother's funeral in April 2002 suggested that deference was by no means in its coffin.

Clearly the issue of deference is complex. Laddish behaviour, cheeky journalism and a refusal to vote do not suggest a politically assertive culture. Attitudes towards the constitution may offer a more fundamental guide and here the 1998 Human Rights Act may be instructive. This offers a means for establishing a rights culture to replace the subject culture preserved in the constitutional monarchy. It has conventionally been held that unlike US or continental citizens, the great mass of the British have little interest in such matters. However, the Joseph Rowntree Reform Trust's large 'State of the

Nation' survey of 2000 registered an increase in rights-based thinking, when compared with a 1995 survey, and it extended well beyond the drawing rooms of Hampstead (Dunleavy et al. 2001: 407–10). Across a wide range of matters concerning their rights, the British were showing more demanding and assertive attitudes. The operation of the Act, a nod in the direction of a written constitution, may signal more fundamental changes to come.

Consensus It can be argued that British political culture is highly consensual; the majority of the population are happy with the liberal-democratic system. The **consensus** can even extend to policy-making, the major parties tending to aim for the centre ground. Yet the political culture is not as seamless and homogeneous as is sometimes thought. Chapter 6 has already explained how the UK was united partly by force, with lingering spatial tensions leading to new devolution settlements. In the case of Ireland, maintaining the union extracted a high price in blood. Beyond this, three other great fissures score the 'one nation' landscape envisioned by liberal-democratic apologists: class, gender and race.

Classes Apart

Defining social class

Generally speaking, social classes categorize people on the basis of such characteristics as family background, occupation, income, manners, accent and privilege. **Class** is essentially about hierarchy and inequality, denoting social divisions similar to 'caste', 'rank', 'degree' and 'status'. It has been considered of greater political significance in Britain than anywhere else in the English-speaking world (Butler and Stokes 1969: 90), although today there are those proclaiming a 'classless society'. There are various bases for defining class, including the following.

> The history of all hitherto existing society is the history of class struggles.
>
> Karl Marx, *The Communist Manifesto* (1848)

Relationship to the mode of production More than any other thinker, Karl Marx made **class** central to his analysis. For him it was determined by the mode of production. Under capitalism there is an essential *dichotomy*: a small upper class (or *bourgeoisie*) owning the capital needed for production, and a large working class (or *proletariat*) with only their labour to sell. The basic relationship between the two is exploitative (see p. 36).

Misery and poverty are so absolutely degrading, and exercise such a paralysing effect... that no class is ever really conscious of its own suffering. They have to be told of it by other people.

Oscar Wilde (1856–1900; Irish author and dramatist), *The Soul of Man under Socialism* (1891)

Social class: Office for National Statistics classes, 1998 (with examples of occupations in each class)

1a   *Large employer*: higher manager, company director, senior police officer, newspaper editor, top football manager
1b   *Professional*: doctor, solicitor, engineer, teacher, airline pilot
2   *Associate professional*: journalist, nurse/midwife, actor/musician, junior police officer, lower manager
3   *Intermediate*: secretary, air stewardess, driving instructor, footballer
4   *Smaller employer*: non-professional self-employed, publican, plumber, self-employed sportsperson, small farmer
5   *Lower supervisor*: craft worker, mechanic, train driver, foreman
6   *Semi-routine*: traffic warden, caretaker, gardener, assembly-line worker
7   *Routine*: cleaner, waitress, road-worker, docker
8   *Excluded*: long-term unemployed and sick, never worked

Occupation Another major figure in the theory of class is Max Weber. While accepting much of Marx's analysis, he argued that other factors were important, particularly the complex structure of the labour market. The capital-owning class contained *rentiers* and entrepreneurs, while the propertyless divided into those privileged with specialist skills and those without. Occupation is certainly a key variable, being generally correlated with a range of other factors – education, accent, social background, leisure activities, lifestyle, housing, and so on.

Official surveys use an occupational classification that was revised in 1998 (for the 2001 census) to reflect the changing social structure: redundant workers setting up their own businesses, increased insecurity of employment, more women in work and the emergence of an 'underclass'. A widely used alternative occupational definition is that devised by the advertising industry, aiming to categorize people according to their consumption patterns.

Social class: Institute of Practitioners in Advertising classification

In its efforts to persuade the right people to covet the right things, the advertising industry uses the following classification, which is widely used in social surveys.

A   Higher managerial, administrative or professional
B   Intermediate managerial, administrative or professional
C1   Supervisory or clerical, and junior managerial, administrative or professional
C2   Skilled manual
D   Semi-skilled and unskilled manual
E   State pensioners or widows (no other earnings), casual or lowest-grade workers and long-term unemployed

Income Income generally shows wide variations between the few high and the many low earners. The early post-war period saw some reduction in income inequality, a trend enhanced by the tax system, but since the late 1970s an unprecedented increase has occurred (figure 7.1). In 1996, the gap between rich and poor was wider than at any time since 1886 (Goodman et al. 1997). The trend continued under New Labour, with the richest fifth of the population increasing its share of national after-tax income to 45 per cent.

Amongst these are the mega-earners. The Royal Commission on the Distribution of Income and Wealth (1976: 10) estimated that there were some 65,000 very highly paid employees in Britain in the 1970s. Globalization, deregulation in the City, privatization and the tax revolution of the late 1980s were to swell this category into a new 'Super Class' (Adonis and Pollard 1997). Glimpses of this new breed were seen in high-profile examples such as 'Superwoman' Nicola Horlick, a working mother and City fund manager earning a reputed £1.15 million, and barrister Lord Irvine, who gave up annual earnings estimated at some £500,000 to take up his position as New Labour's Lord Chancellor. The main drive in the rise of the super-earners was the financial services industry, with its international, US-dominated remuneration regime. In 1996, of some 8,500 people at the top of the private-sector professions, the lowest earners were notching up £190,000 a year, while the chief executives of the hundred largest companies were receiving on average £501,000 in 1995. There are also certain freakishly high, and usually short-lived, salaries earned by entertainers and sports personalities, epitomized by footballer David Beckham on £25,000 a week from Manchester United. The popularity of such celebrities serves to legitimate the culture of inequality. Furthermore, tax breaks given to the 'fat cats' are justified by a theory that everyone else, even those in 'Cardboard City', benefits through the 'trickle-down effect'.

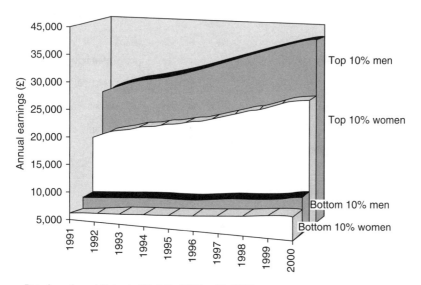

Figure 7.1
Earnings of the top and bottom ten per cent of the working population, 1991–2000.

Source: Data from *Annual Abstract of Statistics* (2001: table 7.23).

Wealth Beyond earnings, there remains a basic dichotomy between a wealth-owning minority (table 7.1) and the great mass. By 1997, the richest fifth of the British population were amongst the best-off in Europe (*Independent*, 15 June 1997). Even amongst the richest thousand, half the wealth (almost £80 billion) is concentrated in the hands of the top 100. Wealth may take various forms, including stocks and shares, property and capital, which is handed down through the generations, though amongst the top thousand featuring in the 2002 *Sunday Times* 'Rich List', almost three-quarters were self-made millionaires. As the new century opened, the millionaires' club was growing at a rate of 17 per cent a year, but the 2002 'Rich List' demonstrated the risks associated with life at the top; the collapse of the dot-com boom had reduced the number of internet millionaires from sixty-two to only thirteen in two years.

Self-assigned class There is also a subjective class structure, reflecting the way people perceive themselves (figure 7.2). The tendency in the post-war era has been for the working class to see themselves as going up rather than down in the world, though millionaire Sir Paul McCartney still termed himself working class. Despite politicians' claims that Britain was becoming a classless society, a BBC/ICM poll in September 1998 showed 55 per cent of people describing themselves as working class and 41 per cent as middle class, proportions that broadly accorded with an objective categorization. However, 25 per cent of those in managerial occupations described themselves as working class, while the same proportion of those in manual jobs felt themselves to be middle class. Only 1 per cent claimed to be upper class, well below the objective assessment of 22 per cent. Yet although self-assigned positions can be at

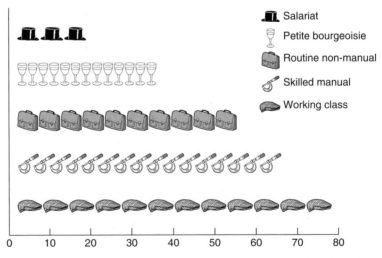

Figure 7.2
Self-assigned class: the percentage in each class identifying themselves as working class.

Source: Data from Evans (1993).

Table 7.1 Distribution of wealth in the UK, 1923–1999 (percentages)

Year	Top 1 per cent	Top 5 per cent	Top 10 per cent
1923[a]	61	82	89
1966[a]	31	56	69
1976	21	38	50
1986	18	36	50
1996	20	40	52
1999	23	43	54

[a]England and Wales only.

Source: Data from Atkinson and Harrison (1978: 159); *Social Trends* (2002: table 5.24).

variance with objective placings, they are important because they influence people's views on key issues such as the welfare state and trade unions, and thus their voting behaviour.

An anatomy of the classes

Britain is often described as rigidly class-divided, and sometimes contrasted with the USA, which is said to be classless. However, these are crude stereotypes: the USA is not without a social elite spanning the generations like an aristocracy, while mobility between classes is certainly possible in Britain. Goldthorpe (1987) found that 53 per cent of a sample of 10,000 British men surveyed in 1983 had changed classes. However, Britain remains particularly class *conscious*. One indication of this is in attitudes towards the redistribution of income and resources: the rich resist it, and the poor favour it, more strongly than in comparable nations (Evans 1993: 133–4). Moreover, despite considerable social mobility in the mid-twentieth century, research shows that opportunities remain dominated by social origins and, unlike the USA, there is no evidence of a more open society (Devine 1997: 74). Although the terms are used loosely, much discussion speaks of a broad threefold division into *upper class*, *middle class* and *working class*.

Is he rich, or is he rich!

The Duke of Westminster not only owns a sizeable chunk of London and large slices of Cheshire, North Wales, the Scottish Highlands, Ireland, Vancouver, Hawaii and Wagga Wagga, he had an income reported to be around £10,800 an hour in 1983 (*Sunday Times*, 20 Feb. 1983). With assets estimated around £4,700 million in 2002, he was back at the top of the *Sunday Times* 'Rich List' (7 April 2002), just ahead of food packager Hans Rausing and the Sainsbury dynasty of supermarket fame, while Labour benefactor Bernie Ecclestone had slipped to fifth place.

The upper class

The British upper class has evolved through a process of fusion and fission that amalgamated the landowning aristocracy, the lesser gentry, the financiers and the bourgeoisie who emerged with the industrial revolution (Scott 1985: 29–35). In 1923, before the Labour Party and the welfare state had made any inroads into the pattern of distribution (table 7.1), this powerful alliance constituted the richest fifth of the population, owning some 95 per cent of the nation's wealth. By 1972, with the welfare state at its peak, the richest fifth still claimed as much as 85 per cent, leaving 15 per cent to be shared amongst the rest (Urry 1985: 59–60). At the end of the twentieth century, 70 per cent of Britain's 60 million acres were still owned by less than 1 per cent of the population, while 77 per cent of the population lived on less than 6 per cent of the land. The holding of wealth is cumulative, since it generates considerable unearned income.

> The stately homes of England,
> How beautiful they stand,
> To prove the upper classes
> Have still the upper hand.
>
> Noel Coward (1899–1973; British actor and playwright)

Members of this class share much in common in terms of background and values. Educated privately through the public school system and disproportionately represented in the elite Oxbridge universities, their intense academic study has been complemented by a sense of training for leadership. Kinship (and old school) ties also ensure that family wealth is augmented rather than dispersed, while accountants and lawyers work assiduously to minimize the effects of inheritance and other taxes. Professional and social life further reinforce commonality. London clubs, golf clubs and the Freemasons preserve a sense of exclusiveness celebrated in ceremonies and great sporting events like the Lord's Test, Ascot, Wimbledon, Cowes, the Boat Race and the Grand National. At all these venues are hallowed places where ordinary folk may not enter: the Long Room at Lord's, the Royal Box, the Royal Enclosure. Only a select few are invited into these places of privilege and they soon subscribe to the accepted values. (Boxer Frank Bruno threatened to leave the country if Labour won the 1997 general election.)

The presence of the upper class is venerated with archaic symbols: a reigning monarch, a fully fledged aristocracy and a host of ancient sinecures such as Lord Lieutenant of the County and High Sheriff. The exclusion process is strengthened by a preoccupation with dress, manners and accent (mocked in Bernard Shaw's *Pygmalion*). These symbols of privilege serve to legitimate the inequality produced by modern capitalism. This explains why the British bourgeoisie sought not to overthrow the bastions of privilege but to ingratiate itself with the old elite through a process of social climbing. The class has shown a genius for survival, assimilating talented or successful members of the lower orders like a vampire sucking the life-blood of the young. This lack of rigid 'structuration' (Giddens 1979: ch. 6) helps to legitimate the system (in theory anyone can become a millionaire, as the dot-com boom demonstrated).

In terms of ideology the upper class exhibits a high degree of homogeneity, though there remains a broad division between the paternalism inherited from Tory traditions – a belief that privilege carries duties – and the hard-nosed whiggish tradition of individualism and competition resuscitated in the 1980s. In addition, much has been made of notions of racial superiority; members of the class saw themselves as shouldering the 'white man's burden' in the great days of empire and of being 'born to rule' (see pp. 193–4). Ideologically their sympathies have generally been towards the right, which has usually meant supporting the Conservative Party, of which many have been members. However, they are equally willing to support Labour if it can deliver the enterprising low-tax regime they desire. Thus David Sainsbury, head of the supermarket dynasty, was an enthusiastic supporter of the New Labour government by which he was ennobled, while the top ten political donors in 2001 were equally divided between Labour and Conservative (*Sunday Times*, 7 April 2002).

> We are forever being told that we have a rigid class structure. That's a load of codswallop.
>
> Prince Edward, quoted in the *Observer* (21 Sept. 1997)

The Establishment Students of politics will undoubtedly encounter this vague but expressive term, popularized in the 1950s (Thomas 1959). **Establishment** denotes a closed group comprising those in control of the leading institutions (public schools, church, monarchy and aristocracy, mass media, traditional professions, Parliament, armed forces, civil service, the City, and of course the owners and managers of industry) (Sedgemore 1980: 11). Many dislike the term, particularly those alleged to be part of it, and it is clearly related to the idea of the upper class, though some would use the term 'elite'. This is discussed further in chapter 17.

> The Establishment talks with its own branded accents; eats different meals at different times; has its privileged system of education; its own religion, even, to a large extent, its own form of football.
>
> A. J. P. Taylor, in *New Statesman* (8 Aug. 1953)

The middle class

Despite his essentially dichotomous view of class structure, Marx did recognize 'middle and intermediate strata'. However, he believed that the obligation to sell their labour, and hence their inability to accumulate capital, would mean that the middle class would ultimately become part of a massive proletariat. This has not happened in Britain (Mandel 1983: 201–2), a fact with very important implications for the legitimation process. The growth of a vast intermediate class can be seen as a process of *embourgeoisement* (see p. 255), which has on the one hand eroded the old upper class, leaving an empty and harmless husk, and on the other, left an insignificant rump of ne'er-do-wells at the bottom, forming an 'underclass' (p. 186).

Much analysis discusses politics and society in these terms, with the intermediate class commonly divided into three – upper, middle and lower – largely distinguished on the basis of occupation. The upper middle class broadly includes the intelligentsia, professional people and managers, termed the 'service class' or 'salariat' by John Goldthorpe (1982) (figure 7.3). The middle characteristically contains the petite bourgeoisie, a tenacious class of small business people who resist the drive to large-scale operation, while the lower middle comprises white- and blue-collar workers, who generally try to espouse middle-class values.

A classless society Many saw the Thatcher era, with its attacks both on the welfare state and trade unions *and* on the old upper-class professions, as the final seal on the creation of this middle-class-dominated society, which enthusiasts, including Tony Blair, prefer to call a *classless* society. There is clearly much in the *embourgeoisement* thesis; capitalism changed dramatically during the twentieth century. However, objections can be raised (see pp. 551–2) and it can be argued that the idea of the classless society contains an element of mythology obscuring the continued holding and control of great wealth by the few (Scott 1985: 38). Indeed, during a decade of Thatcherism 'old money' prospered as never before in the post-war era. Middle-class vulnerability was demonstrated throughout the 1980s and 1990s as professions such as university lecturers, civil servants and doctors were threatened by a government intent upon reducing the tax burden placed upon capitalism. Adonis and Pollard (1997) argue that class barriers actually *increased* during the 1990s.

The working class

This essentially Marxist concept does not actually describe what people do. 'Work' can range from stock-brokerage to road-sweeping and, although condemned to idleness, the unemployed are generally regarded as part of the

> An Englishman's way of speaking absolutely classifies him. The moment he talks he makes some other Englishman despise him.
>
> Professor Higgins, in Alan Jay Lerner's musical *My Fair Lady* (1956)

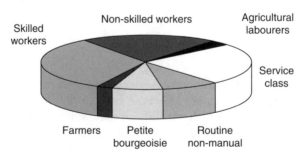

Figure 7.3
Britain's class structure according to one version of Goldthorpe's schema.

Source: Data from Devine (1997: 25).

Thatcher's children?

For some acolytes of the New Right, the era of Thatcherism was seen as the period when Britain became a classless society. At the end of the first decade there existed a large group with no adult memories of full employment, trade union involvement in policy-making and plentiful funds for education, the NHS and welfare state. A MORI poll (May 1989) revealed 'Thatcher's children' as tougher than their parents' generation across a wide spectrum, keener to set up businesses and with a different evaluation of social problems. However, by 1997 the British Social Attitudes Survey found little difference between the generations – all believed income inequality to be too great and that big business exploited its workers (Heath and Park 1998).

---

working class. The essential feature of this class is that its members lack wealth and power. Yet this great majority of the British people can only be designated as a class in the very loosest of senses and it lacks the homogeneity Marx ascribed to it. There are multifarious distinctions within it in terms of race, colour, spatial distribution, income, gender, occupation and, most importantly, in perceptions of the capitalist system.

A shrinking class? The decline of mining and heavy industry, new (post-Fordist) industrial practices and the globalization of the production process have eliminated many jobs and decimated traditional communities. Lockwood (1966) saw this class splitting into three: traditional proletarians such as miners and shipworkers, who showed great class solidarity; traditional deferential workers, with a sense of hierarchy and respect for their 'betters'; privatized workers, with an individualistic view of life and work and upwardly mobile aspirations. These were to become electorally significant from the late 1970s.

Is the working class shrinking? Goldthorpe's (1987) class schema identifies a shrunken working class as the upgrading of employment in a range of occupations has created a new enlarged middle class. In contrast, neo-Marxist Erik Olin Wright (1985) argues that the essential class structure remained unchanged for most of the twentieth century: a large proletariat at the bottom comprising a range of new non-manual but unskilled occupations that stand in the same vulnerable position vis-à-vis capital as the old working class, a small bourgeoisie at the top and an even smaller middle class sandwiched between (figure 7.4). The insecurity of employment for today's blue-collar and routine clerical workers leaves them little different from manual workers (Devine 1997: 219).

> The charm of Britain has always been the ease with which one can move into the middle class.
>
> Margaret Thatcher, in the *Observer* (27 Oct. 1974)

Our human stock is threatened . . . single parents from classes 4 and 5 are now producing a third of all births. If we do nothing, the nation moves towards degeneration.

Sir Keith Joseph, speech to Birmingham Conservatives (Oct. 1974)

Figure 7.4
Britain's class
structure according
to one version of
Wright's schema.

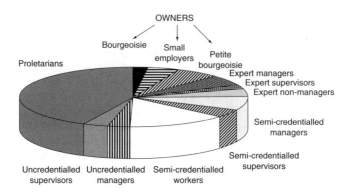

Source: Data from Devine (1997: 21).

Mind the gap: an underclass? Marx also saw a class below the working class – the *lumpenproletariat*. During the 1980s and 1990s J. K. Galbraith (1993) postulated a widening gap between a prosperous majority living securely in a 'culture of contentment' and a depressed minority of the socially vulnerable – the unemployed, low paid, homeless, elderly, handicapped, chronically sick, disabled, ethnic minorities, single-parent families, those with low educational attainments and those dropping out of the 'rat race' of competitive society. They have been characterized by American sociologist Charles Murray (1990) as an **underclass**, a term criticized by Adonis and Pollard (1997) as an elite device concealing the true extent of poverty by implying that it is confined to a small minority. Indeed, economic journalist Will Hutton (1996: 105–10) argued that government policy from the 1990s, deliberately fostering widespread inequality, had resulted in what he termed a 30/30/40 society.

The 30/30/40 society

◆ *Top 40% privileged*: Tenured, secure, full-time jobs or self-employed, a category shrinking by 1 per cent a year.
◆ *Middle 30% structurally insecure*: Part-time work, little protection.
◆ *Bottom 30% disadvantaged*: Unemployed, economically inactive, marginalized.

A report by the independent Joseph Rowntree Foundation revealed the number of people classed as 'very poor' (using some 50 indicators of poverty) to have risen by half a million between 1997 and 2000. The number living below the poverty line (i.e. less than half the national average income) had more than doubled (to over 14 million) since the early 1980s, while child poverty was the third highest among twenty-five developed nations (Gordon and Townsend 2001).

Class and politics

What has class to do with politics? Class is about who has what in society and its political effects resonate throughout the pages of this book. They are felt in voting behaviour, in the media, in the realm of ideas and attitudes, in education, through pressure groups, and even in health. Domination within a wide range of social relationships is often based upon class. Does domination go further than this: can one class collectively dominate the whole of society? In other words, does Britain have a ruling class? This important question is explored further in chapter 17.

The Monstrous Regiment: Sexism in British Society

In turning to the question of gender we are by no means leaving the issue of class because women are predominant in the lower echelons of the class structure (Devine 1997: 44). Moreover, in all classes men tend to dominate women. This remains true despite the fact that from 1979 to 1990 Britain had a woman prime minister. Indeed, other patriarchal societies – India, Israel and Pakistan – have also had women leaders, but they remain lonely swallows showing very little promise of a feminist summer.

> The First Blast of the Trumpet Against the Monstrous Regiment of Women.
>
> Title of pamphlet by John Knox (1505–72; charismatic Scottish preacher)

British patriarchy

British culture is **sexist** and **patriarchal**: a woman's social position is largely fixed by the men in her life, mainly her father and husband. Working-class culture has been particularly male-dominated, with the trade unions bastions of patriarchy. The domination is betrayed in our very language with the repetitious use of the male pronoun: not only have committees largely been headed by chairmen, even God is a man. In the human race we are all *Homo sapiens*; where are the *Femina sapiens*?

The modern pattern of domination by gender did not originate with the capitalism that shapes life today. In many African cultures women spend the day in hard physical labour while the men remain largely idle, Asian civilizations retain rigid sexist traditions and under Muslim law the treatment of women is harsh indeed. As long ago as 300 BC, in an idyll by Theocritus,

---

Mother is the dead heart of the family, spending father's earnings on consumer goods to enhance the environment in which he eats, sleeps and watches the television.

Germaine Greer (Australian-born feminist), *The Female Eunuch* (1970)

Praxinoa, a fine lady, rushes away from a show at the royal palace telling her friend: 'I must be getting back. It's Diocleidas' dinner time, and that man's all pepper; I wouldn't advise anyone to come near him when he's kept waiting for his food' (Seltman 1956: 134). However, male domination and the concept of the family unit have proved functional for capitalism by providing a means for the reproduction and maintenance of labour.

Women and work

> ### The oldest profession?
>
> Even when women have full rights, they still remain factually down-trodden because all house work is left to them. In most cases house work is the most unproductive, the most barbarous and the most arduous work a woman can do.
>
> V. I. Lenin (1870–1924; Russian communist leader), *Collected Works* (vol. XXX: 43)

The multi-faceted subjugation of women is nowhere better illustrated than in paid employment. The growth of capitalism made possible a sharp distinction between two forms of work: the *commodity production* of industry and *domestic production* at home. However, the latter is not usually considered real work at all (Rowbotham 1973: 68) and housewives socialized by the commodity production ethos tend to say: 'I don't have a job'. Figure 7.5 illustrates the extent to which women continue to be classified as 'economically inactive' (a category including housekeeping).

For most women, paid employment must be fitted around the full-time domestic production role, yet this has not significantly altered the basic organization of work practices. The effect is to exclude women from many sections of the labour market (Garnsey 1982: 440). An additional problem is that of the single-parent family. The term is largely a euphemism for families without a

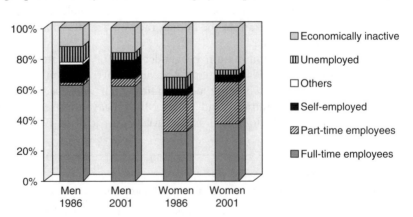

Figure 7.5
Working-age population by economic status, 1986 and 2001.

Source: Data from *Social Trends* (2002: table 4.3).

man, marital break-up or unintended pregnancy usually leaving the children with the mother. The position can be particularly degrading as the need for an income, coupled with an inability to give a full-time commitment, often oblige women to accept menial, low-prestige occupations. Immigrant women, sometimes from particularly sexist societies, are even more vulnerable, often accepting sweatshop conditions and denied unionization. Even professional women can expect to be dominated by their male colleagues, denied promotion by a 'glass ceiling', while those returning to work after child-rearing tend to occupy positions far lower than their qualifications warrant.

The propensity to gravitate towards menial jobs means that, unlike men, women tend to work in a limited number of occupations. Over half are in three service sectors – distributive trades, secretarial and miscellaneous services (e.g. catering, cleaning). They are also found predominantly in caring work such as nursing, primary education and social services, thereby reinforcing the cultural definition of their identity as servers rather than creators. Although changes in employment patterns from the early 1980s saw a rapid acceleration in the recruitment of women into the workforce, this was largely in the flexible, vulnerable, poorly unionized and low-paid service industries. Between 1977 and 1988 the number earning below the minimum wage stipulated in the EC Social Charter rose from 8 million to 9.4 million (*Guardian*, 13 Oct. 1993). By the late 1990s there were over 5 million people working part time, over 80 per cent of whom were women (figure 7.5). The increasing casualization of the labour force had seen women taking low-paid, part-time jobs while their husbands suffered redundancy (Hutton 1996: 106).

Political implications of sexism

Male culture does not welcome women in politics, as was amply demonstrated in the suffragettes' battle for the franchise (pp. 243–4). Women's issues have tended to remain off the political agenda and women themselves have rarely become political activists; far less unionized than men, they may even not support their husbands when on strike. They have been poorly represented on the TUC and, although trade union attitudes have become more sympathetic, there remains much deep-seated sexism. Despite the 1997 influx of women, Parliament remains predominantly a male club (see chapter 12), seen at its most bizarre when pontificating on abortion, viewing the foetus as male property placed in the womb for safe keeping.

During the 1970s, legislation on sex discrimination and equal pay marked the inauguration of a sex equality strategy. However, the legalistic removal of barriers by governments committed to a minimalist state role did little to change behaviour (Forbes 1996). Indeed, policies from the 1980s were particularly bad for women, with much rhetoric on the theme of family breakdown. Women could be blamed for failings such as low educational standards, drug abuse among the young and juvenile delinquency. Social policies shifted the care of the old, chronically ill and handicapped from the state to the family

> Women have served all these centuries as looking-glasses possessing the magic and delicious power of reflecting the figure of man at twice its natural size.
>
> Virginia Woolf (1882–1941; English writer), *A Room of One's Own* (1929)

under a policy termed 'Care in the Community'. The freezing of child benefit payments also specifically targeted women. Labour in power appeared no less harsh in the eyes of critics, with its policy of getting single mothers off state benefits and into work (supported by most of its record new intake of women MPs).

Deeply sexist attitudes vein the state. It will be apparent throughout this book that the world we are examining is one of male dominance. Here there are no female field marshalls, lord chancellors, bishops or heads of privatized industries. The vast majority of cabinet ministers, judges, higher civil servants, MPs, councillors, soldiers and police are still male. Despite becoming Britain's first woman prime minister, Margaret Thatcher was to appoint no other members of her own sex to her Cabinet.

A study of the north-east published in 2000, which was not considered atypical, revealed men comprising 87 per cent of the region's MPs, 77 per cent of its elected councillors, 74 per cent of its housing association members and 66 per cent of the regional arts council. They also made up 87 per cent of the new regional assembly (Durham University 2000). Hence, over eighty years after granting women the vote, the political system still served 'to institutionalise and reproduce inequalities between the sexes' (Lovenduski 1996). Even the NHS is run by men, demonstrating their assumed right to control women's bodies as well as their minds.

Women on top? However, as we saw in chapter 2, feminism is now a serious ideology and the women's movement is part of politics. A number of concessions have been gained in the areas of equal opportunities and pay, and women have been appointed to some high-profile positions: Stella Rimington became head of MI5 and Elizabeth Filkin replaced Sir Gordon Downey as Parliamentary Commissioner for Standards. However, in 2001 both were to depart under clouds, falling foul of whispering campaigns within the male establishment club. A similar fate befell Mo Mowlam, despite the great advances she had made as Northern Ireland Secretary.

A record number of women entered Parliament in 1997 and a record number entered Blair's first Cabinet, rising to seven after his 2001 election victory. However, the most senior positions such as Chancellor, home secretary and foreign secretary remained in male hands. Women have also been involved in some major political affairs, including the 1976–7 strike by Asian women in the Grunwick photographic processing factory over unionization, the Greenham Common encampment against Cruise missiles and the Northern Ireland peace campaign. By the end of the twentieth century, girls were outperforming boys in school and women were more able to pursue professional careers.

Race and Politics

Britain is becoming an increasingly multiracial society (table 7.2), the ethnic minority population having grown from some 3.2 million in 1992–4 to 3.7 million in 1997–9, a rise of 15.6 per cent (*Population Trends*, 2001). The fastest-growing group were the Muslim Bangladeshi and Black African populations (30 and 37 per cent, respectively). Over the same period the white population had increased by only 1 per cent, reaching 53 million. Almost half the entire ethnic minority population is found in the Greater London area, constituting 34 per cent of the Inner London population. Yet there is a deep-seated, indelible **racism** within the political culture. Although many white people may doubt this, few with a West Indian or Asian background could agree with them: race and racism lie at the very heart of their social and economic experience.

What is racism?

The human species may be said to consist of several races distinguished by superficial physical characteristics (size, colour of hair and skin, etc.). These are only broad distinctions: many individuals do not fit the physical type suggested by their racial origins and intermarriage further blurs the picture. Recognition of these differences is not racism. Racism is the practice of discriminating against people on the grounds of race. Some regimes (the European fascists in the 1930s and South Africa in the days of apartheid) have been openly based on the belief that racial differences justify inequality, the implication being that some races are morally or intellectually superior. Apart from being ethically objectionable, this is quite impossible to sustain because of differences in cultural environments. It is about as logically defensible as the distinction Gulliver encountered in Lilliput based upon the method of eating a boiled egg, which resulted in bloody war for 'six and thirty moons' between the 'Big-Endians' and 'Little-Endians'!

Manifestations of racism

Although racism in Britain today does not take the open and violent forms seen in Nazi Germany, the American deep south, or apartheid South Africa, it

Table 7.2 Ethnic composition of the British population, 1996/7 and 2000/1 (millions)

Year	White	Black	Indian	Pakistani/ Bangladeshi	Chinese	Other/ mixed
1996/7	52.9	0.9	0.9	0.8	0.1	0.6
2000/1	53.0	1.3	1.0	0.9	0.1	0.7

Source: Data from *Social Trends* (2002: table 1.4).

Source: Mary Evans Picture Library

permeates every nook and cranny of life. It is found in the membership of clubs and societies, sport, housing, newspapers, employment, education and every-day language. The most openly racist white people have a rich lexicon of derogatory terms ranging from 'our coloured cousins', 'nigger' and 'wog', to the more obscene. Such attitudes are also found in state institutions, with the police and army subject to particular criticism (see chapter 21).

When Hitler and Mussolini were taking power in the 1930s, Britain had its own fascist movement, led by Sir Oswald Mosley. Although making minimal impact, fascist parties have continued to exist, including the National Socialist Movement, the National Front, the British Movement and the British National Party (which won a council by-election in London's Isle of Dogs in September 1993 and captured two council seats in Burnley in 2002). The establishment of an all-white Britain remains their prime goal.

As racist patterns continue, the threat of further resistance, including vio-lence, increases. One result has been for ethnic minorities to turn inwards, living a self-contained existence in decaying inner-city ghettos and abandoning the ambition to participate on equal terms in society. In December 2001, the

> We shall have to start progressively removing their rights. If bloodshed and racial strife are the result, then all I can say is that that is an acceptable price to pay for clearing out the immigrants.
>
> Anthony Reed-Herbert of the National Front, quoted in *The Times* (24 June 1976)

Cantle Report on serious race riots earlier that year in Oldham, Bradford and Burnley revealed ethnic and white communities living separate existences and lacking a sense of common civic identity. The level of feeling had been signalled in the 2001 general election, when two BNP candidates had saved their deposits in Oldham.

It is the young with no experience of a home other than Britain who feel the greatest sense of alienation and despair and who are likely to vent their frustration in riot. By the late 1990s, most major cities had experienced clashes between young blacks and the police. The case against white youths accused of murdering black youth Stephen Lawrence in 1993 was dismissed for lack of evidence, though the Macpherson Report into the affair suggested an underlying racist culture amongst the police (see p. 667).

> In Great Britain racism is smouldering like the funeral pyres in the areas of foot and mouth.
>
> *Stern* (German magazine, May 2001)

The roots of racism

The British have long attributed their supremacy to God, who is frequently enjoined to 'make us mightier yet'. Hence it is not surprising that Jews in particular have been vilified. The late-Victorian poet W. N. Ewer mocked: 'How odd of God, to choose, the Jews', and from Shakespeare's *Merchant of Venice* to Dickens's Fagin they have been depicted as miserly and grasping. Similarly, the Irish (notwithstanding Wilde, Shaw, Joyce, Behan, Heaney et al.) have long been considered inferior.

> British thought and British society has never been cleansed of the Augean filth of imperialism.
>
> Salman Rushdie, in *New Society* (9 Dec. 1982)

The great age of discovery revealed to West European eyes a vast world of 'savages': inferior beings to be tamed, trained, and deprived of their land, culture and property. The seventeenth-century slave trade made the English curiously interested in race. Part of the justification for this abomination was a belief that Africans were so inferior in character and brain that to be enslaved by the white man was actually an improvement! The development of the empire as an integral part of British capitalism (see chapter 4) had a particular significance for today's racist attitudes. The British defeated European rivals in the pillage of the New World, where they subjugated the indigenous populations. By the closing decades of the eighteenth century, once the Indian subcontinent had been retrieved from the French, the empire was the largest the world had ever experienced. Truly they were a master race. Victorian scientists pictured mankind in terms of a great hierarchy, with the white Englishman invariably at the top and the negro just above the ape at the bottom.

Of course the claimed superiority was attributed to the dominant class, not to the lower orders labouring in conditions scarcely better than those of slaves. However, the extension of the franchise obliged establishment forces to seek their support, a seemingly impossible enterprise accomplished through the Disraelian concept of 'one nation' (see p. 279). In this great legitimating myth the empire was invoked as a unifying symbol, serving to bestow splendour on even the most lowly; they were part of the race that ruled the world. This sentiment was to bequeath a lasting sense of **xenophobia**.

> Take up the White Man's burden –
> And reap his old reward:
> The blame of those ye better,
> The hate of those ye guard.
>
> Rudyard Kipling (1865–1936; Indian-born
> British writer), 'The White Man's Burden'

Recognition of this legacy came from Home Secretary Jack Straw in July 2000, when he attributed the hooliganism of English football fans abroad to a distorted sense of patriotism that was part of the 'baggage of empire'. The feelings are not confined to those of a different colour. The general unease with the EU is testimony to a problem many British people have with those from any other country. A 2001 British Council poll of young people in seventeen countries showed these sons of Britannia to be widely regarded not as cool but as arrogant, often drunk and 'xenophobic' (Burke 2001).

The pattern of immigration

> All those who are not racially pure are mere chaff.
>
> Adolf Hitler (1889–1945), *Mein Kampf* (1925–6)

Contrary to the Victorian theory, the British 'race' is in no sense pure; it is a mongrel breed including Celts, Romans, Anglo-Saxons, Normans and Danes that could find no class for itself at a *Homo sapiens* Crufts Show. After 1066 the country was host to further immigration waves: the medieval period saw large numbers of Jewish settlers, at the end of the seventeenth century came the Huguenots escaping persecution in France, and the eighteenth-century Irish famine brought a further major influx. It was never in the British nature to welcome the newcomers. In 1601 Elizabeth I issued a proclamation to remove the country's few black people and a 1605 Act restricted the rights of aliens. However, time generally soothed irate feelings and the immigrants were well integrated, some to become very successful (amongst the most successful were William the Conqueror, William of Orange, the Hanoverians and the Saxe-Coburgs). Intermarriage frequently meant that the only sign of foreign origins was an unusual name, and sometimes even these were changed (the Saxe-Coburgs became the 'Windsors'!).

A new wave of immigration began in the post-imperial era. The 1948 British Nationality Act gave common British citizenship to all Commonwealth citizens, providing a labour source to compensate for shortages at home (Saggar 1992: 97). Workers from India, Pakistan and the West Indies were encouraged through recruitment drives by public bodies such as the NHS and London Transport. Their willingness to undertake uncongenial, low-paid work enabled some traditional industries, such as textiles, to survive in an increasingly competitive world economy. Although the first of the immigrants (mainly men) met with resistance, they were buoyed up by the expectation that, as in the past, they would become integrated. However, such optimism proved illusory. Despite the efforts of bodies such as the Runnymede Trust, fighting for racial equality and social justice, a second British-born generation remained as black as its parents, excluded from better jobs, confined to poor housing in inner-city areas, with inferior education and health care and subject to racially inspired violence.

Problems intensified as the long boom of western capitalism ran out of steam. Unemployment began an inexorable rise amongst the black population (figure 7.6), which was particularly vulnerable to the automation of manufacturing and textile industries. Adding insult to injury, they were seen as one of the *causes* of unemployment.

The break-up of the Soviet Union saw a new wave of immigration as people fled from the horrors of ethnic cleansing, tribal war and economic collapse. Government figures showed 18,000 applications for asylum in the first three months of 2002 – an 8 per cent rise on the previous quarter and a 4 per cent rise on the first quarter of 2001. Whether called asylum seekers, bogus asylum seekers, economic migrants or illegal immigrants, they inflamed the passions of the tabloids and prompted a reaction from politicians in the form of stricter laws, tighter appeals procedures, voucher systems and detention centres. But despite tabloid alarm, the great majority of applications (around 70 per cent) were being turned down.

Institutional racism

Racism can be enstructured into the very institutions of society through laws and habitual practices. It can be found in the legal system, the civil service and educational institutions. The 1999 Macpherson Report highlighted the problem within the police service. David Wilmot, Chief Constable of Greater Manchester, caused considerable shock when he admitted to **institutional racism** within his own ranks (see p. 697).

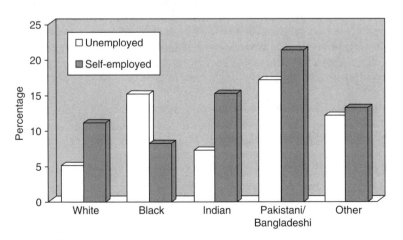

Figure 7.6
Unemployment and self-employment status by ethnic group, 2000/2001.

Source: Data from *Social Trends* (2002: table 4.21 and chart 4.15).

Racism has been institutionalized through legislation, passed by both major parties, designed to restrict coloured immigration. The 1958 Notting Hill race riots marked a grim watershed, leading to the first post-war Immigration Act in 1962. This restricted entry from the black Commonwealth to those able to show they were coming to a specific job, or able to offer a particular skill. Women were subject to strict physical examinations, including a degrading internal virginity test.

The hard reality of the Smethwick election result in 1964 (when an openly racist Conservative using the slogan 'If you want a nigger for a neighbour, vote Labour' won a stunning victory) and increasing anti-black hysteria led Labour to introduce even tougher restrictions in 1965, allowing deportation by the Home Secretary (without a court hearing) of any illegal immigrant of less than five years' standing. A new style of rhetoric, speaking of the 'small crowded island', transformed what had been right-wing views into respectable orthodoxy. Home Secretary Roy Jenkins, hitherto a notable advocate of the humane society, stressed the 'social factor' limiting the number that could be absorbed. In 1968 the Commonwealth Immigrants Act (to stem immigration from turbulent Kenya) was rushed through Parliament in only two days. The Conservatives consolidated the position in 1971 with an Act restricting entry to patrials (those with parents or grandparents born in the UK), while the 1981 British Nationality Act effectively closed the door to non-whites, though keeping another open for 6 million patrials and the 200 million in the EC.

Brothers in law: race relations legislation Attempts to curb racism have been seen in 1965, 1968 and 1976 Acts designed to outlaw discrimination, and the establishment of the Commission for Racial Equality (CRE) to enforce their provisions. The Macpherson Report led to the first new piece of race relations legislation for 25 years. The Race Relations (Amendments) Act (2000) (which came into operation in April 2001) extended existing provisions against racial discrimination to previously excluded public bodies, including hospitals, the prisons service and the police. However, it is debatable how far legislation can change deep-seated prejudices. The CRE is seen by many as a toothless watchdog, serving to legitimate oppressive legislation rather than improve the life experiences of blacks. Others pour scorn on what they term the 'race relations industry' (Banton 1985: vii).

Racism and politics

The politics of Britain logically gives ethnic minorities and working-class whites more reason to unite than divide, yet racism 'appears at its strongest among unskilled working people' (Walvin 1984: 143). Even within the active left there has been a strong vein of racism, particularly evident in the trade unions. Immigrants have been seen as depressing wage levels and taking employment from indigenous workers. The TUC has pressed enthusiastically

> Members of Parliament who represent ethnic minorities – unlike their colleagues who sit for prosperous suburban seats – are always criticised for advancing the claims of their constituents. It is part of the racism which afflicts our society.
>
> Roy Hattersley, *Who Goes Home?* (1996: 284)

for action against illegal immigrants and there is a lengthy catalogue of disputes involving racist behaviour by members and officials. Hence, although Labour has received more solid support from ethnic minorities than from working-class whites, its trade-union roots have inhibited its response. The Scarman Report on the 1981 Brixton riots criticized 'the low level of black representation in our elective political institutions' (Scarman 1981: 16). Yet Labour remained strongly opposed to black sections, thereby denying black people the distinct political voice allowed to women. However, in May 2002 Labour's Paul Boateng made history by becoming the first black member of the Cabinet.

The reality of British political culture means that 'there are votes for the picking in fanning the flames of racial resentment' (Crewe 1983: 263). It has been argued that racism is a weapon of last resort for conservative parties, particularly in the post-cold-war period (Thranhardt 1995: 337). The racist vote was most effectively garnered for the Conservatives by Enoch Powell, whose lurid speeches lamented the submergence of a halcyon English age under the great alien tidal wave. A Gallup poll exposed the hard truth that 75 per cent of the population were broadly sympathetic to his sentiments (Marwick 1982). Fascism had given racism a bad name but Powell made it 'respectable amongst those who saw the Tory party as the epitome of conformist respectability' (Bhavnani and Bhavnani 1985: 150). By the late 1970s, therefore, the National Front had seen its popular support eroded by the Conservatives, who, with their hard-line immigration stance, had stolen its central political message (Saggar 1992: 185).

Powell was known to be greatly admired by Margaret Thatcher, who herself warned of the danger that 'this country might be swamped by people with a different culture' (Sivanandan 1981: 145). Upon becoming Conservative leader she could be seen as 'a poor man's Enoch Powell' (Johnson 1985: 114). While the neoliberalism of the New Right was not itself racist, its authoritarian strand took a hard line on social issues. From here came a 'new racism', its message shrouded in a language of social responsibility. Stressing Englishness, national identity and common cultural history, it attacked multiculturalism (Gordon

> As I look ahead I am filled with foreboding. Like the Roman, I seem to see 'the River Tiber foaming with much blood'.
>
> Enoch Powell MP, on immigration, public speech in Birmingham (4 April 1968)

> The party must learn that holding three or four receptions for Asian millionaires every year does not amount to a race relations policy. Whenever I go to central office the only other black face is the security guard at the door.
>
> John Taylor, defeated Conservative candidate at Cheltenham in 1992 general election (12 Oct. 1993)

and Klug 1986). Norman Tebbit regarded support for visiting cricket teams as a 'test'. In the 2001 election campaign, Conservative leader William Hague spoke of a Britain that was soon to become a 'foreign land', sparking off new accusations that the party was sending out a covert racist message. Indeed, the asylum policies of both Labour and the Conservatives led Liberal Democrat Simon Hughes to accuse them of racism, even lodging a complaint with the CRE.

Hence the claim that there is a gentleman's agreement among politicians not to use race for political advantage may be bogus; racism helps sustain class domination. From the 'one-nation' appeal of Disraeli, Conservatives have vaunted patriotism as more honourable than class loyalty. Yet patriotism is not merely, in the words of Doctor Johnson, 'the last refuge of a scoundrel', it can also be the first refuge of the racist. Unlike that of gender, the racial division has not cut across class. Despite a growing number of upwardly mobile Asians (Saggar 1992: 207), black people belong largely to the working class, so racism weakens working-class solidarity, particularly during economic recession. The depression of the early 1990s saw a tide of racial assaults in London's East End and in other cities. In 2001, it was Bradford and Oldham, places that stood in sharp contrast to the prosperous south-east, that experienced the worst race riots for many years. The general election alarmed many by revealing that, in the privacy of the polling booth, some 16 per cent of Oldham's population were willing to give their support to the openly racist BNP.

> Racism is now beginning to grow in Britain. That was the evidence given to the home affairs select committee by the police, by ethnic groups of all colours and by the government.
>
> Sir Ivan Lawrence (Chairman, Commons Home Affairs Committee), in the *Sunday Times* (3 July 1994)

Covering the Cracks

Britain's deferential, united civic culture is rather more complex and tense than that venerated by liberal-democratic apologists. The working of the polity cannot be explained in terms of a large natural consensus. Class, gender and racial cracks in the social fascia are plastered over with political spin and concealed beneath unwritten constitutional wallpaper. It is in exploring how this is accomplished that one gains the key to the true spirit and genius of the system. This long exploration begins in the following chapter.

Key points

- Political culture is a vague term encompassing history, institutions and attitudes towards the political system.
- Characteristics seen in British political culture include continuity, deference and consensus.
- Beneath the apparent tranquillity fester class, gender and racial tensions.
- There is little to support the thesis that Britain is a classless society.
- Britain has a patriarchal political system in which women have not been encouraged to take part.
- Racism is found in various forms in Britain and is particularly persistent where skin colour prevents long-term assimilation.

Review your understanding of the following terms and concepts

bourgeoisie	institutional racism	sexism
civic culture	meritocracy	underclass
class	middle class	upper class
consensus	patriarchy	working class
deference	political culture	xenophobia
embourgeoisement	proletariat	
Establishment	racism	

Assignment

Study the extract from the *Sunday Times* on page 200 and answer the following questions.

		Mark (%)
1	Suggest reasons why the government 'is highly unlikely to meet its pledge to boost the proportion of women on public bodies'.	40
2	What arguments can you give for achieving a '50% ratio of male and female' on public bodies?	30
3	Why do men predominate on public bodies?	30

Labour's equality target 20 years off

David Cracknell and Rosie Waterhouse

LABOUR is highly unlikely to meet its pledge to boost the proportion of women on public bodies. Ministers reveal in a leaked memo that it will take 20 years to achieve equality.

The admission is made in a private briefing paper drawn up by Patricia Hewitt and Barbara Roche, the ministers for women. It points out that Labour set a target for women to hold between 45% and 50% of all public appointments made by the government by the year 2005.

However, the document, entitled Delivering for Women and dated March 8, confesses that at the current rate of progress "a 50% ratio of male and female would not be reached until 2020".

Whitehall has appointment powers over 30,000 jobs on advisory committees, consumer groups, justice and parole boards, charity executives, review bodies, arts councils and other quangos.

An analysis of government statistics and information in the Commons library shows that there has been a 2.7% increase in female representation on public bodies since 1997, taking the total to about 34%.

The number of women appointed to public bodies by several Whitehall departments has actually fallen since Labour came to power.

©Times Newspapers Ltd, 5 May 2002

Questions for discussion

1 How accurate is it to describe the UK as a cohesive political culture?
2 In what way do you think deference among the British working class contributes to the hegemonic consciousness of the upper middle class?
3 On what grounds can it be argued that the British working class is shrinking?
4 'The rise of the middle classes has rendered redundant the Marxist distinction between the owners of capital and the workers.' Discuss.
5 'Politics is for men.' Discuss.
6 'The post-cold-war wave of asylum seekers has rekindled racism in Britain.' Discuss.
7 'A cohesive society can be multiracial but not multicultural.' Discuss.
8 'Racism is largely a social phenomenon. It does not have any significant effect on politics.' Discuss.
9 'You can change your class, but not your colour or gender.' Discuss the political implications of this.
10 In what ways is Britain's political culture changing?

Topic for debate

This house believes that women have no place in politics.

Further reading

Adonis, A. and Pollard, S. (1997) *A Class Act: The Myth of Britain's Classless Society*.
Argues that, far from diminishing, class barriers are intensifying.

Almond, G. A. and Verba, S. (1963) *The Civic Culture* (reprinted 1989).
Remains a classic text despite criticism.

Almond, G. A. and Verba, S. (eds) (1980) *The Civic Culture Revisited*.
Readings re-evaluate the civic culture in the light of events.

Cahill, K. (2001) *Who Owns Britain?*
Asserts that a conspiracy to keep the land in the hands of the chosen few is a prime cause of Britain's poor economic performance.

Dunleavy, P., Margetts, H., Smith, T. and Weir, S. (2001) *Voices of the People: Popular Attitudes to Democratic Renewal in Britain*.
Reports a ten-year series of opinion polls on constitutional and democratic issues commissioned by the Joseph Rowntree Reform Trust. Finds more support than is commonly supposed for a variety of reforms.

Fryer, P. (1988) *Black People in the British Empire*.
Explores the exploitation of the colonies and presents an alternative view of the place of black people in British history.

Giddens, A. (2001) *Sociology*, 4th edn.
Panoramic introduction illustrates how the discipline of sociology addresses many of the questions important to the study of politics.

Giddens, A. (1997) *Sociology: Introductory Readings*.
Lively readings from a wide variety of sources.

Hobson, D. (1999) *The National Wealth: Who Gets What in Britain*.
A tour de force (1350 pp.) exploring the relationship between money, status and power from the Norman Conquest to New Labour.

Lovenduski, J. and Norris, P. (eds) (1996) *Women in Politics*.
Focusing on Britain, provides up-to-date overview of women's attitudes, behaviour and representation in policy areas affecting them.

Saggar, S. (1992) *Race and Politics in Britain*.
Examines the nature, causes and consequences of racism. Notes link with the political right.

For light relief

Much literature, both from home and abroad, deals with themes that divide societies – class, race and gender.

Martin Amis, *London Fields*.
Surreal vision of London life: four people bound together in a modern urban torment of class, wealth and squalor, destroying themselves within a decaying world.

Billy Bragg, *England, Half English*.
This CD from the most politically engaged of Britain's songwriters addresses the vexed questions of 'Englishness' and nationalism.

Jilly Cooper, *Class*.
Light essay by a proud daughter of the upper middle class.

Edwina Currie, *A Woman's Place*.
According to John Julius Norwich, this 'does for Parliament what D. H. Lawrence did for gamekeeping'.

Henrik Ibsen, *The Doll's House*.
Powerful drama about women's oppression.

Kazuo Ishiguro, *Remains of the Day*.
Moving class novel with powerful political overtones. (Also a film/video.)

George Bernard Shaw, *Pygmalion*.
Witty but subversive comedy on upper-class manners and gender relationships by the Irish genius. (Alternatively, see the less subversive musical film/video, *My Fair Lady*.)

On the net

http://www.sunday-times.co.uk
Via this site you can access the *Sunday Times*' annual Rich List, which has extensive information on changing patterns of wealth distribution.

http://www.ons.gov.uk
The Office for National Statistics is a good source for up-to-date socioeconomic information.

Part II

Mobilizing the Demos

The Greek *demos* means the people as a whole; when they control the government the polity can lay claim to the title democracy. Few polities today would not at least pay lip-service to the notion of democracy, but few fully realize its demanding ideals. Before there can be even a pretence of democracy there must be mechanisms whereby the *demos* will be mobilized to participate in the processes of politics. In this section we evaluate how this is accomplished in Britain. Above all we are interested in fundamental questions concerning the ability of the state to permit genuine and unimpeded entrance of the masses through its portals. Can all enter with equal ease or are there keep-off signs saying 'Members Only', 'Men Only' or even 'Whites Only'?

   We are moving closer to the heart of British politics and encountering some of the very big questions of social life, illuminating not only the nature of the polity we inhabit but the very quality of life. We first look at the way people form the political attitudes discussed earlier. These do not arise spontaneously; they are socially constructed by experience and conditioned through the process we term 'mind politics', a layer of political activity that people encounter before coming anywhere near the ballot box. Chapter 9 examines the most visible mechanism of participation, the electoral system. When everyone has the right to vote the *demos* would indeed appear mighty; or is it? We consider the grudging manner in which the powerful few in Britain extended the franchise to the mass and did so in a way calculated to minimize damage to their own privileges. Chapters 10 and 11 examine the main products of the fully extended franchise, the modern political parties. When these are understood we have some important keys for unlocking the mysteries of the British political system.

8

Mind Politics: What We Think

In this chapter we turn to the processes shaping people's views and attitudes – the politics of the mind. Mind politics arises from the need for social stability. There are various ways of maintaining this, from the brutal use of force and fear, through attempts by the state to ease the effects of inequality (welfare policies), to more subtle psychological processes that discourage the disadvantaged from rebelling. While the British state has not been unwilling to employ force against citizens, it is preferable that people accept their lot with some degree of contentment. In other words, the system must be *legitimated*; the distribution of power and material goods in society, and the form of government, must be seen as being right and proper. People must believe that the political and economic systems in which they live are fair and just. They must feel that their ambitions can be achieved without violence or rebellion. Where there is inequality they must feel that this is justified in promoting the common good as in the case of, say, high wages for skilled surgeons or large profits to job-creating entrepreneurs. We shall see throughout the chapters of this book that legitimation takes place in many ways. Here our focus is on those institutions particularly concerned with what we think. The chapter has four broad sections. The first examines informal political influences encountered through the family, the peer group, religion, school, the arts and the advertising that is so central to our capitalist society. The second section concentrates on a profoundly important source of mass communication: the press. Next we consider broadcasting, perhaps the most potent of the mass media today. We conclude by examining the impact of a development that is reshaping the contemporary world: the revolution in information and communications technology.

Political Socialization

Defining political socialization

The process whereby people acquire their attitudes towards politics is termed **political socialization**. A major flaw in typical studies of political socialization is a preoccupation with voting behaviour, seeking to explain, in the words of W. S. Gilbert:

> How Nature always does contrive
> That every boy and ever gal,
> That's born into this world alive,
> Is either a little Liberal,
> Or else a little Conservative!
> (*Iolanthe*, Act II)

There is much more to the socialization process than explaining the mysteries whereby boys and girls grow up to be Conservatives, Liberal Democrats, Labourites, or even supporters of the British National Party. It is upon the socialization process that the stability of the whole system depends; it determines whether successive generations will vote at all, whether they will be apathetic abstainers, activists, cynics, or perhaps revolutionaries.

A central legitimating feature of a deferential political culture is the notion of the neutral state. This may be promoted by venerating basic constitutional principles such as the rule of law and the political impartiality of state institutions (civil service, police force, judiciary). We shall see in later chapters that the institutions themselves play a part in the socialization process in many subtle ways. However, in addition to the state's direct role in reproducing supportive attitudes we find a range of non-state institutions extending into civil society. In addition, there are institutions specially created to talk to (not to communicate with) the masses: the communications media.

The family

> They fuck you up your mum and dad.
> They may not mean to but they do.
> They fill you with the faults they had
> And add some extra, just for you.
>
> Philip Larkin (1922–85; English poet),
> 'This be the Verse'

The family is the first source of attitude formation we encounter. Despite the role played by mothers, it has been an essentially patriarchal organization reproducing sexist attitudes. Girls have been trained for housework and boys may be induced to feel superior. Xenophobia and racism may also be learnt in this private world. The family is also a power structure in which parents exercise authority, although characteristically on the basis of love. Hence we grow up understanding that authority is generally in our own interests. This can help explain why the political right lays great stress on the family: it helps to reinforce a social organization where a dominant class is accepted in the interest of the whole nation. However, the family can also socialize people into non-capitalist values such as mutual care and equality, which is why it cannot in itself provide a sufficient basis for mind-shaping in a capitalist society.

British family life is changing as a result of the growth of non-white communities, feminism and a greater plurality in social norms. South Asian families traditionally honour family loyalty and conformity, including arranged marriages. This clashes with the liberal competitive environment outside, placing conflicting pressures on children. In families of West Indian origin, although fewer mothers aged 20–45 live with a husband than among the comparable white population, these single mothers gain support from their extended kinship networks (Giddens 2001: 190). Through the influence of feminism, patriarchy is less strong among many younger couples and more domestic chores are shared. Greater plurality in lifestyles produces far more unmarried couples living together and rearing children. There is also more tolerance of gay and lesbian 'marriages'. However, the New Labour government, like its Conservative predecessors, has sought to reaffirm the more traditional family values.

The peer group

Friends and colleagues can also shape our political attitudes. The importance of relationships based on school, work and leisure has been stressed by psychologists such as Mead and Piaget. There are strong social pressures to conform to **peer group** norms in many respects, such as dress, musical taste and attitude towards sex. Since peer relationships are usually based on consent, pressures to conform can be more acceptable than those imposed by parents or teachers. Because of their exclusive as well as inclusive nature, peer groups can engender racist and sexist attitudes. They may also encourage crime, particularly amongst young men, and reinforce drug culture. Falling electoral turnouts amongst the young may also be partly explained by peer group influence.

Religion

Although it is often said that religion and politics should not be mixed, in reality they are rarely far apart. For long most educated people were formally church officials, and leading office-holders such as Thomas Becket, Cardinal Wolsey and Archbishop Cranmer were key political and administrative figures. The English Reformation saw the church formally wedded to the state as the

Church of England, headed by the monarch. Today the bishops sit in the House of Lords and the monarch is crowned in Westminster Abbey.

During the industrial revolution capitalism drew its inspiration from the puritan doctrines of nonconformity. Stressing frugality and saving, these justified the great accumulation of wealth necessary to consolidate their position. However, they saw the Church of England as the religion of the upper middle class and social advancement has often required a switch from nonconformity (Thatcher herself crossed this divide).

From the eighteenth century, with the emergence of the great urban masses, social services were pioneered by the churches, including early ventures into mass education in which nonconformist and Anglican organizations competed for the minds of the population. However, capitalism is about selling dear and buying cheap; it could not operate if people did unto their neighbours as they would have them do unto them. Hence British Christianity has been concerned to explain the divine ordination of inequality in this world ('The rich man in his castle, the poor man at his gate'), with the promise of more egalitarian conditions confined to the next, making a particular virtue of the passive acceptance of one's lot. Marx saw this as a vital cog in the machinery of subjugation and exploitation. Not only has religion socialized people into accepting inequality, it has purveyed patriarchal values. The ordination of the first Anglican women priests in March 1994 was by no means universally welcomed, and within the Roman Catholic Church official doctrine remains implacably opposed.

> Religion is the sigh of the oppressed creature, the heart of a heartless world, just as it is the spirit of an unspiritual situation. It is the *opium* of the people.
>
> Karl Marx, Introduction to *Critique of Hegel's Philosophy of Right* (1844)

Today Britain is a largely secular society with little place for religion (figure 8.1); it is said that faith in science has replaced faith in a God and Sunday shopping has replaced churchgoing. Although most people claim to believe in a God and some 30 per cent profess membership of the Church of England, only around 10 per cent attend church. However, tensions in Northern Ireland (p. 159), the presence of Britain's ethnic minorities, the rise of new religious movements and church leaders' increased willingness to enter the political domain mean that religion has by no means disappeared from politics. Indeed, politicians would be as loath to declare themselves atheists as they would be to profess a lack of interest in football! Often speaking in what critics saw as messianic terms, Tony Blair ascribed his political ideology to Christianity, frequently quoting from the Bible in public utterances. The satirical magazine *Private Eye* featured him as the 'Vicar of St Albion'.

Britain's non-Christian religions The presence of significant numbers of Sikhs, Hindus and Muslims, as well as smaller sects such as Mormons and Rastafarians, has presented new issues for the British polity as religious, racial

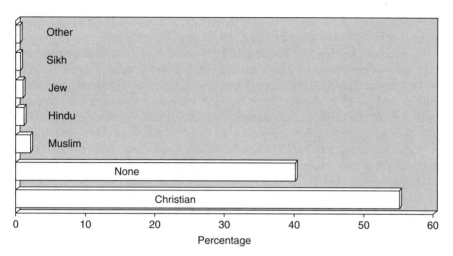

Figure 8.1
A secular society?
Religious affiliation,
2000 (percentages).

Source: Data from *Social Trends* (2002: table 13.19).

and political issues have become enmeshed. Although not essentially a new problem (Britain's Jewish population has long existed within the predominantly Christian culture), the more fervent (sometimes fundamentalist) views can promote clashes. The *fatwa* passed by the Ayatollah Khomeini on author Salman Rushdie over his *Satanic Verses* followed demonstrations and symbolic burnings of the book by some British Muslims. There are also implications for feminism, with some Muslims calling for, and establishing, separate schools for their daughters as a means of limiting their ambitions (Cahanum 1997: 244–7).

The December 2001 Cantle Report on race riots earlier that year (the worst for many years) revealed a strong religious dimension uniting Muslims. Paradoxically, the government, with much support from the Prime Minister, was pressing ahead with a policy of increasing the number of state-funded faith schools, where children would be segregated on the basis of religion. The events of 11 September 2001 further revealed the potential for religion to affect political attitudes, as television screens featured alarming scenes of some Muslims demonstrating fervent approval of the terrorist act and the idea of a *jihad*, or holy war.

New movements The postmodernist scepticism towards Enlightenment thinking and materialism opens the door to the pursuit of eastern religions, forms of meditation, informal variants of Christianity, paganism, and even mystical practices such as astrology. Perhaps social life and politics can never be free of such influences because people are by anthropological nature religious animals. The rejection of established religion can be seen to parallel a rejection of established political institutions and be reflected in new forms of direct action. Indeed, certain versions of feminism and environmentalism also embrace spiritual values.

Turbulent priests? Religion can also demonstrate non-capitalist values; the 11 September attack was seen by many as an attack on the symbols of western materialism. In Britain, the 1980s and 1990s had seen some unexpected political interventions from the Anglican Church, for long regarded as the 'Conservative Party at prayer'. Its leaders began attacking the government's neoliberal policies and its 1985 report, *Faith in the City*, was a damning indictment of conditions in the older industrial cities. In May 1996, Archbishop of Canterbury George Carey, a former prison chaplain, launched a devastating critique of Home Secretary Michael Howard's 'prison works' policy, warning that 'if you treat people like animals, they will respond like animals' (Travis 1996). In 2002, Carey's successor, Rowan Williams, spoke out against Britain's support for US plans to attack Iraq.

Education

Education is simply the soul of society as it passes from one generation to another.

G. K. Chesterton (1874–1936; British writer), in the *Observer* (6 July 1924)

The British school system is sharply dichotomized, the private sector (including the prestigious public schools) preparing the rulers of the future while the state system has aimed to manufacture the smaller cogs in the wheel (Lister 1987: 47). For the most part the latter is shaped by civil servants, many of whom have never darkened the doors of its institutions themselves. In this process of cultural reproduction children learn more than is outlined in the official syllabus; this is the 'hidden curriculum' in which they learn their place in society. Like the family, the school is hierarchical in structure, and ideally teachers and headteachers exercise their authority in the interests of pupils, further legitimating the idea of elite dominance. As an obvious source of social control, the state watches over the system with eternal vigilance.

> A very large part of English middle-class education is devoted to the training of servants . . . In so far as it is, by definition, the training of upper servants, it includes, of course, the instilling of that kind of confidence which will enable the upper servants to supervise and direct the lower servants.
>
> Raymond Williams, *Culture and Society* (1958)

Generations of British children have come to understand their culture through what is alleged to be their country's history. In reality it has largely been the history of the elite: the kings and their conquests. The heroes of school texts are figures like Richard the Lionheart and Henry VIII; of John Wilkes and Thomas Paine children have remained largely ignorant. Although Karl Marx worked in England, and lies buried in Highgate Cemetery, a British child can negotiate the scholastic assault course with little knowledge of perhaps the most influential thinker of the age. Ethnic minorities have challenged the relevance of British history as a basis for understanding their own cultural backgrounds and this has led to some modifications. Yet obliterating the history of

School uniform:
boys at Eton
College

Photo: Times Newspapers Ltd

those from the black Commonwealth is really no stranger than excluding working-class history.

The idea of the state providing education as a *consumption good* to be enjoyed as a gift of citizenship can be at variance with capitalist values, which regard it more as an *investment good* providing training for work. New Labour, with its 'Education, Education, Education' mantra, made much of the link with jobs, renaming the Department of Education and Science the Department for Education and Employment (DfEE) in 1997, and rebranding it the Department for Education and Skills (DfES) in 2001. This kind of philosophy is consistent with an inegalitarian society. A substantial body of research confirms that British education has served to reinforce inequality rather than reduce it (Giddens 2001: 510–15). Of course, many teachers are unhappy with the utilitarian ethos. This accounts for an often tense relationship with government; they have felt poorly paid, placed under increasingly competitive pressures with league tables and associated bureaucracy, and belittled by some politicians.

The arts

Ever since Gutenberg set up the first printing press in Mainz in 1440, the power of literature has been both cherished and feared by the mighty. Although offering a means of legitimating their position by directly shaping mass attitudes, it carries dangerous potential for exposing the privilege of the few to the eyes of the many. Even the idea of a Bible that everyone could read was once seen as dangerous, and radical news sheets circulating during the industrial revolution appeared as an insidious virus in the body politic.

The thoughts of geniuses such as Beethoven, Shakespeare, Tolstoy, Dostoevsky, Dickens, Milton and Shelley can be elevating, but a workforce with a soaring spirit has had no place in the logic of capitalism. It was not until the end of the nineteenth century, when it was realized that industry could no longer function without an educated workforce, that mass literacy became state policy. Yet the results were to disappoint. Critics of the 'uses of literacy' perceived only the rise of a demeaning mass culture usurping the real world of art and (possibly subversive) ideas, offering only a 'candy floss world' and 'sex in shiny packets' (Hoggart 1958). The Frankfurt School of neo-Marxist thinkers argued that undemanding homogenized forms of culture removed from the mass of the people the power to look at the world critically. German philosopher Jürgen Habermas saw this as stifling democracy, replacing the 'public space' in which opinion forms through open discussion with manipulation and thought control.

Advertising

The morality of free-market capitalism is based upon the belief that if everyone buys and sells wisely, according to self-interest, all will be well. The consumer is said to be sovereign. This is questionable in practice because people are generally denied enough information or wisdom to know what is in their own interest. It can be argued that modern capitalism is not at all happy to let people decide for themselves what they want; it is concerned with making them want what is most profitable to produce. Companies devote huge proportions of their budgets not to making products or rendering services but to altering our thoughts. The mega-industry concerned expressedly with getting into our heads and shaping our desires is advertising. Although promoting a particular product, it generally subscribes to the ethos of free-market capitalism and usually favours the political right. However, the political place of advertising in mind politics goes even deeper. We shall see in chapter 9 that it plays a direct part in politics, the parties investing enormous funds to sell themselves to voters.

The Press

The British are great readers (or at least great buyers) of newspapers, circulation figures being the highest in the western world. The British Audience Research Bureau reported 13 million papers bought on weekdays and Sundays in 2000 (Stanyer 2001b: 350). There is less enthusiasm for serious weeklies, where more detailed analysis may be found. However, although these influence the opinions of the intelligentsia, including journalists themselves, the mass readership preference is for lightweight material, with magazines devoted to television the clear favourites.

In addition, there is a recognized division between the quality press (or **broadsheets**) for the middle classes and the **tabloids** for the working class, the latter well outdistancing the broadsheets in circulation and readership; amongst these the lion's share is split between the *Mirror* and the *Sun* (figure 8.2; note that actual readership exceeds sales by a factor of around three).

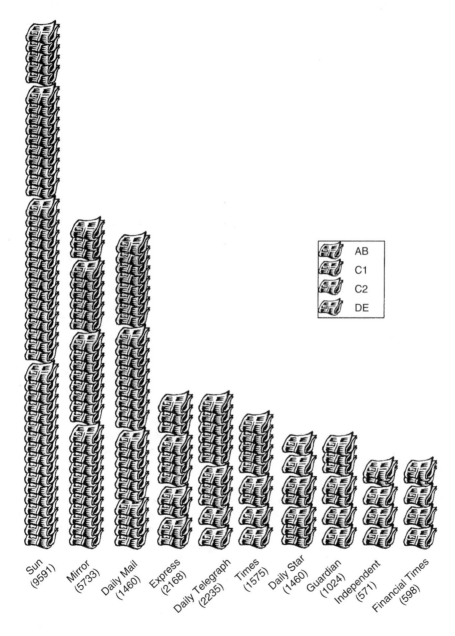

Figure 8.2
National news-paper readership by social class, 2001 (in thousands).

Source: Data from Butler and Kavanagh (2002: table 9.1).

Broadsheet readers are the best informed about politics, are more interested and feel more confident that they can influence things. Tabloid readers have similar views to non-readers, suggesting that tabloids do not contribute much to political knowledge. However, even among the better educated the tabloids are more popular than the broadsheets (Newton 1998: 155).

Because the country is small, the major newspapers are national, producing considerable uniformity of view and centring on London. Provincial morning and evening dailies are in decline, being confronted with 'free-sheets' mainly containing advertising and human-interest stories, force-fed through the letter-boxes of urban households.

Freedom of the press in Britain is freedom to print such of the proprietor's prejudices as the advertisers don't object to.

Attributed to Hannen Swaffer (1879–1962; British journalist)

Partisanship

Part of the process of legitimation is an exhortation of the rights of the **free press** and independent broadcasting. These values were fought for in the eighteenth century against a secretive ruling class, when it was even necessary to smuggle reports of proceedings out of Parliament. A free press is held to be one of the defining characteristics of the liberal state: a democracy must have freedom of speech for its journalists and free access to information for citizens. However, this freedom must logically suggest a capitalist-controlled media because the newspaper industry is itself part of 'big business'; £3.2 billion is spent on newspaper advertisements each year out of a total advertising 'spend' of £9.2 billion (Leys 1998).

> In the tabloids, virtually every Tory has the stature of Winston Churchill, every Labourite is a lying Leninite.
>
> Glenn Frankel (*Washington Post* journalist), quoted in the *Independent* (15 April 1992)

It is only in times of crisis that the state overtly demands that the press become its instrument. In two world wars dishonest reporting was deemed necessary to stiffen people's resolve and the newspaper barons were flatteringly brought into government to ensure their cooperation. Britain has a particularly **partisan** press. Although sometimes critical, newspapers have traditionally spread a generally right-wing message, favouring the Conservative Party and the right of the Labour Party, particularly in its New Labour variant. This has obvious consequences for the political culture. Hence, *The Times* attributed the Conservatives' 1987 election success to 'the good sense of the majority of voters'. There is an extremely close association between newspaper readership and voting, dwarfing many of the other electoral variables (see p. 250). However, not all readers are aware of the bias: the calculatedly yobbish down-market appeal of the *Sun* actually led one-third of its readers to believe it to be a Labour paper (Newton 1986: 324) even before it became one!

What the papers said during the 1992 election campaign

MAJOR DEFIES LABOUR MOBS, *Daily Mail*, 21 March

THREAT OF RETURN TO PICKET TERROR, *Sun*, 24 March

LABOUR TO RATION MORTGAGES, *Daily Mail*, 23 March

THE KICKBACK: THE SECRET TAX THAT WILL ALLOW LABOUR TO REWARD ITS UNION
   PAYMASTERS, *Daily Mail*, 1 April

NAZI RIOTS IN BRITAIN: PR AIDS FASCISTS CLAIMS BAKER, *Sun*, 7 April

BAKER'S MIGRANT FLOOD WARNINGS: LABOUR SET TO OPEN DOORS, *Daily Express*, 7 April

IF KINNOCK WINS TODAY WILL THE LAST PERSON TO LEAVE BRITAIN PLEASE TURN OUT THE
   LIGHTS, *Sun*, Election morning

IT'S THE SUN WOT WON IT, *Sun*, The morning after

As modern governments become increasingly obsessed with 'spin', so the influence of the press worries them more. Yet the extent to which newspaper bias affects voting should not be seen as the central issue. Between elections they exert an insidious influence on attitudes, fertilizing the social soil for the roots of the tree of capitalism.

Content: 'All the news that's fit to print' (motto of the *New York Times*)

Selling newspapers is business and profit maximization means maximizing circulation. This results in a quest for the lowest common denominator, with the tabloids favouring sensationalism, trivialization and titillation. There is also a deep-seated racism in the sentiments and language, which breaks out into hysterical **jingoism** whenever foreign relations become in any way turbulent. In the Falklands war, in an orgy of bellicose press chauvinism, the Argentinians became the 'Argies' and the infamous *Sun* headline 'Gotcha!' gloried in the agonizing deaths of foreigners. Sport evokes similar sentiments: the German teams become 'krauts', while the *Daily Star* headline in March 1998 concerning the French allocation of World Cup tickets read 'FROGS NEED A GOOD KICKING'.

Much day-to-day reporting is preoccupied with the doings of a glitterati of soap stars, super-models, sports personalities and royalty. When Richard Desmond, publisher of *OK Magazine*, bought the *Daily Express* and *Sunday Express* he made no secret of his intention to increase the coverage of 'celebrity stories'. The words of certain acceptable politicians are accorded pride of place on topics upon which they choose to descant. The tabloid coverage of political news is as scanty as the clothing on the pouting models and reporting of events concentrates on the immediate, to the exclusion of background analysis. An IRA bombing, for example, is reported with little mention of the historical context of Ulster politics.

News does not come in labelled packages; it must be selected from a great buzzing mass of reality. What we read as 'news' is what others decide to print, and this crucial exercise of journalistic discretion does not treat all sections of society equally. To understand the reasons for this it is necessary to examine press ownership, journalists, and the issue of regulation.

> Something someone, somewhere, wants to suppress; everything else is just advertising.
>
> Lord Northcliffe's definition of news

Forget all this crap about politicians – who's interested, eh? You only write this bollocks so that you can look good with all your fucking mates in Westminster... The readers don't give a fuck about politics.

Kelvin MacKenzie as *Sun* editor, to his political editor, Walter Terry. Quoted in Peter Chippindale and Chris Horrie, *Stick it up Your Punter!* (1990)

Ownership: the press barons

> I run the *Daily Express* purely for propaganda and for no other purpose.
>
> Lord Beaverbrook, to the Royal Commission on the Press (1948)

The proud boast that the British press is not owned or controlled by the state must be countered with the observation that it lies broadly in the hands of a neoliberal Establishment. Never widely dispersed, ownership narrowed down even further during the post-war era. The celebrated *Times*, founded in 1785, was not intended for the masses. Inescapably an organ of the Establishment (a 'parish magazine' for the upper classes, recording their births, marriages and obituaries), it claimed for much of its life to be a newspaper of national record (offering an objective, definitive account of events). The rise of the 'popular' papers followed the extension of adult literacy at the end of the nineteenth century with the creation of the *Daily Mail* (1896), *Daily Express* (1900), *Daily Mirror* (1903) and *Daily Sketch* (1908). These were the first mass-circulation papers and were to generate vast revenues from advertising, thereby keeping down their prices. They were owned by private individuals who became formidable '**press barons**' wielding awesome power, which was regularly recognized by elevation to the peerage: Alfred Harmsworth (*Mirror*, *Mail* and the *Times*), regarded as the father of modern journalism, became Lord Northcliffe, his younger brother Harold (*Mail*) became Lord Rothermere and the Canadian Max Aitken (*Express*) became Lord Beaverbrook. A second generation included Cecil Harmsworth King, nephew of Lord Northcliffe, who hugely expanded the family empire into the world of magazines and television. A rival empire was headed by Lord Thomson of Fleet (*Times* and *Sunday Times*), a Canadian who had expanded his interests from Canada to Scotland, where he had become a millionaire through commercial television.

What the proprietorship of these papers is aiming at is power, and power without responsibility – the prerogative of the harlot throughout the ages.

Stanley Baldwin (Conservative leader), attacking Lords Rothermere and Beaverbrook in an election speech (18 March 1931)

Modern concentrated ownership, made possible by deregulation from the 1980s, follows the classic advanced capitalist model, with complex transnational conglomerates combining diverse interests in electronic communications, broadcasting, cable TV and the leisure industry. (By 1997 only the Canadian Conrad Black's *Telegraph* titles remained outside a multi-media group.) This renders possible the sustaining of unprofitable titles by cross-subsidization (Thompson 1982). The new-style **media moguls** are typified by Rupert Murdoch of the mammoth News International owning, amongst others, *The Times*, the *Sunday Times*, the *News of the World* and the *Sun*, as well as a number of US papers, including the *New York Post*. Another conglomerate was created in 1996 when the *Express* titles were bought by the Labour-supporting Lord Hollick (ennobled by Neil Kinnock), whose group controlled Meridian and Anglia TV. Although having more independence, the *Guardian*

A place in the Sun

Photo: *The Socialist*

and *Independent* are still caught up in this web of multi-media ownership. The concentration is even found in the so-called local press, once a basis for radical agitation, about half of which has been progressively bought up by a few large companies.

The problem lies in the fact that, despite protestations to the contrary, owners exercise editorial control. Upon buying the *Mirror* Robert Maxwell declared: 'I have invested £90 million. There can only be one boss, and that is me' (Bower 1988). Murdoch conducted a continuing crusade in favour of free-enterprise culture, doing much to enhance the neoliberal project of the right. Such control gives political power. This was recognized by New Labour, and Tony Blair pursued an assiduous courtship. Addressing a jamboree of Murdoch executives on Hayman Island in 1995, he criticized the Major government's proposals for regulating multi-media ownership (Pilger 1998: 468–9). Doors swung open as Blair gained his place in the *Sun*, and indeed the *News of the World*, with articles, usually ghosted by ex-journalists turned **spin doctors** (Scammell 2000: 182), appearing regularly under his name. On BBC TV's 'Newsnight' (17 March 1997), Labour's campaign director Peter Mandelson declared: 'We have earned the *Sun*'s support'. As the 1997 general election approached, the *Sun*'s eve-of-poll headline on 30 April read: 'WHO BLAIRS WINS'. The courtship continued; by the time of the 2001 election virtually all the papers were supporting New Labour's brand of neoliberalism with some openly scornful of Conservative leader William Hague. However, Murdoch's antipathy to Britain joining the euro remained problematic for the government.

Journalists

> Nameless men and women whose scandalously low payment is a guarantee of their ignorance and their servility to the financial department.
>
> George Bernard Shaw on journalists, in *Commonsense about the War* (1914)

While owners have power it is journalists who wield the pen and mouse. They and their editors usually come from middle- and upper-middle-class back-grounds. A career in journalism, with an inside track to the top, ranks high amongst the glittering prizes the Establishment offers bright young Oxbridge graduates. During their careers they get to know leading figures in the arts, business and politics, and are unlikely to bite the hands that can offer them enticing titbits of useful information. Editors in particular live very close to the heart of the Establishment: Geoffrey Dawson, for twenty-nine years editor of *The Times*, moved comfortably in the country houses of the upper classes; one of his successors, William Rees-Mogg, was a pillar of the Establishment; William Deedes, editor of the *Daily Telegraph*, was a Conservative MP; and his successor, Max Hastings, seemed to personify the hunting and shooting set.

The emergence of the succession of **sleaze** cases in the 1990s saw journalists in more challenging mode. *Sunday Times* journalists posed as businessmen in order to trap MPs taking cash for questions and the *Guardian* pursued minister Neil Hamilton, alleging acceptance of payments for questions on behalf of Harrods owner Mohamed Al Fayed. In its sleaze hunt it also indicted Jonathan Aitken, who eventually found himself in prison. New Labour were not to be exempt. In July 1998 Labour staffers-turned-lobbyists, Derek Draper and Roger Liddle, were trapped by journalists posing as businessmen in a 'cash for access' scandal.

Yet while attacking personal misbehaviour, these developments do not challenge the Establishment at a radical level. Although causing some ministerial heads to roll, the real interest of the tabloids is sexual peccadillos. If journalists have radical leanings, the structure of the news industry will largely neuter them. Editors can alter stories, career advancement can be blocked by management and, in the final analysis, recalcitrants can be sacked. The process of career development for those of humbler origins from the provincial press will serve to socialize them into the ways of the Establishment or will filter them out before they reach the precincts of Fleet Street or Wapping.

Members of the political elite, particularly ex-government ministers, frequently turn to journalism as a sideline: Winston Churchill distinguished himself in the field, as does Roy Hattersley. In the USA and continental Europe journalists entering politics must give up their day jobs but in Britain they may do both. At the retirement of a leading Fleet Street editor Mrs Thatcher was able to offer public thanks for a key speech he had written for her (Preston 1997). Use of the media was to reach new heights under New Labour, the Prime Minister and his colleagues producing a stream of regular self-justifying articles in both tabloids and broadsheets.

> He wields far more power than many of the elected politicians at the high table of government.
>
> Andrew Rawnsley on Alastair Campbell, Blair's press secretary, in the *Observer* (1 Nov. 1998)

Self-control: avoiding lying in the *Sun*

The whole point about the concept of a free press is that it is not *regulated*. It is said that in a free society one should have the right to 'publish and be damned'. Those who feel they have a grievance have recourse to the courts and the libel laws. It is argued that rather than **official censorship**, the only acceptable form of regulation is self-regulation. This comes through a Press Complaints Commission (PCC), a body of laypeople and editorial and managerial representatives from within the industry, set up on a voluntary basis to protect their freedom, hear complaints, chastise for misreporting and administer a code of conduct drawn up in 1991. However, critics regard it as a toothless watchdog and it has been made something of a mockery by tabloid reporters plumbing depths of unprofessionalism (fabrication of 'news', malicious character assassination of public figures and the destruction of the lives of ordinary people) that other newspapers could not reach. Rivals have not been slow to follow the coach and horses driven by News International through the PCC gate and, to add insult to injury, some individuals castigated by the PCC, far from being damaged, actually advanced their careers.

Following an enquiry by Sir David Calcutt QC, a statutory framework for the press was proposed in 1993 but a largely united profession was hotly opposed. *Sunday Times* editor Andrew Neil claimed this would make the press 'the poodle of the Establishment' (*Guardian*, 11 Jan. 1993). Further defence came from Lord Wakeham, arguing that the PCC, of which he was Chair, was steadily becoming stronger. In 2001 it heard over 3,000 complaints, twice as many as ten years earlier.

The royal family were to become particular targets of the press, with transcripts of the 'Squidgygate' and 'Camillagate' tapes (conversations between Princess Diana and Prince Charles and their respective lovers) appearing in the tabloids. Watched and photographed incessantly, sometimes secretly as when exercising in a gym, Princess Diana was literally pursued to her death by the *paparazzi*. Instant hypocrisy reigned as they mourned the 'People's Princess', although one US tabloid, *The National Enquirer*, was too late to withdraw its current edition carrying the front page headline 'Di Goes Sex Mad'. This tragic incident concentrated the mind and Lord Wakeham launched an urgent review of the code of practice. This recommended toughening up in five areas: harassment, children, privacy, public interest and intrusion into grief.

JUSTICE and the PRESS

Reproduced by permission of *Punch*

Freedom of the press poses conundrums for democracy. Greater protection for ordinary people against harassment and embarrassment may also allow the high and mighty to evade democratic scrutiny. Again, while official censorship spells totalitarianism, press freedom in a class-based society can allow the wealthy to manipulate the ideas and attitudes of the masses, providing a leverage on the polity regardless of which party reigns. This is political power; it is not difficult to see why Thomas Carlyle called the press the 'Fourth Estate'.

Broadcasting

Television is a major factor in British politics, completely transforming the nature of elections, orchestrating political debate, creating a cult of personality politics, helping to elevate the executive, reducing the role of Parliament and projecting the monarchy into a new era of political theatre. Although radio is by no means dead, television has become the organ of a truly mass culture, the principal means of informing perceptions of the political world (Glasgow University Media Group 1976). Although the working class have a greater propensity to view (table 8.1), in all classes the habit is increasing. The 1997 British Social Attitudes Survey revealed that while 10 per cent of the population watch for less than an hour a day, an equal proportion keep vigil for seven hours. On average the British devote twenty-one hours a week to their screens. Avid watchers tend to form a category similar to tabloid readers – older, on lower incomes and with fewer educational qualifications. However, they tend to watch more news than the better educated, often simply 'falling into it' because the 'box' is always on (Newton 1998: 154).

Table 8.1 Socioeconomic characteristics and TV viewing habits (weekdays)

Characteristic	Watch TV for 1 hour or less	Watch TV for 5 or more hours
Age (average)	43	51
Annual household income (average)	£21,000	£11,000
Age full-time education completed (average)	17.8	15.5
Socioeconomic group (average)[a]	3.2	4.4
Percentage economically active	71	34
Percentage women	53	60
TV news watched (days per week)	3.7	5.7
Percentage regularly reading tabloid newspaper	27	60
Percentage regularly reading broadsheet newspaper	25	1

[a]Using official classification from 1 (highest) to 6 (lowest)

Source: Data from British Social Attitudes Survey (1997: 155).

The power of TV over minds is potentially Orwellian, a fact testified to in advertisers' willingness to contribute currently some £2.6 billion a year to the coffers of the commercial TV (and radio) companies (Leys 1998). Purveying anything from soap powder to soap opera, it is recognized by politicians as a searing spotlight which can heighten their fretful hour on the political stage or consume them like moths near a candle flame. Margaret Thatcher made mastery of the medium her first priority and Tony Blair's easy TV manner was seen as an essential party asset. In news reporting, the projection of visual images suggests a reality greater than that of the printed word, defying scepticism and compelling belief. A Labour Party rally held in the huge Sheffield Arena on the eve of the 1992 general election greatly inspired many of those present. However, in the hands of the TV producers it was to enter folklore as a grotesque miscalculation by leader Neil Kinnock. Action replays of his repeated exultation 'Are we all right!' left the toes of middle England curling with embarrassment.

Evolution

Unlike the press, broadcasters come under two regulatory bodies: the British Broadcasting Corporation (BBC) and the Independent Television Commission (ITC). The BBC is seen as particularly venerable (affectionately known within Establishment circles as 'Auntie'). Established in 1927 as the successor to a private pioneer, the British Broadcasting Company, it has a Royal Charter to broadcast and is financed independently of the Treasury through viewers' licence fees. In its early years, under its legendary Director General Sir John (later Lord) Reith, it built up a reputation for elitism, pomposity and syco-phancy towards the institutions of the state, particularly the monarchy. (It was so much an arm of the Establishment that wireless news readers, though invisible to their audience, wore evening dress, the uniform of the upper class.) The development of television has lessened this, though vestiges remain, as in the reverent tones of commentators at great state or sporting occasions (particularly if attended by royalty), such as the Lord Mayor's parade or Royal Ascot.

The BBC began television broadcasting from Alexandra Palace in 1936 and by 1966 was transmitting to virtually the whole country. It enjoyed a comfort-able monopoly until a traumatic challenge came in the form of commercial TV. If the BBC stood for the high Tory element within the Establishment, commer-cial TV represented its thrusting, free-marketeering spirit. In 1954, after pro-longed political infighting among various factions within the Establishment (Wilson 1961), the IBA (later to become the ITC) was created by the Conserva-tive government to grant licences and (renewable) franchises to regional private broadcasting companies financed by advertising. Its patronage was regal and the franchise to operate commercial TV was described by Lord Thomson (who became a millionaire) as a 'licence to print money'. Although the regional structure implies plurality, the biggest companies belong to massive leisure and media conglomerates, most major programmes are intended for national transmission through a networking system and the main news programmes come from London.

With the creation of commercial TV a new kind of media baron appeared (typified in the gigantic personality of Sidney Bernstein of the Granada empire) from the world of capitalism and competition. They recognized that they could only attract the life-blood of advertising by building up mass audiences, which did little to raise cultural standards. The BBC, though free of this restraint, felt obliged to ape the populist strategy to justify the licence fee; *ratings wars* continually led critics to fear loss of quality. By the 1990s, the Conservative Party with its deregulatory policies had taken broadcasting to the threshold of a new era of viewer and listener choice. Yet the policy had demonstrated 'little interest in ensuring greater diversity of opinions' (Marsh 1993: 347). Satellite dishes and cable promised choice among some 500 channels, making state control more difficult, as was found over the sex channel Red Hot Dutch. Britain found itself at the heart of this global village with the funeral of Princess Diana in September 1997, which proved the biggest TV event in history, the BBC feeding some forty-five broadcasting companies all over the world.

Yet while channels proliferate and audiences are fragmented, ownership becomes more and more integrated, with the media moguls owning TV companies, film studios, publishing houses, film libraries and software companies, as well as newspapers. Murdoch, for example, moved into satellite and cable through his BSkyB TV and controlled Hong-Kong-based Star TV, covering the gigantic markets of India and China. He also acquired a half-stake in Twentieth Century Fox, as well as several US TV stations and the US publishers HarperCollins.

Following further franchise consolidation in 2000, two companies, Granada Media and Carlton Communications, were controlling 91 per cent of the ITV network in England and Wales. In the ratings war both adopted avowedly populist strategies unlikely to increase political reporting or raise BBC standards (Stanyer 2001b: 357). The scope for concentrated ownership was further advanced in May 2002 with a draft Communications Bill proposing the removal of a number of restrictions. This would allow a single company to control ITV and open the way for global giants, such as Disney and AOL Time Warner, to buy into British broadcasting. The way was cleared for Murdoch to bid for Channel Five, although his wider ambitions were curbed by preserving the rule preventing newspaper tycoons owning more than 20 per cent of an ITV licence. In addition, there would be a new super-regulator, Ofcom, replacing nine existing bodies with one, which would include the BBC within its remit.

In this new competitive environment the domestic companies, already losing major sporting events to the wealthy cable and satellite empires with no public service mandate, face an uncertain future. The political potential residing in this multi-media power was demonstrated by Italian mogul Silvio Berlusconi, who used his empire to promote his own political career, becoming prime minister at the head of his own right-wing Forza Italia party.

The impartiality requirement

Both the BBC and the ITC are formally required in their charters to be impartial in their news reporting. However, broadcasting impartiality means impartiality between political parties and interest groups, not between social classes. Indeed a consistent anti-working-class bias in news programmes has been alleged (documented in an extended systematic study: Glasgow University Media Group 1976, 1980, 1982; Eldridge 1993). In industrial disputes middle-class representatives (management or state) tend to receive deferential treatment and are allowed to define the terms of the debate. In contrast, union leaders or young protesters are more likely to be interviewed in a hostile manner, in a setting detracting from their dignity (a jostling picket line, for example). Critics of these conclusions, including some within the TV industry, have questioned their objectivity, arguing that they are based on atypical events (Harrison 1985). However, the key point remains that the idea that TV reporting can be impartial and objective is fraught with difficulty (Eldridge 1993).

For much of the time, despite seemingly heated left–right exchanges, all the points of view presented fit within a consensus acceptable to the Establishment. Views outside the narrow central orthodoxy are rendered 'loony' and even 'unpatriotic'. Although it can be argued that this merely reflects a natural conservatism within British politics, it is equally likely that it contributes to it. In this structuring of political debate the broadcasting media influence not day-to-day decisions between left and right, but the scent in the cultural air we breathe.

Broadcasting journalists Broadcasting journalists are often drawn from the ranks of the press and consequently have similar characteristics and propensities. A tendency towards upper-middle-class domination is strengthened by the high kudos associated with a TV career; it is a prized niche for an Oxbridge graduate. Interestingly, the few TV journalists from ethnic minorities usually speak with particularly impeccable middle-class accents.

Ruling the waves: political interference

The structure of broadcasting is intended to prevent politicians from meddling. Some evidence of independence was seen in January 1998 in a joint BBC–ITC proposal to scrap party political broadcasts and restrict electioneering broadcasts, on the grounds that they bored the audience. However, whenever it appears that the Establishment cannot count on the kind of *reportage* it desires, an underlying conviction that broadcasters should be subservient to the state is forced out into the open.

Patronage The BBC and ITC boards of governors are appointed by government from the bosom of the Establishment. Requiring no particular expertise or knowledge of broadcasting, they reflect the British tradition of amateurism where, in the old cliché, who you know is rather more important than what you know. Each board delegates day-to-day operations to a Director General, whom they appoint. Generally, cautious selection reduces the need for sacking, but should an incumbent decide, like Becket or Sir Thomas More, to turn from his patron and serve a higher god, their martyrdom can be speedily effected. The 1980s saw the Thatcher government roused to fury, culminating in January 1987 with the sacking of Director General Alasdair Milne, a move fore-shadowed in the appointment as Chairman of the Board of Governors of Thatcherite Marmaduke Hussey, who delivered the *coup de grâce* (Milne 1988). He subsequently made the controversial appointment of John Birt, who was to criticize his own journalists for being too robust with politicians. The fact that Birt's successor in 2000 was Greg Dyke, known to have contrib-uted £50,000 to Blair's leadership campaign and general election campaigns (Scammell, 2000: 177), did nothing to quell fears over patronage.

Intimidation Although some journalists aim for a more robust style, they can come under attack. In 1986 Norman Tebbit weighed in heavily against the BBC and Kate Adie for her reporting of the launching of the US attack on Libya from Britain in non-jingoistic terms. John Humphrys of Radio 4's *Today* programme and well-known figures, such as Jeremy Paxman, Andrew Marr and Anna Ford, have all come under fire. In December 2001, Labour Party chairman Charles Clarke accused Humphrys of 'propagating the view that politicians are cynical and basically are not to be trusted, are self-seeking and all the rest of it' (Humphrys 2001).

Direct pressure There are certain formal means whereby governments may influence the media, including D-Notices and the Official Secrets legislation (see chapter 15). However, of far greater importance are the informal workings within the body of the Establishment. Reith laid down the ground rules during the 1926 General Strike, recording in his diary that the government 'know that they can trust us not to be really impartial' (Stuart 1975: 96). He suppressed news that the government did not want broadcast, establishing that 'the vaunted independence of the BBC was secure so long as it was not exercised' (Taylor 1965: 246).

Unwillingness to displease was demonstrated in 1962 when *That Was The Week That Was* introduced a level of popular satire hitherto unseen. Its style was little more than that of an Oxbridge undergraduate revue, part of the middle-class movement that generated *Beyond the Fringe* and the magazine *Private Eye*. However, gamekeepers made effective poachers and the pro-gramme startled deferential working-class viewers reared on the unctuous tones of Richard Dimbleby. Amongst other things it stirred up the Profumo scandal, made the Macmillan government uncomfortable and generally dis-turbed. BBC Director General Hugh Carlton Greene lost his nerve and the programme was taken off on the pretext of an impending general election, which did not actually materialize until 1964.

> What changed between January and March 1987 was not the facts or the quality of the programme but the scale to which the [BBC] governors' political and personal views intruded into the corporation's whole management.
>
> Duncan Campbell, referring to the banning of his controversial programme *Cabinet*, quoted in the
> *Independent* (30 April 1988)

Pressure became much more intense in the 1980s with the Thatcher government's diagnosis of too many liberals in the establishment kitchen. During the Falklands war, mindful of the effect of Vietnam war reporting on the American public (exposing the falsity of official accounts and effectively ending the war), broadcast news of the task force was restricted and the government would not permit the rapid transmission of TV pictures to British audiences (Select Committee on Defence 1982: xiv). In 1985, pressure was placed on BBC governors by Home Secretary Leon Brittan, leading to the cancellation of a *Real Lives* programme which included an interview with a convicted IRA member.

The Broadcasting Standards Authority was established in 1988 under the chairmanship of a pillar of the Establishment, ex-editor of *The Times* Sir William Rees-Mogg. The government insisted it would be concerned only with issues of decency and would not interfere with political content, but opponents feared that once installed it would be but a small matter to extend its remit. By the late 1980s the BBC had become extremely nervous about causing offence. On the eve of the 1992 general election, a *Panorama* programme suggesting that the 'Thatcher Miracle' of the 1980s was a mirage was axed, though the *Sunday Times* (15 March 1992) obtained and published a copy of the script. Another *Panorama* programme, this time on alleged corruption in Westminster Council, was postponed until after the May local government elections following pressure from Conservative Party officials (*The Times*, 25 April 1994).

Evidence of BBC nervousness came under New Labour when, in November 1998, it was to ban staff and guests from discussing the sexuality of Peter Mandelson in its *Any Questions* radio programme after he had been 'outed' by gay journalist Matthew Parris on TV's *Newsnight*. There was anger amongst journalists and one of the guests, Northern Ireland Secretary Mo Mowlam, described the act as 'a serious error on the part of the BBC' and 'insulting'.

> Please will all programmes note that under no circumstances whatsoever should the allegation about the private life of Peter Mandelson be repeated or referred to on any broadcast.
>
> Edict issued to BBC staff, reported in the *Observer* (1 Nov. 1998)

News management Establishment practices have long allowed the government to propagate the official line through the media. A tidal wave of information is washed up on the beaches of Fleet Street and Broadcasting House each day; many journalists live by the source, faithfully trotting out the platitudes from the press releases. So house-trained were the Westminster journalists that officials organized them into a formal club, the **Lobby**, complete with rules and regulations (Tunstall 1970) and assembling in the Members' Lobby, where ministers and spin doctors would throw them unattributable titbits of information. Blair's Press Secretary agreed in March 2000 to end the practice of non-attribution so that 'sources close to the prime minister' became 'Alastair Campbell'. In April 2002 it was agreed that the Lobby would be opened up to other journalists, but members of this exclusive club argued that this would make it easier for the news managers to evade their forensic skills.

From the early 1980s the parties began to take control of the media into new waters. Not only did Thatcher and Blair court Rupert Murdoch, their press secretaries became readily recognizable figures in the political firmament, in turns bullying and cajoling journalists, and furnishing their political charges with carefully crafted 'soundbites'. The Labour Party in opposition had focused on **news management**, with an almost obsessional attention to the way their affairs were reported. Alastair Campbell began to lean on the BBC, complaining, in September 1995, that Tony Blair's conference speech had not been the lead item in the news broadcasts. In government old habits died hard, prompting an exodus of Whitehall press officers (chapter 15). After September 11, the Jo Moore case exposed deep levels of cynicism in news management (p. 487).

> We are dealing with a press that basically wants to do us in.
>
> Alastair Campbell, as Labour Party media chief, *Guardian* interview (17 Feb. 1997)

However, as Richard Hoggart has pointed out, it cannot be assumed that there are no people in broadcasting for whom the goal of genuine neutrality is real (Glasgow University Media Group 1976: xii). The very fact that governments complain and interfere is evidence of this. The establishment of a second commercial channel, Channel Four, a wholly owned subsidiary of the IBA, showed some courage in permitting the airing of non-orthodox points of view, including features with a more than usually left-wing orientation and gay programmes. Although courageous reporting, such as that of Paul Foot, John Pilger or Maggie O'Kane does exist, it can never be taken for granted.

The 'New Media'

The internet

From the time that our ancestors inscribed hieroglyphics on cave walls, technology has shaped communications culture. Marshall McLuhan coined a memorable phrase when he proclaimed that 'the medium is the message'; the way information is conveyed affects what it says. While it has evolved steadily over the centuries, recent advances in information and communications technology (ICT) have generated a breathtaking acceleration, making the internet one of the central drivers of the globalization process that defines the contemporary world. In 1998 the US government began a prolonged legal battle with Bill Gates, creator of the mighty Microsoft empire, and on some accounts 'the richest man in the world'. With a monopoly hold over cyberspace he promised to become perhaps the greatest media mogul of all.

The controllers of the 'old media' were quick to recognize the challenge posed by the new, in which they made huge investments. Newspapers established online versions and broadcasters began to provide internet news reports and interactive sites in which subjects of broadcasts could be further explored. The BBC website soon became one of the largest in Europe, its News Online receiving millions of hits on a newsworthy day. In September 1997, the Press Complaints Commission extended its remit into online material. The symbiosis with the capitalist economy was demonstrated as broadcasters diversified into e-commerce, the BBC's beeb.com offering goods and services linked to programmes on specialist subjects such as gardening and cooking.

The government itself joined the party with its *Knowledge Network*, providing departmental facts and figures. Even the government websites carried advertising, with well-known large companies making significant contributions. There was also the launch of the Number Ten website providing coverage of Prime Minister's Questions in Parliament, lobby briefings, chat rooms and 'good news' stories to win public acclaim.

The latter was the result of government suspicion of press reporting, most of which Alastair Campbell placed in two categories: 'crap and total crap'. In September 2000 the government went further with UKonline, to present news to the British public in the way it wanted it presented. The idea of government controlling the news agenda had previously been tried during the 1926 General Strike, when an official newspaper evoked considerable cynicism; critics, including civil servants themselves, dubbed the new website Pravda.com (Carr-Brown 2001).

We're watching you

The US government (which had initially created the internet for defence purposes) spoke of an 'information superhighway', implying some kind of ordered development. The British government responded enthusiastically to the new media, seeking to promote wide access with a programme to get computers into all schools and schemes to help the poor get online. However, the more appropriate image was of a playground, uncoordinated and anarchic, where individuals inhabit a global world of cyberspace – the world wide web – expanding at a rate of 200 per cent each year. Unlike previous technologies it was interactive. Not condemning people to passivity, it can offer some opportunity to reclaim the public space that sociologists such as Habermas believed to have been eroded. Indeed, mass demonstrations can be planned from activists' studies and bedrooms.

Such developments pose a serious threat to those who wish to control minds and ideas. While the Bible could be banned with relative ease, cyberspace is more difficult to patrol. Will technology be harnessed to create the 'Big Brother' society dreaded by Orwell? The spectres of paedophilia and terrorism are invoked to help justify attempts at official scrutiny and regulation. In July 2000, the Regulation of Investigatory Powers Act, allowing state interception of all emails, became law. Service providers (ISPs) were required to hand over details of people's internet activities. A number of high-profile police swoops demonstrated the penetration of the official eye. Such developments caused concern to the civil liberties lobby but the events of 11 September provided all the justification the government required. Today no one in the UK can send an email or access a website in privacy.

Mind Politics

In shaping our attitudes the agencies of socialization form a rich informational cocktail. Family, education, class background and so on will influence the way we attend to the messages received from advertisers and the media, while what we hear may influence our careers, lifestyle and friendship patterns. This mix forms the ideological bedrock of the political system and its importance cannot be overestimated.

On 1 November 1998 the *Observer* published a list of what it claimed were the 300 most powerful people in Britain, as chosen by a panel of eight worthies (Hutton 1998). Tony Blair headed the list but second and third came two who did not even live in Britain, global multi-media moguls Rupert Murdoch and Bill Gates! Moreover, in fourth place came Peter Mandelson who, prior to his ignominious downfall at the end of the year, had honed the ability to control the media probably more than any British politician before him. Never before had a government entered office with so firm a conviction of the need to monitor and shape public opinion. More than ever the new 'sultans of spin' make modern politics a psychological game – **mind politics**. Yet, while elevating public opinion they downgrade the power of the people's elected representatives in favour of focus groups and advertising gurus.

It is through mind politics that the powerful can make patterns of privilege seem beautiful in the mind of the mass. Although all inegalitarian polities must achieve this if they are to survive, few have done so as smoothly as Britain. On the other hand, Thompson (1995: 42–3) reminds us that passivity can be overstated; the hold of the media does not eliminate the chance for people to form and refine their ideas in the public spaces, be they pubs, clubs or launderettes, or the new spaces created on the internet. The arena of mind politics contains tensions that determine who thinks what, when and how. Our exploration of this psychological dimension of the polity has begun in this chapter but it has not ended; it must continue throughout the book.

Key points

- There is a mental as well as a behavioural dimension to politics. This mental climate shapes the political culture.
- In order for a polity to function there must be some broad consensus on its desirability; it must enjoy legitimacy.
- It is in the interests of those with wealth and power to lead others to share their own views by creating a dominant ideology.
- Attitudes towards politics are developed through a process of political socialization.
- Important agents of political socialization include the family, the school, the peer group, religion, the arts, advertising and the mass media.
- There are many ways in which the powerful can influence the process of political socialization.
- This hegemony is not absolute; ideologies contrary to the one favoured by establishment interests may circulate.
- The world wide web increases the potential for ideas to circulate.
- Politics can thus be seen as a fight for the minds of people as well as for material things.

Review your understanding of the following terms and concepts

broadcasting impartiality	mind politics	press partisanship
broadsheet	news management	regulation
free press	official censorship	sleaze
jingoism	peer group	soundbite
Lobby	political socialization	spin doctor
media mogul	press baron	tabloid

Assignment

In a selected future time period (say a week) choose a prominent political news story and collect press cuttings from both broadsheet and tabloid newspapers. Answer the following questions, quoting extracts to illustrate your points.

		Mark (%)
1	Compare the amount of coverage (column inches or words) given to the story by the tabloids and broadsheets.	20
2	Study the degree of sensationalism found in the tabloids and broadsheets respectively.	20
3	Identify any inconsistencies between the tabloid and broadsheet accounts.	20
4	Look for bias (political, nationalistic, gender based, . . .). Is this more overt in one type of paper than the other?	40

Questions for discussion

1   Identify the main agents of political socialization in Britain and discuss their relative importance.
2   'Political socialization is a process that continues throughout life.' Discuss.
3   'A political culture is more clearly manifest in people's behaviour than in what they say in response to questionnaires.' Discuss.
4   To what extent is the concept of a free press compatible with the freedom of individuals and corporations to own newspapers?
5   'Crusading journalists cannot expect to get very far in a system where newspapers are largely financed by advertising.' Discuss.
6   'The news is not news until it appears in *The Times*.' Examine the political implications of this statement.
7   'The independence of the BBC is secure so long as it is not exercised.' Discuss.
8   How viable is the contention that the British press regulates itself?
9   Discuss whether governments have a right to expect loyalty from the mass media.
10   How do you expect the development of the internet to affect the formation of political attitudes?

Topic for debate

This house believes that the idea of the free press is nothing more than a useful myth.

Further reading

Barnett, S. and Gaber, I. (2001) *Westminster Tales: The Twentieth-Century Crisis in Political Journalism*.
Argues that independent critical political reporting is being undermined by factors such as multi-media ownership, competition and a changing culture of journalism in the interests of the powerful.

Bartle, J. and Griffiths, D. (eds) (2001) *Political Communications Transformed: From Morrison to Mandelson*.
Employs empirical studies to trace changes in the culture of politics and the media since 1945.

Cockerell, M., Hennessy, P. and Walker, P. (1984) *Sources Close to the Prime Minister: Inside the Hidden World of the News Manipulators*.
Written from an insider perspective, the title says it all.

Curran, J. and Seaton, J. (1998) *Power Without Responsibility: The Press and Broadcasting in Britain*, 5th edn.
Introduction to the history, sociology and politics of the media in Britain.

Gibson, R. and Ward, S. (eds) (2000) *Reinvigorating Democracy? British Politics and the Internet*.
Examines how the new information communications technology affects the actions of politicians.

Hoggart, R. (1958) *The Uses of Literacy.*
Argues compellingly that mass literacy has not been used to edify.

Hollingsworth, M. (1986) *The Press and Discontent: A Question of Censorship.*
Details right-wing bias in the press.

Ingham, B. (1991) *Kill the Messenger.*
Memoir by Thatcher's press secretary lamenting the unhealthy state of current affairs broadcasting in Britain.

McNair, B. (2000) *Journalism and Democracy.*
Argues that political communication in Britain is becoming more democratized.

Pilger, J. (1998) *Hidden Agendas.*
Crusading journalist reports the voices that consensual news-definers filter out. Also trenchant critique of media ownership and management.

Thompson, J. B. (1995) *The Media and Modernity: A Social Theory of the Media.*
Analyses the way in which modern societies affect and are affected by the media.

Watts, D. (1997) *Political Communication Today.*
Theoretical perspectives on the role of media in politics as well as interesting anecdotes. Notes the rise of a 'tyranny of the soundbite'.

Wayne, M. (1998) *Dissident Voices: The Politics of Television and Cultural Change.*
Analyses TV portrayal of events over the past two decades, examining its role as a subversive medium.

For light relief

Ray Bradbury, *Fahrenheit 451.*
Nightmare future vision where government firemen burn all books. (Also a film.)

Peter Chippindale and Chris Horrie, *Stick it up Your Punter!*
Frank story of the *Sun.* Contains nudity and strong language!

Barry Hines, *Kes.*
Goes into the mind of a working-class boy and the narrow world it is permitted to perceive.

Henrik Ibsen, *An Enemy of the People.*
Mass opinion is mobilized against a man trying to advance the public good against capitalist interests.

Robin Oakley, *Inside Track.*
Senior BBC journalist recounts anecdotes of his close encounters with the powerful.

John Sergeant, *Give Me Ten Seconds.*
Thoughtful and witty account of major political events and the job of reporting them by ITN political editor.

Michael Shea, *Spin Doctor.*
Fiction close to modern reality. Chilling Machiavellian landscape beyond the eyes and ears of democracy. Author should know: he was the Queen's press secretary.

Orson Welles, *Citizen Kane*.
Classic film exploring personality and motives of newspaper baron.

On the net

The availability of all the broadsheet newspapers on the net (both current and retrospective) enables their treatment of particular political events to be easily studied. The web addresses are all in a similar form (http://www.telegraph.co.uk) and easily obtainable.

http://www.pcc.org.uk
http://www.itc.org.uk
The Press Complaints Commission and Independent Television Commission sites include annual reports, press releases and statistics.

9

The Electoral System: Parsimonious Democracy

In this chapter we scrutinize the machinery supposed to make Britain a democracy, the means whereby ordinary citizens formally participate in politics. The chapter has five broad sections. The first addresses the underlying concept of representative democracy and outlines the mechanics of the electoral system. Next we examine a crucial chapter in British political history, the evolution of the electoral system. This leads to a discussion on electoral behaviour, asking why and how people vote, and noting the impact and relative importance of race, gender, age and class. Section four turns to the behaviour of the politicians and their spin doctors in one of the most visible events in modern politics: the election campaign. We conclude with an evaluation of the electoral system itself and consider the key issue of electoral reform.

Representative Democracy

Democracy and representative government

Over 300 years before the birth of Christ, Ancient Greece consisted of many small self-governing city-states. Adopting a variety of methods and institutional frameworks for conducting public affairs, these presented a unique laboratory for the empirical study of government. As we saw in chapter 1, many of the Greek philosophers, particularly the Athenians, saw democracy as the most desirable form of government, a belief they bequeathed to modern civilization.

In order to be entirely democratic a system of government should permit all citizens to take part in making public policy. There have been examples of such direct democracy: the Greek city-states made some provision for it and early parish government in Britain saw the community meeting in the church precincts to make decisions about such issues as roads, bridges and law and order. The government of the small communities formed by the New England settlers in America was also widely participative in character, as are the Swiss cantons today. Although direct democracy in the modern nation-state has generally been seen as impractical, in an age of advanced technology the use of electronic means of consultation makes it more feasible. In July 1997 the Labour government proposed a 5,000-strong 'People's Panel', a focus group to test public opinion on issues, policies and services. This is 'dipstick' rather than direct democracy and reflects a global trend pioneered in the USA. It was a culmination of the market-driven politics associated with Labour's election campaign.

The Greek city-states were very small and intimate, no larger than around thirty square miles. With a considerable number of slaves, citizenship was restricted to fewer than 20,000; abortion, infanticide and a liberal attitude towards homosexual relationships ensured population control. Yet even these polities were too large to govern themselves directly. A mass forum cannot conduct the kind of deliberation necessary for decision-making; this must be entrusted to a smaller group and, if the democratic ideal is to be protected, the selection of this group, and its **accountability** to the people as a whole, are key issues. The Greek city-states made provision for popular voting, office-holding by rotation and various penalties for unsatisfactory officials. In Athens, candidates were elected to a large panel from which office-holders were selected by drawing lots. They believed that those like Macbeth, with 'high-vaulting ambition', who thrust themselves forward for high office, would be the most unsuitable.

In these devices we see the origins of **representative government**. Although a state may be run by a small group of rulers, not unlike a monarchy or an aristocracy, they are not there by virtue of any personal qualities (birth, wealth, religious status, physical strength or even intelligence) but as *representatives* of everyone else. They act in the name of the people and the people retain the right to control and even remove them.

Representative democracy in Britain

Although Britain formally has a system of representative democracy based on elections, it falls far short of the Athenian ideal. Indeed, for long it was believed by the ruling establishment that only a relatively small proportion of the population should vote. Ordinary people were said to enjoy 'virtual representation' – the aristocracy could be assumed to take the views of all classes into consideration when making decisions. However, the franchise was gradually extended as a result of radical leaders fighting for their rights. Those who regarded themselves as the ruling class became fearful of mass rule, seeking new ways to limit democracy.

This they did by keeping MPs unpaid, charging electoral deposits, developing party machines to dominate elections, refusing to adopt working-class candidates and inhibiting the rise of a working-class party (see chapter 10). In addition, they developed a highly elitist theory of representation in which MPs were supposed to act according to their own discretion, with no particular regard for their constituents' opinions. The view received its most authoritative enunciation by Edmund Burke (1729–97) in a famous address to his constituents in Bristol, when he stressed that what they were to expect from him was not servitude but the exercise of 'judgement and conscience'. This view remains deeply ingrained in British political culture, part of the all-important machinery of deference in which the masses forgo their right to influence the high and mighty. An alternative view of representation is that of the **mandate**, whereby election carries an obligation to fulfil promises made in a **manifesto**. In the reality of modern political life we hear both views expressed, politicians choosing the one that best suits their argument.

The Tamworth Manifesto

A set of electoral promises was first made by the Conservative leader Peel on an historic occasion in 1834 to the 586 electors of his Tamworth constituency. The 'Tamworth Manifesto' marked a new style of campaigning based on the electoral mandate.

Referendums Fear of the mass has also been seen in a disinclination to put questions directly to the people through **referendums**, although continued membership of the EC was decided in this way in 1975 (unlike the Danes, Irish and French, the British were not invited to register their opinion on the Maastricht Treaty), and in 1979 referendums were held on Scottish and Welsh devolution. However, the constitution and political culture are beginning to show signs of change. Further referendums were held on Scottish and Welsh devolution in 1997, and on the London assembly and mayor and the Northern Ireland peace agreement the following year. In his 2001 party conference speech, Tony Blair expressed a strong preference for a referendum on entry into the single European currency during that parliament. Referendums were also making their appearance in local government (see p. 616). Increasingly, opposition parties, pressure groups and citizens will feel able to demand referendums as the idea enters the veins of the body politic.

However, critics argue that, by asking only 'yes' or 'no', referendums may oversimplify issues, be unduly influenced by those controlling information and undermine representative government and parliamentary democracy (Marshall 1997). In all the recent referendums the government obtained the 'Yes' vote it desired. Hence, following the recommendations of Lord Neill's Committee on Standards in Public Life, the Political Parties, Elections and Referendums Act (2000) introduced state funding of £1.2 million, to be shared equally between

Anyone who can claim to understand this issue in simple black and white terms is either a charlatan or a simpleton!

Harold Wilson on EC membership, quoted in Anthony Sampson, *The Essential Anatomy of Britain* (1992: 15)

> I could not consent to the introduction into our national life of a device so alien to all our traditions as the referendum, which has only too often been the instrument of Nazism and Fascism.
>
> Prime Minister Clement Attlee in 1945, quoted in Vernon Bogdanor, 'Western Europe', in David Butler and Austin Ranney (eds), *Referendums around the World: The Growing Use of Direct Democracy* (1994: 34)

the rival campaigns. The government would in future have to remain neutral, no longer using the state machine to promote its own preference.

The electoral process today

The British are frequently invited to the polls. Local elections take place somewhere every year (see chapter 19), elections for the Scottish Parliament and for the Welsh and Northern Ireland assemblies occur every four years, and European Parliament elections at five-yearly intervals. However, electing members to the House of Commons remains the high point in the political calendar. General elections take place around a framework of voters, constituencies and candidates.

Voters Today Britain has a universal **franchise**. With certain exceptions (peers, aliens, bankrupts, imprisoned criminals, people of unsound mind and those guilty of electoral malpractice), all citizens over the age of eighteen are eligible to vote.

Constituencies The basis for representation is spatial; MPs represent areal **constituencies** (659 in 2001, including 17 in Northern Ireland) and a general election is in effect a number of simultaneous contests, each electing one member. Constituency populations tend towards equality (at around 69,000) and population movements are monitored by Boundary Commissions, independent bodies chaired by the Speaker of the House of Commons, which recommend changes every ten to fifteen years. These can have important consequences. Post-war readjustments to reflect declining inner-city populations tended to favour the Conservatives, although the 1994–5 review may have contributed to their 1997 defeat (Johnston et al. 1998) as a number of safe constituencies disappeared or became more marginal. However, some Conservative MPs used the opportunity to move in a 'chicken run' to safer seats.

Candidates Almost any resident British citizen over twenty-one (not eighteen) may stand; the police and armed forces, certain civil servants, judges, and Anglican and Roman Catholic clergymen and those ineligible to vote are all excluded. There are few independents, virtually all clothing themselves in party garb, though in 1997 journalist Martin Bell spectacularly

By-elections

Elections are called in particular constituencies following an MP's death or retirement. These provide a measure of government popularity and allow minority parties to shine. The Conservatives suffered a series of defeats throughout the 1979–97 period, frequently with swings against them in the 20–30 per cent range. Yet although stimulating political debate and media hype, these contests provide a poor guide to long-term trends. The party in power is often victim of a 'protest vote' from those wishing to administer a 'kick in the pants' without dislodging it, and the successful minority parties are usually banished to the wilderness at the next general election.

defeated Conservative Neil Hamilton on an anti-sleaze ticket in Tatton. In 2001, the lone successful independent was Dr Richard Taylor in Wyre Forest, although he registered himself as belonging to the Independent Kidderminster Hospital and Health Concern Party. Independents have little chance unless one or more major parties step down in their favour, as occurred in these two cases.

Each candidate must formally appoint an agent, who ensures compliance with electoral law and will probably also be the campaign manager (organizing canvassing, press conferences and so on). Most agents are well versed in the arts of political intrigue and some are highly professionalized.

Electoral Commission In November 2000 this statutory body was set up to monitor elections. Independent of the government, it reports directly to Parliament via a committee chaired by the Speaker.

General elections A general election follows a number of stages.

1 *Naming the day.* The date is not fixed by law; a government's term of office is merely subject to a five-year maximum. The process is begun by the prime minister asking the Queen to dissolve Parliament.

2 *Mobilizing the electorate.* The Representation of the People Act (1983) sets a minimum of seventeen days between calling the election and the day itself. There is no upper limit but by convention the period is between four and six weeks. During this time, candidates and parties conduct what have become increasingly sophisticated campaigns designed to woo voters (see pp. 257–62).

3 *Determining the result.* Voting in Britain has been the essence of simplicity, an 'X' being placed alongside the name of a single candidate. In this simple plurality system, the candidate with the most votes – the 'first past the post' (FPTP) – is the winner.

In 1997 the voters of Winchester gave Liberal Democrat Mark Oaten victory by only two votes. Unwilling to accept defeat gracefully, his Conservative opponent challenged the validity of the result and a by-election was held. However, perhaps sensing a lack of sportsmanship, the voters endorsed Mark Oaten with a resounding 21,000 majority.

---

4 *Forming the government.* A general election results in the emergence of a government, usually formed from the party with an **absolute majority** in the House of Commons. In a two-party system a simple majority will necessarily be absolute, but with more parties complications set in; the emergence of a *hung Parliament* becomes possible and politicians have to retire to rooms (smoke-filled in less health-conscious times) to consider **coalitions** or party agreements. In 1974, the narrowly defeated Edward Heath (with 297 seats) conducted a tentative flirtation with the Liberals (14 seats) before conceding defeat to Labour (301 seats). By the time he called the 1997 election, John Major headed a minority government dependent on Ulster Unionist support.

Economizing with Democracy: Evolution of the Electoral System

The history of Britain's electoral system is no account of legalistic reform, nor a psephological nightmare of figures, swings and majorities, but a story of violence and political struggle in which the prize was control over the state. Reforms were not born of rational thought or an enlightened desire for democracy on the part of the powerful; they came after a slow and painful political labour. The belief (perhaps misguided) of those calling for reform since the seventeenth century was that entry into the House of Commons would advance their political ambitions. This conviction averted revolutionary challenge to rock the constitutional boat, making British history more tranquil than it might otherwise have been.

A democratic travesty

At the beginning of the nineteenth century the system was a democratic travesty. Of a total population of 16 million, a mere 400,000 were eligible to vote in parliamentary elections. Of the two chambers, the House of Lords was reserved for those of noble birth while the Commons was largely peopled on the basis of patronage and corruption. MPs came from two types of constituency. *Counties* showed no consistency in size or population and the franchise was tied to landownership; each returned two MPs. *Boroughs* were towns that had at some time been granted royal charters. Here franchise rights varied widely and, although some allowed almost universal male suffrage, the scope for malpractice was considerable. In the so-called 'rotten boroughs', the population had shrunk since their days of medieval splendour, leaving a mere handful of citizens (Dunwich had fallen into the sea and Old Sarum had a population of zero). In 'pocket boroughs', rich landowners controlled elections through threats and bribery, while the new thriving and populous industrial towns, many with highly efficient local government institutions, remained starved of representation. Voting was not secret and, since MPs were obliged to be entirely self-financing, candidature was restricted to the wealthy. Parliament was thus held securely in the grip of a landed establishment.

Forces for change

In common with most other institutions, the electoral system was transformed to suit the purposes of the new industrial bourgeoisie. For the emergent class, archaic practices of law, administration and government were not the cherished legacies praised by Burke but barriers to enterprise, trade and social advancement. The clash was typified in the 1815 Corn Law which, by denying free trade, blatantly favoured landed interests over commerce. The bourgeoisie realized that the parliamentary compost required some more earthy additives for the bloom of private enterprise.

Justifying claims for a stronger voice in Parliament through the utilitarian philosophy of the Philosophic Radicals, they called for representative government through rational and fair elections. Although self-interested the bourgeoisie required allies, whom they found in the bottom half of the curious social sandwich in which they were squeezed. Here was a class that they themselves had, in Marx's view, 'called into existence', whose potential for insurrection was made more ominous by the chilling excesses of the French Revolution. It

Source: Mary Evans Picture Library

offered a force that, if harnessed, could drive the piston of reform as effectively as steam power drove their industry.

Wellington's victory at Waterloo in 1815 had produced little relief from the misfortunes that war had heaped upon the poor. Economic slump, the return of soldiers and Irish immigration produced unemployment, destitution and rising costs. The workers were willing to accept the leadership of middle-class radicals working for a reform promising them a voice in Parliament. Agitation operated on a number of fronts, with Hampden Clubs (named after a great seventeenth-century parliamentarian), radical city newspapers, strikes, marches, mass meetings and political discussion classes to prepare ordinary people for rule.

The 1832 Reform Act

Although working-class agitation was easily suppressed by state violence (as in the 1819 Peterloo Massacre), voters felt that the Whigs (see chapter 10) were better able to reduce the tension in the long term. In 1830 they were returned to government after almost fifty years of continuous Tory rule. The scene appeared set for a democratic revolution but once in office they revealed no less a respect for property than the Tories. The difference lay only in their view that factories, machines, raw materials and even the urban labour force could represent property as well as rolling acres in the countryside. In the 1832 Reform Act many small boroughs lost their MPs as seats were redistributed to the more populous counties and new urban kingdoms where the bourgeoisie reigned.

The working class gained nothing. The franchise was parsimoniously extended (from around 500,000 to just over 700,000) to middle-class property-owners (valued at £10 or more a year). MPs remained unpaid, potential candidates faced a prohibitive property qualification, electoral corruption was not eliminated and wealthy individuals could still exert undue control. Of course, the Whigs had never wanted popular democracy; they had dreamed only of a prudent middle-class control over Parliament from which they could command their empire of trade at home and around the world.

Chartism

The radicals' disappointment led to bitterness, violence and renewed calls for electoral reform. In 1836 William Lovett formed the London Working Men's Association, which drew up a *Charter* incorporating the following demands:

1 universal manhood suffrage;
2 annual election of parliaments (to render bribery prohibitively expensive and increase accountability);
3 abolition of the property qualification for candidates;
4 payment for MPs (to enable the poor to serve);
5 equal-sized constituencies (to make all votes of equal weight);
6 secret ballot (to end intimidation).

Working men's clubs developed under the name of **Chartism** but Parliament rejected their demands and those favouring violence rather than argument took the initiative. The government's reaction revealed it to be as willing as its Tory predecessors to use draconian methods involving imprisonment, vigilantes (special constables and spies) and the army. By the late 1840s Chartism was a spent force, battered by the power of the very state in whose government it wished to participate.

The Representation of the People Act 1867

In the 1860s, partly as a result of unease over the American civil war, popular attention again focused upon electoral reform as a means of containing unrest. In 1866 a Liberal reform bill was defeated by a combination of government rebels and Conservatives. The government resigned, to be replaced by a Conservative minority government led by Disraeli who, to the surprise of many, promptly introduced the 1867 reform bill. Dropping the restrictive property qualifications, this enfranchised all male urban householders. In 1868, with around two and a quarter million eligible voters, it was possible to speak of a *mass electorate*. This had far-reaching consequences: to attract mass support

> The politician who once had to learn how to flatter kings has now to learn how to fascinate, amuse, coax, humbug, frighten or otherwise strike the fancy of the electorate.
>
> George Bernard Shaw, *Man and Superman* (1905)

and keep out working-class parties, politicians were forced to take serious interest in social conditions, education and trade union rights.

The 1867 Act further underscored the supremacy of the Commons over the Lords and marked the end of the ascendancy of Parliament over the executive. The so-called 'Golden Age', which began in 1832, was closed by the rise of disciplined parliamentary party cadres (see p. 277), affording ministers a grip over the legislature that the Tudors would have envied. From this time the voters, not the Commons, would choose governments.

The full impact of the reforms could not take effect without certain other measures. The 1872 Ballot Act made voting secret; workers no longer had to risk their livelihoods by opposing their employers' interests. The Corrupt and Illegal Practices Act (1883) reduced bribery and the following year the electorate was almost doubled by the Franchise Act, which introduced virtual universal male suffrage by extending the 1867 provisions to rural constituencies. The Redistribution of Seats Act (1885) had the profound effect of making the working class a majority of the electorate (McKenzie and Silver 1968: 9). However, the franchise was still withheld from certain categories of men, and all women were excluded. MPs were still not paid as such and voters were obliged to select from two competing factions of the elite rather than choose genuine working-class representatives.

Votes for women

Throughout the reform era, the phrase 'one man, one vote' meant exactly that; women continued to be regarded by middle and working class alike as political ciphers. Hence, their struggle for political equality was even greater. Moreover, the number of new voters would be considerably larger than any previous increase, a fact contemplated with consternation by the male establishment and intensifying its resistance.

The achievement of near universal male franchise was a potent catalyst. The idea of a middle-class male monopoly might have irked some of their wives but extending the right to all men, regardless of social status, was even more intolerable. Various associations formed, such as the Nottingham Female Political Union (1838), the Sheffield Association for Female Suffrage (1851) and a Woman's Franchise League (1889). In 1897 Millicent Fawcett sought to unify the movement in the National Union of Women's Suffrage Societies, but the approach was too timid for some and in 1903 Emmeline Pankhurst and her two

> The most important thing women have to do is to stir up the zeal of women themselves.
>
> J. S. Mill, letter to Alexander Bain (14 July 1869)

daughters established the Women's Social and Political Union, which became the most famous instrument of the **suffragettes**.

The movement began with education and propaganda but the pipe-smoking, leather-armchaired Establishment and Asquith's Liberal government were uncompromising and prepared to employ the same state force that had resisted the Chartists. Suffragettes were subject to ridicule, physical attack, forcible ejection from meetings, imprisonment and hard labour. Victorian judicial attitudes were constrained by the mysteries of child-bearing; menstruation was a common explanation for female deviancy and suffragettes were said to be suffering with their ovaries or from spinsterhood (Kennedy 1992). Hunger-strikers were sadistically force-fed through the nose, an ordeal leaving some permanently injured. To avoid creating martyrs, the government passed the notorious 'Cat and Mouse' Act in 1913, enabling it to release weakened hunger-strikers only to reimprison them upon recovery. Yet they could not prevent Emily Wilding Davison's dramatic martyrdom when, in the same year, she hurled herself under the galloping hooves of the King's horse in the Derby.

> Women had always fought for men and for their children. Now they were ready to fight for their own human rights.
>
> Emmeline Pankhurst (1858–1928), *My Own Story* (1914)

War and the franchise Where Asquith would not help the women the Kaiser could. The arrival of an enemy at the gate produced domestic truce and the Pankhursts rallied their supporters behind the flag. On 15 July 1914 they staged their final demonstration, marching down Whitehall to demand not the vote but the 'right to serve'. Their reward was the 1918 Representation of the People Act, which A. J. P. Taylor (1965: 94) describes, with apparently unintended irony, as the victory 'of the radical principle of "one man one vote"'. This gave women the vote and completed the male franchise but it still stopped short of full equality: men could vote at twenty-one but fear that young women might prove radical, engendered by socialist revolutions in Europe, confined their participation to the mature over-thirties (an anomaly not remedied until the 1928 Equal Franchise Act, which was followed by the 1929 Labour victory, perhaps justifying establishment fears). Yet the move added more new voters than all previous franchise acts together. It also gave women the right to stand for Parliament and later that year seventeen did so. Although Lady Astor, amidst some ceremony, made history as the first woman MP, the occasion did not mark the opening of any floodgates. However, the advance of women in Parliament continued to be held back by constituency organizations' unwillingness to adopt them as candidates. Not until the Labour Party introduced all-women shortlists prior to the 1997 general election did the real breakthrough come, with the entry of 121 women MPs, 101 of them Labour. This advance was held in the 2001 election, with Labour women holding only six fewer seats.

War had also led some to muse on the anomaly that, while young people of eighteen could be required to fight and die for the country, they were not entitled to vote for its government. But it was not until the 1960s, with improvements in education at all levels, many more adolescents going up to universities and a prevailing cult of youth, that Harold Wilson, in tune with the *zeitgeist* (to establishment shock the Beatles received MBEs), lowered the voting age to eighteen in the 1969 Reform Act. However, his reward was rebuff in the next general election, though perhaps by a smaller majority than would otherwise have been the case, and in 1974 the young vote helped him back to power (Butler 1995: 69).

The extension of the franchise had been gradual and grudging. The effect of the 1832 Act was to give the vote to a mere 20 per cent of the men in England and Wales. After 1867 this became 33 per cent, reaching 67 per cent in 1884. Full adult franchise was withheld until 1928. No major concession was secured without the threat of violence. How has the universal franchise been used? To answer this we must turn to the study of electoral behaviour.

Electoral Behaviour

People voting

The Philosophical Radicals argued that if everyone voted, governments would be forced to rule for the good of all. Yet universal franchise has not resulted in anything resembling popular rule. Traditional elites have maintained their ascendancy and capitalism has continued its dominance. This conundrum partly reflects the Burkean notion of representation. It may also be explained by the way people have used the vote, the study of which is known as **psephology**.

Why do people vote? Since any single vote, even in a marginal constituency, has a negligible impact, it can be argued that a rational being might be better occupied tending pigeons or reading Shakespeare than entering the polling booth. Some countries (such as Australia) attempt to combat such disinclination by making voting compulsory, but the right to **abstain**, to say 'a plague on both your houses', is itself a democratic freedom. However, according to Johnston and Pattie (1997), 'voluntary' abstainers often belong to the more deprived sections of society, who see politics as largely irrelevant, while 'involuntary' abstainers will only overcome difficulties (e.g. illness) if the local situation promises a close contest.

The decision not to abstain may reflect various sentiments: class solidarity, a herd instinct, a sense of civic duty, or (particularly among women) a tribute to those who fought for the franchise. Voters questioned in a MORI poll for the Electoral Commission (2001) cited habit and civic duty as their main motives (36 and 20 per cent, respectively). Voting is an endorsement of the political system itself; mass abstention would constitute a legitimacy crisis.

However, the proportion of the population staying at home on election day has been rising steadily (figure 9.1). Indeed, at 59 per cent, turnout in 2001 was the lowest since the achievement of universal suffrage in 1928, despite postal voting being more readily available. Although most commentators ascribed the unexpectedly steep fall in turnout to Labour's victory being seen as a foregone conclusion (Electoral Commission 2001: 16), research commissioned

> The returns from voting are usually so low that even small costs [time, energy, etc.] may cause voters to abstain.
>
> A. Downs, *An Economic Theory of Democracy* (1957: 274)

Figure 9.1
Increasing apathy?
Turnout in
post-war general
elections.

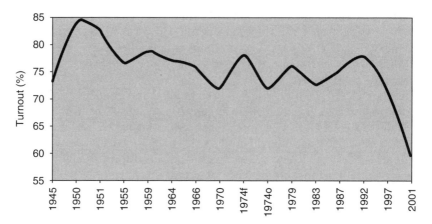

Source: Data from Butler and Kavanagh (2002: table A1.1).

A low turnout is
an indication of
fewer people
voting.

Attributed to US
President George
W. Bush

by the Hansard Society (Diplock 2001) suggested that widespread cynicism and disillusion with the whole political system were the root causes, compounded by lack of knowledge and an inability to make informed choices between the politicians and policies on offer. Many non-voters were not apathetic; they had made a positive decision to abstain.

A BBC/ICM recall poll found turnout to be higher where people felt their vote would make a difference. Local issues can also increase turnout: in Wyre Forest, where Dr Richard Taylor campaigned to keep the hospital at Kidderminster open, it was 68 per cent, while in Brentwood and Ongar, where Martin Bell narrowly failed to remain in Parliament as an independent, it was 67.3 per cent. In its post-election report the Electoral Commission (2001) recommended that voting be made easier through means such as e-voting (internet or mobile phone), polling over several days and easier means of registration. Pilot projects (see p. 628) and an advertising campaign encouraging young voters

Table 9.1 National variations in turnout in the 1999 European Parliament elections

Country	Turnout (%)	Country	Turnout (%)
Belgium	90	France	47
Luxembourg	86	Germany	45
Italy	71	Portugal	40
Greece	70	Sweden	38
Spain	64	Finland	30
Irish Republic	51	Netherlands	30
Denmark	50	UK	24
Austria	49		

Source: Data from *Social Trends* (2002: table 13.22).

demonstrated its commitment to improving turnout. Whether innovative voting methods will make a significant difference remains to be seen. Compared with most of their European neighbours, the British appear to be decidedly unenthusiastic voters (table 9.1).

What do people vote for? Conflicting interpretations of what exactly one is supporting when placing an 'X' on the ballot paper reflect different views on the function of elections. Ostensibly voters are supporting a *candidate*, but even charismatic figures attract a limited personal vote. Most voters feel they actually vote for *parties*, a view reinforced by the theory of the mandate. Alternatively, many see a general election as a presidential-type contest in which they are choosing a prime minister (p. 439).

Stability and volatility

Studies have shown that most people are stable voters, always supporting the same party (Butler and Stokes 1969), while a more volatile minority are described as '**floating voters**'. Since the 1970s, however, an increase in net volatility has resulted in greater support for centrist and nationalist parties (figure 9.2). The explanations for **electoral volatility** and stability are key elements in the study of electoral behaviour and are considered below.

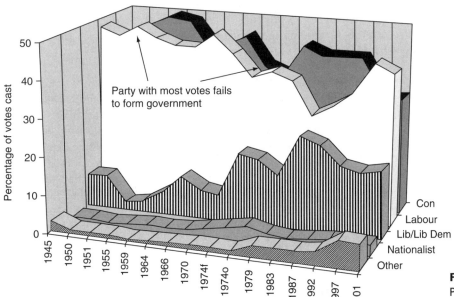

Figure 9.2
Post-war voting trends, 1945–2001.

Source: Data from Butler and Butler (1994: 216–19) and Butler and Kavanagh (2002: table 13.2).

Volatility in the electorate

Gross volatility refers to the total amount of vote-switching, as revealed by large-scale national sample surveys, while *net volatility* represents the final effect. If 10 per cent of Labour voters switch to the Conservatives, while 10 per cent of Conservative supporters move in the opposite direction, the gross volatility would be 20 per cent but the net figure would be zero.

Stable party identification

There are various hypotheses as to why people repeatedly support the same party.

Loyalty Loyalty is fundamental to human existence, producing the cohesion needed to withstand hostile environments. It was not only Dumas's legendary trio who recognized this; unity lies at the very heart of politics, facilitating the formation of associations – basic units of political action. Loyalty towards a political party inspires the **party identification** voting model. Around 80 per cent of voters have identified with a party in much the same way as they take sides in other great contests – the Cup Final, the Grand National or the Boat Race. This model does not postulate that voters act with self-interested calculation; they vote unthinkingly, responding only to vague mental *images* of the parties. In the 1950s and 1960s, when politics reached 'the end of ideology', with little partisan differentiation, there were high turnouts (over 80 per cent) with 90 per cent of voters sticking to their party. According to Butler (1995: 66), 'most citizens vote as they always voted – and usually as their parents voted before them'.

Ideology Within the ideological terrain parties move as much by pragmatism as principle (see figure 2.1 on p. 24). The Conservatives under Macmillan were social democrats but under Thatcher were neoliberals, while Blair's Labour Party effectively dropped the word 'socialist' from its vocabulary. Generally the middle classes are more ideologically polarized than the working class and all three main parties tend to be closer to their middle-class supporters (Crewe 1993: 104). Thatcher's revival of ideological distance between the parties may have accounted for some partisan dealignment (see p. 253) and there were sightings of Essex Man pursuing a rugged individualist lifestyle in the terrain of the south-east. However, despite Thatcher's crusade, voters' ideological positions changed very little and tended towards the left rather than the right (Crewe 1988).

Gender Despite male establishment fears of radicalism, working-class women have traditionally shown a greater propensity than their husbands to vote Conservative. Various explanations have been offered for this. In the first

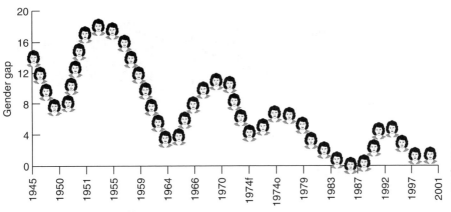

Figure 9.3
Post-war trends in
the Conservative/
Labour gender gap.

Note: This shows the difference in the Conservative/Labour lead between women and men, higher figures
indicating that women are more Conservative than men.

Source: Data from Norris (1996b: table 1) and Butler and Kavanagh (2002: table 13.2).

place, they were less exposed to the forces heightening class consciousness
associated with employment in large industrial undertakings – camaraderie,
unionization and clubs, pubs and sport. An alternative explanation was that
greater longevity gave them more chance to lose the radical fervour of youth
(Hills 1981). Hence Norris (1993) argues that rather than a gender gap one
should consider a gender–generation gap. Both explanations suggest no causal
link between voting and gender as such. Indeed, there are so many differences
between the social experience of men and women that any suggestion that they
vote differently for some biological reason must be highly suspect. Moreover,
the distinction between male and female voting behaviour has diminished
(figure 9.3). The 1979 general election was the first in which more men voted
Conservative than Labour. Margaret Thatcher may have actually antagonized
women. Following her departure, the 1992 general election saw the gender gap
re-open, with Conservative support some 5 percentage points higher amongst
women than men and Labour support 3 points lower (Sanders 1993: 188).
However, in both 1997 and 2001, exit polls showed virtually no difference
between the sexes.

Age The universal franchise was at first limited to those over twenty-one, in the
belief that the young are more likely to question established values and favour
radical policies. Voting tends to confirm this view (figure 9.4), though the
differentials give no cause for establishment alarm and do little to substantiate
Shakespeare's claim. Although the youngest cohort was more Conservative
than Labour in 1992, suggesting the effect of a generation socialized by unbroken Conservative rule, the greatest rise in the Labour vote in 1997 was
amongst the young. However, disappointment may have set in, since an estimated six out of every ten 18–24-year-olds stayed away from the polling booths
in 2001, making them the most apathetic or uninterested age group (Electoral

Crabbed age
and youth
cannot live
together: Youth
is full of
pleasure, age is
full of care.

Shakespeare, *The
Passionate Pilgrim*,
xii

Commission 2001: 15). The increasing potential of older people's votes is shown as Age Concern mounts roadshows and produces glossy brochures to mobilize the elderly (politically speaking), pointing out that as 24 per cent of the electorate they have considerable voter power.

Race Although black people have generally been less inclined to register to vote than whites (Electoral Commission 2001: 15), those of Asian descent are more likely to vote than their white neighbours, while Afro-Caribbeans are less so. In both cases the strong preference has been for Labour. In 1992, some 90 per cent of Afro-Caribbean and 72 per cent of Asian voters supported Labour (Crewe 1993: 102). There are grounds for thinking that non-manually-employed Asians, a growing category, will gradually defect (Studlar 1983), but such predictions may be premature (Saggar 1992: 169). The parties have increasingly courted the ethnic minority vote, though without explicitly focus-ing on race relations or immigration issues. In 2001, however, in emphasizing the asylum-seeker issue, William Hague took what opponents regarded as a covertly racist position, re-igniting long-standing divisions within his party and exposing a deep structural fault-line (Saggar 2001: 759). There was also general unease when two BNP candidates saved their deposits in race-torn Oldham, gaining over 16 per cent of the vote.

Newspaper readership Unlike broadcasters, newspapers can adopt a partisan stance during an election. It is debatable whether readers choose the papers sharing their views or are influenced by their reading (Curtice and Semetko 1994), but the correlation between voting and newspaper choice is strong. One

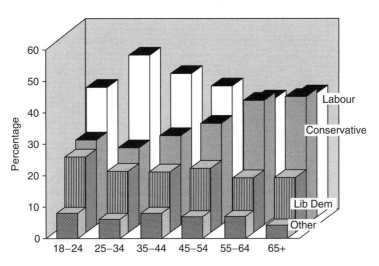

Figure 9.4
Voting by age, 2001.

Note: Percentage in each age group voting for each party.
Source: Data from Butler and Kavanagh (2002: table 13.2).

much feared by politicians is the *Sun*, with its least politically interested but most volatile readership (Miller 1991: 192). Its 1992 post-election boast, 'IT'S THE SUN WOT WON IT', was not merely self-aggrandizement (Harrop and Scammell 1992), and in 1997 and 2001 it again backed the winner.

We saw in chapter 8 how the press has tended to favour the political right, with tabloid support for the Conservatives reaching fever pitch in the 1980s. However, in a surprising turnabout, which could be dated to Black Wednesday (September 1992), the British press became more agents of dealignment than stability as they lined up behind New Labour (Seymour-Ure 1997). The pattern remained much the same in 2001. On the morning of 7 June the *Sun* greeted its readers with the prediction that Blair was poised to win an historic second term, 'and he will do so with *The Sun's* support'. In fact this view was shared by most other papers, with only the *Daily Mail* and *Daily Telegraph* dissenting. Of course it is a moot point as to whether the press had moved to New Labour or New Labour towards the position preferred by the media barons. Blair's courtship of Rupert Murdoch was one of the most compelling symbols of New Labourism. If the party were to disappoint, its new friendships could soon evaporate.

Social class The most durable explanation for party identification has been class. In four successive general elections in the 1960s and 1970s some 80 per cent of the middle class consistently voted Conservative, while about 70 per cent of the working class supported Labour (Gallup 1976). Yet **cross-class voting** – the presence of working-class Conservatives and middle-class Labour voters – shows that class identification has never provided a complete explanation.

The phenomenon of the working-class Conservative is crucial to the pattern of hegemony in British society; without it an upper-middle-class elite could not maintain its supremacy. Although this obvious mathematical truth haunted the nineteenth-century Establishment they need not have lost any sleep, for around one-third of working-class voters were consistently to support a party with its origins in the aristocracy and dedicated to preserving traditional privileges and inequalities. This apparent puzzle has excited various hypotheses.

- *Political deference.* A deferential political culture sees the working class voting for their 'betters', whom they believe to be 'born to rule'. Norton and Aughey (1981: 175) perceive working-class Conservatives as individuals who 'prefer, despite not having . . . privileges, what is known and predictable in the system and who believe that this is how things should be'.
- *Social aspiration.* For many members of the working class the desire for self-betterment is seen in ruggedly individualist terms rather than collectivism. D. H. Lawrence (1950: 119) speaks of his own working-class community in which 'it was a mother's business to see that her sons "got on"'. The individualism in Conservatism can appeal to this sense of aspiration and to 'be Conservative' in a working-class community can, in a snobbish way, represent social improvement in itself.
- *Neighbourhood.* Working-class voters in predominantly middle-class areas show a greater propensity than others to be Conservative. It may be, of course, that people move here because they already hold such values.
- *False consciousness.* Marxists, notably Gramsci (1971), have argued that the working class are led to the mistaken belief that their lowly role in life is in their self-interest, perhaps divinely ordained. This **false consciousness** is fostered through ruling-class hegemony which has forestalled revolution.

However, underlying this debate should be a realization that the British working class has not been driven by strongly left-wing attitudes or egalitarian instincts. There is considerable genuine support for many right-wing positions, ranging from attitudes to race and immigration and the monarchy to council house sales, law and order, trade union reform and social security 'scroungers'. The popularity of Enoch Powell between the 1960s and 1980s testifies to many of these sentiments and the TV character Alf Garnett, a grotesque caricature of the working-class Conservative, evoked ready recognition to become a loved national symbol. New Labour showed a keen awareness of this across a wide policy range.

In contrast, a not insignificant 20 per cent of the middle class (rising to around 30 per cent in 1997 and 2001) have supported Labour. Possible explanations for this include the following.

- ◆ *Intellectual socialism.* The intelligentsia are, by definition, likely to take a reasoned rather than an entirely self-interested view of politics. Much Labour support and leadership has been drawn from this group, with the elitist Fabian movement a significant force from the outset. The Conservatives have fared markedly worse in those Conservative city constituencies (including Oxford and Cambridge) with high concentrations of professional middle classes, university dons and students (Curtice and Steed 1988: 332).
- ◆ *Residual class loyalty.* Not all upwardly mobiles pull up the ladder; some remain faithful to the values of their parents.
- ◆ *Public-sector employment.* Public-sector employees are predominantly middle class and, by the 1970s, comprised around 30 per cent of the workforce. They have a career interest in welfare-orientated policies and a natural antipathy to the right-wing preference for a small state. (An exception is the police force; see p. 669.)
- ◆ *Mistrust of the 'New Right'.* Some 'one-nation' Conservatives were uncomfortable with the neoliberal policies of the post-1979 Conservatives. By branding them 'wets' Thatcher showed little inclination to keep their support, though her successors tried to win them back.

Volatile voting patterns

Non-stable voters are particularly important because, although they may constitute only a small proportion of the electorate, they precipitate the **electoral swings** that can sweep governments from office. A movement of only 3.6 per cent in 1964, for example, served to erase a seemingly impregnable Conservative majority. Increased volatility became a striking feature of the 1980s and 1990s, so that it could be said that 'the majority of British voters no longer readily identify with a political party' (Johnston and Pattie 1996: 299). The 1997 and 2001 Labour landslides suggested that many lifelong Conservative voters had changed allegiance.

Partisan dealignment From 1945 the overall level of class-based voting for both major parties began to fall until over half the electorate was rejecting the class imperative (Crewe 1986: 620). **Partisan dealignment** (figure 9.5) was confirmed using a sophisticated multidimensional definition of class as well as one based simply on occupation (Rose and McAllister 1986). The collapse was particularly injurious to Labour. Between 1945 and 1970 its share of the vote had stood, like that of the Conservatives, at around 45 per cent; by the 1980s it had plummeted to around 30 per cent. Its dramatic recovery in 1997 clearly demonstrated the features of dealignment (Denver 1998: 210), a swing of 10.3 per cent (almost double that of the previous record swing in 1979) indicating high volatility. Of those voting in 1992, almost a quarter had changed allegiance. Class-based voting reached an historic low, with non-manual workers dividing evenly between Labour and Conservative.

Figure 9.5
Partisan
dealignment: class
voting from
1945–1958 to
1992.

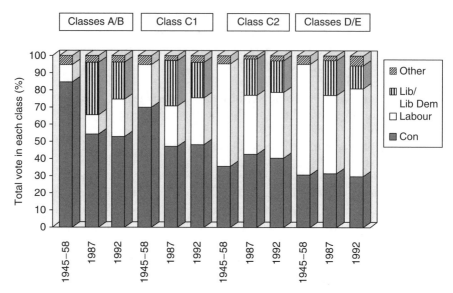

Source: Data from Abrahams (1958), ITN/Harris poll in the Independent (13 June 1987) and Curtice (1997: table 3).

Today, explanations of voting behaviour are more complex than in the days of stability.

The third force The bipartisan model was threatened as a rejuvenated Liberal Party offered electors a third choice. Its share of the vote rose dramatically from 7 to 19 per cent between 1970 and 1974 (see figure 9.2). The SDP further muddied the partisan water when it entered the fray in March 1981. Support for the Alliance remained buoyant (25 per cent in 1983 and 23 per cent in 1987), and as the Liberal Democrats they claimed around 17 per cent of the vote in 1992 and 1997, with this rising to 19 per cent in 2001.

Tactical voting The entry of a third horse in the electoral race opened the door to **tactical voting**: supporting a party, or candidate, that is not the first choice to *prevent* the least-liked being elected. There was some evidence of this during the 1980s: opposition parties that had finished in second place in the previous election generally improved more than those finishing lower (Curtice and Steed 1988, 1992). Newspapers have begun to launch campaigns to encourage tactical voting, advising voters how to get this or that candidate out, and in 1997 a 'Get Rid Of the Tories' (GROT) campaign was orchestrated by Democratic Left. With forty-six seats, the Liberal Democrats were the principal beneficiaries. By 2001 the electorate were showing even greater sophistication. Some, including pop singer Billy Bragg, used the internet to organize 'pairing' arrangements between constituencies whereby voters would effectively 'trade' their votes. An eve-of-election *Observer*/ICM poll (*Observer*, 3 June 2001) revealed hundreds of thousands prepared to vote tactically to keep out Conservatives where the Liberal Democrats were in second place, promising them a possible twenty extra seats. However, the true level and effect of tactical voting remains debatable; results suggested that Labour voters were not switching (Curtice 2001), the Liberal Democrats gaining only an extra six seats. Bragg himself failed to unseat Conservative Oliver Letwin in Dorset West.

Shrinking working class Although working-class loyalty to Labour may have remained solid, movement away from the party during the 1980s may therefore be explained by the class itself shrinking (Heath et al. 1987; see also p. 185). Since the early 1970s the percentage of manual workers in Britain has declined from around 47 to 34, while the proportion of people belonging to the salaried managerial class has risen from around 18 per cent to some 27 per cent.

A new working class The working-class tendency to acquire middle-class values and lifestyles (*embourgeoisement*) was accelerated by the Conservative ethos of aggressive individualism. Ivor Crewe has identified a 'new working class' – owner-occupiers, especially in southern England, in private-sector employment and non-unionized – which may be contrasted with the 'traditional working class', swelling the ranks of the working-class Conservatives (*Guardian*, 15 June 1987). Among the new working class Labour's share of the vote fell from 45 per cent in 1979 to around 34 per cent in 1987. By 1997, however, New Labour, with some support from the *Sun*, had managed to shape its appeal to these key voters.

Geographical cleavage From the 1970s, with a major new shift in the sands of electoral geography, psephologists could no longer speak of a national swing sweeping the whole country. A deep fissure was opening between the predominantly Labour-voting north and the more Conservative south (with a lesser Labour–Conservative divide between the west and the east). The **north–south divide** had been present in the 1930s but had largely been erased in the 1945 Labour landslide (Johnston et al. 1988: 9). Intimations of the renewed division came as nationalist movements in Scotland and Wales gained momentum; regional differentiation continued during the 1980s, reinforced in 1992 by the geography of recession (Pattie et al. 1993). However, although the electoral map of May 1997 left no trace of blue in Scotland, Wales or large areas of the north and south-west, New Labour had begun to shade the south-east red, making the divide less marked.

Sectoral cleavage Since 1945 there has been a fundamental dichotomy between those whose lives are predominantly locked into the public sector (as providers or clients), who tend to support Labour, and those operating largely within the private sector, who are more likely to vote Conservative (Dunleavy and Husbands 1985). From 1979, however, policies such as council house sales and privatization have reduced such dependence on the public sector.

Personality voting A process of 'presidentialization', encouraged by the media (see p. 439), has tended to reduce elections to contests between party leaders (Brown 1992; Mugham 1993; Clarke and Stewart 1995). In 1983 Michael Foot cut a poor figure and in 1987 and 1992 there was some evidence of a Kinnock factor blighting Labour. By contrast, for much of her reign Margaret Thatcher excited personal admiration, and within three months of taking over as Labour leader John Smith's popularity rating had overtaken Major's. From July 1994 Blair consistently dominated, with an average rating of 39 per cent to Major's 19 and Ashdown's 14. His personal ascendancy continued when Hague took the Conservative helm. An *Observer*/ICM poll on the eve of the 2001 general election revealed that, in response to the question 'Who do you think would make the better prime minister?', an overwhelming 67 per cent favoured Blair (*Observer*, 3 June 2001). After the election, a BBC/ICM recall poll found 30 per cent of former Conservative voters giving the beleaguered leader as their reason for not backing the party. Some critics evoked a phrase current in a popular TV quiz programme: 'William Hague, you are the weakest link.'

Shoparound voting The **consumer voting model** sees voters as shoppers in a political market place (Downs 1957; Himmelweit et al. 1985: 70; Rose and McAllister 1986), choosing policies as they choose a powder that 'washes whiter' or a lager to reach inaccessible parts. For example, Saunders (1995: 136) found that Labour's promise to renationalize the water and electricity industries frightened off 'a substantial proportion' of its potential supporters who had bought shares. Generally Labour has fared better in areas such as health, employment and education, the Conservatives traditionally inspiring more confidence in law and order, defence, taxation and the economy. In fact, given the Conservative record on the economy, the electorate's faith was one of the puzzles of British politics (Newton 1993), and by 1997 this had been eroded (Denver 1998: 212). Furthermore, the Conservatives' failure to dent Labour's majority in 2001 was partly attributed to its fixation on asylum seekers and the euro to the exclusion of issues that mattered to people, such as health and education.

Slings and arrows Outrageous fortune between elections can send short-term shock waves through the electorate. Examples include the Profumo affair, the winter of discontent and the Falkands war (curiously Suez did not precipitate a Conservative fall). The sleaze farrago also coloured perceptions in 1997, highlighted by the agreement of BBC journalist Martin Bell, famed for his white suits, to stand as a whiter-than-white anti-corruption candidate against Neil Hamilton, under investigation in the cash-for-questions affair.

It's the economy stupid.

Aide mémoire in the Clinton office during 1992 presidential election

The economy, stupid! There is a long-standing belief that voters support the ruling party if the economy is doing well and shift to the opposition if it is doing badly. This appeared to have been borne out in 2001 (see Sanders et al. 2001). In 1979 the Conservatives came to power after Labour's economic 'winter of discontent' and enjoyed continuing success until 'Black Wednesday' in September 1992 finally sank their reputation for economic competence. By

2001, falling unemployment, income tax pegged and Gordon Brown's reputation for prudence were all strong enough to secure Labour's historic second term.

Feeling good The objective state of the economy, although a key reading on the political barometer, may not accord with voters' perceptions. The notion of the 'feelgood factor' entered journalistic parlance as a measure of the latter. Despite improvements in certain economic indicators, it remained elusive in 1997, confirming Will Hutton's thesis of the 30/30/40 society (see p. 186); under rampant capitalism even those in employment may feel insecure. Thus John Major had the curious distinction of winning in a recession (1992) and losing in an upturn (1997). In 2001 the feelgood factor from economic buoyancy was perhaps helped by England's eve-of-poll win over Greece in a World Cup qualifying match.

Finally, it must be remembered that, despite the considerable body of academic and commercial research since the 1950s, the reasons why people vote as they do remain obscure. Human motives and emotions are not easily unlocked by the researcher with the clipboard. People are not entirely self-interested consumers of policies; 'some form of conditional altruism may be at work' (Gavin 1996: 322). Moreover, views can be manipulated through the processes of mind politics. At election times, this layer of politics comes to the fore in the campaigns the parties wage.

Influencing Voters: Politicians and the Election Campaign

Packaging the parties

Despite its limitations, the consumer voting model is important in a way its proponents may not intend; while it may not entirely account for *voters'* behaviour, it does explain that of the politicians, pundits, parties and the parasitic psephological media, all of whom operate as if it were true. Politicians like to think that the country is enraptured by their comings and goings and make punishing efforts to inform, analyse and persuade in the **election campaign,** one of the most compelling symbols of modern politics. Increasingly, the real campaign is preceded by a phoney one during which the prime minister teases the pundits and opposition over the election date. In both 1992 and 1997 the parties were effectively campaigning well before the starting pistol was formally fired, and in 2001 the foot-and-mouth outbreak made the period of teasing even longer than usual.

Traditionally campaigns involved an unveiling of manifestos, followed by hustings and public meetings, door-to-door canvassing, flattering constituents and kissing sticky babies, with candidates fighting individual constituency battles. Local campaigning and the role of party activists on the nation's doorsteps can still be crucial today (Seyd and Whiteley 1992: ch. 8; Whiteley et al. 1994: 213–18). The Liberal Democrats' successes in 1997 and 2001 were achieved by targeting key seats, often moving reinforcements in from neighbouring constituencies. In 2001, Labour sent its biggest guns to 'battleground' target seats so that, while there was a national swing of nearly 2 per cent to the Conservatives, there was no swing from Labour in its key marginals. Conservative advances were either in seats they already held, or in those where Labour had no chance.

However, more than ever campaigns are conducted by the central party machines, with a sophistication undreamed of a few decades ago. It is a battle of media spin doctors and large-scale advertising, with enormous sums being spent. From 1979 the Conservatives, backed by mighty capitalist enterprises, called the tune. However, learning much from Clinton in the USA, Labour had raised the art to new levels by 1997, operating from its high-tech media centre at Millbank. Indeed, its offensive can be said to have begun the moment Blair took over as leader, with technology, discipline, focus groups, grooming of leaders and news management honed to a fine degree (Kavanagh 1997a). However, the new style of campaigning was leading to increasing concern over the level of national campaign expenditure by the two main parties; by 2001, this was strictly controlled under the 2000 Political Parties, Elections and Referendums Act (see p. 340).

"Oh no — canvassers — pretend we're not in...."

Today politicians have become products to be packaged and sold. Their actions (speeches, interviews and photo opportunities) are planned in detail. What they say, how they dress, their hair-styles, where they go, whom they meet, which politicians or party they attack, which section of the electorate they target, by whom they will be interviewed on television – all is decided for them after careful analysis. Even the manifestos may be written by media men (the 1987 Conservative manifesto was drafted by John O'Sullivan of *The Times*) and the spin doctors have emerged from the shadows, becoming as familiar to *aficionados* as the politicians themselves. Criticized as 'control freaks', they can stifle any real debate, emphasizing personalities rather than policies (Scammell 1995).

> I assume you want to be prime minister. I just want to be an interviewer, so can we stick to that arrangement.
>
> Jeremy Paxman interviewing Tony Blair during the 2001 election campaign, in response to Blair's attempt to change the subject

Campaigns are physically and psychologically gruelling. Politicians rise early, travel daily to and from London, attend frequent strategy meetings, make and remake speeches, give daily press conferences, sweat before television cameras and snatch only a few hours' sleep in each 24-hour cycle. All takes place under the scrutinizing eyes of the media, eager for a gaffe or an encounter with a banana skin. Yet politicians need the media and provide 'battle buses' to carry the journalists around with them. This can be a two-edged sword; eager photographers were on hand in May 2001 to record both the Welsh egg hurled at Labour's John Prescott and the quick counter-punch delivered to the assailant.

Campaigning has taken an increasingly aggressive and negative direction; rather than promoting their own policies, parties attack their opponents. In 1997, Conservative posters had featured Blair with 'devil eyes', while in 2001 Labour portrayed a grotesque vision of Hague with Thatcher's coiffure. Broadcasters, bound by their particular perception of 'balance' as required in the Representation of the People Act, aid and abet by reporting the campaigns themselves rather than fundamental issues (Semetko et al. 1997). They also concentrate on party leaders. In the 2001 campaign, Blair featured in 35.4 per cent of all election news reporting and Hague in 26.4 per cent, while Charles Kennedy was in third place. No other politician reached double figures (Electoral Commission 2001: 19).

Television has become ever more dominant. Although political commercials are not allowed in Britain, slick party election broadcasts use skills developed in advertising. A highly acclaimed production presenting Neil Kinnock, written by Colin Welland and directed by Hugh Hudson (director of the film *Chariots of Fire*), was said to have lifted the Labour leader's rating by 16 percentage points in 1987 (Harrison 1988: 154). However, such campaigns create tensions at party headquarters as the advertising consultants and party officials vie for control (Hollingsworth 1997). When let down by the traditionally Conservative press in 1997, John Major turned to television for salvation, accepting a challenge to a US-style head-to-head debate with Tony Blair (who promptly backed down). In office in 2001, Blair also refused the challenge from Hague for a TV duel.

Throughout all, the public are reduced to passivity. People cannot confront and heckle, as they could at the traditional hustings; a foot projected through the screen will do nothing to register opposition to the relentless talking head, and questioning can only take place vicariously through the medium of the professional interviewer. 'Phone-ins', permitting the public to address politicians directly while others listen, do little to capture the robust spirit of true debate. Questions can be carefully monitored beforehand and an awkward or abusive caller reduced to mute impotence at the press of a button. The spin doctors seek to manipulate and bully the media, so that what appears on the screen is 'politics on the politicians' terms', with little real information dispensed by the 18-second 'soundbite' (Harrison 1992: 170).

In the 2001 campaign interest waned. Sales of several newspapers fell during the month: the *Express* group by 2.8 per cent, the *Sun* by 1.3, the *Mirror* by 1.1 and *The Times* by 0.7. People also voted with their remote controls; while the soap operas maintained their viewing figures, audiences for BBC's 6.00 p.m. news and ITN's News at Ten both fell during the campaign (Deacon et al. 2001: 666–7). However, a new factor also came into play in the 2001 campaign: the internet (see Coleman 2001). While the parties tried e-marketing their policies and the established media provided more detail through their websites, members of the public were also able to take a less passive role by exchanging information and arranging vote swapping and pairing (see p. 254).

Monitoring the campaign

The analogy with selling is extended by the ever-increasing use of market-survey organizations commissioned by the media and the parties to conduct **opinion polls** on voting intentions and related matters (figure 9.6). There are grave dangers in such saturation and some countries ban polling during election campaigns. Sometimes the polls themselves displace real news. Believing with Oscar Wilde's Lady Bracknell that statistics 'are laid down for our guidance', the 'bandwagon effect' may lead people to be swept along like sheep to be on the winning side. Alternatively, supporters may stay away if they see their party is well ahead, while lukewarm voters may be galvanized to assist one falling behind, in a kind of boomerang effect.

Moreover, pollsters may get their predictions wrong. They emerged with much egg on their clipboards as the Conservatives secured their 1992 victory against all expectations (Butler and Kavanagh 1992: 146). Interviewees may have been expressing their disapproval of government policies while still

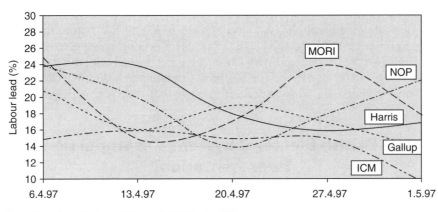

Figure 9.6
An exact science? Labour's lead over the Conservatives according to the last published poll during each week of the 1997 election campaign.

Source: Data from Butler and Kavanagh (1997: table 7.2).

intending to support it in the secrecy of the ballot box (Denver 1994: 163–4). In addition, a late swing to the Conservatives, differential refusal rates, a higher propensity to vote among Conservative supporters and sample bias may all have contributed to the errors (Crewe 1992; Curtice 1996). Hence, the pollsters revised their methods and 1997 was seen as a critical test. When Labour romped home, they claimed to have redeemed themselves. Yet with such a landslide how could they have failed? Ivor Crewe pointed out the need for some modesty. Had the result been narrower (as they usually are), and allowing for the margin of error, some polls would almost certainly have been wrong (Crewe 1997). Between 1997 and 2001 the polls reported a virtually unvarying lead for Labour over the Conservatives, who thus had to fight the 2001 election under a cloud. Since a peak of fifty-seven published nationwide polls in 1992, there was some cooling off, with forty-four in 1997 and only thirty-one in 2001. Yet they remained important and their certainty may have contributed to the low turnout (Crewe 2001; Butler and Kavanagh 2002: 121).

'Sound and fury, signifying nothing'?

Whether the new campaigning trends are desirable or effective is debatable. Familiarity with modern advertising tactics may induce voter scepticism. Short, easy-to-remember messages exorcize all subtlety from discussion and the sheer quantity of coverage may induce torpor and apathy; in 1997 and 2001, increased campaigning coincided with falling turnouts. Finally, the great expense and energy may well be wasted. Although the Conservatives' 1987 campaign was often in disarray they found themselves drinking the champagne with a handsome parliamentary majority, and in 1992, John Major stepped back from the spin doctors' wizardry to take a soap-box into the shopping precincts and gained the last laugh. Although Labour spent over £7 million on press and poster advertising in 1997, many commentators regard this election as one the Conservatives lost by their own disarray (Whiteley 1997). Indeed, in the view of some psephologists, elections are won and lost before the campaigns ever begin (Clifford and Heath 1994: 21). The 2001 result certainly bore this out, with the Labour lead virtually unchanging throughout both its term of office and the campaign itself. The Electoral Commission (2001: 17) concluded that the campaign 'did little to persuade people that their vote mattered'.

The British Electoral System: Disproportional Representation?

The first-past-the-post (FPTP) system is said by its supporters to be quintessentially British, uniquely fitted to the political culture. It is conducive to bipartisan politics, offering electors a clear choice and producing stable majorities, moderate policies and an ethos of strong government. Extremist or frivolous parties are excluded: despite its 30,000 membership in the 1930s, the British Fascist Party did not gain a single seat in Parliament. Stable, single-party governments can count on a full term, enabling them to follow their mandate without compromises through coalition-building or fear of a *coup*. The system also produces a coherent opposition – a 'government in waiting' – and allows a regular alternation of governments. Small, single-member constituencies permit close links between MPs and people and ensure that the interests of far-flung regions are not forgotten in Parliament. Moreover, its simplicity makes it easily understood, voters are used to it and a fairly high turnout is said to demonstrate their satisfaction. However, these virtues are open to question.

> The kind of economy that we are faced with is going to be a market economy, and we have got to make it work better than the Tories make it work.
>
> Neil Kinnock, Labour party conference speech (1988)

♦ *Clear choice.* This idea is belied by the tendency of the two main parties to converge on the centre ground. The post-war consensus was broken only by Thatcher, and it was not long before Labour was moving rightwards across a wide policy range. Even over Europe, the differences were largely *within* rather than between the parties. On the key question of the single currency, both favoured a wait-and-see strategy.

♦ *Strong and stable single-party government.* Throughout the twentieth century Britain experienced some twenty-one years of government by a combination of parties – either a coalition or a National government. There have also been periods when a single party in office has lacked an absolute majority, sustained only by a third-party agreement. Even with a majority, strong government is only possible with disciplined troops; Major was brought to his knees by his Eurosceptics. Moreover, the cabinet reshuffle is a British speciality, belying the claim to long periods of stable government. Only prime ministers are stable.

♦ *Moderate government.* Thatcher demonstrated, to both admirers and critics, that the system did not necessarily prevent a degree of extremism.

♦ *Mandated government.* A victorious party cannot always be expected to execute all its promises as, for example, when the Conservatives jettisoned their 1992 pledge not to increase VAT and Labour reneged on its 1996 vow not to privatize Air Traffic Control.

♦ *Single-party opposition.* For much of the early twentieth century the Liberals coexisted with Labour in opposition. In 1983, the first-past-the-post system was kind to Labour, masking the strength of the centre-party vote. However, with 46 seats in 1997 and 52 in 2001, the Liberal Democrats could lay some claim to be an alternative opposition.

♦ *Regular alternation in office.* Even in the post-war era, when this thesis appeared most plausible, by 1997 the Conservatives had reigned for thirty-five years (figure 9.7) and, once in office, the Blair government successfully gained a second term.

♦ *Close MP–constituency link.* In fact, the dominance of the party machines means that constituencies increasingly find that candidates with few local connections and 'parachuted' from London are foisted on them. Prospective candidates will tote themselves around the country in the search for a seat, sometimes maintaining only a token constituency address.

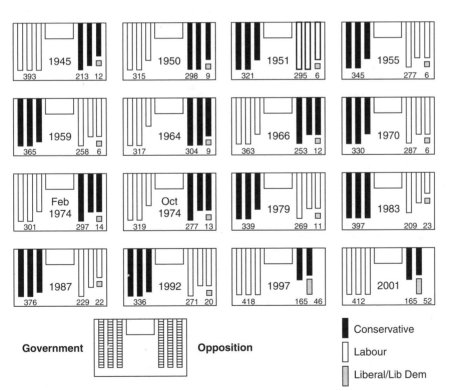

Figure 9.7
Party dispositions in the House of Commons after general elections, 1945–2001.

- *Simplicity.* The choice of **proportional representation** (PR; see pp. 266–9) for elections to the European Parliament, the devolved assemblies and the Greater London Assembly, as well as increasingly sophisticated approaches to tactical voting, give the lie to the claim that the British need simplicity.
- *Popularity.* The record low turnouts in 1997 and 2001 (71.4 and 59 per cent, respectively) did little to substantiate claims that the system was popular.

The case against first-past-the-post

Hence, first-past-the-post has many critics. A 1970s reform campaign orchestrated by academics and politicians gained considerable momentum but came to nothing (Finer 1975), partly through lack of strong public feeling. The two major parties had long resisted reform, but a third consecutive defeat in 1987 concentrated the collective Labour mind. Within the party a vigorous Campaign for Electoral Reform formed, with over 60 MPs and presided over by Professor (later Lord) Raymond Plant, who had chaired a Labour-sponsored working party on electoral reform. Reporting in April 1993 it recommended a regional list system for the European Parliament and a supplementary vote system for the House of Commons (see pp. 266–7). Party leader John Smith promised a referendum if Labour took power, although Tony Blair was more equivocal. However, in March 1997, on the eve of the general election, he struck an historic deal with the Liberal Democrats, and once in office established an independent commission to recommend one proportional system to be pitted against FPTP in a referendum before the next election. Chaired by Liberal Democrat Lord Jenkins of Hillhead, one of the 'Gang of Four' who had dreamed of breaking the mould of British politics (see p. 294), its terms of reference required that the recommendation fulfil a number of criteria:

- broad proportionality;
- stable government;
- extended voter choice;
- maintaining the MP–constituency link.

The inquiry included open meetings across the country where individuals and interest groups were able to put their views. The report, published in October 1998, recommended a system known as AV-plus (see p. 268). Although broadly welcomed by those campaigning for electoral reform, there was no action before the 2001 election and Labour's second huge majority gave it little incentive to move. The problem for reformers is that FPTP always serves the dominant party well. However, as conditions change, with PR now being used more widely, it is necessary to re-evaluate it. Critics allege numerous failings in FPTP, including the following.

◆ *Disenfranchisement.* In a single-member constituency only one set of opinions can ever be represented, leaving many votes 'wasted'. Even votes cast for successful candidates are superfluous where majorities are large, as in many northern Labour seats. Such constituencies remain impervious to national swings and thousands of voters have no influence. Local party oligarchs become the effective electorate (or 'selectorate') through their right to select candidates. (This could be reformed by a **primary election** to choose the candidate.)

◆ *The third-party blues.* Despite gaining widespread national support, third parties may not be in a position to win many constituencies. The Liberal Democrats have been particularly vulnerable. In 1997 and 2001, thanks to targeting and tactical voting, their support became more concentrated but, attracting 19 per cent of the votes, over half that of the Conservatives, their 52 seats (in 2001) fell disproportionately below the Conservatives' 166. Conversely, minority parties with spatially concentrated support can achieve a disproportionate parliamentary presence. In 1997, Scottish and Welsh nationalists together secured 10 seats with only 782,570 votes.

◆ *Over-amplification of opinion change.* It has been estimated that a shift in support from one party to the other of only about 1 per cent will result in a change in Parliament of about 13 seats. Thus, in 1997, a 10.3 per cent swing to Labour gave a 147-seat gain.

◆ *Legitimacy crisis.* Once there are more than two horses in the race, in any constituency, 'winners' may take their seats at Westminster with well over half their constituents having voted against them. In this simple plurality system the absolute number of votes is immaterial, MPs can quite easily be elected with 30 per cent of the votes.

◆ *Disproportionate majorities.* Anomalies at constituency level are transposed to Westminster; since 1935 no governing party has polled over half the votes cast although almost all have enjoyed substantial majorities. With 42.3 per cent of the votes in 1987, the Conservatives were able to push through the poll tax because the system gave them 57.8 per cent of the seats. Ten years later, Labour's 419-seat 'landslide' was a product of only 44.5 per cent of the vote. Blair's lead in terms of votes in 2001 (9 percentage points) was only one point higher than Major's in 1992, which had given him a majority of only 21. Indeed, it is possible for the majority party in Parliament to actually poll fewer votes than the opposition, as in 1951 and February 1974.

◆ *Policy discontinuity.* The fact that government change entails a clean sweep of an entire government threatens policy continuity. Critics cite 'stop–go' policies as a cause of Britain's economic performance in comparison with Western Europe, where continuity is often secured through coalitions in which centre parties remain in power.

◆ *Issue submergence.* The pressure towards bipartism means that voters are offered only two very broad policy *tables d'hôtes*. They cannot choose, say, Labour's education policy and the Conservatives' policy on law and order.

◆ *Limited policy choice*. As the parties converge on the centre ground (see chapter 10), policy differences between them become minimal. Sometimes, on certain crucial issues, such as Europe or the environment, the fissures run largely *within* the parties rather than between them.

◆ *Apathy*. Factors such as those listed above lead to alienation from politics and falling turnouts (see p. 245). In Liverpool Riverside, a mere 33.8 per cent took the journey to the polling booths in 2001. In a cycle of decline, apathy further reduces legitimacy; despite Labour's 247-seat majority over the Conservatives in 2001, only one in four of the eligible electorate had actually placed a cross beside a Labour candidate. Research has shown turnout in proportional systems to be some 9 per cent higher than in the non-proportional (Lijphart 1994).

◆ *A very British peculiarity*. A final anomaly has nothing to do with FPTP as such but lies in the ability of prime ministers, despite being runners in the race, to fire the starting pistol. They will use this *incumbency advantage* to choose the most convenient time. Attlee called the 1951 contest after just one year and Wilson waited only two before consolidating his narrow 1964 victory. Thatcher finely judged the 1983 contest to benefit from the 'Oh what a lovely Falklands war' factor but John Major delayed until 1997, waiting in vain for a 'feelgood' factor. Capitalizing on his high poll ratings, Blair called the 2001 contest after only four years in office.

The alternatives

Many polities use a PR principle, seeking an assembly that mirrors the pattern of support in the country. Thus the Conservatives' 33 per cent of the vote in 2001 would have translated into 217 seats under complete proportionality, rather than the 166 they gained under FPTP. The FPTP system is largely reserved for systems that developed under English influence: the USA, India, Canada, and many states in Africa and Asia. In referendums in 1992 and 1993, the people of New Zealand rejected FPTP in favour of PR.

There are various forms of PR, of which the following are the principal basic models.

Alternative vote (AV) This well-known system is used for the Australian House of Representatives. It cannot produce genuine PR because it operates on the basis of single-member constituencies, but it does ensure that members have an absolute majority by considering the alternative preferences (**preferential voting**) of those voting for minority candidates (figure 9.8).

Supplementary vote This variation on the AV system avoids overvaluing third and subsequent preferences in the redistribution process. It came into

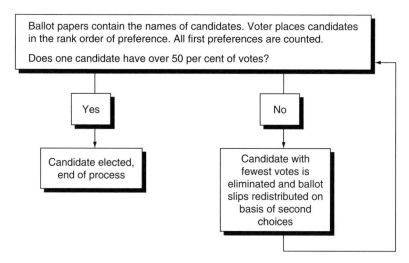

Figure 9.8
The alternative
vote system.

prominence by being recommended by Labour's Plant Report. The ballot paper is the same as in FPTP but voters choose a single second preference. If no candidate wins over 50 per cent of the vote, all but the first two are eliminated and their votes redistributed. This system is used for the election of local mayors (including the London mayor; see p. 616).

Second ballot Instead of voters expressing a second preference, if no candidate secures an absolute majority a second election is held. During the interim period, weak parties may withdraw and others indulge in horse-trading over policies, while voters can think again and abstainers may decide to turn out. The system is used in France, where in the 2002 presidential election the Front National's Jean Marie le Pen finished alarmingly high on the first ballot but was swept aside on the second.

Regional list Widely used in Western Europe, including Denmark, Finland and Belgium, this system is based upon **multi-member constituencies**. Parties prepare lists of candidates, which may be 'open' (voters can indicate their favoured candidates) or 'closed' (voters merely indicate the *party* of their choice and candidates are returned in the list order). The latter increases the power of the party machine and is thus less democratic, a point emphasized by the House of Lords in opposing its use for the European Parliament elections. The percentage vote obtained by each party in each region is calculated and seats are awarded on a pro rata basis. Some systems allow voters to split the ticket between parties.

Additional member (AMS) This system combines single-member constituencies with proportionality. The voter has one vote for the constituency MP and an additional one for a regional list. The balance between the two can vary (it is often around 50–50); the more 'additional' or top-up members, the greater the proportionality. Various versions are employed in Germany, Italy and

> **The multi-member constituency**
>
> This is fundamental to the PR principle. If in a given constituency party X polls 60 per cent of the votes, party Y 30 and party Z 10, a minimum of ten candidates must be returned if strict proportionality is to be observed. This implies that constituencies cannot be small; indeed a 'constituency' may be a large region or, as in the case of The Netherlands, a whole country.

Mexico and it is now used in New Zealand as the 'mixed member proportional' system. It was adopted for the Scottish and Welsh assemblies using the d'Hondt variant (see p. 271).

Alternative vote plus (AV-plus) This combines AV and AMS. Voting takes place as in AMS, but constituency members are chosen by AV rather than FPTP. It was recommended by the Jenkins Commission (see p. 264), which proposed having 80–85 per cent of MPs elected for constituencies (and reducing the number of constituencies to between 530 and 560), with the remaining 15–20 per cent selected from regional lists.

Single transferable vote (STV) With certain similarities to AV, this is probably the best-known PR system. A version was used in Britain between 1918 and 1948, when multi-member university seats existed. It was also recommended by the Kilbrandon Commission on the Constitution for the separate assemblies it advocated for Wales and Scotland, and is used in Northern Ireland for European elections. Although requiring multi-member constituencies (usually three to five MPs), these may be relatively small. Parties may put up as many candidates as there are seats, and voters are thus given considerable choice. The procedure has three main stages.

1   Voters record on the ballot paper their order of preference for candidates.
2   An **electoral quota** (EQ) is calculated using the following formula:

$$EQ = \frac{Votes}{Seats + 1} + 1$$

3   First preferences are counted and those obtaining the EQ are elected. If seats remain vacant, surplus votes for successful candidates are redistributed on the basis of second choices, so that further candidates reach the EQ and no votes are wasted. If all seats cannot be filled in this way, the last candidate's ballot papers are redistributed on the basis of second choices.

Although counting is complicated, in principle the system is simple for voters, who merely number the candidates in order of preference. However, research by Democratic Audit (Dunleavy et al. 1997) found that ballot papers were difficult to understand. The system is used in Ireland, Malta and Australia, but was rejected by the Jenkins Commission as being too great a change from FPTP and outside its remit of maintaining the constituency link.

Signs of change

Britain's adherence to FPTP proved particularly anomalous in the case of the European Parliament, where the purpose is not to form a government (a key argument for FPTP); all other member states used PR. The 1994 elections produced angry complaints from frustrated centre-right leaders. While Europe generally swung to the right, the Socialist group (PES) boosted its representation from 198 to 221, thanks to the disproportionate increase in the number of Labour MEPs (a 4 per cent rise in the vote giving them 17 more seats, whereas PR would have produced around 6) (figure 9.9). Responding to pressure from its EU partners, Britain introduced a regional list system for the 1999 European elections, entailing nine English regions electing 71 MEPs, with Wales and Scotland constituting single regions returning 5 and 8 members respectively. However, the government's choice of closed **party lists** still tended to consolidate patronage in the hands of party machines. While Conservatives and Liberal Democrats ordered their lists on the principle of one member, one vote, candidates on the Labour lists were ranked by caucuses of regional delegates and officials. The result of the election was a trouncing for Labour and a demonstration that small parties can gain a foothold under PR (table 9.2). The Liberal Democrats were particular beneficiaries of the system.

As already noted, devolution has also introduced more PR into the UK. Members of both the Scottish Parliament and Welsh Senedd are elected for four-year terms by AMS. They began with 73 constituency members and 56 from party lists in Scotland, while in Wales the numbers were 40 and 20. The d'Hondt system is used, which gives smaller parties a chance in the list ballot

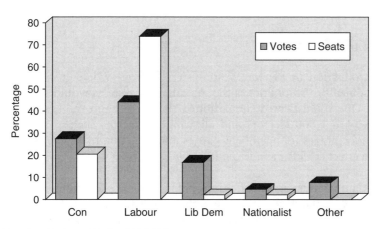

Figure 9.9
The discrepancy between votes and seats in the 1994 European Parliament elections (excluding Northern Ireland).

Source: Data from Butler and Butler (1994: 221).

Table 9.2 European Parliament election results for England, Scotland and Wales, 1994 and 1999

Party	1994	1999
Conservative	18	36
Labour	62	29
Liberal Democrat	2	10
UK Independence	–	3
SNP	2	2
Plaid Cymru	0	2
Green	0	2

Note: Northern Ireland continued to elect its three MEPs by STV.

through a divisor that effectively reduces the vote of parties with members already elected. Thus, as shown in figure 9.10, although Labour secured twice as many votes in the list ballot as its nearest rival in the Glasgow region in 1999, it gained no list seats at all because it already had ten constituency seats. The system even delivered a Socialist member to the Parliament. The Northern Ireland Assembly uses STV to elect its 108 members in order to ensure that all voices are heard (see p. 164). Moreover, PR is also amongst the innovations associated with the 'modernization' of local government, with mayors being elected by the supplementary vote system.

A uniquely British system

Charter88 believes that the strength of AV-plus is that it has been specifically designed to fit in with Britain's political culture . . . if adopted [it] will foster a more productive and efficient style of politics.

Extract from Charter88 press release (Nov. 1998)

Effects of PR in Britain

The introduction of PR for Westminster elections would in all probability revolutionize British politics, although different systems would yield differing results. One sophisticated simulation is shown in figure 9.11, using a mock election with 1,800 electors and allowing for factors such as regional variations, advantages to incumbent parties and targeting by smaller parties. The possible effects of PR include the following.

◆   Campaigning styles would probably become even more centralized. In New Zealand, the reform saw the parties fundamentally changing their strategies, moving from constituency targeting as they sought to maximize votes everywhere (Denemark 1996).

1. Constituency results

Constituency	Party	Constituency	Party
Glasgow Anniesland	Labour	Glasgow Maryhill	Labour
Glasgow Ballieston	Labour	Glasgow Pollock	Labour
Glasgow Cathcart	Labour	Glasgow Rutherglen	Labour
Glasgow Govan	Labour	Glasgow Shetleston	Labour
Glasgow Kelvin	Labour	Glasgow Springburn	Labour

2. Working out the allocation of regional seats

$$\text{Regional figure} = \frac{\text{total number of regional votes for the party in the region}}{\text{number of seats won so far} + 1}$$

	CON	LAB	LIB DEM	SNP	SSP	Elected
Total votes	20,239	112,588	18,475	65,360	18,581	
Seats won so far	0	10	0	0	0	
1st divisor	0 + 1 = 1	10 + 1 = 11	0 + 1 = 1	0 + 1 = 1	0 + 1 = 1	
1st regional figure	20,239	10,235	18,475	**65,360**	18,581	SNP
2nd divisor	1	11	1	2	1	
2nd figure	20,239	10,235	18,475	**32,680**	18,581	SNP
3rd divisor	1	11	1	3	1	
3rd figure	20,239	10,235	18,475	**21,786**	18,581	SNP
4th divisor	1	11	1	4	1	
4th figure	**20,239**	10,235	18,475	16,340	18,581	CON
5th divisor	2	11	1	4	1	
5th figure	10,120	10,235	18,475	16,340	**18,581**	SSP
6th divisor	2	11	1	4	2	
6th figure	10,120	10,235	**18,475**	16,340	9,290	LIB DEM
7th divisor	2	11	2	4	2	
7th figure	10,120	10,235	9,328	**16,340**	9,290	SNP

3. Filling the allocated seats with candidates on the party lists

SNP	LIB DEM	CON	SSP
Nicola Sturgeon	**Robert Brown**	**William Aitken**	**Tommy Sheridan**
Dorothy-Grace Elder	Moira Craig	Tasmina Ahmed Sheikh	Frances Curran
Kenny Gibson	Mohammed Khan	Michael Fry	Rosie Kane
Sandra White	Mary Paris	Mary Leishman	Jim Friel
Maire Whitehead	Iain Brown	Assad Rasul	Ann Lynch
John Brady	Judith Fryer	Rory O'Brien	Robert Rae
Bill Wilson	Matthew Dunnigan	Colin Bain	David McKay
Kaukab Stewart	Clare Hamblen	Murray Roxburgh	Heather Ritchie
Bashir Ahmad	Callan Dick	Iain Stuart	Caroline Moore
Tom Chalmers	Laurence Clark		
Gavin Roberts	James King		
Jim Byrne			

Figure 9.10 PR in action: Glasgow Region, Scottish Parliament election, 1999 using the d' Hondt additional member system.

Note: Candidates elected are in bold type.

Figure 9.11
Simulation of the
1997 general
election under
different electoral
systems.

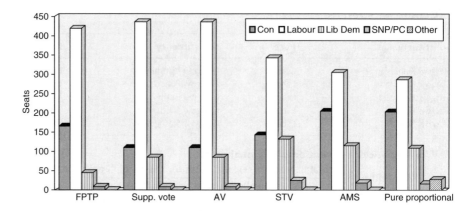

- ◆ Parliamentary representation of minority parties would increase at the expense of the old duopoly. It could also include the rise of disruptive parties such as the BNP.
- ◆ Entirely new parties might emerge onto the national scene (though in the 2001 election, seventy-five parties actually fielded candidates; Electoral Commission 2001: 4).
- ◆ Depending on the system chosen, hung Parliaments and coalition government could become more common. Before long, both the Scottish Parliament and Welsh Assembly had moved to coalition executives (see p. 168).
- ◆ Centre parties, despite minority status, would gain authority and could expect to remain part of successive coalitions. After the first New Zealand election under the new system, the seventeen MPs of the Maori-based New Zealand First party found themselves in a pivotal position.
- ◆ In the longer term, smaller parties might lose their minority status, becoming more attractive once people felt that votes would no longer be 'wasted'.
- ◆ Alternatively, electors might decide that they preferred a two-party system and reduce their support for minority forces.
- ◆ The 'broad churches' of the major parties might fragment into their different factions – Old and New Labour, Eurosceptic and Europhile Conservatives.
- ◆ Turnouts might rise if voters felt their votes would not be 'wasted'.

What the Tories need, did they but know it, is electoral reform. They could then divide into the two parties – European Social Democrat and English Nationalist – that they are.

Andrew Rawnsley (journalist), in the *Observer* (6 July 1997)

A Crisis of Legitimacy?

At the end of the twentieth century Britain found itself with a problematic electoral system. By 1997, the eighteen-year Conservative reign had been the longest since the great Reform Act of 1832. An equally long period of Labour rule would hardly redress the balance. If some people come (as did the Northern Ireland Catholics) to feel the system gives them no constitutional means of influence, a crisis of legitimacy looms. As the new millennium opened, with the record low turnout of 59 per cent in 2001, many critics believed that it was indeed 'Time for a change'.

Key points

- British democracy is based on the principle of representative government, in which a few govern on behalf of the many.
- Representative government may have various interpretations, ranging from the Burkean view to the doctrine of the mandate.
- The evolution of the British system has been slow. Extensions to the franchise were conceded unwillingly.
- The FPTP principle is not proportional but can produce strong, single-party government. It has favoured the continued dominance of the two main parties; this helps explain its persistence.
- The study of voting behaviour has concentrated on seeking reasons why people vote one way or another. Class has been regarded as one of the principal determinants but significant dealignment has occurred since the 1970s.
- Many other factors influence voting, some long term and others reflecting particular circumstances.
- The alternative to FPTP is PR, which was introduced for elections to the European Parliament and the devolved assemblies.
- The 1998 Jenkins Report recommended AV-plus for British general elections, but New Labour's promised referendum on the electoral system has yet to materialize.

Review your understanding of the following terms and concepts

absolute majority	direct democracy	mandate
abstention	electoral quota	manifesto
additional member	electoral stability	multi-member constituency
alternative vote	electoral swing	opinion poll
Chartism	electoral volatility	partisan dealignment
constituency	*embourgeoisement*	party identification
consumer voting model	false consciousness	party list
cross-class voting	first-past-the-post	preferential voting
d'Hondt system	floating voter	primary election

proportional representation	representative government	spin doctor
psephology	sectoral cleavage	suffragette
referendum	simple plurality	tactical voting
regional list	single transferable vote	universal franchise

Assignment

Study figure 9.11 on p. 272 and answer the following questions.

		Mark (%)
1	Which system gives the closest approximation to pure proportionality?	10
2	Which systems would produce coalition governments? Explain why.	10
3	Which systems give the best geographical representation? Explain why.	10
4	Which systems are kindest to small parties? Explain why.	10
5	Is FPTP the least proportional system shown? Explain your reasoning.	10
6	Does this analysis support the view that PR gives undue weight to fringe parties?	20
7	Can it be assumed that people would have voted in the ways shown had one of these systems been in place?	30

Questions for discussion

1 What factors can explain why a substantial proportion of the working class have always voted Conservative?
2 'For all its defects, the British electoral system ensures strong government.' Discuss.
3 Why was the extension of the franchise to the working class so grudging?
4 How important is the concept of the mandate in British politics?
5 What might be the effects of the introduction of primary elections into British politics?
6 How important are class, age and gender in explaining voting behaviour in Britain today?
7 Which system of PR would you consider most suitable for Britain?
8 Why did Labour win the 1997 general election?
9 Why might PR be considered more appropriate for the European Parliament than for Westminster?
10 'The turnout for the June 2001 general election was, at 59 per cent, the lowest since universal suffrage was introduced in 1918.' Discuss possible reasons for this.

Topic for debate

This house believes that proportional representation will revitalize politics in Britain.

Further reading

British Elections and Parties Review.
A more-or-less annual publication including authoritative essays on elections, electoral reform, referendums, etc., and a variety of useful data.

Butler, D. (1995) *British General Elections Since 1945.*
Concise and accessible account of elections and electioneering.

Butler, D. and Kavanagh, D. (2002) *The British General Election of 2001.*
Latest in long line of Nuffield election studies dating from 1945. Lively, accessible and conscious of the politics behind the numbers.

Electoral Commission (2001) *Election 2001: The Official Result.*
First report of the new commission and likely to be regarded as the definitive account; also includes analysis and comment.

Farrell, D. (1997) *Comparing Electoral Systems.*
Gives details and histories of various electoral systems, capturing the flavour of what it is like to vote, with example ballot papers.

Himmelweit, H., Humphreys, P. and Jaeger, M. (1985) *How Voters Decide.*
Explains the consumer voting model and tries to show that attitudinal variables are more relevant than class in explaining voting.

Johnston, R., Pattie, C., Dorling, D. and Rossiter, D. (2001) *From Votes to Seats: The Operation of the British Electoral System Since 1945.*
Examines how, under FPTP, geographical factors help determine election results.

Kavanagh, D. (1995) *Election Campaigning: The New Marketing of Politics.*
Thorough analysis of post-war campaigning strategies tracing the link with media developments and a process of Americanization.

Mugham, A. (2002) *Media and the Presidentialisation of Parliamentary Elections.*
Analysis of press and TV reporting of election campaigns, noting the increasing importance of party leaders.

Norris, P. (1996) *Electoral Change since 1945.*
Accessible overview looking at change and the causes of change.

Norris, P. (ed.) (2001) *Britain Votes 2001.*
Informative account of the 2001 general election by various academics. Examines issues such as falling turnout.

For light relief

Melvyn Bragg, *Autumn Manoeuvres*.
Cumbrians work out their personal and public salvation with passion and deceit during 1970s election campaign.

Douglas Hurd, *The Truth Game*.
A stylish novel by a once-leading politician.

H. G. Nicholas (ed.), *To the Hustings*.
Entertaining election stories.

H. G. Wells, *Ann Veronica*.
Controversial when first published. Relationships between men and women against suffragette background.

Virginia Woolf, *Night and Day*.
A suffragette novel.

On the net

The internet is full of electoral information. During (and after) general elections the broadsheets and the BBC, for example, maintain special sections devoted to the topic. Using any good search engine you will also be able to track down statistics about particular elections. On electoral reform and electoral systems, look at the sites of the campaigning organizations, such as the Electoral Reform Society (http://www.electoral-reform.org.uk) or Charter88 (http://www.charter88.org.uk).

10

The Politics of Power: a Life History of the Party System

This chapter is the first of two on political parties. Although unknown to the constitution, parties dominate the real world of politics; they are symbols of the modern age. The first section examines the concept of the modern mass party. Parties in a democracy should not be seen in isolation; it is in their essential nature to be linked through competition and cooperation. The following sections identify a series of key periods in the evolution of the party system, concluding with an evaluation of British two-party politics.

Defining parties

Any political movement can describe itself as a party, but in a democracy **political parties** are essentially associations with a common set of beliefs and goals, and aiming to take office by constitutional means. Some commentators see the quest for office overriding all else, portraying parties as vote-maximizing machines (analogous to profit-maximizing firms) prepared to pursue any policy that commands support (Downs 1957: ch. 7). While much behaviour bears this out, parties usually reflect ideologies to some extent, though over time they may pick and choose from the ideological cafeteria in the quest for support (see pp. 23–5).

The modern mass party The major British parties are large associations essentially comprising three elements: a parliamentary cadre of elected MPs, a bureaucracy and a large extra-parliamentary army in constituency associations. These **mass parties** evolved as a direct result of extensions to the franchise.

Functions of parties Parties play multifarious roles in political life. Elections are their great celebrations; they energize campaigns, feed the media and mobilize voters. In addition, they organize the life of Parliament; without them the Palace of Westminster would be an empty shell of anachronistic ritual. They also shape popular opinion, set the political agenda, stimulate public debate and, in doing so, help to provide political education. Recruiting people into politics and training them in the Machiavellian arts is another party function; historically Labour has been important in enabling working-class participation. Mass parties also aggregate diverse interests, constructing the compromises that help maintain social stability. When out of government they continue to play a crucial role, providing political opposition: without this, democracy is in peril. In the 1983 election campaign Conservative minister Francis Pym expressed fear of too weak a Labour opposition; similar sentiments were repeated by some commentators after Labour's 1997 and 2001 triumphs.

> No Government can be long secure without a formidable Opposition.
>
> Benjamin Disraeli, *Coningsby* (1844: book II, ch. 1)

The party system

Parties in a democracy do not exist in isolation. The British parties have been inextricably entwined, cross-fertilizing each other with philosophy, policy, strategy and organizational form. They have even made physical contact, to fight or to hold together in the warm embrace of coalition, sometimes even exchanging vital fluids as factions have surged from one to impregnate the other. Each party can therefore only be understood as part of a **party system**. It is usual to classify these in terms of *number* of parties and their relative dominance, thus distinguishing four types.

- ◆ **Multi-party:** more than two parties; governments usually coalitions.
- ◆ **Two-party:** two parties share dominance, each capable of forming an entire government. In reality, minor parties always exist and a more realistic term is *two-party dominant*.
- ◆ **Single-party-dominant:** several parties compete but one stands like Gulliver among the Lilliputians, able to command either an overall majority or remain the dominant partner in successive coalitions.
- ◆ **Single-party:** such 'systems' are unlikely to arise naturally and occur mainly under totalitarian regimes (Nazi Germany, communist Eastern Europe or certain ex-colonial states), usually after the opposition has been eliminated.

Although it is common to characterize Britain as having a two-party system, this must be subject to qualification. There is usually an important third-party presence; indeed, seventy-one different parties actually contested the 2001 election. The system is best understood through its evolution.

Genesis

From the settling dust of seventeenth-century constitutional struggles emerged two parliamentary groupings – the Tories, a landowning cadre avowing fidelity to the King, and the Whigs, devoted to trade and the parliamentary cause. These dominated into the nineteenth century. As **cadre parties** they existed only in Parliament and had little ideology save the protection of self-interest. These primitive organisms were forced under the radical sun, to crawl from the mud of eighteenth- and early nineteenth-century court and parliamentary intrigue onto the hard ground of democracy. The nineteenth-century extensions of the franchise opened the age of the modern mass party.

The Conservatives: the era of Peel and Disraeli

By the 1820s, under the leadership of the Duke of Wellington, the Tories appeared to be collapsing before the radical pressures unleashed by the industrial revolution, fatally vulnerable before any extension of the franchise. However, following the 1832 Reform Act, they experienced an unexpected revival under resourceful leader Sir Robert Peel (1788–1850), who gave them a *raison d'être* beyond self-interest by identifying with Burke's view of conservatism (see p. 40). Asserting tradition over radicalism, it was exceedingly attractive to those whose interests lay in the status quo – the landed gentry. Thus the Conservative Party rose, phoenix-like, from the ashes of the old Tory Party.

However, another crisis occurred in 1846, the party splitting over the repeal of the Corn Laws, which ended tariff protection of agriculture, favouring commerce and industry at the expense of land. Two groups emerged: the more radical one (containing many who had entered Parliament as a result of the 1832 Reform Act), favouring free trade, moved towards the Whigs, with whom they finally merged (forming the Liberal Party). The future of the landed interests again seemed vulnerable but the party was to find a second visionary to lead it from the wilderness. Benjamin Disraeli (1804–81) not only parted the difficult waters of further franchise extensions, he also created an image to carry the party into the era of mass politics.

Disraeli's inspiration was to perceive how the interests of privilege could be allied to those of the ordinary folk whose votes were needed. With a rallying cry of 'One Nation', he stressed the Conservative claim to be the natural guardians of *all* sections of society, evoking the empire as a symbol to unite them as members of a dominant race. The life-saving bond entailed a paternalistic commitment to social reform through Acts regulating the sale of food and drugs, public health, artisans' dwellings, river pollution, factory conditions and trade unions. So effective was the strategy that it was a Conservative government that felt confident enough to extend the franchise further in

> The right honourable gentleman [Sir Robert Peel] caught the Whigs bathing and walked away with their clothes.
>
> Benjamin Disraeli, Commons speech (28 Feb. 1845)

1867. In gaining working-class support Disraeli had laid the foundations for the modern Conservative Party.

However, after his death the future looked bleak as the traditionalists re-asserted their influence. They were saved by the tormented obsession of Gladstone, the Liberal leader, with the Irish question. This split the Liberals in 1886, propelling a group of unionist defectors, led by a radical Joseph Chamberlain, into the Conservative ranks. Subsequently the party acknowledged its commitment to Ireland's link with the mainland by adopting the title 'Conservative and Unionist Party'. The influx returned to the party some Whiggish blood, enabling it to accommodate the rising bourgeoisie increasingly dominating the social order. The Tory and Whig strands offered a formidable electoral potential, which was to become fundamental to the party's remarkable width of appeal.

The Liberals: the era of Gladstone

> You cannot fight against the future. Time is on our side.
>
> W. E. Gladstone, speech on the Reform Bill (1866)

The Liberal Party was a major force for only around half a century. In its heyday it experienced some great periods of office, its social and constitutional reforms standing as its monument. Yet like a figure in classical tragedy, the party (and its leaders) seemed to contain from the first the seeds of self-destruction. The modern party was established in 1859 through the fusion of the old Whigs with the new Radicals and the free-trade faction haemorrhaging from the Tories. This latter infusion provided one of its greatest figures, William Ewart Gladstone (1809–98), whose austere presence, the very antithesis of the polished Disraeli, dominated in the nineteenth century. The rationale of liberalism lay in radicalism and reform (pp. 26–34); impatient with traditional institutions it supported business and commerce through *laissez-faire* and free trade. Beyond the economy there was Irish home rule, nonconformity, parliamentarianism and social reform.

The emergence of mass parties

The two great Reform Acts hardened the fluid parliamentary alliances with a new sense of party discipline, greatly enhancing the leaders' authority. Gladstone and Disraeli forged the characteristic two-party system with its **adversarial** style of parliamentary thrust and parry. It was no longer possible to gain election through corruption and the parties fostered organizations in the constituencies (registration societies) to ensure that all sympathizers would vote. The local associations were also given the crucial responsibility of choosing candidates.

To oversee the local activists two London clubs – the Carlton for the Conservatives and the Reform for the Liberals – became party headquarters and federations of local organizations were established to forge a sense of national unity. The Liberal Registration Association, founded in 1861, was followed in

1867 by the National Union of Conservative and Unionist Associations. The mass membership suggested problems of control: the Conservative Union seemed content to serve the leaders but the Liberal Federation claimed rights over party policy, which Gladstone resisted. Both associations also held annual conferences in which the toilers in the constituency fields could voice their opinions. By the end of the century the mould for the modern system had been cast: parties were ideologically based mass organizations, led by elites, seeking office by courting the electorate.

Challenge to the Established Order: the Rise of the Labour Party

One of the remarkable aspects of franchise reform was the failure of a working-class party to capitalize on the potential in the mass vote – a manifestation of the power of the dominant classes to keep participation as a choice between two elites. They did this by showing some concern for the working class. Conservatives set out their 'one-nation' stall while the Liberals embraced the new liberalism and promoted major social reforms in the early twentieth century (national insurance, pensions, unemployment benefits and employment exchanges). However, a revolutionary ideology was taking shape; Marx's trenchant critique of liberalism meant that things could not remain as they were. Socialist movements were forming and some working-class activists sought to enter the parliamentary stage themselves.

Labour pre-history

The Labour Party was born of a long and painful confinement. Although opposed by establishment forces, the Chartists had argued from the 1830s for a working-class parliamentary voice. In 1869 the trade unions created a Labour Representation League but, although two of its thirteen candidates were returned in 1874, it showed little promise. Some working-class candidates also managed to enter Parliament under the Liberal banner; by 1885 there were eleven Trade Union Liberal MPs. However, the Liberals remained reluctant to cooperate. Keir Hardie, Ramsay MacDonald and Arthur Henderson were all spurned as candidates – had they not been there might never have been a Labour Party.

During the 1880s and 1890s a socialist dynamic came from three associations. At the extreme left was the London-based Marxist group, the Social Democratic Federation (SDF), led by H. M. Hyndman. Of different character was the Fabian Society, founded in 1884 by George Bernard Shaw and the indefatigable social researchers Sidney and Beatrice Webb. It took its name from Quintus Fabius Maximus ('the Delayer'), a Roman general who achieved success by small, cautious moves and delaying tactics rather than reckless bravado – such was the avowed strategy of **Fabianism**. Most important was the Independent Labour Party (ILP), founded in 1893 to pursue moderate socialism and numbering amongst its members Philip Snowden, MacDonald and Hardie. Yet in the 1880s there were only some 2,000 active socialists in the entire country. Despite meagre social improvements, the working class remained content to vote for the elite duopoly and the ILP gained little support. However, a more aggressively socialist New Unionism introduced a new dynamic. In the late 1890s, damaging defeats in large strikes made the case for direct parliamentary representation more compelling.

Emerging from the womb

In 1900, the Trades Union Congress (TUC) made the momentous decision to seek a parliamentary presence. The might of sixty-five trade unions, with their hundreds of thousands of members, combined with the intellectual vigour of the three small organizations to establish the Labour Representation Committee (LRC). Significantly, its strategy was to be in the Fabian tradition: revisionist ('Labourism') rather than revolutionary socialism. At a very early stage the SDF disengaged from the inhibiting embrace.

The Conservative government reacted with intense hostility, portraying the movement as a threat to the constitution and requiring harsh treatment. A series of judicial decisions, culminating in the infamous Taff Vale Judgment of 1901 (holding that unions could be cripplingly sued for tortious acts of members), convinced more unions of the need to combine under the new banner, and one of the movement's key figures, Ramsay MacDonald (LRC secretary), worked to develop a national mass organization.

> MacDonald owes his pre-eminence largely to the fact that he is the only artist, the only aristocrat by temperament and talent in a party of plebeians and plain men.
>
> Beatrice Webb (1858–1943; founder member of the Fabian Society), *Diary* (May 1905)

Labour and the Liberals Although a fundamental principle of the new party was to oppose established elites, an early pragmatic advantage was gained by a secret agreement with the Liberals. Each party would withhold candidates from selected constituencies to unify the anti-Conservative vote. Through this stratagem the new party signalled its entrance onto the parliamentary stage in 1906 with twenty-nine MPs, who together took the title Parliamentary Labour Party (PLP). The election also saw the return of twenty-four Lib–Labs. For the first time there was a formidable working-class phalanx in Parliament. An early success was the 1906 Trades Disputes Act, reversing the Taff Vale Judgment. However, their prime object was to ingratiate themselves with the Establishment by demonstrating *responsible* behaviour (Miliband 1961: 28). At this

ELEVATION.

Wife (of newly-elected Working-Man M.P. to her Visitors). "'OW D'E DO, MRS. FUZBUSH? PRAY TAKE A CHERE, M'UM. THOUGH I HAM A LADY NOW, IT WON'T MAKE NO DIFFERENCE IN MY MANNERS!"

Source: Mary Evans Picture Library

stage the Liberals felt no threat and formed a highly distinguished government, laying the foundations of the British welfare state.

Yet these were turbulent times. The Liberal programme led to a dramatic confrontation with the House of Lords, resulting in the 1911 Parliament Act (see chapter 12) and near civil war over Ireland (see pp. 157–8). Labour became more closely wedded to the Liberals, a development derided by its left wing, which argued for a distinct identity. The first world war provided an opportunity for this.

War and the Inter-war Era

The year 1914 marks the beginning of the Liberals' decline (Wilson 1966). It was the party's misfortune to be in office at the outbreak of war. As prime minister, Herbert Asquith (1852–1928) became the leader of a coalition in 1915 but soon proved unequal to the task. 'His initiative, if he ever had any, was sapped by years of good living in high society' (Taylor 1965: 14) and, following a series of military defeats, he was ousted in 1916 by fellow Liberal David Lloyd George (1863–1945), who formed a new coalition with a Conservative majority.

For Labour, war provided a taste of office and a chance to demonstrate patriotic qualities. It shed its pacifist garb and MacDonald (supported by the pacifist ILP) resigned the leadership to be replaced by Arthur Henderson, who gained influence and was even included in the War Cabinet. However, dealings with international socialism led to his ejection in 1917, leaving him free to prepare for the greater role that Liberal disarray seemed to promise. With MacDonald and intellectuals such as Sidney Webb, Henderson drew up a new socialist constitution, including the famous *Clause Four*, with its commitment to public ownership of the means of production, distribution and exchange. It also recognized the importance of widening party membership, making provision for individuals to join constituency associations in their own right rather than as trade unionists. The 1918 conference formally approved a wide programme, *Labour and the New Social Order*, which was to be the mainspring for policy for the next thirty years (Pelling 1968: 44).

The birth of the 1922 Committee

The immediate aftermath of war proved disastrous for the Liberals. Lloyd George rushed into an opportunistic general election in 1918 by offering further coalition government. Coalition candidates were endorsed with a letter signed jointly by Lloyd George and Conservative leader Bonar Law, dubbed the 'coupon' by Asquith, leader of the independent Liberals, in sarcastic evocation of wartime rationing. Asquith lost his seat and only twenty-eight of his supporters were returned, but Lloyd George had played into the hands of the Conservatives, delivering his own party into a political netherworld.

Though faring badly against what was an anti-socialist alliance, Labour demonstrated its muscle by fielding 361 candidates, a considerable increase on its previous best of seventy-eight in 1910, and the freak circumstances gave little indication of real trends. The coalition proved unpopular and, after a string of by-election failures (mainly gains for Labour), Bonar Law agreed, at a momentous meeting at the Carlton Club in 1922, that it was time to bid farewell to Lloyd George before he destroyed the Conservatives as he had the Liberals. As a by-product, a new institution had been created: the Conservative 1922 Committee.

Labour: a viable government

The Liberals were left in disarray, candidates fighting the ensuing general election as either 'Lloyd George' or 'Asquith' Liberals. Labour's parliamentary strength rose to 142, giving it second-party status. The number of ILP-sponsored candidates reached 32, with an influx of intellectuals giving a wider appeal and more rhetorical virtuosity. It began to attract ambitious young Liberals despairing of the schism within their own party. With increased parliamentary strength, the heady possibility of taking over the reins of government could be contemplated. Ambitions were realized in late 1923 when Conservative prime minister Stanley Baldwin dissolved Parliament over tariff reform. Although the Liberals revived with 158 seats, Labour increased its presence to 191 (39 ILP). The single-issue nature of the election meant that, despite its 258 seats, the government had been rejected. The Liberals felt justified in supporting Labour, which momentously ruled for ten months as a **minority government**. Not surprisingly, so tenuous a period of office produced little reform and was attacked by socialist purists. This was a hard judgement on the leaders, who had been faced with a task hitherto the preserve of those with wealth, position and a solid tradition of parliamentary organization. Labour providing a government was, like the proverbial dog walking on its hind legs, remarkable for being done at all.

Labour versus the Establishment Yet the experience offered a stark illustration of establishment power. The government was undermined with alarmist propaganda and deceit, Anglo-Soviet relations being a particularly sensitive area. The final straw came in the Campbell case. The Attorney General's decision to drop sedition proceedings in a minor case against the editor of a small communist journal was fanned up as evidence of corruption. The Liberals grew nervous, withdrawing their support and forcing MacDonald to dissolve Parliament. The ensuing election campaign saw one of the shabbiest scandals of British politics – the Zinoviev letter (see p. 690). Chilling press warnings that a vote for Labour was a vote for a Soviet system saw the Establishment regain its hold on the tiller.

Yet the value of Parliament to working-class aspirations was underlined in the abysmal failure of the 1926 general strike, which renewed commitment to the Labour Party. With 288 seats it emerged from the 1929 election as the largest single party; it was a turning point in British politics. The Liberals had crossed the electoral Rubicon, the bias of the electoral system beginning to weigh against them. Their future seemed to lie only in some form of union with Labour and a second minority government was formed, though for the Liberals the embrace was to be that of the praying mantis.

> There are no professions he ever made, no pledges he ever gave to the country, and no humiliation to which he would not submit if they would allow him still to be called Prime Minister.
>
> Viscount Snowden on MacDonald, House of Lords speech (3 July 1934)

MacDonald's disgrace However, Labour was also to encounter troubled waters. From the outset the government was severely hamstrung by the Liberals in the Commons and the Conservatives in the Lords. Problems were exacerbated by economic depression, the Cabinet split over expenditure cuts (particularly unemployment benefit) as a condition of international loans and, on 23 August 1931, MacDonald resigned as prime minister. However, the following day he stunned colleagues by accepting the King's invitation to form a Conservative-dominated *National Government*. Together with some followers he was disowned by his party and in the coalition became a prisoner of his Cabinet. He was obliged to fight the next election in the grip of the coalition; 'National candidates' sought a 'doctor's mandate' to heal the country's maladies. Labour fared disastrously with only 46 seats and Conservatives dominated the new coalition. For Labour, these events marked the end of an era, fortunes remaining at a low ebb until 1935. Ex-barrister Clement Attlee (1883–1967) became leader, the first to lack genuine working-class credentials, and although not recovering its 1929 position, the party revived with 154 seats, while the Liberals wandered further into the wilderness.

The close of an era: the second world war   The next war led to Labour's further entrenchment. The party at first refused to join a coalition but later agreed, providing it would not be led by Neville Chamberlain, discredited for his appeasement policy. Thus it could claim to have brought Winston Churchill to power and did well in the apportionment of offices, with Attlee and Greenwood both in Churchill's first War Cabinet of five. Attlee became generally recognized as deputy prime minister.

At the fringe   During the inter-war years a number of small parties emerged. The Communist Party was founded in 1920 though its attempts to affiliate to Labour were rebuffed. Welsh nationalism was reflected in the establishment of Plaid Cymru in 1925. Nationalism was stronger in Scotland, coalescing into a

---

The Liberals: decline and fall

The collapse of the Liberal Party remains one of the cautionary tales of British politics. Despite a landslide victory in 1906 and a period of great reform, a decade after the outbreak of the war it had a parliamentary presence of only forty-two. There is no simple explanation. One historian likened the demise to that of a frail old gent, troubled by a variety of serious ailments (Labour, suffragettes, Ireland), with misfortunes compounded by a meeting with a rampaging bus (the war); his state of health is easy to diagnose but not the actual cause of death (Wilson 1966: 20–1). In this political whodunit a number of suspects may be assembled along with the butler in the drawing room:

◆   a congenital tendency to fragment;
◆   strong personalities whose ambitions overrode party interest;
◆   the prolonged fight with the suffragettes;
◆   the misfortune to be in office at the outbreak of the war;
◆   an inability to adapt to a harsher twentieth-century climate (Dangerfield 1936);
◆   the loss of radical reformers like Chamberlain, Dilke, Churchill and Lloyd George;
◆   a healing of the old social cleavage between landowners and capitalists, who began to unite as Conservatives (Taylor 1965: 172);
◆   failure to embrace leading Labour figures;
◆   a willingness to allow Labour to gather strength through electoral pacts (Wilson 1966: 19);
◆   defections to Labour in the inter-war years;
◆   the British electoral system.

party in 1928. In 1932, Oswald Mosley left the Conservatives to found the British Union of Fascists, which grew to over 30,000 members.

The Era of Consensus: the End of Ideology?

The masters now

We are the masters at the moment – and not only for the moment but for a very long time to come.

Lord Shawcross (member of 1945 Labour government), Commons speech (2 April 1946)

After the war Churchill agreed to an early general election. The 1945 result gave every indication of a revolution in British politics, a Labour landslide producing its first overall majority. The swing in the marginal seats introduced a new kind of Labour MP, drawn from the professions and giving the PLP a broader character. Despite a regime of severe post-war austerity, the government embarked upon an agenda intended to shake the foundations of economic and social life. The aura of office increased the leader's authority, further enhanced by trade union loyalty, but Attlee remained anxious for establishment respect, supporting capitalism, reining in socialistic expectations and even expelling extreme left-wingers.

The popular verdict prompted alarmist talk in middle-class drawing rooms and concentrated Conservative minds, enabling them again to demonstrate the protean qualities that preserved them throughout the era of modern politics. The architect of recovery was R. A. Butler, whose strategy was to challenge Labour at its own game by embracing the new welfare state and Keynesian economics (see p. 513).

By the end of its first hectic term the government was showing fatigue strains; many stalwarts were well past their prime, some stricken with illness and some dead. Furthermore, people were weary of austerity. In 1950 Labour narrowly clung to office but, lacking confidence, Attlee returned to the country the following year. This time, although Labour polled the most votes ever cast for a British party, the idiosyncrasies of the electoral system produced a Conservative majority. Butler had fashioned a bipartisan consensus that began a peace spoken of by the Archbishop of York in Shakespeare's *Henry IV* when 'both parties nobly are subdued, and neither party loser'.

Yet the tranquil consensus interpretation can be misleading; a minority within Labour, led by Aneurin Bevan, were never comfortable pitching the manifesto tent in the middle of the ideological field and prompted enervating infighting. After tenacious resistance, Attlee finally departed in 1955. His replacement, the sternly moderate Hugh Gaitskell, inherited worsening disciplinary problems. Moreover, the supportive trade union old guard was passing on and the largest union, the TGWU, had fallen under the leadership of left-wing Frank Cousins.

Some Conservatives were also unhappy with consensus. When Churchill finally stepped down, party and government seemed healthy and the succession passed to the smoothly aristocratic Anthony Eden. Yet despite an early election success in 1955, domestic problems mounted, and by spring 1956 his popularity rating had nose-dived from 70 to 40 per cent (Butler and Rose 1960: 36). He was certainly in no state to handle the Suez Crisis in 1956 (see p. 112), which traumatized the Establishment and split the party. Retiring in humiliation, Eden left the party in morbid contemplation of loss of office and possibly two decades in the wilderness.

Winds of change: the Macmillan era

> By far the most radical man I've known in politics wasn't on the Labour side at all – Harold Macmillan. If it hadn't been for the war he'd have joined the Labour Party…Macmillan would have been Labour Prime Minister, and not me.
>
> Clement Attlee, quoted in James Margach, *The Abuse of Power* (1981)

Eden's departure exposed the arcane process whereby the Conservatives chose (or rather, did not choose) their leader. Party elders conducted soundings and Harold Macmillan was preferred over the diligent Butler. Yet the choice was to prove inspired. With an Edwardian dilettantism concealing shrewd recognition of the consensus era, he was able not only to rebuild the party substructure but modernize its facade. He also restored self-confidence at home and repaired the damage to Anglo-American relations, earning the cartoonists' moniker 'Supermac'. Yet despite his success the right mistrusted him. In 1960 the Monday Club formed to commemorate 'Black Monday', when he made a celebrated speech on reform in racist South Africa.

> The wind of change is blowing through the continent. Whether we like it or not, this growth of national consciousness is a political fact.
>
> Harold Macmillan, speech in South African Parliament (3 Feb. 1960)

Labour in the wilderness The Suez crisis did not help Labour as expected. Although shocking the intelligentsia, a popular jingoism was shared by many Labour supporters (Pelling 1968: 118). In 1959 the Conservative majority reached 100, a third successive defeat leaving Labour reeling. The post-war inheritance seemed to have been squandered and younger members began to talk of policy revision. In *The Future of Socialism* (1956), Anthony Crosland argued that in an age of affluence public ownership was an anachronism. Gaitskell agreed and confronted the left in a momentous 1960 party conference, where he suffered an heroic failure to remove Clause Four from the party constitution. He was more successful in rejecting unilateral nuclear disarmament as party policy the following year.

> Do you think that we can become overnight the pacifists, unilateralists and fellow travellers that other people are?...There are some of us, Mr Chairman, who will fight, fight and fight again to save the party we love.
>
> Hugh Gaitskell, speech to Labour Party Conference (5 Oct. 1960)

The Night of the Long Knives The government had its own troubles. On 13 July 1962, beset by economic problems and falling popularity, a desperate Macmillan reversed the action of *Julius Caesar*, removing one-third of his Cabinet in the greatest bloodbath in the party's history: 'The Night of the Long Knives'. However, it was the exotic Profumo affair that brought the leader's failing touch to a wider, tabloid-devouring public. The party's image was also not helped by the early 1960s penchant for cynicism and satire. Oxbridge undergraduates began poking fun at the Establishment in the theatre (*Beyond the Fringe*), in the press (*Private Eye*) and on television (*That Was The Week That Was*).

Constitutional change in the Conservative Party

> He is used to dealing with estate workers. I cannot see how anyone can say he is out of touch.
>
> Lady Caroline Douglas-Home, speaking of her father's suitability as prime minister, quoted in the *Daily Herald* (21 Oct. 1963)

> As far as the 14th Earl is concerned, I suppose Mr Wilson, when you come to think of it, is the 14th Mr Wilson.
>
> Sir Alec Douglas-Home, BBC TV interview (21 Oct. 1963)

Macmillan's retirement through ill health in 1963 led to controversy. The patient Butler was again the natural heir, but the aristocratic Sir Alec Douglas-Home was raised from entombment in the House of Lords by renouncing his title. He continued the party's Tory rather than its Whig strain but seemed out of touch with the *zeitgeist*. In the 1964 election campaign, Harold Wilson, Labour's adroit new leader, mocked Home's aristocratic antecedents. Labour won a narrow majority of four; with a different leader the Conservatives

Scandal

The Profumo scandal arose from an intriguing *ménage à trois* involving a defence minister, John Profumo, who resigned in 1963, a high-society prostitute (Christine Keeler), a Russian naval attaché and a host of exotic bit players including Mandy Rice Davies (a prostitute), Stephen Ward (an alleged procurer of ladies for the gentry) and a mysterious man (believed to be a respected pillar of the Establishment) featured in photographs wearing a black mask (and little else). It is doubtful if the public were concerned with the security aspects of the affair. The massive newspaper coverage showed the main interest to lie in the intoxicating contemplation of hanky-panky in high places.

might have secured a fourth term. It was agreed that a ballot of the parliamentary party should become the basis for leadership selection and Home resigned.

The white heat of technology: the Wilson era

> The Labour Party is like a stage coach. If you rattle along at great speed everybody inside is too exhilarated or too seasick to cause any trouble. But if you stop everybody gets out and argues about where to go next.
>
> Harold Wilson, quoted in Leslie Smith, *Harold Wilson: The Authentic Portrait* (1964)

Having acceded to the Labour leadership in 1963 as a result of Gaitskell's unexpected death, Wilson brought a more conciliatory tone. His style was said to have been modelled on the charismatic and youthful President Kennedy.

TARGET PRACTICE

Reproduced by permission of *Punch*

By early 1966 he felt confident enough to ask for a stronger mandate, increasing Labour's overall majority to ninety-six. The influx was predominantly middle-class professionals, reinforcing Wilson's 'white heat of technology' rhetoric. Although the left were dissatisfied, the party began to look more like a 'natural' party of government during this optimistic decade – the 'swinging sixties'. There was some surprise when the government was ejected in 1970 and the glittering decade closed.

On the fringe

The Liberal Party During the consensus era the Liberal Party had been no more than a bit player, to some a buffoon, to others a figure of tragedy. In the bipartisan scenario it had no place, being neither regionally based nor radical.

Northern Ireland parties In 1955 Sinn Féin reappeared as a political force, contesting all twelve seats (although their three successful candidates were disqualified as felons). In 1970 the Social Democratic Labour Party (SDLP) was founded as the moderate vehicle of the Roman Catholic minority. At the same time, cracks began to appear in the Ulster Unionist Party, which had dominated Northern Ireland's Westminster representation: Ian Paisley, standing as a Protestant Unionist, captured the North Antrim seat (see chapter 6).

The Consensus Cracked: the 1970s

Heath: the rise and fall of Selsdon Man

Conscious of Wilson's appeal, the Conservatives applied Newton's Law of Motion to politics by attempting to counter with an equal and opposite force. Edward Heath, the first leader to be elected, was also the first hailing from the party's *petit bourgeois* strain. Although defeated in 1966, he worked to manufacture a technocratic image. A conference of businessmen and politicians at Croydon's Selsdon Park Hotel led to sightings of a new species of *Homo Conservatus* – 'Selsdon Man'. In 1970 Heath pulled off an unexpected *coup*, gaining an overall majority of thirty seats and surprising his own party as much as his opponents.

A long-standing Europhile, he led the nation into the EEC in 1973 and promoted a neoliberal economic agenda at home. However, inflation and rising unemployment led to policy reversals, branded 'U-turns' and taken as evidence of weakness. He also experienced unrelenting union hostility and, in February 1974, called an ill-timed general election to ask 'Who governs?' Although a majority supported him, the electoral system again thwarted voters. Yet Labour lacked an absolute majority and Heath flirted with the Liberals over a possible pact before conceding defeat. The indeterminate situation forced Wilson to return to the country in October, but an overall majority of only three did little to clarify the confusion. The efficacy of two-party politics was beginning to look doubtful.

In April 1976 Wilson shocked his party with his unexpected retirement. 'Making way for an older man', he bequeathed to James Callaghan bad union relations, economic crisis, IMF-imposed monetarism (see p. 513) and public-sector strikes. By-election defeats rendered the government increasingly fragile, until it could be sustained only with the life-support machine of the 1977–8 Lib–Lab pact. All was to culminate in some cold and gloomy months of 1978–9, entering the political record as the 'winter of discontent'. The media and some academics proclaimed a crisis of governability. The government finally lost a no-confidence vote in March 1979 and the Conservatives returned rejuvenated. Again they had used their time in the reformatory of opposition gainfully, emerging ready to take British party politics into a new era.

No such thing as society: the coming of Thatcherism

Any woman who understands the problems of running a home will be nearer to understanding the problems of running a country.

Margaret Thatcher, quoted in the *Observer* (8 May 1979)

Heath's humiliation in 1974 had led to further ordeal by election. On 10 February 1975 he was defeated by Margaret Thatcher, who was to seize radical initiatives on all fronts, the objective no less than a frontal assault on post-war social democratic orthodoxy. She was advised by think-tanks where, outside the formal party machinery, the alchemy of neoliberalism was brewed that was to alter the course of British politics (Riddell 1985: 31).

The 1979 general election was critical. The new leader avowed that (as a woman) she would be permitted just one chance, and the spoils of victory promised riches in the form of a gushing supply of North Sea oil, available for generous tax cuts or increased welfare, according to political fancy. Thatcher also recognized the increasing importance of the mass media and Saatchi and Saatchi were engaged to harness the skills of Madison Avenue. The relationship was to prove symbiotic. For the brothers Saatchi, company stock soared and the general election gave the Conservatives a 60-seat majority over Labour, and Britain's first woman prime minister.

The Thatcher Era: Fractured Consensus or New Centre?

The party begins to swing

Initially the new programme faltered; the Cabinet contained a large contingent of 'wets' inherited from Heath, who impeded progress. Unemployment rose and Thatcher's popularity sank to an all-time low for a prime minister. However, a lifeline came from the South Atlantic. The Falklands crisis (see p. 105) gave her the boost she needed. In an upsurge of popular chauvinism her ascendancy became virtually absolute. The years between 1983 and 1987 saw an ideological flowering, though people spoke not of conservatism but of 'Thatcherism'. The 1987 general election gave the Conservatives a third term with a majority over Labour of 147. However, the pattern of support was becoming increasingly concentrated in the prosperous south-east. In asserting 'there is no such thing as society', Thatcher had renounced the party's 'one-nation' appeal.

Labour in the 1980s

As if on a see-saw, the fortunes of Labour sank as Conservative stock rose. Michael Foot, once a doyen of the left, replaced Callaghan as leader in 1980. Like the New Right apostles, the hard left abhorred consensus; the years from Attlee to Callaghan were depicted as a betrayal. Although the trade unions had shifted leftwards, it was the constituency associations that became key centres for agitation. In 1973 the party had opened its doors to the far left and Militant Tendency had taken control of many local branches. In 1980, they succeeded in widening the leadership electorate beyond the parliamentary party to the wider membership and instigating compulsory reselection of all MPs. For some the pressures had become too great: choosing flight rather than fight, they founded the Social Democratic Party (SDP) in March 1981 to reclaim the centre ground.

Labour's 1983 manifesto was described from the right as 'the longest suicide note in history'. In the final stages of the campaign the party's support began to wilt before the new centrist force and only the quirks of the electoral system ensured its survival (figure 10.1). Foot resigned and Neil Kinnock, who had moved to the centre, was elected leader. Though fighting a much better campaign in 1987, the result was again failure.

On the fringe

In 1985 the Ecology Party relaunched itself as the Green Party and achieved some success in local elections. National Front (NF) support fell away, partly

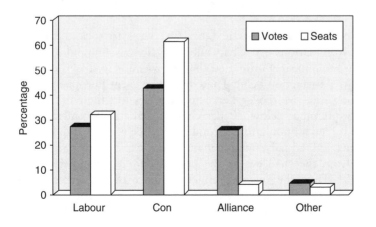

Figure 10.1
Disproportionate representation: votes and seats compared after the 1983 general election.

won over by Thatcher's brand of Conservatism, and internal splits saw the formation of the British National Party (BNP).

The rise of the third force The birth of the SDP, growing from a rib plucked from Labour's breast, appeared as one of the most dramatic party system developments during the 1980s. Dubbed 'the Gang of Four', its leading figures were seasoned parliamentarians. The rhetoric spoke of 'breaking the mould' of adversarial politics and re-introducing consensus through European-style co-alitions (supported by electoral reform). By late 1981, twenty-seven Labour MPs and one Conservative sailed under the new flag and a mass membership of some 70,000 had mushroomed. The fledgling party signalled its presence with some notable by-election victories, two returning Gang of Four members – Shirley Williams and Roy Jenkins.

These developments gave new heart to the Liberals and in 1983 they fought under a common Alliance banner with the SDP, gaining 26 per cent of the vote, only 2 per cent below Labour. Proportional representation would have bestowed around 160 seats, but they received a meagre 23 (figure 10.1). In 1987, they gained 22.6 per cent of the votes and only 22 seats. After this, Liberal leader David Steel opened discussions on complete merger, which took place in March 1988. Paddy Ashdown was elected leader and an all-member ballot adopted the name Social and Liberal Democrats.

The end of an era

New times, new realism It was becoming apparent to Labour leaders that the party was no longer tuned to the march of history. The New Right agenda was recognized throughout Europe by socialist parties in or out of government. Even the USSR had fallen under the *perestroika* of Mikhail Gorbachev, who established a surprising rapport with Thatcher. The hard left saw any attempt to don Thatcher's clothes as a perverse form of transvestism, but a policy of expulsion removed some 200 of them during the 1980s. By 1989 opinion polls were consistently placing Labour above the Conservatives.

The fall of Thatcher Events in late 1990 were to rock the Conservatives. Dramatic resignations by Chancellor Nigel Lawson and Geoffrey Howe (deputy prime minister) intimated that all was not well in Cabinet, the main source of dissatisfaction being Thatcher's lukewarm European vision and her domineering style. Moreover, fierce hostility towards the poll tax had seen her popularity plummet below 30 per cent. A leadership challenge by Michael Heseltine forced a humiliating second ballot (see p. 325) and, after consulting her Cabinet individually, Thatcher made the decision to resign. John Major emerged from the shadows as the new leader, rewarding Heseltine with a cabinet seat. Thus, the longest premiership since 1827, marked by three elect-oral triumphs and dramatic policy advances, was terminated not by the elect-orate nor the party rank and file, but by the Conservative establishment in

The Great Parliamentary Sausage Machine which sucked in public opinion at one end and spewed out popular politics at the other.

Roy Hattersley, retrospectively, on the Labour Listens initiative, in *Who Goes Home?* (1996: 284)

perhaps the most brutal political knifing in modern political history. However, the wound was to fester on into the next era.

> But there was one more duty I had to perform, and that was to ensure that John Major was my successor. I wanted – perhaps I needed – to believe that he was the man to secure and safeguard my legacy.
>
> Margaret Thatcher, *The Downing Street Years* (1993: 860)

The Major Years: Things Fall Apart

Major's succession continued the trend away from the party's aristocratic roots. In contrast to his two main rivals, he had left school at sixteen, experienced unemployment and advanced through local politics. The Major years were extraordinary ones for what had long been regarded as Britain's natural party of government. Without Thatcher's confrontational style or zeal, he seemed a more traditional Conservative. When Thatcher asserted that there was no such thing as 'Majorism' he did not dissent (Norton 1993a: 60). Yet he had accepted a poisoned chalice: his task to please both those who yearned for Thatcherism by other means and those wanting change. The 1992 general election victory was particularly important; like Heath in 1970, he could take considerable personal credit. Yet pragmatism led to vacillation, often described as dithering, and a flimsy majority left him vulnerable to rebel factions. The most trouble-some of these were the Eurosceptics (some even in his Cabinet), whom he described in an unguarded moment as 'bastards'.

Eurobastards Unlike Thatcher's 'wets', Major's enemies were emboldened with a sense of mission and armed by right-wing think-tanks. The fires were fanned by newspaper editors who did little to conceal personal dislike of the Prime Minister (Rogaly 1997). Ratification of the Maastricht Treaty was a tense process (chapter 5) and was not the end of his problems. The humiliation of 'Black Wednesday' (p. 516) was seen as a defining moment of a blighted premiership.

Tensions reached a crescendo in June 1995 when, in an astonishing resigna-tion of the party leadership, Major threw down the gauntlet, demanding that his critics 'put up or shut up'. While heavyweights shrank from the first ballot, Welsh Secretary John Redwood came forward. His demeanour had earned him the moniker of 'the Vulcan' (of the popular TV series *Star Trek*). Although the pretender was held off, with 111 MPs withholding support, Major's endorse-ment was only lukewarm. The vacuum left at the Welsh Office was quietly filled by a figure known mainly for his schoolboy speech at a party conference; unlike his predecessor, William Hague began to learn Welsh. Yet although the rebels had put up, they did not shut up. An EU ban on the export of British beef during the BSE crisis made their voices even shriller.

I'm still here.

Satirist and impressionist Rory Bremner as John Major proclaiming his greatest achievement.

'Back to Basics': low behaviour in high places

There was another zone of embarrassment. In 1993 Major had launched a 'Back to Basics' initiative, extolling traditional morality and social discipline. It could hardly have come at a worse time. Accusations of sexual and constitutional impropriety saw a lengthening roll of shame, including a motley collection for whom 'Back to Basics' meant back to the backbenches. By 1997 some 10 per cent of the parliamentary party had been involved in some kind of scandal (*Observer*, 30 March 1997). Other *causes célèbres* haunted the government. In March 1994 the Public Accounts Committee castigated the 'entanglement' of aid for the Malaysian Pergau Dam project with defence contracts, and the Arms-for-Iraq affair was subject to the 39-month Scott enquiry, which reported unfavourably on ministerial conduct in 1996.

The incredible shrinking majority In addition to by-election losses came defections to Labour and the Liberal Democrats, leaving Major with a majority of only two. The nine Ulster Unionist MPs found themselves in a pivotal position, reducing his room for manoeuvre in an area where he had moved adroitly – the Downing Street Declaration (see p. 162).

A natural party of government? The polls showed the Conservatives entering the 1997 campaign further behind their rival than any party since 1832. With Labour and the Liberal Democrats giving a clear run to journalist Martin Bell in Neil Hamilton's Tatton constituency, it was impossible for the party to put sleaze behind it. In its Euro-angst it appeared to have sacrificed its historic strength – unity. The Eurosceptics were mainly Thatcherites; indeed, as Baroness Thatcher in the Lords, the lady was still amongst them.

New Labour, New Consensus

We're alright!
We're alright!
We're alright!
We're alright!

Neil Kinnock at the 1992 pre-election Sheffield rally

Labour's fortunes had reached a nadir in 1992, a fourth successive defeat leading many to ponder whether Britain had become a one-party state. Some declared Kinnock's triumphalist behaviour at an eve-of-poll rally in Sheffield to have snatched defeat from the jaws of victory (Heffernan and Marqusee 1992), but he had moved the party a long way. He resigned and his successor, John Smith, slid into place to continue the work. In September 1992, two of Smith's biggest critics, Bryan Gould and Dennis Skinner, were thrown off the NEC in favour of two fresh-faced modernizers, Tony Blair and Gordon Brown.

The decline in union membership and the shrinkage of the traditional working class argued for a broader appeal. The spectre of the 'winter of discontent' could be exorcized only by 'modernizing' the relationship with the unions. This was faced at the 1993 conference (see chapter 11), where Smith gained agreement for the one member, one vote (OMOV) principle for candidate selection. The party extended its commitment to Scottish and Welsh devolution, a Bill of Rights, reform of the Lords and a referendum on PR for Westminster.

However, May 1994 saw Smith's fatal heart attack and three leadership contenders emerged: deputy leader Margaret Beckett, Tony Blair and John Prescott. Most importantly, Shadow Chancellor Gordon Brown agreed to curb his own ambition to avoid splitting the modernizing vote. The result came as no surprise, Blair being supported by all sections of the electoral college. The contest had not proved divisive and the scale of the victory endorsed modernization. Harmony was further promoted by the election of John Prescott, trusted by traditionalists, as deputy leader.

Labour Party leaders

1906 Keir Hardie	1921 J. R. Clynes	1963 Harold Wilson
1908 Arthur Henderson	1922 Ramsay MacDonald	1976 James Callaghan
1910 George Barnes	1931 Arthur Henderson	1980 Michael Foot
1911 Ramsay MacDonald	1932 George Lansbury	1983 Neil Kinnock
1914 Arthur Henderson	1935 Clement Attlee	1992 John Smith
1917 W. Adamson	1955 Hugh Gaitskell	1994 Tony Blair

Trust me, I'm a spin doctor

Unlike Kinnock, or even Major, Blair sported no working-class credentials. Educated at Fettes College, Edinburgh, one of Scotland's foremost schools, he had progressed via St John's College, Oxford, to become a barrister, entering Parliament as MP for Sedgefield in 1983. Like all his generation he was starved of office but had shadowed some key areas, including Treasury and Economic Affairs, Trade and Industry, Energy, Employment and Home Affairs. Just forty, and with a barrister's verbosity, a careerist wife (Cherie), two sons and a daughter, he was a spin doctor's dream.

The modernizers had actually been impatient with Smith (Kavanagh 1997b), and if Blair had a model it was that of Labour's arch-enemy, Margaret Thatcher. Master of the soundbite, he spoke of 'fairness not favours' for the unions, no more 'tax and spend' on the economy and, on Labour's other Achilles' heel, he would be 'tough on crime and tough on the causes of crime'. In industrial disputes he studiously withheld support from strikers while seeking the confidence of business leaders, even wooing media baron Rupert Murdoch. The mission was to reassure 'middle England'. Blair was even willing to sound a Eurosceptical note.

Perhaps the most symbolic item of Blair's agenda was the rewriting of the venerated Clause Four, which was looking more dated than ever. On 29 April 1995, at a special conference at Methodist Central Hall, Westminster, where seventy-five years earlier the original clause had been adopted, the party voted two-to-one to back reform. The replacement clause called for 'power, wealth

Table 10.1 The increase in support for the Labour Party, 1992–1996

Category	1992	1996
Members	279,000	400,000
Donors	3,500	71,000
Sponsors	30,000	60,000

Source: Data from Labour Party NEC reports.

and opportunity to be in the hands of the many not the few', but also extolled the 'enterprise of the market'. Although the unions were only narrowly in favour, the constituency parties gave overwhelming support.

Within a year of Blair taking the helm, party membership had risen by 40,000 and continued to increase (table 10.1), and his own popularity dwarfed that of Major and Ashdown (Dorey 1995: 258). He took a tough line with dissidents at both national and local level. In March 1997 the modernization strategy went a stage further, an historic pre-election deal with the Liberal Democrats promising a referendum on electoral reform.

For critics, 'New Labour' showed more froth than substance. The spin doctors dispensed with ideology to follow the beacon of the opinion polls. At their head was Peter Mandelson (grandson of earlier Labour moderate Herbert (later Lord) Morrison), and Blair's press guru, Alastair Campbell. The acid test arrived in May 1997, but the size of the landslide victory, though suggested by the polls, came as a shock. The Conservatives were entirely banished from the Celtic fringes (figure 10.2). Critics argued that their lemming-like behaviour

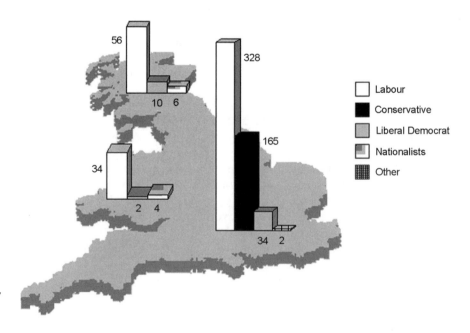

Figure 10.2 Conservative meltdown: the national distribution of MPs after the 1997 election.

had guaranteed a Labour victory, but Labour's modernizers saw it as an overwhelming endorsement. If symbols were needed they were aplenty. At the 1998 Labour conference, avowedly the last at Blackpool, with its old Labour odour of fish and chips, delegates wore name badges sponsored by a supermarket chain (though some refused), while journalists from the radical magazine *Red Pepper* were banned.

Meltdown

The Conservatives' worst defeat since 1832 meant the end for Major; within hours hats were in the ring. However, a record seven cabinet ministers had fallen in the election, including heir apparent Michael Portillo. The final ballot was a bitter contest between the young William Hague and the veteran Kenneth Clarke, in which Euroscepticism took precedence over all else (Alderman 1998). As with the Thatcher and Major elections, it was the least-feared candidate who won (p. 326).

Unlike Labour, the Conservatives did not consider the photogenic qualities of their leader. If Blair was a spin doctor's dream, William Hague, with a flat Yorkshire intonation and said to look preternaturally aged, was perhaps a nightmare. At thirty-six he was the youngest leader since Pitt the Younger, his experience confined to junior positions in social security before becoming Welsh Secretary. Educated at a South Yorkshire comprehensive, he had arrived at Oxford University preceded by a *wunderkind* reputation following his schoolboy party conference speech. Effectively a career politician, he had worked as a political adviser and consultant before winning a 1989 by-election in Richmond, North Yorkshire (adjacent to Sedgefield, constituency of another ambitious politician, Tony Blair).

Thus began what some commentators saw as the Conservatives' 'most futile period of opposition in the last one hundred years' (Collings and Seldon 2001: 624). Hague inherited a broken-backed misalliance with a poor showing in

Table 10.2 The party's over? Attitudes towards the Conservative Party, 1997

Statement	Percentage of respondents agreeing
A party that does not have a bright future	74
A party with very few new ideas	84
A party without a clear sense of direction	75
A party that lacks strong leaders	81
An out-of-date party	77
A party that does not look after the interests of ordinary people	74

Source: Gallup Political Index, October 1997.

Conservative Party leaders since 1900

1900 Marquis of Salisbury	1955 Anthony Eden
1902 Arthur Balfour	1956 Harold Macmillan
1911 Andrew Bonar Law	1963 Alec Douglas-Home
1921 Austen Chamberlain	1965 Edward Heath
1922 Andrew Bonar Law	1975 Margaret Thatcher
1923 Stanley Baldwin	1990 John Major
1937 Neville Chamberlain	1997 William Hague
1940 Winston Churchill	2001 Iain Duncan Smith

opinion polls (table 10.2). With some of his backbenchers showing barely disguised derision (*Sunday Times*, 21 Sept. 1997), his chalice contained more hemlock than had Major's. One of the party's key thinkers, David Willetts (1998), argued that they should learn from their previous major defeats in 1906 and 1945 and embrace the new agenda, but Hague was to cling to much of the Thatcher agenda.

Liberal Democrats: no room in the centre

The Liberal Democrats had enjoyed a string of by-election successes and during the 1992 campaign Ashdown had consistently outscored the other leaders. The party itself rose from 15 per cent in the opening opinion polls to win 17.8 per cent of all votes in the election. Capturing the 'normal' level of third-party support, they remained a serious force, particularly in marginal constituencies (Stevenson 1993: 141). With twenty MPs, a rising membership and a more secure financial position, the party was poised for progress. Further by-election successes provided more cause for optimism. In addition, with two seats in the 1994 elections, there was a breakthrough onto the European stage. (The Greens, with the same percentage of votes, gained none.)

However, Labour's shift had eliminated the vacuum at the centre. Moreover, Labour was raiding their wardrobe as well as that of the Conservatives. Abandoning their policy of 'equidistance', the Liberal Democrats agonized as to how far they should 'snuggle up' to New Labour, as advocated by Shirley Williams and Roy Jenkins, the very people who had wanted to break the two-party mould. Perhaps the party had little future except as a home for the disenchanted (Kavanagh 1996: 44). However, the 1997 result produced the biggest third-party breakthrough of post-war history, their forty-six seats promising to become significant should Labour cohesion melt in the heat of internal friction.

On the fringe

Nationalists The 1992 general election saw nationalist support remaining stable. With four seats Plaid Cymru was one up on 1987 and the Scottish

Nationalists (SNP) maintained their three. A swing of 19 per cent in the Monklands East by-election saw the SNP almost stealing John Smith's old seat. As the Major term progressed, the significance of the Ulster Unionists increased until, just before the 1997 election, they held the balance of power. They were courted not only by Major, but also Blair (*The Times*, 17 Feb. 1997). In 1997, Plaid Cymru held their four seats and the SNP gained another three. However, devolution was to mean a changed climate for the nationalists (see chapter 6).

Single-issue parties Although these are rare in Britain, the strength of Euro-sceptic feeling led to the formation of two parties committed to withdrawal from the EU. The United Kingdom Independence Party (UKIP) set up in 1993 was initially overshadowed by the Referendum Party of wealthy Eurosceptic businessman Sir James Goldsmith. Money (£20 million) tried very hard to talk as citizens were deluged with material, including video tapes, warning of a European super-state. The party's first conference in October 1996 was adorned by famous figures including actor Edward Fox, who had played an early Eurosceptic, the would-be assassin of General de Gaulle, in *The Day of the Jackal*. Yet despite polling over 800,000 votes, the lack of regional concentration meant a trail of lost deposits for most of the 547 candidates. After Goldsmith's death, the field was left open to UKIP, which absorbed many Referendum activists and built up a membership of almost 10,000. In 1999, with the advent of PR for the European elections, it gained three MEPs, but at the 2001 general election, all but six of its 428 candidates were to lose their deposits.

The Greens mainly made their presence felt as a pressure group, greening the agendas of the main parties. As with UKIP, it was PR that gave them real opportunities for a share in power – two MEPs, one MSP and three Greater London councillors were to carry the green flag.

The far left and right Life was bleak on the far left. Britain's Communist Party had declined since the 1950s, relaunching itself in 1991 as the Democratic Left with some 6,000 members – more a pressure group than a party. Militant Tendency and the Socialist Workers' Party also found little resonance with the New Labour mood. In January 1996, former NUM leader Arthur Scargill severed his Labour connections to form a Socialist Labour Party but gained no seats in 1997. At the other extreme, the BNP caused ripples by winning a council seat in east London, in 1993, and in 2001 it was to gain over 16 per cent of the vote in Oldham.

From Butskillism to Blatcherism?

Finally back in power, Labour hit the ground running. The Queen's Speech in May 1997 detailed twenty-two bills covering a wide range of policy areas. Its publicity machine spun added gloss around the package and within a year much legislation had been passed and battalions of task forces were examining numerous other policy options. However, the government had chosen a procrustean bed in its promise to preserve Conservative spending limits. It was certainly unusual for a party to promise to do the same as its opponents! It would be impossible to find a better indication of a return to consensus politics – Thatcherism by other means. The economy would be led by the market, shaped and refined by the state rather than regulated (Gamble and Wright 1997).

The policies were justified variously by reference to Christian values, communitarianism, stakeholding and the 'third way' (see p. 53). Yet New Labour could also be charged with having pursued a Downsian strategy (p. 277) of vote maximization with little regard for principle. The party's old guard, and some left-leaning intellectuals, appeared uneasy with a project that mirrored past 'betrayals' of socialist ideals. However, it could also be argued that New Labour had come to terms with the modern world and would not repeat the mistake of promising much in opposition only to disappoint in office. In a globalizing economy, Blair could argue that debates about the state versus the market were no longer appropriate platforms for economic thinking (Kenny and Smith 1997: 227–8).

> Dear Tony, I can scarcely believe I am writing this letter to you.
>
> Opening of Peter Mandelson's resignation letter (Dec. 1998)

Spinning out of control Yet in the midst of his ascendancy Blair was to be reminded of his mortality. It would have been difficult to have imagined a more destabilizing shock than that of December 1998, when the arch-priest of New Labour was brought down. Peter Mandelson had many enemies inside the party as well as without, and revelations that he had failed to disclose a £373,000 loan from a fellow minister, millionaire Geoffrey Robinson, led to the resignation of both, depriving Blair of two icons of the New Labour project; some said that one had invented it and the other paid for it.

However, after a decent interval Blair brought his trusted confidant back, replacing the discredited Mo Mowlam as Northern Ireland Secretary in 1999. However, when Mandelson was forced to go a second time it began to look like carelessness. This time the issue concerned an application for a British passport for Indian millionaire Srichand Hinduja who had donated £1 million to the Millennium Dome project. In January 2001, with a general election looming, Blair was forced to let his accident-prone colleague return again to the back benches (though his informal presence at the high table remained).

Mandelson was a fervent Europhile and his fall allowed Gordon Brown to lay down tough conditions for Britain's entry into the eurozone (see p. 519), a policy area where the rumour mill found much tension between Chancellor and Prime Minister. The unconcealed ambition of the party was to secure a second term and Brown was happy to be characterized as the iron chancellor; his budgetary watchword was always prudence. With rising house prices, buoyant retail sales and low borrowing costs, the economy delivered the feelgood factor for most people. Under Alastair Campbell, the party maintained a generally good relationship with the press, with many ghosted articles from ministers.

Opposition from the left caused little concern, since the key constituency for New Labour was the territory of middle England occupied by 'Mondeo man'. There were, however, occasional alarm bells, as when Blair's speech to the Women's Institute in June 2000 was interrupted by slow hand-clapping. Opponents claimed this to be a significant straw in the wind but they were, indeed, clutching at straws.

Despite some near scandals over party donations, allegations of cronyism (see p. 588) (Doig 2001) and policy problems in areas such as public transport and the foot-and-mouth crisis, government popularity remained stable throughout the first term at around 48 per cent (compared with 32 per cent for the Conservatives and 16 per cent for the Liberal Democrats). Most striking was the unvaryingly buoyant standing of Blair himself. The Prime Minister thrilled the tabloids by fathering another son, though was embarrassed when his elder son Euan was found drunk in Leicester Square. On the eve of the 2001 general election an *Observer*/ICM poll gave Blair an 18 per cent lead over Hague (50 to 32) on the question 'Who would get the best deal for Britain in Europe?', the one area the Conservative leader had tried to make his own.

The Liberal Democrats Paddy Ashdown had been practising 'constructive opposition' with the goal of a place at the high table of power. However, in January 1999 he stunned his party by announcing his forthcoming retirement. Some believed his decision reflected frustration at a loss of momentum on electoral reform and alliance with Labour, where his ally had been the dis-credited Mandelson. Charles Kennedy assumed the leadership and there was further cooling in the relationship with Labour.

Time to call it a day? With Blair having so successfully plundered the centre-right wardrobe, the Conservatives could find little to wear. Could the party rebuild its membership base without clearly defined and appealing policies (Peele 1998: 145)? It had been a party of empire but this was gone. It had been a party of the Union but had no MPs in either Wales or Scotland, and devolution was now a bitter pill that could only be swallowed. It had been a party of middle-class values but was now mired in sleaze. It had been a party of constitutional stability but Labour was instigating change on many fronts. In its whiggism and neoliberalism it had been a party of world trade but was now set in opposition to the single currency. Indeed, this was the one area where Hague had positioned the party decisively, with a party referendum in September

Liberal/Liberal Democrat Party leaders since 1900	
1900 Henry Campbell-Bannerman	1956 Jo Grimond
1908 Herbert Asquith	1967 Jeremy Thorpe
1926 David Lloyd George	1976 David Steel
1931 Herbert Samuel	1988 Paddy Ashdown
1935 A. Sinclair	1999 Charles Kennedy
1945 Clement Davies	

1998 ruling out the single currency for two parliaments. If a national referendum were to be held on the euro, the party could split asunder. The last time this had happened was over the Corn Laws in 1846, which had been followed by twenty-seven wilderness years.

An historic second term

The 2001 general election was delayed until 7 June by the foot-and-mouth crisis, making the campaigns protracted and wearisome. Voters signalled their interest with the lowest turnout since the granting of the universal franchise. However, New Labour was buoyed by the opinion polls and the press (see p. 261). The polls were right, the 413 seats, gained with only 42 per cent of the vote, meant a loss of only six.

It was an appalling night for the Conservatives, who managed to gain one solitary seat, raising their Commons force to 166. They argued that they had been victims of the very low turnout, but in August the BBC removed this crumb of comfort by publishing a survey of non-voters revealing that, had they gone to the polls, they would have overwhelmingly supported Labour.

The campaign, described by Michael Heseltine as 'extremist and pathetic', had centred largely on Hague's instinctive opposition to entering the eurozone. He had also promised tax reductions, £8-billion cuts in public expenditure, and internment camps for asylum seekers, and had spoken darkly of Britain becoming a foreign land. Critics accused him of bringing racism into the contest and the Liberal Democrats blamed him for racial unrest in some cities. Appearing out of touch on issues such as multiculturalism, marriage and sexual identity, the defeat was a damning verdict on Hague's leadership and he took an immediate decision to resign, securing for himself an unenviable place in history as the first Conservative leader for eighty years not to have been prime minister.

From Ramsay MacDonald to Ronald McDonald: Labour as a party of government Given the party's history, the June 2001 victory was a watershed for Labour and for British politics. Not only was the prized second term secured, it was done in style. Labour appeared to have established itself as a party business could trust, the change symbolized at the September 2001 conference, which displayed the sign of the fast-food chain McDonalds inside the hall. However, this was not the Labour Party of old, and the cost of victory was disenchantment in the old heartlands. Electoral support in the most predominantly working-class areas had fallen by 4 percentage points, while holding up in the middle-class seats (Curtice 2001). At the same time, relations were becoming less harmonious with the trade unions, which were electing more left-wing leaders. The rift was symbolized by John Prescott's decision in 2002, after a lifetime's membership, to leave the RMT in response to demands that he toe the union line in Parliament.

Liberal Democrats

An *Observer*/ICM poll (*Observer*, 3 June 2001) on the eve of the 2001 election revealed hundreds of thousands prepared to vote tactically to unseat Conservatives where the Liberal Democrats were in second place. In the event, a 2 per cent increase in their vote gave the Liberal Democrats six more seats (bringing their total to fifty-two). Their new leader, Charles Kennedy, was judged to have acquitted himself well and erased a reputation for lethargy.

Who's for the poisoned chalice? The Tory leadership election

Hague's decision to fall upon his sword was an additional blow for the demoralized party and plunged it into an unwanted leadership contest using an untried method of election (see p. 326). Within days candidates were marshalling their forces. The most likely heir apparent, Michael Portillo, now back in Parliament, launched his bid with a reception in a glitzy London restaurant. He was joined in the battle by the less than charismatic figures of Iain Duncan Smith, David Davis and Michael Ancram. After much deliberation, the old war horse, Kenneth Clarke, who had languished on the back benches during the Hague regime, joined the race.

With charisma to spare and, despite relative youth, considerable government experience, Portillo exuded an aura of success. With something of Pauline conversion on social policy, a confession of some homosexual experimentation in his youth and a balanced position on Europe, he seemed the man most likely to heal the fatal rift and he began as the tipsters' favourite. However, knives were sharpened as high ambition met low intrigue in the Westminster hothouse. The show of naked ambition, and his style, Spanish ancestry and homosexuality were all cited by his enemies. Those enemies also had friends in the Tory press, which described him as the cannabis and Clause 28 candidate. It was stiletto heels as well as knives when Amanda Platell, Hague's media guru, unveiled her campaign video diary on TV, alleging that Portillo and 'his people' had systematically undermined their fallen leader.

Amidst growing heat, the final ballot on Tuesday 17 July delivered the knockout blow. The two contenders to go before the wider party membership would be Clarke and Duncan Smith. There were strong suspicions that some of the latter's supporters had voted for Clarke to keep Portillo from second place. A shocked Portillo announced his exit from front-line politics. Once again, the 1922 Committee had rejected the candidate most feared by opponents. In the final stages, which involved all party members, things began to get dirty, with two recent leaders attacking each other – Major backing Clarke and Thatcher supporting Duncan Smith. On Thursday 23 August the candidates faced each other in a BBC *Newsnight* debate, but their lacklustre performances made Portillo's rejection all the more poignant.

Victory went to Duncan Smith. It was an extraordinary turn of events; the new leader had been one of the Eurosceptic 'bastards' who had helped make the party unelectable in 1997. In the leadership race Clarke described him as a classic Tory 'hanger and flogger'. Born in 1954, he had joined the party in 1981 and was elected MP for Chingford in 1992, perhaps the natural heir of Norman Tebbit. Indeed, his predecessor was to praise him as a 'normal man', an innuendo to damage Portillo. Son of a Battle of Britain pilot, married to the Hon. Elizabeth Wynne Fremantle, Sandhurst educated and with a military background, he was in social terms a break with the past three leaders. However, his ministerial experience was limited to service as shadow social security secretary during 1997–9.

The new leader's first party conference in October 2001 was overshadowed by the terrorist attack on the World Trade Center. After the humiliating electoral defeat it would have been a low-key affair anyway. Yet, despite his hard right reputation, his message was that the party must cast off the shroud of Thatcherism. Ironically, he sought to paint the party as one with a place for all races, sexes, religions and sexual orientation – very much the agenda of the vanquished Portillo.

Evaluating Two-party Democracy

Under the influence of the first-past-the-post electoral system, a broadly **bi-partisan** politics has evolved in Britain, held by apologists to have features peculiarly favourable to democracy and contrasted with West European multi-partism. Much writing has extolled virtues such as strong single-party govern-ment and alternation of governments in office. Yet these virtuous features can be subject to sceptical review.

The party system in Parliament

The fact that two parties dominate Parliament does not mean that single-party government has invariably been the case. During the twentieth century, Britain experienced some twenty-one years of rule by a combination of parties (see p. 262). Moreover, there have been periods when a governing party has lacked an absolute majority, being sustained only by an agreement with another party; as recently as 1997, Major needed Ulster Unionist support.

The notion that two-partyism produces frequent alternation in office is also unconvincing. Even in the post-war era the Conservatives sustained the claim to be the natural party of government, with the lion's share of office (see figure 9.7). The Labour Party has held office since 1997 and can be expected to make a strong play to continue for a third term. Moreover, the growing strength of the Liberal Democrats since 1997 questions the two-party model itself.

The parties in the country

Looking beyond Westminster, there is even less evidence of a two-party culture. Since the 1970s, the memberships of the centre parties have been by no means inconsequential. They also contain some of the most enthusiastic workers, the Liberal Democrats bringing local activism back into fashion. In terms of electoral support, ever since the emergence of Labour there has been a greater party diversity in the country than at Westminster. Not until the immediate post-war decades did Labour and Conservatives begin to carve up the popular vote, and the period was brought to an end with a groundswell of support for the nationalists and centre parties. In 1983 and 1987 the Alliance polled around a quarter of the total votes, slightly less than Labour (28 and 30 per cent, respectively) and over half the number polled by the victorious Conserva-tives. Another measure of party support is local government, where during the 1980s and 1990s the 'third party' became second to Labour.

The bipartisan nature of Parliament has been in large measure a distortion produced by the electoral system. If Labour honours its pledge for a referendum on electoral reform for Westminster, Britain could come to an historical watershed; this is one of the most significant constitutional issues since 1832. Parties waiting in the wings would hear their cue, soliloquies and dialogues perhaps giving way to turbulent crowd scenes and a rather more colourful *dramatis personae*.

Key points

- A political party is an association formed for the purpose of taking power by constitutional means.
- Although parties often claim to reflect ideologies, the quest for electoral support weakens this link.
- The early British parties were parliamentary cadres.
- Modern parties are *mass* organizations, with thousands of members.
- The first mass parties emerged as a result of franchise extensions.
- The Labour Party was established in 1900 by a merging of the trade unions and certain socialist groups. It was not intended to be a revolutionary party.
- The post-war party system has seen an era of consensus; the cracking of the consensus; the rise of a new centre party and the emergence of a new consensus in many policy areas in the 1990s.
- The view that Britain has a two-party system is simplistic. The two main parties have not shared office equally, and in the country, voting patterns do not mirror the polarization found in Parliament.
- The electoral system is a key factor in creating the two-party system, and a change to PR could be expected to make a difference.

Review your understanding of the following terms and concepts

1922 Committee	Gang of Four	single-issue party
adversary politics	mass party	single-party system
bipartisan politics	Militant Tendency	sleaze
Black Wednesday	minority government	Tory
cadre party	multi-party system	two-party system
consensus	Night of the Long Knives	Whig
Eurosceptic	party system	'winter of discontent'
Fabianism	Profumo scandal	
fringe party	registration society	

Assignment

Study the extract from *Politics* and answer the following questions.

		Mark (%)
1	What is 'Old Labour'?	25
2	'Our values do not change. Our commitment to a different vision of society stands intact. But the ways of achieving that vision must change' (Tony Blair). Discuss.	50
3	Does New Labour put vote maximization before all else?	25

What's new about 'New Labour'?

... Essentially there is nothing new about New Labour. ... That is, the continuities between it and so-called 'Old Labour' are more significant than the cleavages between the two. Times have changed and British social democracy perceived that it needed to modernise itself to catch up with these 'new times'. ... Perhaps one quote from Blair is sufficient to illustrate this: 'Our values do not change. Our commitment to a different vision of society stands intact. But the ways of achieving that vision must change. The programme we are in the process of constructing entirely reflects our values. Its objectives would be instantly recognisable to our founders ...' So the 'arch-modernisers' also emphasise continuities. What is it then, according to them, that makes it different to 'Old Labour'? There is the obvious 'modernisation' element. ... However, there is also the question of *which* 'Old Labour' they are comparing themselves with? If it is the founders of the party and the 1945 Labour government, they cite continuities. However, if it is the corporatism of Wilson and Callaghan ... or the [Bennite period up to the early 1980s] then they are very keen indeed to put as much distance as possible between New Labour and Old.

Extract from Paul Allender, 'What's new about "New Labour"?' *Politics*,
Vol. 21(1), 2001, pp. 56–62.

Questions for discussion

1   Explain the concept of 'party system'. How would you characterize that of Britain?
2   What did Disraeli mean when he spoke of Peel stealing the clothes of the Whigs?

3   Identify the factors that led to Labour supplanting the Liberals as the main challenger to the Conservatives.

4   'The first-past-the-post electoral system will defeat any attempt to establish multi-party politics in Britain.' Examine this statement in the light of developments since the 1980s.

5   Examine the effects of the two world wars on the evolution of the Labour Party.

6   Explain the reasons for the era of party consensus following the second world war.

7   Account for the breakdown in the post-war consensus.

8   How radical was Blair's modernization of the Labour Party?

9   Have the Labour victories of 1997 and 2001 marked a new age of consensus politics?

10   'What if?' Give an account of British politics since 1997 as if the Conservatives had won the election.

Topic for debate

This house believes history shows that a socialist party can never expect power in Britain.

Further reading

Barrett Brown, M. (2001) *The Captive Party: How Labour was Taken Over by Capital.*
Critique of New Labour and its new friends.

Blake, R. (1998) *The Conservative Party from Peel to Thatcher.*
Latest version of classic text.

Crewe, I. and King, A. (1997) *SDP: The Birth, Life and Death of the Social Democratic Party.*
The life and times of the 'Gang of Four'. Explores the role of personalities, rivalries and non-rational factors in the destiny of parties. A large book about a small party!

Kavanagh, D. (1997) *The Reordering of British Politics: Politics after Thatcher.*
A clear mapping of the shifting sands of post-Thatcher politics.

Ludlum, S. and Smith. M. (eds) (2001) *New Labour in Government.*
Examines Labour's modernization project and its link with 'old Labour'.

MacIver, D. (ed.) (1996) *The Liberal Democrats.*
With contributions from academics and party members, this helps fill a gap in the analysis of British parties.

Norton, P. (ed.) (1996) *The Conservative Party.*
Essays by academics and a Conservative MP. Editor's opening chapter probes deeper philosophical grounding.

Pelling, H. and Reid, A. J. (1997) *A Short History of the Labour Party*, 11th edn.
Economical account of the rise of the party with clear narrative.

Rawnsley, A. (2000) *Servants of the People: The Inside Story of New Labour.*
By an astute political journalist. A story those inside might have preferred not told.

Shaw, E. (1996) *The Labour Party since 1945: Old Labour, New Labour.*
Balanced assessment of post-war Labour governments and their commitment to social democracy. Objectively critical of New Labour.

Toynbee, P. and Walker, D. (2001) *Did Things Get Better? An Audit of Labour's Successes and Failures.*
Title says it all. Sometimes yes, sometimes no.

Wilson, T. (1966) *The Downfall of the Liberal Party 1914–1935.*
Probes a key event in modern history.

For light relief

Julian Critchley, *A Bag of Boiled Sweets.*
This autobiography from a perennial backbencher is also a social history of the Conservative Party.

George Dangerfield, *The Strange Death of Liberal England.*
Reveals apparent calm of Edwardian England as a facade concealing seething forces leading towards civil war.

Liz Davies, *Through the Looking Glass: A Dissenter Inside New Labour.*
Old Labour strikes back. One-time member of Labour's NEC, Liz Davies chronicles her bleak experiences amidst 'control freakery' and skulduggery.

Benjamin Disraeli, *Sybil, or: the Two Nations.*
Celebrates the ideas of Disraeli's Toryism; a romance with a Chartist background.

David Hare, *Absence of War.*
Play showing the trials and frustrations of a Labour leader. Said to be based on Kinnock experience.

Scandal.
Video/film of the Profumo affair.

Simon Walters, *Tory Wars: Conservatives in Crisis.*
A light-hearted and entertaining read, packed with inside information exposing the internal machinations, dirty tricks and bitter enmities within a party that some believe may be in its death throes.

On the net

http://www.conservative-party.org.uk
http://www.libdem.org.uk
http://www.labour.org.uk
In addition to current organization and policies, these sites include considerable historical information. Use a search engine or some of the academic political resources sites to track down information on numerous smaller parties.

11

Inside the Parties: Masses, Leaders and Powers Behind Thrones

Having examined the development of political parties and the party system in broad terms we turn inward to the organization and character of the parties themselves. The chapter falls into three main parts. The first section focuses on the anatomy of the mass party organization. The second examines internal party dynamics: cohesion, power relationships, control mechanisms, and the basic relationship between mass membership and leaders. The final sections analyse the location of the parties within the structure of power in society at large, addressing the sensitive issue of funding: who pays the piper and do they call the tune?

Anatomy of the Mass Party

In essence, the main British parties comprise three elements: a parliamentary cadre of MPs, a central bureaucracy and a large mass membership of voluntary workers in the country (figure 11.1). Chapter 10 showed that in the Conservative and Liberal parties the parliamentary cadres came first, while the Parliamentary Labour Party (PLP) was created by the mass movement. The emergence of the Social Democratic Party (SDP) in the 1980s was, like that of the older parties, the result of Westminster-based initiative, but it quickly worked to build a mass membership. The parties have organizational similarities because they all exist in the same environment and must fulfil certain necessary functions to survive. They often show a tendency to copy each other, a phenomenon termed 'contagion'.

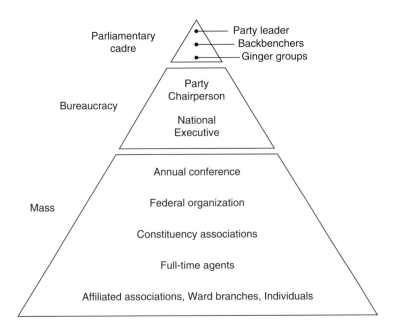

Figure 11.1
The mass party
organization.

The constituency associations

These have been crucial in fighting elections – organizing local campaigns, distributing propaganda, holding meetings, liaising with the local media and canvassing. In addition, they raise funds and recruit people into politics. Each has an organizational structure with a chairperson and executive committee of some kind, and many employ a full-time agent. New Labour took particular care to strengthen the professional core of its constituency parties (CLPs). Probably the most politically significant act undertaken by local associations is the selection of parliamentary candidates (see pp. 328–31), although this is increasingly influenced by the central machines.

> I find most of them boring, petty, malign, clumsily conspiratorial and parochial to a degree that cannot be surpassed in any part of the United Kingdom.
>
> Alan Clark on his local constituency organization, *Diaries* (26 Nov. 1985)

Ward associations The grassroots structure may be further fragmented into ward committees, reflecting the community substructure and based on electoral boundaries. These are often active in the politics of local government and in the 'community politics' approach favoured by the Liberal Democrats.

> There are a fair number of constituency parties in the commuter belt which are run by people who, frankly, might quite properly be labelled neo-fascists.
>
> Unnamed Conservative MP, quoted in S. Ingle, *The British Party System* (1987: 83)

Individual membership In principle anyone can join a political party. Workers are volunteers devoting their spare time to political activity as a hobby or even an obsession; indeed, it is at this level that some of the fiercest zealotry is encountered, from the 'wild-eyed' hard left to the 'goose-stepping tendency'. Of course, by no means all local activists are extremists, though most feel more strongly on issues than the general public (Seyd and Whiteley 1992: 216–17). Membership is also a social activity, involving parties, fundraising dinners and auctions, concerts and so on; the Young Conservatives were traditionally admired as a dating agency and marriage bureau. At one time Conservative associations were controlled by local aristocrats, but they are now largely in the hands of local businessmen and professionals.

Party records are often haphazard and it is difficult to ascertain membership size, which waxes and wanes with the political climate. Throughout the 1970s and 1980s falling numbers tended to leave the zealots in command and in the 1990s party leaders worked to widen membership, Labour being particularly successful (table 11.1), its army of footsoldiers peaking at some 400,000 by 1997. Despite success at the polls, Conservative party membership had plummeted from a high point of three million in the mid-1950s to only a few hundred thousand. The decline was particularly rapid during the eventide of the Major government, membership falling by 40 per cent between 1994 and 1997 (Pinto-Duschinsky 1997). Unlike that of Labour, its membership base was not being renewed; one estimate suggested that over 95 per cent of members were thirty-five or older (Whiteley et al. 1994: 42), the youth membership (Young Conservatives plus students) having fallen from around 34,000 in 1979 to only 10,000 in 1997 (Conservative and Unionist Party 1997: 2). Indeed, by the late 1990s the membership was quite literally dying; sacks of voting slips sent out in September 1997 to endorse Hague's leadership were

Apathy rules?

Political party membership is dwarfed by that of the larger charities, such as the National Trust with almost three million members.

Table 11.1 Membership of the three main British parties, 1997–2002

Party	1997	2001	2002
Conservative*	400,000	325,000	318,000
Labour	405,000	361,000	280,000
Liberal Democrat	103,000	90,000	73,000

*Conservative membership figures are difficult to estimate. The party itself estimated 750,000 in 1996, but Pinto-Duschinsky's survey (1997) suggested 350,000–400,000.

Source: Data from *British Elections and Parties Yearbook 1997*, p. 263; Pinto-Duschinsky (1997) and various online sources.

returned marked 'Deceased'. After the initial euphoria of its 1997 victory, Labour too was losing members steadily, as those who had joined during the 1990s in an effort to oust the Tories gradually became disillusioned and drifted away again. Estimates suggested that by 2002, the membership was only 20,000 above the all-time low of 261,000 in 1991.

Affiliated associations In addition to individual membership, the Labour Party has offered a form of indirect membership whereby associations such as socialist societies and trade unions affiliate, producing an inflated paper membership. The result was often union domination and part of Labour's recruitment strategy was to curb this.

Intermediate-level associations Neighbouring associations may combine for purposes of coordination at area, regional or provincial levels. European elections, with their larger constituencies, also bring adjacent party organizations together.

The federal organizations The constituencies are united through federal associations. The Conservatives form their National Union (see p. 281) while the CLPs constitute the Labour Party as such.

Red flag and blue rinse: the annual conference

Each party holds an annual conference which, in an age of mass communications, is its most important shop window. Although bringing all sections together, it is really a mass membership celebration, a jamboree in which all who have laboured in the fields on behalf of their leaders may draw near to pay homage. **Party conferences** last for several days in the pleasant environs of the seaside at the end of the season but before the weather is too cold to enjoy a publicity-seeking dip. With something of the air of a great sporting event, all takes place before the unblinking eyes of the television cameras, supplemented with a ball-by-ball commentary by the pundits.

The order of play entails a succession of debates on resolutions submitted by members, with speakers drawn from all sections of the party. Formally the Labour and Liberal Democrat conferences have a policy-making role (see below). Voting in the Labour conference has involved a particularly controversial feature – the **block vote**, whereby delegates enjoyed overwhelming influence by casting votes weighted to reflect the size of the membership represented. This was becoming an acute embarrassment and was a key target of the modernization process after the 1992 election defeat (Alderman and Carter 1994).

The appropriate parliamentary leader (minister or shadow minister) will usually conclude a debate, individual popularity being gauged by the length and intensity of the applause. The audiences have their favourites: Michael Heseltine, with his handsome profile and golden mane, was often accorded the

Reproduced by permission of Express Newspapers

adulation of a matinée idol. It is often the more extreme views that gain the plaudits. A Conservative home secretary often has the most difficult time since, however tough the rhetoric, it may not satisfy the demands of the hanging-and-flogging school of penal reform. Michael Howard, however, came close to doing so in the 1990s. Likewise, Labour conferences have often exposed a sharp duality between the parliamentary leaders preaching moderation and trying on capitalist clothes, and the fundamentalist prophets who see sackcloth and ashes as the only garb suitable for those who have repeatedly betrayed the faith. For New Labour, Tony Blair expects most applause; he appeared uncomfortable when a standing ovation erupted at his mention of Mo Mowlam, then Northern Ireland Secretary.

Conferences tend to spill out, both socially and politically, into the surrounding environs. The foyers of conference halls are festooned like bazaars with stands set up by sympathetic pressure groups and stalls selling trinkets and memoirs of party giants or even scandalmongers. Parties of the non-political kind proliferate and there is a brisk business in fringe meetings, where leading figures challenging party orthodoxy and 'managed' out of the main event, such as John Redwood (after his challenge to Major) or Ken Livingstone (under New Labour), can expound their views in an atmosphere often more lively and stimulating than in the official forum. Increasingly the media direct attention here; Michael Heseltine claimed that his fringe appearance in 1988 received 'more serious coverage than for any speech I ever made at a Conservative conference' (Pienaar 1988).

> No member of the conference wants to let down the party in front of the national [TV] audience. Everybody is on his best behaviour, naturally a great aid to the leadership.
>
> Ian Gilmour (Conservative MP), *The Body Politic* (1969: 80–1)

Planning party conferences has become a complex operation (Stanyer 2001a). Conference managers make strenuous efforts to ensure that the boat is not rocked. Conservative leaders for long demonstrated a clear superiority in the art of stage management, employing public relations experts to orchestrate their entrances and exits, though under Major they began to lose their sense of decorum. Receptions for Baroness Thatcher were themselves unnerving, the rapturous acclamation reminding leaders that many lamented her departure. In the Labour Party, speakers often emerged believing that, like justice, the washing of disgusting linen should be seen to be done, preferably using the launderette of television. However, the party learned its lesson; by the 1990s it had acquired consummate public relations skills. Despite his electoral triumph, the 2001 conference threatened some embarrassment for Blair, with renewed union opposition to his privatization plans. However, the attack on the World Trade Center enabled him to replace a speech on this awkward subject with a 'statesmanlike' appeal for national unity in the face of terrorism. Similarly, the Conservatives were able to draw a veil over their recent humiliation at the polls.

All conferences end on an emotional note with a rousing speech from the leader, the content and style of which are regarded as a key test of political virility. Yet although some conferences are momentous, most are soon forgotten (Kavanagh 1996).

The central machinery

The executives As large organizations parties need executives to direct their business. The Conservative Executive Committee consists of around 150, including party officials, representatives of the constituencies and of business interests, MPs and Central Office. Its Labour counterpart is the National Executive Committee (NEC). Its membership is determined by elections from various sections of the party and it elects its own chair and vice-chair. Although constitutionally the servant of the mass party, the NEC's practical role was leadership. Meeting regularly, it had a key position in policy formation, various subcommittees submitting conference resolutions. It also handled disciplinary matters but, under the Blair reforms, these were referred to a new National Constitutional Committee.

However, it could embarrass the leadership; the trade unions were for long able to control a majority and the method of election meant that it could be captured by the left. Hence, a key part of the modernizers' strategy was to reduce NEC power (Lent and Sowemimo 1996: 126–7), and under Blair its

Figure 11.2
Composition of the
Labour NEC, 1997.

Ex Officio Party Leader Deputy Leader General Secretary EPLP leader								
Unions	Socialist Societies	Constituency Parties	Local Government	PLP EPLP	Cabinet	Treasurer	Youth Rep
Elected at Annual Conference. At least six must be women	Elected at Annual Conference (Unopposed)	Elected by all members. Cannot be MPs. At least three must be women	Elected at Association of Labour Councillors. At least one must be a woman	Elected at Annual Conference At least one must be a woman	Nominated by Cabinet	Elected at Annual Conference (Unopposed)	Elected at Youth Conference

composition was changed (figure 11.2). Powerful left-wing party figures are
ruled out because the six elected by the constituencies must not be MPs and
the combined ranks of the PLP and the European Parliamentary Party (EPLP)
are allowed only three representatives. The Cabinet also nominates three, while
the party leader and deputy leader are *ex officio*. However, the leadership was
unable to avert the election of some non-parliamentary left-wingers to the
constituency division in 1998, including Liz Davies, who had been prevented
from standing as a parliamentary candidate in Leeds North East (see p. 330). In
November 1998, the NEC adopted guidelines proscribing the leaking of discussions and obliging members to notify the party's press office before making
public statements about NEC business. Critics bemoaned the leadership's
'control freak' tendencies and Liz Davies resigned.

The Liberal Democrat Federal Executive, under the leadership of the party
president, is responsible for directing, coordinating and implementing party
activities. Responsibility for conference organization lies with a Conference
Committee, while policy proposals are initiated and developed by the Policy
Committee, which draws up election manifestos in conjunction with the parliamentary party.

The bureaucracies These are the professional backbone of the parties. The
Conservatives have their splendid Central Office in Smith Square, where por-
traits of past leaders gaze down from the walls on visitors. The Liberal Demo-
crat headquarters are in nearby Cowley Street, within a stone's throw of
Westminster. Labour's Head Office was for long popularly known as 'Transport House', located in the headquarters of the Transport and General
Workers' Union. In 1980 it moved south of the Thames to Walworth Road
(John Smith House), a building funded by the unions. This was sold in 1995 as
New Labour sought a new image in a state-of-the-art centre at Millbank Tower
on the banks of the Thames. However, by 2002 deteriorating party finances and
rent rises called for some realism and the staff vacated the opulent premises for

a five-storey property in Old Queen Street, Westminster. With a £5.5 million mortgage, the financial strain remained and once again the unions were considering shouldering the burden.

The bureaucracies have a wide range of management and control functions over the voluntary arms, coordinating local activities, providing a link with the leader and giving advice and information. At Westminster they conduct public relations (liaising with the media and advertising and producing party literature), manage the annual conference, organize research and service backbench committees. They also oversee candidate selection policy (such as number of women) and maintain the central list of hopefuls. Most crucially, they control party finances and fundraising.

Conservative Central Office was established in 1870 largely as a personal machine to serve the leader (Pinto-Duschinsky 1972). Significant developments took place between 1906 and 1911 during opposition, when the key position of party chairman (responsible for running the Office) was created, to be held by a cabinet-ranking MP. Although Labour Head Office was created by the NEC and is not formally responsible to the leader, in practice its role is similar to that of Central Office. The smaller parties maintain more modest bureaucratic support, reflecting the lesser demands of their parliamentary cadres.

The parliamentary cadres

At the apex of the party structure sits the parliamentary cadre of MPs, including the leader, the front bench and the backbench organizations (see p. 387). The political mainsprings of Parliament, the extent of their independence from the rest of the party is a key question in political analysis. There are also the European parliamentary cadres, though the Westminster MPs have not been entirely warm in embracing their MEP cousins, reflecting a fear that Parliament's much-cherished sovereignty will be eroded. Indeed, the Euroscepticism of Margaret Thatcher left Conservative MEPs rather in the cold. Labour has shown a more friendly face, making the leader of the European Labour Party an *ex officio* member of the NEC, permitting MEPs to attend Westminster backbench meetings and including them in the electoral college choosing the leader. However, they have shown some willingness to bite the hand that feeds, as when they criticized Blair's reform of Clause Four and his social policies.

The life and soul of the parties: satellite groups

Within and around the main parties is an ever-changing constellation of smaller organizations or ginger groups comprising various combinations of MPs and ordinary members. Although having separate identities, they owe their *raisons d'être* to the parent party, which they often feel an ideological compunction to influence. Usually forming in response to particular events or policies, they can give a party much of its character, claiming variously to be its soul, its conscience, or its ideas bank, though often seen by leaders as unwanted car-buncles or diabolical incarnations requiring surgery or exorcism. John Major suffered greatly from rebellious groups (Ludlam 1996); those who stung him into his 1995 resignation termed themselves the Fresh Start group (though he used a different term). Similarly, in 1998 Blair accused the Grass Roots Alliance of posing as 'critical supporters' while really being 'outright opponents' (*Independent*, 26 Sept. 1998).

Conservative In 1883, the Primrose League was formed in an attempt to keep alive the 'one-nation' spirit of Disraeli (being a reference to his favourite flower), a cause more recently espoused by the Tory Reform Group – established in 1975 to resist the neoliberal forces of Thatcherism. Together with several pro-European groups, the latter became part of an umbrella grouping attempting to develop policies to appeal to the broad mass of the electorate – Conservative Mainstream. The Bow Group, a political research group founded by Conservative intellectuals in 1951 as a counterpoise to Labour's Fabian Society, also professes moderation, disseminating its message through its journal, *Crossbow*. Traditional Christian values are promoted by the Conservative Christian Fellowship, which has strong links with church communities, and the Conservative Family Campaign, with its traditional stance on issues of divorce, abortion and homosexuality.

On the right wing of the party, the Monday Club was formed in 1960 to oppose Macmillan on South Africa. Initially concerned with defence, it went on to adopt a strongly authoritarian position and was accused of dealings with the National Front. The spirit of neoliberalism kindled by Heath led to the establishment in 1973 of the Selsdon Group and the spirit of Thatcherism lives on in the No Turning Back Group (formed 1985) and Conservative Way Forward (1990). There is widespread support for specifically Eurosceptic groups, including Conservatives Against a Federal Europe and the Bruges Group. There is also a rich vein of right-wing think-tanks, including the Centre for Policy Studies, the Adam Smith Institute, the Institute for Economic Affairs, the Salisbury Group (publishing the *Salisbury Review*) and the Conservative 2000 Foundation. Away from the centre are the Young Conservatives and the Women's National Advisory Committee, both with national structures.

Labour There has been no shortage of Labour ginger groups, the most well known being Tribune (propagating its views through the journal of that name). Founded in 1964, it has often been troublesome, but also highly respected and influential, and has included some prominent figures. Thorns in the moderate side have been persistent. The Bevanites were well known, but even the moderate Harold Wilson headed Keep Left and in 1958 Victory for Socialism formed to oppose Gaitskell's revisionism. The 1970s saw the Campaign for Labour Party Democracy and the Labour Coordinating Committee, which sought successfully to gain control of the NEC and instigate reforms in the party constitution.

Militant Tendency believed in a mission to oppose the Fabian tradition, using the Trotskyite tactic of entryism into the party. By the early 1980s, moderates felt its tactics to be seriously damaging and, in a largely symbolic gesture, Michael Foot expelled the five-member editorial board of its journal, *Militant*. Within Parliament, the Socialist Campaign Group was founded in 1982 by disaffected Tribune members as a more radical alternative. During the cold war, CND also penetrated deeply into the Labour ranks.

On Labour's right was the Manifesto Group, established in 1974, though its first two chairpersons went on to form the SDP. From the first the Fabian Society has exerted a profound influence, providing illustrious figures as well as ideas. Although appearing moribund during the 1980s, under Blair it was rejuvenated in a more rightist mode, becoming closely aligned with the Institute for Public Policy Research, set up with union backing in 1989 to pioneer the left's intellectual fightback. A third new force was Demos, a rightish think-tank launched in 1993 by Martin Jacques, formerly editor of *Marxism Today*. Several single-issue groups are also close to Labour, notably the 'Euro-realist' Centre for European Reform and the Constitution Unit. Others, such as Charter88, contributed to the New Labour mood but, with a more radical agenda, remain more distanced from the party.

The Young Socialists organize nationally and tend towards more extreme policies. Some of the party's women also maintain a separate identity as local women's sections, coordinated through a National Labour Women's Conference. However, as feminism began to lose direction in the late 1970s, a number of activists focused on the party itself. The modernization drive gave them a key opportunity (Perrigo 1996), a dramatic breakthrough coming in the all-women shortlists (p. 330). Although Labour remained deaf to calls for special black sections, these began to arise spontaneously during the 1980s. Like the Conservatives, Labour also has a Christian section – the Christian Socialist Movement (founded 1960) – which combines religious and political beliefs concerning peace, equality and justice.

Of course, the most towering external presence for Labour has been the trade union movement, historically its *raison d'être* though greatly reduced under the modernization programme, a matter to which we return later.

Inside the Parties:
Tweedledum and Tweedledee?

Historically, the internal processes and power structures of each party reveal significant differences. Yet it is true that the pressures of modern politics increasingly force them to resemble each other in the quest for power.

Internal cohesion

In a multi-party system each stands for a narrow interest or ideology, thereby promising internal solidarity. However, one of the *raisons d'être* of parties in a two-party system is **interest aggregation** – they have been termed 'catch-all' parties (Kirchheimer 1966). Yet to attract votes they must present a united front and this generates tension between ideology and political expediency. All British parties carry a deep-seated basis for schism; the Conservatives with their traditional Whig and Tory strains (the wet/dry dichotomy under Thatcher), Labour bedevilled by a revolutionary/Fabian divide, and even the centrist Liberal Democrats harbouring Liberal and Social Democrat wings. The way inner tensions are handled constitutes a key focus for analysis; for long, history showed the Conservatives to have been the most successful, Labour continually searching for an antidote to the virulent factionalism coursing through its veins. However, from the early 1990s things began to change dramatically as Labour learned from the Conservatives, who themselves appeared to lose their magic touch.

Social composition Although the Conservatives have always been able to command a wide range of electoral support, their traditional membership came from a narrow and homogeneous social base within the upper middle class and *petite bourgeoisie*. However, the Thatcher era saw a new breed of MP with self-made, meritocratic backgrounds. In April 1988, Major John Stokes, Conservative member for Halesowen and Stourbridge, enquired ironically during Prime Minister's Questions whether 'there is still room in the party for the nobility, the gentry, and the middle class'. Even so, it remains overwhelmingly a middle-class party (86 per cent of membership according to Whiteley et al. 1994: 45–6). Despite the leadership of Thatcher, Major and Hague, its MPs come predominantly from private schools (Baker and Fountain 1996); two-thirds of those elected in 2001 had been privately educated (Criddle 2001: 202). By contrast, Labour has been more a microcosm of society, class tensions being reproduced within its own ranks. However, the New Labour intake of MPs in 1997 showed increased homogeneity around a meritocratic norm, with 75 per cent university educated (see p. 374), a trend continuing in 2001 (67 per cent).

Experience of office A party forming a government is constitutionally and politically pushed towards coherence. The doctrine of collective responsibility, official secrecy, the need for Commons' support and the duty to represent the whole community all conspire to unite. A long history of office gave the Conservatives considerable exposure to these forces. As Labour sought a second term after its 1997 victory, party spin doctors worked strenuously to keep backbenchers 'on message' and were rewarded with another huge majority.

> What a genius the Labour Party has for cutting itself in half and letting the two parts writhe in public.
>
> Cassandra (William Neil Connor; 1910–67; Irish journalist) in the *Daily Mirror*

Ideology Labour has traditionally espoused socialism but this can have a variety of meanings, implying contrasting strategies. Hence, the leadership has regularly sought to reduce the 'red in tooth and Clause Four' commitment to socialism, Gaitskell's attempts to disembarrass the party of this talisman being particularly disruptive. In contrast, the Conservatives' traditional goal has been office rather than ideological purity. Thatcher, however, with her neoliberal crusade, challenged this. MPs who had cut their teeth during her reign learned that politics was the art of confrontation and Major and Hague found themselves at the wheel of an unruly ship. Conversely, Labour under Blair jettisoned much ideological baggage in its bid for power.

Hegemonic consciousness Probably of greatest importance is the fact that the Conservatives regarded themselves (and were regarded by others) as the 'natural' party of government. Even in opposition they tended to remain united, believing office was never far away. By contrast, some Labour members saw the party's role primarily in terms of protest. This was very evident during the early 1980s; the essential project of Kinnock, Smith and Blair was the Sisyphean one of convincing the party it could govern. The achievement of a second term in 2001 marked a major shift in the party's perception of itself.

The imperatives of capitalism An important government role is unifying the competitive and potentially disruptive forces of capitalism. As the party of private capital, the Conservatives traditionally accepted a key responsibility in this respect, forcing members to place a high premium on unity within the party ranks. Recognition of this in the form of 'new realism' during the 1990s (see p. 297) was a key to the New Labour renaissance.

Tendencies and factions A distinction has been made between the concepts of faction and tendency (Rose 1964). A **faction** is a group united across a wide front. Labour has been said to contain two factions broadly differentiated in left–right terms, confronting each other on a wide range of issues and producing a fundamental fault line. In contrast, Conservative disagreements tended not to precipitate the same formations every time. A and B might oppose C on one issue, but on another A and C might unite against B, these fluid **tendencies** never destroying its overall coherence.

However, this mechanism collapsed under Thatcher, who dichotomized the party. By the 1990s, disagreements over Europe were cutting deeply into the Conservative flesh, illustrating an historic problem with foreign relations and reflecting the divide between the old Tory strain emphasizing nationhood and the whiggish element of thrusting commerce. This had produced divisions over the Corn Laws in the 1840s, imperial protection in the early twentieth century, Indian government in 1935, South Africa under Macmillan and Rhodesia in 1965 (Norton 1978). Moreover, with the Bruges Group, No Turning Back and Conservative Way Forward, there was greater factionalism than ever (Kavanagh 1998: 41). Hague talked vainly of reuniting his party, but was to fight the 2001 election opposing the euro, thereby placing his Europhiles in confrontational mode. There was little indication that the party was healing the wound when the 1922 Committee selected representatives of opposite extremes as the two final contenders for the 2001 leadership contest (see p. 306), while rejecting Michael Portillo, the candidate seen as most likely to heal the rift. As the Conservatives began to fight amongst themselves, New

Labour grew new skin over its old scars and claimed the 'one nation' mantle of Disraeli.

Choosing the leader

The selection of leaders and their security of tenure have important implications for a party's culture.

Labour From the beginning, the Labour leadership was elective, with voting initially the exclusive right of the PLP. In theory, leaders were subject to annual re-election but, although Wilson unsuccessfully threw down the gauntlet before Gaitskell in 1960 and Tony Benn challenged Kinnock in 1988, this has largely been avoided. Evidence shows Labour leaders to be more secure than their Conservative counterparts: Attlee was able to cling to office far longer than his younger colleagues wished; Gaitskell, although his reign was turbulent, died with his leadership boots firmly laced; and Harold Wilson was sufficiently secure after fourteen years that his resignation surprised both colleagues and pundits. Even James Callaghan, after stormy battles with the left, was able to depart with dignity. The demise of Michael Foot probably came closest to a Conservative-style hounding from office. He had proved an electoral liability, nicknamed Worzel Gummidge (a scruffy but well-meaning scarecrow featuring in a current TV series) by *Private Eye*.

Left-wing criticism in the 1980s blamed the leadership for shortcomings and at a special conference at Wembley it was agreed that the electoral college choosing the leader and deputy should be widened to embrace the trade unions (40 per cent), the constituency associations and the PLP (30 per cent each). (The left fought unsuccessfully for the whole Shadow Cabinet to be chosen in this way.) However, the new system disappointed reformers by choosing the right's 'dream ticket' of Kinnock and Hattersley in 1983. Paradoxically, the reform actually increased the leader's security in three ways: it gave authority over all sections of the party; the PLP lost any moral right to a vote of no-confidence; and the cumbersome procedure could inhibit challenges.

The 1993 conference agreed further changes, strengthening the power of ordinary constituency members against local oligarchs. Union influence was reduced by making the proportions in the electoral college equal thirds, and both unions and constituency parties were obliged to adopt the principle of 'one member, one vote' (OMOV), thus producing a leadership electorate of millions.

Conservative The process whereby Conservative leaders emerged was for long shrouded in a mystique that would even have puzzled England cricket selectors. The party elders, including the outgoing leader, would take soundings within the party and a new heir would emerge. This was not necessarily corrupt or even irrational; it permitted sensitivity to candidates' qualities and reflected *intensity* of feeling in a way that a simple vote could not. However, the

Table 11.2 Conservative leadership elections, 1965–2001 (number of votes)

Candidate	1st ballot[a]	2nd ballot	3rd ballot	Membership vote[b]
1965				
Heath	150	–	–	
Maudling	133	–	–	
Powell	15	–	–	
1975				
Fraser	16	–	–	
Heath	119	–	–	
Howe	–	19	–	
Peyton	–	11	–	
Prior	–	19	–	
Thatcher	130	110	–	
Whitelaw	–	79	–	
1989				
Meyer	33	–	–	
Thatcher	314	–	–	
1990				
Heseltine	152	131	–	
Hurd	–	56	–	
Major	–	185	–	
Thatcher	204	–	–	
1995				
Major	219	–	–	
Redwood	89	–	–	
Spoiled papers/ abstentions	22	–	–	
1997				
Clarke	49	64	70	
Hague	41	62	92	
Howard	23	–	–	
Lilley	24	–	–	
Redwood	27	38	–	
2001				
Ancram	21	17	–	
Clarke	36	39	59	100,864 (39%)
Davies	21	18	–	
Duncan Smith	39	42	54	155,933 (61%)
Portillo	49	50	53	

[a] Prior to 2001, to win at this stage, a candidate required an overall majority plus a 15% lead over nearest rival.
[b] Turnout 79% in 2001.

Douglas-Home experience discredited the method and in 1965 election by MPs was introduced (table 11.2). Soundings were still to be taken amongst peers and MEPs, and MPs were required to consult their constituency associations. By 1997, with only a rump of 164 MPs remaining to choose Major's successor, there was considerable unease in the constituencies and calls for an OMOV system (Alderman 1998). When this was resisted by the 1922 Committee, disgruntled party officials polled thousands of party members through meetings and telephone banks organized by the Electoral Reform Society. Kenneth Clarke emerged as the firm favourite, but MPs remained deaf to members' voices (and to the consultation requirement), opting instead for William Hague.

Conscious of this, in October 1997 Hague offered members a 'back me or sack me' vote by postal ballot. However, the apparently overwhelming endorsement (80 per cent of the 180,000 members voting) was diluted, being tied to approval of a reform package that few could gainsay. Finally, a special constitutional conference in March 1998 decided upon an electoral college for leadership contests that would include *all* party members, choosing from a shortlist of two determined by a series of ballots of the 1922 Committee. Coming into operation sooner than Hague would have wished, the system introduced new possibilities for disruptive tactical voting by MPs.

The dangers of this were soon to be seen in one of the most openly vicious, and possibly damaging, leadership contests the party had ever witnessed (see p. 306). Although he was clearly the most popular candidate on the first round, the third round showed a bitter determination by opponents to keep Portillo from the final shortlist. Journalists reported Duncan Smith supporters voting tactically for Clarke. With such negative voting, the new leader lacked the aura of legitimacy. Soon derided as the 'quiet man' of British politics, he lacked charisma and appeared unable to heal the party rift. While Portillo turned away from the spotlight, his supporters had not relinquished their hopes and, although remaining on the front bench, David Davis was believed to still harbour gnawing ambition.

The move to election proved highly significant in that it shifted the leadership class basis. First came Heath, son of an artisan (nicknamed Grocer Heath by *Private Eye*), to be followed by grocer's daughter Thatcher, who would probably not have been the choice of the Lords, party elders, Shadow Cabinet or the constituencies (Blake 1985: 320). Major and Hague continued the new pattern of class background, though the election of Duncan Smith saw a reversion to tradition.

The reform also affected the leader's security of tenure. The Conservative tradition of staunch loyalty to a leader when in office was coupled with a reputation for eliminating old warriors that would be envied by the Mafia (Bruce-Gardyne 1984: 22). With the exception of Bonar Law, every incumbent appointed during the twentieth century was either forcibly removed or placed under heavy pressure to go. Like the manager of a league football team, leaders appear safe as long as they deliver victory. Thus, all deposed leaders are tainted with a fatal electoral flaw: for Chamberlain it was Munich, for Eden Suez, for Macmillan the Profumo scandal, for Douglas-Home an unfashionable aristocratic style. Election made removal even easier, opening up the possibility of annual challenges. Heath, whose fatal flaw was the 'U-turn', added to the distinction of being the first elected leader that of being the first to be 'un-elected'. Thatcher's dispatch in 1990 came not because she had lost an election (she was still in power) but because some thought she was *likely* to; the poll tax was her *pons asinorum* (see p. 619). Major was called a ditherer and his undoing was Europe; after the 1997 election he did not need the fabled men in grey suits to tell him it was time to go. Hague's reign was short and without distinction; it was not his failure to win the 2001 general election that prompted his immediate decision to fall upon his sword but the *scale* of the humiliation.

'I must congratulate you on the combination of loyalty and restraint that you have shown in going on television to announce your intention to vote against the prime minister in the Leadership Election.'

'Alan, I'm perfectly prepared to argue this through with you if you'll listen.'

'Piss off.'

Alan Clark on his encounter with Edwina Currie behind the Speaker's chair during the tense moments surrounding the fall of Thatcher, *Diaries* (21 Nov. 1990)

Liberal Democrats Until 1976 the Liberals had followed their traditional practice of allowing the parliamentary cohort, such as it was, to choose the leader. However, following Jeremy Thorpe's resignation over the Norman Scott scandal, party-wide election was instigated. Generally, post-war Liberal leaders appeared secure in office: Jo Grimond left with dignity, continuing as a respected party elder; and although Thorpe's position became untenable, he survived for an astonishingly long time. David Steel, though subject to some rough treatment, remained secure until he voluntarily stood down in 1988 for the SDP merger, at which point Paddy Ashdown was elected as the new party's first leader by a postal ballot of all members. His own resignation, after eleven years of unchallenged supremacy, was both voluntary and surprising. His successor, Charles Kennedy, emerged from a contest of no fewer than five candidates in August 1999 (using the AV system of voting). The Liberal Democrat constitution stipulates that a leadership election should normally be held at least once each parliament, or when a majority of members or seventy-five local associations so demand.

A hollow crown? Although Labour offers its leaders a more secure tenure, this does not necessarily mean they are the more powerful. It may be in the interests of party members to preserve a weak leader in order to enjoy greater freedom to rule from behind the throne. Caesar was slain not because he was weak but because he was powerful. The uncertainty of the tenure makes the party leadership a lonely position, many incumbents becoming brooding and paranoic, and fearing amongst their retinue those who, like the lean and hungry

Cassius in Shakespeare's *Julius Caesar*, lie awake at night and 'be never at heart's ease whiles they behold a greater than themselves'.

Party patronage

Leaders can counter the advantage others have to make or break them by using their own **patronage** powers. Those of Conservative leaders have been almost unbounded: whether in office or opposition, they appoint the front-bench team and the significant officers of Central Office. Thatcher stamped her authority on the party with a thorough shake-up at Central Office. The appointment of party chair has become one of the leader's most significant patronage gifts, though the relationship can be tense. Thatcher had some trouble with her chairmen; with Norman Tebbit in post, she seemed to rely more on advertising experts such as Tim Bell. William Hague appointed erstwhile Thatcher loyalist Cecil Parkinson to signal his political leanings, while in a conciliatory move Iain Duncan Smith initially appointed one of his leadership rivals, David Davis. However, fearing that Davis still nursed ambition for the highest office, within a year he was unceremoniously sacked while on holiday, to be replaced by Teresa May, the first woman to hold the post.

In contrast, the Labour leader has been more tightly circumscribed. In opposition, the front-bench team is elected by the PLP and must be taken into government in the event of a general election victory. However, in October 1993 John Smith broke with tradition by keeping Harriet Harman as shadow chief secretary to the Treasury despite her failure to be re-elected by the PLP. Although the NEC makes appointments to the bureaucracy and is itself elected by the party, leaders can appoint advisers and spin doctors to key positions, a power used increasingly by Blair. Once in office, the restraints on the leader's powers of patronage largely fall away; cronyism was one of the main charges levelled against Blair.

The Liberal Democrats stress their democratic procedures; the party president is elected biennially by all members and a majority of the members of all three executive bodies are elected by the conference.

Candidate selection

To be a genuinely national force a party must field over 600 candidates. Their selection represents a widely based patronage exercise, theoretically giving the constituency associations a key 'gatekeeper' role.

Conservative In theory anyone can apply to be a Conservative candidate; selection committees may be faced with the mammoth task of reducing a list of a hundred or so to a shortlist of around six. These are subjected to scrutiny: interviewed, invited to deliver an address and their profession and lifestyle noted. Those with spouses are preferred and these may be vetted for acceptability on platform and in drawing-room. Throughout the process Central Office presence is felt. Yet although guidelines are issued on candidate policy and a Standing Committee maintains a list of possibles upon which the local associations may draw, local associations have traditionally resisted pressure from above. Thus, when senior figures called for the head of Piers Merchant in 1997, following tabloid stories of an affair with a seventeen-year-old hostess, the Beckenham party defied them with an overwhelming vote of confidence. In like vein, the Tatton Conservatives stood by Neil Hamilton before the 1997 election. Many local parties resented the manner of Thatcher's departure and Major was obliged to appeal to activists not to act against MPs who had supported Heseltine's challenge. Big names are not necessarily favoured: ex-Chancellor Norman Lamont was spurned by eight associations without even an interview before being selected by Harrogate and Knaresborough for the 1997 election. Sir Nicholas Scott argued that his deselection was a result of his pro-European views, though trouble with drink and being found face downwards on the pavement at the 1996 party conference did not help. However, in selecting Alan Clark as his replacement, his Kensington and Chelsea party could not be accused of choosing a less colourful candidate.

Until the post-war Maxwell-Fyfe reforms it was possible for wealthy aspirants effectively to purchase nomination by agreeing to contribute to party funds. A preference for breeding and education remains, with a predilection for company directors and executives (172 stood in 2001, along with 93 lawyers). However, from the 1980s, a new kind of professional politician emerged, working as ministerial advisers and lobby consultants and with no outside experience. Dame Angela Rumbold, who took charge of candidate policy in 1993, reacted against these 'clones', arguing for a return to traditional candidates, but despite her efforts many of the 41 first-timers entering the Commons in 1997 were party *apparatchiks* (Criddle 1997: 196). She had no more success in getting more women selected as 'the blue rinse mafia' dug their block heels in (women comprised 10 per cent of candidates in 1997 and 15 per cent in 2001). Black candidates are even rarer (see p. 377); only 16 stood in 2001. The typical Conservative candidate remains resolutely middle class, middle aged, white, married and male.

Labour Here the selection process has been significantly different. The original lists are considerably shorter because applications are restricted to those nominated by affiliated associations. The NEC maintains a list of approved candidates and has taken increasing interest in candidate selection. This list once distinguished between sponsored and non-sponsored candidates. **Sponsorship** meant that nominating associations met a substantial proportion of election expenses and made a contribution to funds; a powerful inducement to a local association, and the advice of Oscar Wilde to the tempted has often followed. In the post-war era about half the Labour MPs could be described as politically kept men.

Sponsorship did not entail the use of *personal* wealth to gain office, it assisted working-class participation and was in line with Labour's original *raison d'être* of union representation in Parliament. However, it meant that selection was often controlled by union-dominated general management committees and, because the sponsors chose the safer seats, younger and more radical candidates were left with unwinnable ones. It also showed a male bias (Lovenduski and Norris 1994). Hence the system was modified in 1996, with contributions going to the constituency parties in general rather than to candidates. This opened up the possibility of directing resources away from the safe seats to the marginals.

A requirement from 1983 that all Labour MPs undergo reselection each parliament was intended to increase the power of local party oligarchs over the PLP. However, reforms led to this being replaced by one member, one vote (OMOV). To placate the unions, a 'levy plus' system entitled political-levy payers (see p. 387) to participate in voting by 'joining' the party at a reduced rate. At the same time, MPs' security of tenure was strengthened by instigating unopposed reselection if they received at least two-thirds of all nominations.

To increase the representation of women, a 'W' (women-only) list was established in 1989, but perhaps the most dramatic innovation was the agreement in 1993 to establish all-women shortlists for 50 per cent of all winnable seats. Hotly resented in many constituencies, in 1996 it was declared illegal under the Sex Discrimination Act. However, the thirty-eight candidates already selected were unaffected and a further fifteen went on to be chosen for winnable seats from open shortlists, suggesting seismic movements in the party's cultural bedrock. In elections for the Scottish Parliament and Welsh Assembly, Labour paired constituencies, with the intention of having one male and one female candidate. For the 2001 election, women-only shortlists were replaced by fifty-fifty ones and there were suggestions of a backlash against selecting more 'Blair's Babes' (Criddle 2001: 195).

Although black candidates are nominated by Labour, they usually fight unwinnable seats. Prior to the 1997 election a number of acrimonious selection disputes arose in inner cities with sizeable ethnic populations where incumbent white MPs were loath to step aside. In some cases OMOV led to mass signings of new Asian members to influence selection. However, NEC inquiries revealed irregularities, with some names not on the electoral register, some not wishing to be members and some entirely fictional. A number of court cases ensued and candidates were imposed through NEC intervention. A serious case concerned Mohammed Sarwar in Glasgow Govan who, after being elected, faced bribery charges (Criddle 1997: 191–3). However, the 1997 result gave Labour a record nine non-white MPs, increasing to twelve in 2001.

Despite OMOV, Labour's central machine has generally sought a greater influence than Central Office over selection, showing itself quite willing to veto local choices and 'parachute' in favourites, as in the Vauxhall by-election of June 1989 when Kate Hoey was imposed, despite local members' desire for a black candidate. Central dominance increased in the run-up to the 1997 election. There was particular determination to find a seat for Tory-defector, Alan Howarth, despite two failures to make local shortlists. Conversely, in Leeds North East the party refused to endorse the selection of socialist Liz Davies, and in January 2002, *Tribune* editor Mark Seddon was excluded from the shortlist for the Ogmore by-election.

Further intimations of the tight central rein came with the closed lists for the 1999 European elections. Rather than OMOV, prospective Labour candidates were required to go before selection committees in the eleven regions. There was a feeling amongst sitting MEPs that this would be used to rout the left, including those who had opposed the Clause Four reforms.

Liberal Democrats Local associations are responsible for selecting candidates, who are drawn from a national approved list, but an emphasis on community politics has permitted considerable local autonomy. One woman must be on any shortlist of three and for the 1999 European elections the party adopted 'zipped lists' – alternating men and women. Of the party's fifty-two MPs after the 2001 general election, a mere five were women and only one of these sat on the front bench. Yet the 2001 annual conference overwhelmingly rejected quotas for women candidates, something of a setback for Charles Kennedy, who had favoured the proposal. Many of those opposing quotas were themselves women, their sentiment emblazoned across T-shirted Liberal Democrat bosoms: 'I am not a token woman'. As an alternative, delegates opted for a target of 40 per cent women candidates in winnable seats.

Party policy-making: mass rule or iron law of oligarchy?

The ability to shape policy is probably the most significant index of power within a party. There are two extreme models: *top-down*, in which the mass obediently plays follow-my-leader; and *bottom-up*, where they see MPs as parliamentary delegates. The emergence of the local associations in the nineteenth century created fears of mass control. Ostrogorski's famous (1902) study sounded a dire warning that the parliamentary parties had created monsters that would soon undermine representative democracy. Others feared the reverse – that the masses would be denied influence. In the early twentieth century the German/Italian sociologist Roberto Michels enunciated his well-known **iron law of oligarchy**, postulating that within any mass party ineluctable sociological and psychological processes would result in domination by a small elite (Michels 1962). Various related factors influence internal power relationships, including the party's genesis, its constitution, its experience of government, its attitudes towards office and its leader's personality.

Lenin's method leads to this: the party organisation at first substitutes itself for the party as a whole. Then the central committee substitutes itself for the party organisation, and finally a single dictator substitutes himself for the central committee.

Leon Trotsky (1879–1940; Russian revolutionary), quoted in N. McInnes,
The Communist Parties of Western Europe (1975: ch. 3)

Genesis Because the Conservative and Liberal parties originated as parliamentary groupings, the extra-parliamentary organizations were from the first seen as their handmaidens. There was never any reason to address the question of control; it remained within the provenance of the elite. Attempts by Joseph Chamberlain and Randolph Churchill to establish some degree of democratic control within their respective parties came to nothing. However, the conception, birth and growth of the Labour Party implied a quite different relationship. As the offspring of the trade union mammoth, the Labour Representation Committee was essentially subservient. Even the title 'leader' was denied in favour of 'chairman', who was co-equal with the NEC chair.

Party constitutions These formally *prescribe* the internal power structure. Like the country over which it has so long presided, the Conservative Party had no formal constitution but party literature has generally paid homage to the leader's supremacy. However, during the 1980s the party conference began to show some signs of greater assertiveness. Hague secured the endorsement of a formal constitution at a special March 1998 conference, which established a governing board formed from the party's three sections. With an ethics committee and powers to expel MPs, it seemed largely designed to remove the taint of sleaze rather than limit the leader's power.

The Labour constitution imposes an ostensibly democratic pattern of authority, with three centres of policy formation: the PLP, the NEC and the annual conference. Policy, as contained in the *programme*, was to be determined by the annual conference on the basis of a two-thirds majority. In 1945, NEC chairman Harold Laski argued that if Attlee, as prime minister, attended the three-power peace conference at Potsdam his position should be approved by the NEC (an interpretation Attlee rejected; see McKenzie 1967: 330). The authority of the conference declined from the 1950s (Minkin 1980). The six largest unions wielding their massive block votes generally supported the party line. However, as the union leadership moved to the left from the 1970s, fundamental tensions emerged. Beyond practical difficulties for the leadership, the block vote symbolized the union domination alleged by critics and thus became a key target of the modernizers. Reforms from 1993 gave the CLPs parity with the unions. Other constitutional reforms under Blair (such as Clause Four and NEC composition) have further strengthened the leadership.

The Liberal Party constitution was decentralized in 1983, giving a predominantly 'bottom-up' procedure, which was preserved by the Liberal Democrats, making the federal conference sovereign. However, most conference resolutions are drawn up by the party's central Policy Committee.

The experience of government When a party assumes office its leader inherits the supreme powers of the Crown, and when ejected these clouds of glory may be trailed into opposition. This has given an advantage to Conservative leaders. Whenever Labour leaders have experienced power, they too have worn a halo of authority, though such periods have been tantalizingly short-lived, punctuated by lengthy spells in the wilderness, when the steel discipline of office is softened in the heat of internal friction. However, from 1997 Blair developed an iron grip over the party, with dissidents largely silent and most MPs and CLPs remaining 'on message'.

Attitudes towards office Political parties mainly exist to gain office and leaders must frame their manifestos accordingly. If the followers share the hunger for power, there will be little basis for disharmony. The traditional Conservative conviction that they were the chosen ensured that, when displaced by Labour, the mass loyally followed the leadership in radical policy revision. In contrast, the idea of some on the left that it is better to lose than compromise on principle often curbed Labour leaders' rights over policy. By 1997 the party hungered more for office than for pure socialism, becoming voter responsive rather than activist orientated (Kavanagh 1998: 38). At the same time, under Major and Hague the Conservatives seemed to lose the appetite for office, voicing their divisions over European integration regardless of electoral cost.

> Winning is the *sine qua non* and a lot of leeway must be allowed to a leader who is successful at winning.
>
> Ben Pimlott (historian and former Fabian chairman), quoted in the *Observer* (12 Jan. 1997)

The charisma factor Personalities matter in real-world politics. Labour's contentious policy revisionism in the 1950s and early 1960s in part reflected the combative character of Gaitskell, while the relative calm under Wilson can be largely attributed to his ability to pour liberal quantities of oil on the party's sea of troubles. The importance of personality was underlined by Thatcher, with her strident insistence that there was no alternative to her policies, while Major appeared dithering and weak. Blair stamped his personality on the Labour Party in despatching a number of sacred cows to the abattoir, and his photogenic looks and engaging manner produced unparalleled popularity ratings. In contrast, the gods appeared to have been less generous to William Hague. For the Liberal Democrats, leader Paddy Ashdown seemed to personify the new party. Any doubts over its future under Kennedy were dispelled by his showing in the 2001 general election.

A climate of oligarchy Policy determination by the mass party, whether through conference resolutions or in some other way such as postal ballot, has been considered undemocratic because the views of activists may be at variance with 'the mass of those who actually provide the vote' (Butler 1960: 3). McKenzie (1967: 635) argued that such fears were unnecessary, the imperatives of political life (electioneering and governing) providing a procrustean bed forcing parties to become oligarchic. Hence, despite Labour's reforms in the early 1980s, the modernization process diluted the mass voice (Seyd and Whiteley 1992: 218), transforming the party in line with the Michels thesis (Shaw 1996: 219). *The Times* (21 Sept. 1997) was able to conclude that 'Mr Blair's New Labour has become the natural party of deference in which power flows from the top'. In this model the leaders aim to bypass their own mass members to appeal to the wider electorate. We saw in chapter 9 how elections are increasingly conducted from the centre with mailshots and telephone canvassing. The paradoxical result of this is a concentration on the soft vote, those less interested in politics, while parties become increasingly concerned with image rather than substance.

However, beyond power relationships within the parties is another all-important question. There is power behind the party thrones held by those who never draw up manifestos, fight elections or hold high office. This leads us deeper into the labyrinthine world of power.

Who Pays the Piper?

Money can try very hard to talk in politics. In 1997, northern millionaire Paul Sykes promised Conservative candidates up to £3,000 towards election expenses if they were prepared to repudiate their leader's 'wait and see' policy over the single currency; 237 took the wealthy man's shilling (*Guardian*, 30 April 1997). Fighting elections and maintaining an organization are increasingly expensive undertakings. Although parties were required to stick to constituency spending limits, these were routinely flouted by the increasingly centralized campaign techniques because there were no national limits. More was spent during the 1997 campaign than ever before. In the twelve months preceding the election, Conservatives and Labour accounted for £47 million while the Liberal Democrats weighed in with £3 million. Expenditure levels were reduced in 2001, following the Political Parties, Elections and Referendums Act (2000) (see p. 340).

Modern parties cannot operate without vast funds, a hard reality raising some compelling questions about power and democracy. The classic distinction between parties and interest groups becomes blurred; the two are bound together by chains of gold.

Conservative Party

The funding of the Conservative Party was one of the mysteries of British politics. Until 1968 no accounts were published and when they did appear they were economical with ink. Although becoming more detailed in 1993, they continued to conceal the size of private donations. Ex-party treasurer Lord McAlpine admitted in the House of Lords to 'tons' of offshore accounts into which donations were paid (Harrison 1993) and *Business Age* reported some £200 million salted away in a 'slush fund' in three overseas tax havens (Fisher 1994). The party finally published more detailed accounts in November 1998 (see below).

Although much constituency work is directed towards fundraising, at critical points like general elections the broadly capitalist interests of Britain regularly reached for their wallets to achieve what has generally been regarded as a key requirement of successful capitalism – a Conservative government. The party chair and treasurer had the task of rattling the begging bowl before industry, but this was for long as difficult as fishing in a trout farm.

> We need funds and I look to the City of London to give a lead in providing that support which as businessmen they should be prepared to give, in view of our efforts to make their business safe.
>
> Appeal by Conservative leader Stanley Baldwin in the *Daily Telegraph* (2 Feb. 1926)

There were also the intermediaries, associations existing for fundraising purposes, such as the Economic League, British United Industries, and Aims of Industry, which ran the celebrated 'Mr Cube' campaign in 1949–50, featuring a talking sugar lump which successfully saved Tate & Lyle from being dissolved in the thick collectivist tea of post-war nationalization.

> The CBI's character, and perhaps its main *raison d'être*, is geared to a dialogue with government...But it must be emphasised that the CBI is politically neutral.
>
> John Davies (CBI Director General), quoted in I. Gilmour, *The Body Politic* (1969: 351)

Party financing became central to the sleaze scandals of the 1990s. Ian Greer, a lobbyist involved in the cash-for-questions affair, claimed in October 1996 to have raised £750,000 for the party by encouraging donations from businessmen and clients over the previous ten years. He even alleged that ministers had approached him for help with their own election expenses (*The Times*, 7 Oct. 1996).

Party givers Not all donors use intermediaries in bestowing largesse; large companies can inject main line into the veins of the party. The merchant banks are especially important, their directors often being active within the party or its fundraising intermediaries. Almost half the corporate donations have come from banking, insurance, food, tobacco, drink and construction (Scott 1991: 147). Thus munchers of KP nuts, Hula Hoops, McCoy's Crisps, Penguins, McVitie's and Crawford's biscuits were themselves unwitting Conservative benefactors; between 1979 and 1993, United Biscuits, makers of these, headed the list of party givers with a total of £1,004,500. In addition, the party encouraged personal donations with fundraising activities including dinners with ministers and dining clubs such as the Millennium and Premier (see p. 535). Membership fees need not be classed as political donations and range from £10,000 to £100,000. By 1996, a new generation of entrepreneurs who had thrived during the 1980s were coming to the aid of the party with a 25 per cent increase in donations, reducing its overdraft by £2 million to £12 million (*Sunday Times*, 21 May 1997).

Friends abroad A particularly sensitive issue for the Conservatives has been the extent to which they sought and received overseas donations, raising fears that British home and foreign policy might be compromised. A bruising encounter between party chairman Sir Norman Fowler and the Commons Home Affairs Committee in June 1993 revealed millions of pounds secretly donated by governments, or individuals close to them, and foreign businessmen. Major General Sir Brian Wylde-Smith, for twelve years the party's fundraising director, disclosed that they had received £7 million from foreign backers before the 1992 general election (Harrison 1993), and Lord McAlpine (1997) was to report in his memoirs how, a year after retiring as party treasurer, he was asked by John Major to solicit funds from a wealthy benefactor identified as Greek shipping tycoon John Latsis (*The Times*, 3 March 1997). Contributions from Hong Kong ranged from £100,000 to £200,000 and there were even donations from individuals involved in the Yugoslavian civil war, including an associate of human rights violator Radovan Karadžić (Fisher 1997). Mounting fears of foreign influence over policy led to reforms agreed at the March 1998 constitutional conference. The sources of donations over £5,000 were to be revealed and foreign donations rejected. However, in April 1998 party chairman Cecil Parkinson told the Neill inquiry into party funding (see p. 340) that the threat of disclosure had caused overseas funding to dry up anyway (*Independent*, 23 April 1998).

Hard times Yet despite the rich veins of finance it has been able to tap, the party complained of financial difficulties. In 1975 it was £500,000 in debt and by the early 1990s things looked much worse (Whiteley et al. 1994). The 1992 campaign was the first for which it had to borrow from the banks, incurring a deficit of £19 million. It finished the 1997 campaign slightly better – only £10 million in the red. The constituency source, which until the 1980s had provided 20–25 per cent of total funds, was also declining, a trend most marked in Conservative-held seats through a combination of alienation and atrophy (Pattie and Johnston 1996). Even more significantly, the party began to lose its corporate donors. The first list of benefactors giving donations over £5,000 was modest compared with past levels of generosity, showing only thirty-three individual and corporate givers and revealing a party forced to call upon personal loans and gifts from its own senior officers (*The Times*, 21 Nov. 1998).

The Conservatives approached the 2001 general election in poor shape. A report for the independent analysts Labour Research revealed that in 2000 thirty-one companies had donated a total of £359,059, which compared badly with the £2.5 million handed over in the equivalent year of the previous parliament (Summerskill 2000). With backers such as Tarmac, Dixons, Hanson and P&O all deserting ship, and a £9 million overdraft, the party became embarrassingly reliant on donations from party treasurer Lord Ashcroft himself; these totalled around £5m since 1997. Hague was greatly relieved when City entrepreneur Stuart Wheeler, head of the IG betting index, and the philanthropist John Paul Getty Jnr both came up with £5 million, the biggest ever single recorded donations to a British party. Yet times had changed, and a major reason for this was New Labour.

Labour Party

Until 1997, the Conservatives were able to bombard the public with posters, newspaper advertisements and polished election broadcasts on a scale that had regularly demoralized Labour. Traditionally, Labour's funds came from the poorest section of society: under the 1913 Trade Union Act, the unions were entitled to collect a political levy from individual members to form a political fund. Conservative legislation in 1984 requiring union members to opt into the levy (rather than opt out) made it more difficult to collect. This source was for long a political Achilles' heel, ever open to allegations of sinister union pay-masters able to 'buy' positions on Labour's NEC. Although the British Election Study revealed that voters' perceiving the unions as 'too powerful' had declined significantly from 77 per cent in 1979 to 30 per cent in 1992, Labour's modernizers were stung by the taunts. Repeating the new mantra of 'fairness not favours', they sought to loosen if not cut the embarrassing umbilical cord. However, in turning from the devil they knew well they were obliged to court new ones: individual members, private corporations and wealthy benefactors.

The first produced a recruitment drive, the others entailed a search for new friends in the unfamiliar territory of the boardroom. Little could better symbolize the New Labour style. The Labour Business Plan was launched at high-profile dinners with party leaders and donations began to come in from companies including Pearson, Tate & Lyle, the Caparo Group and from wealthy individuals including (the late) Matthew Harding and David Sainsbury. There were also contributions from media and showbiz personalities such as Melvyn Bragg, Mick Hucknell, Lisa Stansfield, Eddie Izzard, Ben Elton and Jeremy Irons. By late 1996 the new sources were accounting for some 25 per cent of income, the party amassing assets of nearly £3 million (Fisher 1997).

The unions were unhappy with these developments, claiming that they still contributed the largest proportion of party income (54 per cent in 1995; see table 11.3). In 1997 the Amalgamated Engineering and Electrical Union showed its muscle by withholding £250,000 from the election fund as a protest against the 'parachuting' of candidates into union-sponsored seats, and in February 1998 the party's largest benefactors (UNISON, the Transport and

Table 11.3 Labour party funding changes, 1986–96 (£ thousands)

Source	1986	1996
Unions	4,419.6	7,729.2
Membership	759.8	1,658.7
Fundraising	359.6	6,309.9
Other	261.0	1,402.2

Source: Data from Labour Party NEC reports.

General and the GMB general union) announced cuts of £400,000 in donations because of the government's policy direction (*Independent*, 23 Feb. 1998). With debts of £3.5 million, plus an overdraft of £4.75 million from the £23-million 1997 campaign, Labour could hardly ignore the implications of these moves.

As the trade unions cut their donations from £12 to £8 million before the 2001 general election, businessmen became increasingly important. On top of the rising rent of its lavish Millbank headquarters and falling membership, the election left the party with debts of £5–6 million. The GMB Union did little to improve the position by withholding £2 million in January 2002 to register its opposition to privatization plans. Lord Sainsbury, the science minister, came forward with an emergency injection of £2 million, raising the estimated total of his donations to something over £7 million. By 2002, donations were making up around two-thirds of the party's income, with the union contribution having shrunk to less than 30 per cent.

Yet this was the New Labour style and Blair was unapologetic. Questioned on a *Breakfast with Frost* TV programme in January 2001 about three £2-million donations (including a cheque from the tax haven of Bermuda), he had claimed to be 'absolutely proud' that successful entrepreneurs and disaffected Conservatives supported Labour. He had also been reported as saying in private that he never again wanted to see Labour outspent by the Conservatives (Marr 1998).

Liberal Democrats

The gargantuan financial appetites of the two major parties leave a centre party with little potential sustenance. Liberal Democrats rely heavily on members' donations and fundraising activities and of necessity must fight lean campaigns (spending only £2.3 million in 1997 and £2.5 million in 2001). Not surprisingly, the party has been critical of large donations and calls for state funding.

Feathers and Favours

Donations have always aroused suspicion of policy rewards and even personal favours, though in practice it is almost impossible to prove a connection. In 1920, Liberal Prime Minister Lloyd George was accused of selling political honours for between £10,000 and £40,000; it was in response to this that the 1925 Honours (Prevention of Abuse) Act made it a criminal offence. More recently, there were allegations that Harold Wilson's resignation honours were paying back favours, and some were not surprised when United Biscuits chairman Sir Hector Lang, often described as Mrs Thatcher's favourite businessman, became Lord Lang upon retirement in 1990. Lord Shackleton, a former member of the Privy Council's Political Honours Scrutiny Committee, told the House of Lords that he believed honours were effectively being bought.

> Nobody gives money to a political party for nothing. They all want their feathers stroked from time to time ... some ... more often and more lovingly than others.
>
> Senior Conservative, quoted in the *Observer* (20 June 1993)

From 1979, around 6 per cent of companies were making donations to the Conservative Party and they received about half of all knighthoods and peerages – statistically unlikely to be an accidental correlation (Bogdanor 1997a). The Labour Party alleged that between 1979 and 1992, eighteen life peerages and eighty-two knighthoods were shared between seventy-six companies donating over £17 million to Conservative coffers, often using 'front organizations'. Amidst much controversy, Michael Ashcroft, Conservative party treasurer, donated £3 million from the tax haven of Belize and was subsequently nominated by William Hague for a life peerage. Conversely, funds may be withheld by organizations unhappy with government policy; BA openly threatened to cut donations to the Conservatives for this reason.

The privatization programme excited further allegations of rewards. It was claimed that eight merchant banks and stockbrokers, contributing a total of £1.4 million in party donations, gained the lion's share of the £1 billion fees paid to the City for advising on the flotations (*Sunday Times*, 17 Nov. 1991). Another source of rewards can be positions on prestigious quangos, offering political power to the unelected (see chapter 18).

Labour could not escape the same kind of charges as those made against the Conservatives; both Sainsbury and Bragg were ennobled within the party's first year in office. Moreover, a great furore arose in November 1997 when the government reneged on a pre-election promise to ban tobacco advertising connected with sport by exempting Formula One motor racing. It emerged that motor racing mogul Bernie Ecclestone had donated £1 million to the party just prior to the election. Moreover, it had apparently requested a further £1 million from him just at the time the government was engaged in EU negotiations over the same issue. On the advice of Lord Nolan the donation was returned and an embarrassed premier 'apologized' on Sunday television. Labour also began to operate a system of blind trusts whereby ministers were supposed to be unaware of who was donating to their private offices. These were denounced by fundraiser Henry Drucker, alleging: 'I don't believe these people would have given a bean unless there were enough nods and winks that Tony was, of course, very grateful' (*Independent*, 30 April 1998).

In January 2002 a new embarrassment arose for Labour over the collapse of US energy giant Enron and the accountancy firm Arthur Andersen, under investigation by the US Congress over allegations of false accounting on a massive scale. It was alleged that a £36,000 reception sponsored by Enron had cleared the way for a takeover of Wessex Water and the ending of a moratorium on building gas-fired power stations. Labour was also alleged to have lifted a ban on Arthur Andersen working for government after its role in the De Lorean scandal. However, Conservative moral outrage looked less convincing when Enron's former European chairman stated that the company had given money to both parties 'in order to gain access'. The Conservatives expressed regret that they had indeed accepted some £25,000.

Unfortunately for Labour, the scandals associated with its fundraising saw businessmen turning away. In the first half of 2002, the Conservatives had received twice as much as Labour. So dire was the position that, in August 2002, as the removal vans drove away from its opulent Millbank centre, Labour had to turn to the unions for a £100,000 emergency injection to meet its bills.

Regulating the paymasters

Although the Commons Home Affairs Committee had recommended regulating donations, Major refused Lord Nolan's request to inquire into this area (*Guardian*, 12 May 1995). However, under Labour, reform began with the 1998 report from Lord Neill's Committee on Standards in Public Life. This recommended a ban on foreign donations, while national donations above £5,000, and local donations over £1,000, should be declared on an open register. Although no restriction was proposed on the size of individual donations, national general election spending should be limited to £20 million per party, with fines for transgressors. Similar restrictions would apply to the new provincial assemblies. In addition, pressure-group spending on behalf of parties should be limited to £1 million, 'benefits in kind' (such as loan of offices) should be declared, blind trusts should be abolished and a scrutiny process should guard against the selling of honours. An independent electoral commission should police the system. The recommendations were broadly accepted and included in the 2000 Political Parties and Referendums Act. The 2001 general election was fought under the new rules, with national party spending capped at £15.8 million per party, a figure seen as unnecessarily high by critics. Estimates suggested that Labour had spent £12–13 million, the Conservatives £9 million and the Liberal Democrats £2.5 million.

However, reforms such as these cannot completely eliminate the problems that arise when finance and politics meet. Wealthy givers will still be sought by parties and rules can be bent or evaded. For many reformists, such as Charter88 (and the 1976 Houghton Committee), only state funding (as in continental European democracies and Canada) will end questionable practices and reduce the impression that influence can be bought.

State funding

Advocates of state funding argue that it would break the link between wealth and political power. It would also allow the state to place social obligations on political parties. Indeed, there is already some public funding, including free delivery of one election leaflet per candidate and free party political broadcasts. State funding also enables opposition parties to function at Westminster (£3,254 for every seat won plus £7.04 for every 200 votes). In addition, there is indirect state aid through postage and research costs (amounting to almost £20 million each parliament).

Yet large-scale state funding is no panacea and raises new questions. What of the smaller parties: what would be the formula for determining the level of funding? Would frivolous parties be eligible? Should the state finance dark forces wishing to undermine democracy or persecute minorities? Should funds be supplemented by private donations? Moreover, the system would be difficult to monitor. There is also a fundamental question of the freedom to use one's money according to personal choice. Although the Neill committee ruled out large-scale public funding, it did make an exception for referendum campaigns (see p. 236).

Masses, Leaders and Powers Behind Thrones

As developments conspire to reduce the role and importance of the mass membership in the British parties, the iron law of oligarchy remains compelling. However, it is clear that the debate over power does not end with internal organization. The need for finance means that there are crucial sources of influence outside the formal party structure. Although for much of the post-war period these were stable, the unions financing Labour and capital financing the Conservatives, the rise of New Labour introduced a new fluidity into the balance of power in today's society. In the next section we move further into the heart of political power by focusing on the central institutions of the state.

Key points

- Modern political parties consist of three elements: a parliamentary cadre, a bureaucracy and a mass membership.
- The question of where the power lies is an important subject for analysis. Michels's 'iron law of oligarchy' asserts that the mass will always fall under a small elite.
- Historically the Conservatives have been less internally democratic than Labour or the Liberal Democrats, allowing greater authority to the leader in patronage, organization and policy-making.
- However, the 1980s and 1990s saw Labour leaders tightening their grip over the mass.
- The Conservative Party has traditionally shown greater internal cohesion than any other. This appeared to have broken down by the 1990s.
- The increasing need for funds makes parties dependent on economic interests and raises profound questions about the public interest and modern democracy.

Review your understanding of the following terms and concepts

affiliated association

all-women shortlist

block vote

candidate selection

Conservative Central Office

constituency association

faction

ginger group

interest aggregation

iron law of oligarchy

NEC

party bureaucracy

party conference

party executive

patronage

sponsorship

tendency

ward association

Assignment

Study the extract from *The Spectator*, and answer the following questions.

		Mark (%)
1	'Above all there were the Thatcherites who never forgave Michael Portillo for turning his back on them after 1997.' Discuss.	25
2	To what extent does this article implicitly condemn the system used by the Conservative Party to elect its leader in 2001?	25
3	'He had too many enemies.' What does this tell us about the way politicians ascend the 'greasy pole'?	25
4	What strengths would Michael Portillo have brought to the Conservative leadership?	25

Questions for discussion

1 Explain how and why parties have varied their methods of appointing leaders.

2 Discuss whether internal party democracy is a necessary condition of a democratic state.

3 What factors have given the Conservative Party its longevity?

4 Compare and contrast the security of tenure of Labour and Conservative party leaders.

5 'Too much power for constituency associations in candidate selection undermines party government.' Discuss.

6 How realistic is it for party policies to be made by means of a 'bottom-up' process?

7 'The financing of the British parties undermines the democratic process.' Discuss.

8 Examine the pros and cons of all-women shortlists in candidate selection.

9 Assess the value of the annual party conference.

10 'Groupings within parties create dysfunctional tensions.' Discuss.

Topic for debate

This house believes that the Conservative Party is no longer the 'natural party of government'.

THE WORST SCRAPE IN TORY HISTORY

WHAT is going on in the Tory party just now is horrible. There was a sense of exultation on Tuesday night in Committee Room 14 as the result of the final round of voting in the parliamentary stage of the Tory leadership contest was announced. But only among those for whom hatred of Michael Portillo was the paramount consideration....

A sense of sadness was the only appropriate feeling as the Tory result was digested in the Grand Committee corridor on Tuesday night. We were watching a tragedy. The Tory party is eating itself. There are those who did not want Michael Portillo to win for good, honourable reasons. And there were those who hated him for disgraceful reasons: the racists and the homophobes and those who simply envied him because he was bigger than they were...

His supporters' belief that they were the victims of a conspiracy deserves to be taken seriously. Their man was the victim of a whispering campaign as relentless as any that Portillo himself is accused ... of masterminding. He had too many enemies. There were allies of William Hague who made certain that every scrap of damaging information about him, however one-sided, was rushed into the public domain in time for the leadership election....

Above all there were the Thatcherites who never forgave Michael Portillo for turning his back on them after 1997. They had well-placed allies in the Tory press, and they used them. Portillo never intended to make Section 28 and cannabis the cornerstone of his campaign. The *Daily Mail* did that for him, with brutal effectiveness...

To get a measure of the hatred, you have only to look at the Ken Clarke vote. Fat Ken put on 20 between the second and third rounds. Almost half of these were votes from calculating right-wingers, determined to ensure the destruction of Portillo by boosting his rival for second place.

Extract from Peter Oborne, 'The worst scrape in Tory history', *The Spectator*, 21 July 2001, pp. 12–13.

Further reading

See also reading for chapter 10.

Bogdanor, V. (1981) *The People and the Party System*.
Critical view of party politics.

McKenzie, R. (1967) *British Political Parties* (first published 1955).
Presents thesis that political constraints force parties to resemble each other.

Michels, R. (1962) *Political Parties* (first published 1911).
Classic statement of 'iron law of oligarchy'.

Muller, W. D. (1977) *The Kept Men*.
Examines trade union sponsorship of parliamentary candidates.

Peele, G. (1991) *British Party Politics: Competing for Power in the 1990s*.
Focuses on the problems of party management and leadership, techniques for marketing parties and party organization.

Riddell, P. (1993) *Honest Opportunism: The Rise of the Career Politician*.
Charts the changing character of the parliamentary parties.

Seyd, P. and Whiteley, P. (1992) *Labour's Grass Roots*; and Whiteley, P., Richardson, J. and Seyd, P. (1994) *True Blues: The Politics of Conservative Party Membership*.
Fascinating empirical analyses of mass memberships.

Willetts, D. (1996) *Blair's Gurus*.
Lively right-wing challenge to a battery of New Labour thinkers (Hutton, Marquand, Kay et al.).

For light relief

Geoffrey Archer, *First Among Equals*.
Ambitious politician attempts to climb the greasy party pole.

Wilfred Fienburgh, *No Love for Johnnie*.
Love, romance and committee meetings in the Labour Party (also a film).

Chris Mullin, *A Very British Coup*.
Labour MP explores (old) Labour's problems in dealing with the Establishment.

Jim Wilson, *The Labour Man*.
Comic novel. Labour has a majority of one, and all depends on Harry Beamish, who, tortured by his socialist ideals and the contradiction between power and honour, disappears.

On the net

See chapter 10.

Part III

Government at the Centre

Significantly we do not arrive at the formal centre of British government until the middle of the book. This underlines the fact that the comings and goings of the high and the mighty by no means represent the whole of the political story. Here we address the most central and exhilarating concepts in politics – official power: who holds it, who uses it, and who is able to influence its exercise. Our search takes us through the most ornate institutions of government (the monarchy and Parliament) to the heart of the Westminster/Whitehall complex, the Cabinet, the prime minister and the higher civil service. Finally, we delve even deeper into the mysteries of power by seeking sources of influence lying below the surface of ministerial pomp in the more shadowy recesses of political life. We shall find that although all may not be as it seems, nothing is without significance; every cam and cog in the machinery of state has a function and our task is to try to discover what that is.

12

Pomp and Circumstance: the Living Dead of the Constitution

In this chapter we meet the more ornate parts of the constitution, the parts visitors come to see and which are shown on the postcards they send home. These include the monarchy with its robes, jewels and golden coaches, and the Palace of Westminster housing the two chambers of Parliament – the House of Lords and the House of Commons. Here we see much flummery lovingly preserved from bygone ages, a celebration of the much-vaunted continuity of the British constitution. However, although as lifeless as the waxworks at Madame Tussaud's, like the mystic ritual of high church and courts, the ceremonial is by no means without significance. It induces respect and reverence for authority; it is the living dead of the constitution.

The physical setting

Parliament formally comprises the monarchy and two legislative chambers – the House of Lords and House of Commons – with their very tangible presence as the picturesque Palace of Westminster. One of the major landmarks of London, situated grandly on the bank of the Thames at the end of Whitehall, it is a popular tourist destination, around a million visitors a year queuing to be conducted on guided tours and purchase trinkets marked with the prestigious portcullis logo (also found on its official notepaper).

The beautiful architecture is not merely ornamental, it is deeply symbolic. Following severe damage by fire in 1834, it was restored in the Gothic style to reflect the belief that Britain's civil liberties stemmed from medieval achievements. The two chambers have a cathedral-like aura, intimidating all but the initiated. Around them a labyrinth of corridors, quadrangles and staircases leads to offices, committee rooms, smoking-rooms, tea-rooms, and of course bars. MPs can be seen variously talking in intimate clusters, meeting groups of eager constituents, playing host to interest-group representatives or lobbyists, or lying low in places of refreshment trying to avoid such encounters.

The chambers are surprisingly small and could not seat all members if they were to descend simultaneously. This is quite deliberate; another opportunity to rebuild was presented by the German Luftwaffe in 1941 but the decision was taken to retain the sense of intimacy conducive to debate. Unlike most chambers, the benches are arrayed in a confrontational manner (figure 12.1) and, in the Commons, the front ranks are two swords lengths apart, commemorating an age when the thrust and parry of debate could be more than figurative.

The evolution of Parliament

The three elements of Parliament represent the great estates of the realm which have fought over the centuries for control of the state: the Crown, the aristocracy and the common people. Its origins lie in the assembly of Anglo-

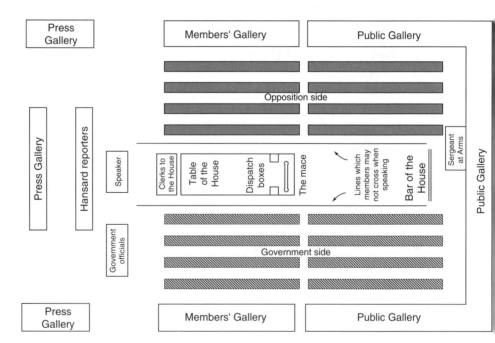

Figure 12.1
Chamber of the House of Commons.

Saxon kings which met as the *Witangemot*. In Norman times kings governed assisted only by their officials, although the country was divided into territorial units ruled by barons whom the kings would summon as the *Magnum Concilium* for discussion, advice and to raise money. The barons demanded more control, securing this through the Magna Carta signed at Runnymede in 1215. Herein lies the origin of the House of Lords.

The House of Commons was conceived in the kingly practice, from the thirteenth century, of calling additional meetings of the less-important local representatives, the commoners (knights from the shires and burgesses from the incorporated towns), as a further source of revenue. They would assemble humbly before the monarch, who would tell them how much was required and dispatch them to find it, leaving the aristocracy to discuss important matters of state. However, the Commons, recognizing its potential power, began making demands. When expensive wars forced Edward III (1327–77) to summon frequent parliaments, they took the opportunity to attach a list of reforms when accepting the tax demands. At the beginning of the fifteenth century Henry IV agreed that grants of money would only be initiated in the Commons, recognizing the lower house as part of Parliament.

This hold over the purse-strings saw the gradual erosion of the monarch's position. Coming soon after the profligate Henry VIII (1509–47), Elizabeth I (1558–1603) recognized the reality and was careful to court Parliament. However, the Stuarts lacked the Tudors' realism and Charles I sought to govern without parliamentary consent by raising taxes directly from towns ('ship money'). By this time the Commons had become powerful enough to oppose him and events led to the Civil War (1642–6) between the Royalists (Cavaliers) and the parliamentarians (Roundheads). It resulted in Charles losing not just the Crown but a head upon which to rest it. Britain entered upon a brief period as a **republic** (1649–60) with the Puritan Oliver Cromwell supreme as 'Lord Protector'.

The Restoration in 1660 saw Charles II return in glory from exile but things were to be different. He was a *constitutional monarch*, constrained by Parliament. The anniversary of his father's execution was marked by a grizzly ceremony in which Cromwell's disinterred corpse was hung on the infamous gallows at Tyburn. Yet James II could not accept the limitations and further skirmishes culminated in the Glorious Revolution of 1688, which placed William (of Orange) and Mary (daughter of James II) on the English throne, their powers clearly restricted in the 1689 Bill of Rights. It was not until the 1701 Act of Settlement that the subordinate position of the monarchy was satisfactorily established, made easier by the fact that the Hanoverian line (established in 1714) had little interest in British affairs.

The upper house had also been abolished during the republic and was reinstated at the Restoration. In the 1689 settlement the Commons concerned itself with commerce while the Lords attended to affairs of state, including foreign policy, subject to the convention that money supply was in the sole gift

> I would rather hew wood than be a king under the condition of the king of England.
>
> Charles X of France (1757–1836)

of the Commons. However, the Commons remained under the control of aristocratic and royal factions, both exercising a corrupt influence on elections and nominations. It was the great nineteenth-century Reform Acts that delivered the *coup de grâce*, through the moral authority given to the Commons by the popular vote.

Yet the message was not immediately clear to their lordships. In 1883 they rejected the second Irish Home Rule Bill and the reforming Liberal government of 1905 found eighteen of its bills rejected. Matters came to a head when Chancellor Lloyd George, needing £16 million in extra revenue to finance the planned social programme as well as build *Dreadnought* battleships, determined that the money should come principally from taxing the landed interests, against whom he had been conducting a campaign. His 1909 'People's Budget' was rejected by the Lords, precipitating a constitutional crisis in which a reluctant monarch, weakened by 'four gargantuan meals a day together with endless wine, brandy, whisky and cigars' (Cross 1963: 106), was told he might be forced to create sufficient new government-supporting peers to swamp their lordships' opposition. The outcome was the 1911 Parliament Act, which not only legalized the convention regarding financial legislation but reduced the Lords' veto over other legislation to a power to delay for two years (shortened to a year in 1949 by the Labour government, nearing the end of its life and fearful of the fate of its steel nationalization bill).

The Monarchy

Constitutional monarchy means that although the Queen may be said to *reign*, she does not *rule*. Perhaps the monarchy's last dying gasps were heard under Victoria. Initially influenced by her consort Albert (who took his authority seriously) and later encouraged by the flattering Disraeli, she made several efforts to exert the royal prerogative. It was the lot of the austere Gladstone to school the Queen in her role and cut the modern pattern of British democratic kingship (Magnus 1963: 42–7). Today the monarch formally continues to hold hundreds of prerogative powers, the extent and scope of which are largely determined by convention. They range widely, covering appointments, legislation, emergency powers, and summoning and proroguing Parliament, but are generally exercised on advice (usually prime ministerial) and conflict has been rare since the beginning of the twentieth century.

Why study the monarchy? Some commentaries on British politics and sociology omit the monarchy. This may be intended to betoken a jettisoning of meaningless symbolism in order to focus on the world of reality but it is a mistake, betraying a short-sighted and superficial vision. The monarchy affects modern politics by being a significant element in political culture.

> The use of the Queen, in a dignified capacity, is incalculable. Without her in England, the present English government would fail and pass away.
>
> Walter Bagehot, *The English Constitution* (1867: ch. 2)

Characteristics of the monarchy today

Today Buckingham Palace, the main royal residence, stands at the end of the Mall in some 40 acres of gardens. Together with Horse Guards' Parade, Westminster Abbey and the Palace of Westminster, all within a cannon's shot of each other, it is part of a baroque Disneyland of the past, gradually becoming overgrown by a towering office-block jungle. Inside the palace, courtiers and flunkeys, with titles and sometimes costumes of a bygone age, perform the tasks of running the monarchy industry. Many are themselves nobly born and treasure their families' links with the sovereign, passing the positions down through the generations. Today's monarchy is distinguished by certain characteristics.

Hereditary No one votes for the British Head of State. Although faltering from time to time, the succession is based on inheritance, Elizabeth II being the fortieth monarch since the Norman Conquest.

Ceremony While Britain is not alone as a constitutional monarchy (Luxembourg, the Netherlands, Belgium, Spain, Sweden, Denmark and Norway are the same), it is unique in the degree to which the pomp and **ceremonial** have been preserved. (The Scandinavian royals have been slightingly dubbed 'bicycling monarchies' because of their exorcism of ostentation.) The British monarchy, although never able to match the French in its extravagant prime, can on great occasions in the royal life-cycle (births, weddings and funerals) reach a scale only matched in Hollywood epics.

Political neutrality Although informed on a weekly basis by the prime minister, the Queen remains above the political fray. She does not vote; neither is she expected to express partisan opinions.

Familial Like the Mitchells of the East End or the Archers of Ambridge, the Windsors of Belgravia present to the public an extended family supported by a galaxy of bit players. Indeed, the Queen was faced with a similar challenge to that of Snow White's mother, her personal popularity (measured as 'the member of the royal family you would most like to meet') falling from 34 per cent in 1981 to 19 per cent in 1987, while the Princess of Wales became fairest of all.

Expense The monarchy does not come cheap. In 1761 George III agreed to surrender the income from the Crown Estate (worth some £95 million a year today) in exchange for a regular grant from Parliament – the Civil List – to cover expenditure relating to the monarch's official duties. Although remaining constant for a considerable time, it was revised under Elizabeth II to keep pace with inflation. Other expenses include the upkeep of five palaces and the travel costs of up to 2,500 official engagements annually, which are met by Grants-in-Aid from Parliament. One of the most ostentatious sources of expenditure was the royal yacht *Britannia*, which was not replaced under New Labour government.

In addition there is the Privy Purse, primarily used to cover official expenditure not met from the Civil List. The Queen's private expenditure is met from her own considerable personal fortune, its precise size subject to much speculation. Estimates of £100 million and upwards in 1993 were said by the Lord Chamberlain to be 'grossly overstated'. Although her property includes two royal residences, Sandringham and Balmoral, certain 'inalienable' items are held not as private property but on behalf of the nation (though most of the nation will never see them). These include the internationally renowned art collection, heirlooms in the Queen's jewellery collection and the Crown Jewels.

For long the Queen's income was exempt from tax and death duties, giving her a touch similar to that of King Midas and enabling her to outdistance all aristocratic rivals (some of whom, even after the second world war, were actually richer than the king). While they were collecting the tickets for the exhibitions and zoos on their estates, the wealth in the royal coffers continued to grow. When part of Windsor Castle (which was not insured) was destroyed by fire in November 1992, the Conservative government's immediate response was to shoulder the £50-million repair burden. However, this uncharacteristic generosity with taxpayers' money provoked controversy, and from 1993 the Queen joined her subjects as clients of her tax inspectors. The money for the restoration was raised by opening Buckingham Palace to a fee-paying public. In addition, the Civil List was cut to the bone, leaving only the Queen herself, the Duke of Edinburgh and the Queen Mother. A city accountant became guardian of the royal finances. The parliamentary annuities paid to the remaining members of the royal family to enable them to carry out official duties (totalling some £1.5 million) are now repaid to the Treasury by the Queen. In 2000, she agreed that the Civil List should be frozen until 2011 at the 1990 level of £7.9 million. However, further controversy followed the Queen Mother's death in 2002, when the contents of the will were not revealed and no death duties paid.

Popularity Before the second world war, shaken by the abdication crisis, the future of the monarchy was uncertain, but the war itself and the post-war era, with the coronation, weddings, many royal offspring and even dramatic marital disasters, saw the public appetite for its 'dignified' constitution grow to gargantuan dimensions. The period following the death of Princess Diana in

1997 led to a belief that the Queen's popularity was plummeting, but 200,000 were to file past the Queen Mother's coffin as it lay in state in Westminster Hall in April 2002, while around a million lined the streets for the funeral procession. The Golden Jubilee celebrations of 2002 saw thousands at concerts in Buckingham Palace, while millions turned out around the country as the Queen proceeded on her jubilee tour, confounding predictions that the event would prove an embarrassing flop.

If Her Majesty stood for Parliament – if the Tory Party had any sense and made her its leader instead of that grammar school twit Heath – us Tories, mate, would win every election we went in for.

Alf Garnett, in Johnny Speight's TV series *Till Death us do Part*

The functions of the monarchy

The monarch's functions are both practical and symbolic, including the following.

- *Ceremonial*. The expectations of British kingcraft were virtually defined by Walter Bagehot in 1867. He argued that 'the masses of Englishmen are not fit for an elective government; if they knew how near they were to it, they would be surprised and almost tremble' (1963: 97). The monarchy was the keystone in the dignified facade concealing the real processes of government from the uncomprehending masses (particularly women).
- *Symbol of national unity*. As a tangible object of veneration the monarch can symbolize the unity of society in a way that a party leader cannot. Patriotism can become xenophobia and it may be prudent if it can be channelled off in support of a constitutional icon.
- *Head of the armed forces*. Members of the royal family frequently hold ceremonial military ranks and the armed forces and police are constitutionally servants of the Crown, supposedly symbolizing their independence from politics.
- *Head of the Commonwealth*. This is an area where the Queen's authority is not controlled by the prime minister. Indeed, it was widely reported in 1987 that she was displeased by Thatcher's opposition to sanctions against apartheid South Africa.
- *Head of state*. Monarchy or not, any system of government requires a large element of formality, from entertaining foreign leaders to opening hospitals and presenting awards. Without a sovereign, the role of Head of State falls on elected leaders, perhaps fattening their egos or removing them from real politics.

◆ *Fidei defensor.* The Reformation established the Anglican Church with the monarch at its head as 'defender of the faith'. Many royal ceremonies have a religious nature, including the coronation itself. However, with increasing multiculturalism Prince Charles has spoken of being the defender of the *faiths* and in June 2002 the shoeless and garlanded Queen paid her first visit to a Hindu temple during her jubilee tour.

◆ *Virtual regality.* It can be argued that the royal family can add colour to the lives of people with otherwise drab existences, thereby helping to maintain social stability.

◆ *Moral leadership.* The presentation of the monarchy as a family has been seen as a basis for giving the public a moral example.

The throne behind the power Beyond the largely ceremonial functions is the possibility that monarchs can exert real influence. Unlike prime ministers they are not troubled by popular opinion, elections, party infighting and rivals for power. Enjoying office for as long as they remain alive, their experience can be a source of wisdom. Although believing a republic had insinuated itself beneath the folds of a monarchy, Bagehot asserted a famous trio of royal rights: to be consulted, to encourage and to warn. In 1884 even Gladstone formally thanked Queen Victoria for her 'wise, gracious and steady exercise of influence' (Magnus 1963). When Elizabeth II celebrated fifty years on the throne in 2002, she had worked with ten different prime ministers, giving her more experience of public life than any political figure. This influence is likely to be greatest over non-ideological issues (Bogdanor 1996a), particularly the Commonwealth, a point borne out by former prime minister James Callaghan:

> the Queen's initiative on Rhodesia [openly disapproving of Ian Smith's declaration of UDI] was a perfect illustration of how and when the Monarch could effectively intervene to advise and encourage her Ministers . . . with complete constitutional propriety. (Callaghan 1987: 382)

Moreover, in conditions of constitutional crisis powers may go beyond Bagehot's modest assessment. Few would deny that the monarch would be justified in intervening if events 'subverted the democratic basis of the Constitution' (Jennings 1959: 412). Even in less dramatic circumstances the powers to dissolve Parliament and appoint the prime minister could become real. Although no dissolution request has been refused since before the 1832 Reform Act, this could happen if, in the words of Sir Alan Lascelles (former private secretary to George VI and Elizabeth II), 'the existing Parliament was still vital, viable and capable of doing its job' or if the monarch 'could rely on finding another prime minister who could [govern] . . . with a working majority' (Hennessy 1994). Peter Hennessy (1994) suggests that since 1949 the possibility of such powers being used has loomed on at least five occasions: in the spring of 1950 when the general election cut Attlee's majority from 146 to 6; in

July 1953 when Churchill and Eden were seriously ill; in January 1957 following Eden's post-Suez resignation; in October 1963 following Macmillan's resignation; and in March 1974 when the narrowly defeated Heath attempted to do a deal with the Liberals.

The hollow crown

While supporters of monarchy extol its virtues and agnostics dismiss it as harmless sideshow, republicans point to more disturbing aspects.

Out of touch The life experience of the Queen, despite her known enthusiasm for *Coronation Street*, can hardly be said to have brought her into contact with the feelings of ordinary people. Her personal circle has remained largely within the aristocracy. According to a BBC report (25 Feb. 1998), Prince Charles apparently managed to complete a nine-day trip round Central Asia in 1996 without once saying hello to the small press party with him.

> Kings are not born, they are made by artificial hallucination.
>
> George Bernard Shaw, *Man and Superman* (1905)

Vulgarization If Bagehot were to return he would have cause to rue the day he praised the virtues of royal ceremonial. Today the masses gape through the vulgarizing lens of the tabloid press. The 'Royals' have been elevated to the status of show-biz celebrities and hounded all over the world by the *paparazzi*, aptly named the 'rat-pack'. The intense scrutiny led the Queen to label 1992 her *annus horribilis*.

Falling popularity According to one opinion poll, less than half the population support the monarchy; the proportion thinking the country would be worse off without the royals fell from 70 per cent in 1994 to 48 per cent in 1997 (*Guardian*, 12 Aug. 1997). Indeed, November 2002 saw the Jubilee year disintegrating into yet another *annus horribilis* with the trial of Paul Burrell, former butler to Princess Diana, accused of theft after her death. In announcing that he had confided his intention to remove items, the Queen effectively ended the trial. Yet her intervention appeared bizarre and speculation in drawing rooms and tabloids talked of a ploy to prevent embarrassing disclosures of palace life.

A dysfunctional family The idea that the royal family could exert an uplifting moral force was to become almost risible. In an earlier era Princess Margaret had denied herself marriage to Group Captain Peter Townsend because he was divorced, yet by 1996 she and three of the Queen's children were themselves divorced. Moreover, the romance that had enchanted millions disintegrated in a moral morass in 1992 when first the 'Camillagate' and then the 'Squidgygate' tapes allowed the world to hear the fairytale couple on their mobile phones murmuring sweet nothings to others. The public who had cheered along the wedding route were to discover that the royal establishment had allowed the heir apparent to make a cynical marriage for the purpose of royal procreation. Charles's mistress, Camilla Parker-Bowles, had sat calmly in row three during the glittering ceremony in Westminster Abbey (Holden 1997).

> Because we do not have the guts to sweep the monarchy away, we shall do the only thing we dare. We shall mock them until they wish they had never been born.
>
> David Hare, playwright and polemicist, in the *Guardian* (24 May 1993)

Democracy as deception: **panem et circenses** Bagehot's views reflected a widespread elite fear of the extending franchise but, where J. S. Mill argued for more political education, he preferred constitutional sleight of hand. Like the emperors of imperial Rome, the elite would provide bread and circuses to divert popular attention from affairs of state. However, a political culture that values deception is one that can tolerate secrecy and even lies.

Legitimation of inequality Unlike other constitutional monarchies, Britain's does not stand alone; it is the tip of an aristocratic iceberg of inherited wealth and titles, the survival of which is one of the political wonders of the world. This legitimates elitism and maldistribution of wealth, helping to keep the social soil fertile for capitalism.

A neutrality myth? Finally, the convention of political neutrality is open to question. It is partly a consequence of the two-party system in which the sovereign is not asked to exercise discretion in the choice of prime minister or the dissolution of Parliament. However, royal leanings can be discerned. Disraeli's 'one nation' Conservatism made the Crown one of its symbols. To be a patriotic member of society entailed support for the Crown, loyalty that could be expressed by voting Conservative. Indeed, the Queen is head of the Anglican Church, long described as the Conservative Party at prayer.

Peter
Mandelson:
You're a secret
Blairite.
Prince Charles:
I gather Mr Blair
is a secret me.

Sunday Times
(15 June 1997)

On the other hand, former Australian prime minister Bob Hawke disclosed that the Queen had argued with Thatcher on policy and Ben Pimlott's 1996 biography prompted tabloid headlines: 'The Queen's a Lefty'. Legend has it that, as a student at Cambridge, Prince Charles had asked the Master of Trinity if he could join the university Labour club, and in 1988 he criticized Conservative social policy. In 1997 he wrote to Blair noting their shared agenda. Indeed, a September 2002 leak revealed a long-running correspondence with the Lord Chancellor and Prime Minister expressing his views on matters of public concern, ranging from the Human Rights Act to foxhunting.

The problem has increased as the royals move into commercial life, as was revealed by the *News of the World*'s publication in March 2001 of a transcript of a conversation between the Countess of Wessex (Prince Edward's wife, formerly Sophie Rees-Jones) and a reporter posing as an Arab sheikh client of her public relations company. Betraying strongly Tory sympathies, she called

Gordon Brown's budget 'Pap', and mocked Blair's 'impromptu' speech after Princess Diana's death. She subsequently resigned from the company.

How long to reign over us?

Death of a princess The monarchy debate was thrust to the front pages with the death of Princess Diana. She had spoken of being the 'queen of people's hearts' and her funeral became her tragic coronation, provoking an unprecedented mass outpouring of grief. Yet this was no demonstration of love of royalty. Many were offended by protocol that forbade the flying of the flag at half-mast and by the Queen remaining at Balmoral. Only after government intervention was a public rather than a private funeral agreed.

While the royal family tried to reclaim Princess Diana in death, repeats of her astonishingly frank 1995 *Panorama* interview reminded people of her unhappiness. Rejected and effectively banished on her divorce, stripped of her royal rank, she became 'a totem of protest against that ringfenced elite that has quietly run Britain from gentlemen's clubs and secret societies' (Holden 1997). Whether the monarchy should be abolished or reformed, few could imagine it remaining unchanged.

Abolition While abolition, and even execution, has been the principal basis for constitutional evolution (until the first world war monarchy was prevalent throughout Europe), Britain's relatively smooth transition to democracy has

A people's princess: flowers left by mourners at the gates of Buckingham Palace after the death of Princess Diana

Photo: Times Newspapers Ltd

never produced a sustained call for republicanism. Although the 1997 Labour government's wide-ranging constitutional reform programme implied republicanism, the death of Princess Diana changed the climate. There was even talk of Labour spin doctors advising the Queen and fears that she would be booed at the funeral proved unfounded.

Attitudes to the monarchy following the death of Princess Diana

Which of these options for the monarchy would you prefer?
Continue in its present form: 12%
Continue but be modernized: 74%
Be replaced with a republic when Queen dies: 5%
Be replaced with a republic immediately: 7%

Observer/ICM poll in the *Guardian* (17 Sept. 1997)

Reform: New Labour, New Monarchy? Princess Diana was no republican; she herself had a hereditary title and wanted her son to be king. However, she had begun to forge a new and popular style, suggesting that the institution could be modernized. What are the alternatives?

She was always trying to get across to people like us.

East London girl, on Princess Diana, quoted by Simon Jenkins in *The Times* (3 Sept. 1997)

- ◆ *A bicycling monarchy.* A scaling down to Dutch or Scandinavian proportions would entail less ostentation and less attention to 'minor Royals'. Jack Straw, as Labour's home affairs spokesman, had affirmed such a vision. Yet for many this would destroy the magic.
- ◆ *A hands-on monarchy.* Princess Diana's style was to pay more attention to meeting ordinary people while retaining the glitter. The personal frailty and humanity she displayed revealed a public longing for a more humane and caring monarchy. Although this approach did not meet with Palace approval, the Queen's eve-of-funeral broadcast declared that 'lessons would be learned'. However, such a transformation might prove difficult for a family schooled in the art of the stiff upper lip rather than the gentle touch.
- ◆ *A fresh-start monarchy.* With Prince Charles's rehabilitation by no means certain, some have seen Prince William as the great hope. With his mother's looks, he carried her imprimatur. There was considerable popular approval for such a move, 53 per cent of those polled in September 1997 feeling that the crown should pass to him (*Guardian*, 17 Sept. 1997). While this could set the republican cause back a generation, it would require a self-denying ordinance from Charles. This appeared unlikely as the royal family sought, with the aid of spin doctors, to rehabilitate itself, and Camilla Parker-Bowles was increasingly seen at royal events. In 2002, the seventy-six-year-old Queen announced that she was indeed long to reign over us; there would be no retirement.

In defence of monarchy

There is a place for constitutional monarchy in the modern world. In a democracy, it is generally good for politicians to be kept down to size. They are supposed to represent the interests of others and should be restrained from self-aggrandizement. Thatcher's style in the late 1980s was criticized by some as inappropriately imperious and usurping the role of the real queen. Without a monarchy some other institution would be required as head of state. Certain functions could perhaps be handed to the Speaker of the House of Commons, but the Speaker is also a politician. For most abolitionists the solution lies in some form of presidency, elected either by the people or Parliament. However, this would mean battles over the succession. Thomas Hobbes (see p. 26) argued for the hereditary principle to avoid this.

The monarchy's uncertain future is tied in with a host of other variables, including the demise of press deference, the demand for a written constitution, the future of the Commonwealth and Britain's place in Europe. However, the institution has shown considerable flexibility in surviving over the centuries. There is perhaps more to the debate than constitutional logic. As Bogdanor states:

> If the conjunction of monarchy and democracy may seem a contradiction, it would be well to bear in mind Freud's aphorism that it is only in logic that contradictions can not exist. (Bogdanor 1996a: 421)

We have become a grandmother.

Margaret Thatcher, sounding regal

On the whole it is wise in human affairs and in the government of men, to separate pomp from power.

Winston Churchill, speech in Ottawa (1952)

The House of Lords

Beneath the monarchical tip of the iceberg has long floated an edifice of ancient privilege – a fully fledged aristocratic class of titled lords and ladies, sighted on special occasions and in special places such as the royal enclosure at Ascot, Cowes and, most visibly of all, in the House of Lords. It remained one of the most curious of the anomalies in British public life, defying any rule book of democratic and secular politics. The general atmosphere of the upper house has been seen as somnambulant, likened to a mausoleum or adduced as evidence of life after death.

If, like me, you are over 90, frail, on two sticks, half deaf and half blind, you stick out like a sore thumb in most places, but not in the House of Lords.

Harold Macmillan (Lord Stockton), quoted in the *Observer* (19 May 1985)

The composition of the House has been, and remains, a highly contentious issue. It has been seen as deeply undemocratic and became a principal target of New Labour's reforming programme (see pp. 362–7).

Politics in the House of Lords

Though cryptically referred to in the Commons as 'the other place', the Lords is linked to the Commons by a short corridor. Despite the leisurely atmosphere, the House has come to work harder over the past fifty years (Shell 1994: 734). Sittings take place from Mondays to Thursdays for about thirty weeks a year, usually between 2.30 and 7.00 p.m. Only towards the end of the session do they meet on Fridays. The central throne is reserved for the monarch and debate is chaired by the Lord Chancellor, sitting on the traditional 'Woolsack', which symbolizes national prosperity through trade. In November 1998 there was agreement on some minor reductions to the pomp surrounding the office, allowing the Lord Chancellor to dispense with breeches and tights in favour of trousers at certain less ceremonial times, though traditionalists feared the office was losing its dignity.

> This is a rotten argument, but it should be good enough for their lordships on a hot summer afternoon.
>
> Civil servant's note on a ministerial brief, read out by mistake in Lords debate;
> quoted in Lord Home, *The Way the Wind Blows* (1976)

Debates are rarely acrimonious and the Lord Chancellor does not pretend to be independent, often leaving the Woolsack to join the cut and thrust. The party machines have been less dominant than in the Commons, around a fifth of members sitting as independent **cross-benchers**, often having renounced former allegiances (table 12.1). Of the regular attenders, Conservatives (even before reform) did not have an outrageous majority but if all had descended they would have swamped the House. These were the 400 or so 'backwoodsmen' and, when the trumpet sounded, they forsook their estates to answer the call, as they did in 1968 to vote against a trade ban on Rhodesia and in 1998 to defeat New Labour's proposed closed-list system for EU elections. Peers who had never voted before, and who did not even know their own leaders, were to be found wandering in bewilderment around the precincts of Westminster.

Table 12.1 Political allegiance in the House of Lords (November 1998) prior to the first stage of reform

Type of peer	Conservative	Labour	Lib Dem	Cross-bench	Other
Life	173	158	45	120	9
Hereditary	302	18	24	202	87

Source: Data from parliamentary website (accessed Nov. 1998). Excludes peers without writs of summons (68) and bishops (26).

The House of Lords is not the watchdog of the constitution; it is Mr Balfour's poodle. It fetches and carries for him. It barks for him. It bites anyone that he sets it on to.

David Lloyd George, House of Commons speech (21 Dec. 1908)

Peer pressure: the functions of the House of Lords

The House of Peers, throughout the war,
Did nothing in particular,
And did it very well.

The Peers in Gilbert and Sullivan's *Iolanthe*

Generally speaking, second chambers can represent various interests, provide parliamentarians who are more independent of the executive, exercise a veto and share the burden of parliamentary duties (Russell 2001). The House of Lords does each of these to varying degrees and in varying ways.

Criticism The Lords have been able to demonstrate a freedom of expression not found in the Commons, speaking out where elected mortals favour discretion. Unlike MPs, they are less dependent upon further patronage and often beyond the age of ambition, at least in this life. Since the early 1970s the House has made greater use of select committees (see p. 403), the most significant being those on the European Communities and Science and Technology.

Informed debate Although the **hereditary peers** represented a narrow interest, the presence of **life peers**, appointed because of some particular expertise (from the professions, the arts, industry or academia), can at times sustain a high level of debate, while the bishops have injected a moral dimension.

Legislation The Lords can share the parliamentary burden by scrutinizing bills, proposing amendments and tidying up legislation passed in haste in the lower house. Bills may also be introduced in the Lords (see p. 393).

Restraint of the executive Although not having a full veto, the Lords can check the executive. With less party discipline, there can be more sense of a separation of powers, and over recent decades the Lords have become more assertive (see p. 394). The power to delay non-financial legislation can force a government to think again (and a full veto remains in the case of any government seeking to extend its life beyond five years). In December 2001, to the frustration of Home Secretary David Blunkett, considerable changes were made to the Anti-terrorism Bill, rushed through in the wake of the 11 September attack.

Potentially draconian powers in areas such as police snooping into private (including medical) records were curbed and the proposed crime of incitement to religious hatred was thrown out.

Judicial decision-making One function not common to upper chambers, but remaining central to the living constitution, is that of final court of appeal. This is not performed by the House as such but by the Law Lords headed by the Lord Chancellor (see p. 632).

The end of the peer show: a reluctant revolution

One of the main problems with the Lords has been its composition. Traditionally, membership was based on hereditary right; certain people were 'born to rule', a distinction acquired by emerging from a particular womb following an aristocratic impregnation. To this principle was added, through the 1958 Life Peerages Act, another equally undemocratic one: life peers (who could not hand down their titles) were appointed by the prime minister, thus reviving the House with a transfusion of fresh (though not always young) blood. This system could have been purpose-built to produce maximum controversy yet it proved remarkably resistant to change. In 1998 the House contained around 760 hereditary peers (mainly Conservatives) and nearly 500 life peers. In addition, there were 26 Anglican bishops and 28 Law Lords. It was indeed a House of Lords, for they outnumbered Ladies by around 13:1.

Almost a century earlier Lloyd George, who regarded the Lords with contempt, had intended the 1911 Parliament Act to be a stop-gap, a prelude to a revolution. However, despite much huffing and puffing, for long no wolf emerged with the constitutional lung power to blow the House down. Although people looked to Labour for action, they did so in vain, the party barking in opposition but unwilling to bite in office. A 1968 white paper announced some half-hearted reforms but the subsequent Parliament (No. 2) Bill was dashed on the rocks of an unholy alliance between two unlikely bedfellows – Enoch Powell (favouring the status quo) and Michael Foot (favouring the constitutional bulldozers).

In 1988, Lord Scarman, one of the Law Lords, called for a strengthened upper house to resist encroaching prime ministerial dictatorship, and Labour's 1989 policy review proposed an elected second chamber. This policy was also advocated by the Liberal Democrats and Charter88, which envisaged much stronger powers to initiate, revise, delay and even veto legislation. Labour's 1997 manifesto promised reform and, once in office, Blair began to redress the Lords' inbuilt Tory domination, his first Honours list containing thirty-one 'working' Labour peers. Expected to attend regularly, they included a glittering array of leading industrialists, writers and media figures. The Liberal Democrats gained eleven new working peers and the Conservatives five.

In October 1998 a two-stage timetable for real reform was announced. First, the hereditary peers would be removed, but after a deal brokered by Viscount

Cranborne, Leader of the Conservative peers, ninety-two hereditary peers, elected by their own number, were allowed to remain. Moreover, a further ten were immediately reprieved with life peerages. In the case of life peers, the prime minister's sole right of nomination was to be reduced, with an independent commission recommending some non-political appointments. The second stage of reform was to be considered by a Royal Commission under Conservative peer Lord Wakeham and a white paper suggested four options:

1 fixed levels of representation for interest groups and professional associations;
2 direct popular election;
3 indirect election with members seconded from the devolved institutions, including the Scottish, Welsh and Irish Assemblies, local authorities and the European Parliament;
4 a mixed chamber comprising elected and nominated members.

The Wakeham report Reporting in January 2000, Wakeham saw the role of the upper house as a 'revising and deliberative assembly – not seeking to usurp the role of the Commons'. In other words, the Lords was to be kept in the state of impotence to which its previous lack of legitimacy had consigned it. With no hereditary peers, the chamber would comprise 550 members, some elected and some nominated. However, direct election would be used for only a 'significant minority' (the majority of the Commission favoured eighty-seven), to represent the regions, with the great majority being appointed by an independent commission, selecting from all sectors of society without reference to party. Other proposals included a statutory minimum of 30 per cent women, a 'fair' representation of ethnic minorities and the broadening of the range of religious representation.

The government's response There was some expectation that the report would gather dust on the shelves of the Westminster libraries, allowing the ninety-two hereditary peers to avoid the chill winds of change. However, a November 2001 white paper (Lord Chancellor's Department 2001a) suggested that Wakeham's recommendations would largely be followed. However, beneath the rhetoric was one highly significant departure. Although the hereditary peers would go, and 20 per cent of the new chamber would be popularly elected, only 20 per cent would be chosen by an independent cross-party commission. The remaining 60 per cent would enter on the basis of party patronage – in effect, the life peerage system writ large, particularly as the prime minister would make the lion's share of the nominations (to reflect party strengths in the Commons).

The proposals evoked a barrage of criticism from the opposition parties, the Commons Public Administration Committee and the government's own supporters. Lord Wakeham lamented that his 'hard-fought consensus' had been abandoned (Tempest 2002). The result was a government climbdown, with Leader of the House Robin Cook announcing in May 2002 yet another review.

Tony's Cronies

Photo: Charter88

A joint committee of MPs and peers would produce further proposals, to be put to a free vote in both Houses. Although critics welcomed the abandonment of the white paper proposals, there were fears that the issue had again been kicked into the long grass.

The debate

The Lords reform debate has never been conducted in a political vacuum since party interest was never absent. Labour has enhanced its reformist credentials, and ejecting the hereditary peers eliminates a key source of Conservative opposition. The hereditary peers had indeed mounted a number of revolts since 1997.

The Conservatives might of course have been expected to support the preservation of ancient institutions. However, Iain Duncan Smith responded with an even more radical suggestion – a 300-strong Senate with 80 per cent elected. In this apparently selfless behaviour he was aiming to outflank the government in reformist zeal. However, the wind was taken out of his sails by party members, particular anger coming from those who had already been ennobled, including ex-Foreign Secretary Lord Howe and ex-Chancellor Lord Lawson (Watt and Ward 2002). The Liberal Democrat call for a predominantly elected house chosen by STV was also self-serving, reflecting their quest for increased representation.

However, the debate goes beyond party interest. The principal alternatives – direct election, patronage, selection by independent commission and the hereditary principle – each have strengths and weaknesses.

The people's choice: direct election Election is the basis for populating most upper houses. This is based on democracy, the right of people to choose and remove those involved in their government. Moreover, only elected members can be said to be truly representative of the people. Election can also ensure balanced geographical representation and offer a form of participation. Hence, it bestows legitimacy, an essential condition of stable government.

> Why we think that, unlike France, India, Germany... God knows where, we can't have an elected upper house that works I don't understand.
>
> Baroness Shirley Williams, speaking on BBC TV's *Newsnight* (9 Jan. 2002)

Yet valid objections have been made to an elected Lords.

- ◆ *'Gridlock'*. Two houses of comparable legitimacy would be liable to the stalemate sometimes seen in the USA. The government shared with Wakeham the view that a largely elected house would be a recipe for 'damaging conflict' (Lord Chancellor's Department 2001a: para. 11.6).
- ◆ *Competition*. Elected members representing constituencies would compete with MPs as the people's trouble-shooters.
- ◆ *Party domination*. An elected chamber would mean the end of the cross-bencher, with candidates lining up behind manifestos. The Lord Chancellor argued before the Commons Public Administration Committee: 'If you convert it to an elected house the whips will take over'.
- ◆ *Professionalization*. Election might also bring in a new wave of professional politicians with little experience of the wider world, losing the variety of expertise and experience given by the life peerage system.
- ◆ *Unnecessary*. Being largely a talking shop and, unlike the Commons, not the source of the government's authority, the House may not require the legitimacy of election.

Royal favourites: patronage A strong argument for prime ministerial patronage comes from the life peerage system, which brought to Parliament knowledge and experience from the arts and media, science, sport, law, banking, industry, and so on. Moreover, the practice does not mean a neutered House; the interim reform, slashing the Conservative majority and increasing Labour's representation, did not reduce obstructionism (see p. 394). Indeed, there is no certainty that appointees will remain loyal. The voting record after Blair's first year revealed only three-quarters of the 'working peers' to be regular supporters.

Patronage can be very useful to a government. Sitting MPs can be moved 'upstairs' to make room for a new face in the Commons, as was suspected when Labour's Roy Hughes (ennobled in August 1997) relinquished his Newport seat to Conservative defector Alan Howarth. Indeed, key figures can be brought into government without confronting the electorate at all, as when Thatcher made David Young Secretary of State for Employment and Blair brought in long-time friend Lord Falconer as Solicitor General.

However, patronage has many critics.

- *Party domination.* Some cite the case of Canada, where an appointed second chamber is generally seen as a government poodle. On the *Breakfast with Frost* programme in November 2001, Lord Wakeham lamented: 'I wanted an end of Tony's cronies'. It also allows career politicians, as opposed to those with wide experience, an undemocratic way up the greasy pole.
- *Thwarting the democratic process.* Patronage enables ministers to overcome rejection by the electorate, as when Lynda Chalker, transmogrified into Baroness, remained at Overseas Development despite the adverse judgement of her constituents in 1992.
- *Political rebirth.* Figures of yesterday receive an elixir of everlasting political life. In June 1992, Margaret Thatcher entered the chamber, along with many of her former Cabinet, although her Commons opponent, Michael Foot, true to his principles, became the first Labour leader since 1935 to spurn the honour.
- *Prime ministerial power.* For most critics the loudest complaint concerns prime ministerial power. A monarchical hangover, patronage allows them to act like kings, rewarding favourites, donors of funds and doers of favours.

Appointment by commission Like patronage, appointment by independent commission could bring in expertise and experience not available to the Commons. It could also produce a large number of independents and lessen the opportunities for corruption. However, critics question the true independence of an appointments commission.

- Who will appoint its members?
- Would their role become politicized?
- Would the chamber become populated with more of the great and the good, establishment figures with little understanding of the NHS waiting list and the dole queue?
- Despite experience in their own specialized fields, would independents lack the political antennae to survive in the febrile atmosphere of Westminster? There have been examples of outsiders being introduced only

to fail dismally, both in the chamber and in the corridors, tea-rooms and bars where the subtle 'art of the possible' is practised.

Born to rule: the hereditary principle Can anything be said in the modern age for a system based on the principle of superior genes? It is not entirely irrational to argue that a belief that one is born to rule can create a good leader. Plato advocated training the guardians from birth and Hobbes supported hereditary monarchy. Compared with the life peers, their hereditary brothers had less reason for sycophantic behaviour and their road to Westminster did not involve the compromises and backroom skulduggery required of party *apparatchiks*. Whether those prepared to fight for office are best fitted for it is indeed debatable. The ancient Greeks believed that such people were, by definition, the least trustworthy, preferring instead to draw lots for office. Today we choose juries on a similar principle. It can also be argued that those with great wealth are free from the temptations to corruption. They need not court favours and do not fear sacking.

There are, of course, arguments against the hereditary principle.

◆   We would not, for example, make a woman a brain surgeon merely because her father was one. Empirically it would be hard to find overwhelming evidence for aristocratic supremacy in the fields where talent and intelligence matter.
◆   Seen as a relic of a bygone age, the hereditary principle was rejected by the Royal Commission, the white paper, the Liberal Democrats, the reformist lobby and even the leader of the Conservative Party. Perhaps the most remarkable thing is that it was able to persist into the twenty-first century.

The chains of history

Why did the preservation order remain so long on this aristocratic edifice? Perhaps establishment interests found symbolic value in one of the remaining bastions that only the select (or the selected) might enter. A key element in British political culture, Britain's upper house symbolized hierarchy and exclusion, reminding the mass where they belonged – on the outside. As their Lordships finally shuffled from their red leather benches, reformists could claim that Britain was taking one more timid step into the modern age.

The House of Commons

The third element in the parliamentary triumvirate is the only one that may be called democratic. Seating 659 members chosen by popular election, the House of Commons is also the chamber of the prime minister, the leading ministers and opposition front bench. However, although the site where Britain's political Titans confront each other on a daily basis, it is by no means free of flummery and ceremony.

Parliamentary mumbo-jumbo

The Commons embraces Westminster ritual from the very beginning with the annual opening of Parliament. Black Rod, the officer responsible for maintaining order in the House of Lords, carrying an ebony cane for the purpose, summons the Commoners to hear the Queen's Speech. All is conducted in Norman French. When he approaches the lower house the doors are slammed in his face (because in 1642, the last time the Commons allowed the monarch in, he arrested five members). Undeterred, he gives three solemn knocks, the doors are opened and the MPs, led by the prime minister and opposition leader, advance in pairs like a *corps de ballet* towards the 'other place'. The flummery of the State Opening engages 'ladies of the bedchamber' in long evening dresses and officials with Ruritanian titles such as 'silver stick in waiting'. MPs are required to swear an Oath of Allegiance to the Crown. This is a problem for anyone professing republican principles and some Labour MPs do so with tongue in cheek. Two Sinn Féin MPs, elected in 1997, were denied office space at Westminster for their refusal.

In understanding Commons discourse there are various arcane terms requiring translation. The 'usual channels' means consultation between party whips; in the chamber MPs should refer to each other as honourable friends or honourable members for this or that constituency, and they vote by trooping through division lobbies. Members raising a point of order in a division do so wearing an opera hat. Privy Councillors (cabinet and ex-cabinet members and leading members of the opposition parties) enjoy certain privileges: 'right honourable', rather than 'honourable', they receive precedence in debate. New Labour came to power promising to end such flummery, but past experience has seen many Young Turks seduced by the ritual of the club.

I think...that it is the best club in London.

Mr Tremlow on the House of Commons, in Charles Dickens's novel *Our Mutual Friend* (1864–5)

The Speaker

At the centre of Commons life is the Speaker, who chairs debate. Yet there is more to the role than this: adorned with wig and black robes, the Speaker presides over a variety of solemn ceremonies often held in his or her official baroque residence within the Palace of Westminster. Although now considered an honour, the position was once unenviable, entailing facing the monarch on behalf of MPs; a newly elected Speaker thus makes a show of resistance before being forced into the chair by colleagues.

I have neither eye to see, nor tongue to speak here, but as the House is pleased to direct me.

William Lenthall, in the House of Commons on 4 January 1642, in reply to Charles I asking if he had seen five MPs whom he wished to arrest. A classic statement of the Speaker's role

The Speaker is elected by MPs, usually from the ranks of well-respected uncontroversial figures. Mrs Thatcher, in an unprecedented move, tried to treat the office as one within her patronage. Although she did not get her way, when Bernard Weatherill was elected in 1983 his authority was weakened (Heffer 1988). The election of his successor, Betty Boothroyd, the first woman Speaker, was a landmark.

The 300-year-old procedure was no less archaic than the office and its dress. A nominee was put forward and then, if there was a rival, an amendment proposed, a debate would follow and MPs would vote. If there were further rivals the process would be repeated for each, following a list ordered by the Father of the House (p. 373). A recent convention that the office alternate between the two major parties was broken in October 2000 when Labour's Michael Martin was chosen to replace Betty Boothroyd. Conservatives felt cheated and the list became unusually long, with eleven candidates making

> Piss-up in a brewery? This lot couldn't organise an orgy in a massage parlour, or a sit-in at the Parker Knoll factory.
>
> Simon Hoggart on the election of Speaker Martin, in the *Guardian* (24 Oct. 2000)

the process tortuous, if not ludicrous. As a result the Commons agreed in March 2001 that future Speakers would be elected by secret ballot.

The Speaker is attended by the Sergeant at Arms, equipped with sword and mace. Responsible for maintaining order, he will eject the unruly, including MPs banned by the Speaker, and could imprison enemies in the clock tower of Big Ben. Each day the Speaker leads a dignified procession into the House following the Sergeant, and during debate the mace rests on the table at the centre of the chamber. Michael Heseltine etched his name in parliamentary folklore by brandishing it in the face of the Labour enemy; only by prostrating himself before the House the following day did he gain forgiveness. When Labour's Ron Brown made a similar gesture he refused to apologize and the whip was withdrawn for three months, the sternest punishment imposed for twenty-five years.

In debate, the Speaker must shed political affiliation and call members fairly, and with due weight to their expertise, interest and status. Conservatives questioned the impartiality of speaker Martin (Jones 2002) and in October 2001 he caused shock by proclaiming his personal view on policy (abandoning vouchers for asylum-seekers). The Speaker also gives rulings on points of procedure, emergency debates, money bills and **parliamentary privilege**. The latter are rights and immunities from court action granted to MPs to ensure free debate. Thus, for example, in 1987 Ken Livingstone could accuse Conservative Airey Neave (later killed by an IRA bomb in the Commons car park) of nursing knowledge of treasonable activities practised by Britain's security officers in Northern Ireland (Pienaar 1987).

The Speaker also keeps discipline. Although there are often raucous scenes, turbulence is nothing new. Conservative opposition to Lloyd George's 'People's Budget' produced uproar, giving the reaction of Labour backbenchers in 1988 to Chancellor Lawson's 'rich people's budget' the air of the proverbial vicarage tea party. Where MPs persist in bad behaviour the Speaker will 'name' them, whereupon they are banned for a prescribed period. Thus in July 1992 Dennis Skinner was ordered from the House for refusing to withdraw the unparliamentary term 'wart' as a description of Agricultural Secretary John Gummer. The Speaker is generally accorded great respect. In December 1995 Betty Boothroyd summoned the Conservative Chief Whip for a serious dressing-down after a whispering campaign against her by his MPs.

However, from his contentious beginning, Michael Martin continued to court controversy. Critics within his own party alleged that he was putting the brakes on reform. Others claimed that his strong Glaswegian accent was difficult to understand, but defenders alleged this to be snobbery. Some thought it inverse snobbery when, in November 2001, he sacked an experienced secretary for being 'too posh'. However, it was his role in the Filkin affair that caused most raised eyebrows (see p. 380).

The timetable

The life of a *parliament* is the period between two general elections, which must not normally exceed five years. This is divided into annual *sessions* commencing each autumn, punctuated by *recesses* (holidays) over Christmas, Easter, Whitsun and summer. A Daily Agenda (formerly the Order Paper) outlining each day's events (see p. 399) is the responsibility of the Leader of the House, liaising with the Opposition, and is also available on the internet.

At one time debate regularly continued into the small hours as an *all-night sitting*, but recent modernization efforts have reduced their frequency. The 1994 reforms included Wednesday-morning sittings (for backbencher-initiated debates), no sittings on ten constituency Fridays, and rearrangements of business to reduce all-night sittings, and from January 2003 the normal working day has ended at 6 or 7 p.m. On Fridays, sittings usually adjourn by mid-afternoon, enabling MPs to return to their constituencies.

'The best club in London': an MP's job

The House has for long retained the characteristics of a Victorian establishment club, with bars, smoking-rooms and leather armchairs. Most MPs are back-benchers, the name indicating where they sit on the green leather rows behind the leading figures in their parties. A useful quality is to be 'clubbable', to be able to mix easily and enjoy a good joke. While parties separate them, MPs can form cross-party friendships, with clubs for activities ranging from skiing and football to chess and jazz. However, the club ethos was challenged in May 1997 with the entry of a veritable regiment of women. Many changes were demanded, such as the earlier end to the working day, though calls for breastfeeding in the chamber and replacing the rifle range with a creche went unheeded.

The times they are a-changin'

New, younger MPs of both sexes have, probably, brought more sex into Parliament.

> Liberal Democrat MP Dr Evan Harris, leading calls for condom machines in the Commons, in the *Guardian* (13 March 1998)

There is no job description for an MP, each must make of it what they will. Some do much, some little. Those yearning to ascend the 'greasy pole' must define their role in conformity with a culture of obedience (see chapter 13). There is little glamour in this. If they seek the limelight with a controversial article or a challenging speech they run the risk of incurring displeasure. Some may experience a sense of *ennui* and spend time in the many tea-rooms and bars, sometimes appearing 'tired and emotional' (MPs are never drunk) and sometimes even falling into casual adultery. Some will continue with their professional careers, but the 'full-time' MPs have two stages upon which to act, one in Westminster and one in their constituencies.

Parliamentary matters Wednesdays excepted, 'full-time' MPs spend their mornings dealing with correspondence, sitting on committees, meeting constituents and receiving lobby groups. They work in premises round about (the Norman Shaw Building, Abbey Yard, Parliament Street and Millbank), and in the corridors and bars of Westminster. In the afternoons and evenings they may attend debates in the main chamber, meet fellow MPs, feed information to the press, gossip and plot; Parliament is a hot-house of rumour, character assassinations, secret agreements and broken confidences.

Constituency matters MPs represent geographical areas, by which titles they courteously address each other, and can find much employment in dealing with their constituents' concerns. This is an area largely free from the straightjacket of party discipline and it has increased significantly (Norton 1994) with the growth of the welfare state, MPs' role in the ombudsman system, increased volatility amongst voters and the need to secure readoption by local parties. It has also been encouraged by the rise of the Liberal Democrats with their community politics approach, the creation of the civil service agencies and the neoliberal view of citizens as state customers. The influx of women could also be expected to give a higher priority to constituency work (Norris 1996c). MPs themselves have encouraged developments, advertising regular surgeries, developing websites and holding public meetings. While 'to be a good constituency MP is still...downgraded by the ambitious' (Mitchell 1994: 703), the careerist may find in the constituency dimension a means to attract attention and gain fuel for parliamentary questions and adjournment motions. Yet there are costs. MPs are not trained counsellors, social workers or civil rights lawyers. Moreover, the deflection from the Westminster role may be welcomed by an executive eager to swell its power. Critics impugned such a motive when, in 1998, Labour leaders produced contracts laying down the amount of constituency work expected of MPs.

> Being a backbencher is really a very good job; ... and if they've got intelligence and guts and a good relationship with their constituents then it's a better job than in most parliaments of the western world.
>
> Michael Foot, interviewed by Bill Jones in *Talking Politics* (vol. 9, no. 3)

Honourable members

Who are these people who purport to represent their fellow citizens? Placing them under the microscope we find they can differ from the general population in various ways.

> A Parliament elected by the universal suffrage of voters grouped according to geographical areas is about as truly representative as a bottle of Bovril is a true representative of an ox.
>
> Eleanor Rathbone, in the *Observer* (29 March 1931)

Age The Commons tends to mirror the mature population, the 40–60 age group being best represented and Labour tending to be the older party. The longest-serving member enjoys the title 'Father of the House' and, with no compulsory retirement age, there is competition for the honour. One reason for ripe age is the need to demonstrate ability (in business, the professions, academia, trade unions or local government) in order to impress a selection committee. In 1970, the local Labour oligarchs of Merthyr Tydfil decided that at eighty-three their candidate, S. O. Davies, was beyond his best. Although resisting their slight by winning handsomely as an independent, his death shortly afterwards gave them what would in other circumstances have been the last laugh. With an average age of forty-five, the class of '97 lowered the age profile significantly, with Christopher Leslie, at twenty-four, the baby of the House. There was little change to the pattern in 2001 (figure 12.2).

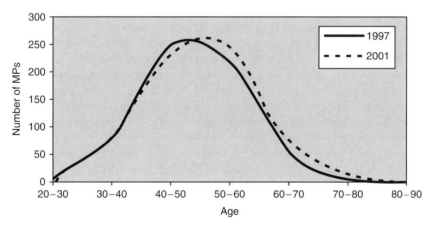

Figure 12.2
Age profile of MPs, 1997 and 2001.

Source: Data from Criddle (1997: 203; 2002: 199).

Figure 12.3
Educational
background of
MPs, 2001.

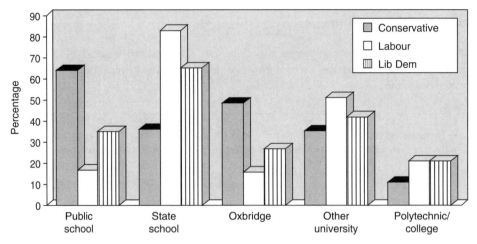

Source: Data from Criddle (2002: 202).

Education Increasingly MPs tend to be among the better educated, some 68 per cent of the 2001 intake being graduates (Criddle 2002: 202). Labour's graduate count has more than doubled, from 32 per cent in 1945 to 67 per cent in 2001. For much of the post-war period the majority of graduates were from Oxbridge and this proportion remains high, despite an increase in those from other institutions (figure 12.3). Traditionally the public schools provided the pre-university education for the great majority of Conservatives (mainly Eton, Harrow and Winchester), but during the 1980s this began to change, with more from the meritocratic state grammar school assault course (Burch and Moran 1984). However, by the end of that decade the party had reverted to its tradition of social exclusivity (Baker and Fountain 1996). Ex-public-schoolboys have also not been absent from Labour's ranks.

Occupation Occupational backgrounds stretch Conservative and Labour MPs further apart (table 12.2). Since 1945 both parties have included a high proportion (around 45 per cent) classed as professional, though in the case of Labour these have mainly been teachers and academics. Despite its business-friendly image, less than 10 per cent of New Labour MPs have business backgrounds; this can be compared with around a third of Conservatives. Indeed Conservatives are not merely businessmen, they are *big* businessmen. Of the 273 company directors elected to Parliament in the first three decades following the second world war, no fewer than 245 were Conservatives. The working class is virtually unrepresented on the Conservative benches and is declining sharply in Labour's ranks (from over 40 per cent in 1945 to 12 per cent in 2001). However, unlike their Conservative siblings, Labour MPs are often first-generation middle class with working-class parents (Cowley 2001: 826). In terms of occupation, the Liberal Democrats are now the most socially representative party.

Table 12.2 MPs' occupational backgrounds, 2001 (rounded to nearest whole percentage point)

Occupation	Conservative	Labour	Liberal Democrat
Professions			
Law	19	7	11
Education	4	24	23
Publishing and journalism	8	8	7
Civil service and local government	1	7	6
Armed services	7	< 1	0
Other	8	5	11
Business and management			
Company directors/senior executives	29	4	25
Other	7	4	2
Miscellaneous white collar[a]	1	18	2
Politicians/political staffers	11	11	7
Manual	1	12	2
Other	4	0	2

[a]Includes occupations such as trade union officials, social workers and voluntary-sector employees.
Source: Data from Criddle (2002: 204).

Political experience Many MPs cut their political teeth in local government; of the new intake in 1997, 70 per cent of Liberal Democrats, 64 per cent of Labour and 25 per cent of Conservatives had been councillors. Another indication of increasing professionalization is early work for political parties as 'staffers' (researchers or consultants). The 2001 parliament contained 44 Labour staffers, 18 Conservatives and 4 Liberal Democrats. Labour has always relied on a considerable body of trade union grounding and has also become a home for student union ex-presidents.

Sexual orientation If the House is representative of the wider population in this respect, then a number of gays and lesbians must choose life in the parliamentary closet. After the 2001 general election, the *Guardian* recorded eight openly gay or lesbian MPs, including Labour's Ben Bradshaw and Chris Smith. Generally, such admission does little to enhance a political career. Indeed, when Conservative David Ashby lost his libel case against the *Sunday Times* over allegations of homosexuality, he was removed by his constituency, complaining 'they are behaving like Smithfield meat-porters – love the Queen Mum and bash the queers' (Criddle 1997: 197). Portillo's confession of early homosexual experience may have actually cost him the Conservative leadership in 2001 (see p. 306). Homophobia is of course as inappropriate in a democratic parliament as is racism or sexism. In 1998, following the Ron

Davies Clapham Common farrago, gay journalist Matthew Parris 'outed' Peter Mandelson on television. Shortly afterwards, Nick Brown came out under threat of exposure by the *Sun*, which also ran the headline 'TELL US THE TRUTH TONY – ARE WE BEING RUN BY A GAY MAFIA?' However, a *Guardian* poll (10 Nov. 1998) revealed public attitudes becoming more relaxed about gay MPs and ministers. Of course, heterosexuals can also deviate from sexual norms, as the press, ever zealous in their democratic responsibilities, will inform us.

> The House of Commons is not so much a gentleman's club as a boy's boarding school.
>
> Shirley Williams (SDP politician), on Granada TV (30 July 1985)

Gender It is a democratic anomaly that only a small proportion of MPs have been women (figure 12.4). Not becoming eligible for election until 1918, the first three all represented seats formerly held by their husbands. The poor record leaves Britain out of step with many other western democracies. In Sweden, for example, around 40 per cent of MPs are women. In 1928, when franchise equality was gained, suffragette Millicent Garrett Fawcett declared: 'Our cause is a long way from full success'; today the Fawcett Society continues her mission. The 300 Club has that number as its goal for women MPs, while Labour's Emily's List (Early Money Is Like Yeast) was launched by Barbara Follett in 1993 (who herself won Stevenage in 1997) to give women candidates independent financial resources. She was also credited with getting Labour women out of jeans and donkey jackets and into smart suits. However, although women actually join political parties in similar numbers to men, they have not tended to seek nomination and have not been favoured by selection committees.

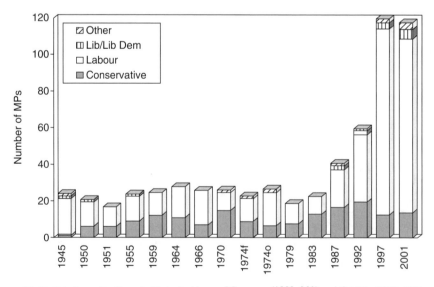

Figure 12.4
Women MPs, 1945–2001.

Source: Data from *The Times Guide to the House of Commons* (1992: 282) and Criddle (2002: 196).

So what will your husband do for sex if you get the job?
How is your husband going to get his evening meal if you're at Westminster?
You should be wearing red. Are you wearing red knickers?

Questions asked of women at local candidate selection committees, reported in
R. Watson and M. Kite, 'Most unwanted', *The Times* (1 Aug. 2000)

The 1997 breakthrough, with 120 women elected, doubled the previous number. However, any applause belonged largely to Labour, the Conservatives returning only 13, the Liberal Democrats 3 and the SNP 2. This reflected Labour's short-lived policy of all-women shortlists (see p. 330). In Parliament, New Labour women began forming networks to work together (Lovenduski 1997: 719). However, although immaculately turned out, they promised little that was radical and the media were soon mocking 'Blair's Babes' and the 'Stepford Wives'.

The total number of women MPs fell by only two in the 2001 general election, Labour's complement dropping from the high of 102 to 95, while, the Liberal Democrats gained two and three Northern Irish parties gained one each. Although the main parties had fielded a total of 381 women candidates, they proved reluctant to place them in target seats. Labour had set itself a goal of 50 per cent women MPs but, realizing that this would entail large-scale male self-sacrifice, revised this down to 30 per cent in January 2002. However, the Queen's Speech in 2001 had promised a potential watershed in British politics: a pledge to legalize positive action towards the selection of women candidates (Lovenduski 2001).

Monstrous regiment or Blair's Babes? Tony Blair with some of the 101 Labour women MPs, May 1997

Photo: Times Newspapers Ltd

Race Racism has held back the representation of ethnic minorities, parties tending not to field black candidates for fear of losing votes. In 1979 the Conservatives broke an all-white tradition with two Asian candidates and the 1987 election produced four black Labour MPs. The total increased to six in 1992 (five Labour, one Conservative) when John Taylor's nomination for Cheltenham in 1992 caused much controversy in the local Conservative association; he lost the formerly safe seat. In 2001, the three major parties fielded 66 ethnic minority candidates (Labour 22, Conservatives 16 and Liberal Democrats 28). However, of the 56 who were not sitting MPs, only 3 fought winnable seats. The election produced an all-time high of 12 ethnic minority MPs, but at 2 per cent it fell some way short of the 6–7 per cent in the population at large.

Amateurs or professionals This issue goes to the heart of democracy, being concerned with what kind of people become MPs. Before 1911 they were expected to give their services freely, unsullied by pecuniary motivation. Reflecting an historic establishment fondness for amateurism this meant that, as on the county cricket and rugby union fields, only the wealthy were welcome. Until as recently as 1964 MPs received only the equivalent of part-time salaries, working- and lower-middle-class members often being unable to eat in the Westminster dining-rooms. In July 2001, amidst considerable criticism, MPs voted themselves substantial rises, beyond an independent review board's recommendations. A motion proposed by Chris Mullin to link their pay to that of nurses and teachers was crushingly defeated. A further 2.5 per cent rise in 2002 brought their basic pay to over £55,000 a year (table 12.3). Yet effective representation requires the participation of all classes. When rich MPs oppose higher salaries they threaten democracy (Batty and George 1985: 171). Moreover, low salaries can leave weaker MPs open to temptations.

Dishonourable members: private interests and public confidence

Some MPs have not seen the work as a full-time job. Conservatives have characteristically held company directorships, worked in the professions

Table 12.3 Parliamentary salaries, 2002

Position	Salary (£)	Position	Salary (£)
Prime minister	171,554	Leader of the Opposition	119,979
Cabinet ministers	124,979	Junior ministers	91,358
Speaker	124,979	Backbench MPs	55,118

Sources: Various.

(often law), or been large-scale landowners. When James Prior was ejected from the Thatcher Cabinet he soon re-emerged in public view as chairman of GEC, while Cecil Parkinson joined the boards of no fewer than nine companies after resigning in 1983. Some, often Labour, supplement their incomes by journalism. It is argued that working keeps MPs in touch with the real world, though it is debatable how many ordinary people inhabit the boardrooms of industry, the Inns of Court, or even the inns of Fleet Street and Wapping.

In addition, MPs have long been associated with interest groups, Conservatives particularly with business interests and Labour with promotional groups and trade unions. So overt is the practice that the Speaker will often choose MPs to speak not on the basis of constituencies, but because of the interests they are known to represent (Roth 1981: xxvi). However, from the late 1970s developments took a dangerous turn.

Registering interest There are two levels of concern over MPs' outside interests. First, there is the possibility that they will lack time for the job. Indeed, multiple interests appeared to be associated with safe seats, where members need spend less time courting their constituents (Norris 1996b). Secondly, there is a fear that they may favour sectional interests over the public interest. The Poulson affair, involving prominent Conservative Reginald Maudling, led to the establishment of a Register of Members' Interests in 1975. This revealed a growing profession termed 'parliamentary consultant'. Initially there were only twenty-eight, working for a total of thirty-three organizations, but by 1995 the Nolan Committee (see below) listed 168 MPs holding between them 356 consultancies. Although most lead to financial gain, Tony Banks registered his twelve jars of honey from the London Beekeepers Association!

The 1980s saw a new growth industry: commercial lobbying firms, existing expressedly for the purpose of approaching MPs on behalf of clients, some, such as Ian Greer Associates, even advertising in *Dod's Parliamentary Companion*. These firms actually began to employ MPs, so that instead of being lobbied they would do the job themselves. Despite journalistic concern, the Commons Select Committee on Members' Interests showed no haste to adjust its rules of disclosure; MPs were not required to record payments received, give details of their own shareholdings or name the interests represented by their lobbying forms. Although the rules were tightened, allegations of widespread corruption and venality at the heart of government began to circulate during the 1990s (Wintour and Pallister 1995). The final straw came when two Conservative MPs were trapped by *Sunday Times* journalists posing as businessmen offering £1,000 for a question in Parliament. Some suspected this was only the tip of an iceberg. Further disclosures resulted in the resignation of one junior minister, Tim Smith, and the sacking of another, Neil Hamilton. Rising public concern led to the establishment in October 1994 of the Committee on Standards in Public Life, a standing body, chaired first by Lord Justice Nolan.

Reporting in May 1995, Nolan concluded that the Register was inadequate. To combat the deadly sins available to MPs he set out seven Principles of Public Life and a draft code of conduct. While outside interests were to be permitted, their financial value was to be declared and paid parliamentary work for lobbyists should cease. An independent Parliamentary Commissioner should police the system, though with final judgements remaining with Parliament.

As prime minister, Major immediately accepted the report's broad thrust though some bitter debates ensued. In November 1995, with votes split 322 to 271, MPs grudgingly agreed to reveal outside earnings. In addition, all paid advocacy would be banned and a Select Committee on Standards and Privileges established. Sir Gordon Downey (ex-Comptroller and Auditor General) took up the position of Parliamentary Commissioner for Standards, to advise and investigate complaints from MPs and the public.

However, the commissioner has fewer powers than the Ombudsman or the Comptroller and Auditor General with respect to sending for persons and papers, taking oral evidence, publishing findings and imposing sanctions; these powers lie with the Standards and Privileges Committee. Hence, the commissioner operates within the framework of the 'Westminster club' and a government can control the committee through its majority (Woodhouse 1998). An example of how the system could be subverted came when John Major prorogued Parliament in time to prevent publication of the 'cash-for-questions' report before the 1997 election.

The system's weaknesses were starkly exposed when Elizabeth Filkin took over from Downey. Frustrated at every turn, she was accused of 'nit-picking' and her complaints were often disregarded by the Standards and Privileges Committee. She felt she was the victim of 'unchecked whispering campaigns and hostile press briefings'. Most surprisingly, Speaker Martin, the figure responsible for good conduct, was accused of bullying. He criticized her publicly and forbade publication of a letter she had sent him about MPs' obstructive behaviour (Cracknell 2001). A particularly controversial case concerned Labour minister Keith Vaz, accused, amongst other things, of misleading Filkin over payments to his wife by the millionaire Hinduja brothers over immigration issues. Some MPs even accused Filkin of racism. The final insult came when her three-year term expired; the Commons commission chaired by the Speaker decided that rather than renew her contract she should reapply – effectively a sacking. She was replaced by Philip Mawer, an ex-civil servant and leading lay figure in the Church of England; critics alleged that he would prove more of a poodle than a watchdog.

Those in favour of stronger controls were not holding their breath. The June 2000 white paper, *Raising standards and upholding integrity: the prevention of corruption* (Home Office 2000), had included a draft Corruption Bill prepared by the Law Commission. This would close a legal loophole dating from the 1689 Bill of Rights that gave MPs immunity from public prosecution. However, finding time for it in the legislative programme did not appear to be a top priority.

In this chapter we have introduced the three great estates of the realm. To different degrees they are all parts of the dignified constitution, serving to legitimate the exercise of power. The extent to which they do this is under question; each has reached a state of crisis marked by profound public dissatisfaction and calls for reform abound. However, there is more to the life of Parliament than representing the three estates. The reality today can only be understood by reference to its processes and internal power structure. We turn to these in the following chapter.

Key points

- All polities contain ceremonial elements, though Britain is particularly rich in this respect.
- Bagehot took an exceedingly elitist view of such ceremony, believing its purpose to be that of keeping ordinary people in the dark about the real process of government.
- Britain has a constitutional monarchy but the idea that the monarchy is above politics can be questioned.
- The death of Diana, Princess of Wales created a crisis for the monarchy.
- The House of Lords, with its composition based on breeding and prime ministerial favour, is a relic of an undemocratic age.
- Any reform of the Lords runs the risk of constitutional turbulence.
- Any idea that the Commons is a microcosm of society is questionable. The working class, women and racial minorities have been long under-represented.
- The 1990s saw the prestige of the Commons plunge, with widespread perceptions of venality.

Review your understanding of the following terms and concepts

appointments commission
backbencher
bicameral
Black Rod
ceremonial
Civil List
constitutional monarchy
cross-bencher
division lobby
hereditary peer
honourable member
Leader of the House

life peer
Lord Chancellor
mace
Magnum Concilium
mumbo-jumbo
Order Paper
'other place'
parliamentary privilege
Parliamentary
  Commissioner for
  Standards
patronage

Privy Councillor
Register of Members'
  Interests
republicanism
Restoration
right honourable member
Select Committee on
  Standards and Privileges
Speaker
usual channels

Assignment

Study the extract from the *Independent* and answer the following questions.

		Mark (%)
1	What inference do you draw from the publication date of this article?	5
2	What advantages might there be from a chamber selected on the same principle as a jury?	15
3	What alternative methods for selecting members of the upper house can you suggest?	20
4	Why does an elected, or partly elected, upper house threaten the Commons?	30
5	What are the dangers of appointing members to the upper house on the basis of patronage?	30

Questions for discussion

1 Consider the consequences for British politics if the monarchy were to be abolished?

2 In what sense was the death of the Princess of Wales a crisis for the monarchy?

3 'Without the attentions of the media the British monarchy would die.' Discuss.

4 Why do you think the process of government is surrounded by ceremony and display?

5 What changes in Parliament and policy can be expected from the 1997 influx of women MPs?

6 'Parliament cannot be described as a representative assembly if its composition is not a microcosm of British society.' Discuss.

7 Examine the pros and cons of MPs having outside jobs.

8 Has Parliament adequately protected itself against sleaze?

9 'The development of the MP's constituency role detracts from the constitutional role of the Commons.' Discuss.

10 Evaluate reform proposals for the House of Lords.

Topic for debate

This house believes that the abolition of the House of Lords is a prerequisite for social reform.

'People's Lords' to replace hereditary peers

Exclusive

By Charles Suter,
Constitutional Affairs
Correspondent

A CABINET committee drawing up plans for the abolition of hereditary peerages has proposed their replacement with temporary "People's Lords", according to documents leaked to *The Independent*.

Under the changes, existing hereditary Lords will stay in place until they die. Their seats will then be taken by "ordinary citizens" chosen at random in a system similar to jury service.

The new "People's Lords" will serve for fixed terms of one, five or fifteen years. It is expected that the first citizens to be elevated in this way will take their seats in time for the Millennium celebrations at the end of next year. There will be no change to the system of life peerages.

The committee, chaired by the Prime Minister and including Peter Mandelson, Lord Irvine and constitutional experts – was established soon after last May's Labour landslide.

Confidential minutes seen by *The Independent* reveal the committee examined the possibility of replacing the House of Lords with an elected second chamber, similar to the US Senate.

The idea was rejected because the committee was worried that "even a partly elected Upper House would challenge the democratic legitimacy" of the Labour-dominated Commons.

There were also fears that outright abolition of the Lords would bring renewed and direct pressure on the Monarchy itself – something which new Labour is keen to avoid.

The document details discussion of the "middle way" which Labour hopes will "preserve the stability and continuity" provided by the inherited peerage.

By allocating seats in the second chamber by lottery, appointments to the Lords will "remain beyond the political fashions of the day".

At the same time, the removal of the hereditary element will get rid of an "out-of-date principle which is an affront to the sensibilities of a modern inclusive and increasingly classless democracy".

According to the plan, the "Lottery Lords" will be chosen by computers using the electoral roll. Citizens selected to serve in the Lords will be paid a salary "commensurate with their current earnings with an additional element of compensation"

for their period of office. Attendance will be mandatory, though as with jury service it will be possible to seek exemption.

Systems will be introduced to ensure that equal numbers of men and women are elevated to the peerage. The young, together with members of ethnic minorities "and the just plain average" would have an equal chance of gaining a seat in the second chamber and thus an opportunity to scrutinise legislation, suggest changes and draft new clauses and amendments.

Opponents of the plan were quick to register their protest. Professor Pamella Benlott of London University, an influential new Labour intellectual, said: "The British constitution is fragile. Hereditary peers have centuries of inbreeding in their blood. The fact that many Lords are congenital idiots is a subtle and unique part of the constitutional settlement with which Tony will tinker at his peril."

Henry Masingbird-DeMonforte, who as 27th Earl of Thanet can trace his ancestors back to Harold Haffacanute, warned of a "mass uprising along the lines of the Countryside March... but more violent" if new Labour took his seat away.

Independent, 1 April 1998

Further reading

Bagehot, W. (1963) *The English Constitution* (first published 1867).
Highly elitist and disdainful of the masses, but contains enduring truths about the relationship between the rulers and the ruled, and the place of symbolism in politics.

Bogdanor, V. (1997) *The Monarchy and the Constitution*.
Accessible academic analysis of the monarchy in politics. Ultimately a defence of the institution.

Cannadine, D. (1992) *The Decline and Fall of the British Aristocracy*.
Title tells all.

Judge, D. (ed.) (1983) *The Politics of Parliamentary Reform*.
A varied collection. Opening chapter takes a neo-Marxist view, noting that reforms that succeed are those legitimating the rule of the economically powerful.

Norris, J. and Lovenduski, J. (1994) *Political Recruitment: Gender, Race and Class in the British Parliament*.
Examines relative dearth of women, black and working-class MPs and discusses whether the social bias in the political elite matters.

Pimlott, B. (1996) *The Queen: A Biography of Elizabeth II*.
Divides long reign into key periods: from fairytale to nightmare.

Russell, M. (2000) *Reforming the House of Lords: Lessons from Overseas*.
A comparative examination of upper chambers.

Shell, D. (1992) *The House of Lords*.
Perceptive overview.

For light relief

Julian Critchley, *Palace of Varieties*.
An entertaining insight into an MP's role by one of its mavericks.

Edwina Currie, *A Parliamentary Affair*.
Obsessive ambition, eroticism and political intrigue.

Frances Edmonds, *Members Only*.
A sharp and witty analysis of the Commons as seen by a feminist.

Anthony Holden, *The Tarnished Crown*.
Express columnist and keen monarchy watcher with paradoxically republican sympathies.

Andrew Morton, *Diana: Her True Story*.
Book which put the cat among the corgis on the break-up of the fairytale marriage.

Sue Townsend, *The Queen and I*.
Life for the royal family on a council estate.

On the net

http:/www.royal.gov.uk
The monarchy's website.

http://www.parliament.uk
Parliament's home page has links to the Commons and Lords and an enormous amount of information on parliamentary history, customs and procedure.

13

Parliament: Not to Reason Why

In this chapter we turn from the overtly ceremonial and structural aspects of Parliament to its more active functions, focusing mainly on the House of Commons. We begin by noting the overwhelming dominance of political parties, before turning to three central parliamentary functions: legislation, debate and scrutiny of the executive. After this we consider how parliamentary proceedings are brought to the attention of the mass population in whose name Parliament operates. We conclude by trying to look behind the formal trappings to clarify Parliament's essential role today.

Parliament's procedures are scrupulously regulated by its Standing Orders. However, these make no mention of the most pervasive source of influence within the chambers, committee rooms and even the bars and terraces – the political parties. Journalist Martin Bell, entering as an independent on an anti-sleaze ticket in 1997 was, in his white suit, a lone figure. This torch was carried on after June 2001 by Dr Richard Taylor, representing Wyre Forest.

The idea that Parliament has its own distinct identity is really part of the dignified constitution; such life it has is breathed into it by the political parties through their front-bench teams, forming the government and the shadow government respectively, and their massed backbench ranks. What is the *raison d'être* of such dominance? For the majority party it is nothing less than producing and sustaining a government; for the others, the less heroic role of opposing and waiting.

The Parliamentary Parties:
Sustaining Government

In Britain we believe we have a democratic government, yet no one voted for it as such; citizens choose only MPs. The government emerges as the creation of the House of Commons. Does this mean that the Commons is master of the government? The doctrine of parliamentary sovereignty would seem to imply this, but the reality is rather different. Because the government is formed from the party that can count on majority support within the Commons, its survival depends on its MPs. Their loyalty becomes, quite literally, a matter of political life or death. Far from being a check on the executive, party discipline makes the House its servant. This fact dominates Westminster life, with profound implications for the way Parliament performs each of its functions.

Today party leaders are invariably from the Commons; in earlier times they came from the Lords, but Salisbury, who retired in 1902, was the last of this breed. In 1906, after a landslide victory, the leading Liberals in the Commons – Asquith, Grey and Haldane – plotted (unsuccessfully) to dispatch their leader, Campbell-Bannerman, to the Lords, knowing that this would neuter him and allow Asquith in the Commons to become *de facto* prime minister (Cross 1963: 14–15). In 1963, Douglas-Home had to renounce his peerage and enter the Commons before he could become prime minister.

Backbench organizations

Backbench organizations meet regularly once or twice a week. The Conservatives form the 1922 Committee (see p. 284). Its chairperson, who is elected annually, retains direct access to the leader and is always a commanding party figure. Proceedings are conducted informally with few rules, day-to-day affairs being organized by an executive committee of around fifteen, also elected annually. When in government the party leader and ministers are not members, the former attending only rarely, the event usually something of an occasion. In 1965, the Committee assumed the key function of electing the party leader, though in 1998 this was reduced to selecting a shortlist to be placed before the mass membership (see p. 326).

The Labour Party formed its near-equivalent in 1923 as the Parliamentary Labour Party (PLP). This is not exclusively a backbencher group; the leaders are also members, as are the party's MEPs. When in office it elects a chair, but in opposition the party leader takes control and the front-bench team is elected annually as the 'Shadow Cabinet'. The leader and deputy were once elected in this way, but since 1980 the PLP have formed one element in a wider electoral college (see p. 324). When in office, a parliamentary committee with one-half government representatives and one-half elected by the PLP acts as a channel of communication between leader and backbenchers.

The vicissitudes of the electoral system have left third parties at their weakest on the parliamentary stage and their organization is more informal. At one time it was unkindly said that the Liberals could hold their meetings in a telephone kiosk, but with fifty-two members after the 2001 election the Liberal Democrats could laugh at the joke.

In the upper house things are more relaxed but all three parties have a leader and chief whip. The near-equivalent of the 1922 Committee is the Association of Conservative Peers. Labour peers may attend PLP meetings but also meet separately.

There remains an element of mystery about the workings of the backbench organizations. Although the PLP agreed to press reporting of its meetings in the 1970s, there is no constitutional requirement that they conduct their affairs before the public gaze. The 1922 Committee practises its rites behind closed doors and sinister stories have circulated, some of the earlier ones started, not surprisingly, by Lloyd George. On balance, the evidence is that, although having less formal authority, it receives a more studious ear from party leaders than does the PLP. Even Thatcher observed the tradition. Loss of confidence can see ministerial heads roll, as may have been the case in the resignations of several of Major's ministers in the 1990s. The dispatch of Thatcher in 1990 demonstrated just how brutal the Committee can be.

Policy-making

Backbenchers form party committees specializing in particular policy areas, regions of the country and items of legislation. In opposition, there is some feeling in the PLP that votes should be binding on the front bench, a possible conflict avoided by the Conservatives since shadow ministers often chair the committees themselves. Committee influence is always weaker when a party is in government as the leaders become more remote. Not wishing to antagonize their troops, however, they generally take soundings on the general mood through the whips. Heath's reputation for aloofness contributed to his downfall. The all-male club atmosphere of the House placed Mrs Thatcher at a disadvantage, though she encouraged cabinet colleagues to act as her eyes and ears in the bars and corridors.

The culture of obedience

> I always voted at my party's call,
> And never thought of thinking for myself at all.
> I thought so little they rewarded me,
> By making me the leader of the Queen's navy.
>
> Sir Joseph Porter in Gilbert and Sullivan's *HMS Pinafore*

The role of backbench MPs today is largely one of humility, their lot to follow rather than lead. The motive for such obedience is ambition; careers are advanced through the patronage of those above. The first advancement a backbencher can expect will be as a parliamentary secretary or a junior minister (or shadow minister) at one of the lesser departments; continued obedience is required to reach further rungs on the ladder. Discipline is even stronger for government members. Indeed, in free votes prime ministers may still expect loyalty from this 'payroll vote', as John Major did over abolition of corporal punishment in state schools in November 1996. Those entering the House later in life and not expecting to ascend far up the greasy pole may lack the incentives to grovel, yet such members rarely exhibit radical tendencies.

> The principle of Parliament is obedience to leaders. Change your leader if you will, take another if you will, but obey No. 1 while you serve No. 1, and obey No. 2 when you serve No. 2. The penalty of not doing so, is the penalty of impotence.
>
> Walter Bagehot, *The English Constitution* (1867)

The mavericks A small category of MPs, scorning the party leaders and placemen, will speak their minds and can be more influential than their docile colleagues. Enoch Powell, for example, caused both major parties to harden their lines on immigration, while the Eurosceptics influenced attitudes towards European integration. Sometimes these mavericks spend their earlier years as orthodox careerists. Powell was Minister of Health in 1962, and Michael Heseltine, who was poised at the crossroads between orthodoxy and Mavericksville in the late 1980s, was to return as a pillar of the Major government. Fiery Welsh radical Aneurin Bevan succumbed to the warm embrace of orthodoxy for a time as the siren of office beckoned, while Tony Benn strayed progressively from the centre throughout a long career. Indeed, mavericks are not always without ambition, and a rebellious stand on a populist issue may prove popular (Pattie et al. 1994). Harold Wilson resigned from the government in 1951 over NHS charges but by 1964 was prime minister, and Iain Duncan Smith, a Euro-rebel under Major, became party leader in 2001. On the other hand, MPs really falling foul of the leadership can be expelled from the party. Under New Labour, Dennis Canavan and Tommy Graham suffered this fate, as did Ken Livingstone, expelled for running as an independent in the London mayoral election. Gwyneth Dunwoody proved such a thorn in the New Labour side that attempts were made to prevent her chairing the transport select committee (p. 406).

Uncritical mass Newer MPs are more likely to toe the line than the old stagers. With only 62 rebellions in 941 votes in its first three years, Labour's 1997 contingent, replete with newcomers, was the most loyal of the post-war era. Of the pre-1997 vintage, 32 per cent rebelled at least once, compared with only 25 per cent of the freshers. The new women proved the most loyal of all, with a 14 per cent rebellion rate (White 2001). It can be argued that this level of obedience was a product of widespread agreement amongst Labour MPs and a belief that they could exert influence behind the scenes (Cowley 2001: 827). However, in contrast to the young and ambitious, Gwyneth Dunwoody had turned 70 by 2001 and was the oldest-serving woman MP, while Tam Dalyell, another Labour maverick, had actually become Father of the House.

> I am unique among MPs in that I can say when I don't know. I can say I've changed my mind and I can say I've made a mistake. That's what being independent is about. The mistakes I make are my own mistakes and they are not forced on me by a party whip.
>
> Martin Bell, in 'On being an independent MP', *Talking Politics* (13(1), Summer 2000)

The mechanics of discipline A key figure in **party discipline** is the chief **whip**, aided by assistants. In the Conservative Party the leader makes the appointments but Labour's whips are elected by MPs. In both cases, however, their loyalty is to the leadership, ensuring that members will be in the House to vote as required (the title comes appropriately enough from the world of the hunt where the 'whipper in' is charged with the management of the hounds). The whips circulate weekly memorandums outlining the pattern of business and showing the relative importance of the votes by underscoring the request to attend with one, two or three lines. A 'three-line whip' indicates top priority, with grave consequences for backsliding, ranging from a dressing-down in the chief whip's office to a 'withdrawal of the whip' (a form of excommunication, to be restored only when the offender has purged his political soul). Labour has proved far more likely to use stern measures, even resorting to expelling rebels. In 1954 the whip was withdrawn from Bevan and seven of his supporters on the left.

Stern measures do not always work. In November 1994, eight Conservatives abstained over the European Communities (Finance) Bill, which the Major government was treating as a vote of confidence. The government scraped home and the whip was withdrawn from the rebels. However, far from becoming pariahs, as 'the whipless Tories' they were to enjoy a collective notoriety, gaining much media attention. The whip was restored the following April with little sign of atonement.

> **Dead certainties**
>
> As chief whip in the Wilson government, Edward Short had sick and unconscious members wheeled through the division lobby while hooked up to oxygen tubes.
>
> Reported in the *Observer* (26 Feb. 1989)

The constituency associations can also be part of the machinery of obedience. Of the seven left-wing rebel MPs voting against Eden over Suez, four failed to secure readoption as parliamentary candidates. In the 1960s, Wilson employed canine imagery to warn Labour rebels that although every dog might be permitted one bite, he should not forget that his constituency 'licence' would need renewing. Among the Conservatives, Sir Anthony Meyer, who had the temerity to challenge Thatcher for the party leadership in 1989, suffered deselection soon afterwards. In January 1997, the Reigate association deselected sitting MP Sir George Gardiner, a Eurosceptic who had described Major as a ventriloquist's dummy for the chancellor. He subsequently alleged Central Office influence, asserting on BBC Radio's 'World at One' (28 March 1997) that the constituency chairman was 'taking orders daily'. However, by the 1990s, some Conservative associations appeared to becoming less supportive of the leadership: the 'whipless Tories' were buoyed by local support, while Neil Hamilton, under investigation for sleaze, was retained by his Tatton party, despite being an embarrassment to party leaders.

While we were in opposition Humphrey Atkins had been a most objectionable Chief Whip, and had marked my card. . . . he gave me a spastic 'dressing down' for smashing one of the House telephones. . . . 'We don't do that sort of thing'.

Alan Clark, *Diaries* (1 Jan. 1990)

Disciplining the Lords Party discipline has been more relaxed in the upper house and cross-voting can be acceptable. Despite dignified titles (the chief government whip is the Captain of the Gentlemen at Arms and his deputy the Captain of the Yeomen of the Guard), they had few sticks with which to fright the souls of old warriors and, in the days of hereditary peers, few carrots to dangle before the eyes of those who already owned much of the country.

Three-line whips are very rare, and if I get 150 peers in to vote, using a really strong two-line whip, I am doing jolly well.

Lord ('Bertie') Denham (Conservative chief whip in the Lords),
in the *Independent* (27 April 1988)

We'll swing together Yet in the final analysis backbenchers and leaders are in the same boat; discipline is in everyone's interest. The fratricide under Major contributed to the Conservatives' disastrous result in 1997, many finding themselves expelled from the 'best club in London'.

Making Laws

Parliament is the British legislature, free to make any law it chooses and subject to no legal restraint from any other constitutional body. It is in this that its sovereignty is manifest. Although this supremacy is constrained by EU membership, it is always free to secede. However, we shall find that in practice this supremacy is not all it seems.

Bills All Acts of Parliament begin life as **bills** which, broadly speaking, are of two kinds.

- *Private bills* are introduced by some body (a local authority or public corporation) wanting some special power in the form of a *by-law*. These were common in the nineteenth century as the local bourgeoisie (as councils or ad hoc authorities) sought new powers to develop the industrial cities.
- *Public bills* constitute the lion's share of all legislation, becoming the normal laws of the land. Although most are government bills, some are introduced by private members.

The legislative process

All bills travel a lengthy **legislative process** (figure 13.1). Normally this was completed within a single session, otherwise they were 'lost' and had to start from the beginning in the following session. However, following the Modernization Committee's 1998 report, certain bills may be 'rolled' over, a practice increased from 2003. The first to be so treated was the Financial Services and Markets Bill, carried over into the 1999–2000 session. If necessary, the

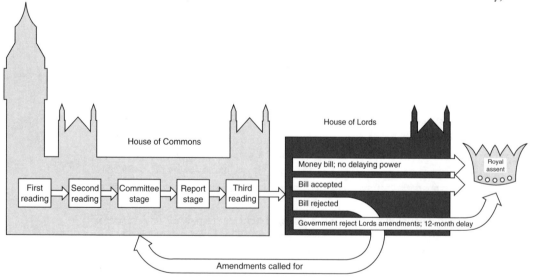

Figure 13.1 The legislative process.

legislative process can be accelerated (the 1911 Official Secrets Act was rushed through the Commons in one day, as were the 1998 Landmines Bill and the 2000 Northern Ireland Bill re-imposing direct rule).

Bills pass through both Houses, usually originating in the Commons but sometimes in the Lords. With its packed programme, the 1997 Labour government introduced several major pieces of legislation (including the Crime and Disorder Bill, the Higher Education Bill and the Human Rights Bill) in the Lords.

The typical process includes the following stages in the Commons.

◆ *Pre-legislative scrutiny.* Consultation documents and white papers often precede major legislation to permit widespread discussion. Increasingly, governments release draft bills for pre-legislative scrutiny by select committee and in May 2002 it was agreed to make specialist staff available to assist MPs in this.

◆ *First reading.* This is a formality when the bill is introduced by its sponsor who, in the case of government bills, is a minister. The House orders the bill to be printed and sets a date for the second reading. The bill is prepared by parliamentary draughtsmen with the exactitude of lawyers. Although a second reading is rarely denied, this can happen, and was the fate of the Shops Bill (on Sunday trading) in April 1996.

◆ *Second reading.* The broad principle of the proposed legislation is debated, but modifications are not permitted.

◆ *Committee stage.* The bill is considered clause by clause, sometimes leading to proposed amendments. Meetings take place 'upstairs' in a **standing committee**. The term is a misnomer since, when a bill has been considered, the committee disbands, allowing no opportunity for MPs to build up specialist expertise. Membership (16–50) reflects party balance, giving the government the last say. For matters of major constitutional importance, as with the Scottish and Welsh devolution legislation, this stage can take place before a Committee of the Whole House.

◆ *Report stage.* The committee reports back to the full House, which debates the clauses in detail. Amendments may be made, but most are introduced by the government as a tidying-up function. Voting usually follows party lines but, if the government's own supporters stand up, the boat may begin to rock. Thus, in April 1988 the Conservative majority was slashed to a humiliating twenty-five in the report stage of the 'poll tax' bill.

◆ *Third reading.* This final Commons stage is nowadays largely a formality. There is no debate unless a matter of particular political importance arises, in which case six members must table a motion. No amendments are permissible.

House of Lords From the Commons the bill proceeds to the Lords, to follow a similar route. Generally no serious challenge is expected: if amendments are made, the bill returns to the Commons, but if these are rejected the Lords are expected to comply gracefully. Moreover, in the case of manifesto commitments, the Salisbury Convention requires that the Lords will never frustrate the will of the elected House. Only if a government was clearly acting unconstitutionally (say, attempting to extend its life beyond five years) would continuing opposition be justified. Hence, the constitution allows the Lords little substantive influence. Thus, for example, despite receiving an eloquent and informed mauling by Lord Lestor QC and the Law Lords, the Commons reversed all amendments to the 1993 Criminal Justice and Public Order Bill (Klug et al. 1996: 547–8).

Yet their Lordships have not been powerless. Under the 1949 Parliament Act, they have the right to delay non-money bills for twelve months. Again, the very process of returning a bill with amendments takes time and, before the provision for bills to 'roll over' (see above), delay could amount to government defeat, particularly towards the end of a session when a legislative backlog has built up. Moreover, defeats in the Lords can be embarrassing to governments, generating adverse publicity. The 1980s and 1990s saw greater assertiveness, beginning with a notable defeat in March 1980 over school transport charges. Over a hundred defeats caused Thatcher, according to one peer, 'to scream and kick her legs in the air' (Gunn 1988). Conservative Home Secretary Michael Howard proved particularly accident-prone as shifting alliances of former home secretaries, judges, police officers, bishops and opposition peers ravaged his police reforms and penal programme.

New Labour fared no better, with some thirty defeats in each session up its 1999 interim reform. Indeed, astonishing events in 1998 suggested that Conservatives peers, using tactics reminiscent of those seen during the 1909–11 crisis (see p. 350) were prepared to ignore the Salisbury Convention. In July 1998 the Higher Education Bill was so batted back and forth that it was termed 'Wimbledon in Ermine'. Similar treatment greeted attempts to lower the age of homosexual consent. The European Parliamentary Elections Bill, at the very end of the 1997/8 session, suffered five defeats. Here the introduction of closed lists could be seen as a constitutional matter, but most agreed that such draconian action was unwarranted. Finally the 1949 Parliament Act was invoked and the bill was passed in the following session after the Lords' delay. Significantly, the 1999 interim reform did little to stem the tide, with thirty-six defeats in the first session, some on flagship measures. Contrary to expectations, ejecting the battalions of hereditary peers appeared to have lessened the need for self-restraint (Cowley and Stuart 2001: 244).

Hence, it can be seen that, while having the appearance of technical modernization, the 'roll-over' reforms have considerable political impact in strengthening the hand of the executive against the Lords, and therefore against Parliament itself.

La Royne le veult.

Norman French formula for the Royal Assent

Royal Assent The Queen formally approves the bill, whereupon it becomes an **Act of Parliament**. This stage has been entirely ceremonial since Britain became a constitutional monarchy; the royal assent was last withheld in 1707.

Restrictions on legislative influence

Governments have become adept at limiting legislative influence during the passage of a bill. In 1902, standing orders were introduced enabling the government to decide what subjects could be raised and for how long they would be discussed (dubbed 'Balfour's railway timetable'). Both front benches accept this curtailment, the opposition recognizing that they too may enjoy the advantages when in government, and negotiations between them are conducted by the whips through 'the usual channels'. Devices curtailing debate include the following.

◆ *Committees.* The committee stage excludes the majority of MPs from detailed discussion. Infuriated by lack of time allowed for the Criminal Justice and Police Bill in March 2001, Shadow Home Secretary Ann Widdecombe and three colleagues staged a sit-in at the committee stage.
◆ *Closure motions.* These permit the House to agree that the vote be put without further discussion.
◆ *The guillotine.* While tedious speakers are not decapitated, the debate itself is put under the blade at a government-determined time. This frequently arouses opposition accusations of steamrollering, as in the case of the bill for the devolution referendums in June 1997.
◆ *The kangaroo.* Only a limited number of the proposed amendments are discussed, 'hopping' over the others like the antipodean marsupial.
◆ *Delegated (or secondary) legislation.* Much legislative power is given to civil servants to frame detailed clauses through statutory orders and regulations. Although freeing Parliament from 'technical details', as long ago as 1929 the Lord Chief Justice Lord Hewart (1929: v) feared the dangerous 'pretensions and encroachments of Bureaucracy', in which he discerned a 'new despotism'. Most Acts conferring such powers contain provisions for Parliament to consider **delegated legislation** and pass affirmative or negative resolutions.

Promises of modernization New Labour established a Modernization Committee to propose Commons reforms and monitor developments. It produced an early report on the legislative process in July 1997 and the decision to allow certain bills to carry over from one session to the next was one of its recommendations. In February 2002, Leader of the House Robin Cook sent a memorandum to the committee suggesting extending the scope of this provision. Other issues on the agenda for legislative reform include:

◆ a more open and formal programming of legislation determined by the standing committees;
◆ increased pre- and post-legislative scrutiny;
◆ more effective use of the committee stage;
◆ chairs able to limit the length of speeches;

- committees able to reconvene during later legislative stages;
- removing constraints on times of sittings and standing committees to operate during recess.

Private members' legislation

It is here that Parliament comes nearest to a policy-initiating role, yet nothing better betokens the humility of MPs than the provision made for them to introduce bills of their own. In each session a mere ten Fridays are reserved for **private members' bills**, during which time they must attempt to negotiate the legislative hurdles. Demand outstrips the niggardly supply of opportunity and a ballot (drawing lots) selects the first twenty. Moreover, of these lucky ones, fewer than half will ever see their bills discussed, let alone complete the obstacle course to become an Act of Parliament. The reefs upon which their bills can founder are various.

Procedural problems Friday is the day when many return to their constituencies and there is a danger that the House will not be quorate. Malevolent opponents may 'talk' the bill out, preventing debate from closing, as happened to Labour backbencher Mike Foster's attempt to ban foxhunting in March 1998, despite a 250 majority in favour on first reading. Between 1967, when David Steel steered his abortion bill through, and 1988, when David Ashton introduced another on the same subject, no fewer than fifteen private members' bills on abortion law fell foul of procedural devices.

Government attitude If a government wishes, it can put various spanners in the legislative works. It may mobilize its majority to strangle a bill at birth, or it may be more devious. In May 1994, a bill on rights for the disabled was derailed by feeding selected MPs a large number of amendments prepared by civil servants, forcing it to run out of time. Lady Olga Maitland earned a stern rebuke from the Speaker for her part in the ploy. Alternatively, if it welcomes the measure, a government can make time available. This is a convenient means of passing legislation with which, for reasons of discretion or cowardice, a government may not wish to be associated – say, homosexual law reform or abortion. Sometimes a government will make known a number of topics upon which it would welcome legislation.

Government takeover A government may induce a member to drop a bill in order to bring in a similar one of its own, as in the case of the 1965 Health Services Complaints Act. Similarly, in 1996 Labour MP Janet Anderson drafted a bill with police support to make stalking punishable by up to five years in jail. Believing its scope too wide, the government withheld support, promising to produce its own proposals 'at the earliest opportunity' (*Guardian*, 10 May 1996). This tactic may be used to water down a proposal, as with the 1988 reform of the Official Secrets Act.

Despite the restrictions, some MPs use the opportunity to demonstrate parliamentary flair and make their mark, as did Roy Jenkins (obscene publication), David Steel (abortion law reform) and Margaret Thatcher (admission to public meetings). Even if a bill meets an ignominious end, MPs have had an opportunity to publicize their views and stimulate debate, as with Foster's failed foxhunting bill.

Legislation from Europe

EU membership produces an alternative source of law affecting British subjects. Critics see this as a dramatic affront to parliamentary sovereignty and MPs have sought some element of control. In May 1974 a sixteen-member Committee on European Secondary Legislation was established to examine draft proposals submitted to the Council by the Commission. However, unable to question proposals it can only recommend their submission to a standing committee or the House. Even here no amendments can be made; the House debates it as a 'take note' motion in the hope that ministers will reflect its views in Brussels. Matters are additionally complicated because the Westminster and Brussels timetables are not synchronized and proposals may surface during a recess. The Lords also has a European scrutiny committee, working through seven specialist subcommittees. Unlike its Commons counterpart, it may discuss the merits of a proposal and call upon expert witnesses. However, debates are again confined to 'take note' motions. In practice the Commons committee has proved unpopular with MPs but, rather than testifying to the dominance of Brussels, this is a symptom of the might of the British executive. In Denmark, for example, the Folketing has secured far greater powers to influence its own government's position in Brussels.

The value of the legislative process today

The legislative process bestows the official seal of approval. Ordinary people can rest in their beds secure in the knowledge that the laws affecting their lives have satisfied their elected representatives, rather in the way that a car might pass its MOT test. Or can they? If vehicles were examined in the way MPs examine legislation, the roads would be littered with wrecks. Scrutiny of this order produces only a false sense of security. The constitutional brakes may be failing and the wheels about to come off, yet Parliament is as rigorous as the mechanic in the back-street garage with pockets full of greasy folding pictures of the Queen.

Although outwardly the process remains essentially that of the nineteenth-century 'Golden Age', it has become in large measure part of the dignified constitution. Like all such ceremonial its value lies in its ability to beguile and deceive. Although the legislative process may not have *policy-making* significance, it remains of considerable *political* significance as a means of legitimation. It would, however, be mistaken to conclude that all stages of the process are as empty as the Royal Assent. Parliament fulfils two useful roles: *publicity* and *criticism*. Although imperfect, and capable of being subverted, these are not to be entirely dismissed as contributions to democracy.

Debates in Parliament

A second major parliamentary function is debating issues of the day; indeed the essence of Parliament's role is debate ('parliament' derives from the French *parler*). On certain occasions debate can continue into the small hours although, since 1994, the government has used its 'best endeavours' to avoid such late-night sittings. Practice has varied over the years, with various experiments and attempts at modernization, and includes opportunities such as the following.

- ◆ *The **Queen's Speech***. Delivered in the House of Lords at the beginning of each session, this catalogue of proposed legislation (written by the prime minister) is debated over the following five days.
- ◆ *General government debates*. The government will normally devote around fifteen days each session for debate on topics of its choice. In this way it can test ideas, hear views on green or white papers, and outline its position.
- ◆ *Opposition Days*. Originally called Supply Days, these are twenty occasions when the choice of topic is determined by the opposition parties (seventeen to the largest and three to the second largest). The aim is to attack the government.
- ◆ *Estimates Days*. Since 1981, three days have been set aside each session for debating the Estimates, the topics chosen by the Liaison Committee (see p. 504).
- ◆ *Adjournment debates*. On four days a week, a half-hour debate at the end of the sitting traditionally allows the House to consider grievances. Backbenchers must ballot for this opportunity to choose the motion, often concerning some constituency matter, which is answered by a minister. The final adjournment debate before a recess is a larger affair, the motion selected by party leaders.
- ◆ *Wednesday morning debates*. Three Wednesday mornings are now devoted to select committee reports, the remainder being used to debate issues raised by backbenchers (see the Daily Agenda opposite).
- ◆ *Emergency adjournment debates*. A government may propose the adjournment of business at the beginning of the day to debate an emergency, such as the Gulf war of 1991.
- ◆ *Emergency debates under Standing Order No. 24*. Here an MP can ask for an adjournment to debate a 'specific and important matter that should have urgent consideration'. The Speaker only agrees if convinced of the urgency and such debates are infrequent. Their value lies in

Early Day Motions

Citizens may read that their MP has put down, or signed, an Early Day Motion, though may never see any record of the debate. This puzzle arises because 'Early Day Motion' is today a colloquial term for a notice of a motion for debate with no expectation that it will ever take place. A number of such motions are tabled each day, enabling MPs to record their feelings on a subject and gauge support. One signed by sixty-nine of his backbenchers in June 1992 gave John Major a forbidding warning of his Eurotroubles to come. Sometimes much can be achieved. In November 1994 an Early Day Motion forced Michael Heseltine to drop Post Office privatization plans.

forcing discussion of issues that the government might wish to avoid. One such debate was held on the GLC Fares Fair case.

◆ *Private members' motions*. In each session a number of Fridays are reserved for motions put by private members. Although constituency matters may be raised, debates often centre on government policy.

Empty debate

Despite the opportunities, commentators have criticized the way Parliament uses its debating powers.

Blind loyalty Debate is rather a misnomer. There is little real cut and thrust and speakers tend to read from prepared briefs, rarely responding to previous points and not even remaining in the chamber to hear how others respond. Final votes reflect not the qualities of wit or wisdom but party loyalty.

An extract from the Daily Agenda for Wednesday 20 January 1999

9.30	Prayers
Afterwards	Adjournment Debates:
	Mr Tony Worthington: Cairo conference on population and development – five years on
11.00	Mr Tim Boswell: Horticultural industry
12.30	Mr Stephen Twigg: Sentencing policy in road death cases
1.00	Mrs Jacqui Lait: Disposal of Health Services Accreditation
1.30	Mr Gareth R. Thomas (Harrow West): Developing social enterprise (until 2.00 p.m.)
2.30	Oral Questions to the Secretary of State for Northern Ireland
3.00	Oral Questions to the Prime Minister[*]
3.30	Private Notice Questions, Ministerial Statements (if any)
Afterwards	Greater London Authority Bill (Clauses 1 to 4 and Schedules 1 and 2): Committee [2nd allotted day] (may continue until 10.00 p.m.)
At the end of the sitting	Adjournment Debate: Education funding for South Gloucestershire (Steve Webb) (until 10.30 p.m. or for half an hour, whichever is later)

[*]From January 2003, Question Time starts at 12 noon.

Backbench frustration At all times front-benchers are preferred. In calling members the Speaker is supposed to look to those with particular expertise or interest, but frequently MPs are left seething at not having been called. The inexperienced spend fruitless hours preparing speeches never delivered. In 1988 backbenchers openly attacked Speaker Bernard Weatherill for being over-conscious of the rights of Privy Councillors (Heffer 1988).

Superficiality Debate can emphasize meretricious rhetorical skills. Members performing stylishly may triumph over less articulate, but more sound, colleagues. Deputy Prime Minister John Prescott's problems with the English language led to much mockery from the opposition. The parliamentary style, with the confident accent spiced with the Shakespearean quotation, can seem particularly ill suited to working-class politicians. However, the Glaswegian cadences of Speaker Martin somewhat modified the upper-class tone of the House.

Ill-mannered The televising of Parliament brought into shocked viewers' homes scenes of booing, fist-waving and shouting down, often likened to a bear garden. Indeed, the Speaker's cry of 'Order, Order' became the 'signature tune' of the broadcasts.

Weak in substance Debates tend to be of a low quality (the Lords often giving a more informed treatment of a subject). Ministers rely blindly on a crutch of bureaucracy (providing statistics, arguments and information), while the opposition struggles to build its case on the basis of outside advice, intuition and invective.

The empty chamber Backbenchers do not always support each other well; once opening speeches have been made they drift from the chamber, sometimes to their offices, sometimes to places of refreshment, re-emerging only to cast their all-important votes. Absenteeism was made even easier by a 'deferred vote' system introduced in December 2000, allowing them to submit a printed sheet showing their voting intentions on selected issues for the following week without even entering the chamber. To critics this was a sop to the new influx of women MPs, many of whom were unhappy about long hours. Traditionalists, seeing it as a thin end of the wedge to sideline Parliament, were refusing to hand in the slips (Black 2000).

The Modernization Committee's 1998 report on conduct in the chamber addressed some of these problems. Questions and answers were to be brief and members were called upon to respond to comments of previous speakers and, having spoken, to remain in the chamber. It was also suggested that the Speaker cease to give Privy Councillors precedence. To ease pressure on time, from November 1999 additional debates have been held on Tuesdays, Wednesdays and Thursdays in the ancient banqueting chamber, Westminster Hall. Usually on non-controversial issues, these are chaired by special deputy speakers who, unlike the Commons Speaker and deputies, do not relinquish their political identities.

Yet despite some reform, debates in Parliament are likely to take the form of a party clash rather than a dialogue between executive and legislature. In the effort to hold the executive more effectively to account, Parliament has sought other means. It is to these that we now turn.

Scrutiny of the Executive

It is said that the price of freedom is eternal vigilance; the idea that Parliament should scrutinize the executive remains a key aspect of its rationale. MPs probe through **parliamentary questions** and through an updated version of an ancient instrument – the select committee.

Questions in the House: a fretful hour

One of the few opportunities MPs have to shine is during **Question Time**: every day (except Fridays) government members face an hour of questions on their areas of responsibility. A relatively modern innovation, it began in the nineteenth century as a means of strengthening Parliament against an enlarging executive. The occasion can prove testing to ministers. Although answers are prepared by civil servants (work in the upper echelons of a department can come to a virtual standstill while this is done), the hour receives keen media attention and those who falter may be earmarked as political liabilities; for junior ministers it can be make-or-break time.

Ask me another

In July 2002 it was revealed that Tory MP John Bercow had tabled an average of 121 written questions a week (annual cost £565,278), the longest running to 10,195 words.

Oral and written answers Questions may, at the choice of the member, receive an oral answer in the chamber or a written one (indicated by an asterisk on the order paper). With almost 50,000 questions tabled each session, about three-quarters receive written answers. The distinction has considerable importance. Written answers can be prepared by civil servants in the name of the minister and arouse little media attention. With oral answers, ministers are forced to become personally involved, which gains publicity and allows further probing through supplementary questions.

Supplementary questions Ministers cannot get away with merely reciting a civil servant's brief; they must also be prepared to deal with follow-up questions. Skilful MPs will lure the minister to the dispatch box with an innocuous question, only to unsheathe a rhetorical stiletto. Supplementaries have steadily increased, reducing the number of questions answered each day from around sixty in the 1920s to around twenty. This leaves some forty questions unanswered in the House, although they will be printed (together with written answers) in the following day's *Hansard* (the report of parliamentary proceedings). Successive Speakers have urged members to cut supplementaries, but this reduces their power and is resisted.

Prime Minister's Questions The highlight occurs on Wednesdays at 12 noon, when for half an hour the prime minister stands at the dispatch box. Parliamentary broadcasts frequently place this at the top of the bill. There are more oral questions for the prime minister than any colleague, ranging widely over issues of the day. Sometimes these can be deflected to the responsible minister but, to prevent this, members adopt the strategy of asking very specific personal questions, enquiring into the prime minister's immediate plans and engagements, and following this up with their real concern. Nowadays most MPs merely table their questions as 'engagements'. Subsequent 'engagement' questions are not even answered once a reply has been given to the first. Although Wilson, Thatcher and Blair have all appeared to revel in the opportunity to enthuse supporters and ridicule opponents, Question Time can be fraught with danger.

Question Time in question The present system owes much to Balfour's reforms at the beginning of the twentieth century, which were intended to restrict rather than encourage debate. Amongst other things, he instigated the *written answer* and limited the time for oral questions. By replacing two fifteen-minute sessions for Prime Minister's Questions with one of thirty, Tony Blair was seen to be further weakening the system. Various other problems remain.

- *The rota*. Particular ministers come to the dispatch box on certain days only and oral questions require a fortnight's notice. Thus issues become 'stale' and a backlog develops.
- *Written answers*. These are used increasingly (a daily average of over 100). However, although providing much detailed information, they cannot be subject to spontaneous debate.
- *Time*. Despite various suggestions for improvement (an extended question hour, Friday sessions), Question Time remains a very inadequate fifty-five minutes.
- *Evasion*. Ministers have an increasing capacity to evade by claiming that a matter lies outside their control (local government, civil service agencies and the NHS, for example). They may also refuse on matters of security, including policing, or on 'public interest' grounds. Prime ministers are also guilty of this (Dunleavy and Jones 1993; Burnham et al. 1995).

> *Andrew Mackinlay*: Does the Prime Minister recall that, when we were in opposition, we used to groan at the fawning, obsequious, softball, well-rehearsed and planted questions asked by Conservative members of the right honourable Member for Huntingdon [Mr. Major]? Will my right honourable friend distinguish his period in office by discouraging such practices – which diminish Prime Minister's Question Time – during this Parliament? Furthermore, in view of the rather depleted official Opposition, will he encourage rather than discourage – without fear or favour, and without showing partiality or affection – loyal Labour backbenchers who wish to seek and provide scrutiny and accountability in this place?
>
> *The Prime Minister*: I fully respect my honourable friend's independence of mind, and shall do my very best to ensure that he retains it.
>
> Exchange between Labour backbencher and Tony Blair during Prime Minister's Questions (3 June 1998)

◆ *Party domination.* Despite MPs' alleged freedom at Question Time, the parties insinuate their tentacles. Governments can 'plant' questions, detailing tame backbenchers to ask what they want asked, or crowd out opposition questions. This reached a new low under Blair, forcing Speaker Boothroyd to complain of 'sycophantic questions'; the new women were particularly 'helpful' in this respect (White 2001).

Scrutiny by committee

Much of the work of Parliament is done by committees. Many of these are **select committees** drawn from all parties to fulfil some function on behalf of the House. Thus the Procedure Committee regulates its internal working, the Committee on Standards and Privileges (established November 1995 to replace the Privileges and Members' Interests committees) guards ethical standards and oversees the work of the new Parliamentary Commissioner for Standards (see p. 380), and the Modernization Committee considers reform. Select committees are also involved in policy issues (in the nineteenth century they functioned rather like royal commissions) or are used to gather information. In addition, they are increasingly being used to consider draft bills prior to the first reading.

One of the most successful has been the Public Accounts Committee (PAC), created in 1861 to examine the departmental accounts. This provided a model for a pattern of reform, beginning in the 1960s, to improve MPs' ability to scrutinize the executive. Committees were established with the power to 'send for persons, papers and records' and hold public hearings. However, the major advance came under the 1979 Conservative administration, which created twelve committees to cover the major spending departments. Superior to anything seen before, they could choose the topic for investigation, call for persons and papers and were served by a staff. They were also able to receive written and oral evidence from ministers, civil servants, local government officials and other interested parties, including pressure groups, and could appoint advisers to prevent witnesses pulling the wool over their eyes.

House of Commons: Select Committees, 2001–2002

Departmental	**Non-departmental**
Culture, Media and Sport	Accommodation & Works
Defence	Administration
Education & Skills	Broadcasting
Environment, Food & Rural Affairs	Catering
Foreign Affairs	Chairmen's Panel
Health	Deregulation & Regulatory Reform
Home Affairs	Draft Communications Bill*
International Development	Environmental Audit
Northern Ireland Affairs	European Scrutiny
Science & Technology	Finance & Services
Scottish Affairs	Human Rights*
Trade & Industry	Information
Transport, Local Government & the	Liaison
Regions	Modernization
Treasury	Procedure
Welsh Affairs	Public Accounts
Work & Pensions	Public Administration
	Selection
	Standards & Privileges
	Standing Orders
	Statutory Instruments*

* joint with Lords

Established for the complete duration of a parliament, they could not be disbanded by government. Membership, reflecting party strength, would be kept small (around eleven), with chairs shared between parties and the system overseen by the Liaison Committee (comprising the committee chairs). Some were to produce stinging reports: the Treasury and Civil Service Committee was particularly scathing of economic policy in the 1980s. The creation of the provincial assemblies was to further increase the scope for scrutiny by committee; on 5 April 2001, Minister for Europe Peter Hain became the first Westminster minister to appear before a Scottish parliamentary committee.

A mandarin's charter However, if the executive conceded with one hand it took with the other. A hitherto unknown assistant secretary in the Civil Service Department secured modest immortality in May 1980 by codifying some earlier guidelines as the Osmotherly Rules: a hitchhiker's guide to the committee galaxy designed to keep officials out of trouble on hazardous voyages through Westminster. The black holes of questioning into which civil servants should not allow themselves to be lured included:

◆ advice to ministers;
◆ interdepartmental policy exchanges;

◆ matters of political controversy;
◆ confidential information supplied by firms or individuals;
◆ delicate information concerning foreign powers.

Furthermore, in no circumstances were MPs to receive extracts from cabinet papers or to be told anything about cabinet discussions. Decision-making details were also to be clasped to the bureaucratic bosom. These guidelines could be seen as a mandarin's charter and gave an indication of the official view of Parliament's place in government.

The Westland affair This affair, which shook the Thatcher government to its foundations in the mid-1980s, provided a case study in the fragility of the system. The issue concerned the leak by the Department of Trade of a letter from the Solicitor General criticizing Michael Heseltine, who was at odds with the Prime Minister over how to save the Westland helicopter company. The Defence Committee launched an investigation. However, in January 1986 the government prevented key civil servants (Colette Bowe, John Mogg, Bernard Ingham and John Mitchell) from testifying, Thatcher claiming 'major implications for the conduct of the government and for relations between ministers and their private offices' (*The Times*, 31 Jan. 1986). In their place the Permanent Secretary at the Department of Trade, Sir Brian Hayes, was sent in to play a straight bat. When reminded of the committee's unqualified power to investigate, he unabashedly referred to a memorandum of guidance to civil servants produced by Cabinet Secretary Sir (later Lord) Robert Armstrong, saying in effect that although a committee may get a horse to the water, the minister can still forbid him to open his mouth.

Subsequently, Sir Robert Armstrong was asked by the Prime Minister to conduct his own enquiry (bordering on a farce since he must have known who was responsible before starting; see Hennessy 1990: 305) and after this he too went before the committee to obfuscate. Thus Parliament was never to know the extent of Downing Street's involvement in what Armstrong admitted to be the 'discourtesy, impropriety, and unwisdom' of the leaked letter (Evans 1986b). The committee's report was a damning indictment of those involved in the cover-up. Yet the sabotage did not end there; the Conservative majority on the committee delayed publication until the eve of the summer recess, thereby muzzling debate. No US executive could have got away with such evasion; Thatcher avoided a British Watergate.

For a Prime Minister to sit there for half an hour and allow the Secretary of State [Leon Brittan] to mislead the House was a most extraordinary procedure.

Roy Jenkins, at the time of the Westland affair, in the House of Commons (13 Jan. 1986)

Problems with select committees The Westland affair did not bode well for the committee system and foreshadowed a number of areas of difficulty, including the following.

- ◆ *Composition*. Appointments are made by the Committee of Selection on the advice of the whips. Major's administration infuriated its own backbenchers by removing a raft of independently minded (i.e. awkward) members from committees by 'inventing' a rule that no MP could serve for over twelve years. Nicholas Winterton, struck off the Health Committee, which he had chaired, accused the whips of 'saying free speech and an independent mind can have no role in Parliament' (*Observer*, 12 July 1992). After its June 2001 election triumph the Blair government sought to remove Gwyneth Dunwoody and Donald Anderson from their positions as chairs of the Transport and Foreign Affairs committees respectively; both had proved critical of the government. However, MPs (including the Leader of the House) were so incensed that they resisted and, to government embarrassment, the two were reinstated. The Liaison Committee has called for appointments to be placed in the hands of an independent panel of MPs, but this has remained a pipe dream (Lansdale 2001).
- ◆ *Prime ministerial reticence*. Prime ministers (and former prime ministers) have been reluctant to appear before select committees. Following the Pergau Dam scandal in 1994 (concerning government aid for the Malaysian dam being tied to arms contracts), Baroness Thatcher refused to appear before the Foreign Affairs Committee. After 1997, the New Labour government took to publishing an 'annual report' detailing its achievements. When the Liaison Committee suggested that it might question Tony Blair on these, he declined on the grounds that a convention existed that prime ministers did not appear. His argument that Prime Minister's Question Time provided an adequate forum was hotly contested by the Public Administration Committee (Sherman 2001), and he eventually relented, appearing before the Liaison Committee for the first time on 16 July 2002.
- ◆ *Intimidation*. Some committee members, conscious of their careers, are easily frightened. In May 1998, Labour's Diane Abbott accused Denis MacShane, PPS at the Foreign Office, of intimidating both members and chairman of the Foreign Affairs Committee investigating the arms-to-Sierra-Leone affair. As a member of the committee, her own questioning was regarded as disloyal to the government (*Sunday Times*, 24 May 1998).
- ◆ *Misplaced loyalty*. Some appear to agree that loyalty to party bosses comes before Parliament. The Foreign Affairs Committee report on the arms-to-Sierra-Leone affair was leaked to the Foreign Secretary before publication and Labour member Ernie Ross was forced to resign from the committee as a result. Further investigations revealed Labour MPs on other committees guilty of similar offences.

◆ *Government pressure.* Under the Major government, whip David Willetts attempted to influence the Members' Interests Committee in its investigation into the cash-for-questions scandal. Called before the Committee on Standards and Privileges, his evasive answers were seen as 'dissembling', and he was forced to resign in December 1996. Evidence later emerged that attempts to influence select committees were widespread (*Independent*, 14 July 1997).

◆ *Non-cooperation.* After the Willetts affair there were reports of Conservative whips evading scrutiny and shredding notes on file. In investigating the arms-to-Sierra-Leone affair in 1998, the Foreign Affairs Committee found its access to papers blocked by Foreign Secretary Robin Cook. In January 2002 Lord Birt, Blair's special adviser responsible for 'blue skies' thinking, refused to appear before the Transport Committee, claiming that Department of Transport officials were better qualified to answer questions.

> Everyone thought it was very harsh on David Willetts. All he was doing was his job.
>
> Former Conservative whip, in the *Independent* (14 July 1997)

Scrutiny and the constitution Given their paucity of resources (staff, advisers, expenses for witnesses, time and formal powers), the committees can be said to have achieved much. They have produced hundreds of reports, publicized some important issues and sometimes influenced government policy. However, they work under a major constitutional handicap. Across the Atlantic congressional committees exert considerable sway, their chairpersons nationally recognized figures able, as British television viewers witnessed in the Watergate, 'Irangate' and Monica Lewinsky hearings, to put the US executive on the spot. However, British committees could never operate with the same authority. Congress is set within a constitutional separation of powers (see p. 69); in Britain the Cabinet and prime minister dominate the House from which the committees come. All the formidable powers the government has to control Parliament can be used to limit its committees.

Moreover some (such as Enoch Powell and Michael Foot) have argued that the whole development is misguided. Parliamentary debate is traditionally wide ranging, concerned with points of broad principle. The micro-level scrutiny of the committees may lose sight of the ideological wood for the trees. In this view, the argument that MPs require more information in order to be better at their jobs may be fallacious.

Reporting Parliament: the Fourth Estate

> Burke said that there were Three Estates in Parliament; but, in the Reporter's Gallery yonder, there sat a *Fourth Estate* more important far than they all.
>
> Thomas Carlyle (1795–1881; Scottish essayist and historian),
> *Heroes and Hero Worship* (1841)

Whatever its faults, Parliament remains the nation's central democratic forum. Even though debate rarely leads to direct policy change, it can have a longer-term influence by shaping public opinion. The mechanism for reporting Parliament is therefore crucially important.

Problems of reporting Parliament

Although all debates and discussion are faithfully reproduced in *Hansard*, the vast majority of people wishing to follow the proceedings of Parliament do so through the mass media. There are certain problems with this.

◆ *Selectivity.* It is impossible to cover everything said in this palace of a million words. Journalists must be selective, seeking the essence of a speech or debate.

◆ *Simplification and trivialization.* In the tabloids single-syllable words are *de rigueur,* while the broadsheets have a tradition of amusing 'Parliamentary Sketch' columns, often highlighting the antics of the more bizarre and exotic parliamentary creatures.

◆ *Sensationalism.* In the quest for circulation, any suggestion of scandal will take precedence over serious news. In October 1998, Welsh Secretary Ron Davies's strange encounter on Clapham Common crowded out debates on the devastation caused by hurricane Mitch. Able ministers, such as David Mellor and Stephen Byers, can even be hounded from office. Broadsheets and broadcasters are not immune from this criticism.

◆ *Bias.* Right-wing bias has seen editorial selection generally favouring the Conservatives or centrist Labour case, with 'Rowdyism' on the left being reported in lurid detail.

◆ *News management.* Much reporting merely relays information disseminated by ministers, press secretaries and spin doctors through press releases and the exclusive club of Westminster journalists known as the Lobby. Although not all are tame, journalists can still be subject to the black arts of news management. The Lobby system allows the executive to set the news agenda with authoritative statements (see p. 227). In April 2002 it was agreed that the Lobby would be opened up to *all* journalists. Leader of the House Robin Cook proclaimed this as a move towards greater transparency but members of the exclusive club argued that it would make it easier for government spokespersons to take 'soft questions' from non-specialists and avoid those from the awkward squad.

The media can reduce the status of the House by encouraging statements outside its precincts under the eyes of the cameras. This can catch opponents unprepared and evade critical debate. Even Enoch Powell, a fervent parliamentarian, was guilty of such behaviour. In March 1998 the Speaker admonished Labour '*apparatchiks*' for playing a public relations role for ministers. Although the ministerial code of conduct (refreshed for the 2001 parliament) laid down that policy statements should first be made to the Commons, *not* the media, it was soon clear that this was not happening. A number of important policies, including the use of private operators to run failing hospitals, a linking of grammar schools with comprehensives and changes in immigration and asylum rules all appeared in the press and on the BBC's *Today* programme before being announced in Parliament. However, in February 2002, in the face of fierce criticism, the Prime Minister's spokesman stated baldly that the code would be followed 'only where practicable' (Sherman 2002b).

The Times has made many ministries. When, as of late, there has been a long continuance of divided Parliaments, of governments which were without 'brute voting power', and which depended upon intellectual strength, the most influential organ of English opinion has been of critical moment.

Walter Bagehot, *The English Constitution* (1867: ch. 1)

Live from the Commons: broadcasting Parliament

No technological innovation has had a greater impact on the political life of the nation than the unblinking eye. Campaigning is now mainly a television art and between elections politicians feature regularly in news stories, as chat-show guests and hosts, and on phone-ins and 'question time' programmes. Viewers may even be taken into their homes to share their Christmas festivities and hear them singing carols with their families. Yet the cameras for long remained out of the House.

In March 1976 the Commons agreed in principle to sound broadcasting, though this was not to be the thin end of the television wedge. It was another ten years before the Lords agreed to submit to the cameras and the historic first live television broadcast from the Commons took place on Tuesday 21 November 1989 with the debate on the Queen's Speech. Although officially an experiment, the cameras had come to stay, both in the House and in the committee rooms. Today, debates can be seen in their entirety on the parliamentary channel.

The debate When the British Parliament finally agreed to experiment, Australia, Austria, Belgium, Canada, France, Greece, Holland, Italy, Japan, West Germany and the USA had all accepted the principle (*Sunday Times*, 14 Feb. 1988). What was the reason for the reticence? Opponents argue that it highlights the 'worst' aspects of debate, encouraging members to play to the gallery. Moreover, as with sports coverage, editing concentrates on 'highlights' in the quest for ratings. In 1998, *Yesterday in Parliament* was removed from Radio 4's FM frequency for fear of losing listeners (part of a process termed 'dumbing down' by its critics). The counter-argument is that, having been courted for their votes, people should be allowed to witness the results of their choices.

Moreover, in a televisual age, if the cameras did not enter the House, coverage would be confined to studio confrontations between academics, journalists and a chosen few media politicians or ex-politicians: not public debates but private debates upon public matters.

Official reticence is hardly surprising in the most closed and secretive political culture in the western world, where democracy, unlike justice, has been deemed better for not actually being seen. In Westminster, the public gallery is small and usually full of sightseeing tourists. This was very convenient for those who wished to emasculate the people's representatives. Today the public gallery contains some 54 million at home and even a worldwide audience. However, with jeering MPs and an expanse of empty green leather benches, people do not always like what they see (Norton 1997: 364–5).

From Golden Age to Golden Sunset?

An incessant theme of post-war debate has been the reform of Parliament, the underlying critique centring on its inability to bridle, or even effectively scrutinize, the executive. While formally regarded as sovereign, it is rather like the aged parent of an arrogant son, grown beyond discipline.

The Golden Age of Parliament

It is sometimes contended that, from its origins, Parliament has never been strong vis-à-vis the executive, and that it is not in the nature of the British constitution that it should be. However, there was a 'Golden Age', between the 1832 and 1867 Reform Acts, when MPs really mattered. This was before the parties began to dominate, when governments were genuinely vulnerable to being turned out of office without a general election (as in 1852, 1855, 1858 and 1866), and ministers could be individually censured and forced to resign. MPs controlled the organization of the House and could shape policy through debates. Information could be demanded from government, and select committees would conduct authoritative investigations and even draft legislation. During this period the legislative process began with a formal request for leave to introduce the bill, justification being required before a first reading. Second and third readings, and the committee stage, were genuinely critical scrutinies in which MPs set their own time and secured amendments. Gladstone's financial reforms subjected public expenditure to real control.

Today MPs are members of their parties first and of the House second. Despite some attempts at modernization, the unity of Parliament remains like that of a gigantic pantomime horse in which two ill-matched thespians wrestle with each other about who should be the head. What was vividly revealed during the Major government was that the greatest check on the executive comes not from Parliament as such, but from the government backbenches.

Friendly fire: will the real opposition stand up!

If a party has consolidated the executive hold over Parliament it can also imperil it. It is within the parties that the real executive/legislature tension can be seen (Brand 1992). A government's own backbenchers can become an effective opposition. This important facet in appreciating the role of Parliament has been a key theme in a continuing analysis by Philip Norton. From the 1970s MPs appeared to be becoming less disciplined, resulting in a greater incidence of government defeats. Heath (1970–4) experienced six such setbacks, three on three-line whips. The 1974 Labour government suffered no fewer than fifty-nine defeats, although there were special circumstances, including fragile majorities, minority government and the uneasy Lib–Lab pact.

The Conservatives' success in broadening their social base brought in young meritocrats displaying less instinctive loyalty. They helped make Major's government increasingly vulnerable. Not only were there serious defeats, often at the hands of the Eurosceptics, there was a vote of confidence and even Major's exasperated resignation as party leader. Following his sacking in the face of hostile backbench rumblings, Norman Lamont spoke in June 1993 of a government 'in office but not in power'. As his majority dwindled, Major's hands became tied over his Northern Ireland initiative and even individual MPs could take advantage; Sir John Gorst warned in December 1996 that his vote was conditional on a hospital closure threat in his constituency being removed.

A secure majority does not guarantee peace since backbenchers may feel free to air their consciences without real damage. In 1964, when Labour had the barest of majorities, Wilson could enjoy loyal support, but after his 1966 victory the left began to make demands, particularly on defence issues. Similarly, the seemingly impregnable Thatcher governments experienced many challenges (over matters as varied as rate-capping and charges for dental and optical tests) and some backbench victories were gained (the 1986 Shops Bill and the 1982 amendment to the immigration rules). Dramatic revolts in April 1988 over the poll tax and housing benefits also forced government concessions.

However, after Major's uncertain reign, Blair's government was to reassert the position of the executive through unprecedented attention to party discipline. MPs were allegedly being kept 'on message' by spin doctors; in March 1998 Tony Benn reported in *Tribune* that Labour backbenchers regularly received faxed personalized press releases ready to be sent unchanged to their local newspapers.

A new MP entering the chamber with Winston Churchill remarked that it was time to face the enemy. 'No', came the reply; the facing benches contained the 'opposition', the 'enemy' sat behind!

Not while I'm alive he ain't!

Ernest Bevin's alleged reply to the remark that minister Herbert Morrison was his own worst enemy

---

One MP told me that four of his colleagues had refused to take part in a charity swim because it would mean removing their vibrating bleepers for an hour.

Labour MP, reported in *Index on Censorship* (1998, no. 5: 57)

Bloody good
news for
democracy.

Speaker Bernard
Weatherill, on
government
defeat on a three-
line whip over its
Shops Bill to bring
in Sunday trading;
quoted in the
Independent
(24 Dec. 1987)

Hence, the power to check the executive, while real, is contingent: limited by a government's majority, the willingness of MPs to toe the line and the effectiveness of internal party discipline. This is not the constitutional check of a genuine separation of powers. Indeed, its fragility was demonstrated over the damning findings of the Scott Report when 'a majority of MPs voted, in effect, to be repeatedly misled by civil servants', demanding no ministerial heads even though the executive had subjected the House to a barrage of lies and deception (Norton-Taylor et al. 1996: 197).

Significantly, it is often the House of Lords, largely free from the straitjacket of party discipline, that, despite its constitutional limitations, provides the greatest resistance. In June 2002, for example, after a threat by the upper house to block the proposals, Home Secretary David Blunkett was unable to extend the powers of state 'snooping' under the Regulation of Investigatory Powers Act to seven government departments and local authorities.

Reform and talk of reform

The scale of the problems facing the Commons can be measured in the length of the catalogue of possible reforms (see, for example, Norton 1997). After the 1997 Labour victory the Modernization Committee produced a succession of reports covering areas such as the legislative process, select committees, scrutiny of European legislation, voting procedures, the parliamentary calendar and the conduct of debate. However, while promising to streamline procedures, these offered no greater controls on the executive. Indeed, Blair's 'modernization' of Prime Minister's Questions, strengthening rather than weakening his position, was done without consulting the House.

Inhibitions to reform All hope of reform must come up against the 'great ghost' of the constitution. Bagehot saw virtue in the Commons' *fusion* with the executive, the constitution's 'efficient secret'. Yet it was this, together with party discipline, that was to render parliamentary sovereignty so palpable a fiction. The very disease renders the House unable to administer the medicine. Only the executive has the power to effect change, but why should it connive to reduce its omnipotence? Governments may be enthusiastic about rearranging the deckchairs but will they alter the course of the Titanic? In the USA, where there is genuine separation of powers, Congressional leaders are not members of the executive, neither do they depend on executive patronage for advancement; these are the conditions required for a genuine check on the executive. Clinton, for example, was subjected to unremitting hostility and lost some of his most cherished legislative ambitions.

Moreover, one can doubt MPs' real commitment to a stronger role. Some are happy enough to engage in constituency work or pursue their business interests, leaving their leaders to govern, while the new breed of young professional politicians see their future not on select committees but as front-benchers, and they must court the patronage of their leaders. In the constituencies, most associations do not expect their MPs to rock the boat and, for the general public, executive domination is entirely compatible with a political culture that admires strong government. Many would be disturbed to find their representatives continually frustrating the executive. Thatcher enjoyed much adulation and Tony Blair swept to victory as a dominant leader, even professing admiration for the lady and wearing much of her finery. Finally, the establishment of the Nolan Committee, the appointment of a Parliamentary Commissioner for Standards and the white paper on preventing corruption (Home Office 2000) all cast doubt on the ability of this 'mother of Parliaments' to guarantee its own integrity, let alone that of the executive. Furthermore, when Elizabeth Filkin, Parliamentary Commissioner for Standards, was in effect sacked, it suggested a Parliament not only unable to scrutinize ministers but unwilling to let anyone else do the job.

Denouement: a deeper function exposed

If Parliament is flawed with respect to its key roles, what then is its function in modern politics? Perhaps the answer lies in Bagehot's analysis of the value of monarchy: outward display serving to beguile the masses, leaving the real process of government in the hands of a political elite. Perhaps this reading can help explain the Commons. Politicians of all hues, representatives of powerful interests, the media and civil servants, all pay unctuous tribute to the idea of parliamentary sovereignty.

It is crucially necessary for the economically and politically powerful that the House of Commons *should* have this apparent centrality in British political life, because it stands alone in the constitution as the embodiment of democracy. Without it there would be little to justify the exercise of state power. More than any other institution, it can foster a popular belief that ordinary folk control their rulers. In other words, it is one of the most powerful legitimating devices in the political system. In the following chapter we shall look deeper into the modern executive that so dominates the political landscape.

Key points

- Parliament is largely energized by political parties, with little real identity of its own as the collective voice of the people.
- Party discipline, the absence of a separation of powers and the tendency of the electoral system to bestow absolute majorities mean that parliamentary sovereignty is effectively hijacked by the executive.
- The principal functions of Parliament may be said to be legislation, debate and scrutiny of the executive. In all these the executive holds the whip hand.
- EU membership produces an alternative source of legislation, limiting parliamentary sovereignty.

- Because it is the forum of popular debate, the reporting of Parliament is constitution-ally significant.
- There are latent powers in Parliament that under certain circumstances a government's backbenchers can use.
- To an extent Parliament serves to conceal the reality of power in Britain.

Review your understanding of the following terms and concepts

Act of Parliament	*Hansard*	Question Time
adjournment debate	legislative process	scrutiny committee
backbencher	legislature	select committee
backbench organization	Liaison Committee	standing committee
bills, private and public	Opposition Day	supplementary question
delegated legislation	parliamentary question	whip
Early Day Motion	party discipline	written answer
emergency debate	private member's bill	
'Golden Age' of Parliament	Queen's Speech	

Assignment

For this assignment you must refer to *Hansard*, the record of parliamentary debate. Do this in your library or on the internet (www.parliament.uk). Look up the debate on 'Parliament and Politics (BBC Coverage)' which took place on Wednesday 21 October 1998 beginning at 11.00 a.m. (column 1215). Answer the following questions.

		Mark (%)
1	What kind of debate is taking place?	5
2	What parliamentary device had been used by Nigel Evans to show his concern over BBC policy?	5
3	Summarize in around 500 words the case against the BBC made by Paul Tyler.	20
4	Which MP lends support to the BBC? Assess the validity of his argument?	10
5	Why do backbenchers place a particular value on regional broadcasting?	20
6	Upon what grounds does David Winnick assert that 'the BBC is treating Parliament with utter contempt' (column 1218)?	10
7	What does Richard Allan mean by a 'reality lag' (column 1228)?	10
8	Consider the validity of the BBC's argument that parliamentary broadcasting should be reduced if it is found boring by the mass audience.	20

Questions for discussion

1 Explain the way in which the Labour and Conservative backbenchers organize in Parliament.
2 What factors account for the high level of party discipline in the Commons?
3 'The legislative process was designed for the mid-nineteenth-century Parliament and is nothing more than an anachronism today.' Discuss.
4 Evaluate Parliament's role with respect to EU law-making?
5 What is the value of the parliamentary question today?
6 Evaluate the opportunity for, and value of, private members' legislation.
7 How important today is Parliament as a forum for debating current issues?
8 To what extent can select committees enable MPs to control the executive?
9 Consider the pros and cons of televising Parliament.
10 What Commons reforms do you consider necessary?

Topic for debate

This house believes that the modern House of Commons is little more than a part of the dignified constitution.

Further reading

See also reading for chapter 12.

Adonis, A. (1993) *Parliament Today.*
Stresses Parliament's role as a focus of national attention.

Brand, J. (1992) *British Parliamentary Parties: Policy and Power.*
Illustrates how intra-party tension constitutes the real executive–legislative tension.

Hansard.
Official reports of proceedings (available in libraries and on internet).

Hansard Society (1993) *Making the Law: Report of the Commission on the Legislative Process.*
Examines the question of reform of the Commons.

Norton, P. (1993) *Does Parliament Matter?*
'Yes', says one of Britain's leading authorities.

Richards, P. G. (1970) *Parliament and Conscience.*
Illustrates the backbencher's role in legislating on sensitive issues of morality.

Peter Riddell (2000) *Parliament under Blair.*
Finds the Blair government unwilling to admit to the diminishing power of Parliament.

Rush, M. (2001) *The Role of the Member of Parliament since 1868.*
Analysis of the socioeconomic transformation of the Commons from the mid-nineteenth century.

For light relief

Tony Banks, *Out of Order.*
Parliamentary anecdotes from a colourful MP.

Hilaire Belloc, *Mr Clutterbuck's Election.*
Satire on early-century political life.

Michael Dobbs, *House of Cards.*
Follows the progress of evil chief whip, Frances Urquhart, who will stop at nothing for power. Fictional of course. Available on video.

Greg Knights, *Right Honourable Insults.*
Tory MP of Tony Blair: 'He's so vain he'd take his own hand in marriage', and so on. Hundreds of wicked insults from the experts.

Matthew Parris, *Great Parliamentary Scandals.*
Entertaining mapping of the moral swampland of British politics over four centuries.

Howard Spring, *Fame is the Spur.*
Labour politician's rise to power and subsequent disillusionment.

On the net

http://www.parliament.uk
Parliament's home page includes links to *Hansard*, select committee reports and the progress of bills through the legislative process. Many MPs now also have websites of their own.

14

The Heart of Government: of Cabinets and Kings

In this chapter attention turns from the elected assembly to the relatively small group of MPs who head the executive arm of government, and to the environment in which they work. The complex territory around the cabinet system comprises individual actors (officials, spin doctors and advisers, junior ministers), committees of politicians and officials, and institutional structures. Together this network constitutes Britain's core executive. The chapter comprises two broad sections. The first begins by examining the nature of cabinet government and its evolution in Britain. Next we begin to map the anatomy of the core executive, identifying a range of associated political debates. In the second section we turn to one of the most compelling questions of modern government: the role of the prime minister. Is it, or is it not, becoming more presidential in character? Alternatively, does Britain have cabinet government: collective rather than singular, the principle of rule by the *one* having been repudiated in the long series of constitutional struggles against monarchy? Or is the modern core executive so complex that neither answer can be appropriate? This chapter tells us much about the living constitution, revealing a dense network of relationships and dependencies in which power is diffuse and found in many guises.

Defining the executive head

Every state has a centre of political authority. Decisions made here determine how we live, how we are educated, our health, our employment and perhaps, where war is concerned, how we may die. Formally the head of the British system of government comprises the prime minister and around twenty other senior ministers, most heading ministries. This is the **Cabinet**, which works through weekly meetings in the Cabinet Room at the prime minister's residence, 10 Downing Street, a familiar backdrop for the comings and goings of the important and self-important. The Cabinet has also become integrated into the EU and can be expected to become more so. Ministers operate at the very heart of the decision-making process in the Council of Ministers, while the prime minister sits on the European Council, sometimes assuming its presidency.

The Cabinet and the government Journalists often write as if the terms 'Cabinet' and 'government' are synonymous. In the eighteenth century this was largely true but today the Cabinet is but a small part of a complex web comprising over two hundred politicians, forming a hierarchy ranging from secretaries of state to junior parliamentary private secretaries assisting ministers (figures 14.1 and 14.3). This web of power extends even further to embrace

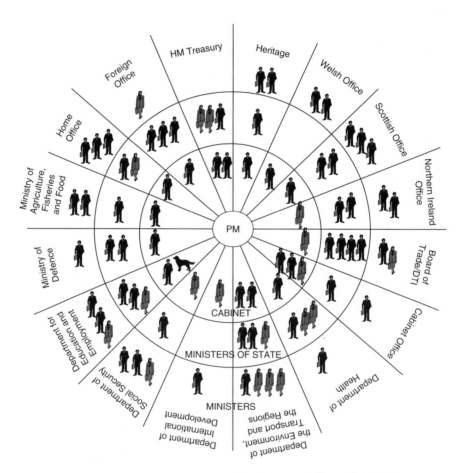

Figure 14.1
The Cabinet stands at the centre of a web of government.

Note: This example shows Blair's 1997 government.

the senior public servants at the heads of the departments of state and executive agencies to form the '**core executive**' (Dunleavy and Rhodes 1990).

An Anatomy of Cabinet Government

What is cabinet government?

The Ancient Greek philosopher Plato believed that rule by a divine 'philosopher king' would be the most perfect form of government. However, this could only exist in an ideal world; in reality it would deteriorate into the *worst* form – tyranny. Regimes that have terrorized populations have characteristically been dominated by single rulers – tyrants, dictators and demagogues, their very names synonyms for oppression. Constitutions are designed to prevent tyranny; this is what the English sought to do in 1215 and 1689 and the Americans in 1787. After Stalin the Russians vowed they would never again permit one person so much power. Yet the British executive, inheriting the powers of the monarch and able to dominate Parliament, knows no constitutional constraints. Hence, faith in **cabinet government** is crucial.

Cabinet government entails the sharing of authority, with decision-making based upon discussion and compromise. However, this self-moderating form of government is only protected by conventions and these are among the most fragile in the constitution. If there is a document to be consulted, it is *Questions of Procedure for Ministers*, finally released in 1992 after some fifty years of official secrecy. However, the dry passages of dos and don'ts of this ministerial highway code say little about the politics of power. For this reason, one of the most crucial questions in modern British politics is whether cabinet government is real or just one more myth in our slippery and elusive constitution.

> In the multitude of counsellors there is safety.
>
> *Proverbs, xi: 14*

Evolution of the Cabinet

The history of the Cabinet cannot be traced as a continuous line linking a distant past indissolubly to the present. The modern Cabinet owes much to political forces generated by the rise of capitalism and is linked with the nineteenth-century constitutional reforms. It is certainly true, however, that monarchs have always surrounded themselves with small bands of loyal advisers and confidants and this helps explain the structure of the modern executive and the culture of power within it.

The Privy Council By the sixteenth century the practice of monarchical consultation had become institutionalized in the Privy Council, a body that had itself evolved from a council of royal advisers in Norman times (the *Curia Regis*). The following century saw the Civil War and the republican period with government through *executive committees*. This proved unworkable, but after the Restoration, when Charles II sought to re-establish what he believed to be his divine right to rule alone, he found the Privy Council difficult and resorted to a smaller group, a committee of the council. This was called the 'cabinet' as a term of abuse, a synonym for 'cabal' – a devious, inner group. The modern Cabinet remains constitutionally a committee of the Privy Council, members retaining the title 'right honourable' for life. Consigned to the dignified part of the constitution, the full Council nowadays meets only rarely, to mark great state occasions such as the sovereign's marriage or death.

The Glorious Revolution In 1681 Charles II dissolved Parliament, establishing an alternative 'Oxford Parliament'. The ensuing struggle led to the 'Glorious Revolution' of 1688, resulting in the flight of James II (who had acceded in 1685), and his ultimate replacement by William (of Orange) and Mary. Matters of state were transacted in the full Privy Council and, to prevent royal influence, ministers were excluded from Parliament. However, this principle was soon abandoned because Parliament wanted ministers in its midst for questioning. Had it been retained, Britain would have developed a separation of powers and a significantly different constitution. As it was, membership of Parliament, rather than being forbidden, became an essential requirement of office, thereby clearing the way for a *fusion* of powers – Bagehot's 'efficient secret' of the constitution.

The Act of Settlement Later anxiety about the succession, resulting from the death of Queen Anne's son, was allayed in the Act of Settlement (1701) establishing the Hanoverian succession. George I and George II are said to have shown little interest in British politics between 1714 and 1760, thereby allowing the Cabinet to become increasingly dominant, but there were also more fundamental forces at work. Ministers had in fact met in the absence of the monarch during Anne's reign (1702–14), and when George III attempted to reassert a degree of royal authority in 1784 he was castigated as unconstitutional; the roots of the modern Cabinet had taken hold. Hence, five years before the French revolution, George III made the last appearance of a monarch in the Cabinet. The monarch reigned but the Cabinet had effectively hijacked the royal prerogative. It did not, however, possess all the essentials of its modern counterpart.

- ◆ Responsibility was to the Crown rather than to Parliament, so that it was possible to govern without a majority.
- ◆ Parliamentary groupings (Whigs and Tories) were only loose coalitions, making it possible for a Cabinet to contain representatives of both and enjoy cross-party support in the House.
- ◆ Cabinet members were responsible only for their own ministries and quite prepared to attack each other's policies.
- ◆ The resignation of the First Lord of the Treasury (the prime minister) did not mean that other ministers also had to depart.
- ◆ A significant number of MPs owed allegiance to neither 'party' and could be courted through patronage and bribery.

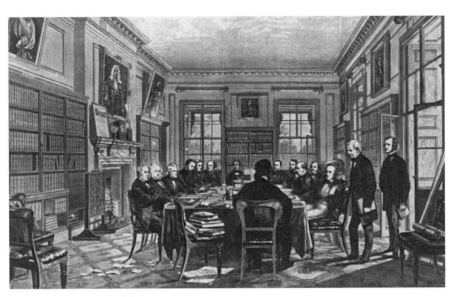

The Cabinet Room
in Downing Street,
1870

Source: Mary Evans Picture Library

The industrial revolution The rise of the industrial bourgeoisie in the nine-teenth century challenged the *ancien régime*; the new men entered Parliament through the extended franchise and dominated it through party discipline. This added a second dimension to the power of the Cabinet.

◆ Cabinets became more tightly knit with members drawn from one party only.
◆ Members accepted collective responsibility for policy.
◆ So long as their backbenchers remained loyal, governments enjoyed a degree of supremacy unknown since the Tudors.

Here was the modern Cabinet: relatively autonomous and drawing authority from various constitutional and political sources, including its lineage to the Privy Council, its inheritance of the prerogative powers of the Crown, and its domination of the constitutionally sovereign Parliament.

Collective responsibility

The constitutional basis of cabinet government is sometimes said to lie in the doctrine of **collective responsibility**, which implies a form of collective decision-making. Interpreted variously by participants and commentators, it generally implies the following features.

◆ All (or several) members play a part in formulating policy.
◆ All members support each other in public (even if privately disagreeing).

♦   Any member unable to lend support should resign.
♦   Cabinet proceedings are regarded as confidential (though resignees earn the right to a resignation speech revealing their reasons).

The convention probably originated in the eighteenth century when ministers sought to strengthen their hand vis-à-vis the monarch by sticking together. Today its prescriptive force lies in the ideal of collective decision-making as a curb on power. However, in reality it is honoured more in the breach than the observance.

Now, is it to lower the price of corn, or isn't it? It is not much matter what we say, but mind, we must all say *the same*.

Attributed to Lord Melbourne (1779–1848; Whig prime minister), quoted in Walter Bagehot, *The English Constitution* (1867: ch. 1)

Collective responsibility or collective expediency? An important reason for the doctrine's persistence is political expediency (which is why we even find it applied to the Shadow Cabinet). A united front has proved a valuable asset. Indeed, the collective cloak can be thrown over all members of the government, usually encompassing around one-third of the parliamentary party. In 1983 Nicholas Budgen, a mere assistant whip, resigned over the provisions of the Northern Ireland Bill, while in April 1994 Jonathan Evans resigned as a Parliamentary Private Secretary over a disagreement on local government reform in Wales. The doctrine can thus be a basis for party discipline, giving the government a 'payroll vote' that can be relied upon by the whips.

However, submerging differences can be stressful. Once in opposition, former Home Office minister Ann Widdecombe, in a passionate Commons speech, revealed the tension between her and the Home Secretary over the dismissal of prison service chief Derek Lewis. Michael Howard was never to shake off her declaration that he was a man with 'something of the night' about him. Again, Geoffrey Howe's momentous resignation speech, marking the beginning of the end for Thatcher, revealed anguish submerged beneath a famously ovine exterior when he lamented the futility of

trying to stretch the meaning of words beyond what was credible, of trying to pretend there was a common policy…(House of Commons speech, 13 Nov. 1990)

In practice, cabinet leaks enable journalists to reveal much cabinet disagreement. A number of Major's ministers remained in the Cabinet while indicating variance over the EU. Indeed, when arch-Eurosceptic John Redwood resigned in 1995, it was to challenge for the leadership rather than express dissent.

"Our minutes are going to make pretty boring reading in 30 years' time with no one ever dissenting."

Reproduced by permission of *Punch*

Cabinet structure

Within the cabinet hierarchy, the seniormost members hold titles such as Home Secretary, Chancellor of the Exchequer, Foreign Secretary, or Secretary of State for this or that. Generally ministers are not expected to have specialist knowledge. Indeed regular reshuffles positively discourage this; they are generalists rather than specialists. The status of a position can vary with circumstances and personalities. When Howe was made deputy prime minister it was seen as an insult, but when Heseltine took the position under Major, some even saw him as the *de facto* prime minister. Under Blair, however, John Prescott was never to enjoy the same status, with critics alleging that he was a cover for the *real* deputy, the non-elected Alastair Campbell. The post of Northern Ireland secretary was regarded as something of an incubus, but in 1998 Mo Mowlam became a heroine.

A Cabinet can also contain ministers without portfolio, their responsibilities reflecting a prime minister's priorities. This appointment was used for a time by Tony Blair to include Peter Mandelson, with a responsibility for coordinating and presenting policy.

Composition Cabinets were traditionally drawn largely from the social elite, a large proportion having aristocratic backgrounds. However, in both major parties there has been a steady increase in the *petit bourgeois* element (figure 14.2). In terms of education, ministers have been by no means typical of those they govern, a high proportion having attended public school (particularly Eton) and Oxbridge (Guttsman 1963). However, Blair's first Cabinet contained only four Oxbridge alumni (including Blair himself). A further four came from Durham, three from Edinburgh and ten other provincial universities were also represented. Ron Davies enjoyed the distinction of being the first cabinet member from a polytechnic (Portsmouth).

Like Parliament, the Cabinet has been largely a male preserve, women often having had only a token presence. Ironically Thatcher showed no desire for female company and Major's first Cabinet contained no women. Blair began with five, rising after his 2001 victory to a magnificent seven. There was also a new attitude. While the older women, like fifty-eight-year-old Margaret Beckett, were content to do the job on men's terms, the younger representatives, such as Patricia Hewitt and Tessa Jowell, sought to change the rules, integrating motherhood into their working lives (Sieghart 2001). Significantly, Hewitt combined her post of Trade and Industry Secretary with that of Minister for Women.

A minister reaching cabinet rank will normally be experienced in government. However, Blair's first team began at a considerable disadvantage as a result of an unusually prolonged period in the wilderness. There had, however, been some relaxation of the rules preventing opposition access to Whitehall to allow contact with permanent secretaries and agency heads from January 1996. Other preparations included seminars at Oxford University to receive the collective wisdom of retired mandarins and ex-Labour ministers.

> We still thought in terms of appointing a statutory woman. 'Who should she be?' asked Ted [Heath]. 'Margaret Thatcher', was my immediate reply.
>
> James Prior (Conservative cabinet member), *A Balance of Power* (1986)

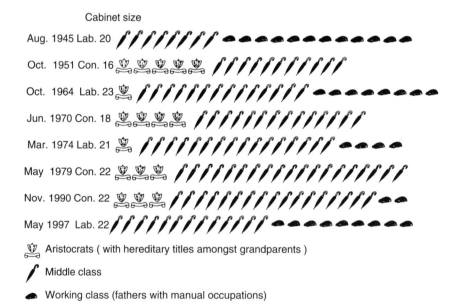

Figure 14.2
Social composition of incoming Cabinets, 1945–1997.

Cabinet size

Aug. 1945 Lab. 20

Oct. 1951 Con. 16

Oct. 1964 Lab. 23

Jun. 1970 Con. 18

Mar. 1974 Lab. 21

May 1979 Con. 22

Nov. 1990 Con. 22

May 1997 Lab. 22

♛ Aristocrats (with hereditary titles amongst grandparents)

/ Middle class

◗ Working class (fathers with manual occupations)

Source: Data from Butler and Butler (1994: 66), *Dod's Parliamentary Companion* (1998), Waller and Criddle (1997) and various on-line information sources.

Size The size of the Cabinet is no mere technicality; it has implications for the way it works. Eighteenth-century Cabinets contained around five to nine members, which grew to twelve to fifteen in the following century and by Asquith's time had reached twenty-three, whereupon the figure remained constant (figure 14.3). Today the law allows for twenty-two salaried members. Although this might not seem very large, it is so by international standards. The mighty US president, for example, surrounds himself with only around ten colleagues. Critics generally believe British Cabinets to be too large for effective collective decision-taking but various pressures tend to increase size.

- *Growth in the public domain*. Since the nineteenth century, government has taken on many more areas of responsibility. Wilson defended his Cabinet of twenty-three on the grounds that it was 'inconceivable that important sectors of our national life should be excluded' (Walker 1972: 35).
- *Bureaucratic pressure*. Representation in Cabinet remains politically important to departments as they compete for resources.
- *Interest group pressure*. Outside Westminster, groups see in cabinet composition indications of a government's priorities. Doctors, farmers, trade unionists, and so on, all look for visible confirmation that they are recognized.
- *Parliamentary pressure*. Leading party figures such as, say, John Prescott or Gordon Brown, usually have bands of supporters in the House pressing for their inclusion.
- *Party faction*. A prime minister will try to appease factions of party opinion; hence Major's inclusion of the troublesome Eurosceptics.

Critics allege that large Cabinets can be slow and cumbersome; vulnerable to factionalism (Thatcher's were characterized as 'wets' and 'drys'); liable to leak –'The more you have,' said Harold Wilson, 'the more people can be got at' (Hennessy 1986: 149); and lacking a strategic vision as ministers develop departmental tunnel vision. Reformers advocate some form of slimming down.

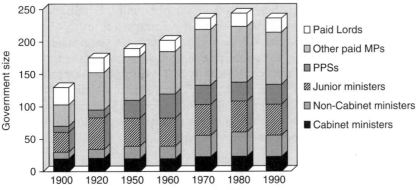

Figure 14.3
The increasing size of peacetime governments.

Source: Data from Butler and Butler (1994: 66).

Blair's War Cabinet, 8 October 2001

John Prescott, Deputy Prime Minister
Jack Straw, Foreign Secretary
Geoff Hoon, Defence Secretary
Gordon Brown, Chancellor
David Blunkett, Home Secretary

Clare Short, International Development
  Secretary
Robin Cook, Leader of the Commons
Admiral Sir Michael Boyce, Chief of the
  Defence Staff

- ◆ *Policy Cabinets*. One of the most discussed models is the **Policy Cabinet** advocated by Leo Amery (1947), who served under Bonar Law and Baldwin. He argued for around six members, each free of departmental ties, to take an overarching strategic perspective. Ex-Chancellor Nigel Lawson put forward a similar proposal in 1993.
- ◆ *War Cabinets*. The exigencies of war have produced some enforced experiments. In 1916, Lloyd George's War Cabinet contained five members, as did Churchill's in the second world war. Even the skirmish with Argentina in the 1980s saw the fleeting emergence of a War Cabinet. In the tense period following 11 September, Tony Blair operated unilaterally until, bowing to pressure, he created a War Cabinet of eight.
- ◆ *Policy Cabinets in peacetime*. The nearest peacetime version of the model was Churchill's 1951 experiment. In a Cabinet of sixteen he appointed three non-departmental 'Overlords'. This is generally regarded as a failure, with a return to 'normal methods' two years later (Daalder 1964: 110–18). There was speculation in early 1997 that a 'super minister' system might be reintroduced by Blair to oversee large programmes such as welfare reform and transport (Grice 1997), but after the 2001 election these empires were disbanded.
- ◆ *Inner cabinets*. While outward forms remain, informal evolution takes place beneath the surface. One such has been the rise of what has been termed the **inner cabinet** – a small group of ministers closest to the prime minister, meeting independently and informally. Burch and Holliday (1996) found key decisions regularly being made in this way in the mid-1990s. This can threaten genuine cabinet government, but has proved irresistible to most prime ministers. Major's inner group varied with the matter under consideration (what Gordon Walker called partial cabinets). Under Blair, a 'big four' emerged to include John Prescott (Deputy Prime Minister), Robin Cook (Foreign Secretary) and Gordon Brown (Chancellor), which took the momentous decision to cede power over interest rates to the Bank of England.

Yet the policy cabinet principle assumes that strategic thinking can be separated from day-to-day departmental matters. Douglas Wass, ex-joint head of the civil service, questioned this in his Reith Lectures: 'In my experience of adminis-tration I have found it almost impossible to think constructively about general policy issues if I have not been involved in particular practical cases' (1984: 29).

Cabinet committees

Keeping the people informed

He agreed that no Prime Minister has ever explained why the numbers and membership of Cabinet Committees were kept secret. Why were they? I asked.

There was a long pause. 'Erm,' said the former Secretary to the Cabinet. 'Well. Erm. Are we on the record or off the record?'

'On the record.'

'Then I think I'd rather not go into that.'

Lord Hunt (ex-Cabinet Secretary), interviewed by Michael Davie in the *Observer* (11 Oct. 1987)

Modern cabinet government in Britain is enmeshed in a dense network of committees and subcommittees (table 14.1), the growth of which is one of the most significant post-war constitutional developments. Yet it long remained cloaked in secrecy, with accounts pieced together from memoirs, leaks, press guesswork, and occasional parliamentary statements. In 1972 Patrick Gordon Walker gave some clear indications in his book *The Cabinet*, Mrs Thatcher acknowledged them in the House in 1983 and the following year *The Times* published a detailed list. Finally, in 1992, the Whitehall ribcage, if not the flesh, was detailed in X-ray, with the official release of full details, including terms of reference and membership. These are now readily available on the internet.

In principle, committees are created to assist the Cabinet, which remains the 'parent' body. There are two broad categories – ad hoc and standing committees.

Ad hoc committees Created for specific problems, these have only ephemeral lives. The first was established in 1855 to handle the Crimean war, to be followed by others concerned with aspects of foreign policy. Towards the end of the nineteenth century, with a massive tide of legislation, more committees emerged to formulate policy and draft bills. They remain very important. In 1984 an ad hoc committee addressed the abolition of the GLC and the metro-politan counties, and Thatcher controlled strategy towards the 1985–6 miners' strike in this way. In June 1997, Social Security Secretary Harriet Harman chaired a committee to promote women-friendly policies across Whitehall. Labour's raft of new policy initiatives required a range of committees, such as those on constitutional reform and welfare-to-work.

Table 14.1 Cabinet committees and subcommittees, 2002

Committee	Chair
Economic and Domestic Affairs Secretariat	
Criminal Justice System (CJS)	Home Secretary
Crime Reduction (CJS(CR))	Home Secretary
Nations and Regions (CNR)	Deputy Prime Minister
Domestic Affairs (DA)	Deputy Prime Minister
Adult Basic Skills (DA(ABS))	Education and Skills Secretary
Active Communities and Family (DA(ACF))	Home Secretary
Drugs Policy (DA(D))	Home Secretary
Equality (DA(EQ))	Min. of State, Cabinet Office
Fraud (DA(F))	Chief Secretary, Treasury
Energy Policy (DA(N))	Deputy Prime Minister
Older People (DA(OP))	Work and Pensions Secretary
Rural Renewal (DA(RR))	Environment, Food & Rural Affairs Secretary
Social Exclusion and Regeneration (DA(SER))	Deputy Prime Minister
Economic Affairs, Productivity and Competitiveness (EAPC)	Chancellor of Exchequer
Employment ((EAPC(E))	Chancellor of Exchequer
Environment (ENV)	Deputy Prime Minister
Green Ministers (ENV(G))	Environment, Food & Rural Affairs Secretary
Local Government (GL)	Transport, Local Government and Regions Minister
Legislative Programme (LP)	Leader of Commons & President of Council
Panel on Regulatory Accountability (PRA)	Minister for Cabinet Office and Chancellor of Duchy of Lancaster
Public Services & Public Expenditure (PSX)	Chancellor of Exchequer
Electronic Service Delivery (PSX(E))	Chief Secretary, Treasury
Local Public Service Agreements (PSX(L))	Transport, Local Government and Regions Minister
Science Policy (SCI)	Trade & Industry Secretary
Biotechnology (SCI(BIO))	Leader of Commons & President of Council
Welfare Reform (WR)	Prime Minister
Children & Young People's Services (MISC9)	Chancellor of Exchequer
	(continues)

Standing committees Dating from a later period, the first of these was the highly successful Committee of Imperial Defence (CID), with its network of subcommittees. Its creation in 1903 marked a watershed in cabinet government. Concerned with particular areas of policy (education, defence, the economy, and so on; see table 14.1), standing committees have continuing existence.

Table 14.1 *(continued)*

Committee	Chair
Millennium Dome (MISC10)	Transport, Local Government and Regions Minister
Wembley Stadium (MISC12)	Foreign Secretary
Animal Rights Activists (MISC13)	Home Secretary
Manchester Commonwealth Games (MISC15)	Culture, Media & Sport Secretary, plus Minister for Cabinet Office and Chancellor of Duchy of Lancaster
Illegal Work & Managed Migration (MISC16)	Home Office Minister
E-Democracy (MISC17)	Leader of Commons & President of Council
Universal Banking Service (MISC19)	Work and Pensions Secretary
Civil Contingencies Secretariat	
Civil Contingencies (CCC)	Home Secretary
Central Secretariat	
Constitutional Reform Policy (CRP)	Lord Chancellor
Incorporation of European Convention on Human Rights (CRP(EC))	Lord Chancellor
Freedom of Information (CRP(FOI))	Lord Chancellor
House of Lords Reform (CRP(HL))	Lord Chancellor
Consultative Committee with Liberal Democratic Party (JCC)	Prime Minister
Overseas and Defence Secretariat	
Defence & Overseas Policy (DOP)	Prime Minister
Northern Ireland (IN)	Prime Minister
Intelligence Services (CSI)	Prime Minister
European Aerospace & Defence Industry (MISC5)	Trade & Industry Secretary
Conflict Prevention in Sub-Saharan Africa (DOP(A))	International Development Secretary
Conflict Prevention outside Sub-Saharan Africa (DOP(OA))	Foreign Secretary
International Terrorism (DOP(IT))	Prime Minister
Protective & Preventive Security (DOP(IT)(T))	Home Secretary
European Secretariat	
European Issues (EP)	Foreign Secretary
World Summit on Sustainable Development (MISC18)	Deputy Prime Minister

Source: Cabinet office website.

Composition and functions The committees characteristically include a core of cabinet ministers, some junior ministers and civil servants attending as the secretariat or in their own right. Sometimes outsiders are included. Tony Blair caused some consternation in July 1997 by announcing a new cabinet committee chaired by himself and including five Liberal Democrat MPs, amongst them leader Paddy Ashdown, to focus on issues of mutual interest, including the constitution. To veteran MP Tony Benn this was 'the beginning of the end' of party government.

Government by committee? Some committees have exceedingly high status, often chaired by the prime minister or another senior minister. The great 1944 Education Act was largely the product of a committee led by R. A. Butler. In 1967 Wilson formally enhanced their status, decreeing that matters should only be reconsidered by the Cabinet with the agreement of the chairs. Mrs Thatcher herself chaired committees on the economy and other key areas and Blair's reforming constitutional committees were chaired by Lord Chancellor Derry Irvine, who enjoyed an exceptionally close rapport with the Prime Minister. Although their role is recognized in *Questions of Procedure for Ministers*, there remains an underlying fear that they reduce the Cabinet to a rubber stamp, leaving no room for ministers to discuss each other's policies or take an overall strategic perspective. In the view of Whitehall-watcher Peter Riddell (1997), under Blair 'the full Cabinet has lost even its residual role as a court of appeal or as a forum for discussing big issues'.

Most of my work when I was Minister of Education was done outside the Cabinet, and hardly referred to the Cabinet at all.

Lord Butler, interviewed by Norman Hunt (later Lord Crowther-Hunt)
in the *Listener* (16 Sept. 1965)

Civil service committees The system of cabinet committees is paralleled by one of official committees that prepares the ground. There is a danger here that decisions may really be made before the politicians actually meet, with ministers being given briefs that foreclose their options.

The Cabinet Office

Over the past twenty years power has seeped from cabinet committees in a process of informalization and centralization around the Number Ten complex. Central to this is the Cabinet Office. The cabinet territory is by no means the exclusive preserve of politicians. Civil servants, and some outsiders, exert a dominant presence through this key department of some 2,000 lying at the epicentre of power. It is organized into sections and units responsible for various aspects of government business, such as the machinery of government, senior public appointments and top management. Its role has increased during the past two decades as various new specialist units have been added, enlarging it by some 300 per cent (Burch and Holliday 1996).

The Cabinet Secretariat

A key part of the Cabinet Office is the **Cabinet Secretariat**. With the exception of its head, the **Cabinet Secretary**, the 200 or so civil servants comprising the secretariat are seconded from other departments and there is much competition for these prestigious positions within the super-elite of the service. Its ostensible functions are similar to those of any other secretariat: circulating information to the Cabinet and its committees, preparing and distributing papers and agendas for meetings, advising on procedure and taking minutes (conclusions). The cabinet secretary conveys decisions to departments and monitors their implementation. These functions give the secretariat great political significance. Its role in establishing compromise solutions that enable ministers to present a unified front, both domestically and to the EU Council of Ministers, affords considerable influence (figure 14.4).

Agenda for the Cabinet meeting of 1 August 1963

1	Future pensions increases	6	Policy towards South Africa
2	Incomes policy	7	Butter imports
	Construction industry	8	Commercial policy
3	Foreign affairs		Barley imports
	United Nations	9	Commercial policy
4	Commonwealth and Colonial Affairs		Jute imports
5	Finance for the United Nations in the	10	Welfare services
	Congo		School meals

Evolution Until the early twentieth century it was traditional for the Cabinet to work informally with no agendas or minutes and no officials present. The only records were notes and personal letters from prime minister to monarch or diary entries (Gladstone's diaries are a particularly rich source of information). Sometimes ministers were unclear about outcomes, their civil servants being obliged to deduce what might have been decided. This seeming madness had some method: meetings were regarded as highly secret and the involvement of non-elected outsiders as unconstitutional. However, the first world war was to undermine such constitutional niceties. When Lloyd George took over he commandeered the much admired secretariat of the CID, including its head, Maurice Hankey, for the War Cabinet. Housed in huts in the garden of 10 Downing Street it became known as the 'garden suburb'. After the war the innovation was reappraised; opponents associated it with Lloyd George's overbearing style and the Treasury saw it as a rival in Whitehall. However, the 1918 Haldane Report on the machinery of government recommended its retention.

As the main architect of the secretariat Hankey deserves an honoured place in the bureaucratic hall of fame. Remaining to serve five very different prime ministers (Lloyd George, Bonar Law, Baldwin, Ramsay MacDonald and

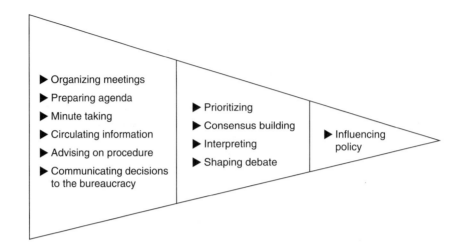

Figure 14.4
Administrative
functions have
political
implications.

Chamberlain) in a variety of circumstances (war, reconstruction, coalition and both Labour and Conservative administrations), he demonstrated the value of the new machinery. Today the cabinet secretary is frequently described as the most powerful civil servant in the country. Since 1983 he has been formally designated Head of the Home Civil Service. In addition to Herculean formal responsibilities, cabinet secretaries can find themselves in politically sensitive trouble-shooting roles, as was Sir Robert Armstrong over the 'Spycatcher' and Westland affairs and Sir Robin Butler over the Scott enquiry and alleged breaches of the rules on MPs' outside interests.

Critics accused Sir Richard Wilson, reportedly personally selected as Sir Robin's successor by Tony Blair, of undermining civil service impartiality (Heathcoat Amory, 2001). He found his name in the tabloids after a controversial lunch in July 1998 with MP Keith Vaz and the Hinduja brothers, whose business dealings gave cause for concern. In another case, minister Geoffrey Robinson accused Sir Richard of acting politically in attempting to push him from office following adverse publicity regarding his business activities, and he was also involved in the very political inquiry that led to Peter Mandelson's resignation. Indeed, he was said to have done much to centralize power within the Cabinet Office, helping to make it a prime minister's department (see p. 445).

> Now that the Cabinet's gone to its dinner,
> The Secretary stays and gets thinner and thinner,
> Racking his brains to record and report,
> What he thinks what they think they ought to have thought.
>
> Anon., quoted in S. S. Wilson, *The Cabinet Office to 1945* (1975)

139

Printed for the War Cabinet, November 1942.

SECRET.   Copy No. 48

W.M. (42)

159th Conclusions.

TO BE KEPT UNDER LOCK AND KEY

It is requested that special care may be taken to
ensure the secrecy of this document

WAR CABINET 159 (42).

*CONCLUSIONS of a Meeting of the War Cabinet held in the Prime Minister's
Room, House of Commons, S.W. 1, on Thursday, November 26, 1942, at
12·30 P.M.*

Present :

The Right Hon. WINSTON S. CHURCHILL, M.P., Prime Minister (*in the Chair*).

The Right Hon. C. R. ATTLEE, M.P.,   The Right Hon. ANTHONY EDEN, M.P.,
Secretary of State for Dominion   Secretary of State for Foreign
Affairs.   Affairs.

The Right Hon. Sir JOHN ANDERSON,   The Right Hon. ERNEST BEVIN, M.P.,
M.P., Lord President of the Council.   Minister of Labour and National
                                       Service.

The Right Hon. HERBERT MORRISON,
M.P., Secretary of State for the Home
Department and Minister of Home
Security.

The following were also present :

The Right Hon. Sir KINGSLEY WOOD, | The Right Hon. VISCOUNT CRANBORNE,
M.P., Chancellor of the Exchequer. | Lord Privy Seal.

The Right Hon. Sir ARCHIBALD | The Right Hon. Sir STAFFORD CRIPPS,
SINCLAIR, Bt., M.P., Secretary of | K.C., M.P., Minister of Aircraft
State for Air. | Production.

The Right Hon. ERNEST BROWN, M.P., | The Right Hon. BRENDAN BRACKEN,
Minister of Health. | M.P., Minister of Information.

The Right Hon. Sir WILLIAM JOWITT, | The Right Hon. JAMES STUART, M.P.,
K.C., M.P., Paymaster-General. | Joint   Parliamentary   Secretary,
                                   | Treasury.

Mr. W. WHITELEY, M.P., Joint Parliamentary Secretary, Treasury.

Secretariat.

Sir EDWARD BRIDGES.
Mr. NORMAN BROOK.

CONTENTS.

[24681—1]

176

Social Services.   THE War Cabinet had before them a Summary of the Report
The Beveridge   by Sir William Beveridge on Social Insurance and Allied Services
Report.   (W.P. (42) 547), and considered the date of publication of the Report
Question of   and what statement the Government should make as to their attitude
Publication.   in regard to it.

(Previous   The War Cabinet's conclusions were as follows :—
Reference:
W.M. (42) 153rd   (1) The Report should be made available to Members of
Conclusions,   Parliament at 3 P.M. on Tuesday, the 1st December,
Minute 5.)   and released to the Press for publication in the morning
                          newspapers of Wednesday, the 2nd December. (Arrange-
                          ments should be made by the Minister of Information to
                          allow Editors to have copies, in confidence, in advance
                          of publication, so as to enable them to study the Report.)

                     (2) No objection should be raised to Sir William Beveridge
                          broadcasting on the Report after publication.

                     (3) The Paymaster-General, in the Debate on reconstruction
                          matters, should make a statement on the following
                          lines :—

                          The questions dealt with in the Report were
                          of great interest, and the Report itself was a
                          notable contribution to their study. Time, however,
                          would be required for detailed examination of the
                          recommendations by all those concerned, including
                          the Government and their advisers.

                          An undertaking should be given that the
                          Government would be prepared to make some general
                          statement on the position after Parliament had
                          reassembled in the New Year.

                          A reminder should be added that, not only must
                          the practicability of the recommendations contained
                          in the Report be examined, but also that the Report
                          must be considered in relation to the main measures
                          which would have to be taken over the field of
                          reconstruction as a whole, not forgetting what was
                          necessary to maintain international security.

                     (4) The Chancellor of the Exchequer and the Paymaster-
                          General were asked to prepare a statement on these lines
                          and to submit it to the Prime Minister.

Offices of the War Cabinet, S.W. 1,
November 26, 1942.

Minutes ('Conclusions') of the Cabinet meeting
of 26 November 1942, which discussed the
Beveridge Report (PRO document reference
CAB 65/28)

The minutes: how they run Initially Hankey kept near-verbatim accounts,
attributing opinions and attitudes to individuals. Criticized as unconstitutional,
this was modified to include only a general view of the debate, making
it possible to use the 'conclusions' as the directions for civil service action.
This practice places the secretariat in a pivotal position, with disturbing possibilities. In a break during a meeting, Richard Crossman examined the notes of
Cabinet Secretary Sir Burke Trend and was shocked to see that the report of the
Prime Minister's position was 'not the substance of what he had said, and if it
had been the substance he would have divided the Cabinet' (Crossman 1975:
103–4). Michael Heseltine complained that the Prime Minister prevented
discussion on certain matters and 'insisted that the Cabinet Secretary should
record my protest in the Cabinet minutes', yet when circulated 'no record of my
protest' was to be found (Heseltine 1986: 2). Under Blair the quality of the

minutes changed, with much important business transacted elsewhere and a more informal flow of discussion. The secretariat were left to write things up as best they could so that some non-cabinet ministers (and no doubt future historians) found them among 'the least important part of their weekly reading' (Hennessy 1998: 11).

From substance to shadow

Even less known to the constitution than the Cabinet is its shadow on the opposing front bench at Westminster. Often ignored in studies of government, the **Shadow Cabinet** constitutes a ready-made governmental cast waiting in the wings; its members are shadow ministers with shadow portfolios and the leader is the shadow prime minister. It is a particular feature of a two-party system, where a foetal government will lie curled in the womb before the general election.

Evolution In the eighteenth century parliamentary factions would organize into groups to oppose those in office (Turner 1969). If a government seemed likely to fall, lists of possible ministerial teams would begin to circulate. The relatively frequent fall of governments meant that there were always ex-ministers in Parliament able to provide well-informed criticism; thus the 'ex-Cabinet' is the natural forebear of the Shadow Cabinet. Once a general election meant the removal of a government *en bloc*, it followed that a new one must be ready to emerge overnight (Punnett 1975: 144).

The Shadow Cabinet today Although the difference between shadow and substance is that the former has no executive responsibility, in many respects they function in a similar manner: holding meetings, appointing specialist committees and practising collective responsibility and secrecy (and suffering leaks). In September 1992 Bryan Gould resigned to voice his support for a referendum on the Maastricht Treaty, complaining that the Shadow Cabinet was a 'gag and a straightjacket', and in 1998 Hague was to sacrifice two senior Shadow Cabinet members over his anti-single-currency position.

Shadow Cabinets are valuable to democracy. Americans see little of any alternative president until the campaign period and do not see the Cabinet until well after. In Britain, Her Majesty's Opposition is an alternative government displayed on the shelves of the Westminster supermarket. The role is officially recognized with salaries for the opposition Leader and chief whip. Yet its value is reduced by lack of information; ex-mandarin Sir Douglas Wass (1984) argued that it should be power-assisted with a special department.

The Central Policy Review Staff 1970–1983: RIP

No student of cabinet government can ignore Edward Heath's 1970 experiment. The Central Policy Review Staff (CPRS) was baptized with this dry title by Cabinet Secretary Burke Trend who, belying his own name, found the US term '**Think-Tank**', preferred by Heath, rather too racy for bureaucratic sensibilities. However, the media preferred Heath's choice. Heath briefed the infant CPRS on the lawn of 10 Downing Street, recalling how he had seen 'Cabinets which all the time seemed to be dealing with the day-to-day problems' with 'never a real opportunity to deal with strategy' (Heath 1972: 5). With its multidisciplinary composition drawing representatives from academia, industry and the civil service, it was to be a small unit in the Cabinet Office, its role to:

◆ provide ministers with wide-ranging information to prevent departmental 'tunnel vision';
◆ offer advice on policy alternatives;
◆ promote interdepartmental cooperation;
◆ help determine relative priorities;
◆ provide continuing performance review in the light of overall strategy.

The career of the CPRS However, after the honeymoon years, the CPRS experienced an erratic rake's progress, its function varying according to the government in office. Its leaked report on the future of the NHS under private insurance forced Thatcher to her impassioned 1982 conference declaration that the service was 'safe with us'. She did not promise the same to the think-tank, and after her re-election the axe fell (Fry 1986: 98). Its demise was little mourned; resented by bureaucrats, it was often ignored by ministers. Yet with ministers burdened by departmental duties and little time for strategic thought, Wass (1984) regarded something like this as essential to genuine cabinet government.

Son of CPRS The CPRS saw something of a rebirth when, towards the end of its first term, the Blair government created a Strategy Futures Group within the Cabinet Office. Headed by Geoff Mulgan, political adviser and co-founder of the think-tank *Demos*, its remit was to look ten years ahead and coordinate policy across departments. Its members would each head satellite strategy units in the departments. Comprising young civil servants, management consultants and academics on short-term contracts, they were to 'think the unthinkable' and produce radical policy agendas. Whether they would fare any better than their predecessor in the Whitehall village remained to be seen.

Cabinet government: dead or sleeping?

Clearly the idea that Britain is governed by a tightly knit team is grossly simplistic; it is hard to discern where any particular decision is actually taken. The modern Cabinet is but one body in a labyrinthine network at the core of the state. It can be argued that it is little more than a fiction, a device whereby senior ministers share responsibility for tricky decisions. Cabinet meetings are mere formalities during which senior ministers may even sit working through a pile of their own papers (*Guardian*, 29 Sept. 2001). It is now time to replace the wide-angle lens with a microscope and peer more deeply into the heart of state power. In particular, we must address a crucial debate of the modern era: the position of the prime minister.

When I was a minister I always looked forward to the Cabinet meeting because it was, apart from the summer holidays, the only period of real rest which I got.

Nigel Lawson, quoted by Michael White in *the Guardian* (29 Sept. 2001)

The Prime Minister: Elective Dictatorship?

Who is the prime minister?

The prime minister is not elected as such but is asked by the monarch to form a government on the basis of being able to command a majority in the Commons. Normally this means the leader of the majority party, yet this has been less common than is usually realized. Although Britain had only three fully fledged coalition governments in the twentieth century, all in times of national emergency, governments with a single-party majority held office for a total of only fifty-six years. Under a coalition or party pact the prime minister is most likely to be the leader of the largest party, although the minority partners might influence the choice. Thus Labour refused to serve under Chamberlain in 1940 and in 1987 David Steel of the Alliance declared that serving in a Thatcher-led coalition would be 'inconceivable'.

The circumstances of political life mean that prime ministers will usually be of mature years, with substantial political experience (table 14.2). In 1964, however, Labour's thirteen years in the wilderness meant that Wilson had only been Secretary for Overseas Trade and President of the Board of Trade and Mrs Thatcher's experience amounted to but four years as Secretary of State for Education and Science. In 1997 Tony Blair came to the office, like MacDonald in 1929, with no ministerial experience whatsoever. Lack of experience can be compensated for by youthful vigour: Mrs Thatcher took the reins at the relatively young age of fifty-four but, at forty-three, Blair was a veritable infant prodigy. On the other hand, when Callaghan moved from 11 to 10 Downing Street in 1976, he had at sixty-four reached the age where most people stop working and turn their attention to growing vegetables.

Table 14.2 Age and experience of prime ministers since 1895

Name (and party)	Date of first coming to office	Age	Years in Commons before becoming PM
Salisbury (Conservative)	1895	55	15 (+ 19 in Lords)
Balfour (Conservative)	1902	53	28
Campbell-Bannerman (Liberal)	1905	69	37
Asquith (Liberal)	1908	55	22
Lloyd George (coalition)	1916	53	26
Bonar Law (Conservative)	1922	63	22
Baldwin (Conservative)	1923	56	15
MacDonald (Labour)	1924	58	14
Chamberlain (Conservative)	1937	68	19
Churchill (coalition)	1940	65	38
Attlee (Labour)	1945	62	23
Eden (Conservative)	1955	57	32
Macmillan (Conservative)	1957	62	29
Home (Conservative)	1963	60	15 (+ 13 in Lords)
Wilson (Labour)	1964	48	19
Heath (Conservative)	1970	53	20
Callaghan (Labour)	1976	64	31
Thatcher (Conservative)	1979	54	20
Major (Conservative)	1990	47	11
Blair (Labour)	1997	43	14

Evolution of the office It was the Hanoverians, through lack of kingly interest in things British, who allowed Sir Robert Walpole (1676–1745), the First Lord of the Treasury, to fill the power vacuum. He is usually cited as the first prime minister, though the term was used abusively, to deplore his dominance over his colleagues. After his fall in 1742, his immediate successors were denied the same authority. However, by the time of William Pitt the Younger, the position had become firmly established by constitutional convention.

Yet to accept a cabinet leader was not to confer supremacy. The purpose of the historic constitutional struggles had been to curb monarchy, not replace one with another. Early prime ministers were regarded as only *primus inter pares* (first among equals). Indeed, when highlighting the significance of the nine-teenth-century Cabinet, Bagehot placed little stress on the role of the prime minister. Subsequent developments saw a shift in the balance of power, so that in 1963 Richard Crossman argued in the introduction to a reprint of Bagehot's great work that

> ...the post-war epoch has seen the final transformation of Cabinet Government into Prime Ministerial Government. (Crossman 1963: 51)

The prime minister as president

This question is central to an understanding of modern British government. Real-world **presidential government** takes various forms; some presidents share power with a prime minister, as in France, while others, as in Germany, are mainly symbolic, rather like the British monarch. However, exponents of the 'presidential prime-ministerial' thesis think in terms of a powerful model such as that of the USA, where incumbents stand in a particular relationship with the other political structures.

◆ *The state*. The president is head of state, holding some key powers.
◆ *The people*. Presidents are in effect directly elected in a country-wide constituency, enjoying a popular legitimacy greater than that of any other person or institution. Moreover, they remain in direct contact, regularly addressing the nation on television over the heads of other institutions.
◆ *The Cabinet*. Members are not elected but appointed by the president on the basis of personal choice.
◆ *The bureaucracy*. The upper echelons of the bureaucracy are appointed by the president on the basis of political sympathy.
◆ *A personal department*. Presidents are served by a formidable White House staff, providing powerful intellectual and political support.
◆ *The legislature*. Presidents are not members of Congress and their position is independent of its support.

Yet despite their personal ascendancy, presidents face certain *restrictions*. The separation of powers allows the judiciary to examine the constitutionality of executive actions and Congress can block presidential legislation and veto certain appointments. They also rely on their cabinets; in the post-11-September crisis, George W. Bush was calling regular meetings, and relying on his defence secretary to travel to the Middle East and Asia to negotiate and build alliances.

The constitutional position of British prime ministers appears to bear little relationship to that of US presidents: they are not heads of state and not directly elected; their cabinet choice is restricted to members of their party in Parliament; they are not independent of the legislature; they depend upon their position as party leaders to hold office; their bureaucracy is permanent rather than politically appointed; and there is no 'Department of the Prime Minister' like the White House staff. However, our examination cannot end with the formal constitutional position; on the contrary, this is where it begins.

Head of state

Although this position is formally held by the monarch, in many respects the prime minister functions as a head of state. The important prerogative powers of the Crown are only exercised on prime ministerial advice. Moreover, meetings with other heads of state allow some of the gloss to rub off, Thatcher characterizing her encounters with President Reagan as meetings of 'two heads of state'. Regular European Council summits enhance this impression. Early in his premiership Blair came to the presidency of the European Council and journalists began to speak of 'President Blair' with some irony. A hagiography on *Blair's 100 Days* by a Labour staffer even employed the term as a chapter title (Draper 1997). At the death of Princess Diana it was Tony Blair, rather than the Queen, who expressed the nation's sorrow.

The populist connection

Although prime ministers are elected only as ordinary MPs, political practice provides an increasingly **populist** link with the nation (figure 14.5).

General elections It can be argued that modern general elections are effectively contests between party leaders. Before the 1987 election Mrs Thatcher proclaimed '*I can handle a big majority*' and in the 1997 campaign, Blair challenged Major to a US-style face-to-face televised debate (only backing down when the latter accepted). The result is that prime ministers can claim a personal mandate.

The media Throughout the world, the media have transformed politics, making demagogy more feasible; at the touch of a button presidents can address nations. Prime ministers' press offices have become increasingly dominant in politics, feeding journalists with a 'carefully filtered version' after cabinet meetings (Hennessy 1986: 5). As the term 'spin doctor' gains currency, government becomes the art of communication and prime ministers' press secretaries have risen to become their closest confidants (see p. 445).

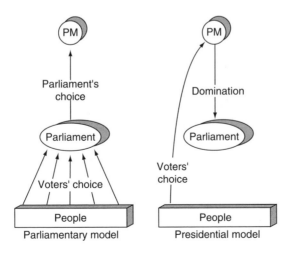

Figure 14.5
Choosing the prime minister.

On 15 June 2000, Blair began a new style of regular televised press briefings from Number Ten, very much in the manner of presidential briefings from the White House.

Opinion polls The increasing application of market research techniques tends towards personalization, dwelling on the ratings of party leaders. Despite his upper-middle-class background, Blair played the common touch. In managing the aftermath of Princess Diana's death in 1997 he finely judged the popular mood. After five years in office his popularity rating had hardly fallen (and had been a key factor in the 2001 victory).

Image-politics Further presidentialization comes from the politics of image, ex-film actor President Reagan representing the apotheosis of this trend. Wilson modelled himself on the youthful President Kennedy but Mrs Thatcher carried image-making well beyond anything practised by her predecessors: following the advice of publicity experts she altered her hairstyle, expression, clothes and even the pitch of her voice. The failure of both Kinnock and Hague has been attributed at least in part to image, while Blair's charisma may have led Gordon Brown to stand aside in the 1994 Labour leadership contest (see p. 297). Blair, known to have been an amateur thespian in his youth, appeared to mirror much of the style of Clinton. The Labour government began to promote a 'Cool Britannia' image with parties at Number Ten for showbiz personalities.

> Quite suddenly, he who had been looked upon as something of a bore became both a formidable debater and a funny speaker…He once told me that he set out deliberately to make himself amusing, writing out his jokes in longhand, late at night.
>
> Alan Watkins on Harold Wilson, in the *Observer* (19 Oct. 1986)

Weak and hopeless.

Norman Lamont on John Major, quoted in *The Times* (29 Jan. 1994). He claimed to have been misquoted but was absent from Major's honours list in July 1997.

Political culture Finally, it can be argued that the British actually prefer strong figures at the helm. 'Churchillian' is a term of approbation and, while Thatcher and Blair were applauded, Major's willingness to consult was often seen as weakness. British history is replete with examples of great individuals – from kings and generals to explorers and social reformers; there are no 'great' committees or working parties to stir the imagination. Even the Knights of the Round Table and the Merry Men of Sherwood Forest had leaders who were by no means *primus inter pares*. At the time of the 1997 general election, 79 per cent thought Blair to be a 'strong leader' (Denver 1998: 212).

The cabinet connection

This relationship lies at the heart of the debate and contains various facets.

Creating the Cabinet Unlike the president, the prime minister cannot make wide-ranging choices from social, commercial, industrial and academic life, ensuring a team of trusted allies. However, the restrictions are not inhibiting. The appointment of the Cabinet from amongst parliamentary colleagues is a powerful source of patronage, giving an iron grip over all those wishing to attain, or keep, high office. Moreover, the life peerage system allows non-MPs to be brought in (see p. 366). Thus Blair made Derry Irvine, his ex-head of chambers, Lord Chancellor. With the right to hire comes the even more devastating power to fire. Her Majesty's ministers hold office at her first minister's pleasure and those incurring displeasure can have their careers abruptly terminated; by the late 1980s the benches behind Thatcher rattled with the bones of ex-ministers. Blair's reshuffles were believed to be designed to curb the advance of his ambitious Chancellor, Gordon Brown, by removing some of his allies.

Cabinet meetings The conduct of meetings remains securely under the prime ministerial thumb, with control of the agenda giving the power to decide what is discussed. Wilson was able to prevent debate on devaluation and Mrs Thatcher avoided economic strategy and the decision to purchase the Trident missile system. Blair prevented full-scale debate on the euro, economic policy and missile defence. Indeed, he was reported as dispensing with formal agendas 'in the sense of an item by item discussion', preferring to choose the order in which topics were discussed during the meeting (Hennessy 1998: 11).

Furthermore, as chairperson the prime minister decides who shall speak, when and at what length; dissident voices can be limited or studiously ignored. Even seating can be manipulated: Heath placed the *ingénue* Margaret Thatcher at an inconvenient position, from which she found it difficult to interject, and Lord Home (1976: 192) tells how Macmillan avoided having the 'steely and accusing eye' of Enoch Powell facing him across the table. The prime minister can also decide the frequency and length of meetings; under Blair they were reported to be cursory affairs, taking place once a week on Thursdays, often for little more than forty minutes. Finally, prime ministers can define precisely what was decided through their prerogative to sum up and shape (or doctor) the content of the all-important cabinet minutes (known as 'conclusions').

> This is not a collective government. We have to accept that the old model of Cabinet government is as dead as a doornail.
>
> Whitehall insider to Peter Hennessy (1998: 12)

Cabinet committees Cabinet committees might seem to offer ministers key positions of influence. However, it is the prime minister who manages the network – appointing members, designating chairs and chairing those critical to major initiatives. In 1979 Thatcher took control of the 'E' committee on the economy, packing it with sympathizers. The committee handling the poll tax under her chairmanship kept opponents in the dark as it 'acquired a jargon-laden life of its own' (Howe 1994: 602–3). The main Thatcher strategy was to reduce the role of the *standing committees* and work more through *ad hoc* groupings which she could dominate. The gestation of the Next Steps programme, NHS reform and the poll tax all took place beyond the Cabinet and its formal committees. Ministers lose any right to attend informal meetings and, when no minutes are taken, outsiders cannot be privy to discussions. This style was reproduced under Blair. He also ensured that Minister without Portfolio Peter Mandelson, although not initially a cabinet member, was on most of the important groups.

Collective responsibility When ministers feel they are inadequately consulted they have constitutional grounds for complaint. Yet today the doctrine decrees little more than that all support the prime minister or resign. Blair's first Cabinet was tightly bound and Harriet Harman and Frank Dobson were rapped over the knuckles by Alastair Campbell, his press secretary, for stepping out of line.

> If the basis of trust between Prime Minister and her Defence Secretary no longer exists, there is no place for me with honour in such a Cabinet.
>
> Michael Heseltine, after his resignation over the Westland affair, quoted in *The Times* (10 Jan. 1986)

The inner cabinet Here is one of the most significant sources of the modern prime minister's power. Government has become both more centralized and more informal and inner cabinets more dominant. Thus can prime ministers encircle themselves with cronies. The 'wets' in the first Thatcher Cabinet were soon countered by a loyal band of her supporters. John Major liked to consult with close colleagues unilaterally to gain their support before cabinet meetings. The inner circle may even include people not in the Cabinet itself. In his second term, Blair's closest confidants included Jonathan Powell (chief of staff), Alastair Campbell (director of communications), Lord Guthrie (former chief of the defence staff) and Sir David Manning (a career diplomat emerging as a White-House-style national security adviser). In addition there was his personal assistant Anji Hunter and, despite official banishment from the circle of power after his resignation (see p. 302), Peter Mandelson was never far away. There were reports that Chancellor Gordon Brown, Foreign Secretary Jack Straw and Defence Secretary Geoff Hoon found themselves sidelined from much discussion (Perkins 2001).

Unilateral action Prime ministers can sometimes take momentous decisions virtually alone. Attlee's decision to develop a nuclear capability did not come before the Cabinet. Similarly, in 2002, amidst tension within the country and his own party, Tony Blair made the decision to support the bellicose stance of US President George W. Bush towards Iraq.

Policy initiative Prime ministers have no specific portfolios and can range freely over policy, choosing to act in successful or 'sexy' areas. Thatcher was closely associated with the economy and later with Europe, although Major searched in vain for a 'big idea'. Blair's enthusiasm to seize the wheel from his cabinet colleagues ranged from the foot-and-mouth crisis to the NHS. However, it is in foreign affairs that premiers can find the greatest scope to act presidentially; Thatcher will forever be associated with the Falklands war. Blair intervened over Kosovo, Sierra Leone and missile defence. Northern Ireland was another area where he upstaged his minister: despite her earlier work, Mo Mowlam became a bystander as Blair and Jonathan Powell effectively took over the sensitive negotiations. Blair's most dramatic opportunity came with the attack on the World Trade Center on 11 September 2001 and the 'war on terrorism'. The once august Foreign Office appeared in decline as he effectively installed an alternative foreign policy directorate in Number Ten (Oborne 2001). The one area Blair kept out of was the fiefdom of his rival for power, iron Chancellor Gordon Brown.

The official connection

When US presidents take office they sweep like new brooms through every nook and cranny of the White House. While their wives have traditionally changed furniture and wallpaper, they have changed the people, some three or four thousand of them. This is the **spoils system**, giving awesome power to reward, bribe and command. In contrast, incoming prime ministers are faced with a marble face of public bureaucracy, constitutionally as permanent as the Sphinx. Or are they? The idea that the public service is beyond the reach of political manoeuvring is but one more myth of British public life.

'One of us' Though less dramatic and sudden than the presidential shake-out, prime ministers are able to control key positions and distribute considerable prestige and power. These powers were originally inherited from the monarch and since Walpole's day have been used to enhance prime ministerial standing (figure 14.6). Positions within the prime minister's gift include:

- ◆ honours (peerages and knighthoods);
- ◆ state offices (armed forces, church and judiciary);
- ◆ government posts (from senior ministers to parliamentary private secretaries);
- ◆ ministerial advisory posts;
- ◆ top jobs beyond Whitehall (in water authorities, the NHS, nationalized industries, tribunals, royal commissions and committees of enquiry, the BBC, a diversity of quangos, and so on);
- ◆ party offices;
- ◆ Whitehall (although seen as conventionally immune from the web of patronage, from the 1980s even this came under threat (see p. 485).

Moreover, with no parliamentary or judicial vetoes, the prime minister is not accountable for these appointments in the way that a president is. Early beneficiaries of the Blair regime were quickly dubbed 'Tony's cronies'.

Figure 14.6
In an age of patronage to make Walpole blush, the tentacles of prime ministerial patronage reach deeply into the state machinery.

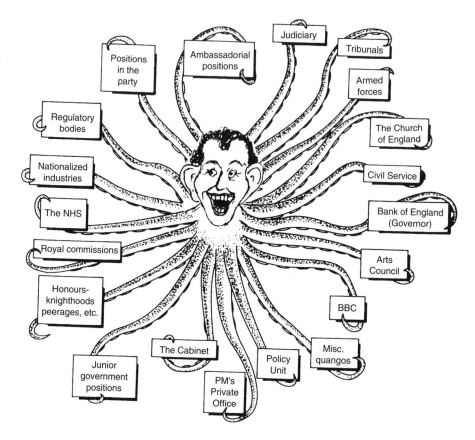

Positions in the party
Ambassadorial positions
Judiciary
Tribunals
Armed forces
The Church of England
Civil Service
Bank of England (Governor)
Arts Council
BBC
Misc. quangos
Policy Unit
PM's Private Office
The Cabinet
Junior government positions
Honours- knighthoods peerages, etc.
Royal commissions
The NHS
Nationalized industries
Regulatory bodies

Shaping the machine In addition to making appointments, the prime minister shapes the very architecture of government, thereby determining what it is capable, or not capable, of doing. The administrative skyline can be transformed overnight. Wilson created a Department of Economic Affairs (DEA) and the Civil Service Department (CSD) to usurp Treasury power, while the CPRS was Heath's brainchild. The CSD and CPRS both perished under Thatcher. Civil service agencification proceeded apace under Major. Michael Heseltine and John Prescott were both given new administrative empires to symbolize their enhanced status as deputy prime ministers.

In 1997 Tony Blair quickly began to take a firm grip on the government machine, much as he had done with his party. The number of ministerial advisers increased, cabinet committees were reduced in number and inter-departmental taskforces, headed by ministers and staffed by civil servants and outsiders, were to be created on an ad hoc basis to handle major policy initiatives such as the welfare-to-work package and constitutional reform (Timmins and Kampfner 1997).

A prime-ministerial department?

Unlike the US president, prime ministers do not have their own departments. They appear to stand alone against cabinet colleagues powered by high-octane information and advice from their bureaucratic forces. Yet this is a misleading picture; today's prime ministers are buoyed up by various agencies.

Personal offices Prime ministers have personal offices containing staffs of around 100, comprising the following:

◆ *Private Office*. Housekeeping functions, managing day-to-day affairs.
◆ *Political Office*. Responsibility for party and constituency matters.

Press Office Recent decades have brought into prominence a new and dominant political presence, the prime minister's press secretary. Described as 'communications', the function was more frequently labelled 'news management'. Thatcher's Bernard Ingham became better known than many politicians and his belligerent style was replicated by Blair's Alastair Campbell, who was soon being accused of news management on an even greater scale (sometimes by Ingham). Both were reported to have briefed against their respective prime ministers' colleagues (for example, Geoffrey Howe was described as a 'semi-detached member' and Gordon Brown as 'psychologically flawed'). In July 1997 Blair revised *Questions of Procedure for Ministers*, already a severe straitjacket, to insist that all ministerial speeches, press releases, interviews and media appearances be cleared with his press office.

> They have got to know I'm running the show.
>
> Tony Blair defending the right of his press secretary to call ministers to account, quoted in the *Sunday Times* (26 April 1998)

Number Ten Policy Units. Wilson introduced a policy unit in 1974 to assist in policy-making. Thatcher needed such a unit more than her predecessors and the succession of eminent figures she brought to head it became well known. It was the Policy Unit that produced Major's 'big idea' – the Citizen's Charter. However, under Blair this arm of government was made even stronger. In opposition, key strategists had laid plans for a government with a steel centre and this included an enhanced Number Ten policy force (Mandelson and Liddle 1996). There was press speculation that the Policy Unit was assuming supreme importance in Whitehall, vetting all green and white papers and watering down proposals that might prove unpopular.

   In December 1999, an answer to a House of Lords question revealed that the staff in Number Ten had grown by 50 per cent (Sherman 2002a). An 'Organogram' produced by Downing Street showed a triumvirate of Alastair Campbell, Jonathan Powell and Baroness Morgan (who replaced Blair's trusted Anji Hunter when lured away by BP) presiding over the political and civil staff of Downing Street. It was admitted that twenty-seven special advisers and 175 other staff were on the Downing Street payroll. There was also a new Number Ten Policy Directorate and a Forward Strategy Unit (with the curiously meteorological remit of 'blue skies thinking'). The changing culture was symbolized by the Chief Whip, traditionally housed in No. 12 Downing Street, being moved out to make way for the profusion of units sprouting from Number Ten. Senior civil servants were obliged to see their advice overturned by 'policy wonks' only a few years out of Oxbridge.

The Cabinet Office The Cabinet Office is increasingly seen as a bureaucratic shell within which a further battery of new units can be housed. The result has been a blurring of the lines of accountability and responsibility between the Cabinet Office and Number Ten. The units have played an increasingly import-ant role in policy, undermining both the Cabinet and its committees. Thatcher's Efficiency Unit, under businessman Sir Derek Rayner, was of enormous signifi-cance. From this acorn grew such initiatives as the Ibbs Next Steps programme (see chapter 15).

Under New Labour, policy units in the Cabinet Office proliferated, with one for most new initiatives, and a minister for the Cabinet Office was created (popularly known as the 'Cabinet Enforcer'). The Orwellian-sounding Social Exclusion Unit included representatives from five Whitehall departments as well as from business, local government and the police. After the 2001 election, a bewildering game of musical chairs saw units begetting units and more advisers than ever before. The Performance and Innovation Unit, Blair's per-sonal think-tank, moved from Number Ten to the Cabinet Office, having first spawned the Forward Strategy Unit to replace it. The Delivery Unit and the Office of Public Services Reform had heads located along the corridor in Downing Street. Political journalist Peter Riddell (2001) noted a striking simi-larity to the arrangements in the White House.

The Office of Public Services Reform Originally the Civil Service Department and responsible for civil service management, this was moved from the Treas-ury into the Cabinet Office in July 1998, giving the prime minister additional influence as the minister for the civil service. In this role he was assisted by the cabinet secretary, who is also Head of the Civil Service. From this position managerial reforms, often challenging the traditional civil service ethos, can be pushed through.

The Cabinet Secretary Unlike his colleagues, the prime minister does not have the services of a permanent secretary. However, the cabinet secretary (see pp. 431–2) can become very close to being one (Walker 1972: 54). From the beginning Lloyd George relied heavily on Maurice Hankey. Sir Burke Trend, who served from 1963 to 1973, denied that he was 'the Prime Minister's exclusive servant' (Hennessy 1985) but worked closely with Wilson, accom-panying him, for example, to Washington as an equal and opposite force to Nixon's Henry Kissinger (Wilson 1974: 947).

Thatcher established an exceptional rapport with Sir Robert Armstrong – her 'oracle' (Hennessy 1986). Indeed, critics questioned whether his loyalty exceeded that of a neutral public servant, the select committee on the Westland affair worrying that so close a confidant should simultaneously be the head of the civil service. Under Blair, Sir Richard Wilson, who produced the hasty report that led to Peter Mandelson's second resignation, was adjudged by a leading journalist to have become 'immersed in New Labour's presentationally driven culture' (Rawnsley 2001). Blair envisaged the secretariat as a 'Whitehall whip', driving the state machine as never before (Grice 1997). Wilson's successor, Sir Andrew Turnbull, showed himself well attuned to New Labour's approach to management (see p. 490).

External think-tanks and advisers Prime ministers can also look outside for advice and support. Thatcher maintained contact with a number of right-wing intellectual groups, including the Centre for Policy Studies, the Institute of Economic Affairs and the Adam Smith Institute. The weight she gave to the views of economic guru Sir Alan Walters led to Chancellor Nigel Lawson's resignation. Blair turned to bodies such as the Fabian Society, the Policy Studies Institute and Demos, often placing New Labour wrapping around Thatcherite policies (Pilger 1998: 83).

> I resigned on a matter of fundamental principle, because it seemed to me that the Prime Minister [Wilson] was not only introducing a 'presidential' system into the running of the government...far too often outsiders in his entourage seemed to be almost the only effective 'Cabinet'.
>
> Lord George Brown, *In My Way* (1972)

What's in a name? If the British prime minister were to have a department it would, perhaps more than any other development, 'symbolise the shift from cabinet to prime ministerial government' (Jones 1983: 84). However, the ability of prime ministers to establish think-tanks and policy units at the drop of a hat or handbag leaves them with all the support they need. Blair was able to ensure that members of his Policy Unit and Efficiency Unit sat 'on all the comprehensive expenditure review teams' (Hennessy 1998: 15). This may explain why, despite repeated speculation as new leaders take office, the temptation to establish a formal department is resisted. The existing arrangements (figure 14.7) offer a *de facto* department, while formalization would invite accusations of presidential self-aggrandizement.

However, the merging of the Office of Public Services Reform into the Cabinet Office, with the prime minister adding the title of Minister for the Civil Service to that of First Lord of the Treasury, may have moved this a step nearer (Kellner 1998). Tony Wright, chairman of the Commons Public Administration Select Committee, declared: 'there is a prime minister's department in all but name, with a growing capacity to drive policy from the centre'.

POLITICAL OFFICE

Chief of Staff

Political appointees

Managers and advisers

Helpers with PM's constituency affairs

Links with backbenchers

PARTY POSITIONS

Government Chief Whip (Commons)

Captain of the Gentlemen at Arms (Chief Whip Lords)

Whips teams

Leader of the House

PRESS OFFICE

Press Secretary

Director of Communications

Civil servants

Political appointees

'Spin doctors'

News managers

POLICY UNIT

Head of Policy Unit

Political appointees

'Policy wonks'

'Blue skies' thinkers & 'thinkers of the unthinkable'

PRIVATE OFFICE

Personal Principal Private Secretary

Civil servants; 'high fliers' on secondment.

Organizers of the PM's diary, links with Whitehall, engagements, etc.

CABINET OFFICE		
OFFICE OF PUBLIC SERVICES REFORM	**CABINET SECRETARIAT**	**CROSS-CUTTING ISSUES UNITS**
Minister for Public Services Reform	*Cabinet Secretary & Head of Home Civil Service*	*Directors of cross-cutting units ('Tsars')*
Permanent Sec.	High-powered civil servants in various secretariats, e.g.	Social Exclusion
Specialist groups, e.g.	Economic & Domestic	Women & Equality
Better Government Team	Defence & Overseas	Performance & Innovation
Efficiency & Effectiveness Group	European Affairs	Anti-drugs
Efficiency Unit	Constitution	etc.
Next Steps Team		

Figure 14.7   A Prime Minister's department?

> [Tony Blair] has torn up the constitution and become far more presidential than any other Western leader. We don't even have the checks and balances they have in the US.
>
> A 'senior liberal Democrat', quoted in MacAskill and White (2001)

The Westminster connection

Finally there is a relationship in which the prime minister is constitutionally stronger than the president. We saw in chapter 13 how, with a fusion rather than a separation of powers, the British executive dominates the legislature and the prime minister gains from this.

Leader of the House The parliamentary timetable, the committee network, the process of reform and so on are the responsibility of the Leader of the House. However, until 1915 the prime minister held this position and today makes the appointment from the party faithful; the two work hand in glove. New Labour's modernization strategy clearly reflected the Blair agenda and the changed format of Prime Minister's Questions came without parliamentary debate.

Debates Prime ministers can appear to be adroit parliamentary performers but the odds are heavily stacked in their favour. With extensive civil service back-up, most dominate the House. Alternatively, they can make institutional changes to reduce debate, which helps explain a long-term decline in their accountability to the Commons (Dunleavy and Jones 1993).

Power of dissolution Like Samson, the prime minister can bring down the temple on all heads, sending members off to the country, perhaps to lose their seats. Wilson made a dissolution threat after a near-mutiny by George Brown and others over the supply of British arms to South Africa, as did Major during the passage of the Maastricht Bill.

The culture of obedience As we saw in chapter 11, the British parties fall inexorably under Michels's iron law of oligarchy. Unlike presidents, prime ministers are leaders of their parties. Thatcher's dominance was legendary and Blair soon established an iron grip. In November 1998 a leaked document showed the Labour leadership seeking to prohibit the members of its NEC (which included some of an 'old Labour' disposition) from expressing disagreement in public.

Sharks and banana skins

There can be no doubt that Britain's ancient, ambiguous and elusive constitution leaves a formidable armoury in the hands of the prime minister.

However, in the real world of politics, where personalities and interests clash, the weapons can be double-edged. Although popularity can confer authority, public opinion can be fickle; a poor showing in the polls can damage, as Thatcher discovered in November 1990. Neither is the Cabinet always compliant. Unlike presidential appointees, its members are career politicians who, like Macbeth, entertain vaulting ambitions of their own. Within the Cabinet sits the likely heir apparent and plots and rumours of plots against the prime minister are regular features of political reportage. Major's colleagues – Heseltine, Clarke and Howard – were serious rivals, as was a lean and hungry Cassius in the form of John Redwood, who picked up the gauntlet in 1995 (see p. 295).

Even the seemingly impregnable Blair had reason to lie awake at night when Paul Routledge's biography of Gordon Brown revealed that, although standing aside in the leadership battle (see p. 297), brooding ambition continued to gnaw at the Chancellor's heart. Indeed, Blair had to accept something of a dual administration, with considerable power over the domestic agenda lying in Brown's hands (Oborne 2001). The relationship bore comparison with the mid-nineteenth-century partnership between Lord Palmerston, whose interests lay overseas, and his Chancellor Gladstone, who placed his iron grip over public finance at home. Significantly, the latter was to wear the crown as one of Britain's greatest prime ministers.

Cabinet selection is subject to political constraints and there will be a core of senior MPs with strong followings who cannot be omitted. Moderate Labour leaders have been obliged to endure some unwelcome company from the left. After the 1990 leadership election Major could hardly exclude rivals Hurd and Heseltine. Again, the fear of prime ministerial displeasure does not afflict all. Thatcher's wealthy Foreign Secretary, Lord Carrington, could afford an outspoken line.

The opportunity to butcher can also be questioned. Macmillan was weaker after his 'Night of the Long Knives' and the weight of Thatcher casualties built up a body of discontent waiting only for the demoted Howe to produce one of the most bitter denunciations in modern history and precipitate her downfall. Major feared sacking colleagues; in his victory reshuffle, following the unwanted leadership contest of July 1995, he might have been justified in some radical surgery but did not feel up to removing the carbuncle of Euroscepticism.

Neither is collective responsibility always the gag it might seem. Most prime ministers feel plagued by leaks and Thatcher was to lament in her memoirs the lack of some 'good men and true'. Even access to the media can provide rope for a noose; only the telegenic can prosper. Sir Alec Douglas-Home's cadaverous features were no asset before the cameras and Major's grey persona and monotone defied the image-makers while proving irresistible to satirists. Even Blair's 'Cool Britannia' initiative became too cool for comfort in February 1998 when Danbert Nobacon, of the band Chumbawamba, emptied an ice bucket over Deputy Prime Minister John Prescott at the Brit Awards. Moreover, Samson did not come out of Gaza well and the power of dissolution may still lie more in the threat than the use. An election precipitated by a cabinet crisis

Cooling Britannia: John Prescott doused by Danbert Nobacon with the contents of an ice bucket at the Brit Awards, February 1998

Photo: Times Newspapers Ltd

would suggest unfitness to rule. When Major brandished the weapon he appeared more desperate than strong.

What of Michels's iron law ensuring support from the ranks? The Achilles' heel of the prime minister is the party. Having been elected by the people, a president's security of tenure is absolute. Only upon some gross misdemeanour (such as Watergate) should the process of impeachment roll into action (events surrounding the Monica Lewinsky affair were exceptional). In contrast, prime ministers occupy their positions only as long as the parliamentary party is prepared to back them. Thatcher was once praised by colleague John Biffen as 'a tigress surrounded by hamsters'. However, on Wednesday 21 November 1990, the hamsters were to devour her. Perhaps as a consequence, Major lived amidst constant rumblings of discontent and rumours of challenge.

Destiny and disposition

Hence, the prime minister's powers are potential, their reality depending upon two factors: *prevailing contingencies* and the *personality* or character of the incumbent.

The contingency factor Like sportsmen and businessmen, politicians need a helping hand from Lady Luck; the circumstances surrounding prime ministerial tenure are largely a matter of fortune. Attlee was obliged to reign during the years of post-war austerity while Macmillan inherited the years of plenty.

Gaitskell's untimely death gave Wilson his big chance (although in office he suffered extensive economic restrictions), Heath was forced into humiliating U-turns amidst world economic crisis and Callaghan was squeezed by the IMF and undermined by those upon whom he most relied – the trade unions. Major reaped the bitter harvest of a fractious party and an overheated economy, but for 'Black Wednesday' he could not entirely blame his stars; as Chancellor it was he who had persuaded a reluctant Thatcher to enter the ERM at a fatally high rate. Victory in the World Cup and the Beatles may have helped Wilson, contributing to the feelgood factor, and he distributed honours appropriately. Tony Blair surfed on the crest of a wave of fortune. Coming to the party leadership through the untimely death of John Smith, he led a party united by weariness of opposition and faced a flagging Conservative Party. Upon victory in May 1997 he inherited a relatively healthy economy and a popular mood for a change of cast.

Particular circumstances will call for different styles; an individual can seem right for one situation but wrong for another. Wars have been of particular significance. Asquith and Chamberlain were unequal to the challenge while Lloyd George and Churchill thrived, though in the aftermath they were less sure-footed. Suez proved to be Eden's downfall. In contrast, the Falklands war saved the unpopular Thatcher, her inflexible style reinvented as 'resolution'. Blair was quick to align himself with Clinton's sabre-rattling in the Middle East, and the events of 11 September 2001 saw him donning the accoutrements of a president.

Another card in the hand of fate is the parliamentary arithmetic. While Thatcher and Blair sailed on buoyant majorities, Major's twenty-one-seat margin in 1992 soon haemorrhaged with a succession of disastrous by-elections, leaving little scope for manoeuvre.

The personality factor Weber noted charisma as a significant source of power and Asquith etched his name in the textbooks by declaring that the office of prime minister is what the holder makes of it. All prime ministers will share a fondness for power; having risen up the greasy pole they are likely to possess political skill, ambition and a desire to dominate. However, each is unique, and the informal nature of the office permits infinite scope for interpretation. This helps to explain why the debate remains unresolved and of unquenchable interest.

In the early post-war years, incumbents interpreted their role cautiously, content to preserve the constitutional status quo. Macmillan is credited with having been surprisingly radical but Labour leaders were repeatedly accused of wilting in the face of the Establishment. However, things were to change under Thatcher. Even before coming to office, the effect might have been anticipated.

> No political leader that I have ever known has been less dependent upon the advantages and trappings that attend high office for the impact she made; and none more dependent on the force of her own character and mind. (Cosgrave 1978. xx)

Interviewed in the *Observer* (25 Feb. 1979), she appeared to reject the very principle of cabinet government: 'As prime minister I could not waste time having any internal arguments'. In this era, personalized politics in Britain came of age. The state relentlessly asserted its authority under a philosophy that bore the name 'Thatcherism'. A child reared during these years would be unable to understand why William Pitt (the Elder) was compelled to resign in 1761 because the majority of his Cabinet refused to support his policy towards Spain.

Major brought a quite different personality, having 'all the charisma of a provincial bank clerk' (Charmley 1998: 124). Without Thatcher's confrontational style or zeal, he was to be plagued by accusations of weakness, and many believed his deputy Michael Heseltine (sitting on fourteen cabinet committees) to be the real prime minister.

In opposition Blair had certainly not looked *primus inter pares* as he stamped his modernizing imprint on his party, even rewriting the totemic Clause Four. *Sunday Times* columnist Andrew Grice (1997) was not alone amongst Westminster-watchers in prophesying that 'the overwhelming influence on Blair in power will be Labour's arch-enemy, Margaret Thatcher', whose style he professed to admire.

> He has real star quality. There were few enough Tories on *EastEnders* – there is one less now.
>
> Barbara Windsor on seeing Tony Blair at Labour's election gala, quoted in the *Observer* (26 April 1998)

A Monarchical Culture?

The last twenty years of the millennium saw a testing of the ambiguities, myths and conventions that had long misted any clear vision of the British constitution, and upon which apologist textbooks have preferred to turn a benevolently blind eye. It became clear that Britain's ancient monarchical lineage was no mere curio; it held deep implications for contemporary politics. Cabinet powers are derived from the royal prerogative, a power supposed to come from God. Together with a hijacking of the supremacy of Parliament, this bestows an authority surpassing that of monarchs of old. Constitutional authority Anthony King (2001: 1–21) draws a distinction between 'power-sharing' and 'power-hoarding' regimes. The Netherlands is an example of the former; Dutch ministers serve *with* not *under* their prime minister, cabinet members come from various parties, and meetings last a long time and really make policy. British cabinet meetings today take a little over thirty minutes.

Recent decades have shown that the much-vaunted freedom from an overweening executive depended not upon checks and balances but upon conventions of moderation. A driver blind to the political road signs and speed limits could career on a dangerous course. Thatcher took the constitution at its face value, extending 'the repertory of available styles' at the disposal of the office (King 1985: 137). Did her unceremonious fall vindicate this unwritten highway code? Hugo Young declared: 'finally the system, which says that this is cabinet and not prime ministerial government, reacted. There was a point beyond which it declined to be flouted' (*Independent*, 23 Nov. 1990). Yet she had enjoyed an astonishing eleven years of supremacy and when the fall came it was precipitated not by constitutional checks but by a nervous party cadre suspecting that its leader had passed her electoral sell-by date.

The Blair regime was careful to protect this one Achilles' heel with an astonishing level of party discipline in Parliament. In the 'war against terrorism' he could position himself shoulder to shoulder with Bush without consultation and without setting up a war cabinet. Critics saw an alarming impatience with Whitehall and Westminster procedures as he appeared single-handedly to be using the royal prerogative to take the country into war.

The tercentenary of the Glorious Revolution was celebrated in 1988 in a most muted manner (privatization of the steel industry receiving far more publicity). In marked contrast to the French celebration of 1789 the following year, the British appeared to see little to applaud in the notion of freedom from tyranny. With the monarchical character of the British constitution laid bare, Charter88 declared:

> No country can be considered free in which the government is above the law. No democracy can be considered safe whose freedoms are not encoded in a basic constitution.

Unlimited power is apt to corrupt the minds of those who possess it.

William Pitt the Elder (1708–78), House of Lords speech (9 Jan. 1770)

However, although rich in the resources of constitutional and political power, prime ministers operate in a wider environment, which imposes numerous constraints. A complex web of interrelating structures and processes extends out to encompass the departments of state and even the security and intelligence services (Dunleavy and Rhodes 1990). From outside the executive terrain figures such as journalists, media moguls, business magnates and trade union leaders also penetrate the shell of the core executive. Dispersed throughout this network, power becomes elusive and fluid and the answer to the question 'where does it lie?' can never settle simply upon either Cabinet or prime minister (see Smith 1999). Hence, issues concerning the working of the cabinet system do not tell us all we need to know about policy and power. The next chapter takes us further into this labyrinthine world.

Key points

- Formally speaking, Britain has cabinet, as opposed to monarchical or presidential, government. This means government based on discussion, compromise and moderation.
- This system is recognized constitutionally in the convention of collective responsibility.
- The modern Cabinet works through a system of committees.
- Cabinet government in Britain cannot be appraised without considering the office of the prime minister, who is formally constrained by a *primus inter pares* convention.
- The prime minister is able to control the composition of the Cabinet and its method of working.

- Control over the machinery of government allows a prime minister to have much of the administrative back-up and advice that a personal department would offer.
- In important respects the prime minister is potentially more powerful than a typical president in a democracy because there is neither separation of powers nor a written constitution to restrain the executive.
- The last two decades of the twentieth century saw British government become more centralized and more informal; both developments enhance the prime minister's authority.
- However, there are still constraints and prime ministers vary in their capacity to exploit the position.

Review your understanding of the following terms and concepts

cabinet committees	Efficiency Unit	populism
cabinet government	elective dictatorship	presidential government
Cabinet Office	executive arm of	Privy Council
Cabinet Secretariat	government	Shadow Cabinet
Cabinet Secretary	inner cabinet	spoils system
Central Policy Review Staff	patronage	War Cabinet
collective responsibility	Policy Cabinet	
core executive	Policy Unit	

Assignment

Study the extract from the *Independent* on page 456 and answer the following questions.

		Mark (%)
1	Why is it said that Tony Blair can have few trusted friends?	25
2	What do you think is Gordon Brown's purpose in 'networking' within the constituencies and trade unions?	25
3	Discuss the pros and cons of newspaper articles carrying Tony Blair's name being ghosted by journalists.	25
4	Consider the possible dangers of Blair surrounding himself with non-elected 'cronies'.	25

Questions for discussion

1 Outline the essential features of cabinet government.
2 Critically evaluate the role of the Cabinet Secretariat in British government.

Tony's cronies: the A-list

AFTER he waves off the Gallaghers at the end of the next glittering Downing Street bash, the Prime Minister might do worse than to pick up *Alan Clark's Diaries* for his bedtime reading.

There are few signs of blood yet, of course, but who can Tony Blair really trust? Who are in the charmed circle that he can draw around him with confidence, knowing that they have no one's best interests at heart but his own?

Labour's first year has brought just one big surprise in this department: one name notably absent from the list is Gordon Brown. Of course the Chancellor is still a close political contact of the Prime Minister, and the two men still meet very regularly. But the publication of a biography revealing Brown's bitterness over the 1994 deal which, he feels, deprived him of the leadership, has left its scars. Recent networking by the Chancel-

lor with constituencies and the unions has been interpreted as an attempt to garner support.

In other areas, though, there have been no such surprises. The few men regarded as closest to Mr Blair know well that if and when the blood begins to seep, it will probably be mixed with their own.

Alastair Campbell, the Prime Minister's press secretary, has been a constant and loyal aide, pulling together speeches and – most memorably – helping to craft the killer soundbites with which Mr Blair is apt to carry off the headlines. The "people's princess" line which struck a chord after Diana's death almost certainly had some of his magic worked into it.

Other loyalists who owe their senior positions to the Prime Minister include Peter Mandelson, the Minister without Portfolio, and Lord Irvine, the Lord Chancellor. Both still enjoy close and regular contact with Mr Blair.

Other former Labour staffers who have made the transition include David Miliband, Peter Hyman and Liz Lloyd, all of whom now reside in the Number 10 policy unit. While Mr Miliband is in overall charge, Mr Hyman has a significant input into Mr Blair's speeches and Ms Lloyd briefs him each week for Prime Minister's Questions.

Geoff Mulgan, centre-left guru and founder of the Demos think tank, has been brought into Downing Street to oversee the Social Exclusion Unit, expected to be a major driving force in terms of policy direction over the next few years. Other recent acquisitions include two journalists, David Bradshaw from the *Daily Mirror* and Philip Bassett from the *Times*, who have been appointed to the new Strategic Communications Unit and who are often the true authors of the Prime Minister's newspaper articles.

Fran Abrams

Independent, 30 April 1998

3　Discuss the function of the Shadow Cabinet in British politics.

4　How important is personality to the authority of the prime minister?

5　By what means is the British prime minister able to establish a direct link with the public? How significant is such a link?

6　How far is 'news management' a legitimate role for the prime minister's press secretary?

7　Compare and contrast the leadership styles of John Major and Tony Blair.

8　In what ways would the establishment of a prime-ministerial department alter the process of government in Britain?

9　How might the British cabinet system be reformed?

10　'The real question is not whether or not the powers of the British prime minister are presidential, but how far they are monarchical.' Discuss.

Topic for debate

This house believes that the British love a strong leader.

Further reading

Benn, T. (1979) *Arguments for Socialism*.
A stimulating essay expressing extreme distaste for presidential-style premiership.

Burch, M. and Holliday, I. (1996) *The British Cabinet System*.
Well-crafted case studies showing the increasing centralization of power.

Foley, M. (2000) *The British Presidency*.
Title leaves no doubt where the author stands on the key debate; the Blair premiership is seen as the 'clinching proof'.

Hennessy, P. (1986) *Cabinet*.
Lively account by academic and master journalist with an intimate knowledge of the geography of the corridors of power.

Hennessy, P. (2000) *The Prime Minister: The Office and Its Holders Since 1945*.
Charts the gradual move towards presidentialism with a vividly empirical account of premierships in an unfailingly engaging and accessible style.

Lawson, N. (1993) *The View from Number 11: Memoirs of a Tory Radical*.
Challenging account of some of the Thatcher years by notable resignee, with some thoughts on the nature and reform of cabinet government.

Mandelson, P. and Liddle, R. (1996) *The Blair Phenomenon: Can New Labour Deliver?*
New Labour, New Cabinet. The blueprint for executive power straight from the arch-spin doctor's pen.

Pimlott, B. (1992) *Harold Wilson.*
Rehabilitation without hagiography of a key post-war prime minister.

Rhodes, R. A. W. and Dunleavy, P. (1995) *Prime Minister, Cabinet and Core Executive.*
New and previously published pieces examining the centre of the web of power in Britain.

Rose, R. (2001) *The Prime Minister in a Shrinking World.*
Charts the changing nature of the office since 1945. Examines the paradox that, while power at Westminster increases, power on the world stage diminishes.

Smith, M. (1999) *The Core Executive in Britain.*
Emphasizes the fluid network of relationships around Britain's cabinet system.

Young, H. (1989) *One of Us.*
Excellent account of Thatcher in government. Clever punning title sets the tone.

For light relief

Peter Bradshaw, *Not Alan Clark's Diaries.*
Entertaining parody from *Evening Standard* feature, but read the real thing first (see below).

Alan Clark (1993) *Diaries.*
An irreverent account of Whitehall and Westminster life and beyond.

Michael Dobbs, *To Play the King* and *Final Cut.*
Sequels to *House of Cards.* Evil chief whip Frances Urquhart becomes prime minister and his eventful career reaches a dramatic conclusion. You may like this, I couldn't possibly comment. Available on video.

Douglas Hurd, *The Shape of Ice.*
Novel from a once-leading politician about political life in a Cabinet with a dominant woman and a weak dithering prime minister. Any resemblance to real people is entirely coincidental of course.

Nicholas Jones (2001) *The Control Freaks: How New Labour Gets its Own Way.*
No holds barred and lively critique of New Labour's media manipulation by a BBC political correspondent.

Sue Townsend, *Number Ten.*
A satirical tale of fictional prime minister Edward Clare from an author best known for the Adrian Mole books.

On the net

http://www.number-10.gov.uk
http://www.cabinet-office.gov.uk
Two websites at the heart of government. You can even have a virtual tour of Number Ten.

15

The Village of Whitehall: of Ministers and Mandarins

In this chapter we move to the engine room of the modern state – the central government bureaucracy, constitutionally part of the executive arm of government. We first detail the anatomy of the modern civil service and its evolution. Next we examine the bureaucrats who rub pin-striped shoulders with ministers in the process of government. What kind of people are they? Do their life experiences resemble those of the people they serve? From this we turn to a contentious issue that has characterized this world of power: official secrecy. This leads to the key debate on the influence of the bureaucrats: are they really the 'obedient servants' they claim at the end of their polite letters? We conclude by assessing the impact of the reforming gales gusting through the corridors of power since the 1980s.

An Anatomy of a Bureaucracy

The British **civil service** is the central government **bureaucracy**, its function in the great liberal-democratic scheme of things to serve faithfully the people's elected representatives. Writers in the apologist tradition have had no difficulty in believing this to be the case, depicting the bureaucrats in the way seventeenth-century painters portrayed the nobility, in romantically idealized poses without warts or wrinkles. Thus E. N. Gladden (1967: 199) notes: 'On its record of public service it stands unchallenged, setting an example that the lesser breeds of official strive, almost hopelessly, to emulate'. This tradition of approval is partly explained by the fact that many writers (like Gladden) are themselves ex-members. Sir John Hoskyns, an outsider brought in by Mrs Thatcher to shake up this comfortable world, observed:

No one is qualified to criticise ... unless he has first hand experience of working in it. But if he *has* worked in it, then there is a convention that he should never speak about it thereafter except in terms of respectful admiration. (Hoskyns 1984: 4)

The constitutional position of the civil service is said to entail three related characteristics.

> Empires fall, ministries pass away but bureaux remain.
>
> Duc d'Audiffret-Pasquier (1823–1905; French statesman)

◆ *Permanence*. Political storms may rage and politicians be swept in and out of office but the bureaucrats cling like pin-striped limpets to the solid grey rocks of Whitehall. They are career civil servants, not political appointees.

◆ *Neutrality*. Taking no sides, and favouring no class, civil servants are above the sordid world of politics, the very embodiment of the liberal-democratic ideal of the *neutral state*.

◆ *Anonymity*. Ministers alone are *responsible* to the outside world (through Parliament) for departmental actions. Civil servants remain in the shadows, neither named nor blamed when issues are debated.

However, the myths and ambiguities clouding the British constitution are nowhere more evident than in the role of the civil service. In this chapter, we must try to substitute a microscope for rose-tinted lenses, first setting the scene by identifying our specimens and the environment in which they civilly serve.

The civil servants

Not all state employees are civil servants. They may broadly be defined as servants of the Crown working in a civil (non-military) capacity and not

The ornate facade of Whitehall: the New Home and Colonial Office, 1875

Source: Mary Evans Picture Library

holding political or judicial office. Said unkindly in caricature to be rarely civil and never servile, they are popularly thought of as grey, passionless beings who sometimes exercise discretionary power over our lives. They, and the study of them, are often characterized as rather boring, which may well be precisely what the Establishment likes the masses to think; people do not look too closely at boring subjects. However, despite evident efforts by some writers to avoid over-exciting their readers, the role of the civil service in our lives is certainly not a boring subject; it is about nothing less than running the state we inhabit. When examining the balance of power in society, its role must be central to analysis.

Civil servants may be broadly dichotomized as industrial and non-industrial. Thus, although the civil servant of popular imagination wears a suit and carries a rolled umbrella, many are obliged to roll up their shirt sleeves, others have stripped to the waist in government dockyards and the exotic Quentin Crisp entitled his autobiography *The Naked Civil Servant* because, when posing for students in state art colleges, he wore nothing at all. Today the industrial civil service (primarily employed by the Ministry of Defence) has shrunk to minute proportions. The non-industrial service broadly comprises three main elements: the *Administrative Group*, a category of *specialist groups* containing experts such as scientists, doctors and lawyers, and a set of departmental classes employing *specialists* in areas such as taxation.

From the mass of workers at its base to its tiny elite pinnacle (figure 15.1), the service is a social microcosm. However, our principal focus is on the 1 per cent at the top, those whose daily lives bring them into intimate contact with the highest and most mighty in the confident world of the Establishment. These comprise the **mandarin** class. Named after the officials in imperial China, they sit at the top of what, from April 1996, has formed the Senior Civil Service, comprising some 3,000 members from what used to be known as grade 5, or Assistant Secretary and above. Although there is now some limited open competition for Permanent Secretary vacancies, members form a closed caste networking across departmental boundaries (Mountfield 1997: 309). At the apex sit the departmental permanent secretaries, the apotheosis of the mandarinate.

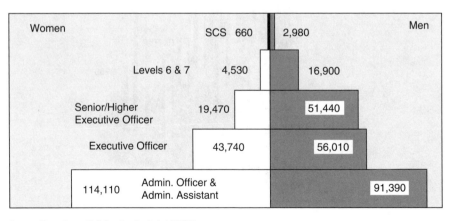

Figure 15.1
The civil service hierarchy: full-time staff in post by grade in the non-industrial civil service, April 2001.

Source: Data from *Civil Service Statistics* (2001).

From *mander*, to command, 'mandarin' is not a Chinese word; it was used to describe the officials (*Khiouping*) by the Portuguese colonists at Maca'o. Mandarins were appointed on the basis of imperial birth, long service, illustrious deeds, knowledge, ability, zeal and nobility.

The structure of the civil service

Following nineteenth-century reforms (see p. 466), the civil service grew steadily. In 1900 membership stood at around 50,000 but growth was promoted by two world wars and the emergence of a complex welfare state, reaching a peak of 763,000 in 1976. With a changing political climate the number fell to 459,000 in 1999, rising slightly thereafter.

The great historic departments at the centre of government (Treasury, Foreign Office and Home Office) stand in the environs of Whitehall, the dignified corridor surveyed by Nelson from his vantage point in Trafalgar Square and leading to the Palace of Westminster. Their origins lie in the royal household. The newer departments, concerned with issues such as social security and education, reflect the changing role of government and inhabit less grand areas of the metropolis.

Outside London is a national network of civil servants, many working in semi-autonomous **executive agencies** (figure 15.2), leaving a central core around Whitehall of some 50,000 (the size of the service in 1900). Formerly offices of the central departments, the agencies were **hived off** from 1988 onwards under the 'Next Steps' initiative. By 2001, over a hundred of them were employing three-quarters of all permanent civil servants. A related change has been the increasing casualization of staff, numbers rising from 11,100 in

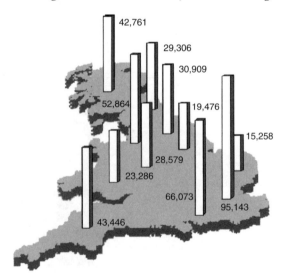

Figure 15.2
The national distribution of civil servants, April 1996.

Source: Data from *Civil Service Statistics* (1996).

1976 to 19,600 by 1997, though by 2001 they had fallen somewhat to around 14,000. Similarly, to cope with the loss of permanent staff there has been a steady increase in part-timers, from 31,000 in 1976 (4 per cent of employees) to almost 73,000 in 2001 (14 per cent).

The EU impact Membership of the EU makes increasing demands on Whitehall. Although there is no special department of European affairs, those departments closely involved (Treasury; Environment, Food and Rural Affairs; Education and Skills; Trade and Industry) have established dedicated EU sections. While the Treasury and Cabinet Office are the traditional leaders, in an internal power struggle the Foreign and Commonwealth Office (FCO) has found a lifeline to arrest its declining importance. Mandarins meet in committees to take a strategic perspective and over all sits a special EU Committee to coordinate policy. Some members serve on the UK Permanent Representation at Brussels and once breathing its heady air can be accused of 'going native', becoming disdainful of the Whitehall world as they act on the larger stage of European summitry (Sampson 1992: 40–1).

The politics of structure Structure is no technical matter lying outside politics. The beauty of the unwritten constitution is that it can be forever reinvented at prime ministerial whim, usually for some political purpose. Indeed, the very creation of the modern civil service was itself a political project. During the 1960s and 1970s a fashion for departmental fusion created new giant departments such as Health and Social Security (figure 15.3). This provided empires for prominent politicians and enabled governments to remove certain controversies from the public eye by resolving them within Whitehall. By the mid-1970s the climate began to change and the giants were dismembered, but within days of Labour taking office in 1997, John Prescott's Department of Environment, Transport and the Regions (DETR) was born – a giant empire created to satisfy the political ambition of the Deputy Prime Minister (Dunleavy et al. 2001a: 406). However, this was short lived as the environment was hived off and the Department of Transport, Local Government and the Regions was born. The embarrassing resignation of Transport Minister Stephen Byers in 2002 saw further fragmentation and Local Government and the Regions came under the grandiosely named Office of the Deputy Prime Minister.

The merging of education and employment in 1995 could be seen as a statement of educational philosophy, suggesting that education was a service providing workers for the capitalist economy. This went further in Blair's second term to become the Department for Education and Skills; employment, having barely got comfortable in bed with education, was whisked away to join pensions. The creation of the Department of the Environment, Food and Rural Affairs (DEFRA) in 2001 was effectively an environmental takeover of the Ministry of Agriculture, discredited by the BSE and foot-and-mouth fiascos. Food scares had also led to the creation of the Food Standards Agency in 1999. This looked like an attack on food producers and these mighty interests lobbied energetically to water down the initiative.

Figure 15.3
Departmental
fusion and fission:
the rise and fall of a
giant.

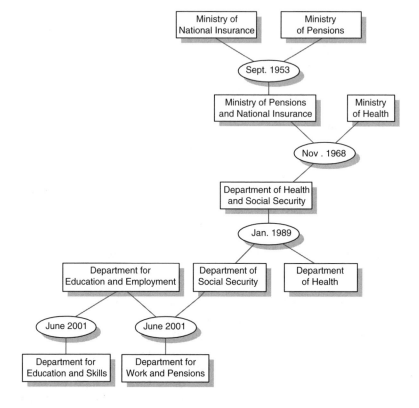

A Civil Service Department created in response to the Fulton Report (see p. 471) to control management and effectiveness was abolished by Thatcher in 1981, its functions drawn first into the Treasury and then in 1994 into an Office of Public Service. This became responsible for agencification, itself a reform with major political implications (see p. 489).

The genesis of the modern civil service

Like many institutions the civil service owes much to its evolution. Orthodox accounts stress the nineteenth-century reforms, which are said to have replaced the corruption of an old aristocratic order with rational administrative principles. Less readily acknowledged is the fact that these reforms made this powerful state institution the property of the bourgeoisie.

Its ancestral roots lie in the courts of Anglo-Saxon kings who required clerks to accompany them around the realm (Stenton 1941: 349). As officers of the royal household, their functions persisted through episodes of constitutional turbulence, some offices, such as the Chamber and the Wardrobe, gradually giving way to newer ones. However, there was no single service and many positions were little more than sinecures, with appointments made through

> I was asked to copy some lines from *The Times* newspaper with an old quill pen, and at once made a series of blots and false spellings. 'That won't do, you know,' said Henry Freeling to his brother Clayton. Clayton, who was my friend, urged that I was nervous and asked that I might be allowed to do a bit of writing at home and bring it as a sample on the next day... With a faltering heart I took this on the next day to the office... But when I got to 'The Grand', as we used to call our office in those days, from its site, St Martin's le Grand, I was seated at a desk without any further reference to my competency. No one condescended even to look at my beautiful penmanship.
>
> Anthony Trollope (1815–82; English novelist), *Autobiography* (1883)

nepotism and bribery. Civil servants were often the sons of the aristocracy too dull to survive in any other walk of life such as church, law or army. Trollope's autobiography recounts his own selection process. Salaries were supplemented by bribes and gifts, a practice well documented by Samuel Pepys, who served in the Admiralty in the mid-seventeenth century.

> Going out of Whitehall, I met Capt. Grove who did give me a letter directed to myself from himself; I discerned money to be in it and took it, knowing, as I found it to be, the proceed of the place I have got him... But I did not open it till I came home to my office; and there broke it open, not looking into it till all the money was out, that I may say I saw no money in the paper if ever I should be Questioned about it. There was a piece of gold and 4/- in silver. So home to dinner with my father and wife.
>
> Samuel Pepys (1633–1703; diarist and naval administrator), *Diary* (1 April 1663)

The rise of the industrial bourgeoisie Eighteenth-century radicals lamented the failings of the service and a campaign for reform emerged under Burke and Fox. However, it was the new industrial bourgeoisie that fashioned the modern service. A critical element was the experience of empire, where the model for reform was found: the Indian Civil Service (ICS), which had evolved from the East India Company to become a complex instrument of British colonial rule. It was manned by the brightest sons of the bourgeoisie, who would take the passage to India, reigning there as the epitome of the over-dressed, over-confident Englishman (depicted by writers such as E. M. Forster). It is clear from the fading sepia photographs that the adventure was luxuriantly pleasurable and exceedingly good for the ego.

The young bureaucratic conquistadors prepared themselves to rule a race about which they knew little, in a climate for which they were singularly ill suited, by means of the newly revived public school system with its umbilical link to the universities of Oxford and Cambridge. Under the stimulus of men like Thomas Arnold of Rugby, these schools became forcing houses for transforming the sons of rough-talking businessmen into scholars and (more importantly) gentlemen. They sought to place a stamp of superiority on their alumni through the study of the classics, team games and a hierarchical prefect system which, while appearing sado-masochistic, simultaneously stressed a natural right to rule and passive obedience. The ICS used examinations in selecting candidates, and the classics, the intellectual diet of the universities, were seen as the best indication of excellence. As **generalists**, with no practical skills, successful candidates confidently sailed away to command a vast subcontinent. The ICS seemed to the bourgeoisie to offer the very best model upon which to reform the home administration.

The Northcote–Trevelyan Report (1854) This report, the result of an enquiry established by Gladstone, set out the blueprint for radical reform. Its driving spirit was Sir Charles Trevelyan, a zealous member of the ICS. The report recommended that the separate departments be amalgamated to form a single *home civil service*. The work was characterized hierarchically, from clerical drudgery, through a range of executive tasks, to the intellectualism of policy-making. Recruitment was to reflect these distinctions in appropriately Platonic terms: men of iron would labour at the lower levels, while the upper echelons were reserved for the men of gold forged on the public school–Oxbridge anvil.

Merit would replace patronage and nepotism. Yet in this praiseworthy ideal lay the key to a bourgeois capture of the service. The examinations would be geared to the Oxbridge syllabus and neither aristocrats nor the working classes could match the sons of the bourgeoisie on such territory. The report was warmly welcomed by Gladstone: the class he represented would have 'command over all the higher part of the civil service, which up to this time they have never enjoyed' (Morley 1903: 649). The old guard were not blind to the writing appearing on their decaying walls, Queen Victoria worrying where 'the application of the principle of public competition is to stop' (Magnus 1963: 118).

The twentieth century The fact that the civil service took this shape is by no means remarkable: it was fashioned to serve a new political order. What *is* remarkable is that, as society changed during the twentieth century, the model persisted. Even an era of reform instigated by Thatcher, including the Next Steps initiative (which undermined the Northcote–Trevelyan principle of a single service), could not penetrate the bastions of the mandarinate (see p. 491).

The Culture of Whitehall

Following the nineteenth-century reforms the civil service evolved its own particular culture which preserved its elitist character. It has been likened to an Oxbridge college, with much attention to status, ritual displays of courtesy, esoteric speech codes involving Latin phrases and much cricketing jargon, and a general air of superiority.

Social make-up: unrepresentative bureaucracy?

Post-war mandarins have been asked to run a complex welfare state. Do they know what it is like to sit at nights with a loved one in pain on an NHS waiting list? Have they known unemployment, discrimination or harassment by the forces of law and order? How far has the service reflected the society it serves in terms of gender, race and social class? Has the selection process aimed for a representative bureaucracy?

Gender The civil service has not welcomed women into its ranks. The Victorian era was marked by overwhelming male hegemony, shown in all-male London clubs, limited education for girls and a male House of Commons elected by a male electorate. While their opportunities in the service have improved (no longer forced to retire if they marry), women have remained grossly under-represented at the upper levels (see figure 15.1). Their value has been seen to lie in performing routine tasks as administrative assistants and casual employees. Of the part-time staff, almost 95 per cent are women. Although the Crossman diaries conferred a modest fame upon Dame Evelyn Sharp, the first woman Permanent Secretary, she remained a rare bird.

Diary of Jim Hacker: Oct. 27th

'How many Permanent Secretaries', I asked Sir Humphrey, 'are there at the moment?'

'Forty-one I believe.'

A precise answer.

'Forty-one,' I agreed pleasantly. 'And how many are women?'

Suddenly Sir Humphrey's memory seemed to fail him. 'Well broadly speaking, not having the exact figures to hand, I'm not exactly sure.'

'Well, approximately?' I encouraged him to reply.

'Well,' he said cautiously, '*approximately* none.'

J. Lynn and A. Jay, *The Complete Yes Minister* (based on TV series) (1981: 355)

In 1994 the government made its fourth five-yearly report to the UN Human Rights Committee, claiming 'significant progress for women at all levels of the Civil Service since 1984'. However, while 29 per cent of those in the glittering diplomatic service were women, only 3 per cent had reached ambassadorial level. At the upper reaches of the mandarinate (grades 1–4) women held only 9 per cent of the 652 jobs and only 2 of 34 permanent secretaryships. Six departments remained skirt-free zones, while the Ministry of Defence numbered only 2 women among 60 senior staff. Elizabeth Symons, leader of the First Division Association (the senior mandarins' 'union'), criticized the government for failing in its 1991 Opportunity 2000 commitment to fill 15 per cent of senior posts with women (*Independent*, 17 Oct. 1994). A new target of 35 per cent was set by the 1999 Wilson Report (see p. 490).

In opposition Labour had published grandiose plans for a Ministry for Women in 1986. However, in government this was scaled down to a Women's Unit with responsibility for 'gender mainstreaming' throughout Whitehall, calling upon departments to consider women's needs in policy-making. Yet this did not guarantee influence and the results disappointed. The government appeared to place greater emphasis on its Social Exclusion Unit, with which the Women's Unit was to be merged to form a Women and Equality Unit (Squires and Wickham-Jones 2002).

Race The prospects for ethnic minorities in the upper echelons remain bleak (figure 15.4), despite the target of 3.2 per cent at SCS level by 2005, proposed in the Wilson Report. In October 1997 Labour MP Keith Vaz, in a report based on replies to parliamentary questions tabled between May and July 1997, described a failure to recruit Asians as a 'national shame'. The Foreign Office and the Ministry of Defence were singled out for particularly poor records.

Social class Nowhere has the Northcote–Trevelyan legacy been more evident than in the class make-up of the mandarinate. Moulded from the same establishment clay as the heads of industry, commerce, the City, the army, the church and ancient professions, they attended the same schools and universities (Kellner and Crowther Hunt 1980: 193; Theakston and Fry 1989: 132), join the same London clubs (the Athenaeum and the Oxford and Cambridge being particular favourites) and meet at the same house parties. Class bias has been reinforced by working-class graduates' disinclination to apply, reflecting the deferential British culture and low expectations of success (see p. 469). It is sometimes pointed out that there has been an increased tendency for civil servants to come from 'minor' public schools – hardly a social revolution! However, the appointment of Sir Andrew Turnbull as Cabinet Secretary in 2002 represented some degree of change. Unlike his three predecessors (who had spent their schooldays at Harrow, Eton and Radley College, respectively), he was a product of the state system (Enfield Grammar School) and under clubs in his *Who's Who* entry he listed Tottenham Hotspur!

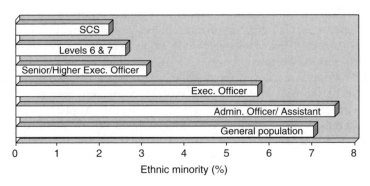

Figure 15.4
Ethnic minorities in the civil service and the general population, April 2000.

Source: Data from *Civil Service Statistics* (2000).

Socialization Although there has been some increase in the number of state school entrants, in coming from the diligent middle classes they may be pursuing personal ambition rather than social reform. Moreover, despite meritocratic procedures, career advancement requires informal patronage from above and the ambitious will need to catch the eye of their superiors (Richards 1996: 665). Consciously or unconsciously they will assume the colours of their environment, joining the right clubs, attending the right parties and adopting the right speech codes.

'Yes Permanent Secretary'

There are those who are always on the side of authority and quite exceptionally adept at formulating the answer that will be most acceptable to those at the top. It is no secret that they get on better than those who are outspoken and speak their minds.

E. N. Gladden (retired civil servant), *Civil Services of the United Kingdom* (1967: 199)

Age There has been one modest change in the characteristics of top officials during the post-war decades and this is towards relatively younger appointments, which may reflect the drive towards managerialism (see p. 489). However, the Whitehall village is still largely inhabited by the white, middle-class, middle-aged male (Rhodes and Weller 2001).

Skimming the milk: selecting mandarins

The selection process is the key to understanding mandarin culture. Northcote–Trevelyan established that potential mandarins would enter directly into a closed upper elite – the Administrative Class. This at once removed the inconvenience of working through the ranks and precluded aspirants rising from the lower strata. Subsequent reforms maintained this principle; today a Policy Management Programme (formerly the Fast Stream) provides a gilded staircase to the top. From the start entrants inhale the oxygen of power, meeting and even advising ministers. Competition is intense: 7,000 applied for just 115 vacancies in 1994 (*Financial Times*, 25 Oct. 1995). After a filter of written tests a small number proceed to several days of interviews and work simulations where subjective assessment searches for ill-defined 'right qualities'. Elite cloning has enabled the service to reproduce in its own image.

Between 1965 and 1986, Oxbridge entry swelled to 75 per cent (Theakston and Fry 1989: 132). When in 1993 Cabinet Secretary Robin Butler told the Treasury and Civil Service Committee that public school entry had fallen to 51 per cent he was, like his predecessor Robert Armstrong, being 'economical with the truth', casting his net over a far wider area of the service than is usual in defining the mandarinate. An *Economist* analysis (19 March 1994) of the 'true mandarinate' found that, of twenty permanent secretaries, sixteen (80 per cent) had been so educated and fourteen (70 per cent) were from Oxbridge. These proportions remained remarkably stable throughout the twentieth century. Although the mandarins frequently talk of revamping their image, scepticism amongst redbrick graduates must die hard. In June 1996 the government revealed that of Leeds University's 349 applicants in 1995, just 2 per cent entered the fast stream – compared to 10.6 per cent of Oxford applicants. Meanwhile, universities with strong science backgrounds (such as Aston and Brunel) had no successful candidates at all (*Financial Times*, 13 June 1996).

Vetting An additional safeguard against social infiltration has been through security vetting. Although officially a means of excluding communists and fascists, interest has focused rather more on those with leanings towards the former (Miliband 1984: 103).

Promotion Progression to the highest levels, while subject to various 'object-ive' meritocratic processes, including the work of the Senior Appointments Selection Committee, is really controlled through a secretive, club-like process at the highest level of the mandarinate. At an early career stage individuals suitable for advancement will be identified and apparently meritocratic pro-cedures will be but a facade to legitimate their rise (Richards 1996). Some challenge came to this cosy process in the 1980s (see p. 485).

The expertise of the mandarins: gentlemen versus players?

The social bias in the upper echelons is defended with the argument that the criterion is brains, the apparent class domination arising because the best and brightest issue from the loins of intelligent and successful parents. Yet severe doubts have been expressed about the mandarins' expertise. While doctors attend medical schools and lawyers study law, Britain's mandarins, in sharp contrast to the practice in many other countries, have remained almost un-touched by the disciplines relevant to their work (sociology, economics, civil engineering, and even social and public administration).

It is argued that high-level work requires *generalist* rather than *specialist* abilities, a preference redolent of the nineteenth-century reforms. Yet in truth the reformers had little choice; it was classics that the public schools and universities taught, so it had to be classics for the examinations. Had practical subjects been examined, the 'barbarians' from the urban technical colleges might have entered the establishment gates. This approach could work during the nineteenth century, with the state's minimalist 'night-watchman' role, but the post-war era brought government into new areas of economic and social life. Britain slipped behind its main competitors as civil servants wrestled with problems they did not understand, their cultivated air of superiority concealing shallow dilettantism (Balogh 1968). The retention of the generalists' hegemony was justified variously. Only they knew their way around the Whitehall system, only they could understand the (equally generalist) minister's mind; that is, the best people to lead the blind would be the blind. Legitimation came in a doctrine which condescendingly declared that experts must be 'on tap not on top'.

The Fulton Report: anything but action The arrival of a Labour government in 1964 promised an attack on both social exclusiveness and amateurism and a committee was soon established under Lord Fulton. Its 1968 report castigated the 'cult of the amateur' yet, of over a hundred recommendations, one was politely declined – that entrants should possess *relevant* degrees. This seemingly small reservation effectively sabotaged the enterprise. Ten years later the Commons Expenditure Committee saw little evidence of change and disenchanted high-flier Clive Ponting (1986: 85) reported how in 1983 four of the senior officials responsible for the entire defence budget of £18 billion 'were all classicists who had read Greats at Oxford'. By the 1990s, the generalists' promotion prospects were still considerably brighter than those of the specialist (Richards 1996). Although a 1996 white paper (Cabinet Office 1996) contained a resolution to increase the proportion of fast-stream recruits with science backgrounds from 20 to 33 per cent, David Willetts, as junior minister in the Cabinet Office, insisted the drive was not intended to reduce the chances of Oxbridge generalists.

Mandarins in the hereafter: life after Whitehall

Mandarins have not feared retirement; indeed some greet their professional demise with the relish of Christians in Foxe's *Book of Martyrs*, so certain are they of paradise to come. The close of a career brings rather more than a pocket watch; titles have been dispensed twice a year in the honours lists. These awards reflect status reached rather than any particular contribution; the most senior can expect peerages. Although the practice was curbed by Major and Blair, the rewards do not end with ennoblement. Though gone, the mandarins are not forgotten, their names are entered upon the revered list of the great and the good from which are chosen the heads of university colleges, quangos and government commissions. Their value lies in assiduously cultivated conformity; they can be relied upon not to rock the establishment boat. Thus was Sir Thomas Legg (a long-serving 'Sir Humphrey' and Garrick Club member) brought in to investigate the arms-to-Sierra-Leone affair in May 1998.

There is also a tendency, once the winter of retirement threatens, for some to migrate like starlings to the warm climes of the private sector in merchant banks and industry (Balogh 1968: 21). In the 1980s, public service could increasingly be seen as a prelude to private gain (Doig 1984) and senior mandarins could feel considerable anguish if they had not ensured that when the Whitehall door closed another was ready to open. Amidst much controversy, the ex-head of the civil service, Sir William Armstrong, became chairman of Midland Bank.

The real concern here is that civil servants in key positions will be 'inclined to take a general view of things not awkward to large private interests' (Balogh 1968: 23). In 1994, amidst controversy, Sir Duncan Nichol, NHS chief executive, joined the board of BUPA, Britain's largest private health care organization. In the same year Richard Thomas went from the Office of Fair Trading to Clifford Chance, an influential lawyer-lobbyist firm. It is not difficult to see why an unrivalled knowledge of the workings of Whitehall should be prized by private interests, including multinational companies.

Although some restrictions have ben introduced, these remain light. For two years after leaving the service mandarins' appointments are subject to an independent vetting body, but its declarations are only advisory. In June 1994 the Public Accounts Committee disclosed that a senior Home Office official responsible for privatizing the Wolds prison had joined Group Four less than twelve months after it had won the five-year contract to run the prison with a remarkably uncompetitive bid.

Secrets of Success

I know that's a secret, for it's whispered everywhere.

William Congreve
(Restoration dramatist), *Love for Love* (1695)

Whitehall may be characterized as an incestuous 'village'. The inhabitants of Whitehall-on-Thames have their own private world of shared experiences 'united by coherent patterns of praxis' (Heclo and Wildavsky 1974: 2). This image is particularly apposite with respect to sharing information with outsiders: the locals like to keep themselves very much to themselves. Yet the mandarins are supposed to serve the world outside and if they are miserly with information they threaten democracy. The issue is thus central to the analysis of British government.

Information and power

Endemic throughout British society, secrecy, rather than flagellation, is perhaps the real *vice anglais*. It is a necessary instrument of a dominant elite; ignorance among the masses helps maintain deference. It is no small irony that the Privy Council, a respected constitutional building block, actually means *secret council*. Official information has long been seen as the property of the high and mighty, who have been as likely to distribute it as they have their land, money and capital. The civil service, as keeper of the keys to the informational vaults, has been able to make British government one of the most closed in the world.

Not only is secrecy bad for democracy, it can be bad for the health. We have been denied information about the air we breathe, the food we eat and the harmful effects of medicinal drugs. There are countless examples. Relatives of soldiers meeting accidental death, mistreated hospital patients, victims of Gulf war syndrome and pursuers of justice on various fronts have all met the wall of official silence. Richard Lacey (1997), a scientist who worked strenuously to highlight the BSE threat (and whose own career was undermined in the process), was to dub MAFF 'The Ministry of Truth' in evocation of Orwell's visionary nightmare of official deception, *Nineteen Eighty-Four.*

Beyond the state lie powerful forces with their own interests in a government that can keep a secret (see chapter 17). When junior health minister Edwina Currie warned in December 1988 of the danger of salmonella in egg production, she angered the National Farmers' Union and was forced to resign. In 1993 it emerged that the government was holding back the names of five brands of soft drink known to have levels of patulin, a carcinogenic toxin, above the World Health Organization's safety level. To Maurice Frankel, director of the Campaign for Freedom of Information, this was another example of government succumbing to 'the unbearable temptation to work problems out in secret with industry' (*Guardian*, 11 Feb. 1993).

There is no shortage of some kinds of information, bland material likely to mislead, confuse and obscure. The civil service is a giant information processing plant, producing each week thousands of memos, answers to parliamentary questions, **white** and **green papers**, and streams of data on the state of society, the economy and the international situation *ad infinitum*. The creaking shelves of 'Government Publications' in any university library present precipitous mountain faces that only the most intrepid (or foolhardy) attempt to scale. Today a seeker after information can go to the government websites and download further voluminous official details at the click of a mouse (see p. 228). Yet all this can be seen as part of a legitimation process: much turgid material disgorged from the Whitehall intestinal tract has served to mask the true level of **official secrecy.**

Official Secrets Acts

Having enacted them in 1889, 1911, 1920, 1939 and 1989, Britain is extremely good at passing Official Secrets Acts. The most restrictive element in this corpus was for long the infamous Section 2 of the 1911 Act, which made it a criminal offence for *any* Crown servant to disclose without authorization *any* information learned at work. It was also an offence to receive such information and the claim that disclosure was in the **public interest** was no defence. Ironically, the 'public interest' is the basis upon which government itself justifies withholding information. Moreover, in the Ponting case the judge, following an earlier House of Lords judgment in *Chandler* v. *DPP* (1962), ruled that the public interest could only be defined by the government, thereby opening the door to political interpretation. The jury was not impressed and surprised many by acquitting Ponting.

Section 2 was a 'catch-all' provision or a blunderbuss: a civil servant could be imprisoned for disclosing the colour of Whitehall toilet paper. Originally intended as a form of press censorship, it was rushed through a Parliament fearing war with Germany. In 1971 it was reviewed by the Franks Committee which declared it 'a mess' (Franks 1972: para. 88). Yet for those wishing to keep things under wraps the 'mess' was extremely useful. Thus Sarah Tisdall, a Foreign Office clerk, was sentenced to six months' imprisonment in March 1984 for leaking to the *Guardian* information on the arrival of US Cruise missiles in Britain. As in the Ponting case, the prosecution appeared merely to be revenge for political embarrassment.

The 1989 Official Secrets Act finally laid to rest the infamous Section 2 but did little to open Whitehall's doors. No past or present employee of the security services could disclose anything about their work and there was no public-interest defence. Those charged under the old system would still have been prosecuted.

In another case, former MI5 officer David Shayler leaked information to a Sunday newspaper in 1997 revealing, amongst other things, that MI5 kept files on future Labour ministers and MI6 had been involved in a 1995 plot to assassinate Libyan leader Muammar Gaddafy. For a time he evaded prosecution by living in France, where a Paris court refused the UK's extradition request. He returned to fight his case in court but in September 2001 the Court of Appeal rejected his application to use a defence of public interest. However, it did recognize a need for some form of defence. In a landmark ruling, the court stated that a 'defence of necessity' should be allowed in cases where a person leaking information had no other choice in trying to expose wrongdoing, but it did not consider this to apply in Shayler's case.

Beyond Official Secrets Acts

The wall of secrecy contains more than official secrets acts. The Franks Committee reported sixty-one statutes criminalizing the disclosure of information but none punishing unnecessary secrecy. In addition, the thirty-year rule laid

"What rankles is that, after years as a civil servant, one has never been trusted enough to be put in a position from where, if one wished, one could have passed on state secrets."

Reproduced by permission of *Punch*

down in the Public Records Act consigns forty categories of government papers to the state vaults; the period during which they gather dust may be extended at the discretion of the Lord Chancellor. Another restrictive tool reached the front pages in the arms-to-Iraq affair, when Public Interest Immunity Certificates (PIICs) were issued to prevent the release of documents embarrassing to the government, even though they were vital to the defendants in the Matrix Churchill trial.

It might be expected that MPs would enjoy special rights to information. Indeed, a House of Commons Public Service Committee report (1996: para. 32) called upon the executive 'to provide full information about and explain its actions to Parliament'. However, armed with their Osmotherly rules (see p. 404), mandarins have kept their lips as well locked as their briefcases and filing cabinets in the face of scrutiny committees. In its section on ministerial accountability, the Scott Report on the arms-to-Iraq affair cited seven examples of ministers failing to give information, while an archaic practice was used to impede the Commons Foreign Affairs Committee's investigation of the shipment of arms to Sierra Leone in 1998. It could be argued that Parliament could compel disclosure through its power to punish for contempt, but this is impeded by party discipline.

Anthony Wright: Did ministers behave in ways that ministers ought constitutionally not to have behaved?

Sir Richard Scott: I have said so, yes.

Anthony Wright: Was Parliament denied information that Parliament constitutionally ought to have been provided with?

Sir Richard Scott: I think so, yes.

Sir Richard Scott answering Labour MP Anthony Wright before the House of Commons Public Service Committee (HC 313-III, 1995/6, paras 378–80)

Official secrecy and the media

Official secrecy legislation plays a major part in keeping things from the media. However, there is an additional means of controlling the reporting of matters pertaining to defence. Introduced in 1912 after the 1911 Official Secrets Act, it was an alternative to formal censorship, though its admirers call it 'responsible journalism'. **D-notices** are issued by a Defence Press and Broadcasting Committee, comprising representatives of the media and senior civil servants. For example, after the 11 September attacks in 2001, editors and broadcasters were asked to 'minimize speculation' about any forthcoming military action. However, although it has been used to hide establishment embarrassment, this non-statutory gentleman's club system has never been as useful to governments as the official secrets legislation. Indeed, during both world wars it was effectively suspended. With modern terrorist-type warfare and the rise of the internet and radio scanning, it can appear something of an Edwardian anachronism.

A further government control over journalists was the lobby system. Journalists stepping out of line and citing sources could have their membership cards removed. New Labour's reforms to this in 2002 made it even easier for awkward journalists to be avoided (see p. 408), and the art of 'news management' to be practised. Of course not all journalists are lobby hacks and Whitehall poodles. Some crusade in the cause of the unauthorized version and papers can rebel; the *Guardian* and *Independent* both withdrew from the lobby during the Thatcher years. Sometimes a more accurate account of events may be gleaned from maverick publications such as *Private Eye* and *Red Pepper*.

A la recherche du temps perdu: political memoirs

Political memoirs rarely threaten security yet the attempts to suppress them have been reminiscent of 'Carry On' films, the goal usually being to avoid embarrassment in high places. Probably the most important of these were the diaries of Richard Crossman (1975–7), published posthumously from his taped account of the Wilson government. Whitehall tried in vain to prevent publication and during the debate a further secret was revealed – the existence of unwritten 'guidelines' on memoirs, ruling out various subjects such as cabinet discussions and civil service advice. This gentleman's agreement entailed the cabinet secretary inspecting proposed memoirs. Despite objections, the Crossman diaries emerged and for the first time a full-blooded account of Whitehall life surfaced (Barberis 1996: 264). The *Spycatcher* case represents the apogee of memoirs furores, the government literally pursuing its prey to the antipodes. Here it was possible to argue that national security was involved because author Peter Wright had worked for MI5. However, the absurdity arose from the book's free circulation throughout the capitals of the western world while the po-faced servants of the Establishment were trying to conceal it from the eyes of their own people.

> What I wanted to do was to show Wilson that we'd got him and that we wanted him to resign.
>
> > Peter Wright, referring to a secret MI5 file on Harold Wilson in TV interview,
> > reported in the *Guardian* (14 Oct. 1988)

Memoirs or diaries were to become almost commonplace from Labour politicians, the chroniclers including Harold Wilson, George Brown, Barbara Castle, Tony Benn, Roy Jenkins, Denis Healey and Roy Hattersley. Conservatives also took up their pens, Alan Clark's uninhibited revelations in 1993 raising many eyebrows. Nigel Lawson's *View from No. 11*, detailing souring relations with his next-door neighbour, was to be answered with several autobiographical tomes from the ex-Prime Minister herself. By the 1990s, memoirs, often conveniently packaged for the party conference season and newspaper serialization, had become big business and critics lamented the sight of ex-ministers 'on the make'. With a few notable exceptions, the accounts were largely self-congratulatory and rather turgid, shedding little new light on the inner workings of government.

The lure of publishers' royalties has seen non-elected political figures also trying their literary talents. A memoir by former SAS chief Sir Peter de la Billière was followed by a flood of bestsellers by former troopers. However, the most astonishing case was that of former head of MI5, Stella Rimington. In fact, with no damaging revelations, *Open Secret* was something of a paean to MI5, but the code of secrecy was an article of faith and the one-time establishment insider found herself out in the cold. Detecting more than a whiff of sexism in her treatment, she told of her 'stiff bollocking' from Cabinet Secretary Sir Richard Wilson (*Observer*, 9 Sept. 2001).

A right to know: towards a Freedom of Information Act

If we look to other countries we find an emphasis not on the state's right to conceal but on the people's right to know. After the second world war, the UN declared this 'a fundamental human right'. Denmark, Sweden, Norway, France, Holland, Australia, Canada, Finland, New Zealand and the USA all passed laws giving a presumptive right of access to government-held information. Those wishing to withhold must make their case in the courts (Birkinshaw 1991). Calls for a British **Freedom of Information Act** have come from libertarian groups such as the Campaign for Freedom of Information (established in 1984) and Charter88. However, governments fought shy and private members' bills introduced in 1978, 1981, 1984 and 1992 met with little encouragement.

As an alternative came a feeble compromise, the 1977 *Croham Directive*, an attempt to encourage departments to publish the background information for major policy studies. With delicate irony it was itself a 'confidential' document and had to be leaked (Ponting 1986: 205)! One of its effects was an increase in official smoke-screening with uninteresting information. The Citizen's Charter initiatives of 1991, relaunched by New Labour as Service First in 1998, also made available some limited information on public services. In 1992, details of cabinet committees were finally released, followed by *Questions of Procedure for Ministers*. Ironically, this cabinet rule-book was updated by Blair in 1997 to strengthen his control over the dissemination of information by ministers (Hennessy 1998: 17).

In July 1993, prompted by judicial criticism over the Kirk Sancto case (a soldier's accidental death) and a private member's bill with wide all-party support, the 'Open Government' initiative was unveiled (Cabinet Office 1993). This included a code of practice to be policed by the ombudsman. Taking effect the following year, it offered more details on policy-making but contained many exemptions. People were offered information as consumers of services rather than as citizens (Raab 1994).

In 1997, the New Labour government incorporated the ECHR; Article 10 promised new rights to citizens and a white paper on Freedom of Information duly emerged in December 1997. This introduced an independent Information Commissioner with powers to compel official release and a new criminal offence of evading disclosure or destroying records. However, after this initial enthusiasm New Labour was to disappoint. Things did not augur well when David Clark, the responsible minister, became a casualty of Blair's first cabinet reshuffle, and freedom-of-information policy was transferred first to the Home Office and then to the Lord Chancellor's Department. A Freedom of Information Act, a considerably watered-down version of the white paper, finally entered the statute book in November 2000. Its passage was marked by much criticism from bodies such as the Campaign for the Freedom of Information and by a backbench revolt. It was condemned by the Public Administration committee for not creating a presumption in favour of disclosure (figure 15.5).

Categories subject to exemptions under the 2000 Freedom of Information Act

Information supplied by, or relating to, bodies dealing with security matters	Law enforcement	Health and safety
National security	Court records, etc.	Environmental information
Defence	Audit functions	Anything provided in confidence
International relations	Parliamentary privilege	Legal professional privilege
Relations within the UK	Formulation of government policy, etc.	Commercial interests
The economy	Anything prejudicial to the effective conduct of public affairs	Prohibitions on disclosure
Investigations and proceedings conducted by public authorities	Communications with the Queen, etc., and honours	

In addition there were exemptions on information accessible by other means or intended for future publication.

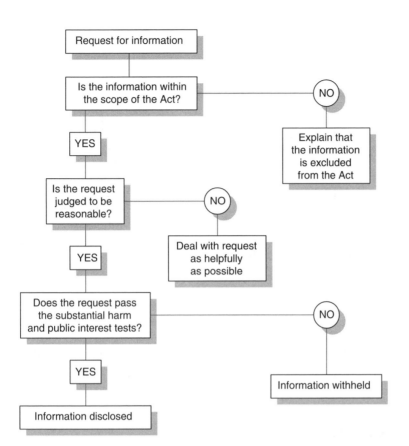

Figure 15.5
Processing an application under the Freedom of Information Act.

A principal point at issue was the draconian list of exemptions, apparently allowing government to conceal just about anything. Of particular concern was the restriction on information relating to policy formulation, thus denying the public knowledge of arguments surrounding decisions, and of advice given by officials advisers and interest groups that might have been consulted. Ministers and officials argued that openness here would inhibit frank discussion. A second bone of contention was the failure to give the Information Commissioner power to demand release on the grounds of public interest. Some limited concessions were gained but the government did not give way on any major point.

A measure of New Labour's true enthusiasm to inform was shown by obstructive behaviour on the part of several ministers in the face of demands for information (see p. 656). Elizabeth France, appointed as the first Information Commissioner, lamented that, despite the open government rhetoric, there was still a long way to go. Additional frustration came when the Lord Chancellor announced that the Freedom of Information Act would not become operative until January 2005. Infuriated critics noted that such legislation in Canada, New Zealand, Ireland and Australia had come into force within twelve months (Campaign for Freedom of Information 2001). Complaints came from a frustrated Elizabeth France, and in 2002 she announced her decision not to seek reappointment.

A right to tell: towards a whistleblower's charter

When public servants feel a government is compromising the public's right to know, what are they to do? In the USA a code of ethics enjoins officials to put loyalty to country above that to persons, party or government. However, the British 'good chap' theory of government denied any need for such checks. Yet from the 1980s confidence began to wilt as affairs such as Ponting, Tisdall, Westland, the Pergau Dam and Matrix Churchill highlighted the ethical dilemmas facing civil servants. The First Division Association (FDA) pressed for a US-style code and a reluctant government finally complied in January 1995, allowing any official faced with a crisis of conscience to appeal to a Civil Service Commissioner. Sir Michael Bett was appointed to the position and by June 1996 the FDA was pursuing several 'serious incidents' of allegedly improper ministerial conduct (*Financial Times*, 26 June 1996). Yet critics remain unsatisfied, arguing for a statutory whistleblowers' charter (Birkinshaw 1997). The issue also interested Lord Nolan, who argued in his first report on standards in public life that public servants should have a right to complain anonymously without going through the management structure.

Political public information

Government spending on advertising was planned to increase by twice the rate of inflation from £109 million in 1988/9 to over £120 million in 1989/90. Civil servants complained that they were encouraged to 'expound half-truths, produce dodgy material and leak in the Government's interest' (*Sunday Telegraph*, 2 April 1989).

A monarchical inheritance

The key to the informational constipation that seizes up the bowels of government is not restrictive legislation but the culture that has engendered it. State information belongs to the Crown not the people, the thirteenth-century Privy Councillor's Oath, lovingly preserved, making secrecy a constitutional rule. Such monarchical disdain permitted Cabinet Secretary Sir Robert (later Lord) Armstrong to boast in the Australian courts of his 'economy with the truth' and allowed minister William Waldegrave, in March 1994, to defend his position in the arms-for-Iraq affair by claiming it was at times proper to lie to Parliament.

Power in Whitehall: Obedient Servants?

The liberal constitution portrays politicians as being in charge in Whitehall; otherwise the whole edifice of democracy becomes a sham. Around the turn of the century German sociologist Max Weber, a liberal troubled by the decline of liberal culture, noted an inexorable trend in developed states:

> It is obvious that technically the large modern state is absolutely dependent upon a bureaucratic basis. The larger the state . . . the more unconditionally this is the case. (Weber 1978: 971)

Fearing a body politic trussed in red-tape he outlined a theoretical *ideal-type* bureaucracy recruited on merit, bound by impersonal rules and playing defined roles which resulted in a politically neutral, disciplined hierarchy under the control of the elected government. Apologists for the British system see in the civil service much of this model and Weber himself was one of its admirers.

The assumption behind the idea of an obedient bureaucracy is that there is a clear distinction between politics (**policy-making**) and administration (**policy implementation**). The **politics–administration dichotomy** underlies much writing on public bureaucracy and was enunciated in 1887 by Woodrow Wilson who, concerned about corruption in American public life, argued that administration should be divorced from political skulduggery. Yet the distinction is untenable in practice. In the first place, policy can only be made in the knowledge of how it will be implemented. Secondly, no public servant implements policy like a robot; all instructions must be interpreted in the light of particular circumstances. In other words, the policy is being modified. Finally, in their advisory relationships with ministers, the mandarins exert considerable influence at the epicentre of the policy-making process.

Individual ministerial responsibility

Lying at the very heart of liberal democratic theory, the doctrine of **ministerial responsibility** articulates the relationship between minister and department. Because they are elected, it is ministers alone who are *responsible* to the outside world (through Parliament) for departmental actions. Various corollaries follow: civil servants should not themselves speak publicly, they must remain anonymous and, when praise or blame is apportioned, it must fall on the minister who should, in cases of serious error, resign. In the words of the House of Commons Treasury and Civil Service Committee: 'Ministerial preparedness to resign when ministerial responsibility for failure has been established lies at the very heart of an effective system of parliamentary accountability' (1994: para. 133). A shining example of this was the resignation in 1954 of Sir Thomas Dugdale in the Crichel Down affair (see p. 653), in which officials had behaved improperly.

> My husband has saved your service from being torn to pieces.
>
> Lady Dugdale, to Head of the Civil Service Sir Edward Bridges after her husband's
> resignation. Quoted in letter from G. L. Wilde, Dugdale's principal
> private secretary, to the *Daily Telegraph* (20 May 1998)

However, despite its detailed exposition, the convention is largely illusory. Mandarins are increasingly to be found addressing the media, their roles overtly politicized, even their names becoming well known. Cabinet Secretary Sir Robert Armstrong found his a household word through his trials and tribulations in the *Spycatcher* affair, while his successor, Sir Robin Butler, hit the headlines variously: approving a £4,700 payment towards Chancellor Norman Lamont's legal costs for evicting a sex therapist from his London home, appearing before the Scott enquiry and even featuring on the BBC's *Desert Island Discs*. Not only named, they can also be blamed. In the Westland affair, Collette Bowe enjoyed an unsought hour of notoriety as an instrument in the devious political stratagem, her anonymity broken by Leon Brittan in attempting to protect himself (Birkinshaw 1988: ch. 4). In 1972, the governor of Holloway Prison was publicly rebuked by the Home Secretary for an 'error of judgement' in taking Myra Hindley for a walk. In 1996, Nicholas Soames blamed civil servants for not making him aware of research on Gulf war syndrome, and in September 1998 the BSE enquiry blamed senior civil servant Elizabeth Acridge for advising John Gummer to reject scientific advice to establish a computer base for tracking cows.

Moreover, ministers are loath to atone by accepting the loaded pistol. In the Maze Prison breakout case, Northern Ireland Secretary James Prior sweated it out, securing the resignation of the prison governor instead. When Lord Carrington took the honourable way out after the Foreign Office failed to foresee the Falklands crisis, he appeared a relic of another age. Indeed, he would be an exception in any age; Finer's (1956) classic study of cases dating from the mid-nineteenth century shows how rarely the convention is honoured.

Moreover, by the 1990s it appeared that ministers did not resign, even if *they themselves* were culpable. A key event was 'Black Wednesday' in September 1992 (see p. 516). After the humiliating collapse of his economic strategy and the loss of some £4 billion, Chancellor Norman Lamont continued his economic stewardship. In November 1994, the High Court condemned the giving of aid (£234 million) towards the Malaysian Pergau Dam project, which had been tied to arms deals, arms that might well be deployed against the very people supposedly being helped. Select committee investigation revealed that Foreign Secretary Douglas Hurd had ignored civil service advice that this was 'a very bad buy'. A politician of the old school, Hurd considered his position but in the end did not go. Even more surprisingly, no heads rolled after the Scott inquiry into the Matrix Churchill affair, despite direct criticism of Attorney General Sir Nicholas Lyell, whose actions could have sent innocent men to jail.

Centralizing power – decentralizing blame The agencification of the civil service had profound consequences for ministerial responsibility. The North-cote–Trevelyan structure – unified, hierarchical and rule-based – had been held to stand for integrity and probity against corruption. Critics found numerous problems in the new structure, including poor coordination, duplication, waste, institutional complexity, barriers to communication, information concealment, loss of experience, reduced public participation, impaired central coordination and ultimately loss of accountability (Rhodes 1994). In September 1997, with retirement looming, Robin Butler, Cabinet Secretary and head of the civil service, voiced his own concern at an Economic and Social Research Council conference that agencification 'obscures and blunts the democratic accountability of ministers' (*Financial Times*, 25 Sept. 1997). As in the case of the old public corporations, MPs found themselves frustrated by ministers refusing to answer questions on the grounds that they were no longer responsible. There is, however, an element of discretion in this; thus in May 1998 Home Secretary Jack Straw announced his willingness to answer prison questions.

In 1993–4 widespread criticism of the Child Support Agency resulted in the resignation not of a minister but of its chief executive. Even greater controversy arose over the Prison Service Agency (PSA) as riots, breakouts and problems over IRA prisoners led to buck-passing. The 1995 Learmont Report on the Parkhurst Prison breakout chronicled 'mind-numbing bureaucratic incompetence' (*The Times*, 18 Oct. 1995). Home Secretary Michael Howard, claiming the matter to be 'operational' and therefore not within his responsibility, promptly sacked PSA head Derek Lewis. Lewis protested that he was being scapegoated and that his operational independence had been undermined by detailed 'breakfast, lunch and tea' interference, including an insistence that the Parkhurst governor be sacked (*Guardian*, 18 Oct. 1995). (Home Office Minister Ann Widdecombe was later to substantiate Lewis's account.)

Ministerial responsibility appears to be in a state of crisis. For politicians, the question of resignation is determined by political expediency, not constitutional imperative. Generally those who go, do so not for accountability issues but for sexual peccadillos or personal impropriety, often destroyed by tabloid reporting. Mandelson's first departure was due to the undisclosed loan from Geoffrey Robinson, and the second to an indiscreet phone call in the Hinduja case. Where policy or administrative failings are exposed, an ability to 'tough it out', sometimes at the expense of civil servants, becomes a mark of government virility. Transport Secretary Stephen Byers hung on for a long time, despite worsening rail chaos, before being hounded out by the media in May 2002. Thatcher, Major and Blair all stood by colleagues against calls for resignation. At the same time, ministerial frankness before Parliament has come seriously into question.

Mandarins and ministers: 'Yes Minister'?

What of the relationship between mandarins and their political masters? Are they the compliant instruments of Her Majesty's Government? Some agree that they are. Attlee is a widely quoted apologist, always finding them 'perfectly loyal...That's the civil service tradition, a great tradition. They carry out the policy of any given government' (Williams 1969: 79). In evidence to the House of Commons Expenditure Committee (1977: para. 1877), Edward Heath avowed that in his experience civil servants were definitely all 'under ministerial control', while Harold Wilson declared that any minister unable to master his civil servants 'ought to go' (para. 1924). On gaining office, Richard Crossman confided to his diary:

> Now at last I was a Minister in charge of an important Department and I could take decisions [and] lay down the law. (Crossman 1976: 293)

'Yes Minister, but...' Yet there is reason to doubt the passive civil servant thesis since they have numerous advantages over ministers:

- highly educated, long experienced and street (or corridor) wise to the ways of Whitehall;
- with access to information and the ability to control its flow to the ministerial desk;
- well connected with powerful outside interests impinging on the departmental portfolio;
- armed with detailed historical knowledge of departmental policy;
- more numerous than the ministers and able to collude informally and in committees (of which there are hundreds) within and across departmental boundaries;
- with security of tenure;
- from the confident classes who assume a right to rule.

Moreover, even if blessed with the wisdom of Solomon and the strength of Hercules, the width of a departmental ambit means that no minister (or ministerial team) can possibly be aware of everything going on. Civil servants are thus indispensable: they give advice, answer parliamentary questions, write speeches, arrange meetings, draft memos and reports and generally organize ministers' lives.

It is not surprising, therefore, that an alternative body of evidence comes not from government publications or officially sanctioned memoirs but from exposés. Crossman's *Diaries* reveal how, from an initial state of euphoria, he was to feel he had, as if in a horror movie, sought refuge in the very room where the vampire was hiding; the accounts of his enervating battles with Permanent Secretary Dame Evelyn Sharp should not be read by those of a nervous disposition. Other chroniclers (Benn, Castle, Hattersley) give equally frank insights into bureaucratic power.

There are also civil servants who have come out of the bureaucratic closet. Brian Sedgemore, first a mandarin and then an MP, was uniquely qualified to illuminate the private world of public policy. From him we learn of the

> Victor, if you go on arguing with me I'm going to crawl under the table and chew your balls off.
>
> Denis Healey (Defence Secretary) to General Sir Victor Fitz-George Balfour
> (Vice Chief of the General Staff) in discussions on Northern Ireland;
> reported in Roy Hattersley, *Who Goes Home?* (1996: 80)

... arrogant and subtle way in which they dealt with ministers ... developing departmental policies which weak ministers could call their own, using delaying tactics, skilfully suborning powers of patronage that belonged to ministers. (Sedgemore 1980: 26)

For Kellner and Crowther-Hunt (1980) the mandarins were nothing less than 'Britain's ruling class'. Through these sources we enter a world making that of Sir Humphrey Appleby and Jim Hacker seem tame. A House of Commons Expenditure Committee report (1977: para. 137) confirmed that 'some departments have firmly held policy views ... When they are changed, the department will often try and reinstate its own policies through ... the erosion of the minister's political will'.

Politicizing Whitehall?

The power of civil servants was to produce a reaction from politicians and, from the early 1980s, much debate centred on the possibility that the service was becoming **politicized**. While there was no comparison with the US system, where an incoming president sweeps out thousands of officials in order to install a completely new team, significant changes were occurring.

One of us? Thatcher's radical agenda was to send tremors through Whitehall. She needed to break the legendary capacity to resist and began to take an unprecedented interest in senior appointments, asking whether, ideologically speaking, those due for advancement were 'one of us'. In this she was assisted by Cabinet Secretary Sir Robert Armstrong, with his additional role as head of the civil service. Prudent careerists recognized that 'if you can't beat 'em', there remained only one sensible thing to do. A salutary case was that of William Ryrie, a Treasury official with the misfortune to cross swords with Thatcher when she was leader of the opposition. Once tipped as a future cabinet secretary, his career was forever blighted (Richards 1996: 666). Ex-mandarin Lord Bancroft noted the rise in the Whitehall 'grovel count' (*Guardian*, 12 Nov. 1985) as monetarists and managerialists began to emerge from the closets. By the end of the decade, over two-thirds of the mandarinate had been newly appointed and critics feared politicization. Government defector Emma Nicholson (1996: 196), veteran of three ministries, noted in her memoirs how 'permanent secretaries can now lose their jobs so that a ministerial favourite can be brought in'.

Civil servants were even found doctoring figures by 'redefining' unemployment and directly falsifying returns (*Guardian*, 29 March 1997). In the Scott inquiry they confessed to drafting inaccurate, misleading and 'clearly wrong' ministerial replies. The run-up to the 1992 election saw NHS chief executive Sir Duncan Nichol publicly defending government health policy while attacking Labour. In 1994, the *Observer* (24 April) reported the Cabinet Secretary advising departments to avoid anything controversial until after the local and European elections. The civil service was becoming 'so close to party politics that lines were constantly being crossed over, even redrawn' (Nicholson 1996: 196).

> The Civil Service is slowly being destroyed. Unless the Government changes course, we'll go right back to the 19th-century days of nepotism, corruption and incompetence.
>
> John Sheldon (General Secretary of the National Union of Civil and Public Servants), quoted in the *Independent* (7 Nov. 1994)

Advising ministers The use of **ministerial advisers** is another way of countering civil service influence. However, in Whitehall they encountered a wall of impeccably polite intransigence. Only during the heat of two world wars did such 'outsiders' make any impression and they were quickly demobbed once normal service resumed. Economist Thomas (later Lord) Balogh, brought in by Wilson in 1964, found himself effectively frozen out. In 1970, Heath's team of businessmen encountered similarly cold pin-striped shoulders. The 1974 Labour government permitted cabinet ministers two advisers each but their experiences were also frustrating.

However, from the 1980s the climate changed. Advisers and think-tanks became as well known as the politicians they served, hard-line monetarist Alan Walters a familiar face on television screens. The new factor was determined Downing Street backing and the advisers began to turn the tables. The FDA made an official protest that even junior ministers were rejecting official advice, sometimes adding emphasis with the 'F word' (McKie 1994), and civil servants began to feel pressure to say what ministers wanted to hear (Plowden 1994). The privatization programme saw government turning outside the civil service to commercial consultants such as Price Waterhouse, their work seeing the light of day in the form of government white papers (Ward 1993). This could be seen as the privatization of policy formation.

> To give spurious intellectual justification to the Secretary of State's political prejudices.
>
> Maurice Preston's mock job description as adviser to Roy Hattersley, Secretary of State for Prices and Consumer Protection, in Roy Hattersley, *Who Goes Home?* (1996: 169)

The New Labour government welcomed much of the remodelled Whitehall architecture, including the use of political appointees. Although Robin Cook was prevented from appointing his mistress, by June 1997 Labour had fifty-three advisers paid from public funds, an increase on the Conservative's thirty-eight. The ethos of neutrality also came under attack. In February 2000, the Cabinet Secretary warned Alastair Campbell regarding comments about the Conservative Party. In the battle between the government and Mayor of London Ken Livingstone over the London Underground, an official in the Department of Transport, Local Government and the Regions (DTLGR) was moved by Jo Moore, adviser to Transport Secretary Stephen Byers, for refusing to take part in a campaign to slur Bob Kiley, Livingstone's transport expert.

The DTLGR soon found itself at the centre of an even greater controversy, which was to stand as a cautionary tale. At the heart of this was Jo Moore's infamous email of 11 September 2001, sent within an hour of the attack on the World Trade Center, and suggesting to civil servants that the tragedy could be used to bury 'bad news'. Despite widespread calls for her resignation, including one from Tony Wright, chairman of the Public Administration Select Committee, Byers continued to value her services for several more months.

The events left ill-feeling within the department and in February 2002 a leaked email from civil servant Martin Sixsmith, head of communications, suggested that Moore had wanted to slip out more bad news under cover of Princess Margaret's funeral. What followed was an imbroglio of intrigue, bullying and back-stabbing, drawing in Permanent Secretary Sir Richard Mottram and Downing Street. Claims by Byers that Sixsmith had resigned along with Moore in February 2002 were repudiated. While the Speaker cautioned MPs against use of the word 'liar', the minister later conceded that he had been 'misleading'. With the backing of the Prime Minister, Byers was able to resist immediate demands for his head, but he was a dead man walking towards resignation, which came in May 2002.

> **The black art of spin**
> It is now a very good day to get anything out we want to bury.
>
> Email from Jo Moore, 11 September 2001

Oh! Sir Humphrey!
We're all f*****. I'm f*****. You're f*****. The whole department's f*****. It's been the biggest cock-up ever and we're all completely f*****.

Permanent Secretary Sir Richard Mottram to a colleague during the Sixsmith–Moore affair, quoted in the *Sunday Times* (24 Feb. 2002)

When governments change

The left had long doubted civil service neutrality, Harold Laski arguing that it only appeared neutral because the political system never threw up radical governments of the left. He predicted that the civil service would be unable to serve under such a government. In the event the challenge came from the right, and throughout the Thatcher and Major years questions were asked as to how the civil service would be able to work with Labour afterwards. Would a set of hard-nosed free marketeers have to be pensioned off? Some claimed that the Rolls Royce neutrality was still intact. Robin Butler had declared: 'If my position wasn't acceptable to an incoming government that would weaken the tradition of impartiality' (Williamson 1995). In the Major government's eventide one ex-mandarin observed:

> No one at the moment . . . is going to waste time putting up a paper on trade union rights . . . But all a Labour minister will have to do is ask for a full range of options and they'll get them. (Timmins and Kampfner 1997)

In the event there were indeed some problems. The new mastery of public relations acquired by Labour in opposition left the official information service particularly exposed. Civil servants complained to the Cabinet Secretary about ministers politicizing press releases and eight press officers soon resigned. However, in ideological terms the coming of New Labour posed few problems since, in line with Laski's argument, the system had once again not thrown up a radically left-wing government. But there could be no guarantee that an incoming government would always share the agenda of its predecessor. At some point the proportion of outsiders could reach a level where 'the policy commitments of its senior figures will have made it unacceptable to the main alternative government' (Bogdanor 2001: 12). Indeed, Labour reached the end of its first term with seventy-five political appointees in place and, rather like the US system, all were paid off prior to the general election. They were back at their desks after the few weeks spent campaigning for the party (Pyke 2001), but many commentators felt the civil service to be undergoing a revolutionary change, albeit subtly manifested.

Managing the Mandarins: Reinventing Government?

Despite their backgrounds it does not follow that mandarins lean to the political right; the newer departments associated with the welfare state have a vested interest in its maintenance. Hence, a body of rightish thought (**public choice theory**) depicts bureaucrats as profligate users of public money, intent on enlarging their empires and 'over-supplying' their services (Niskanen 1973). The 1980s and 1990s saw attempts to curb this through a 'new public management' movement. The process was portrayed by ministers as 'reinventing government', following the title of a book by US authors Osborne and Gaebler (1992). Reform proposals began to strike at the foundations of Whitehall like Exocet missiles, the momentum maintained by the Office of Public Service.

Private lessons A major theme in civil service reform has been the belief that it can learn from the private sector. Such calls came from the 1961 Plowden

Report and the 1968 Fulton Report, and were exemplified by Heath's 'Selsdon Man' approach in 1970 (see p. 291), but all initiatives were skilfully neutralized by the mandarins, who preferred the intrigue of managing their ministers to the more prosaic task of managing their departments.

However, Thatcher moved with greater zeal on the **managerialism** front than any predecessor. Sir Derek Rayner of Marks and Spencer became head of an Efficiency Unit in 1979. He had already served as one of Heath's disillusioned businessmen and knew the wily ways of Whitehall. A system of 'scrutinies', with teams of young civil servants probing established practices, achieved more than any previous initiative (Hennessy 1990: 619). In the changing climate, the environment became inhospitable to traditional bureaucratic life-forms; at jolly parties at Number Ten, permanent secretaries learned to hold their views, like their vols-au-vents, close to their chests. In addition, management consultants were brought in at various levels. They did not come cheap. A report by the Efficiency Unit in August 1994 revealed Whitehall spending on consultants to have quadrupled between 1985 and 1990 to over £500 million. Critics were sceptical of the quest for efficiency, which seemed to threaten the traditional ethos of public service (Chapman and O'Toole 1995).

> Now, can you tell these bozos about the real world?
>
> Reported remark of Conservative minister to group of businessmen with reference to his civil servants, quoted in the *Independent* (17 July 1994)

Agencification: accountability or accountancy? A feeling that the Rayner reforms had not gone far enough led to a further report (Efficiency Unit 1988). Popularly known as the 'Next Steps' report, this presaged full-scale agencification (p. 462), a principle that had made limited impact, although it had been suggested in the Fulton Report. Although a structural change, part of a process of 'hollowing out' the state (Rhodes 1994), its essential purpose was managerial (Elcock 1991: 236–42). The new chief executives, on fixed-term contracts, were given considerable managerial freedom. They were able to introduce performance-related pay and short-term contracts; civil servants were to be 'deprivileged'. Yet critics argued that democratic government imposed restrictions on the extent to which public-service managers should be granted autonomy (Elcock 1991: 188).

Culture shock: bringing in talent The Northcote–Trevelyan reforms had centralized recruitment through an independent Civil Service Commission. However, in 1991, in a seismic challenge to Whitehall culture, the government abolished this for some 95 per cent of appointments. Recruitment was to be conducted by the departments and agencies themselves, although they could engage the services of a newly created Recruitment and Assessment Service, which retained responsibility for fast-stream recruitment. Amidst heated controversy, the agency went on to be privatized in 1996 as Capita Group plc. Describing this as 'the sale of an ethos' (*Guardian*, 20 Dec. 1995), ex-mandarin Lord Bancroft mobilized 124 peers to defeat the plan in the Lords, while academic Richard Chapman (1996) saw both 'tragedy and farce' in a profound government disregard for civil service ethical values.

The outcome was a variety of terms and conditions of employment, with private-sector-style contracts. Only the top echelons successfully resisted the change (see below). There was also a drive to recruit from the private sector. By 1999, some 25 per cent of senior posts were being advertised and this was expected to rise to 35 per cent (Cabinet Office 1999a: 30). Critics saw this as another prong in the attack on the tradition of political neutrality (Bogdanor 2001: 12).

Market-testing: reinventing or abandoning? A further Efficiency Unit report led to a white paper (Treasury 1991) introducing '**market-testing**'; civil servants had to compete with private firms for the work they had already been doing. Thatcher had earlier argued that agencification was an alternative to privatization, and those just settling into agency life felt demoralized. Moreover, the Treasury and Civil Service Select Committee noted that in 1992/3, £768-million worth of activities out of the £1.119 billion subjected to market-testing was contracted out without any in-house bid having been allowed (*Independent*, 25 Nov. 1994). By 1996 the process had eliminated some 34,800 posts (*Civil Service Statistics* 1996: 8). One American computer company, Electronic Data Systems, reached the point of controlling more than half the government's IT services (*Guardian*, 10 April 1997). The minister responsible argued that 'the government's job is to steer not to row' (Hencke 1992). One bizarre consequence was a proposal by the Ministry of Defence in January 1996 to sell off Admiralty Arch. Critics feared constitutional landmines in the path ahead: private contractors, anxious to win or keep contracts, would lack motivation to question government policies in the national interest. It was suggested that this was not reinventing government but abandoning it (Painter 1994).

Modernizing government In 1999, the Labour government published its *Modernising Government* white paper (Cabinet Office 1999b). Claiming to be as radical as the Next Steps programme, it outlined developments for the next ten years, continuing the theme that private-sector management was the recipe for public-sector improvement. Next came the Wilson Report (1999) from Cabinet Secretary and Head of the Civil Service Sir Richard Wilson. Repeating the private sector mantra, it recommended leadership, business planning, performance management and the employment of more outsiders. *The Times* (16 Dec. 1999) detected a smoke-screen for greater politicization. Others feared an erosion of permanence and unity and dilution of the public service ethos (Greenwood et al. 2002: 91).

Plus ça Change: Room at the Top

At the beginning of the twenty-first century, Britain's civil service appeared to stand at a crossroads, its traditions of neutrality, permanence and anonymity in question. The boast that Whitehall provided a 'model for the world' had become less credible. The increased use of advisers invites comparison with the French *ministerial cabinet* system, political appointments and career advancements suggest some leaning towards the US spoils system, while agencification is redolent of the Swedish bureaucratic structure.

However, in a constitution moulded through evolution rather than revolution, the idea that the architecture of the central state can be 'reinvented' in less than two decades invites caution. Did the reforming hurricanes whistling along the corridors of power penetrate the closed offices of the mandarinate at the very heart of the state? Radical ministers such as Michael Heseltine had certainly wanted to shake up this elite world with short-term contracts, market-testing and large-scale appointments from outside on the 'revolving door' principle.

However, after much fevered consultation the Efficiency Unit (1993) produced the Oughton Report on recruitment to the top three grades. This was to prove a 'classic civil service holding operation' (Theakston 1995: 154) in which the mandarinate would survive as a 'Senior Civil Service' of around 3,500, encompassing posts at grade 5 and above. There would be no market-testing or privatization and, although accepting some opening of top appointments to national competition (Michael Bichard came from local government to head the Benefits Agency, moving in 1995 to become permanent secretary at the Department of Employment), the service would continue to 'grow its own timber'. Little change was heralded in the white paper *The Civil Service: Continuity and Change* (Cabinet Office 1994a), which showed more enthusiasm for the former than the latter, and a review of fast-stream recruitment (Cabinet Office 1994b) declared that this gilded staircase, renamed the Policy Management Programme, should remain. In February 1999, a little-publicized written answer announced that the management of the programme would return from Capita to the Whitehall fold (see Chapman 2000).

Employing the reasoning of public choice theory, Dunleavy (1991; see also Dowding 1995) accounted for the outcome with a 'bureau-shaping model'. In conditions of financial restraint, rather than maximize their empires, senior officials will try to shape their own bureaux as small agencies, removed from the actual delivery of policy and insulated from the chill winds of cuts. The paradoxical implication of this was, as Andrew Marr noted (*Independent*, 14 July 1994), that the mandarins' interests came to coincide with those of anti-statist politicians. The mandarins had dug their heels in as they had over all previous reforming initiatives and avoided the fate they had visited upon hundreds of thousands of their more lowly colleagues. The nineteenth-century model of the mandarinate has survived two world wars and the Keynesian revolution. It remains a limb of a formidable Establishment and, despite bold words from reformers, it is not time to write its obituary.

Key points

- The civil service is a key part of the executive, headed by the elected government through a system of ministerial posts.
- The modern service was born in the mid-nineteenth century, when the bourgeoisie used their new political and economic power to gain control of the state.
- Civil servants are said in liberal-democratic theory to be permanent, politically neutral and anonymous. All these features can be critically questioned.
- The mandarin class has traditionally enjoyed a significant role in shaping policy.
- Studies have demonstrated that the bias in favour of the public school and Oxbridge candidates deliberately sought in the nineteenth-century reforms has been broadly maintained.
- Whitehall has for long been characterized by secrecy. Reforms are slow.
- Despite their social backgrounds civil servants are not necessarily right wing and have a considerable stake in the welfare state.
- The 1980s and 1990s saw some major assaults on the traditional Northcote–Trevelyan model with agencification and managerialism. However, at the elite pinnacle the mandarinate emerged largely unscathed.
- The Labour government of 1997 did not have a radical agenda and, as before, found little problem in working with the service as it found it.

Review your understanding of the following terms and concepts

agencification
bureau-shaping model
bureaucracy
bureaucratic power
Citizen's Charter
civil servant
D-notice
Freedom of Information Act

managerialism
mandarin
market-testing
meritocracy
ministerial adviser
ministerial responsibility
official secrecy
policy implementation

politics–administration
   dichotomy
public choice theory
public interest
Senior Civil Service
specialist and generalist

Assignment

If you are able to do so, visit the Public Record Office at Kew (a short walk from Kew Gardens underground station). Locate the Cabinet Minutes (Conclusions) section and look up reference CC(63)39 relating to the meeting held on 20 June 1963. Locate agenda item number 3 on the Resignation of the Secretary of State for War. Answer the following questions.

		Mark (%)
1	What is the affair under discussion?	5
2	Why can this assignment not refer to the minutes pertaining to a recent event such as, say, the 11 September attack?	5
3	Why are the cabinet minutes referred to as 'Conclusions'?	20
4	How far do you feel that this account captures the true flavour of the stormy events under discussion? Seek out some contemporary press reports to assist you.	40
5	What objections to a select committee inquiry does the Cabinet raise? To what extent do you think these are justified?	30

Questions for discussion

1 How useful is it to characterize the world of Whitehall as a village?
2 What factors lead to the view that civil servants will tend to dominate ministers in their professional relationship?
3 'Individual ministerial responsibility is a convention honoured more in the breach than in the observance.' Discuss.
4 How did the Northcote–Trevelyan reforms reflect the power structure of nineteenth-century British society?
5 Examine the constitutional and administrative implications of civil service agencification.
6 What might be the long-term effects of introducing a 'spoils system' for appointing top civil servants in Britain?
7 Discuss the pros and cons of ministers using personal advisers.
8 Discuss whether the composition of the civil service should reflect the demographic profile of the country at large.
9 Explain the nature and causes of secrecy in British government.
10 What developments lead to the assertion that the British civil service is becoming politicized?

Topic for debate

This house believes that the model of the British civil service is no longer able to meet the needs of the modern state.

Further reading

Barberis, P. (ed.) (1996) The Whitehall Reader.
Short readings from academics, politicians and officials, giving various angles on debates, both current and perennial.

Crossman, R. H. S. (1975–7) *Diaries of a Cabinet Minister.*
Published posthumously, this frank account forced the establishment door a little further open.

Elcock, H. (1991) *Change and Decay: Public Administration in the 1990s.*
Sustained critique of the quest for efficiency, effectiveness and economy in the public domain. Latter half contains extracts from key sources.

Fry, G. K. (1995) *Policy and Management in the British Civil Service.*
Lively approach to the civil service, giving a scholarly summary of basic information, and with a critical edge.

Greenwood, J., Pyper, R. and Wilson, D. (2002) *New Public Administration in Britain.*
Details the anatomy of the British state with authority, while remaining accessible.

Hennessy, P. (2001) *Whitehall,* 2nd edn.
Revised edition of a classic study, which shows how the grey men of Whitehall must be of central interest to political scientists.

Hoskyns, J. (2000) *Just in Time: Inside the Thatcher Revolution.*
Raging attack on alleged obstructionism, negativity and complacency of the Whitehall mandarins by one of Thatcher's managerial evangelists.

Mallalieu, J. P. W. (1941) *Passed to You Please.*
A short early polemic against overweening officialdom, with a penetrating introduction by Harold Laski.

Osborne, D. and Gaebler, T. (1992) *Reinventing Government.*
Work by US authors inspiring (or justifying) much British civil service reform.

Page, E. (2001) *Governing by Numbers: Delegated Legislation and Everyday Policy Making.*
Delves into the almost hidden world of delegated legislation and notes how junior ministers, mid-ranking civil servants and pressure groups can exert great influence behind the headlines.

Rhodes, R. A. W. (ed.) (2000) *Transforming British Government, Volume 1: Changing Institutions; Volume 2: Changing Roles and Relationships.*
Monumental and definitive product of a five-year ESRC study to map the changing contours of the UK central state.

Rhodes, R. A. W. and Weller, P. (eds) (2001) *The Changing World of Top Officials: Mandarins or Valets.*
Illuminating comparative analysis puts the Whitehall mandarins in a wider context.

Rimington, S. (2001) *Open Secret.*
Memoir by the ex-head of MI5.

Rogers, A. (1997) *Secrecy and Power in the British State.*
Argues that state secrecy perpetuates elite rule.

Theakston, K. (1995) *The Civil Service Since 1945.*
Concise account of the period, demonstrating the ability of the mandarins to thwart the reformers most of the time.

Theakston, K. (1999) *Leadership in Whitehall*.
Very readable portraits of nine 'Sir Humphreys' of Whitehall. Notes how they work and how times changed during the twentieth century.

For light relief

E. M. Forster, *A Passage to India*.
A study of English manners, arrogance and racism in the Indian Civil Service.

J. Lynn and A. Jay (1981) *The Complete Yes Minister*.
Edited version of the television series. Perhaps not as astonishing as the real thing in the form of the Crossman *Diaries*, but shorter. Also available on video.

Giacomo Puccini, *Tosca*.
More corrupt officialdom, set to music.

William Shakespeare, *Measure for Measure*.
Corrupting effects of high office as a state official uses power to seek sexual favours.

C. P. Snow, *Corridors of Power*.
While some find passion in action and sex, Snow finds it in the ambitions and memos of the men in pin-striped trousers. Title added a term to the English language.

On the net

http://www.ukonline.gov.uk
The starting point for a vast amount of government information, with links to all departments and agencies, but beware of those spin doctors (see p. 228).

http://www.civil-service.gov.uk/index
There's no shortage of information about the civil service, from statistics to career opportunities.

16

Getting and Spending: the Politics of Public Expenditure

It is impossible to understand politics without appreciating the financial dimension. Much of the controversy around who gets what, when and how in society comes down to questions of money. The Chancellor of the Exchequer, the keeper of the nation's purse, is the second most powerful cabinet figure and the prime minister is formally titled First Lord of the Treasury. This chapter has four main sections. After examining the nature of public expenditure and its associated institutions, we consider the processes involved, including the fixing of public spending levels, the raising of money and the public accounting process. Next we note how public expenditure has been used as an instrument of economic management within the capitalist economy. The final section assesses the extent to which the approach to public expenditure can be seen as a factor contributing to Britain's post-war pattern of economic decline.

The Nature of Public Expenditure

At its simplest, **public expenditure** is the money used by the agencies of the state in its multifarious operations from waging war to emptying the nation's dustbins. Its absolute level is beyond intuitive grasp – total government spending for 2001/2 was in the region of £392 billion; almost 40 per cent of gross domestic product (GDP – the total annual output of the economy). The lion's share is raised through taxation, supplemented with borrowing and trading enterprises. Since 1994 the government has also sponsored a national lottery to raise money for sport, the arts and charities, though this is run by Camelot, a private, profit-taking company, rather than the state (making it unique within Europe). Thus the state draws money from society, passes it from one agency to another, and

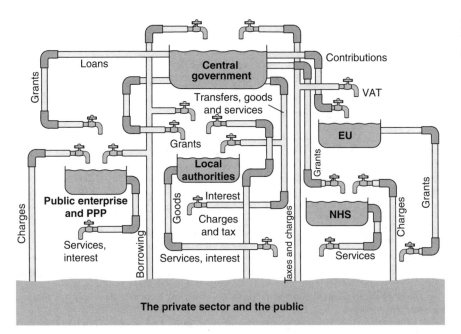

Figure 16.1
The flow of public expenditure.

returns it to society as services and grants in a complex network of financial flows (figure 16.1).

Public expenditure can also be thought of more philosophically as an expression of community – one of the most important factors in our survival on earth. A polity is cemented by public expenditure: ensuring national security, preserving its culture and guaranteeing social rights through welfare policies. The collective nature of our psyche is denied by *individualists*, who object if the richer are taxed to assist the poorer. Margaret Thatcher even asserted that 'there is no such thing as society' (Kingdom 1992). From this stems much heated political debate concerning relative priorities (figure 16.2). Although centring on technical, dry-sounding processes, this leads to decisions affecting the quality of all our lives.

> No man is an Island, entire of itself; every man is a piece of the Continent, a part of the main.
>
> John Donne (English poet), *Devotions* (1624)

Trends in public expenditure

Public expenditure grew inexorably throughout the twentieth century, a ratchet effect ensuring that gains during emergencies were never fully relinquished afterwards. Until the first world war it had stood at around 15 per cent of national income, but by 1918 had climbed to over 50 per cent, stabilizing at around 25 per cent through the 1920s and 1930s. The second world war exerted further pressure, driving it up to 75 per cent, and it subsequently settled at around 35 per cent from 1950 until the mid-1960s. At this point further dramatic growth occurred, both in real terms and as a percentage of the GDP, peaking in 1975 at 48 per cent, a time of economic crisis when the IMF

Figure 16.2
Public support for
government
expenditure in
various policy
areas, 1985–1996.

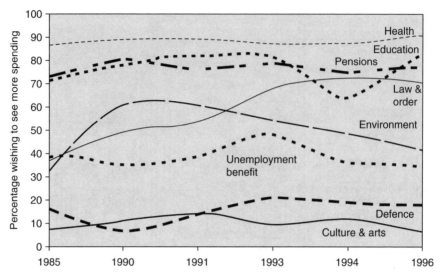

Note: The figure shows the percentage of respondents thinking that there should be more spending in each particular area.

Source: Data from *Social Trends* (1998: 121).

demanded cuts (see p. 513). By the late 1980s it had fallen, to stabilize around 40 per cent, where it has remained to the present.

The institutions

Although expenditure concerns all aspects of government, its control lies with two of the most powerful state institutions – the Treasury and the Bank of England.

The Treasury Originally the Keeper of the Royal Purse, Her Majesty's Treasury stands closest to power both geographically and functionally. Its political head, the Chancellor of the Exchequer, is the prime minister's next-door neighbour in their much-sought-after terrace. Controlling almost every sinew of the body politic, its permanent secretary, along with the cabinet secretary, reigns supreme in Whitehall.

The Treasury employs the best and brightest of the mandarinate, working in various sections specializing in the spending of particular departments. Notwithstanding its overweening importance, it is a small and intimate department of just under a thousand staff, its ambience creating a tightly knit community. An aroma of politics pervades each committee meeting and each informal exchange in the fabled corridors of power. Personal relationships constitute key channels of communication; trust between colleagues is cemented over long acquaintance and counterpoised with mistrust and suspicion of outsiders. Within this village, orthodoxies emerge as unchallengeable wisdom, contributing to a 'Treasury view' – a set of attitudes towards policy and the proper medicine for this or that malady – which will tend to influence all decision-making in Whitehall and Westminster. Despite the enhanced importance of the Cabinet Office, the Treasury has managed to retain much of its hegemony, able to go beyond conventional economic management to exert a profound influence on policy in areas such as social security, education and health (Deakin and Parry 2000).

The good Treasury man is an able amateur... He relies on ability to argue, to find internal contradictions, to pick out flaws in arguments whose substance he has not fully mastered and whose subtleties he can only be dimly aware of.

H. Heclo and A. Wildavsky, *The Private Government of Public Money* (1974: 60)

Who are those with such dominance? They are called the 'Treasury men', a very special breed. Although their work sounds technical, they have been by tradition dilettantes *par excellence*, hand-picked from the very cream of civil service applicants, often with no specialized knowledge of economics, accounting, or any of the policy areas in which public money is spent. Even within the Treasury the average time spent in any particular policy area is but a fleeting two years, so that they 'are clearly exposed to little danger of losing their amateur status' (Heclo and Wildavsky 1974: 65). Apologists will argue that the reason the Treasury men can move so lightly between policy areas is their renowned Rolls Royce minds; they are the exotic orchids of the Whitehall hothouse, cultivated in the fertile soil of Oxbridge.

The Bank of England The Treasury often works in collusion with another formidable institution which, although not part of the civil service, lies at the heart of the governing establishment. Nationalized in 1946, the Bank remains formally autonomous, nestling away from Whitehall as 'The Old Lady of Threadneedle Street' in the bosom of the historic square mile forming the City of London. Its appearance as a veritable palace, served by pink-coated flunkeys, is appropriate, for in the political life of the country its role is indeed regal.

This is the government's bank, holding its account and with a prime responsibility for implementing financial policy. On the domestic front it acts as the government's agent, managing the note issue and the national debt. In international matters it is similarly close to government, dealing in foreign currencies and maintaining the value of the pound, buying and selling gold, and engaging in international discussion on financial and trade policy. It also stands at the centre of the nation's financial community. As the central bank it is the bank of banks, holding the cash reserves of the clearing banks, providing facilities that an ordinary customer might expect from the High Street bank and acting as a channel of communication between them and the Treasury.

Yet despite its overwhelming importance to the nation, the Bank has never been a passive servant of government; on the contrary, it has often appeared the master, effectively shaping policy through its advice. It can even be seen as a pressure group, using its relationship with the Treasury on behalf of the banking sector against industrial capital and pressing its preference for high interest rates (Marsh and Locksley 1987: 223). In addition, the legendary secrecy of the British state is here amplified by the claims of necessary confidentiality, keeping out any prying eyes from Parliament, the media and even the government. Generally, what is known about the Bank is what it wants to be known, information being purveyed through its own carefully edited publications. Some light was allowed in when, in April 1994, Chancellor Kenneth Clarke agreed to the publication of the minutes of his monthly meetings with Governor Sir Edward George. These revealed considerable tension between the two, with the Chancellor resisting interest rate rises.

Given this enormous power, one must ask who is in control and whether they are likely to be responsive to the needs of society. The Bank is formally under a Court, consisting of the governor, a deputy governor and sixteen directors, twelve of whom are supposed, in a quasi-democratic manner, to represent various interests throughout society. However, they come overwhelmingly from the white male establishment galaxy, with public school–Oxbridge backgrounds and top jobs in multinational giants and the world of high finance. One token trade union representative sits like the timid dormouse at the Mad Hatter's tea party. The New Labour government promised to make the Court more widely representative.

The governor is a key figure, even grander than the head of the Treasury, moving in the world of the most powerful, feted by millionaire capitalists, delivering speeches declaiming his views and theories, conferring with government and in times of crisis exerting a domineering presence. Despite the dignity surrounding the office, the position is profoundly political. The Wilson government learned very soon of this power. In its first year of office, being unpopular with the financial sector, it suffered in the face of malicious speculation against the pound, and Lord Cromer demanded that the government, notwithstanding its manifesto commitments, make all-round expenditure cuts. Wilson records:

> In January 1965...I told him that Government expenditure was committed far ahead; schools which were being built, roads...were part-way to completion... Was it his view, I asked him, that we should cut them off half-finished...The question was difficult for him, but he answered, 'Yes'. (Wilson 1974: 62)

The political salience of the position was recognized by Thatcher, who brought in Robin Leigh-Pemberton, chairman of National Westminster Bank, an overtly political appointment of an 'outsider' resulting in considerable furore (Keegan 1984: 197–8). In 1993, after two stormy five-year terms, he was replaced by his deputy, Eddie George, known as 'steady Eddie' because of his cautiously monetarist views (*Guardian*, 23 Jan. 1993).

When Gordon Brown acquired the keys to Number Eleven in 1997, some major changes were made. With the line between banks, securities firms and insurance companies becoming blurred, limitations in the regulatory competence of the Bank had been humiliatingly exposed in two major banking scandals: the collapses of BCCI and Barings Bank. Supervision of the commercial banks was given to a new City 'super regulator', based on the Securities and Investments Board. The Bank also lost the job of managing the government stock to the Treasury (*Financial Times*, 22 May 1997). However, it gained a crucial new responsibility: while the Chancellor would continue to set inflation targets, interest rates would be set by the Bank, to reflect expert assessment rather than political expediency. Meeting monthly and taking decisions by majority vote in the Bank's committee room, overlooked by a portrait of Sir Montague Norman (a legendary but eccentric governor from 1920 to 1944), a nine-person Monetary Policy Committee led by the governor makes the decisions, which are also scrutinized by the Treasury Select Committee. There is, however, a political advantage from the Bank's independence: it relieves chancellors of responsibility.

The purposes of public expenditure

Intuition suggests that the purpose of state expenditure is, like that of a household, to finance its activities. Figures 16.4 (p. 510) and 16.6 (p. 515) show how this can take two forms: providing services and redistributing income through transfer payments (table 16.1) to individuals (say pensions or student grants). Another purpose is less self-evident and has no analogue with family budgeting. The colossal scale of state finance means that government is able to use its taxation and spending muscle to influence the economy in what is termed **fiscal policy**. When post-war governments have made their getting and spending

Table 16.1 Income redistribution through taxation and benefits

	Poorest 20% of households	Richest 20% of households
Original income	£2,430	£41,260
Benefits	+ £4,910	+ £1,200
Income tax, national insurance and council tax	− £1,130	− £10,480
Indirect taxes	− £1,930	− £5,090
Value of benefits in kind (NHS, education, etc.)	+ £3,950	+ £2,310
Final 'income'	£8,230	£29,200

Source: Data from *Social Trends* (1998: table 5.20). Figures are averages per household in each category.

decisions, economic objectives have been as much in their mind as the services the money is to fund. The following sections consider these two purposes in more detail.

Paying for the State

In figure 16.1 (p. 497) a number of taps interrupt the financial flows, and a key question considers whose hands are on these. The issue has been at the heart of British constitutional history and remains at the epicentre of modern political debate.

Controlling public expenditure: developing the machinery

We saw in chapter 12 how public expenditure was the key to increased parliamentary control over the executive. The sovereign's crown was hollow without funds, and as Parliament became the effective payer of the piper it sought to call the royal tune. By the time of Elizabeth I it had acquired a control over taxation that was to be consolidated in the Glorious Revolution of 1688. Since then, Parliament has remained nominally in control of public finance, although as we are about to discover, today this is seen as largely a fiction.

" Oh, Mabel, is it not dreadful ?   What a miserable place to bring up such a lovely dog !"

Source: Mary Evans Picture Library

> [The capitalist bourgeoisie] has accomplished wonders far surpassing Egyptian pyramids, Roman aqueducts, and Gothic cathedrals...It draws all nations into civilisation...has created enormous cities...rescued a considerable part of the population from the idiocy of rural life...and...has created more massive and more colossal productive forces than have all previous generations together.
>
> Karl Marx, *The Communist Manifesto* (1848: ch. 1)

Further important reforms came in the 1780s under the stimulus of Pitt and were intended to simplify public accounting and strengthen parliamentary control. Of particular significance was the creation of the Consolidated Fund in 1787, amalgamating a complex muddle of accounts into one, into which all state revenue would flow and from which all expenditure would be drawn. This is in effect the government's bank account and is lodged with the Bank of England. The modern system of public finance is largely a nineteenth-century invention, fashioned by the industrial bourgeoisie as part of its greater creation – the liberal-democratic state set in the capitalist economy.

> The public be damned. I am working for my shareholders.
>
> William Henry Vanderbilt (1821–85; US millionaire railway owner), refusing to answer a reporter asking questions on behalf of the public

The Protestant work ethic and the ethos of parsimony When the early capitalists acquired wealth, they did not use it extravagantly like the merchants and landowners of old but, like Dickens's Ebenezer Scrooge, tended towards frugality. In this way they could invest in yet more capital and amass wealth quite beyond their needs for personal survival. The cumulative effect was to consolidate the position of the capitalists and their families, who formed an increasingly dominant class. The importance of this was stressed by sociologist Max Weber, who attributed it in large measure to religion – to Protestantism and Calvinistic puritanism. The Protestant work ethic, in Weber's view, explained the ascendancy of capitalism in Western Europe by adding religious zeal to the lure of profit. This parsimony was to inform the approach to public expenditure. The prime goal was to become that of Victorian prudence – a *balanced budget* as advocated by Mr Micawber.

> Annual income twenty pounds, annual expenditure nineteen nineteen six, result happiness. Annual income twenty pounds, annual expenditure twenty pounds ought and six, result misery.
>
> Mr Micawber in Charles Dickens's novel *David Copperfield* (1849–50)

Against this background, the key figure in a series of rigorous reforms was Gladstone who, as Chancellor, determined that government finance should be as tightly controlled by the bourgeois paymasters as were their own prudently managed businesses. The aim was to evolve a system that would tax capitalists' profits as little as possible, taking just enough to keep open the trade routes and contain the potentially unruly masses at home. The system was conceived in terms of an annual cycle that would balance expenditure and taxation.

The Gladstonian cycle

> It is the mark of a chicken-hearted Chancellor when he shrinks from upholding economy in detail... He is not worth his salt if he is not ready to save what are meant by candle-ends and cheese-parings in the cause of the country.
>
> W. E. Gladstone, quoted in F. W. Hirst, *Gladstone as Financier and Economist* (1931)

Through Gladstone's reforms Parliament was (nominally) given the kind of control over the economy that a Victorian husband would want over his family, overseeing three basic housekeeping functions:

1 granting of prior approval to planned expenditure (the estimates process);
2 considering the ways and means of raising the sum required (the budgetary process);
3 checking that all past expenditure had been conducted in a proper manner (the accounting process).

Prior approval: who gets what, when, how in Whitehall?

Supply procedure of the House of Commons: flogging a dead mouse? In constitutional theory the Crown asks for Supply and the House considers whether to grant the amount requested or allow only a reduced level; it would never gratuitously offer to increase it. Today of course the Crown means the government ministers. The position suited the parsimonious founders of the liberal state, and eighteenth- and nineteenth-century reforms saw the examination of the Estimates (of the year's expenditure) consuming much House time, with each departmental vote being moved separately and amendments to reduce even small items. Between 1858 and 1872 the Estimates were reduced seventeen times. Yet despite talk of a golden age this period was tantalizingly brief, the process soon becoming little more than ritual. Government majorities could generally override all opposition and debates were used not to scrutinize the Estimates but to criticize policy. Governments ceased to care which Estimates were debated and allowed the choice of topic to pass to the opposition.

> In prehistoric times there might have been some [parliamentary] control over the expenditure but there certainly has not been in my parliamentary experience.
>
> Arthur Balfour (Conservative prime minister) in 1905, quoted in Heclo and Wildavsky, *The Private Government of Public Money* (1974: 242)

Some reformers were unhappy and attempts to strengthen the House's role in expenditure matters included the creation of an Estimates Committee in 1912 (replaced with a Select Committee on Expenditure in 1970). Following the 1961 Plowden Report, a Treasury-inspired Public Expenditure Survey (PES) process aiming to consider expenditure and the anticipated level of resources was instigated. This was intended to produce major debates on expenditure white papers looking five years ahead. However, from the first the debates fell flat, the process not inaccurately described in the House as 'flogging a dead mouse' (Heclo and Wildavsky 1974: 199–251). The Procedure Committee decided that evolved practice represented the wishes of the Commons and in the early 1980s Supply Days became Opposition Days, with three days reserved for discussion of the Estimates with topics selected by the Liaison Committee.

Does this mean that departmental spending decisions escape the ears, eyes and teeth of any constitutional watchdog? The answer is 'No'. A key instrument in the eighteenth- and nineteenth-century reforms was the Treasury, which became accountable to the Commons for all departmental expenditure. At first its authority increased hand in hand with that of Parliament but, as the latter waned, the Treasury star rose; by the mid-nineteenth century it was no longer the junior partner.

Whitehall: blood on the carpet Beneath the charm and courtesy of the Whitehall 'village' there is, as in Agatha Christie's St Mary Mead, an undercurrent of gossip, competition, mistrust and sublimated violence. 'Who gets what' is the purpose of the interdepartmental battle, and allocating funds is 'the most pervasive and informative operation of government' (Heclo and Wildavsky 1974: xii). From the early 1960s the Treasury remit was extended to the full range of public expenditure, including the NHS, nationalized industries and local government.

A process of negotiation entails a protracted series of 'bilaterals' between each department and the Treasury, having more in common with a north African *souk* than a rational decision-making process; yet the outcome is nothing less than the policy of Her Majesty's Government. The bilateral nature of the encounter is very significant, enabling the Treasury to 'divide and rule', and there is often blood on the carpet as mandarins and ministers fight their corners. Much of the haggling is done by the Chancellor's second in command, the Chief Secretary to the Treasury. A glimpse into this taut world was offered in 1994 by the leaking of a letter from Chief Secretary Michael Portillo to Michael Heseltine, President of the Board of Trade, strongly attacking his spending (*Guardian*, 30 July 1994). Arbitration comes from a 'star chamber', a powerful cabinet committee on Public Services and Expenditure (PSX) containing one-third of the Cabinet itself.

Treasury power increased under formidable New Labour Chancellor Gordon Brown. In 1998 he introduced his Comprehensive Spending Review (CSR) by which he hoped to end the annual infighting. Less of an innovation compared with the PES regime than government propaganda claimed, this would set Departmental Expenditure Limits (DEL), plans rigidly fixed for three years ahead. Negotiations with the department would no longer be in terms of what money was wanted, with only a hazy notion of how it would be used. They would focus on 'outcomes' and departments would have to argue on the basis of what they planned to do with the money. The result would be agreed 'performance service agreements' (PSAs) upon which they would be judged by the Treasury and the PSX cabinet committee. In addition, to discourage rash spending at the end of each year, departments would be allowed to carry surpluses over into the following year. The Treasury also set up interdepartmental committees to consider expenditure (such as crime reduction) not falling within any one department. Certain expenditures, not easily subject to DELs, remained as Annually Managed Expenditures (AMEs). The result of the CSRs are announced in the July of the appropriate year; the first came in 1998, covering the period 1999/2000–2001/2, the second (for 2001/2–2003/4) in 2000, and the third (for 2003/4–2005/6) in 2002. Each has a one-year overlap with its predecessor.

However, the reforms could not be expected to eliminate cut-throat competition. Indeed, the prize was now the bigger one of a three-year financial commitment. In the run-up to the first review, Brown was reported as incensed by Foreign Secretary Robin Cook's unwillingness to make savings to enable more spending on education and welfare (*Sunday Times*, 24 May 1998). In early 2002, the blood ran from the carpets of Whitehall onto the streets when Brown pre-empted colleagues with a prior public announcement that the NHS would be his top spending priority, prompting retaliatory speeches stressing the need for spending on defence, crime, education, and so on. In the event, the July 2002 review made generous provision for other services as well, with education the biggest gainer. The role of the Chancellor in allocating funds in this way thus puts him in effective command of most government activity, making him a formidable rival to the prime minister.

The budgetary process: who pays what, when, how?

The second operation in the control cycle entails raising the money – the **budgetary process** – through various forms of taxation (see figure 16.4; p. 510). Constitutionally the government's right to tax must be renewed by Parliament annually; this is why the Chancellor presents the Budget. Taxation may be direct or indirect.

Direct taxation falls upon individuals or organizations. This includes inheritance tax (on assets left after death), capital gains tax (on profit made in selling certain assets) and corporation tax (on company profits). Most important is income tax. Introduced in 1799 as a temporary measure to fund war against France, it has become a keystone of the system, a rise of 1p in the rate netting some £1.6 billion a year. Direct taxation can be used to redistribute income in the manner of Robin Hood; when a greater proportion is taken from the rich than the poor the system is termed 'progressive'. National Insurance contributions are also effectively a direct tax, which means the true income tax rate is higher (and less progressive) than it appears.

Indirect taxation is tied to goods and services and includes excise duties levied on items such as alcohol, tobacco and petrol. VAT falls across a wide range and is the best known (part of the take goes to the EU). Although rates on commodities can vary (some are zero rated), they fall equally on all, regardless of means, and are therefore 'regressive'. Thus a move from direct to indirect taxation favours the rich.

Although the bulk of taxation is levied by Westminster, the Scottish Assembly has limited powers, as do local authorities (chapter 19). In the latter case there has been much central interference through capping and reform. The poll tax, though direct, was a regressive tax, but its replacement, the council tax, being tied to property values, has a more progressive character. Although the national lottery (figure 16.3) is not a tax, the heavy odds against winning have led some to declare it a tax on stupidity! The proceeds going to 'good causes' count as general government revenue, available to reduce public borrowing (see below) and finance capital projects. In 1997 the Labour government began using some of this for certain items of NHS expenditure. With an estimated 90 per cent of adults having played and around £94 million spent weekly, it has been acclaimed a success.

The budget The budget is prepared over the course of the financial year deep in the bowels of the Treasury by high-powered committees. Although working below the level of the public eye, the door is opened to thousands of interest groups. The proposals are embodied in the Finance Bill and the Chancellor, with the aid of a private secretary and various experts, drafts the Budget Speech – the focal point of Budget Day. Parliament gives automatic approval to the proposals, though days of debate follow and the Finance Bill proceeds upon a ritualistic voyage through Parliament.

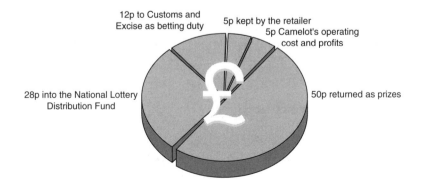

12p to Customs and Excise as betting duty

5p kept by the retailer

5p Camelot's operating cost and profits

28p into the National Lottery Distribution Fund

50p returned as prizes

Figure 16.3
Where each pound spent on a lottery ticket goes.

Convention permits Chancellors alcoholic refreshment during their speech, a privilege
not extended to other MPs. Denis Healey drank brandy, Sir Geoffrey Howe took a gin
and tonic, Nigel Lawson a mixture of wine and Malvern water but austere Scot Gordon
Brown chose mineral water.

Ostensibly, the reason for budget secrecy was market sensitivity. In 1947,
Hugh Dalton inadvertently divulged information to a lobby journalist on his
way to deliver his budget speech and later resigned. However, the traditional
period of *purdah*, when Chancellors retreated behind a veil of silence, has been
largely abandoned. Indeed, in an age of media manipulation, eve-of-Budget
leaks have become almost *de rigueur*. A substantial part of the 1996 Budget was
leaked to the *Daily Mirror*, although it was not published. Under Gordon
Brown the veils of secrecy were seemingly discarded. In March 1998 he gave
a pre-Budget interview and by 2002 he was outlining much of his Budget policy
in speeches to business leaders.

The budget and politics In practice, taxation is used for a variety of politically
motivated purposes, including redistributing income, curbing pollution, influencing behaviour (e.g. reducing smoking or car use), regulating the economy
and offering election bribes. Conservatives have proclaimed themselves to be
the party of low taxation while Labour has endured a tax-and-spend reputation. The eighteen years of Conservative government from 1979 were partly
sustained by judicious pre-election Budgets. Yet overall taxes did not fall. In
1978/9, the year before Thatcher took power, tax revenue was 34 per cent of
GDP; in 1994/5 it was 36 per cent. However, there had been a significant shift
from income tax to indirect taxation. This is the key. Although perhaps the
fairest, income tax is visible and unpopular. Hence New Labour fought the
1997 election promising no rises; one of its leading figures, Clare Short, was
sternly reprimanded for suggesting that people like her should pay more. Only
the Liberal Democrats promised to increase income tax (to go towards education). However, Labour's 1998 Finance Bill contained a novel feature designed
to prevent future Chancellors offering pre-election goodies: a Code for Fiscal
Stability. This entailed the 'golden rules' that borrowing should only be for
capital investment and the ratio of public debt to GDP should be kept at a
'prudent' level. In the 2002 Budget, Labour effectively broke its self-denying
ordinance on income tax by raising national insurance contributions to fund a
massive increase in NHS spending.

Calling the executive to account

Finally there is the accounting process, checking that the money has been used as
Parliament formally agreed. In 1861 Gladstone established one of Parliament's
most effective scrutiny instruments, the Public Accounts Committee (PAC).

Budget bites

In a media era Chancellors have adorned their Budgets with titles.

Nigel Lawson (1983–9)
1987 A Budget for Success
1988 A Tax Reform Budget
John Major (1989–90)
1990 A Budget for Savers
Norman Lamont (1990–3)
1992 A Budget for Recovery
1993 (March) A Budget for Sustained Recovery and a
     Budget for Jobs
Kenneth Clarke (1993–7)
1993 (November) The Budget of a Responsible
     Government

1994 A Budget for Jobs
1996 A Budget for Lasting Prosperity
Gordon Brown (1997–)
1997 (July) Equipping Britain for Our Long-term Future
1998 (March) New Ambitions for Britain
1999 Building a Fairer Society
2000 Prudent with a Purpose: Working for a Stronger
     and Fairer Britain
2001 Investing for the Long Term
2002 The Strength to Make Long-term Decisions:
     Investing in an Enterprising, Fairer Britain

Its membership of around fifteen specialist MPs reflects party balance in the House but the chair is always taken by a prominent member of the opposition.

Since 1866 it has been assisted by a unique constitutional figure, the Comptroller and Auditor General (C&AG), a servant of Parliament with the twin tasks of regulating the release of funds from the Consolidated Fund and auditing the departmental books. In 1983, the C&AG's department became the National Audit Office (NAO), its remit extended beyond Whitehall to other public bodies, such as the NHS. Local government comes under the supervision of the Audit Commission.

In 1996/7 the C&AG and his staff of 750 audited 465 accounts covering over £500 billion. Any department or organization which has its accounts 'qualified' by the NAO – there were twenty-eight in 1996/7 – may be investigated by the PAC, which has the power to call ministers and civil servants to explain themselves. The PAC has claimed many scalps. Headlines were prompted in September 1993 when it reported on an inquiry criticizing the royal family for lavish spending of £20 million of taxpayers' money on royal palaces.

Problems with the audit The PAC has the advantage of enjoying the goodwill of the Treasury, its parsimonious concerns making it more accommodating to requests for information than is customary towards select committees. However, it would be a mistake to conclude that the watchdogs are unfettered.

The contracting out of many services to the private sector and creation of thousands of quangos create a zone of public expenditure which the NAO cannot reach. In addition, the Audit Commission lost the right to monitor opted-out schools, which appoint their own auditors. Moreover, wasteful turf wars are fought between the NAO and the Audit Commission. For example, the former audits the Metropolitan Police and the Department of Health, while

Figure 16.4
Getting and
spending: receipts
and expenditure
(general
government
spending), 2001/2
(pence in every
pound).

Receipts

28   Income tax

8   Corporation tax

16   National Insurance
contributions

2   Stamp duties

16   VAT

6   Fuel duties

4   Alcohol and
tobacco duties

7   Other taxes, royalties
and duties

5   Business rates

4   Council tax

1   Interest and dividends

5   Gross operating
surplus and rent

−1   Other items and
adjustments

Expenditure

13   Education

19   Health and personal social
services

3   Transport

1   Housing

3   Environmental services

6   Law & order

6   Defence

1   International development

3   Trade & industry

2   Agriculture, fisheries,
food & forestry

1   Culture, media & sport

28   Social security

4   Central administration
& EC payments

6   Debt interest

4   Accounting &
other adjustments

Source: Data from *Public Expenditure Statistical Analysis 2002/3* (Cm 5401: table 3.6) and *Public Finances Databank* (April 2002; table C4; accessed via www.hm-treasury.gov.uk).

the latter looks at local police authorities and NHS trusts. The departmental performances with respect to the new three-year PSAs also escape parliamentary scrutiny, and the Treasury Select Committee has pressed for a role in monitoring outcomes. The committee also called for more information on the PSAs and for the involvement of the NAO (HC 485, 1999/2000), a call resisted by the Treasury, wishing to retain ownership of the PSAs.

The NAO itself comes in for criticism. The PAC has complained that it is too chummy with departments, never publishing a criticism without first obtaining Whitehall approval. Indeed, although Parliament's position was somewhat strengthened by being given a voice in the appointment of the C&AG, all have been former mandarins and, although they consult the PAC, the choice of inquiries is entirely theirs. In 1992 the C&AG persuaded the PAC chairman to suppress an NAO inquiry into allegations of bribes to secure a £20 billion Al Yamamah arms deal with Saudi Arabia, leaving committee members furious. Hence, the PAC often has to rely on whistleblowers and journalists for evidence of wrongdoing. Only after a series of parliamentary questions did the NAO begin to investigate the Pergau Dam affair, four years after the event.

Indeed, the NAO appears somewhat old-fashioned in style. Some argue that it should be modernized along the lines of the US General Accounting Office and made to serve Parliament as a whole rather than just the PAC (*Economist*, 10 July 2000). It can be contrasted unfavourably with the Audit Commission (see p. 621), which is more confrontational in its relations with those it audits. Public finance expert Tony Travers argues that the regime should resemble that of the rail regulator and should not be afraid to court public controversy (*Public Finance*, 19 Nov. 1999).

Who audits the auditors? Finally there is the question of auditing the auditors. The NAO's budget is approved annually by a Public Accounts Commission of nine MPs, while the Audit Commission is subject to the oversight of the NAO, but in practice this has never gone beyond a cursory glance. The PAC has argued that the Audit Commission should report to parliamentary select committees rather than to ministers (*Economist*, 10 July 2000).

The cycle of control established by Gladstone, modified, supplemented and criticized, has tenaciously survived. Has it proved adequate for the needs of the post-war era? We examine this in the following section.

Managing Capitalism

The national economy is the totality of a myriad of purchases, sales, borrowings, investments, decisions, promises and contracts that people make in their daily and corporate lives. To the classical economists (see p. 30) it was a delicate mechanism that governments should leave well alone. Expenditure on welfare, for example, would disturb the balance by reducing people's incentive to work and (through taxation) would eat into the profits needed to fuel enterprise. Hence public expenditure was seen as a necessary evil to be limited at all times.

Despite an embryonic welfare state, this cheeseparing approach survived into the twentieth century; indeed the inter-war years are sometimes called a golden age of Treasury control. Economic depression resulting from the failures of capitalism enabled it to practise a firm **monetarist** policy (controlling inflation by limiting the quantity of money in the economy) and keep down public expenditure in the belief that industry and world trade could only flourish if there was confidence that the currency would hold its value. Yet the depression persisted, threatening the state's legitimacy. The classical economists had argued that unemployment would automatically correct itself by precipitating a fall in wages, which would restore the demand for labour. Yet although wages fell, unemployment persisted. With the spectre of the Russian revolution and the 1926 General Strike, Marx's prophecies of inevitable crisis, culminating in the collapse of capitalism, gained ominous plausibility.

Rescuing capitalism: the coming of Keynes

However, an alternative diagnosis and prescription was offered by John Maynard Keynes, appearing like a knight in armour as the saviour of capitalism. In his *General Theory* (1936) he argued that, contrary to the Gladstonian view, **macroeconomic** budgeting for the state was not the same as the microeconomic budgeting of firms or households. Constantly aiming for a balanced budget was inappropriate and potentially harmful to the economy and employment.

Keynes refuted the classical economists' view that the free market would automatically eliminate unemployment. Left to itself it could reach a point of equilibrium (where aggregate supply equalled aggregate demand) *below* full capacity, thereby creating unemployment. The economy rested upon the fragile flower of confidence; falling wages, far from restoring full employment, would have the opposite effect. Less could be bought, less would need to be made, would-be entrepreneurs would lack the confidence to invest in new projects and, in a downward spiral, more jobs would go. The slumps of the inter-war years seemed ample verification of the theory.

The solution was for the state to step in where private investors feared to tread. Government should use public expenditure as a means of increasing the level of aggregate demand (**demand management**), spending money on public works such as roads and hospitals. The effect would be to stimulate demand throughout the economy, with more roads requiring more materials, machinery and so on, in a multiplier effect. Of course, if the government financed its expenditure by increasing taxation there might be no increase in aggregate demand because citizens' expenditure would fall. However, it could be financed by borrowing from those citizens with savings who were afraid to invest, creating a *budget deficit*. Alternatively, in times of prosperity a *budget surplus* could be created by reducing expenditure while raising taxes, to repay the national debt. This strategy had the momentous implication that the hallowed goal of the *balanced budget* would no longer be sacrosanct.

Although Keynes was scorned, the experience of the war years seemed to confirm his theories. Massive government expenditure on arms virtually erased unemployment and there was also an enormous increase in direct government intervention in various walks of life. In the dark days of war, politicians made a raft of welfare state promises.

The years of plenty: the Treasury loses its grip

Hence the post-war decades of the long boom of western capitalism saw public expenditure used for the quite new purpose of managing the national economy: stabilizing the trade cycle and maintaining full employment. In addition, key industries were brought into state control by nationalization (see chapter 18). Forceful spending ministers were able to push through costly programmes with no necessary fiscal implications. Moreover, in the expanded welfare state, people did not appear to mind paying more taxes. It seemed that the boom would last for ever; the capitalist economy could be permanently protected from its own propensity to crisis. Although Britain was still a capitalist country, the market was no longer forbidden territory to the state and the nineteenth-century Treasury ideals were rendered anachronistic.

The principle of economic management was further advanced in 1961 with the establishment by a Conservative government of a National Economic Development Council (NEDC – known as Neddy). A consultative body embracing labour, capital and government, this was a timid entry into the area of **economic planning** and corporatism (see p. 544). In 1964, the Wilson government created a purpose-built Department of Economic Affairs (DEA) to usurp the Treasury's role and work with Neddy.

The restoration of the Treasury However, with the end of the long boom (see p. 90), the 'hidden hand' of Adam Smith began to push up his creaking tombstone. Inflation reached an alarming 24.7 per cent in 1975, but unemployment, defying the Phillips Curve (which postulated an inverse relationship between the two), continued upward. The state appeared unable to service its existing debts and the concerted call from the IMF, the City, the financial markets, the Governor of the Bank of England and the media pundits was for a return to the Victorian principles (Keegan 1984: 88). The cry came echoing back from Whitehall, where the Treasury stood like a rock emerging glistening beneath the retreating Keynesian tide.

In 1975 Labour Chancellor Denis Healey was obliged to turn humiliatingly to the IMF for large-scale loan support. It came with strings attached; he was forced to exert further controls over the money supply, cut public spending, trim public borrowing and raise interest rates (which reached a record 15.5 per cent). In 1976 James Callaghan measured up the corpse of Keynesianism for the Treasury undertakers in his fateful declaration to the Labour conference: 'We cannot now, if we ever could, spend our way out of a recession'. Monetarism was on the agenda before Thatcherism became a word in the economic lexicon.

Public expenditure under Thatcher: the end of Keynes

When Margaret Thatcher took up residence in Downing Street, Treasury control in the Victorian sense experienced its rebirth. Despite the years of plenty, and the global nature of the crisis, the view was that Keynesianism had failed. While Labour had reluctantly relinquished the economic reins, the New Right government dropped them with relish as it 'rolled back' the state. Collectivist tendencies gave way to individualism, balancing the books became the key budgetary consideration and public expenditure was again to be regarded as a necessary evil. In the Treasury, Keynesians were hunted like medieval witches, prudent young bureaucrats quickly deciding that they had really been closet monetarists all the time (Ponting 1986: 102).

Applying monetarism The policy differed from that prescribed by monetarist guru Milton Friedman. He argued that the level of public expenditure and taxation did not have an important effect on the economy; the key was to control the rate of increase in **money supply**. However, the Thatcherite agenda also had moral and social goals, including a particular determination to reduce union power and cut welfare state expenditure. The initial strategy had two broad thrusts: controlling the money supply and, preferring the advice of Polonius in *Hamlet* that 'borrowing dulls the edge of husbandry' to that of Keynes, reducing the **public sector borrowing requirement** (PSBR). The PSBR could be seen as increasing money supply and causing **inflation**. Moreover, money borrowed by government was not available to the private sector where, contrary to Keynes's view, it would be used more productively.

The failure of monetarism Yet monetarism did not work as promised. The average growth of M3 sterling (a measure of money supply) was actually higher in the period 1979–85 than it had been at any time under the previous government. At the same time, there was a huge loss of industrial capacity and a high price to be paid in terms of unemployment (figure 16.5). Until 1984, investment and output were actually below 1979 levels, and their subsequent climb was

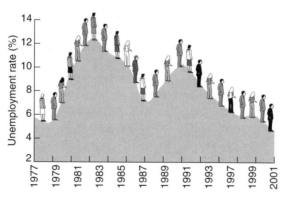

Figure 16.5
Unemployment
trends, 1977–2001.

Source: Data from *Annual Abstract of Statistics* (various years).

> The major tenet of free market economics – that unregulated markets will of their own accord find unimprovable results for all participants – is now proved to be nonsense.
>
> Will Hutton (neo-Keynesian economist), *The State We're In* (1996: 237)

sluggish, well below the OECD average. The balance of trade moved adversely and the growth in the economy actually went into reverse in 1980 and 1981; it was never significantly better than that of rival economies (*Guardian*, 29 May 1987).

By 1985, the Chancellor had effectively abandoned monetarism. Target-setting gave ground to the use of *interest rates*, which were increased to hold down money supply by decreasing borrowing and encouraging saving. Paradoxically, public expenditure rose each year throughout the 1980s as cuts in infrastructure spending and services were counterbalanced by increased welfare, health and social security costs caused by unemployment and poverty (Mullard 1997: 272). Income support for the unemployed dwarfed all other categories, reaching almost £45 billion in 1987/8 (figure 16.6).

With tax reductions and easier access to credit, Chancellor Nigel Lawson was able to engineer a consumer boom in the economy, which helped the Conservatives win the 1987 general election. However, the balance of payments plunged into deficit from mid-1987 as a decimated productive base at home sucked in imports. By 1989, Britain was running its largest ever trade deficit.

Wednesday's child is full of woe Throughout the crisis years a time-bomb had been ticking in the form of the drive towards European economic and monetary

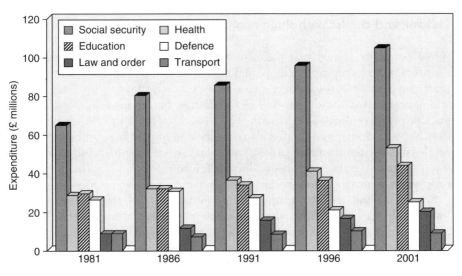

Figure 16.6 Public expenditure for selected policy areas, 1981–2001.

Source: Data from *Social Trends* (1998: table 6.20) and *Public Expenditure Statistical Analysis* (Cm 5401: table 3.6).

union. Although Britain had remained outside the exchange rate mechanism (ERM), business leaders felt that floating exchange rates left them at a grave disadvantage and the City, most economists and the opposition parties favoured entry. Chancellor Nigel Lawson agreed and, from the mid-1980s, had pursued a covert policy of 'shadowing' the Deutschmark; a kind of DIY ERM membership. Unneighbourly tension between 10 and 11 Downing Street led in October 1989 to Lawson's resignation over Thatcher's refusal to sack her economic adviser Alan Walters, who declared the European monetary system 'half-baked'. Finally Thatcher conceded that sterling would enter when 'the time was ripe'. The 'right time' arrived under new Chancellor John Major in October 1990, the eve of the Conservative Party conference.

In the event the time was to prove quite wrong. With Britain experiencing rising inflation, a large balance of payments deficit and heading towards recession, the pound entered at an unsustainably high level. Efforts to hold sterling's value (including high interest rates) proved disastrous to the economy. This atmosphere of panic drove Conservative MPs to the astonishing butchering of their leader (see p. 294). Ironically, her replacement was the very man who had taken Britain into the ERM. Tumultuous events were to follow.

Selling of overvalued sterling by foreign-exchange speculators saw the Bank of England frantically buying in an effort to protect its ERM position. The doomed rescue operation cost some £18 billion and the government's economic strategy was entirely discredited on 16 September 1992 as Britain made an ignominious withdrawal from the ERM, a day to enter political demonology as 'Black Wednesday'. The PSBR, which had actually gone into a surplus of £15 billion in 1988/9, sank into a deficit of £50 billion in 1993/4, forcing post-election tax increases and high political cost.

Labour and the 'stakeholder economy'

Neo-Keynesians argued that the neoliberal era had elevated selfishness and distorted business priorities; companies aimed to grow not by increasing investment, innovating or expanding markets, but by swallowing up rivals. The willingness of shareholders to sell to the highest bidder forced companies to put short-term returns above growth. The weakening of the unions, leading to a 'flexible' workforce, had created a vast wasteland of part-time and temporary employment without worker protections. Market-testing introduced insecurity into private and public sectors at all levels (Hutton 1996: 327). Tougher rules on unemployment benefits recalled the harsh Poor Law reforms of 1834. A furore over the 'fat cats' heading the privatized utilities, their remuneration linked to share prices, highlighted new levels of income inequality. All had taken place against a background in which direct taxation had been made much less progressive (figure 16.7) and greater weight placed on indirect taxation.

Labour rhetoric in opposition echoed much of the critique, and Tony Blair began to refer to the 'stakeholder society' – in which the business and financial communities accept social obligations towards their employees and society at

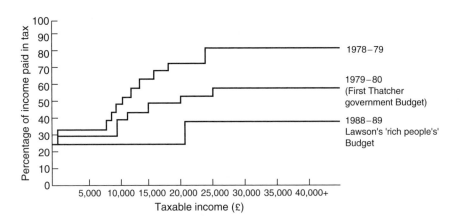

Figure 16.7
The changing income tax profile during the 1980s.

large, as well as to shareholders (see Kay 1993; Hutton 1996: ch. 12). Upon coming to office in 1997 New Labour quickly declared its intention to reverse the EU Social Chapter opt-out, legislate for a minimum wage and breathe new life into a number of corporatist-style bodies (see chapter 18).

However, keen to appear respectable in the eyes of the City, policy soon revealed much continuity with that of the immediate past, Gordon Brown's Budgets betraying little nostalgia for Keynesianism. Stressing the fight against inflation and tight restraints on public spending and borrowing, he revealed a Gladstonian passion to 'balance the books' and adhere to his 'golden rules'. Policy on capital expenditure breathed new life into Major's Private Finance Initiative (see p. 579). There was to be no renationalization, no change in the balance between direct and indirect taxation, and a pledge to stick to Conservative spending targets for the next two years. The widening gap between rich and poor was no longer seen as a problem. A 'Welfare-to-Work' scheme aimed to promote a work ethic.

The global factor

This chapter has explored some of the mechanics of public finance and the government role in the economy. However, as chapter 4 explained, the economy of the modern nation-state is located within a global economy, which imposes strict limits on the ability of governments to control or manage. Decisions by transnational corporations and financial institutions such as the World Bank can thwart the designs of a Chancellor of the Exchequer. Defining events such as the Suez crisis, the IMF loan and Black Wednesday all testify to the might of economic forces beyond national control. Two particular factors cast shadows over Labour's second term: the events to become known as 9/11 and the delicate question of the eurozone.

11 September Prior to the fateful day in 2001, three factors were already troubling the global economy: the end of the hi-tech dream with crashing dot-com shares, rising oil prices and interest rate increases. For the UK there was also the foot-and-mouth crisis, threatening both agriculture and tourism. The attack on America was worsening what was already a precarious situation.

Within Britain Gordon Brown faced his sternest test. A MORI poll showed economic optimism at its lowest level since the recession of 1980 (*The Times*, 27 Sept. 2001). Yet while City analysts expected the worst, figures published in early 2002 by the Office for National Statistics demonstrated that the economy had defied the sharpest downturn in the world outlook in 20 years. It had continued growing for nine and half years, by far the longest expansion in the post-war period, placing Britain at the top of the G8 growth league, comfortably above the 2.25 per cent forecast by the Chancellor. Considerable buoyancy had come from robust growth in the services sector, offsetting the downward drag from manufacturing. Industry leaders saw as a key factor the freedom given to the Bank of England and its prompt action (Denny 2002). In what could be seen as a sea change in British politics, Brown had gone a long way to making Labour a party that industry could trust. Yet the cost of success was growing mistrust from trade unions (see pp. 549–50).

A single European currency: a fistful of euros The granting of Bank independence had another important aspect: it brought Britain into line with EU partners and reflected Maastricht Treaty requirements for joining the eurozone. This latter promised to be the biggest economic decision Britain would make in the post-war era, with considerable limitations on any government's ability to manage the national economy. When eleven of the EU partners formally adopted the euro on 2 May 1998, Gordon Brown set five economic tests that should be met before the government would hold a referendum and recommend a 'Yes' vote. Many pundits declared the tests largely meaningless and based on imponderables, and ministers Peter Hain and Charles Clark

Heads or tails? No euros please, we're British

Photo: European Parliament

The five economic tests

1 Would joining create better conditions for firms making long-term decisions to invest in the United Kingdom?
2 How would adopting the single currency affect our financial services?
3 Are business cycles and economic structures sufficiently compatible for Britain and other EU members to live comfortably with euro interest rates on a permanent basis?
4 If problems emerge, is there sufficient flexibility to deal with them?
5 Will joining help to promote higher growth, stability and a lasting increase in jobs?

---

intimated that ultimately the decision was political rather than economic. However, prospects of a referendum concentrated minds and demanded that people take sides.

Within the main parties only the Liberal Democrats were unreservedly enthusiastic. While Tony Blair was positive, his Chancellor remained cautious. Other supporters included the Foreign Office (with an instinct to seek membership of any prestigious international club), the Treasury (since joining would pose no direct threat to taxation powers), the unions (seeing advantages in a 'social Europe' in the prevailing neoliberal climate), the CBI (recognizing the trading benefits and the reality that some 70 per cent of business legislation already came from Brussels), the City (doing a huge amount of business in the dollar and yen and not wishing to be left out in the cold) and finally the Celtic fringe (seeing the possibilities of increased independence as thriving statelets).

Mainstream Conservatives opposed the euro, with Hague campaigning for the 2001 general election on a 'Save the Pound' slogan. His replacement, Iain Duncan Smith, as a leading Eurosceptic was no less implacable in opposition, while from the sidelines Thatcher's antipathy grew more shrill. Horrific scenarios were painted by some members of the party, evoking visions of neo-Nazi domination. Beyond the Conservatives, opponents of entry included Sir Edward George, fearing relegation to branch-manager status. Arguably the most important factor was global media mogul Rupert Murdoch, owner of *The Times* and the mass-circulation *Sun*, who stood to lose out under a powerful pan-European regulatory regime with its desire to limit cross-media ownership. Blair's warm words on the launch of the euro at the June 1998 Cardiff summit earned the *Sun* headline: 'THE MOST DANGEROUS MAN IN BRITAIN'. Not surprisingly, opinion polls at the time showed a large majority with no love for the new currency. However, in Labour's second term there were signs of change. One straw in the wind was a BBC *Panorama* debate on 24 March 2001 that invited viewers to vote on the question: 'Should Britain enter the euro in this parliament?' With 45 per cent saying 'yes' and 48 per cent saying 'no', the result was surprisingly close.

No euros please, we're British: debating the single currency

The case for

A single currency eliminates the considerable expense of currency transactions, facilitates comparisons between costs in different countries and eases travel. By removing the temptation of competitive devaluations it can inspire business confidence, stability and growth over time. Without the possibility of devaluations, firms are forced to keep costs, wages and prices down to remain competitive, thereby reducing inflationary pressure. Currency speculation and the nightmare of Black Wednesday are ruled out. The euro will in all probability develop into a reserve currency rivalling the dollar. There are also political implications, eurozone members achieving a greater collective weight in world affairs. At an emotional level it is a potent symbol of political union. It can also contain the dominance of a leader economy, in this case Germany and the Bundesbank. For weaker economies, full EMU offers a means to gain control, not lose it (George 1991: 188).

The case against

States must sacrifice some economic sovereignty, accepting common objectives such as interest rate and inflation targets. The Bank of England cedes power to the European Central Bank. The exchange rate is no longer available to regulate competitiveness and some control over monetary and fiscal policy is surrendered. The system can be dominated by a leader economy at the expense of weaker states. There is also the possibility that economic convergence will lead on to convergence in social policy, justifying the suspicion of 'socialism via the back door', a fear voiced in Thatcher's notorious Bruges speech. Beyond rational argument, some reservations reflect a deeper emotional unease at losing the 'British way of life' that even shades into xenophobia.

Public Expenditure and Long-term Economic Decline

Britain has experienced a prolonged period of economic decline since the pomp of its nineteenth-century imperial splendour. Chapter 4 examined this in terms of the orientation of the ruling class towards the wider globalizing economy. However, beyond these exogenous factors are endogenous ones, and various hypotheses are advanced by left and right. Here we consider how far the patterns and traditions of public expenditure management in Britain have in themselves contributed, identifying three likely suspects:

- ◆ the institutional setting;
- ◆ the competitive pattern of Whitehall decision-making;
- ◆ a failure to incorporate key economic interests into the process.

The institutional setting: Victorian institutions in a Keynesian landscape

The two key institutions associated with public finance – the Treasury and the Bank of England – are august establishments imbued with nineteenth-century liberal values. For critics they have lain at the heart of the problem. Their dominance has meant that nineteenth-century values have lingered like the smell of stale tobacco smoke in the redecorated constitution of the post-war era. Both could be but poor instruments for Keynesianism, placing a 'dead hand' on public expenditure in general, with little thought for industry, employment, the wider economy or the welfare state. Whatever the economic problem – falling pound, rising pound, balance of payments crisis, inflation or unemployment – the response was invariably a deflationary package. The result was a series of what were termed 'stop–go' policies. When the economy expanded, imports were sucked in, the trade deficit widened and the Bank of England would step in to buy sterling with foreign currency in order to maintain its value as an international reserve currency. As the foreign currency reserves fell, deflation would be introduced (a 'stop' period) to reduce imports. However, this caused unemployment, calling for the economy to be stimulated (a 'go' period) and the cycle would begin again. As a result, the post-war Keynesian period could be described as 'the revolution that never was' (Hutton 1986).

The pound in your pocket

From now on the pound is worth 14 per cent or so less in terms of other currencies. It does not mean, of course, that the pound here in Britain, in your pocket or purse or in your bank, has been devalued.

Harold Wilson's speech after devaluation of the pound (20 Nov. 1967)

Although removing the possibility of electorally motivated juggling, the independent fixing of interest rates by the Bank may not in itself remedy the defects critics see in the economy. Will Hutton (1996: 298) has stressed the need for a deeper cultural change in which the financial community sees itself as 'a servant of business rather than as its master', with banks and their customers showing more commitment to the success of industry and less hunger for dividends, accepting lower rates of return on investments and allowing longer terms for repaying loans.

Competitive decision-making in Whitehall

Linked with the dominance of the Treasury and Bank has been the Whitehall method of reaching spending decisions. Despite formally accepting the

You never have
debates about
ethics or morals
here, just about
saving money.

Patrice Claude,
London
correspondent of
Le Monde, quoted
in *the Observer*
(11 March 2001)

Keynesian package, the Treasury missed its historic opportunity to become an economic coordinator. The PES reforms did not eliminate competitive infighting, and the Treasury persisted in trying to reduce expenditure, regardless of the merits of individual policies. New Labour's Comprehensive Spending Reviews and talk of 'joined-up government' did little to remove the ethos of competition. This style of economic management has reflected an inability to see the state as something over and above sectional interests; it is a manifestation of the Victorian legacy of individualism. In this respect, British government has compared unfavourably with the French, where the Commissariat Général du Plan aims to coordinate departments in line with an overall economic policy. Hence, the creation of the DEA proved but a short-lived experiment.

Failure to incorporate key economic interests into policy-making

This same ethos prevented the successful implantation of institutions designed to bring together the key interests: finance, industry and labour (see chapter 17). Remaining arm's-length quangos, Neddy and the 'little Neddies' were never well integrated into the machinery and the Cinderella DEA was killed off by the ugly sisters, the Treasury and Bank, daughters of the penny-pinching Gladstone. The Industrial Reorganization Corporation and National Enterprise Board, lacking both powers and funds, were unsuccessful in the late 1960s and 1970s respectively. Further failure came with incomes policy, union antagonism costing Labour the 1979 general election. The lack of harmony was graphically illustrated in the fate of Heath's Industrial Relations Court, which existed for only three years. Under Thatcher the declared policy was to end consultation with economic interests. While New Labour began to speak of forging a new consensus in a 'stakeholder society', the weakened trade unions reacted with suspicion. They were particularly alarmed when, at the March 2002 Barcelona summit, Blair aligned himself against the rest with two of Europe's most right-wing leaders, Silvio Berlusconi of Italy and Spanish prime minister Maria Aznar. The three became known as 'the BAB axis' as they called for economic deregulation and opposed employee protection laws. TUC General Secretary John Monks accused Blair of being 'bloody stupid' (Black 2002).

The hands-off state

> The British state is so imbued with the liberal philosophy... that sustained, coherent, and disinterested arbitration and sponsorship of the economy is extremely difficult, if not impossible.
>
> Will Hutton, *The Revolution that Never Was* (1986: 196)

All these factors lead to the conclusion that British governments have not used their financial role in the best interests of the economy at large. The persistence of liberal values has meant that, from the time of the Liberal social programme of 1906–14, governments have been willing to help the losers in a capitalist economy with welfare measures but have remained unwilling to interfere with the freedom of businesses to pursue their self-interest. However, decisions that seemed rational to individuals (say continuing with outmoded technology rather than risking new investment) were, contrary to the claims of Adam Smith, not in the overall interest. Britain declined to become a 'developmental' state in the manner of the dynamic post-war economies (Marquand 1988: 121–3). The result is a state that has always been subservient to the market order, with a persistent legend of minimal government etched into its institutional masonry – never open enough to engage in dialogue with industry, never coordinated enough to plan, and never autonomous enough to manage.

Key points

- The public sector is held together by a financial web; few political questions can be addressed without attention to the financial dimension.
- Public expenditure is money spent by the state, its scale is enormous and most is raised by taxation.
- Public expenditure is also an expression of our propensity to live collectively in a community; paying taxes is a duty of citizenship.
- Her Majesty's Treasury presides over a set of financial controls fashioned in the nineteenth century.
- Because of its great magnitude, public expenditure cannot but influence the rest of the economy. This allowed post-war governments to intervene in the capitalist economy in pursuit of social goals.
- By the mid-1970s, with the end of the long boom, the New Right emerged to restore Victorian principles.
- The Thatcher government generally failed in its goal of reducing state expenditure: money supply grew, firms went bankrupt, and unemployment and interest rates soared.
- In retrospect it can be argued that Keynesianism was never really practised. The ethos of the minimal state and the half-hearted involvement of key interests prevented the central control found in more successful competitors.
- The New Labour government of 1997 made a virtue of continuing much of its predecessors' economic policy.
- Joining the European single currency would have considerable implications for the government's role in the economy.

Review your understanding of the following terms and concepts

Audit Commission
'Black Wednesday'
budgetary process
C&AG
capitalism
Consolidated Fund
demand management
direct taxation
economic planning
fiscal policy
indirect taxation
inflation

Keynesianism
laissez-faire
macroeconomics
mixed economy
monetarism
money supply
National Audit Office
national debt
National Lottery
prior approval
progressive taxation
Protestant work ethic

Public Accounts Committee
public expenditure
public expenditure survey
   process
public sector borrowing
   requirement (PSBR)
regressive taxation
single currency
stakeholder society
supply process
transfer payments

Assignment

Study the extract from the *Economist* and answer the following questions.

		Mark (%)
1	'Both proved lethal to their parties.' Evaluate the case for this assessment of the chancellorships of Roy Jenkins and Nigel Lawson.	20
2	Discuss the extent to which a budget must always be something of a gamble.	20
3	Why is it argued that tax increases have had political potency?	20
4	'Gladstonian orthodoxy' or 'a resurgence of inflation'? To what extent is Gordon Brown's approach likely to make either of the alleged mistakes of his two distinguished predecessors?	40

Questions for discussion

1   'Public expenditure is a reflection of our propensity to live communally.' Discuss.
2   Outline the Gladstonian cycle of financial control. What were its principal objectives?
3   How can government use its powers of spending and taxation to manage a capitalist economy?
4   How effective is Parliament in controlling public finance?
5   Explain how the monetarist approach to the economy differs from that advocated by Keynes.

The budget

Gordon's gamble

The chancellor is taking unnecessary risks to save the National Health Service

IN THE past 40 years there have been at least three intellectually formidable chancellors of the exchequer – Roy Jenkins, Nigel Lawson and, now, Gordon Brown. Each has exerted an easy domination over Whitehall's brainiest and most powerful department. Within government, each conducted policy on his own terms. Despite or, perhaps, because of this, Mr Jenkins and Mr Lawson both proved lethal to their parties: the former because he insisted on Gladstonian orthodoxy on the eve of an election; the latter because he allowed the resurgence of inflation that led in the end to the Tories' decline and fall. Might Mr Brown be going the same way?

For a man whose favourite words are "prudent" and "cautious", Mr Brown is taking some big risks. Perhaps his huge self-confidence and delight in command, which give him the air of a man who has come to believe himself invincible, have turned him into a gambler.

In purely economic terms, the budget looks just about prudent. Although Mr Brown's forecasts are optimistic, especially his belief that Britain's ability to grow over the long term is now a full quarter of a percentage point higher than it was before Labour entered office, they are not reckless. Nor is his fiscal policy likely to frighten the horses: public sector net debt as a proportion of GDP is expected to stay roughly constant for the next five years, while the budget deficit will remain modest. Tax as a proportion of GDP will continue to climb, but it will not be much higher than when Margaret Thatcher was prime minister.

A cynical reading of the budget might suggest that Mr Brown is not taking political risks, either. He may be raising taxes now to cut them just before the next election. After all, that is what he did in the last parliament. But the figures and the rhetoric he has produced, committing the government to whacking year-on-year increases in spending on the National Health Service, suggest otherwise.

...Part of Mr Brown's gamble is that to help pay for this unprecedented increase in funding – a 43% rise after inflation by 2007 is projected – he is raising the tax rate on the earnings of people in work, thus breaking the spirit of repeated government promises not to increase income tax. Although he is calling this an increase in employees' National Insurance Contributions, it's a distinction that will elude most of those paying it. Mr Brown believes that because Labour is now trusted to spend this money responsibly, tax increases have lost their political potency. Maybe, maybe not.

The Economist, 20 April 2002

6   What is meant by the 'dead hand of the Treasury'? Discuss its effect on the post-war economy.
7   Explain the shift from direct to indirect taxation since 1979. Is it likely to be reversed?
8   What role is implied for government in the idea of the 'stakeholder economy'?
9   Examine the pros and cons of allowing the Bank of England to set interest rates.
10   Assess the political significance of 'Black Wednesday'.

Topic for debate

This house believes that the 'failure' of Keynesianism is a result of institutional factors in the British state rather than inherent defects in the approach.

Further reading

Some of the reading for chapter 4 is also relevant to the issues discussed here.

Friedman, M. and R. (1985) *The Tyranny of the Status Quo.*
Collaboration between the influential monetarist guru and his wife laments the failure of the Thatcher regime to control money supply in the manner prescribed.

Gamble, A. (1990) *Britain in Decline*, 3rd edn.
Traces various explanations for decline, stressing the importance of global influences.

Grant, W. (1993) *The Politics of Economic Policy.*
Accessible and wide-ranging account of forces shaping economic policy.

Heclo, H. and Wildavsky, A. (1974) *The Private Government of Public Money.*
A unique book, showing those involved in the public finance processes as real people.

Holt, R. (2001) *Second Amongst Equals: Chancellors of the Exchequer and the British Economy.*
Lively account of post-war economic policy, with a penetrating examination of the performance and capabilities of 20 holders of this powerful office.

Hutton, W. (1996) *The State We're In.*
In the traditions of Keynes and J. K. Galbraith, a sustained critique of the 'universal imposition of the market principle and decay of our political system'. Contains a comprehensive and stimulating reform agenda.

Keegan, W. (1984) *Mrs Thatcher's Economic Experiment.*
Written by an economic journalist, this account contains the flavour of the real-world politics lying behind all expenditure policy.

Marquand, D. (1988) *The Unprincipled Society.*
Erudite yet accessible critique of Britain's failure to manage its economy.

Mullard, M. (1993) *The Politics of Public Expenditure.*
Examines the political climate in which public expenditure decisions are made.

Thain, C. and Wright, M. (1995) *The Treasury and Whitehall: The Planning and Control of Public Expenditure 1976–1993.*
Monumental study explaining the structures and political forces underlying this key aspect of politics.

For light relief

Hilaire Belloc, *Pongo and the Bull.*
The power of money and the moneyed classes.

Tim Renton, *Hostage to Fortune*
Intrigue in Threadneedle Street by ex-Conservative minister. The Chancellor of the Exchequer and Governor of the Bank of England plot downfall of prime minister.

H. G. Wells, *Tono-Bungay.*
Biting comment on an entrepreneurial society with nothing of value to sell.

Tom Wolfe, *Bonfire of the Vanities.*
Satire on the US world of capitalist high finance and its penetrating social implications.

Brassed Off
Film/video with moving account of social consequences of deindustrialization which is seen as politically motivated.

On the net

http://www.hm-treasury.gov.uk
The Treasury's home page provides links to a wealth of information on all aspects of public expenditure, the budgetary process and the state of the economy, in addition to details of the institution itself.

http://www.bankofengland.co.uk
The Bank of England home page will lead you to information on the Bank's history, organization and role, and an extensive range of economic and financial statistics. There is even a section entitled 'Funny Bank Stories'.

Both these sites will also lead you to information on the single currency.

17

The Politics of Influence: Who Gets What, When, How?

In this chapter we move beyond both the formal institutions of government and the overtly political structures to uncover the more shadowy forces in politics – the powers behind the throne. Where 'real power' lies is the greatest conundrum of the study of politics. We find repeatedly that the apparent puppetmasters are themselves dangling on yet further strings stretching away out of our sight in an infinite regression. The chapter falls into three main sections. The first introduces the concept of group politics and defines the types of groups to be discussed. The next identifies major theoretical approaches to this study, analysing the theories of pluralism and corporatism. We also consider the neoliberal view that the group approach distorts the political process. Finally we go beyond the group approach to examine elitist and Marxist views of power in society.

The Group Approach

In 1978, a number of protesters hurled from the public gallery of the House of Commons foul-smelling bags containing a substance later described as of 'agricultural origin' onto the heads of cowering members. In February 1988, to the alarm of the seated aristocracy, a hoard of Amazon women abseiled into the House of Lords and others appeared uninvited on a BBC news broadcast. The names 'Swampy' and 'Animal' became familiar to all but the most apathetic news followers in 1997, as they holed in beneath ground earmarked for new roads and airport runways. Such behaviour knows no class boundaries. Groups of ramblers defy enraged lords armed with shotguns, while a letter thanking the Duke of Edinburgh for his support is delivered to Buckingham Palace by protesters opposing legislation banning hand-guns. Almost daily the news media report on the activities of protest marchers, eco-warriors, parent demonstrators and hurlers of eggs at the high and mighty. The name of professional **lobbyist** Ian Greer, involved in the 'cash-for-questions' imbroglio in 1996, was probably more widely known than that of many MPs. Although the constitution makes no provision for activities such as these, they are events in politics. It is clear that our study does not end with constitutions, parties and Parliament.

Once a government has been elected the formal involvement of citizens in policy-making ends. MPs return joyfully to Westminster, the ballot boxes are stacked away in town hall vaults, and returning officers and vote counters return to their desks. To be sure, a government will take cognizance of public opinion during its term of office, may even form focus groups to test ideas, but such consideration places the population in a position of passivity and can hardly be dignified as participation. Representative democracy does not formally allow people to make policy; it merely permits them to choose between elites. However, in practice popular involvement is not confined to elections, it continues through the activities of pressure groups.

A key founding figure in group theory was Arthur Bentley, an American economist who realized the limitations of studying policy only in terms of institutions and office-holders. For Bentley, the process of government was essentially about the activities of organized groups; his major work, first published in 1908, averred compellingly that 'when the groups are stated, everything is stated' (1967: 208).

> Get up, stand up. Stand up for your rights. Get up, stand up. Never give up the fight.
>
> Bob Marley (1945–81; popular singer), *Get up, stand up* (1973)

Definitions

Pressure groups appear in many guises, raising various *definitional issues*, such as the following.

Interest groups and pressure groups Although essentially different, these two terms are often used synonymously. However, an **interest group** is an association with a shared interest or concern, while a **pressure group** is one actively attempting to *influence* government. The latter term carries sinister connotations of factions seeking to subvert the democratic process and was probably coined by US journalists as a term of abuse. Some modern writers (particularly those in the pluralist tradition – see below) tend to favour the more innocent-sounding 'interest group'.

Groups and individuals The logic of the group approach to analysis is to downgrade the role of individuals. This makes sense in that one vote is likely to have less influence than a group campaign. However, it obscures the fact that groups usually have dominant leaderships (Salisbury 1969), reflecting Michels's iron law of oligarchy. A study of the British 'poverty lobby' revealed that out of thirty-nine groups concerned with income maintenance policy, around half were controlled by a political entrepreneur (Whiteley and Winyard 1984).

Similarly, leaders of economic groups are often powerful movers in the political firmament. In the early post-war decades, giants of the CBI and the TUC, as well as a variety of industrial and trade union figures, featured in the national news as visibly as ministers. Thus, groups need not eliminate personality politics; they can actually fuel it by adding to an individual's political weight, sometimes at the expense of the democratic voice of members.

> The reasonable man adapts himself to the world: the unreasonable one persists in trying to adapt the world to himself. Therefore all progress depends on the unreasonable man.
>
> George Bernard Shaw, *Man and Superman* (1903)

Groups and parties Definitions usually stress a fundamental distinction between groups and parties.

◆ Unlike parties, pressure groups do not seek to enter government, they wish only to influence policy.
◆ Pressure groups have only a limited range of policy interests; parties are concerned with the entire government remit. This is sometimes expressed in terms of different *functions*; groups *articulate* interests and parties *aggregate* them.
◆ Parties tend to be clearly located along the ideological spectrum but pressure groups may seek links at many points and try to gain access to a government of any political complexion.

Although useful, this distinction breaks down under scrutiny. The differences should be seen in terms of tendencies rather than clear orientations. We saw in chapter 11 that the Labour and Conservative parties have historically been wedded to particular interests. Some pressure groups do indeed fight elections: environmentalists as the Greens, anti-abortionists as the Pro-life party and Eurosceptics as the Referendum Party or as UKIP (see p. 301). Some also aggregate interests as peak organizations (see below), while the Real World Coalition was a rainbow alliance of over thirty of the UK's leading environmental campaigning organizations (Jacobs 1996).

Types of pressure groups

An important dichotomy distinguishes groups on the basis of the interest they fight for. Although the nomenclature varies, the distinction is fundamental.

Promotional groups The policy goal of **promotional groups** is beyond self-interest and they are sometimes called *cause groups*. Thus, for example, the Royal Society for the Prevention of Cruelty to Children, the Society for the

Protection of the Unborn Child and, say, the Antivivisection Society fight for those unable to defend themselves. Others pursue ideological or moral goals; Liberty is concerned with civil rights while Greenpeace fights for the planet. Generally speaking, membership is open to any concerned individual and they may attract zealots. Thus members of the National Viewers and Listeners' Association (NVLA) expose themselves to long unselfish television vigils in their mission to purify the airwaves. Some groups are by their very nature limited; the Campaign for Homosexual Equality tends to attract homosexuals, while the diversity of feminist groups consists mainly of women. Many do not devote all their time to politics. The Automobile Association, for example, serves its members in a wide variety of ways, only becoming politically active when motorists' interests are threatened.

The number of cause groups rose during the 1980s and 1990s, reflecting a disenchantment with traditional politics, a greater interest in the politics of direct action, welfare cutbacks and increasing environmental concerns. The *Directory of British Political Organisations* lists over 200 concerned with the environment alone (Mercer 1994). Indeed, the groups not only aim to influence government, they may also direct their attention at other centres of power – international associations, the EU and private corporations – as when Greenpeace took on the mighty Shell over the Brent Spar oil rig. Such action became more appropriate as a neoliberal government cut back the state to leave more quality-of-life issues to the market.

Sectional groups Individual self-interest is the motive for much economic and political activity and this is reflected through **sectional groups**. Sometimes called *economic groups*, membership is generally restricted. The trade unions are a notable sub-category. Their importance was heightened by the enormous growth of the industrial public sector, making the government a large-scale employer, but has been reduced following extensive privatization. On the employers' side, there are business associations reflecting various sectors, and even multinational firms. Both unions and employers' associations combine into **peak organizations** – the Trades Union Congress (TUC), the Institute of Directors and the Confederation of British Industry (CBI) – to press their collective demands. Another category comprises *professional associations* such as the British Medical Association (BMA) and the Law Society.

The promotional/sectional distinction is blurred in practice with some promotional groups, such as Alcoholics Anonymous or the Prisoners' Wives and Families Society, concerned largely with the interests of members and some sectional groups often pursuing wider goals for society (health, education, justice and so on).

The policy bazaar: bargaining with power

Generally governments are not unwilling to talk with groups. Indeed, commissions of inquiry, consultative documents, green papers, white papers and draft

You're never too
young for politics:
campaigning against
child poverty

Photo: Helen Stone/End Child Poverty

bills encourage participation. This is partly because the groups themselves can have powerful bargaining counters in terms of expertise and veto power.

Expertise Many groups are expert in particular fields – farming, medicine, nature conservation – and the state bureaucracy is generally deficient in specialism. When new problems arise it is likely that voluntary organizations will be first with the expertise and information. Thus, as AIDS began its fateful march through the population, the Terrence Higgins Foundation clearly understood the problem better than the mandarins. Businessmen know how to promote trade, Sustrans can map out the best cycle routes and so on. Indeed, where expertise is not brought in the result can be policy failure, as with the poll tax, or the introduction of attainment-testing in schools.

Veto power The NHS needs doctors, education must have teachers and only farmers can implement agricultural policy. In addition, the regulatory character of much EU legislation (setting standards for companies) requires considerable cooperation. To secure compliance, government concessions may be necessary. The 1971 Industrial Relations Act, for example, failed owing to trade union unwillingness to play ball. A group's leverage increases in proportion to its monopoly status. The BMA was in an immensely powerful position when the NHS was created and threats of non-cooperation were constantly rumbling. Of course circumstances can change. The National Union of Mineworkers (NUM) appeared mighty when its strike unnerved the Heath government in 1974, but during the 1980s its power was broken by the formation (with government encouragement) of an alternative union and the exploitation of other fuel sources. In September 2000, tractors and lorries blocked motorways as a combination of farmers and road hauliers threatened to bring the country to a standstill.

The cost of influence Bargaining is a two-way process: by permitting a group to enter the decision-making forums, a government obtains an opportunity to sell its policies. For the group representatives the price of involvement can be 'responsible behaviour' and some commitment to sell a policy to members.

Talking to power

To communicate their views to government groups require some channel of access. These range from influencing the public at large to direct talks with decision-makers. Beyond the domestic institutions there is also the path to the EU. A growth industry of professional lobbyists has emerged to direct those seeking to influence, with advice on PR and arrangements ranging from lavish receptions to quiet after-dinner discussions.

The public A favourable climate of public opinion is in a group's interest and there are numerous ways to achieve this. The director of the Child Poverty Action Group declared 'coverage in the media is our main strategy' (Whiteley and Winyard 1984: 35). The press is critically important, though less helpful to groups of the left, for whom biased reporting may be harmful. Some major left-wing demonstrations may even go unreported. Moreover, in an era of mass communications, power over public opinion can be a function of wealth. Rich interests may enlist the services of the advertising industry – the professional persuaders – to reach parts of the national subconscious that others cannot reach. In the early 1990s the nuclear industry assiduously massaged its public image, its infamous Windscale site became Sellafield and costly TV commercials enticed the public onto guided tours. Less well-endowed groups are usually obliged to adopt more robust tactics – marches, demonstrations and sometimes violent confrontations.

Traditional post-war political analysis had suggested that such tactics amount to an admission of weakness and, although eye-catching, generally end in failure. A case of 'not waving but drowning', groups often resort to direct action because they are denied access to other channels. Certainly the activities of groups such as animal rights campaigners (who, amongst other things, attacked the managing director of Huntingdon Life Sciences with baseball bats) sometimes lose rather than gain public support. However, from the suffragette movement to the women peace campaigners at Greenham Common, major advances have been made by more raucous forms of action. Moreover, globalization has brought to British eyes the more extravagant tactics employed elsewhere. In France, for example, a branch of Marks and Spencer was kept open after direct action by threatened workers. Road blockades by lorry drivers, airport standstills, bomb threats and, in 2000, the poisoning of the river Meuse by workers facing redundancy in the town of Givet show the increasingly less deferential British new vistas of direct action. The decision over the Brent Spar oil rig, the ban on hand-guns, changes in the law on foxhunting and concession to fuel tax protesters suggest increased willingness to take to the streets and, indeed, the motorways.

Parliament Groups may launch onslaughts with mass demonstrations outside the Palace of Westminster and MPs may be lobbied, besieged in their constituencies or deluged with persuasive mail. Some will be sympathetic to particular groups; deaf MP Jack Ashley campaigned with fervour on behalf of the handicapped and David Alton pursued the anti-abortionist cause. Groups try to cultivate long-term relationships with MPs and peers, even appointing them to honorary positions in their associations. The relationship can be symbiotic, a reputation for specialist knowledge serving as a basis for catching the Speaker's eye and impressing the whips. The general showpiece debates on issues chosen by the front benches afford few opportunities for backbench influence, but the committee stage of legislation can be more useful; proposed amendments, even if defeated, gain valuable publicity. Private members' bills

1996 in United Britain, Great Kingdom...

Conservative Party	
Labour Party STREET PARTY! Democrats	

Representation of the Peoples Act 1996
This ballot paper conforms to the standards laid down by the Electoral Reform Society and is registered under Subsection a), Paragraph iii) of the You Mark a Cross On a Piece of Paper Once Every Four Years Meanwhile We Make a Right Pig's Ear of Things and Get Rich Act 1996, Patent No. 37649801.

Get away from it all this Summer!

Music, children's area, info-stalls, art, magic, poetry, food, sunbathing, volleyball, clowns, acrobats, street theatre, trapeze artists, debates, instant beach & a prize for the best fancy dress...

A FESTIVAL OF RESISTANCE

**Meet 12 Noon, Saturday July 13th
Broadgate, next to Liverpool St Station
Reclaim the Streets**

provide a unique (though limited and expensive opportunity) to shape legislation; Friends of the Earth and the Green Party both played a significant part in the early drafting of the 1997 Road Traffic Reduction Bill. The upper house is not exempt from attention; its function of 'tidying up' bills affords a chance for one last-ditch stand.

It is sometimes argued that promotional groups are more interested in Parliament than are the economic giants, but this is far from true. Indeed, it is possible to view the Houses as *functional* chambers where the members sit as representatives not of constituencies but of corporate interests; the 'Honourable Member for Harrods', or even 'Lord Channel Tunnel'. Wealthy interests also employ MPs as parliamentary consultants or avail themselves of the services of the professional lobbyist (Jordan 1991). The establishment of the Register of Members' Interests did little to discourage developments and in the 1980s and 1990s the British public were to learn a new piece of political terminology – sleaze – while their gaze was turned into the deeper recesses of power (see p. 379).

> Don't let the buggers get you down.
>
> Inscription on watch given by Michael Mates MP to fugitive businessman Asil Nadir, upon whose behalf he had lobbied

Parties The orthodoxy that groups will seek friends anywhere in the ideological landscape is questionable in certain cases. The ideology of many promotional groups gives a partisan leaning. Welfare groups like Age Concern or Shelter expect more from a leftish party while business interests and the law-and-order lobby traditionally expect a better crack of the whip from the right. Moreover, the traditional Siamese pairings of labour and capital with the two major parties demonstrate all the complications associated with the funding relationships (pp. 334–41). However, it takes two to tango and the parties themselves will attempt to court interest groups by tailoring their manifestos to their needs. In this way New Labour danced towards the business interests in the 1990s.

The government Direct lines to ministers at the heart of state power might seem the most promising of all channels. The Major government proved there was no such thing as a free lunch by creating the Millennium Club, offering businessmen (membership fee £10,000) the opportunity to meet ministers at lunches, receptions and private functions, while the Premier Club (membership fee £100,000) opened the door to the Prime Minister and senior cabinet colleagues (Cohen 1997; Fisher 1997). The discovery in July 1998 that former Labour staffers turned lobbyists, Derek Draper and Roger Liddle, were also offering access to ministers for cash caused considerable embarrassment.

The more powerful groups can *demand* meetings with ministers if so moved. Even under Thatcher, when consultation styles came to resemble that of Greta Garbo, the presidents of the royal colleges of surgeons, physicians, and obstetricians and gynaecologists demanded a summit meeting as the NHS careered towards crisis in early 1988. Again, when the 1988 Local Government Bill (Clause 28) banned the 'promotion' of homosexuality by local authorities, distinguished actor Ian McKellen sought a meeting with the arts minister.

However, although their clients often long to pass through the door of Number Ten, lobbyists advise against such close encounters. Their value is largely symbolic; they are ritualistic exchanges unlikely to result in policy change. One weakness is the incitement of media interest. Bernie Ecclestone's *tête-à-tête* with Tony Blair in 1997 may have brought home the bacon for Formula One racing but there was considerable embarrassment for both (p. 339). An increasingly sought-after channel of access is the growing number of high-profile ministerial advisers. When Labour took power in 1997 these attracted increasing interest; figures such as Dan Corry at the Department of Trade and Industry, Ed Balls at the Treasury and Geoff Norris at the Downing Street Policy Unit became increasingly popular within the shadowy world of the lobbyists, and even known to the public.

Whitehall Demonstrations may catch the headlines and lunches with ministers carry kudos, but it is dealings with the Whitehall mandarins that often prove the most potent sources of influence. The grey-suited professional lobbyists moving oleaginously about the corridors of power aim to keep out of the spotlight. It is here that the bargaining counters of the groups are most valued and where the symbiosis of mutual need is most apparent. Consultation can shape the content of official publications, green papers (putting ideas on the political agenda) and white papers (declaring government policy). This influence is greatest because it is conducted below the level of public awareness. The village of Whitehall does not encourage sightseers and those welcomed to tea may rest assured that the curtains will remain drawn; the genteel residents will not betray their secrets even to Commons select committees (see p. 475). The group–mandarin duet sings even more *sotto voce* in the making of statutory instruments, where discussion concerns details of actual legislation.

> Recently I had to do a job on the road issue and the civil servant I wanted to talk to wouldn't meet me. So I arranged for our MP to draft something like twenty written questions, questions which I knew he would have to do the work of answering. He soon got the message. You might call that blackmail. I call it a triumph for democracy.
>
> Douglas Smith (a lobbyist of Martin Dignum Associates), quoted in the *Guardian* (31 Oct. 1978)

The European Union The EU, drawing on corporatist continental traditions, sees employers and unions as 'social partners', an approach institutionalized through the ECOSOC (see chapter 5). This offers a further focus for British pressure groups, sometimes a more receptive ear than their own government. There are many hundreds of groups lobbying at Brussels over issues such as trade, agriculture, food, commerce and the service industries. Many form transnational alliances; the CBI and the TUC operate through the European employers and unions bodies (UNICE and ETUC). As the flow of directives from the Commission increases, more and more associations are drawn into the consultative web. Interests go beyond the industrial to include human rights, children, consumer protection and the environment. Calls to Brussels for stricter regulation of drinking water and bathing beaches brought the British government before the European Court over its failings.

Groups may approach the EU institutions directly or try to influence the national government's stance at Brussels. It is symptomatic of the embryonic stage of European federalism that the indirect route is the more popular. Yet there are risks; the government may be forced to let a group down by making concessions in the Council. Groups choosing the direct line may talk to the European Parliament and ECOSOC, though it can be a mark of weakness to concentrate effort here. The key Brussels access point is the Commission – not the commissioners themselves but the 'Eurocrats' operating within the dense committee network. Here groups will find an open door and be invited to participate at very early stages in the policy process. Like governments, the Commission has a voracious appetite for advice and expertise. In addition, talking to interests enables it to combat the charge of faceless undemocratic Euro-officialdom. However, the grave danger of lobbyist involvement with unelected institutions was thrown into stark relief in the March 1999 report of the 'Committee of the Wise', which led to the Commission's resignation (see p. 131). Amongst this catalogue of bureaucratic shame were accounts of the corrupt awarding of contracts and even suspicions of Mafia involvement.

Explaining Group Politics

The politics of influence takes us beyond the constitutional theory of electorates, parliaments and cabinets and different theoretical perspectives are required. These take us close to the heart of the power structure within the polity.

Pluralism

Much orthodox British study in the liberal-democratic tradition subscribes to a generally **pluralist** view of politics. The operation of groups is believed to remedy some shortcomings in representative government, including the following:

- a single vote can hardly be said to constitute participation;
- the principle of one vote each fails to recognize the variation in the intensity with which views are held;
- people are denied influence between elections;
- manifesto promises can be broken mid-term;
- minority voices are generally unheeded.

The modern variant of the theory is largely a US import deriving from Bentley. Although he saw group activity as a necessary and inescapable feature of *any* political system, subsequent thinkers developed the theory as a hallmark of liberal democracy. It was not merely a *description* of the way things were, but a prescription of how they *ought* to be. Robert Dahl wrote extensively on the theory in the USA. Coining the term **polyarchy**, he regarded it as no less than a completely new theory of popular sovereignty in which groups help to exert the checks and balances so central to the US constitution (Dahl 1956). In Britain, interest in pluralism, which had been present since the rise of the trade unions (exercising thinkers like Cole, Tawney, Russell, Laski and the Webbs), was reinforced by American commentators on the British scene, such as Samuel Beer (1965), and entered into the mainstream liberal-democratic orthodoxy.

The tenets of pluralism This benign system, complementing representative democracy, may be portrayed as follows.

- The right to join groups is a mark of a free society.
- Groups provide a more effective means of participation than elections.
- Public policy is the outcome of group forces acting against each other. This resembles the mathematical vector diagram, where the *resultant* reflects the combined effect of forces (figure 17.1). Thus the system tends towards a state of equilibrium, with all forces having some effect on the outcome.
- The point where the forces act is the government, which is an impartial referee, its role 'the balancing of group pressures' (Richardson and Jordan 1979: vii).
- No single group will dominate because, as in Newton's law of motion, for every force there is an equal and opposite to counterbalance: the roads lobby will generate an anti-roads lobby and so on.

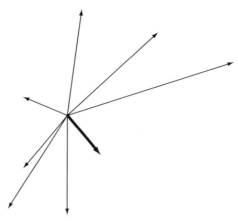

Figure 17.1
A vector diagram.

Note: The lines represent the magnitudes and directions of forces acting at a point. They produce a resultant (the bold arrow) which is the sum of their directions and magnitudes; thus every force is taken equally into account. This is analogous to a pure theory of pluralism.

- Competition will not threaten the integrity of society because each individual tends to belong to several groups; a loss on one front will be balanced by gains elsewhere.
- The larger the group the more influence it will have, thereby maintaining the majoritarian principle while not silencing minorities.
- People with intense feelings on an issue will tend to exert more pressure than the apathetic, thereby countering the insensitivity in the one-person-one-vote principle.
- Those with a common interest, but not organized, will be accommodated because the government and other groups will regard them as *latent groups* ready to mobilize.
- Policies, as the product of bargaining and compromise, will tend to be moderate, fair to all, and conducive to social stability. Another leading pluralist, Charles Lindblom (1959), noted how a process of 'partisan mutual adjustment' resulted in **incrementalism** – small policy changes rather than great unsettling leaps.

This of course is an abstract model; the idea of government as a cypher or mere referee is unrealistic and was specifically rejected by Beer (1956) in the heyday of the theory in the mid-1950s. However, a weak role for government is necessary to the theory. Thus when the mighty Shell did a U-turn in 1996 over the disposal of the Brent Spar oil platform following action by Greenpeace, the government, although voicing disapproval, was little more than a bit player in a drama where two multinational organizations competed for public support. Lively (1978: 191) suggests two interpretations of the government role: the *arbiter* model (government with enough power to ensure that the groups play by the rules) and the *arena* model (government as one of the participants in the game). Dahl and Lindblom themselves came to accept a somewhat more directive role of government under the label neopluralism.

> With all its defects, [pluralism] does nevertheless provide a high probability that any active and legitimate group will make itself heard effectively at some stage in the process of decision.
>
> Robert Dahl, *A Preface to Democratic Theory* (1956: 150)

The policy community Neopluralists give a more practical picture of the arena in which the groups bargain. In each policy area are ministers, civil servants, professional lobbyists and groups in mutual dependencies (figure 17.2) termed variously policy communities, **subgovernments** or **policy networks**. While the network image can be accommodated in other theoretical perspectives (Smith 1993: 74), it is mainly applied by those of a pluralist leaning. The communities are highly fluid, actors entering and exiting as issues change. Although in some respects members may be rivals, they also work

Figure 17.2
The pressure group world in terms of policy communities or subgovernments (simplified view).

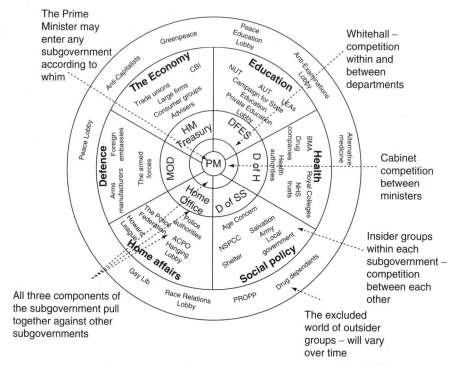

together against other policy communities in pursuit of a greater share of public resources (Richardson and Jordan 1979; Rhodes and Marsh 1992). Communities themselves may intersect (Grant and MacNamara 1995). Over the BSE crisis communities around the Ministry of Agriculture, Fisheries and Food and the Ministry of Health presented a united front with the British beef interests (Winter 1996: 60–1).

> When I was at the [Health Education Council] . . . the Ministry of Agriculture was in there like a ton of bricks acting virtually as a lobby for the National Farmers Union.
>
> Dr David Playfair (former Director General of the HEC), quoted in
> the *Independent* (17 Dec. 1988)

Networks also form at EU level through vertical alliances comprising national ministries, European parliamentary committees, Eurocrats, politicians and professional lobbyists, as well as the pressure groups themselves (Scharpf 1988: 270). Close relationships develop between the favoured interest and the relevant directorates and there is rivalry between directorates in advancing the claims of their clients.

Evaluating pluralism

Few would quarrel with pluralism's stress on the role of groups in politics. However, their uniqueness to liberal democracy is questionable; they also form under totalitarian regimes. Indeed they can be seen as *undermining* democracy; Rousseau believed factions subverted the General Will. They can also be internally undemocratic with unelected leaders whose views may be at variance with those of members. Very few associations have procedures for consulting members. Moreover, the largest groups are not necessarily the winners, tightly knit associations (the City, the BMA) often having a degree of influence entirely out of proportion to their democratic weight, while groups with vast memberships – teachers, nurses and miners – have suffered successive defeats. Beyond these considerations is the geometry of the Establishment, determining which forces intersect at the centres of power and who has friends in high places.

Friends in high places: insiders and outsiders Pioneering British studies, such as those of the BMA (Eckstein 1960), the CBI (Grant and Marsh 1977) and the National Farmers Union (NFU) (Self and Storing 1962) (as well as the majority of smaller case studies and various symposia on the subject), have concentrated on groups that are largely successful, respectable and legitimate. These are **insider groups**, part of the Establishment. Relationships here can be relaxed and informal, extending beyond tea and sympathy in Whitehall's corridors of power to G&T in the exclusive clubs and restaurants of London, and even to weekends in country houses where the high can meet the mighty. For the mandarins, public service can be followed by private gain when, upon retirement and duly knighted, the ex-mandarins can take up lucrative appointments with those with whom they have been doing business (pp. 471–2). Needless to say, such a warm embrace is not extended to all; those in the underground tunnels, in raucous demonstrations or on the cold picket lines are the **outsiders**.

In practice the dichotomy between insiders and outsiders is not clear cut; there are a multiplicity of positions along a notional spectrum determined by various factors.

- ◆ *Public esteem.* The BMA has always gained mightily from the natural veneration that society accords healers. On the other hand, groups espousing causes such as, say, the legalization of cannabis or Radical Alternatives to Prison, can be safely snubbed by a government ever conscious that it will be judged by the company it keeps.
- ◆ *Stage of development.* New groups often start as outsiders, sometimes resorting to 'non-responsible' behaviour. However, insider status may well be the ultimate goal, in return for which a code of good behaviour will be accepted. By the end of the 1990s the anti-roads lobby was beginning to come in from the cold as gridlocked motorways fulfilled its prophecies.

- ◆ *Ideology.* Where group and government ideologies clash, it is likely that neither will wish to be seen holding hands with the other. By choosing to remain outside the pale a group avoids any moral burdens of self-restraint and may kick more violently against the pillars of the Establishment.
- ◆ *Social positioning.* It helps to know the right people. The middle classes are generally better placed, the representatives of some groups resembling civil servant clones, often from the same schools (public) and universities (Oxbridge). Sharing norms, values and interests, they will not only speak the same language, they will do so with the same accent.
- ◆ *Wealth.*   Money can talk in many accents. Wealthy associations such as the CBI or NFU can spend much on entertaining, lobbyists, public relations consultants and image-building. Among promotional groups, unpopular causes (say ex-prisoners, drug addicts) have problems raising funds, while others (say animal and child welfare) enjoy a Midas-like touch.
- ◆ *Economic leverage.* Certain interests (private industrial sectors, banks and the City) enjoy a pivotal position in the economy; governments of all complexions must therefore cater for their needs. Labour governments can be so concerned to reassure on this front that they often subordinate their social programmes.

Charitable giving
The top five cancer raised almost £600 million in 2001, and the National Trust alone over £200 million.

Governments will vary over the interests they favour but for the most part the insider groups will be those close to the heart of the Establishment. They are welcomed in by governments of the centre right, be they Conservative or Labour. The TUC experienced a back-slapping 'beer-and-sandwiches' heyday under the Wilson government, a frosty cold shoulder from Thatcher and only a stiffly formal handshake from Blair. Yet the deaf ear to unwelcome voices is one of the hallmarks of totalitarianism, for an absence of alternative views threatens democracy.

There can also be insiders and outsiders at EU level. From its inception, the idea of a federal Europe has offered a tantalizing glimpse of new forms of power to banks, international financiers and mighty multinationals. The vision of a giant market-place like that of the USA was tempting indeed; today every major company has offices in Brussels. More than other interests, these largely bypass the European Parliament in favour of the Eurocrats, whom they fete with lunches and entertainment. The desire to contain this globalization of power is one of the reasons for calls to make the EU institutions more democratic.

Neopluralism The inequalities clearly manifest in society lead some to reject the theory altogether and look to alternative approaches, stressing the operation of the capitalist economy or the elitist nature of human society (see below). However, others retain a pluralist orientation, while accepting that real-world outcomes can never have the perfection implied in pure pluralist theory. Sometimes termed **neopluralism**, this thinking underlies much analysis of Western liberal democracies.

Does pluralism make might right? Critics would allege that group activity does not result in equity. Like the Ancient Greek Thrasymachus, pluralism allows that 'might is right'. Anti-roads protesters proved little match for a roads lobby of hauliers, engineers, motorway caterers and the bankers behind them. Yet it can be argued that the purpose of government is to control the rich and powerful (Scattschneider 1960); weak game wardens can be profoundly dangerous when the wildlife park contains marauding beasts. In his farewell address, President Eisenhower warned of the menacing growth in America of a 'military-industrial complex' actually threatening the sovereignty of government. Of course, this idea of weak government fits snugly within the general liberal-democratic suspicion of the state. As a kind of political *laissez-faire* it removes moral responsibility from the state for outcomes; you cannot accuse the referee if you lose the game. This culture can induce the poor to blame themselves rather than the system.

Pluralism, with its tendency towards small-scale change, can be said to produce a static society. Thus Labour governments are not able to bring about anything resembling a socialist revolution. Dahl and Lindblom (1976) came to accept in their later work that group politics does not take place on a level playing field. However, preserving the normative aspect of the theory, they argued that a democratic constitution should aim to counter the power of capitalist interests by maximizing group participation and listening to the weak as well as the strong (Dahl 1985). An alternative interpretation of group politics – **corporatism** – gives a much stronger role to government.

Corporatism

This is an approach to government with long European antecedents and became interesting to British scholars during the 1970s as the limitations of pluralism were exposed. Here, government works in deliberate collusion with certain major interests in society. Corporatism is identified with the fascism of the 1930s and this unpleasant aftertaste is expunged by the term **neocorporatism**. Philippe Schmitter (1974) distinguished two forms – state corporatism and *societal corporatism* – the latter arising naturally within a society and, unlike the former, *not* a feature of oppressive government. For some, a neocorporatist style of government is the answer to the wasteful competition generated by pluralism. It can appear as a great cure-all for national problems, engendering a classless camaraderie allegedly seen in times of war (indeed, the two world wars were great corporatist periods for Britain).

The tenets of corporatism Societal corporatism is the variant to be found in modern liberal democracies and has the following characteristics.

- ◆ Politics is seen in terms of groups but they are cooperative rather than competitive.
- ◆ Government is not a passive referee; it decides who shall be invited into the consultations and has clear views on policy.
- ◆ Groups may even be created by government to represent interests it wishes to work with.
- ◆ The interests included tend to be capital and labour, the result being **tripartism**, a *pas de trois* of government, trade unions and employers.
- ◆ Those included tend to monopolize the right to represent their interest.
- ◆ Sometimes groups join together as peak organizations to facilitate consultation.
- ◆ Special corporatist institutions can be created to bypass the formal constitution.
- ◆ The relationship is reciprocal: not only do groups influence policy, government can influence groups, forcing them to modify their demands and gaining their cooperation.

A climate of corporatism In the early twentieth century Britain encouraged institutionalization among bodies representing labour and capital as a means of securing state legitimacy. There was an attempt to set up a National Industrial Conference in 1919 and subsequently efforts were made to create a 'Parliament of Industry' (Middlemass 1979: 372). The post-war consensus saw renewed corporatist tendencies; the trade unions combined under the TUC, and the employers under the CBI. Government established a number of tripartite institutions, particularly the National Economic Development Council (Neddy) in 1961. In the mid-1970s, the Manpower Services Commission, the Health and Safety Commission, and the Advisory, Conciliation and Arbitration Service were established on a tripartite basis. In addition, there were hundreds of advisory and **consultative bodies** concerned with particular industrial sectors and policy areas. Various policies also had a corporatist flavour, particularly over prices and incomes, and the 1975–8 'social contract' gave labour and capital a voice in many domestic policies in exchange for cooperation.

The tendencies were not restricted to the capital–labour duet. In specific policy areas certain groups enjoyed particularly easy access to government while others were excluded. Thus the BMA, the NFU and the National Union of Teachers were welcomed in, while the ancillary medical professions, the environment lobby and smaller teaching unions shivered in the cold.

However, this was never fully blown corporatism and by the mid-1980s the age appeared to be past. Schmitter, who had once believed in the historical necessity of corporatism, was quick to note a dramatic revolt in Britain among Conservative and capitalist interests after the mid-1970s (Lehmbruch and Schmitter 1982). The decay came in the face of economic crisis. Heath's confrontation with the miners was a defining moment and the collapse of Callaghan's 'social contract' showed that Labour had lost its trump card – trade union cooperation.

The seeds of failure This form of corporatism was essentially a consensus-era product, the *ménage à trois* proving most fragile when it should have been most valuable – in economic crisis. Under these circumstances:

◆ unions were liable to opt out once the benefits of full employment were no longer available to compensate for the concessions to capital;
◆ employers became disenchanted with rules and constraints as profits fell;
◆ militants on both sides favoured confrontation rather than cooperation;
◆ large firms and unions preferred dealing directly with government rather than corporatist institutions;
◆ radical governments of the right found the corporatist embrace inhibiting.

Questioning the logic of group action

Some theorists question the group interpretation of politics in both descriptive and prescriptive terms, doubting whether groups are as natural as Bentley asserted or as desirable as pluralists claim. By applying the methods of classical economic theory to political analysis, public choice theory attempts to explain political decisions (public choices) in terms of self-interested actors. Olson (1968) suggests that rational individuals will not become active in a group merely because it is fighting for a collective interest that they share. They can do just as well by sitting back and letting others do the work. In the school choir it is easy enough to open the mouth soundlessly and enjoy the free meal after the concert. This is the problem of the 'free-rider'.

Thus the idea that people tend to form groups (or even parties) to protect their common interest is fallacious; groups that do exist have formed for some other reason. This, for Olson, is the explanation of the success of the capitalist interests: 'the multitude of workers, consumers … and so on are organized only in special circumstances, but business interests [corporations, banks, the City] are organized as a general rule' (Olson 1968: 143). Groups in the first category must develop strategies for recruiting and retaining members. They must offer **selective incentives** (insurance, free T-shirts etc.), or use coercion such as a closed-shop arrangement or intimidation. Being artificial, they lack cohesion and remain essentially weak. This can also explain the failure of workers to unite for revolution in the way prophesied by Marx.

However, political scientists study a real world of passion and emotion, not the abstract terrain inhabited by 'economic man'. It may be true that one more person joining, say, Greenpeace will not alter the course of history, but it will give a psychic satisfaction. In the same way, many people join trade unions because they believe in the movement, seek camaraderie and see strength through numbers. As for the explanation of the success of capital in terms of superior organization, this is simplistic, ignoring the slope of the capitalist playing field.

On the prescriptive front Olson (1982) further argues that the presence of artificially created groups holds back economic growth. Hence commentators believed Britain to have reached a state of '**pluralist stagnation**' by the late 1970s as a result of governments' willingness to listen and bargain with union leaders (Beer 1982: 31). This thesis appealed to the New Right, with its deep antipathy towards union involvement in government.

A post-corporate era?

With talk of government overload, hyper-pluralism and pluralist stagnation, as well as the demonizing of the 'winter of discontent', the 1979 Conservative government spoke a rhetoric of 'enemy within' rather than of partnership. The high steel railings erected across Downing Street were symbolic; the cosy days of beer and sandwiches at Number Ten were over. The result was bitter confrontation with the steelworkers in 1980, the railwaymen in 1982 and, most dramatically of all, the miners in 1984–5. A series of Acts weakened the unions, removing legal immunities for collective action and outlawing secondary picketing. The closed-shop laws were relaxed and compulsory secret strike ballots enabled the more deferential mass to reject the leadership advice on action. Legislation brought the courts into the arena and some unions found their funds sequestrated on a crippling scale.

By the end of Thatcher's reign the political role of the unions had virtually disappeared (Marsh 1992: ch. 4). Figure 17.3 chronicles the decline. Not only was there no more beer and sandwiches, the government also appeared less interested in wine and pâté with the CBI. Traditional insider groups, including the Institute of Directors, the CBI, the Bar Council, the Law Society, the Royal Colleges, the BMA and the NFU all had unpalatable dishes thrust down their throats, with little consultation over the menu.

Yet the anti-corporatist drive had mixed results. Ignoring expertise in framing policy initiatives imposed high costs in terms of ill-drafted legislation and policy failure in areas such as the core curriculum and the NHS internal market. Criticism from alienated groups reduced public confidence further. Moreover, while it may have been possible to exclude them from the consultation chambers they remained central to the implementation process, where they could often put the brakes on radical initiatives (Marsh and Rhodes 1992: 181). The most dramatic failure was the poll tax; conceived with zero consultation, the outcome extracted a heavy toll on the government and the Prime Minister herself (Butler et al. 1994).

However, the exclusion was not absolute. Some post-war machinery survived, the TUC and CBI remained on a host of intermediate-level bodies and the sense of alienation was reduced under Major (Norton 1993a: 62). The number of consultative documents rose (though response times were very short), access for the BMA improved and local government associations detected greater willingness to listen (Baggott 1995a: 498). The *dirigiste* Michael Heseltine became President of the Board of Trade. Yet with deep symbolism Neddy was abolished in early 1993, its responsibilities passing to the Department of Trade and Industry. Consultation was conspicuously lacking in a number of important policy areas, from pit closures to police pay and conditions.

Corporatism by other means Paradoxically, the government's policies produced other forms of corporatism. Various public–private partnership schemes created a new consultative network, while compulsory competitive tendering, market-testing and the growth of the quango state (chapter 18) further extended the involvement of private business in the business of government. This exercise of patronage tended to spurn the left so that, for example, the subject groups of the National Curriculum Council excluded local authorities and teachers' unions while including independent schools and right-wing pressure groups (Baggott 1995a: 487). Further tendencies towards back-door corporatism came through consultation with think-tanks and private consultants, particularly over the privatization launches.

When one doors closes Yet developments were to demonstrate the ubiquity of groups; if denied access at one point they will seek another. One target was the EU. Encouraged by the Social Chapter and the globalizing economy, the unions looked more to Brussels, often strengthening cross-national links (Farnham

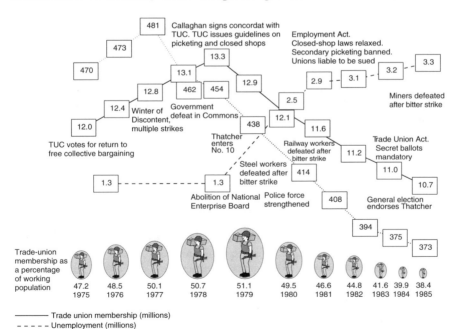

Figure 17.3
The death of corporatism.

Source: Data from *Social Trends* (1988: tables 4.19 and 11.8).

1996: 597). Other promotional groups made the journey across the channel; the European Commission's environmental directorate received many more letters from Britain than any other country (*Economist*, 13 Aug. 1994). At home there was a dramatic rise in the lobbying of Parliament, a development enhanced by opportunities to appear before select committees (Norton 1997: 360).

The denial of access also increased direct action; if the *vox populi* could not be heard in the chambers of state it would be heard in the streets. A turning point may have been marked by the successful campaigns against the poll tax, suggesting a Leviathan lying dormant in the generally inert mass. Similarly, Heseltine's pit closure programme was derailed by large-scale demonstrations, and a campaign waged by the parents of the children shot in Dunblane in 1996 resulted in the banning of hand-guns; even royalty could not prevent the tide of feeling. Amidst increasing disruption people not only took to the streets, environmentalists risked death on the high seas, critical-mass cyclists risked rage on the roads, and anti-motorway and airport runway demonstrators took to the trees and tunnels. Daniel Hooper (aka Swampy) emerged from underground in Devon before the TV cameras and walked unpunished from court in 1997 to become a folk hero and a welcome guest on chat-shows. Thatcher's attempt to restrict access to government had uncovered new and perhaps dangerous regions in the complex map of power.

The recourse to direct action continued under New Labour. A 250,000-strong Countryside March descended upon London in February 1998, pledged to save the 'British country way of life', particularly the hunting of foxes. Organized by a 'Countryside Alliance', funding came from some of Britain's biggest companies, the Duke of Westminster and even America's shooting and hunting lobby (*Independent*, 26 Feb. 1998). In March 1998 the government refused to make time available for Mike Foster's private member's bill to ban foxhunting, despite earlier pledges.

September 2000 saw what one authority described as the pressure politics event of the year (Grant 2001: 337). Direct action by farmers and road hauliers sent government popularity reeling and forced concessions on fuel tax. Grant

---

THANKS TO ALL THOSE WHO HELPED US DO OUR WORK IN 1998
Shell for deciding to recycle the Brent Spar...at last.
John Prescott for agreeing not to dump any oil installations in the ocean.
Japan for becoming the 26th nation to ratify the Antarctic Treaty.
Michael Meacher for agreeing to ban toxic and radioactive discharges from the sea by 2020.
EU fisheries ministers for banning 'wall of death' driftnets.
Peter Mandelson for not putting PVC on the Millennium Dome roof.
...OK, so we had to run campaigns against some of them first – but thanks anyway.

Extract from front cover of Greenpeace, *Annual Review 1998*

discerned a fundamental challenge to the orthodoxy that quiet Whitehall negotiations with insider groups was the dominant mode of effective pressure politics. Indeed, prior to this, farmers and road hauliers would have been seen as
insider groups *par excellence*. Developments seemed to suggest that large-scale
disruption, or its threat, could yield results. Yet this would produce a costly way
of forming policy in which ultimately 'everyone would be worse off' (Grant
2001: 348). However, there could be no doubt that the more covert forms of
consultation continued under New Labour, some of them proving controversial
when donors to party funds appeared to benefit from policies (see p. 339).

New Labour: old corporatism or new social partnership?

Part of Labour's modernization process had been a fundamental revamping of
its relationship with the unions. The promise of 'fairness not favours' ruled out
any return to the 1970s; the talk was of a new 'social partnership'. Moreover,
this was a reality that the 'new unionists' – those sympathetic to 'New Labour',
including TUC leader John Monks – were prepared to accept (Farnham 1996:
597). By 2002, however, with changes in union leadership, the withdrawal of
union funds and an increasing incidence of public-sector strikes, the partnership was looking distinctly shaky.

In opposition, Labour had made strenuous efforts to gain the approval of
establishment interest groups. The 1996 annual conference marked the coming
of the new style with champagne receptions and working breakfasts between
business leaders and leading party figures. Stands were erected by such powerful interests as the Institute of Directors, BA, the British Bankers' Association,

Road hauliers
blocking the M4 in
protest at fuel
prices

Photo: Times Newspapers Ltd

Lloyds, and even defence contractors. Tony Blair paid each a courteous visit in front of the television cameras. Within its first weeks of office Labour had made a number of corporatist-style appointments embracing establishment figures. David Simon of BP was to consider competitiveness in Europe and Martin Taylor, chief executive of Barclays Bank, was appointed to head a task-force streamlining the welfare state.

The 'social partnership' was no reincarnation of Neddy, with its alleged veto on policy; government would remain firmly in the driving seat, supervising a range of advisory groups, such as the Low Pay Commission, embracing not only the CBI and TUC but other players considered central to economic success. An advisory group on competitiveness included Adair Turner, head of the CBI and John Monks of the TUC, as well as the heads of major companies, including Nissan, Glaxo, BP and Guinness. For some of the older-thinking unionists, the social partnership seemed to offer too much to business interests and did not seek sufficient influence over company management. A key area of early dissent concerned union recognition in the workplace, the government appearing loath to force the CBI to match union concessions.

The access to the Prime Minister enjoyed by figures like Bernie Ecclestone and Rupert Murdoch demonstrated Labour's extraordinary respect for private power. After one year in office, an official register of firms and their clients (set up at the request of Sir Gordon Downey) revealed an exodus of former Labour staffers to the world of influence, almost all major lobbying companies employing at least one. The interests represented included arms dealing, the tobacco industry and firms involved in genetic engineering. Alarmingly, these were being wooed by party fundraisers (*Independent*, 24 March 1998).

Corporatism has never been highly developed in Britain. Some crucially important interests, particularly the City, remained outside the corporate institutions, and even those included never entirely eschewed competitive behaviour, making self-interested decisions which were bad for the economy as a whole (Marquand 1988: 121–3). Grant (1984: 130) saw 'a weakly developed system of corporatist interaction . . . coexisting with a . . . healthy and important pluralist system'. This raised the question: 'Which issues are decided in which way?' Cawson and Saunders developed the dual state thesis, suggesting that economic issues tend to be settled in a closed corporatist style affording much power to capitalist interests, while those broadly concerning welfare emerge from a more open pluralist process (Cawson 1986: ch. 7). However, the economic implications of the welfare state blunt this distinction. The 1997 Labour government justified many welfare policies in terms of Treasury, rather than social, considerations. For Middlemass (1979: 371–85) the system contains a 'corporate bias', reflecting a *desire* on the part of government to insulate itself from pluralism in order to best meet the needs of capitalist interests.

Critics see the world of participation like an exclusive golf club, fine for members but not so good for those beyond the fairways. Although trade unions enter this exclusive world, this may represent little more than the opportunity to act as caddies, with no invitations to the bar. For much of the time the main requirement from them was to suspend their *raison d'être* and hold down wages (Mullard 1993: 235–6). Whether corporatist or pluralist, some interests seem to come out winners and some losers.

From 1979 Britain became an increasingly unequal society, by 1995 the most unequal in the western world. To some this outcome is desirable, to others it is morally defective, but regardless of the ethics, why does it happen? It is necessary to open yet another door in the labyrinthine world of influence and go beyond the group approach.

Beyond the Group Approach

Although an examination of organized interests tells us much about the politics of influence, it cannot explain everything. Why are some interests more advantaged than others? Is this but a *symptom* of a more fundamental architecture of power. To search for the explanation, we must examine big questions about the *structure* of society. Two broad perspectives that help to illuminate this are the **elitist** and the **Marxist**.

Elite theory

This approach, sometimes termed 'scientific elitism', was pioneered at the beginning of the twentieth century by a school of Italian thinkers now known as the classical elitists – Mosca, Pareto and Michels. They agreed with Marx that the institutions of liberal democracy did not work in the way claimed by apologists; the masses tended to be dominated by the few, who ruled in their own interest. However, unlike Marx, they did not see the economic base of society as the sole cause; the processes, inevitable and ineluctable like laws of nature, were present in all forms of society. The talented people in all walks of life would inevitably come out on top and, having done so, would preserve their supremacy by *collusion* with each other. This elite power is *cumulative*, new generations coming along and finding silver spoons in their mouths. The elite gains control of the state by dominating the parties, securing the elective offices and monopolizing key official positions; it becomes a ruling class. For right-wing commentators this is not only natural, it is desirable. Key positions are held by those best fitted for them. However, to critics the ever-present danger is that the elite rules in its own interest rather than that of the whole society. Elite theory was rejuvenated in the 1950s by those sceptical of pluralism. Floyd Hunter's famous (1953) study argued that a small coherent corps of wealthy people dominated both the social and political life in a US city, while C. Wright Mills argued that the pluralist belief in automatically balancing forces was more 'ideological hope than factual description' (1959: 126n).

Many chapters in this book suggest that, with its aristocracy and monarchy, public schools (still expanding), Oxbridge institutions, exclusive London clubs, the Freemasons and so on, Britain's social culture is replete with elitist features.

This is both symbolized and reinforced in the unique and elaborate honours system. Titles continue to be inherited by those in the upper classes, with lesser ones bestowed upon the chosen from the upper-middle class. Life peerages have enhanced elite power with seats in Parliament for those who come far nearer the royal box than the ballot box. The elite structure has been maintained by a class system which, while permitting some 'short-range' mobility (Giddens 1973: 181–2), has kept most in the same class. A study by *The Economist* (19 Dec. 1992) revealed that, despite meritocratic rhetoric from the grocer's daughter and circus performer's son who had become prime ministers, the education and social background of the top 100 people had changed very little. Two-thirds of the group had been to private schools and over half to Oxbridge. They were also overwhelmingly male and white. Only one woman had made it into the group without going to Oxbridge – Elizabeth II!

Yet the idea that the rich and successful are able to cohere and collude is questionable. There is rivalry and bitterness within the upper and upper-middle classes, much of it arising from economic competition under the name of *individualism*. The quest to understand the balance of power and privilege is clearly not yet over.

Marxist perspectives

For Marx, the key driving force in politics was a struggle not between groups but between classes. The Marxist perspective argues that, under capitalism, the state always operates in the interests of the owners and controllers of capital. Today economic globalization means that this class is transnational and its power within any single state is amplified (see chapter 4). There are, however, many schools of thought with conflicting views on how this domination is effected. At one extreme, the state may be said to be controlled through the conspiratorial activities of the capitalist class – an instrumental perspective. At the other extreme, the structural perspective holds that the state is compelled to act in favour of the business and financial interests by virtue of the logic of capitalism.

The instrumental perspective The view of the state as an instrument of the ruling class is a feature of classical Marxist analysis and Marx's description of the government as a 'committee for managing the common affairs of the bourgeoisie' is regularly cited. The **instrumental** perspective can be supported in many ways, beginning with the manner in which, during the nineteenth century, the rising bourgeoisie reformed the state machine. Since then the senior civil service, armed forces, judiciary, and so on, have largely recruited from the same establishment soil that nurtures the financiers and businessmen. Gramsci saw the ruling class using these key positions to shape the dominant ideology so that the masses would be content and not threaten the revolution predicted by Marx. The penetration and funding of the Conservative Party (and increasingly New Labour) and the ability of a right-wing press to deliver sympathetic governments are further testimony to capitalist domination. Ministers may

> There is a high degree of homogeneity among the members of the dominant class...They constantly cross each other's paths in an incessant round of meetings, lunches, dinners, functions, and ceremonies, and as members of boards, commissions, councils, committees and institutions of the most varied kind.
>
> Ralph Miliband (Marxist scholar), *Capitalist Democracy in Britain* (1984: 7)

themselves take up company directorates upon retirement. The extensive use of patronage offers yet further ways to strengthen the influence of the business and financial communities through the quangocracy. We have seen how Labour's victory in 1997 came only after systematic courtship of capitalist interests and a loosening of its union ties (chapter 10).

Contrary to the pluralist argument that political and economic competition limit group power, there is evidence of coherence, if not collusion, within the capitalist class. At the head of Britain's largest companies are the directors, often sitting on the boards of several companies: in 1976, eleven men held 56 of the 250 top directorships in Britain, as well as many others in smaller companies (Scott 1985: 44). In 1988 the boards of the top 250 companies contained 290 multiple directors (Scott 1991: 79). Class solidarity is further promoted by intermarriage and various methods of excluding outsiders, including private education, freemasonry and inimitable accents.

In addition, although their interests can sometimes diverge (Marsh and Locksley 1983: 21–52), the split between industry and finance is now a myth: 'In terms of both ownership and control, banks, traders, and producers have come closer together the last 60 years' (Scott 1985: 45). The split is between big business and finance on the one hand and medium and small business on the other, with the former dominating (Scott 1991: 151). The fusion of finance and industry produces an 'inner circle' of finance capitalists at the heart of the state, dominating the top levels of the major cohesion-promoting institutions: the Association of Chambers of Commerce, the Institute of Directors, the British Institute of Management and the CBI. Unseem (1984) argues that world recession from the 1970s saw an intensification of the political activity of big

---

Egg on the face of power

On 24 December 1988 the *Independent* revealed that the boards of the large food and poultry feed manufacturers, producing most of the eggs sold in British supermarkets, included a number of ex-cabinet ministers and top civil servants (Sir Peter Carey, permanent secretary at the DTI, 1976–83; John Biffen, former leader of the Commons and a senior Conservative MP; and former Cabinet Secretary Lord Hunt). Another big feed supplier had donated nearly £10,000 to Conservative funds in the 1987 election year. Little wonder that the government agreed to compensate egg producers for lost sales during the salmonella scare. Little wonder that the person responsible for alerting the public (Edwina Currie) disappeared from the ministerial firmament.

business, with the inner circle representing a City view on behalf of the whole financial and business community on key matters of economic policy. The Thatcherite 'big bang' transformed the City, an influx of foreign capital extending links to a global financial community.

The structural perspective However, although it may capture a deep truth about the *essence* of the state under capitalism, the committee metaphor should not be taken literally. The idea that a class consciously makes the state an entirely compliant instrument is open to question. Indeed it can be argued that the very existence of state institutions (Parliament, the executive, bureaucracies, and so on) promises some degree of autonomy because these develop interests of their own. This is part of the public choice theorists' explanation for the expansion of social democracy, producing a large empire-building bureaucracy. Many public servants have a firm ideological commitment and regularly vote Labour (p. 253). In the twilight of the Major government one Conservative minister remarked ruefully that, while some top mandarins might pose problems for Labour, the grades below 'all read the *Guardian* or the *Independent*' (Timmins and Kampfner 1997).

In addition, politicians are highly ambitious and keen to remain in office. If the demands of capitalists were to threaten or inhibit their ability to do this they could be expected to resist. Some writers even believe that liberal-democratic states can actually be highly insensitive to the needs of capital. Crouch (1979: 27) argues that 'two of the most remarkable facts...are, first, the extent to which their ruling class mistrust the state and try to limit its activities, and second, the relative responsiveness of the polity...to working class demands'.

However, the structural perspective argues that the state must perform certain functions if the capitalist economy is to survive. It must protect profitability and facilitate private capital accumulation. The state depends on the prosperity of capitalism for its tax income (Grant 1987: 239–40). This interpretation was advanced by the Marxist scholar Nicos Poulantzas (1973), who conducted a long-running debate with Ralph Miliband. In this view, far from appearing as an instrument of the capitalist class, the state must be able to show a degree of real autonomy in order to:

◆ provide services (health care, education, roads, legal services and so on) that it is unprofitable for capitalists to provide;
◆ promote homogeneity within the capitalist class to prevent it destroying itself, reconciling the fundamental conflict between finance capital, monopoly capital and non-monopoly capital;
◆ ensure political stability by absorbing potentially disruptive demands from the underprivileged and ethical pressure groups;
◆ keep welfare spending low enough to guarantee profitability;
◆ legitimate the capitalist system by promoting an ideology espousing inequality as for the good of all.

The instrumental model is *voluntaristic*, allowing individuals choice in their behaviour, while the **structural** one is *deterministic*, seeing them as puppets or role-players. In the latter case politicians are driven by the imperatives of capitalism as the actor playing Hamlet is driven by Shakespeare's script. Although both perspectives can be seen in Marx, the French philosopher Althusser (1969) believed the structural to be the more important. In real-world states we find elements of both; people have some choice but they are constrained by the system.

Questioning the Marxist perspectives

The Marxist interpretation is not welcomed by politicians and writers in the liberal tradition.

The managerial revolution thesis It has been argued in one version of elite theory that a managerial revolution has swept through the capitalist system. The old-style capitalists have been displaced by a diverse body of anonymous shareholders, allowing control of capital to pass to a new managerial class of meritocrats, well educated but of lower social origins and without the same close identification with those controlling the state (Burnham 1942).

However, Marxists deny that power *has* passed to neutral meritocrats, asserting that it remains with the old dominant class, although the latter has undergone an internal transformation. In the first place, although a new ladder of meritocracy may exist, it is also open to the sons and daughters of the upper class, and they still have the best chance of ascending. Moreover, the position of meritocrats remains insecure; they can easily land upon the head of a snake and slither down to square one. Again, the meritocrats operate largely at the level of middle management, leaving the traditional elite members, with power based on ownership of property (and shares), in the boardrooms and in strategic control. Astonishingly, between the 1850s and the 1970s (when Britain was transformed into a social democracy) the proportion of chairmen of major companies with upper-class backgrounds remained stable at around 66 per cent (Stanworth and Giddens 1974). In addition, the old upper class is sufficiently permeable to absorb outstanding aspirants from the lower strata who, with

> Do you suppose that you and half a dozen amateurs like you, sitting in a row in that foolish gabble shop, can govern Undershaft and Lazarus? No my friend: you will do what pays us. You will make war when it suits us, and keep peace when it doesn't ... When I want to keep my dividends up you will discover that my want is a national need.
>
> Andrew Undershaft (wealthy industrialist), addressing his MP son-in-law in
> Bernard Shaw's *Major Barbara* (1907)

artificially cultivated upper-class mores, become '*plus royaux que le roi*' and neutered as potential agents of social change. Finally, although companies are no longer in the hands of the old-style capitalists, there remains a small class with large personal shareholdings, so that control of capital remains in the hands of the few: in the view of Scott (1991: ch. 4) 'still a ruling class'.

Moreover, the managers' power is dwarfed by that of the finance capitalists, moving in the world driven not by commodities and production but by banks and ledgers. These come from various walks of the Establishment, including politics, the civil service and industry, and most have titles. Holding multiple directorships, they unify the business system (figure 17.4). Their strength is enhanced beyond measure through economic globalization, de-regulation of finance and the formation of the almighty TNCs with their ever-present threat to desert any country which does not cater for their needs (chapter 4).

Bureaucratic power The idea of class domination of government can be countered by the argument that the civil service is a neutral machine, safeguarding the public interest. Some Marxists accept bureaucratic power as a source of state autonomy. However, civil service recruitment and socialization processes have long tended towards harmony with establishment interests (see p. 468). Upon becoming Cabinet Secretary, Sir Robin Butler was immediately proposed for membership of the Athenaeum, Brookes and the Oxford and Cambridge – exclusive clubs that enable the great to meet the good (Paxman 1991: 313). Moreover, unlike the USA, Britain offers no public interest defence for a bureaucrat going public on an issue of concern (see p. 480).

Welfare statism It may be argued that the post-war rise of social democracy, with a wide range of policies designed to ease the conditions of the working class, is hardly evidence of upper-class domination. Yet this may be countered with an argument that the **welfare state** serves the interests of capital by socializing the costs of production, furnishing a body of healthy and reasonably well-educated workers and maintaining social harmony through legitimation (Gough 1979). Moreover, if the economy runs out of steam, a *fiscal crisis* arises as the tax-borne cost of welfare erodes profitability (O'Connor 1973); when this occurs, the capitalist interests will soon rein in the welfare state. This appeared to happen with the collapse of the long boom in the mid-1970s when doctors, for example, once insiders, found themselves on the outside as NHS budgets were squeezed in the interests of tax cuts. The New Labour government continued the squeeze, Blair proclaiming an end to the 'something for nothing culture' at the time of the 1998 Queen's speech. When Chancellor Gordon Brown announced increased expenditure for health and education in 2002, the press hailed the move as 'Gordon's Gamble' (see p. 525), many predicting the beginning of the fall of the government.

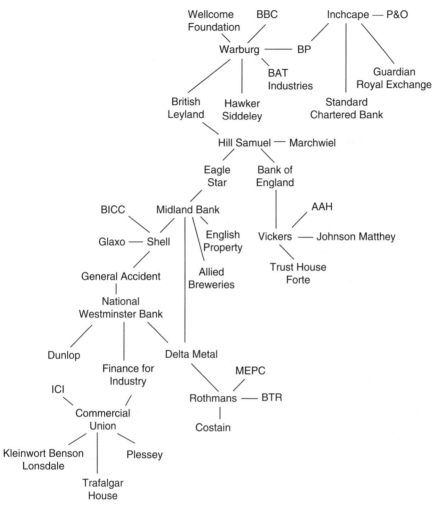

Figure 17.4
Top company links,
1976.

Source: Scott (1985: figure 2.5).

Who Gets the Loot?

Explanations of power in society range from the most benign version of plural-ism to class-based elitism. All devalue the role of the democratically elected government, representing an important corrective to the accounts that see formal institutions as the beginning and end of political life. Power is a complex mystery. One way to solve it is to use the technique of Hercule Poirot and see who gets the loot; to repeat the question at the beginning of this book: who gets what, when, how? Although from the late 1970s the corporatist institutions became overgrown with creepers and the path to Whitehall gathered moss, Lawson's 1988 Budget placed the loot in the wallets and handbags of the wealthy at the expense of the rest. By 1995 some 25 per cent of the male workforce was unemployed or not making themselves available for work. Between 1979 and 1996, the proportion of households with no working adult partner had risen from 6 to 16 per cent. At the other end of the scale, a 1998 survey revealed forty-nine directors of British companies to be earning over £1 million a year (Hobson 1999: 557). As inequality steadily increased, Will Hutton (1996) depicted the emerging social divide as the 30/30/40 society (see p. 186).

Nothing represents communal welfare so clearly as public health, yet with powerful lobbies associated with areas as varied as agriculture, convenience foods, tobacco, drugs manufacture and trunk roads, many issues have arisen (from salmonella and BSE to railways neglect, pesticide use, pollution, road congestion and tobacco advertising) in which governments have appeared slow to defend the public interest. The case of BSE placed the issue in sharp focus. Evidence presented to the inquiry in April 1998 showed that regulations to prevent the catastrophe could have been put in place in the mid-1970s but had been thwarted by lobbying from rendering firms (*Guardian*, 30 April 1998). In 1990, Agriculture Minister John Gummer displayed rather bizarre loyalty to producer interests, giving the nation the poignant image of his small daughter munching a beefburger on prime-time television. The Southwood Committee set up to investigate the issue refrained from recommending a ban on the use of cattle offal in food, not for scientific reasons but because they felt politically it was a 'no-goer' with the MAFF (Winter 1996: 163). Despite much rhetoric about establishing an independent Food Standards Agency, it was not until early 1999 that firm proposals were announced.

In broader terms governments have responded to the City preference for short-term dividends and capital gains, free international capital flows, stable exchange rates and tight monetary controls. The general economic interest is sacrificed as companies are constrained to boost share prices through wage cuts, downsizing and takeover bids rather than long-term investment. Labour came to power in May 1997 and, if the capitalist interests at home and abroad needed a sign, the government gave it in pledging to stick to the Conservatives' spending targets for the next two years. The Welfare-to-Work scheme aimed to promote a work ethic; 'life on the dole' was not to be an option. Labour had learned the lesson that socialism in a capitalist economy meant life in opposition. The party claimed it had made a new pact with the people; for critics it was a Faustian pact with capital.

Yet in the shadowy world of power, policy is made in many ways. Sometimes mass opinion can sway a government, sometimes election promises must be honoured, sometimes pluralistic bargaining takes place. Feminists and environmentalists, for example, have certainly secured some victories. However, the argument that the most important areas are under elite domination (as C. Wright Mills concluded for the USA) is compelling. The pattern of economic power moulds the space in which politics is enacted. The struggles of those representing the poor and underprivileged resemble that of Sisyphus, whose torment in hell is forever to push a great boulder to the top of a hill, from which it will invariably roll down again.

Key points

■ The politics of influence takes place behind the formal scenery of the constitution; it is largely the domain of organized interests.

■ Promotional groups advance broad principles while sectional groups protect their members.

■ Groups have bargaining counters in the form of resources governments need.

■ Points of access to the political system include public opinion, Parliament, political parties, the executive, the bureaucracy and the institutions of the EU.

■ Not all groups enjoy equal access; some are insiders and others outsiders.

■ Two principal theories explaining group politics are pluralism and corporatism, although there are a number of variants of each.

■ Some theorists see group involvement as unnatural, distorting the allocation of resources within society.

■ Elitists and Marxists look for even deeper sources of power within the polity.

■ On the basis of the question 'Who gets what?', the system mainly operates in favour of the large-scale owners and controllers of capital.

Review your understanding of the following terms and concepts

bourgeoisie	Marxism	pressure group
corporatism	neocorporatism	promotional group
determinism	neopluralism	public choice theory
dual state thesis	outsider group	ruling class
elitism	peak organization	sectional group
incrementalism	pluralism	selective incentives
insider group	pluralist stagnation	structural power
instrumental power	policy community	subgovernment
interest aggregation	policy network	tripartism
interest group	polyarchy	voluntarism

Assignment

Study the extract from the *New Statesman* (on p. 560) and answer the following questions.

		Mark (%)
1	Are young people today apathetic, or have they just found new ways of participating beyond the ballot box?	30
2	'The anti-capitalist movement has realised that it cannot trust the corporate media to see beyond establishment interests.' Discuss.	30
3	Is the traditional view that outsider groups might occasionally be powerful but insider groups are more effective at influencing decision-makers still true today? Illustrate your answer with examples from, and beyond, the extract.	40

May Day 2001

What shape will the deliriously anticipated May Day protests in London take? Will there be hijackings, kidnappings, pillaging and plunder? Let's consider what actions have been publicised already. There's to be a veggie-burger hand out by the Mcdonald's in Kings Cross, a picnic in Victoria Embankment Gardens, and a city of cardboard hotels will be built on Mayfair. There's to be a Critical Mass cycle ride from Liverpool Street....There'll be protests against third world debt outside Coutts and the World Bank office.

There'll be a picnic against privatisation on the Elephant and Castle roundabout, and a protest in Earl's Court against Accommodata, the contractor that the Home Office uses to house refugees. At Oxford Circus there'll be drummers, jugglers and dancing...

If there is any violence, it is far more likely to be the result of an irresponsible press that has unquestioningly printed stories fed it by the Metropolitan Police. We have been warned that, on May Day, we need only be standing around looking a bit shifty to be sent straight to jail.

The anti-capitalist movement (or as Naomi Klein terms it, the 'pro-democracy movement') has realised that it cannot trust the corporate media to see beyond establishment interests. They must 'become the media' themselves. ...

Many campaigners have been using the internet to create their own news channels: go to www.indymedia.org.uk to read alternative accounts of the May Day protests. This is a democratisation of the media: anyone can post their own news stories, audio, video or picture files.

Extract from Andrew Barley 'Protest: a short but definitive guide'. This is taken from an article which first appeared in the *New Statesman*, 30 April 2001, pp. 24–5.

Questions for discussion

1 'In the analysis of politics, pressure groups rather than institutions are the key actors.' Discuss.
2 What problems are likely to face a group advocating a reduction in car use?
3 'Pressure groups are a natural extension of the liberal-democratic state.' Discuss.
4 'Groups that resort to loud public campaigns are revealing impotence rather than strength.' Discuss, with examples.
5 Is British corporatism dead?
6 'Rational people do not join pressure groups.' Discuss.

7 'In all societies power will tend to be held by a small elite.' Discuss in the British context.

8 'A committee for managing the affairs of the bourgeoisie'. What does this say about government under capitalism?

9 'Pressure groups distort the popular will.' Discuss with examples of government policy.

10 Compare and contrast different theories of power in society.

Topic for debate

This house asserts that direct action is the most effective way for ordinary people to participate in politics today.

Further reading

Baggott, R. (1995) *Pressure Groups Today.*
Up-to-date introductory text.

Bentley, A. F. (1967) *The Process of Government* (first published 1908).
The classic text.

Bottomore, T. (1964) *Elites in Society.*
Good introduction to elite theory.

Grant, W. (1995) *Pressure Groups, Politics and Democracy,* 2nd edn.
A comprehensive introduction, including group activity at the EU level.

Jordan, G. (1991) *The Commercial Lobbyists: Politics for Profit in Britain.*
Authoritative account of the rise of professional lobbying.

Lehmbruch, G. and Schmitter, P. (eds) (1982) *Patterns of Corporatist Policy-Making.*
Comparative insight with some seminal contributions.

Mazey, S. and Richardson, J. (1993) *Lobbying in the European Community.*
Examines the new focus for pressure-group activity.

Miliband, R. (1984) *Capitalist Democracy in Britain.*
A classic neomarxist perspective on power in society.

Olson, M. (1982) *The Rise and Decline of Nations.*
The politics of influence from a public choice theorist.

Scott, J. (1991) *Who Rules Britain?*
Asks if there is still a ruling class in Britain. Traces industrial and financial dynasties and answers 'Yes'.

For light relief

Ben Elton, *Gridlock*.
Comic novel about the nightmarish power of the roads lobby.

Jeremy Paxman, *Friends in High Places*.
Britain's most acerbic inquisitor of the high and mighty making enemies in high places.

Frederick Raphael, *The Glittering Prizes*.
A nostalgic view of a privileged world where success comes as of right to scions of the Establishment.

George Bernard Shaw, *Major Barbara*.
Explores with humour and insight government–industry relations, exposing greed and hypocrisy.

On the net

With its anarchic nature, the internet is a natural medium for all kinds of groups, from the mainstream to the more outlandish, to promote their particular viewpoints and encourage participation in their campaigns. The One World site (http://www.oneworld.org) gives access to over 350 organizations working for global justice, while the two main environmental organizations, Greenpeace (http://www.greenpeace.org.uk) and Friends of the Earth (http://foe.co.uk), concentrate on saving the world. More narrowly, the recently formed Countryside Alliance (http://countryside-alliance.org) promotes the interests of rural people (including field sports). You can also access the sites of the peak organizations representing employers (http://www.cbi.org.uk) and labour (http://www.tuc.org. uk) in their negotiations with government.

Part IV

The Outer Reaches of the State: Worlds Beyond Whitehall

The media construction of British politics is generally centralist in orientation; it is around the precincts of Westminster and Whitehall that the heat of policy-making is generated. However, when we refocus through a wider-angle lens we find a variety of institutions which, while responsible for making and implementing much state policy, operate with varying degrees of freedom from the central institutions of government and the system of democratic accountability to Parliament.

These bodies include the civil service agencies already encountered in chapter 15. However, in this section we move even further from the centre to examine four areas: a diverse category known as quangos, the system of local government, the agencies of law and order and the judiciary. Why are these functions distanced from the central state? In the case of the quangos we shall see that there is a variety of reasons for taking matters out of the hands of politicians. In the case of local government, the intention is for local democracy to supplement that of Parliament. The distancing of law and order from the central state prevents the emergence of a police state, and with the judiciary the purpose is to give effect to the constitutional principle of the separation of powers.

Yet in moving from centre stage we are by no means leaving the world of politics. We shall argue that **arm's-length administration** is often part of a strategy to 'technocratize' important matters out of politics and hence out of the public domain. In addition, we find in the grey, twilight part of the state much scope for the dangerous exercise of political patronage.

18

Arm's-length Administration: Quasi-autonomy, Quasi-democracy

We begin exploring the non-Whitehall territory with a constitutional rag-bag that defies clear classification and, under the acronym 'quango', sounds more like something Alice might have encountered than part of the machinery of government. Bodies in this category share little in common other than their freedom from the machinery of ministerial control and parliamentary accountability. The chapter is something of a pot-pourri, comprising four main sections. The first introduces the category as a whole, identifying some important subgroups. In the second section we examine a very special group: the institutions comprising the National Health Service. Next we consider the lessons of the largely defunct category of nationalized industries, which were given the special constitutional status of public corporations. Their difficulties and contradictions typify those of quangos in general. The fourth section considers the programme of privatization and the problems thrown up by the creation of a new generation of special regulatory bodies. We conclude by evaluating the implications of shadowy state territory at the fringes of democracy.

Introducing the Quango

Although not officially recognized in Whitehall, scholars and politicians use the acronym **quango** for Quasi-Autonomous Non-Government Organization. The term is employed rather loosely and often pejoratively; some might prefer the *Daily Telegraph*'s 'Quite Unacceptable And Nasty Government Offshoots'! Officials sometimes call them non-departmental public bodies. An alternative term is QGAs (Quasi-Governmental Agencies), while a report by Democratic

Audit catalogued the vast panorama of what it termed 'extra-governmental organizations' (EGOs) (Weir and Hall 1994). Although set up by government, often on a statutory basis, they are bodies operating with some degree of freedom from democratic control and accountability. Usually funded from the national exchequer, they are run by boards appointed by ministers from the nation's trusted worthies; not only 'great and good', they are generally white, middle class and male.

There are a number of reasons for this administration at 'arm's-length'.

- ◆ *The evolutionary pattern.* Many important state functions (e.g. education, housing and medical services) grew up at the periphery rather than at the centre.
- ◆ *The policy–administration dichotomy.* There is a normative belief that policy-making and implementation should be separated, the latter being entrusted to the arm's-length agency.
- ◆ *Commercialism.* When the state becomes involved in commercial activities the traditional institutions and rules are seen as inappropriate.
- ◆ *Expertise.* Many areas of policy require knowledge and experience beyond the scope of politicians and bureaucrats (e.g. drug safety, the environment, the school curriculum).
- ◆ *Artistic and technical matters.* It has been felt that pin-striped bureaucrats and popularity-seeking politicians are ill-equipped to make judgements about distributing funds to the arts and sciences.
- ◆ *Personal morality.* Certain areas of life are felt to be beyond political judgement (e.g. race relations or film censorship).
- ◆ *Freedom.* A fundamental plank of liberal democracy is that certain state functions must be free from political control (e.g. broadcasting, police and justice).
- ◆ *National security.* In the interest of security, certain matters are kept beyond the eyes and ears not only of Parliament but even of ministers. The security services operate with few restrictions, sometimes at the fringes of legality.
- ◆ *Efficiency.* It is often more rational to provide services through locally based bodies able to respond to local conditions.
- ◆ *Democracy.* If democracy is to be real it should go beyond mere voting to allow people to participate directly.

Arm's-length agencies may be broadly classified as follows.

Judicial These are mainly tribunals and inquiries, of which there are many hundreds (see chapter 20).

Advisory A peculiarly British institution, known variously as advisory councils, working parties, boards, royal commissions, standing conferences or task forces, these are created to examine specific problems and make recommendations, though their use is often seen as a government ploy to avoid action.

Classified as temporary or permanent, **advisory bodies** have lain thick on the ground – in 1979, the Pliatzky Report (1980: 1–2) identified over 1,500 but they were cut back under Thatcher. The temporary group includes the large, prestigious royal commissions addressing major issues such as the reform of local government or the police, their deliberations often taking several years and sometimes heralding momentous changes. The permanent category is larger and includes some major bodies advising on matters such as the safety of drugs; but many, such as the White Fish Authority, have worked diligently in the cobwebbed backrooms of the state. The Blair government placed renewed emphasis on the task force, the species multiplying rapidly at the epicentre of government. Examples included the Social Exclusion Unit and the New Deal Task Force.

Consultative These are corporatist forums such as Neddy, designed to bring together ministers, civil servants and representatives of interests. They had their heyday during the consensus era, declined under Thatcher and began to make a comeback under Blair (see pp. 549–50).

Crown Bodies These are charged with the management of institutions such as the royal palaces, the British Museum, the National Gallery and Kew Gardens.

Commercial After the second world war a special public body was created to operate the nationalized industries: the **public corporation**. Although these industries have largely returned to the private sector, the principle of freeing state bodies to act commercially has advanced since the early 1980s.

Regulatory These agencies protect citizens from abuses such as exploitation, pollution and racial and sexual discrimination. They are common in areas such as hygiene, building standards, safety at work, the use of pesticides and quality of food. Regulation is an alternative to public ownership, particularly in conditions of natural monopoly, and a new generation of regulatory agencies grew up with privatization.

Self-financing A new kind of body developed from the late 1980s as a result of civil service agencification: the self-financing regulatory agency (SEFRA). These inspect, regulate and award licences to companies, aiming to pay their own way by charging fees. Examples include the Medicines Control Agency, the Data Protection Agency and the Driver and Vehicle Licensing Agency.

Executive These actually administer some public service: disseminating information (tourist authorities, the Health Education Agency), distributing public funds (the education funding councils, the Arts Council) or delivering a service (NHS trusts). Pliatzky identified almost 500, but they became even more evident following the Thatcher government's creation of a 'new magistracy' (see p. 602 and Ridley and Wilson 1995). Police authorities effectively belong in this category. If housing associations, grant-maintained schools,

"*The committee on women's rights will now come to order.*"

Reproduced by permission of *Punch*

colleges and universities are added, the number of **executive bodies** soars to well over 4,000.

Sick of Democracy: the National Health Service

The National Health Service (NHS) is a very special case of arms-length administration. While much political activity sees the main goals in the battle for 'who gets what' in material terms, health is far more important to the quality of our lives. Yet curiously Britain's NHS, employing more people than any other organization in Western Europe, accounting for a huge proportion of GDP (6.9 per cent in 1995) and likely to be used by virtually every citizen in their journey from cradle to the grave, was placed beyond democratic control. The explanation for this conundrum lay in the politics of its creation.

> Everyone – rich or poor, man, woman or child – can use it. There are no charges … no insurance qualifications. But it is not a charity.
>
> Ministry of Health leaflet, on the eve of the birth of the NHS (Feb. 1948)

Genesis

In 1942, in the darkness of war, the Beveridge Report, *Social Insurance and Allied Services*, emerged as the blueprint for a welfare state. It espoused the New Liberal concept of *positive freedom* (see p. 33) from the 'evil giants' of want, ignorance, idleness, squalor and disease. The last of these would be felled by a comprehensive health service, free to all. A 1944 white paper, which enjoyed widespread support, outlined a unified service under local government and coordinated by a health minister. However, the passing of the mood of wartime emergency saw bitter political infighting. The doctors resented the idea of control by local councillors and a threat of non-cooperation finally carried the day. The result was a system run by appointed health authorities (Klein 1989: 95). Local government retained only the responsibility for community health care, and in 1974 this too was also lost to the health authorities.

> They neither speak as elected representatives nor do they have the expertise of their own officials. And their attitude to the secretary of state and the department is necessarily pretty subservient – they want to keep their jobs.
>
> Barbara Castle (Labour Minister of Health) on health authority chairs,
> *The Castle Diaries 1974–6* (1980)

The New Right reforms

The problem of medical dominance was recognized by the Thatcher government, alarmed at the NHS appetite for finance. However, the solution was to move even further beyond the arms and eyes of democracy. During the 1980s, under a 'general management' initiative, managers (often from the private sector) were brought in at all levels, their decisions to reflect economic criteria rather than democratic demand or clinical judgement. Even more fundamental changes followed a 1989 white paper introducing the 'internal market', which replaced central resource allocation to hospitals with competition between them. A whole new raft of quangos emerged as hospitals and community health care units became self-governing NHS trusts, under appointed boards, and groups of general practitioners became 'fundholders', receiving a budget with which to purchase care from the trusts. The Blair government promised to end the internal market but the changes were more to terminology than substance.

> Physicians of the utmost fame,
> Were called at once; but when they came,
> They answered, as they took their fees,
> 'There is no cure for this disease'.
>
> Hilaire Belloc (1870–1953; British essayist and poet), *Cautionary Tales*

Problems with the NHS: doctor knows best One of the key arguments for arm's-length administration is the involvement of experts, and the medical profession are experts *par excellence*. The structure of the NHS allowed a health policy community to evolve in which the profession played a dominant role (figure 18.1). Inevitably, the result was widespread acceptance of a 'medical' model of health care that reversed the old adage to say cure was better

Figure 18.1
The central arena
for health service
politics.

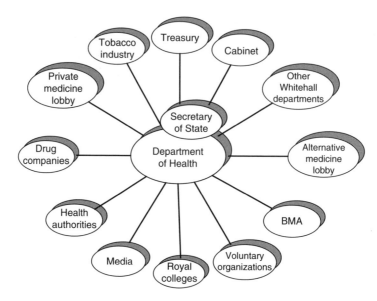

Tobacco industry · Treasury · Cabinet · Private medicine lobby · Other Whitehall departments · Secretary of State · Drug companies · Department of Health · Alternative medicine lobby · Health authorities · Media · Royal colleges · Voluntary organizations · BMA

than prevention. Policy entailed the expansion of expensive hi-tech hospital medicine, to the relative neglect of social and public health measures (including attacking poverty and polluting industries) that might have reduced illness in the first place. Patients, denied a democratic voice, were subjected to a paternalistic regime in which 'doctor knew best'.

Prescriptions for a cure

Various instruments have been introduced to remedy the lack of accountability, including local community health councils, a complaints procedure and a Health Services Ombudsman. There was also an increasing tendency for people to resort to the courts. To critics, these underlined the problem rather than solved it, and the call was for more democracy. The original local government model was recommended by the 1979 Merrison Royal Commission and in 1993 the Institute of Health Services Management argued for local authority involvement within the internal market set-up (Hunt 1995). In 1995 the independent Commission for Local Democracy (see p. 624) called for health authorities themselves to be directly elected. Lord Nolan suggested that the Audit Commission publish public interest reports on NHS bodies at its discretion.

> As to the cause of our illness
> One glance at our rags would
> Tell you more. It is the same cause that wears out
> Our bodies and our clothes.
>
> Bertolt Brecht (1898–1956; German dramatist and poet), 'A Worker's Speech to a Doctor'

Nationalizing Industry

Health care was not the only area to be nationalized and placed beyond the conventional mechanism of accountability in the post-war years. Large-scale advances in state ownership of industry occurred in two waves. The first, immediately following the war, encompassed coal, electricity, gas, rail, road haulage, air transport and steel. (The Bank of England was also nationalized at this time.) The second began in the mid-1960s under both Labour and Conservative governments, largely through state purchase of shares in a wide range of undertakings. This was not a capitalist economy but a **mixed economy**. The motives for state ownership were also mixed, and by no means all anti-capitalist.

Motivations for state ownership

The reasons for **nationalization** were partly ideological principle and partly political expediency, the left being more favourably disposed for a number of reasons.

- *Socialist doctrine*. Nationalization represents an attack on capitalism, central to the Labour Party constitution until expurgated by Blair.
- *Market imperfections*. Keynes showed that the free market alone did not produce the optimum allocation of resources; nationalization is one means of regulating it.
- *Power within society*. Large-scale owners of capital have great political power. Public ownership is a means of strengthening the democratic voice.
- *Protection of workers*. Industrial relations in the coal and rail industries were particularly bad. The state could prove a model employer.
- *Security*. Certain industries were adjudged too important for state security to be left in private hands. Similar considerations applied to atomic energy and the exploration of the North Sea for mineral fuels.
- *Natural monopolies*. Some industries (such as power and railways) were regarded as necessarily monopolistic and therefore the public had to be protected from exploitation.

Natural monopolies

In some industries, such as rail, power supply or telecommunications, the cost of creating the infrastructure is so high that companies will not enter unless sure of a profit. Because competition drives down profit, companies will tend to amalgamate or die. Two or more cannot exist side by side so a 'natural monopoly' will tend to emerge. Government must accept this reality and seek ways of regulating it to prevent abnormal profit and consumer exploitation rather than try to enforce competition with anti-monopoly laws.

Although the principle was ideologically anathema to capitalist interests, in practice there were advantages. The owners of outdated plant and machinery were not only relieved of the responsibility for modernization, they received generous compensation. Moreover, in an era that was Keynesian rather than socialist, most industry still remained in private hands and could benefit from state control of the **natural monopolies**. Table 18.1 shows the extent of the mix in the economy on the eve of the collapse of the post-war consensus.

However, the question of management became a key issue and an orthodoxy emerged that this could hardly be entrusted to Whitehall mandarins with little knowledge of industry, trussed in red tape and socialized in a culture of detailed parliamentary accountability. The quest to combine public accountability with commercial freedom led to the evolution of a new kind of arms-length agency – the public corporation.

The concept of the public corporation

In 1908 a Port of London Authority had been set up to manage London docks and the Labour government of 1929–31 had created a London Transport Passenger Board; both had considerable autonomy. A prominent figure in establishing the latter was Transport Minister Herbert Morrison, who outlined the model of the public corporation in *Socialism and Transport* (1933). Although connected to government through a sponsoring department, it was not subject to the full rigour of ministerial control or parliamentary accountability. Its management structure would broadly resemble that of a private industrial undertaking, although the board was appointed by ministerial patronage and responsible not to shareholders but to the nation. The key actors in this set-up were the minister of the sponsoring department, the chair of the board, Parliament, and a set of consumer councils established as watchdogs.

Table 18.1 The mixed economy at its height: the share of the big nine nationalized industries in the UK economy, 1975 (percentages of total)

Industry	Output	Employment	Investment
Post Office and Telecommunications	2.8	1.8	4.5
Electricity Board	1.5	0.7	2.9
British Airways	0.3	0.2	0.4
Coal Board	1.5	1.2	0.9
British Rail	1.2	1.0	1.0
National Bus Co.	0.2	0.3	0.1
National Freight Corporation	0.2	0.2	–
British Gas	0.8	0.4	1.7
British Steel	0.8	0.9	2.0
Total	9.3	6.7	13.5

Source: Data from McIntosh (1976).

Problems with the nationalized industries The key was to combine commercial freedom with public accountability; to secure that most illusory of human desires – the best of both worlds. Ministers were responsible for broad policy but the boards were to be free to make day-to-day management decisions. However, ministers were empowered to intervene in the 'national interest' and this meant that chairmen were to be regularly frustrated in their commercial designs. Factors leading governments to interfere included:

- the initial need to promote rapid post-war economic reconstruction;
- a desire to use the industries for management of the economy;
- a tendency to emphasize social interest at the expense of commercial performance, leaving some in need of huge government subsidies;
- a tendency to manipulate the industries for political advantage (such as holding down prices before elections).

The result was a blurring of the roles of boards and ministers, making it difficult for Parliament to pin ministers down. The national interest and commercial effectiveness were never successfully reconciled.

State shareholdings

An alternative form of nationalization was to become the main instrument after the initial phase. The principle was by no means new; government had acquired an interest in the Suez Canal in 1875 and shares in British Petroleum (BP) were used to guarantee naval oil supplies during the first world war. Such arrangements were more congenial to private capitalists, allowing maximum managerial independence to company directors.

The most important motive for this wave of nationalization was rescuing capitalist disasters rather than public control over industry. In 1966 Labour established an Industrial Reorganization Corporation (IRC) with capital of £200 million to promote industrial development through state share purchase, but much of its effort went into merely supporting lame ducks and it was abolished in 1970 by the Conservatives. The end of the long boom and the mid-1970s oil crises brought new problems and, returning to office in 1974, Labour established an even more comprehensive policy of state aid. A National Enterprise Board (NEB) was set up in 1975 as a more powerful successor to the IRC and shares were acquired in over twenty companies. However, the Thatcher government reversed the trend, giving lame ducks specific time limits to restore their plumage and winding down the NEB.

State share purchase: the problems This policy was always controversial. The left saw it as propping up capitalism at a time when its frailties were being exposed, while the right viewed it as creeping statism. The firms themselves found it difficult to pursue profits when the government was seeking social (employment) as well as commercial objectives. Finally, the transfer of substantial funds to the private sector raised constitutional questions of responsibility, since Parliament had little ability to scrutinize private companies (Mitchell 1982).

Privatization: the Full Circle

The 1979 general election introduced a government committed more firmly than any of its predecessors to the view that public corporations should function profitably. State ownership was at a peak, producing 10.5 per cent of GDP, employing some 1.75 million, with an annual turnover of £55 billion and annual investment of around £7.5 billion. As part of the general strategy to reduce the PSBR and control inflation, medium-term financial targets were set and tight restrictions placed on grants and borrowing. Ministers took a Pontius Pilate interest in a number of disputes over wages and job losses. The power of patronage was used to replace Labour appointees with ideological sympathizers from the private sector or ex-civil servants. Yet tinkering with the system did not go far enough. A radical solution began to brew in the cauldrons of the New Right think-tanks that was to redraft the political agenda – **privatization**.

The case for privatization

Broadly meaning the transfer of a state-owned undertaking into private hands, privatization offered the following advantages:

◆ consumer sovereignty through breaking the state monopolies;
◆ greater efficiency through the profit motive and shareholder pressure;
◆ reduced public expenditure through the ending of state subsidies;
◆ reduction in the PSBR;
◆ worker ownership through shareholding;
◆ no political interference in management;
◆ a sense of *real* ownership for the shareholding public rather than the *illusion* of ownership given by nationalization.

Generally these arguments came from the right, the policy having several political advantages for the Conservatives. By increasing the private sector it served the interests of capital. Furthermore, short-term cash gains from the sales (figure 18.2) generated colossal government income (almost £90 billion by 1997) to fund tax reductions. The beneficiaries of these were largely in the higher tax brackets; those buying the lion's share were thus twice blessed. In addition, the policy offered a populist power base for the Conservatives, who claimed to be transforming society into a *shareholding democracy*.

Privatization can take various forms. Where the state holds shares in a company these may be sold. A public corporation can be converted into a limited company through a flotation of all, or some, of the shares. Alternatively,

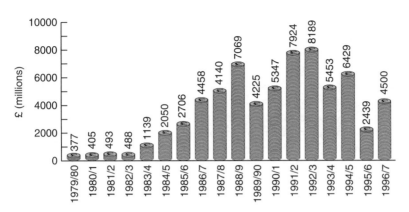

Figure 18.2
Un embarras de richesses?
Privatization proceeds, 1979–1997 (£ millions).

Source: Data from Treasury (1997: table 3.13).

the undertaking may be fragmented into a number of companies, each sold separately. The purchasers may be members of the public, employees from within the industry or, sometimes, certain preferred bidders. Other policies, such as introducing private competitors through deregulation, contracting out and creating public–private partnerships (PPP), are also loosely regarded as forms of privatization. From 1979 all forms were to be seen.

The pattern of privatization

The steel industry had been denationalized by the Conservatives as early as 1951 but was later reclaimed by Labour. A Labour government itself made nods in the privatization direction when, during the 1976 sterling crisis, it sold part of the stake in BP to achieve the expenditure cuts demanded by the IMF. However, it was the Thatcher government that made privatization a central policy. First its holdings in BP, Cable and Wireless and British Aerospace were reduced. Next the National Freight Corporation went to a management-led buy-out. A major watershed was reached with the sale of 50 per cent of the equity of British Telecom (BT) for £4 billion. As the first large-scale public monopoly to be shifted it generated a clamorous demand from small investors. Jaguar Cars, Enterprise Oil, Sealink Ferries and the British Gas onshore oil wells followed. The sale of British Gas in 1986 represented an even bigger operation than BT. The only cloud on the horizon was the intense opposition to the privatization of the water industry, postponed until after the 1987 general election for 'technical reasons'.

The 1987 stock-market crash did not stay the fall of the auctioneer's hammer or stem the cascade into the Treasury vaults. Only the Post Office remained stubbornly public after a backbench revolt in November 1994 forced a government retreat. Ten years after gas privatization, the number of private shareholders had more than trebled to 10 million (Miles 1996). The programme had generated a growth industry in itself as merchant bankers, stockbrokers, advertisers and lawyers grew richer from lucrative opportunities to advise, conduct sales and underwrite share issues.

The privatization trawl went well beyond the industrial to the very fabric of the state (figure 18.3). In the civil service and local government, market-testing and compulsory competitive tendering saw a large range of functions (from catering to financial services) move into the hands of private companies. One would not have been surprised to wake up to find Britain conducting war by means of a contract with the 'British Army PLC', or receive a parking ticket from 'British Police Ltd'. After 1992 it became possible to be 'sent down' to a private-sector prison rather than one of Her Majesty's. The question asked was not 'Why should this industry be privatized?' but 'Why should it not be?' For enthusiasts the years were euphoric, with soaring profits (table 18.2) for the privatized concerns (some with debts written off).

However, the public was becoming more sceptical: a 1989 MORI poll showed almost all prospective privatizations evoking hostility. For many the most controversial case was the hasty disposal of British Rail by the Major government, at what critics regarded as knock-down prices, in time for the 1997 general election. In a complex arrangement, the entire track network was

Table 18.2 Shareholder profits in the privatized industries: average annual percentage increase in share prices from launch date to November 1996

Year of launch	Name	Annual % increase (mean)
1981	British Aerospace	45
	Cable & Wireless	108
1982	Amersham International	39
1983	Associated British Ports	142
1984	Enterprise Oil	18
	BT	15
1986	British Airways	44
	Rolls Royce	5
	British Airports Authority	33
1988	British Steel	4
1989	Water companies	23
1990	Electricity companies	33
1991	National Power	32
	Powergen	46
	Scottish Hydro-Electric	5
	Scottish Power	8
1992	Forth Ports	128
1993	Northern Ireland Electricity	15
1996	British Energy	14[a]
	Railtrack	31[a]

[a]Share price increase in first 6 months.

Source: Data from the *Guardian*, 23 Nov. 1996.

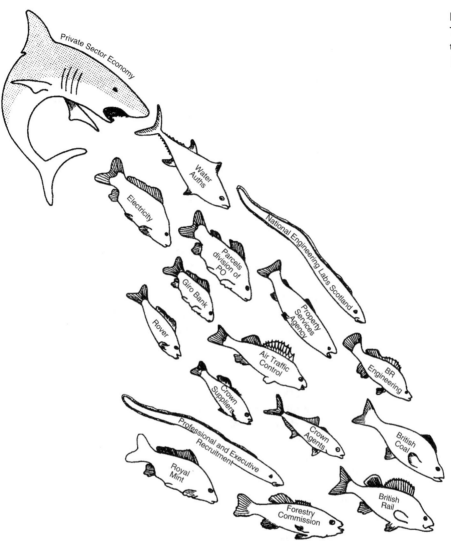

Figure 18.3
The privatization
trawl into the
1990s.

placed in the hands of one company, Railtrack, while the train services were leased to a number of train-operating companies by a franchising authority.

As in many other cases, Labour had promised to renationalize but, upon coming to office in 1997, discovered a new enthusiasm for privatization, pushing ahead on various fronts. There was even to be some privatization of the Post Office. The partial privatization of Air Traffic Control aroused much opposition, the Commons Transport Select Committee, chaired by Gwyneth Dunwoody, declaring this to be 'the worst of all possible options' for ownership and structure. The case of the London Underground was also contentious, since deliberations coincided with the reorganization of local government in London (see chapter 19) and the election of Ken Livingstone, Blair's candidate from hell, as London Mayor. Livingstone opposed government plans to raise finance

Our air is not for sale.

Andrew Smith MP (Labour transport spokesman) on the proposed sale of Air Traffic Control, speech at Labour Party conference (Oct. 1996)

through a PPP, which bore much similarity to the increasingly discredited railways model, proposing instead a £13-million bond issue. The result was a bitter battle of claim and counter-claim, with spin doctor Jo Moore (see p. 487) orchestrating a whispering campaign against Bob Kiley, the world expert appointed by Livingstone to run the tube. Livingstone challenged in the courts but lost because the government had laid down that his Underground responsibilities did not take effect until the issue had been settled.

Mammoths and fat cats: problems with privatization

Critics saw the policy broadly as serving elite interests: giving to a few that which belonged to the many. Early in the programme Samuel Brittan (1983) had argued that an ethical form of privatization would be the equal distribution of free shares to the public, who of course already owned them. The sheer cost of the programme was another cause for concern; at £1.4 billion, rail privatization topped the bill (*Guardian*, 3 Aug. 1998).

In the case of the natural monopolies there are special problems. In April 1995 the combined profits over the previous year for gas, electricity and water jumped by 40 per cent, to a record level estimated at £7.7 billion (Smith 1995), suggesting an abuse of monopoly status. Share prices soared (see table 18.2) and public indignation was further roused by the share options and fat-cat salaries with which the executives rewarded themselves. The water companies incurred particular public anger as reservoir levels fell while dividends and top salaries rose. In 1995 Yorkshire Water was losing 103 million gallons a day through leakage, almost a third of the total distributed, while its chairman had enjoyed a pay rise and perks of 169 per cent since privatization; the £11 million being spent to control leaks appeared meagre. Rail operating companies were widely criticized for late running, cancellations and dirty carriages and in 1998 some of their new owners became millionaires by doing no more than selling on their companies, which they had bought at knock-down prices.

However, the low quality of the track and rolling stock was highlighted by serious rail crashes at Paddington and Hatfield, forcing a programme of track replacement that led to further chaos, an unmanageable £6.6 billion debt, and calls for widespread renationalization. In October 2001, Transport Secretary Stephen Byers unexpectedly announced a decision to take Railtrack into administration; it would be run by government officials until a new form of ownership could be devised. In March 2002 he announced its takeover by a government-appointed not-for-profit company bearing some resemblance to a public corporation – Network Rail. This had no shareholders and would be

---

In the country that invented the train, a journey ... often has the same effect as a visit to a dominatrix. One is tortured, humiliated and abused – and all at the price you would expect to pay in a red light district.

Comment in Germany's *Stern* magazine (May 2001)

Off the rails: the Paddington train crash, October 1999

Photo: Times Newspapers Ltd

financed through bonds, with interest paid by the operating companies and profits reinvested. Its first chairman, Sir Ian McAllister (formerly chairman of Ford UK), headed a board of six executive and six non-executive directors. All were to be paid and enjoy performance-linked bonuses. The board was to be responsible to stakeholder groups such as passengers and operating companies.

Public–private partnership (PPP)

By the beginning of the twenty-first century the public appeared overwhelmingly against further privatization (*Times*, 3 Sept. 2001). However, since the early 1990s governments had become interested in other means of involving private business in the business of the state. There were termed **public–private partnerships**. While privatization represented the takeover of a public asset, a PPP was more of a merger between a public body and a private company. The most common form was the **private finance initiative** (PFI).

Governments and local authorities had for long used private contractors to build roads, schools, prisons, hospitals and so on. Such capital projects would usually be financed by borrowing, with repayment over many years funded through taxation. However, from the Thatcher era, public sector borrowing was to be anathema. In 1992 the Conservatives launched a new flagship policy, a way of building and maintaining capital projects without borrowing. Under PFI, the contractors raise the finance themselves, build and maintain the facility, and rent it to the public sector. At the end of a contracted period it is owned by the state.

The pattern of development By the time New Labour took office, some £9 billion worth of deals had been struck. However, wrangles over contracts had seen the initiative running out of steam. Although sceptical in opposition, Tony Blair made clear his conviction that private companies were often better run than state bodies. By early 2002 an avalanche of new deals had been struck. There were eight new private prisons (with more planned), huge road schemes like the Thames crossing and the Birmingham relief road, a £16-billion upgrade of the London Underground and a £13-billion Strategic Tanker Aircraft. The NHS was a particular target, with six major projects completed and a further sixty-two in the pipeline. Local authorities were also being urged to use PFIs for schools. In the Treasury a task force was created to drive the initiative forward. It was replaced in 2000 by Partnerships UK, a private-sector-led PPP to advise and even provide development funds to get companies involved.

Public service, private profit: problems with PPPs There was much enthusiasm from the City for this 'third-way' form of private involvement, which offered considerable profit to the financiers who advised, lent money, or invested. It was estimated that trade in public services could ultimately net the private sector an extra £30 billion a year. In the eyes of apologists everybody won – the public sector was relieved of borrowing while gaining the financial and managerial expertise of the private sector.

However, the initiative was intensely political, with disquiet within the government ranks and public sector unions. There was concern about employees being shifted into the private sector, with a loss of employment rights and benefits such as pensions and child care. An additional worry was that companies would compromise on quality and cut jobs in the quest for profit. Some critics feared that the public service ethos was being diluted. Others argued that government enthusiasm was based on a misguided assessment of the superiority of private sector expertise. Indeed, there were some major PFI disasters. Some projects, such as the management of the housing benefit system in Lambeth and various IT projects in the NHS, hit the headlines as high-profile failures. A Passports Agency deal with Siemens produced a massive backlog of applications, threatening people's businesses as well as their holidays.

It was also alleged to be a very bad deal for taxpayers. The true level of costs was masked in the same way that unscrupulous salesmen lure the gullible into long-term commitments on the 'never never'. The traditional method of borrowing had always allowed the public sector, being 'gilt edged', to secure more favourable rates than the private sector. Moreover, the 'rent' charged by private contractors had to allow for profit as well as debt repayment. For example, the total cost to the NHS of a PFI allowing a consortium to build and maintain a hospital could run to £900 million (£30 million a year for thirty years), while the traditional borrowing option would have cost only £180 million (Cohen 1999). The GMB union claimed that in some cases, such as Fazackerly prison in Liverpool, the initial cost could be recouped within two years, leaving 23 years of pure profit.

The extent to which PPPs will provide Britain's public services remains questionable. With the health and education sectors representing some 13 per cent of GDP, the potential rewards for the private sector are huge, but union opposition and the full realization of the longer-term bill promised to impose limits.

Regulating the Natural Monopolies

In the absence of competition, when natural **monopolies** are privatized government must find other ways of protecting the national interest. Significantly, this question of **regulation** remained well away from the front pages during the privatization process. However, it was to become increasingly salient as problems emerged. Various instruments are available to government.

Creating competition

In some areas competition can be introduced. For example, the Department of Transport's road construction designs department was hived off to fifteen private consultancy firms and a competitor for BT's business services emerged in the form of Mercury, a consortium formed by the privatized Cable and Wireless, BP and Barclays Merchant Bank. Other companies also began to make inroads into the telecommunications market.

Breaking the natural monopolies into competitive units was not initially favoured, being less attractive to buyers and likely to lower the sale price. However, in 1988 the electricity industry was offered as two separate operations, generation and transmission, the former sold as two companies and the latter parcelled out regionally. Similarly, the water industry was offered as ten separate regional companies and British Rail was broken up by separating track from train operation and selling the freight and parcels services outright. In early 1996 British Gas split into two, Transco dealing with the pipeline business while British Gas Energy embraced retailing and supply. However, artificial fragmentation can never produce the degree of competition demanded in the perfect market model.

Existing regulatory machinery

At the time of privatization there were several regulatory instruments available.

- ◆ *Existing regulatory quangos*. Regulation has increased in Britain to such an extent that some commentators speak of the rise of the regulatory state (Moran 2001). There is regulation within the public sector with consumer councils and ombudsmen, and there is also regulation of, say, schools and hospitals, with league tables and through bodies such as OFSTED. Many areas of social life are regulated, from conditions at work to race relations and sex discrimination. A number of watchdog bodies are also concerned with the private sector (the Office of Fair Trading and the Monopolies and Mergers Commission – the MMC) and these could be used to police the new Leviathans. Under the 1998 Competition Act the MMC was replaced by a Competition Commission to toughen controls and bring the UK into line with EU competition law. However, with their wider-ranging remits, such bodies cannot develop the necessary level of detailed understanding.
- ◆ *Fiscal instruments*. The taxation system can influence companies through carrots and sticks, but this relies heavily upon the concerns themselves providing information, and entails the problems and costs of analysing it.
- ◆ *Special laws*. Although privatized companies are legally indistinguishable from private ones, it is possible to prescribe a special framework within which they operate. However, critics see this as blunting commercial instincts.
- ◆ *Special articles of incorporation*. It is possible to amend certain articles of company law (such as outlawing takeovers in early life, proscribing foreign ownership and blocking disposal of assets without ministerial consent). Such arrangements were made in the cases of Cable and Wireless and British Aerospace.
- ◆ *Ministerial intervention*. In the final analysis ministers can step in. Thus in April 1996 President of the Board of Trade Ian Lang vetoed takeovers of electrical companies by PowerGen even though the MMC had been satisfied, and in 2002 Transport Secretary Stephen Byers took Railtrack into administration.

The golden share A government may retain one special share in a privatized industry. Although nominally only worth £1, the '**golden share**' gives it the power to outvote all other shareholders on national-interest issues. This was used from the early days of the privatization programme. However, it is not in the free-market spirit; it could even be used by a left-wing government to restore state control without the inconvenience of renationalization. Golden shares were held in National Power, PowerGen, British Energy, Rolls Royce, British Aerospace, National Grid, Transco, Cable and Wireless, Scottish Power, Scottish Hydro and Northern Ireland Electric. However, governments seem loath to use them and the 1997 Labour government actually relinquished its golden share in BT.

New regulatory bodies

Special regulatory bodies were familiar players on the American scene but were a novelty in Britain. The first to be established was the Office of Telecommunications (OFTEL) to watch over BT by laying down conditions (a universal service including uneconomic rural areas) and controlling price increases. The early auguries did not suggest a firm regime; the government's avowed intention was to keep the regulation as light as possible (de Jonquieres 1983). When the licence for OFGAS was published in December 1985 it gave a decidedly hands-off role. Apart from abuse of monopoly powers and serious miscalculation, the setting of prices was left entirely to the company, constrained only by a price formula in the domestic market (to be revised every five years):

$$RPI - X + Y$$

where RPI = retail price index; X = an arbitrary figure designed to squeeze efficiency from the company; and Y = an allowance for increasing costs as North Sea supplies become tighter.

   Special regulatory agencies began to proliferate. OFFER was created to regulate the electricity industry and OFLOT to regulate Camelot, the lottery operator. The water industry posed particularly difficult problems because of public health considerations. An Office for Water Services (OFWAT), headed by a director general, was established and the National Rivers Authority (later the Environment Agency) given a remit to monitor pollution.

Problems with regulation

Debate over the role of the new regulatory bodies has come to replace that over the relative benefits of public corporations or privatization (see Thatcher 1998). Are the regulators too timid or too interfering? Either way, there is

THE ECONOMIST FEBRUARY 25 1989

the underlying issue of the accountability of this new breed of unelected officialdom.

Amalgamations and technological innovations Even when split up, the gravity of natural monopoly tends to draw companies back together through amalgamations or hostile takeovers. Vertical integration within the electricity industry began to take place between generators and distributors and there were even mergers between gas and electricity suppliers, threatening a wider monopolistic hold than under public ownership. Technological innovations can erode the boundaries between industries so that, for example, gas and electricity increasingly compete in the same market. This leaves the single-industry regulators unmatched to the structure and struggling to keep up – hence the formation in 1999 of OFGEM, a unified Office of Gas and Electricity Markets regulator.

Agency capture Regulators are vulnerable to becoming not watchdogs but tame guard-dogs of the industry. Even before the lottery came into operation Camelot was feting the regulator. When Ian Byatt, director general of OFWAT, urged the government in July 1993 to renegotiate EC sewage and drinking water standards for fear of putting up water prices, Friends of the Earth accused him of 'using legitimate public concern about rocketing water bills as an excuse to . . . let the water companies off the hook' (Bannister 1993). Other examples followed, many concerning the railways. The danger of **agency capture** could be reduced by replacing individual regulators with boards or a regulatory commission covering a number of utilities.

Bullying When regulation bites, the companies usually retaliate and try to undermine the regulator. The proposal by gas regulator Claire Spottiswood for new controls aiming to cut some prices by up to 20 per cent within a year led to an angry reaction from the company and she was forced to retreat. The kind of reforms favoured by the companies include reducing the regulators' discretion and giving rights of appeal against decisions. Some argue that the regulators should be removed and competition law strengthened, with the utilities being treated like any other company.

Accountability The fundamental problem is that unelected regulators escape democratic accountability. The Comptroller and Auditor General has argued for greater openness and a right of appeal for dissatisfied consumers (National Audit Office 1996: 38–40). Other reform proposals include increased ministerial powers to overrule regulators, defined appointment procedures, greater parliamentary powers over appointments and a select committee to scrutinize the system.

Government attitude Government ideology will set the climate in which the regime operates. Free-market enthusiasts have little appetite for it, even when health is involved. Speaking in Parliament on the tobacco industry, Thatcher stressed that 'we should be very slow indeed in thinking of imposing statutory

Friends of the Earth protest outside the Environment Agency to draw attention to the cosy relationship between polluters and regulator

Photo: Jennifer Bates/Friends of the Earth

regulation' (Goodin 1986). The whole purpose of privatization is to prise the fingers of the state off the ball. In late 1989, when the US giants General Motors and Ford were bidding for Jaguar, Nicholas Ridley, as Industry Secretary, threw in the government's golden share gratis, surprising even the bidders. Under Labour there were suggestions of a tougher line; the water authorities were ordered to reduce leaks, with new targets being set by OFWAT, while the rail regulator's powers were increased and a tighter licensing regime imposed on Railtrack.

> The Government has never made any secret of the fact that it would consider relaxing the law if authorities are having temporary problems ... The water authorities cannot meet the [anti-pollution] standard overnight.
>
> Department of the Environment spokesman, quoted in *Daily Telegraph* (12 Nov. 1988)

The ubiquity of politics The networks around different services and functions contain producers, consumers, ministers, officials, MPs and the regulators themselves. In addition, a host of groups call for cleaner air, purer water, better public transport, and so on. There are also directives from Europe, itself the centre of a further lobbying network. All is watched by the media, keen to report late trains, polluted drinking water and fat-cat salaries. It is impossible to argue that privatization has depoliticized the operation of the public utilities.

Quangos in Politics

It is clear that a system of governance that has set great store by secrecy and evading accountability is attracted by the concept of a shadowy world of quasi-democracy. It is 'a means of farming out government functions based on distrust of the public, the belief that they are best left as passive consumers' (Hirst 1995: 358). Yet any idea that quangos can take matters out of politics is fallacious. Indeed, they tend to operate in acutely sensitive areas: unemployment, race relations, atomic energy, inner-city riots, police violence, local government reform, education, the NHS, university grants, the arts, railways, water supply, broadcasting, and so on.

Quasi-democracy is criticized from left and right. The left view with misgivings the reduction in accountability while the right fear the insidious extension of state tentacles. The wide disparity of bodies in this category makes generalization difficult, but key areas of debate include the following.

Scale The unending debate over what is or is not a quango arises in part from attempts by government to minimize the number and by critics to maximize it, the latter frequently evoking the term 'explosion'. Conservative MP Philip Holland established a reputation as a quango hunter, publishing *The Quango Explosion* in 1978 and *Quango, Quango, Quango* in 1981. In 1992/3 conservative estimates suggested a figure of 5,573, but if advisory bodies, Next Steps agencies and tribunals were included the figure approached 7,000 (Weir 1995: 306). Scale is not only a question of numbers; in 1992/3 quangos were responsible for some £46.6 billion, almost a third of central government expenditure (Weir 1995: 306).

Representation Generally members of quangos are chosen from the great and the good – those white, middle-class, middle-aged males carrying the 'safe pair of hands' kitemark. This bias obviously discriminates against the lower social classes and ethnic minorities. It has also tended to ignore women, though moves to strengthen their representation resulted in an increase from 23 to 30 per cent between 1991 and 1993. By the mid-1990s, NHS trusts comprised 39 per cent women, a third of them holding the chairs. However, some were wives of prominent Conservatives, likely to represent party and husband rather than women. Moreover, only 2 per cent of Training and Enterprise Councils were chaired by women and no Urban Development Corporations (Sperling 1997). Lord Nolan argued that quango membership should be representative of the whole community.

Is he really suggesting that one should engage in a series of silly questions to all the people on quangos as to what their political affiliation might be? Are you or have you ever been a Conservative – is that the sort of society the Hon. Gentleman wants?

John Major on the Nolan Report, quoted in the *Guardian* (12 May 1995)

Accountability This is a key issue in the debate over the arm's-length state (Weir and Hall 1994). Not elected and not subject to the Access to Meetings Acts, most quangos can assemble behind closed doors and need not expose their documents to the withering sunlight of scrutiny. The nationalized industries saw ministers influencing policies while evading responsibility in Parliament, and the same accusations are made over the operation of the Next Steps agencies, the NHS and many other quangos. When the Lottery Commission turned down Virgin's bid in favour of Camelot in December 2000, although Camelot had been rejected earlier, commission chairman Sir Terry Burns could not be called to account for his decision in Parliament.

Without accountability any system of government is open to corruption, or charges of corruption. Some high-profile scandals (the Welsh Development Agency, Wessex and West Midlands health authorities) linked the world of quasi-democracy with the wider allegations of sleaze and venality gnawing at the heart of the British state.

Power and paternalism: we know what you need The arm's-length state has important implications for the exercise of power by elevating the 'expert' over the elected representative. Policy in areas such as drugs use, BSE, poverty, the arts, and so on are shaped by task forces and commissions on the grounds that they know best. The example of the NHS illustrates how professional power can serve its own interests (Illich 1975: 165). Indeed, the medical vision of health also served capitalist interests (Navarro 1976).

The unhealth industry

Cigarettes provide government with one of their biggest and most reliable sources of revenue: they create tens of thousands of jobs in hard economic times; they present a healthy surplus on the balance of payments; they help the development in Third World countries where tobacco is grown.

Peter Taylor, *The Smoke Ring* (1984: xix)

Patronage: of placemen and toadies Patronage is as old as the constitution itself. However, the aim of democracy is to prevent rulers, be they monarchs or presidents, from placing favourites in positions of power and prestige. Yet postwar nationalization saw governments seeking to ensure that boards and chairmen reflected their own ideologies. In 1977, under Labour, the 39 members of the TUC General Council shared 180 public appointments (Stewart 1995: 229). By the 1990s, it was the Conservatives in the dock. Lady Denton, a junior trade and industry minister with responsibility for 804 public appointments, confessed to never knowingly appointing a Labour supporter (*Independent on Sunday*, 23 March 1993). The press became replete with stories of party placemen, while academics (Morgan and Roberts 1993) declared Wales to be under an 'inner circle' of Conservative quango kings. Although patronage was built into the NHS from the beginning, the new trusts greatly enlarged its scope. In March 1986 Conservative Central Office carried out a vetting process designed to root out any who had resisted funding cuts; sixty-two were earmarked for non-reappointment (*Guardian*, 19 March 1986).

Concerns such as these led the Commons Public Accounts Committee in 1994 to place the matter within the remit of the Nolan Committee and its recommendations included the following:

- all appointments to executive non-departmental public bodies or NHS bodies should be made after advice from an independent panel;
- at least one-third of a body's membership should be independent;
- an independent Commissioner for Public Appointments should regulate departmental appointments procedures and publish annual reports;
- the Public Appointments Unit should be taken out of the Cabinet Office and placed under the Commissioner;
- all secretaries of state should make annual reports on their appointments;
- candidates should report any political activity undertaken during the previous five years (Nolan 1995).

The government's response was to produce a code of practice and create a Commissioner of Public Appointments within the Cabinet Office. With some irony the first incumbent was one of the great and the good – Sir Len Peach, former NHS Chief Executive. He made an early appearance before Parliament's Public Service Committee to state that from July 1996 over 8,000 ministerial appointments would be made on merit through open competition and political allegiance would be a matter of public record. For critics this did little to address the problems of the unelected untouchables of the quango state (Hall and Weir 1996).

New Labour was soon accused of cronyism as its supporters, often 'celebrities' in their own right, began to populate its task forces. During its first term a report from Commissioner for Public Appointments, Dame Rennie Fletcher, concluded that health boards were being systematically packed; since June 1997, 318 Labour councillors had been appointed and only one Conservative. Opposition leader William Hague argued that the trusts were full of 'placemen and toadies'. In September 2001, Gavyn Davies became chairman of BBC. This was the first appointment under the Nolan rules, the position was advertised and the recommendation came from an independent panel. Yet this did not avert a storm; he was a known Labour sympathizer whose wife ran the Chancellor's private office.

'Snouts in the trough' The nature of politics makes it unrealistic to argue that party appointments should disappear. However, critics stress a difference between ideological sympathizers and donors of funds. Is patronage used to

reward party support? In 1986 the vice-chairman of the Health Education Authority, often concerned with regulating industries likely to harm health, was also director of a market research firm with interests in the tobacco and alcohol industries. Moreover, he had the distinction of having made the eighth largest company donation to the Conservative Party (*Guardian*, 19 Feb. 1987). In the 1990s, of the 450 directors on the boards of the companies in the FTSE-100 Index making donations to the Conservative Party, as many as 150 were appointed to quangos. Only 50 appointments had been made from the remaining 480 directors of companies *not* making donations (Fisher 1997).

Once in power, New Labour was soon subject to a host of criticisms that party fund-givers were gaining positions of power. At the BBC Gavyn Davies would work closely with Director General Greg Dyke, who himself had given some £50,000 to the Labour Party. To Labour's critics, its House of Lords reform proposals (see chapter 12) promised to make it the biggest quango of all.

Who's afraid of the quango?

The problems of quangos have led to a debate (see Skelcher 1995), with various models for reform suggested that go beyond the Nolan principles. Although the diversity means there is unlikely to be any single answer, various ideas have been canvassed:

- more functions given to a revitalized elected local government;
- the establishment of a regional tier of government. It was hoped that Welsh devolution would lead to a 'bonfire of the quangos';
- greater powers for the voluntary sector;
- limitations on the number of public positions an individual may hold;
- public advertisements for posts;
- a register of interests and affiliations of appointed members;
- a written constitution to reduce executive manipulation.

Whatever happens, quangos are unlikely to become an endangered species. They offer governments some extremely useful facilities, enabling them to wash their hands of embarrassing matters, disclaim responsibility for unpopular policies, evade parliamentary scrutiny and keep areas off the political agenda. Patronage power also provides a large bag of goodies with which to encourage and to repay favours. We find that the great, the good, and the sometimes pompous move in and out of quangos from the other peaks of social, academic and economic life, names tending to reappear on this or that council, working party and advisory body with some predictability. Virtually all can be counted upon to favour an establishment line; if they develop a maverick streak they can be removed as easily as they were appointed. Even the Director General of the BBC is not immune, as Alasdair Milne found to his cost. Hence there remains in British public life today more than a little whiff of early-nineteenth-century corruption and nepotism (Hood 1979: 40).

Key points

- Quangos are state-created bodies deliberately placed at arm's length from the institutions of democracy. They may be broadly classed as judicial, advisory, consultative, commercial, regulatory and executive.
- There are various reasons for the view that certain areas are best placed outside politics.
- The Thatcher government came to power promising a large-scale cull but ended up presiding over a quango explosion.
- The creation of the NHS as a quasi-autonomous system was an institutional recognition of medical resistance to political control.
- Nationalization of industry represented a major experiment in arm's-length administration.
- The public corporations were intended to combine state control with commercial freedom but were never entirely successful.
- The Thatcher government tried to erase the problems associated with nationalized industries by privatization, but this solution bequeaths a new set of problems of regulatory quangos.
- Quangos survive despite much criticism because governments of all complexions find them politically useful.

Review your understanding of the following terms and concepts

accountability	health authority	public finance initiative (PFI)
advisory body	medical model of health	public health
agency capture	nationalization	public–private partnership
arm's-length administration	natural monopoly	QGA
consultative body	NHS trust	quango
EGO	patronage	regulation
executive body	privatization	regulatory agency
golden share	public corporation	state shareholding

Assignment

For this assignment you need to log on to the House of Commons website at www.parliament.uk/commons and go to the page of Select Committee publications on the internet. Selecting the Public Administration Committee for the 2001–2 Session, go to Thursday 7 March 2002. Select questions 1–19 and 54–65. Here you can read evidence to the Public Administration Committee from Dame Rennie Fletcher, Commissioner for Public Appointments, and singer/songwriter Billy Bragg on the subject of public appointments and patronage. Study this and answer the following questions.

		Mark (%)

1   Describe Dame Rennie Fletcher's account of the way public
    appointments should be made (see question 13 onwards).   10
2   Evaluate Dame Rennie Fletcher's defence of her interpretation
    of her role as increasing the appointment to public bodies
    of women, people from ethnic minorities, the disabled and
    younger people against the criticism that this 'was none
    of her business'.   30
3   Discuss the following statement: 'Underneath the elaborate
    process that should take place in a public appointment there
    may be an informal, unreported process going on whereby
    there is a nod and a wink between the civil servant and the
    minister and a list accidentally left on a desk with names on
    it... rather than the formal process' (question 16).   30
4   'Chairman, I look – no disrespect to you all – at you in your suits
    and ties and I sit here in my Clash t-shirt. What I am saying is,
    if I were a Muslim woman and I looked at the body politic as
    represented where would I see myself. I would not see myself
    there at all... the majority of us do not see ourselves
    represented' (Billy Bragg, question 58). Discuss.   30

Questions for discussion

1   Compare and contrast right-wing and left-wing attitudes towards quangos.
2   Discuss the problems associated with the use of patronage in appointments to public boards.
3   How has the autonomy of the NHS influenced its policy-making style?
4   'The diversity in quango forms makes it impossible to consider them as a single category.' Discuss.
5   Outline the basic structure of the public corporation. Why was such a model considered necessary?
6   'Regulation of the natural monopolies must encounter the same conflict between commercial pressures and the public interest as did the public corporations.' Discuss.
7   Evaluate the role of advisory bodies in British government and politics.
8   Account for the longevity of the quango in British public life.
9   How could the 'quango state' be made more democratic?
10 'The use of quangos brings expertise into the service of the state which would not otherwise be available.' Discuss.

Topic for debate

This house believes that while the people of Britain voted for Tony, they did not vote for his cronies.

Further reading

Bishop, M., Kay, J. and Mayer, C. (eds) (1995) *The Regulatory Challenge*.
Readings on an increasingly important topic.

Graham, C. (2000) *Regulating Public Utilities: A Constitutional Approach*.
Describes the emerging system of regulation, looking at political and constitutional factors such as ministerial accountability.

Holland, P. (1981) *The Governance of Quangos*.
Quangos seen as an insidious extension of the state tentacles.

Jenkins, S. (1995) *Accountable to None: The Tory Nationalisation of Britain*.
Sharp polemic exposing an impatient *dirigisme* leading to the destruction of local government and the extension of the quango state.

Klein, R. (1989) *The Politics of the National Health Service*, 2nd edn.
Lively account stressing how NHS structure serves medical interests.

Wall, A. and Owen, B. (2002) *Health Policy*, 2nd edn.
Examines the development of the NHS up to the present day.

Weir, S. and Hall, W. (eds) (1994) *Ego Trip: Extra-Governmental Organisations in the United Kingdom and their Accountability*.
Articles on the contemporary quango threat.

Young, A. (2001) *The Politics of Regulation*.
Examines the rationale of privatization and the accountability of the regulators; notes the complexity caused by mergers.

For light relief

George Bernard Shaw, *The Doctor's Dilemma*.
Written forty years before the creation of the NHS, this play explores the power of the medical profession.

On the net

http://www.ofwat.gov.uk

http://www.ofgem.gov.uk

http://www.rail-reg.gov.uk

http://www.oftel.gov.uk
These are just some of the websites of the regulatory agencies that control the natural monopolies. Log on to ukonline.gov.uk to access many other agencies and non-departmental bodies.

19

Local Government: the Grass Roots of Democracy

The media construction tends to see in Westminster, Whitehall and the Cabinet the holy trinity of political life, but this places the political thermometer too near the radiator of London. Throughout history it is in local rather than central government that ordinary people have encountered much of the reality of the state. A vast range of important services (including roads, law and order, education, water supply, housing, hospitals and social security) were pioneered here. This is also a level of government where many ordinary people can experience democracy at first hand by electing, or being elected to, local councils. After defining local government and local governance, the chapter charts its evolution. Next we examine what local authorities actually do. However, not all locally administered services are provided by elected local authorities, and the third section outlines the wider world of local governance. Beyond this we discuss local politics, identifying the principal actors in the municipal drama. This leads on to the question of organization, management and leadership. Throughout, we will be conscious that every breath local authorities take is polluted with a Dickensian fog drifting from London, not least in the crucial area of finance, which forms the subject of the sixth section. We conclude with the controversial question of central–local relations.

Local government, democracy and local governance

As the self-government of subnational territorial units of the state, some form of **local government** is found in virtually all developed polities as a complement to central government, and is generally seen as a sign of a healthy democracy – a check on state power. Indeed, eliminating local government is generally taken as a symptom of totalitarianism; it was an early casualty of Hitler's rise in Germany. Modern local government has the following characteristics:

♦ democratic control by locally elected representatives who form the council;
♦ power to levy taxes;
♦ clearly delineated territorial boundaries;
♦ large permanent bureaucracies;
♦ responsibility for a wide range of services;
♦ a legal *persona* as a **body corporate** – the **local authority** in the name of which all activities are carried out.

When we speak of **local politics** we go beyond formal structures to the complex processes of settling differences and reaching compromises over community issues that can take place in the streets as well as in the town hall. It involves local elections, parties, pressure groups, media and local opinion. It can also involve a world of intrigue and power struggles between politicians and bureaucrats within the debating chambers and corridors of municipal power.

The term **local governance** draws attention to the fact that the elected local authorities that form the main focus of this chapter are by no means the only providers of local services. There is a wider range of bodies operating locally including various quangos, voluntary societies and private organizations working in partnership with (or sometimes in competition with) the elected authority. The range of bodies has increased from the 1980s and increasingly the elected council is seen as the strategic guide in the development of community services rather than the actual provider (see Ruddat and Rennie 2000). In this development some see a threat to local democracy with the rise of what has been termed the 'new magistracy' (see below).

Evolution

The spirit of local democracy

Local government has a long history and from the first there has been a tension between the centre and the locality. Its evolution saw a twin-track development, with two traditions – centralist and localist – that continue to colour modern debate.

♦ The *centralist tradition* arose from the ruling needs of royal authority. The key territorial unit was the **county** (sometimes small kingdoms). Kings would impose local agents, sheriffs and Knights of the Peace, who became Justices of the Peace (JPs), to collect taxes, recruit soldiers, keep order and dispense justice.
♦ The *localist tradition* developed in an organic, evolutionary way as communities sought to provide collective services such as roads and

poor relief for themselves in the **parishes** and **boroughs**. Also part of the localist tradition were guilds, developing from the twelfth century as associations of craftsmen and merchants. Their interests lay in orderly, well-conducted town life and they lent a strong dynamic to civic administration; guild halls often became in effect town halls.

By the mid-eighteenth century local government was a patchwork counterpane. The centralist and localist traditions had coalesced into a two-tier system, with counties containing parishes of various sizes and status, operating under the eye of the JPs and local landed interests, and boroughs (often controlled by the guilds) with royal charters granting them independence from county jurisdiction.

The industrial revolution: a municipal revolution

The social upheavals of industrialization destroyed this pattern as massive urbanization drew people from the countryside to spawn huge teeming communities around the factories, the like of which had never been seen before. This did not necessarily happen in those market boroughs where municipal institutions were well established. Often sleepy rural hamlets were traumatized by a range of social and economic problems quite beyond the administrative capacity of the *ancien régime* of squirearchy and JP. Housing was hastily erected with little thought for comfort or sewerage. With its privy middens, the urban ecology was better suited to bacteria than to people; disease of epidemic proportions was as much part of life as the dense smoke belching from the factories. Gross inequalities generated by the new economic system promised crime (dark alleys were fertile ground for footpads and prostitutes) and threatened public order. The harrowing spectre of the French Revolution and its aftermath haunted the bourgeoisie, leaving them in a state of perpetual fear of the Frankenstein's monster they had created – a vast new social force, the urban working class.

The initial response was necessarily localist. The capitalists required a strong passive workforce, good roads, freedom from disease, public transport, a degree of education, street lighting and law and order. This was accomplished by establishing a range of ad hoc bodies and reforming the system of local government.

Ad hoc bodies These were essentially boards of leading citizens (often elected by ratepayers) established to provide some particular service, sometimes gaining the statutory right through private Acts of Parliament, sometimes following a public Act. The movement gained momentum, producing a network of boards responsible variously for services such as the poor law, burial, gaols, asylums, sanitation, water supply, roads, street lighting, hospitals, civic improvement and education.

Municipal reform This had a more lasting effect. Following the 1832 Reform Act, which increased the power of the Liberal Party, a number of important official inquiries were conducted into the state of the municipal institutions. The Elizabethan poor law was reformed in 1834 to reflect Benthamite 'less eligibility' principles. An inquiry into local government was deeply critical of administration by the old landed classes and the Municipal Corporations Act (1835) modernized the system with prudent accounting, elections and a widening remit of efficient services.

> The truth, Sir, is that we have a chaos as regards authorities, a chaos as regards rates, and a worse chaos than all as regards areas.
>
> G. J. Goschen, House of Commons speech introducing bills to reform local government (3 April 1871)

Later Local Government Acts (1888 and 1894) extended the new model to the counties. The original intention was for a unified system covering the whole country based upon counties, with a second (subordinate) tier responsible for certain defined functions. However, the efficient (mainly Liberal) municipal corporations resented losing autonomy to the (mainly Conservative) counties and lobbied strongly to amend the 1888 bill, and all boroughs with populations of over 50,000 were permitted to remain independent as county boroughs (figure 19.1). The Act met the unique needs of the huge London conurbation with an entirely new administrative county, under a London County Council (LCC) (figure 19.2), with a second tier of twenty-eight metropolitan boroughs (established in 1899) and three county boroughs. The curious system was a recognition of the facts of social and economic life. It was, as Redlich and Hirst stated

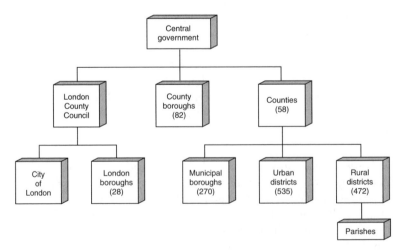

Figure 19.1
The local government structure in England and Wales at the end of the nineteenth century.

Note: Actual numbers varied slightly.

in a classic work of 1903, 'a system...condemned by logic...[but] approved by experience' (1970: 115).

> The County Councils are likely to prove stronger and more exacting than local sanitary authorities have been, though here it must be recollected that manufacturers who find it convenient to pour their refuse into the nearest rivers will be very apt to seek a place on the County Councils.
>
> Leading article in *The Times* on the prospects for the new county councils (23 Oct. 1888)

The 'Golden Age' As the modern pattern became established, the responsibilities of the ad hoc bodies and voluntary societies were gradually taken over (not without resistance and infighting). In addition, the authorities bought out the various utility companies (water, tramways, electricity and gas). With municipal schools, hospitals, bathhouses, parks, improved roads and pavements, libraries, museums, art galleries and even public conveniences, the late nineteenth century can be seen as the high point of local government. The energy of capitalism was harnessed with municipal endeavour. Joseph Chamberlain was able to build a national reputation through his modernization of the city of Birmingham. The economic elite were also the political leaders; Gothic town halls, the cathedrals of the age, testify to the importance placed by the Victorian capitalists upon their municipalities and, indeed, upon themselves.

Into the twentieth century: reappraising the pattern

Although the nineteenth-century boundary pattern reflected the prevailing patterns of life, there was no mechanism to accommodate subsequent demographic development and it remained in a Victorian time warp. As the twentieth century progressed, railways, trunk roads, aeroplanes, telecommunications, radio and television enlarged the territory in which people lived their daily lives. The traditional heavy industries that urbanization had served went into decline and the urban–rural dichotomy was blurred as towns increasingly interacted with their hinterlands.

Reforming the Great Wen The problems of London were the most acute; the LCC area and surrounding counties had experienced enormous population growth, imposing heavy housing demand and traffic congestion. In 1957 the Conservative government set up a Royal Commission under Sir Edwin Herbert to drive through a wall of intransigence erected by the local authorities and the Labour Party (fearing loss of its control over the LCC). This recommended a drastic redrawing of the 1888 boundaries, massively expanding the area from 75,000 to 510,000 acres, raising the population from just over 3 million to well over 8 million, and engulfing parts of Kent, Surrey and Essex, as well as the

Figure 19.2 The Greater London reforms.

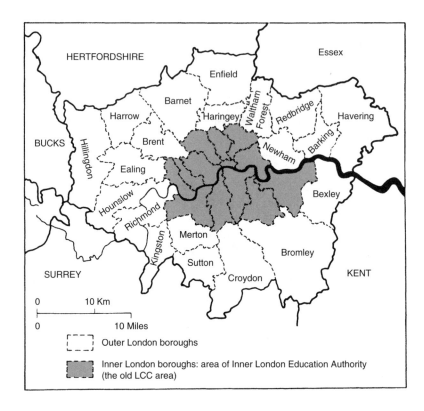

whole of Middlesex (figure 19.2). The newly staked territory would be divided into 32 boroughs (plus the City of London), with functions shared between two tiers. In 1963 a new Greater London Council (GLC) emerged, with responsibility for area-wide functions (housing, major roads and traffic management); it soon gained public transport by taking over the London Passenger Transport Executive.

The 1974 reform In 1964 Labour came to office and Richard Crossman, Minister of Housing and Local Government, set up the Royal Commission on Local Government chaired by mandarin Lord Redcliffe-Maud. Reporting in 1969, it criticized the complex maze of over a thousand authorities, recommending replacing it with a simple **unitary system**. However, the 1970 general election gave an unexpected victory to the Conservatives, who sniffed out a number of malodorous political rats in the scheme. In particular, a single-tier model, integrating rural areas with the densely populated urban strongholds, risked the new areas falling under Labour control.

The 1972 Local Government Act therefore preserved the two-tier principle, and in 1974 the 58 counties of England and Wales were recast in the form of 47 shire counties and 6 metropolitan counties (covering the major conurbations of Greater Manchester, Merseyside, Tyne and Wear, West Yorkshire, South Yorkshire and the West Midlands). With populations between 1 and 2.7 million, these were based on the GLC model. The vital functions of water supply, sewerage and community health were lost to new water and health authorities.

A further revision was even more overtly political. The metropolitan counties and the GLC were seen during the 1980s as hotbeds of socialist insurrection. Conservative patience finally snapped and the decision was taken to 'streamline' them (Department of the Environment 1983). This meant abolition, their functions being absorbed by their districts, which thus became unitary authorities, and by appointed boards. London became unique in the world as a capital city without a strategic authority.

Into the twenty-first century

Wiping away the tiers After the fall of Thatcher in 1990, Michael Heseltine, as John Major's Environment Secretary, placed reform back on the agenda. In 1992 a Local Government Commission was established under Sir John Banham to consider structural reform. Wales and Scotland were to be examined by their respective Secretaries of State. The government's political hope was to end Labour's domination of the massive Strathclyde region of Scotland, and certain English counties such as Nottinghamshire, by replacing them with smaller, Conservative-winnable, unitary councils (Game 1997: 6).

At first it appeared that some 100 new authorities would emerge, encompassing over two-thirds of the population outside the English metropolitan boroughs (which were already unitary). However, opposition unearthed through Banham's consultative process resulted in considerable watering down of the proposals. By 1998 the map had settled at 34 counties, divided into 238 districts, and only 46 new unitary authorities (table 19.1). However, in Scotland and Wales the move to a unitary system was indeed made. Regions

Table 19.1 The decline in the number of local authorities, 1994–8

	England								
	Non-metropolitan				**Metropolitan**				
Year	**Counties**	**Districts**	**New unitaries**	**London**[a]	**Metrop. boroughs**	**Scotland**	**Wales**	**NI**	**Total**
1994	39	296	0	33	36	65	45	26	540
1995	38	294	1	33	36	65	45	26	538
1996	35	274	14	33	36	32	22	26	472
1997	35	260	27	33	36	32	22	26	471
1998	34	238	46	33	36	32	22	26	467

[a]Including City of London.

(including Strathclyde) and counties (such as Gwent) vanished overnight. The government claimed that services would be closer to the citizen. However, with fewer councils (table 19.1) and the number of councillors cut by almost a third, this was difficult to sustain. The exercise was criticized for its lack of rationality (Stoker 1993: 4) and some suspected a government smoke-screen obscuring a fundamental weakening of local democracy (Leach 1998: 35).

Full circle London and the metropolitan boroughs (already unitary) had remained untouched by these changes. However, the great wheel of reform moved to complete a circle when, on 7 May 1998, the Labour government held a referendum on a new elected strategic top-tier authority for the Greater London area – effectively restoring the GLC and, even more radically, introducing an elected mayor. The issue was not seen as particularly controversial (it was supported by the three main political parties) and although the people voted 'Yes', turnout was distinctly underwhelming. However, the process of electing the mayor was to generate much more heat (see pp. 614–15).

In England, the future of the local government structure cannot be divorced from another development, that of regionalism (see chapter 6). In Wales and Scotland, where devolution has taken place, the system is one of unitary authorities, and the establishment of elected regional assemblies in England would probably sound the death knell of the counties. The New Local Government Network, a New Labour think-tank, has argued for a system of sub-regional super councils with Barcelona as a prime exemplar (Filkin et al. 2000). However, some forty years of structural tinkering has done little to revitalize local government, suggesting that the real problem is the relationship between local and central government (Leach 1998). We return to this later (pp. 622–4).

What Does Local Government Do?

Local authorities are by no means entirely free. They are subject to the legal doctrine of **ultra vires** (beyond the power), which means that, however well intentioned, they cannot exceed those powers given to them by Parliament. An action that may be legal for an individual (say giving children free ice-cream) will not be legal for a council. This is largely an Anglo-Saxon model; in many countries authorities have a 'general competence' to act on their own initiative. Although Section 111 of the 1972 Local Government Act does allow authorities to do things 'incidental, conducive or calculated to facilitate the discharge of their functions', doubts over how far this may go restrict its application.

The strength of free peoples resides in the local community. Local institutions are to liberty what primary schools are to science.

Alexis de Tocqueville (1805–59; French writer and politician),
Democracy in America (1839)

Yet local democracy is meaningless if it is not linked with important services. Parish government today is of little more significance than maypole dances performed on village greens. Yet if it had important functions, it would, as in France, be a central feature of communal life. Although interesting the Webbs in the 1920s, few studies of local government have stressed the political importance of function; today this complacency is being shattered in politically charged debate.

Classifying functions

Local authorities are *multi-functional*, to be distinguished from *ad hoc* single-purpose bodies. They can provide most state services required by ordinary people from womb to tomb, which may be broadly classified as follows:

- *protective* – fire and police services, consumer protection;
- *environmental* – roads, transport, planning, refuse collection and re-cycling;
- *personal* – schools, social services, housing;
- *recreational* – parks, sports facilities, theatres, art galleries, libraries;
- *commercial* – markets, restaurants, transport;
- *promotional* – employment creation, tourism, economic regeneration;
- *regulatory* – implementing regulations and monitoring standards (national and European).

Allocating functions within the state

Is there any clear rationale explaining the division of functions between local and central government? There are few theories to underpin such a discussion. A basic premise of any rational explanation must be that services where local knowledge, local participation and sensitivity to the popular will are important should be provided locally. However, other rational arguments can dictate otherwise.

- *Equality.* From a socialist perspective, it would be unfair if, for example, the hospitals in one area were better than those in another. This calls for central administration to ensure equality.
- *Efficiency.* Some services are better, and more economically, adminis-tered over wider areas. Indeed, several functions have been transferred to central government or unelected regional boards; electricity and gas supply, water and sewerage, hospitals and income maintenance were all at one time in local government hands.

However, beyond rationality comes politics and it is in the realm of the political that the issue is often settled. Central government may use its power to shape the allocation of functions to its own advantage. Although the rise of the all-purpose authority was seen as the beginning of modern local government, the 1980s saw some turning back of the clock. Thus, for example, local government lost a number of functions to Whitehall or to unelected local bodies in the 1980s in what was essentially a battle between left-wing councils and a right-wing central government (see below). This movement saw growing acceptance of the philosophy of local governance.

The Wider World of Local Governance

A 'new magistracy'?

This term was coined by John Stewart (1992, 1995) in evocation of a bygone age when local bigwigs had ruled the towns and cities. The 'new magistracy' emerged in three principal ways:

- ◆ local authority appointees were removed from boards upon which they had previously sat;
- ◆ local government functions were transferred to appointed quangos;
- ◆ bodies were allowed to opt out of local authority control.

By the late 1990s local authorities had ceased to make appointments to health authorities or the family health service agencies running the GP services. Self-governing trusts had been created to run hospitals and community health care services. Housing Associations had to a considerable extent taken over public housing, while Housing Action Trusts and Urban Development Corporations had assumed many urban development functions. Training and Enterprise Councils were responsible for many educational and economic development matters. Grant-maintained schools, sixth-form colleges, colleges of further education and what were once the polytechnics had come under appointed boards, financed by nationally appointed funding bodies, and from 2002 all 16–19 education was funded through local Learning and Skills Councils. Control of the police had been lost to new police authorities (see chapter 21). In 1997 there were over 5,000 local quangos but only 445 local authorities, a situation reflected in the employment pattern (figure 19.3).

What kind of people form this shadowy magistracy? Estimated at around 66,000, they outnumber elected councillors by three to one (Hall and Weir 1996). Sharing many of the characteristics of councillors, they are of course not elected, though one in ten has stood in a local election (Skelcher and Davies 1996: 20). They have fewer similarities with the populations they serve, tending to come from local business communities. Politically many claim to be independent but there have been allegations of jobbery: 'patronage . . . as well as the desire by the government to see greater private sector involvement, all contribute to the possibility of one set of political interests predominating' (Skelcher and Davies 1996: 20). Critics have alleged a 'democratic deficit' and

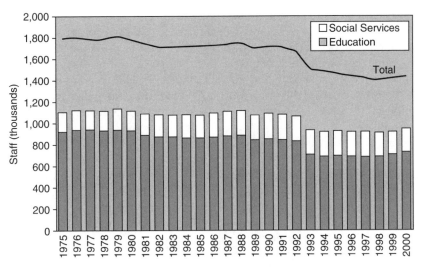

Figure 19.3
Local authority
staffing
(England only),
1975–2000.

Note: Totals and numbers employed in education and social services departments.

Source: Data from *Local Government Financial Statistics England* (1996: table 8.2) and *Annual Abstract of Statistics* (2001: table 7.8).

loss of popular accountability. Those serving on the boards look to central government for their reappointment, further promotion, or even a CBE, and since the local electorate pass no judgement on their stewardship, the new magistracy has no particular reason to satisfy the communities it serves.

The rise of the 'new magistracy' took place on a salami-style basis, a constitutional revolution by stealth resulting in a hotch-potch of organizations with little overall coordination – the very thing the nineteenth-century municipal reformers had sought to eradicate. Local authorities looked to the 1997 Labour government to restore some of their functions. Various consultation documents were followed in July 1998 by a white paper, *Modern Local Government: In Touch with the People* (DETR 1998a). This spoke vaguely of the duty of local authorities to 'promote the . . . well being of their areas'. It stated that 'the more a council demonstrates its capacity for effective community leadership, the greater the range of extra powers which should be available'. Around a hundred 'beacon councils' were designated as examples to the rest. However, the emphasis continued to be on working in partnership with private sector agencies rather than returning functions to local government.

The enabling authority: government by contract

The fact that local government is responsible for a service does not necessarily mean it should deliver it; responsibility may be '**contracted out**' to the private or voluntary sectors. Such a practice was by no means new but, following the

1988 Local Government Act, it became a principal goal of central government policy, with compulsory competitive tendering (CCT) required for an ever-widening range of functions, from refuse collection to professional, legal and accounting responsibilities. A foretaste of the market-testing wave that was to hit civil servants, it meant that council employees had to compete with the private sector. Sharing the same roots as privatization, the policy had a clearly ideological thrust and was strongly advocated by right-wing and New Labour think-tanks.

Local responses varied with political disposition, but in virtually all authorities the culture was changed (Audit Commission 1993b). The 'care in the community' initiative added impetus in 1993 by asking local authorities to make use of private and voluntary-sector residential homes in taking over NHS responsibility for a range of categories, including the chronically sick, the elderly and the physically and mentally handicapped. In 1996 the principle was extended to the provision of social services.

Although critical in opposition, once in government New Labour maintained the CCT principle, rebranding it 'Best Value' and requiring authorities to consider new national performance indicators when awarding contracts. In addition, they were encouraged to extend PFI (see p. 579) into areas such as school building and maintenance. Supporters argued that the use of the private and voluntary sectors cost less and that contracts and various citizen's charters would safeguard the public interest. Critics, including the local authority associations and various professional bodies, feared job losses, worsening conditions of work, damage to the corporate approach and a loss of accountability. There were also worries that the search for profit would lower the quality of services and increase risks of fraud and corruption (Doig 1995: 104).

Municipal pomp: the first council of the Royal Borough of Kensington – elected November, 1900

Source: Mary Evans Picture Library

The Local Political Environment

Each local authority is a miniature political system populated by politicians, bureaucracies, electorates, parties and interest groups.

The council

Sitting like local parliaments, councils are formally the linchpins of local politics. Full meetings in the council chamber usually take place once a month although, like Parliament, any idea that this is a decision-making body is a myth. Today many council chambers split along party lines, disciplined Westminster-style voting reducing many members to backbencher status. The power structure within councils can vary, but increasingly the leading council-lors of the majority party dominate in the form of a cabinet. Changes promoted by central government have enhanced this development (see pp. 612–16).

Choosing councillors: local elections

Local elections are of great constitutional significance. Dicey justified parlia-mentary supremacy on the basis of the popular election and, unlike any other state actors, councillors can claim a similar legitimacy. They serve four-year terms and are elected by first-past-the-post to represent subdivisions of the area (wards), which often return three members. Counties, London boroughs, some unitary and shire districts and all parishes have whole council elections every four years. Metropolitan districts, some unitary authorities and some shire districts elect one-third of the council each time, with three elections in every four-year cycle.

Local electoral behaviour This often betrays the centralism within British politics (Newton 1976: 19), with voters often casting a judgement on central government, which the media tend to emphasize. Because national govern-ments are often at their lowest ebb in mid-term, local elections tend to show a swing to the opposition party at this time. Hence, the unusually long period of Conservative government in the 1980s and 1990s subjected the party to a painful near-death by a thousand cuts at local elections, with heavy losses (often to the Liberal Democrats) in their traditional south-eastern heartlands. By 1996 they were bereft of any representation whatsoever on more than fifty councils and, on many others, including six metropolitan authorities, they were down to one solitary member.

Turnout A much-discussed issue is the relatively low turnout (often below 40 per cent), the lowest of all the EU countries (figure 19.4). Those favouring centralism invariably take this as evidence that people do not value local democracy. However, in many areas one party enjoys so entrenched a position

Figure 19.4
Average turnout in
sub-national
elections in the EU
(percentages).

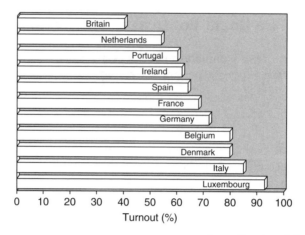

Source: Data from Rallings et al. (1996).

that a rational person might not bother to vote. In urban areas Labour have traditionally dominated while the Conservatives have had green wellies securely planted in the mud of the shires. Lack of publicity, the rise of the 'new magistracy' and central domination also help to explain low turnouts. A further factor is the relatively large size of ward populations (figure 19.5). Rallings and Thrasher (1994) concluded that factors helping to increase turnout include a close contest, elections by thirds, single-member wards, small ward populations and middle-class social profiles. However, these effects were very small, suggesting that more deep-seated causes were at work.

High turnout is generally seen as a sign of a healthy democracy and the 1997 Labour government opened debate on ways to improve matters. Various suggestions have been canvassed, such as the following:

- annual election (by thirds) in *all* authorities;
- more effective means of registering voters;
- mobile polling stations located at places of work, colleges, hospitals, supermarkets, railway stations and other places where people congregate;

Figure 19.5
Ratio of councillors
to population in
selected West
European
countries, 1994.

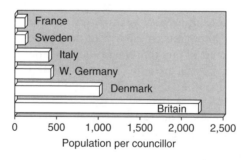

Source: Data from Wilson (1994).

- ◆ electronic voting;
- ◆ weekend polling;
- ◆ proportional representation.

Some of these were tried in subsequent local elections but none seemed to make a very dramatic difference to turnout.

The local elections of May 2002 saw 31 authorities experimenting with some new form of voting or counting, often involving computers. The reform that might prove most significant would be the introduction of PR, which would produce more close contests (Rallings and Thrasher 1994). This is used for elections to the Greater London, Welsh, Scottish and Northern Ireland assemblies (see chapters 6 and 9), and the supplementary vote system is used in the election of the new mayors (see p. 614). However, central government showed no enthusiasm for PR in the election of ordinary councillors.

Beyond the ballot box It is also possible to increase popular interest through various other forms of participation including:

- ◆ citizens' juries, bringing together groups of twelve to sixteen selected as representative of the community to consider an issue in depth (usually over three to five days);
- ◆ focus groups of approximately twelve to twenty people brought together to give in-depth responses to a particular question;
- ◆ deliberative opinion polls involving debate on an issue prior to voting;
- ◆ standing citizens' panels comprising a stable sample, statistically representative of the population, to act as sounding boards;
- ◆ area-based neighbourhood committees;
- ◆ interest- and user-group forums;
- ◆ tenants' and residents' groups;
- ◆ referendums;
- ◆ public question times at council meetings;
- ◆ interactive technology using the internet to inform and ascertain people's views.

Such methods, which several councils had been pioneering long before, have many similarities with market research. In opposition, the Labour Party had used them extensively to tailor its popular appeal and saw a continuing use for them in government. The 1998 white paper stressed councils' 'duty to consult local people about plans and services' and promised 'power to hold local referendums'. Another white paper appeared in December 2001 entitled *Strong Local Leadership: Quality Public Services* (DTLGR 2001), to be followed in June 2002 by a Draft Local Government Bill, which, amongst other things, confirmed the power of local authorities to hold advisory referendums on matters relating to finance or services.

The calibre of councillors

The question of councillors' calibre is frequently addressed (it is less commonly asked about MPs). The subtext of this enquiry suggests a traditional elite suspicion of the entry into politics of ordinary folk: like the dog walking upright, it is an unnatural occurrence requiring some explanation. These issues were addressed by the Maud Committee on management in local government (1967) and the Widdicombe Committee (1986a) (see also Barron et al. 1991).

The belief that the calibre of councillors has fallen since the nineteenth century unites middle-class politicians, academics and Whitehall mandarins. It has two basic strands – *class* and *centralism*. The class case notes the retreat of the old landed and industrial elites from local affairs. Academic case studies (such as Birch 1959) argued that the managerial revolution in British capitalism meant that local industry was no longer controlled by local people, separating economic leadership from political leadership to the detriment of quality. It was this local vacuum that allowed socialist activists to enter politics. Hence the lament is in part an attack on increased mass participation (Kingdom 1991: 119–36). The centralist case, put by J. S. Mill amongst others, is that local activists lack the sophistication of their Westminster counterparts. This concern is certainly not dead. In 1998 Labour introduced interviews and tests for sitting and would-be councillors. Thus, for example, in October 1998 Rotherham mayor Ron Windle, despite over twenty years' council service, was one of those who failed and agreed not to stand for re-election.

> Labour representatives usually make excellent councillors, because they are much more severely criticised than their middle-class colleagues. It is possible for a middle-class councillor to sit on a municipality for twenty years in a condition of half-drunken stupor without exposure and defeat at the polls; but Labour councillors receive no such indulgence.
>
> George Bernard Shaw, *The Commonsense of Municipal Trading* (1908)

A changing breed The 1974 local government reform signalled a change in the composition of many urban councils and a new breed emerged – younger, more self-confident and better educated. A number of councillors in all parties became nationally known through news programmes and chat shows. Increasingly the municipal route became the path to Westminster, many, such as David Blunkett, going on to pursue distinguished careers. John Major himself had risen from humble origins through the local government ranks.

Political parties

Although modern local government is dominated by parties, study of them has been rather neglected. Neither the Maud nor the Bains reports (1967 and 1972, respectively) regarded them as central and their tone was disapproving. However, by 1986 the Widdicombe Committee was able to report high levels of party dominance in the town halls, with strict party-line voting in council and committee (1986b: tables 2.3 and 2.5).

Opponents of local parties often evoke a mythical age when independents supposedly ran councils, yet local parties have long existed. Even before the nineteenth-century reforms, electoral battles would take place to secure control of both ad hoc boards and boroughs. However, it was Labour, without the advantages of wealth and position, that needed local organization. This was deeply feared; the old Liberal and Conservative adversaries sometimes formed anti-Labour alliances, behaving like Tweedledum and Tweedledee when confronted by a

> monstrous crow as black as a tar-barrel,
> Which frightened both our heroes so,
> They quite forgot their quarrel.
>
> (Lewis Carroll, *Through the Looking Glass*: ch. 4)

Local national parties Today the term 'local party' is largely a misnomer. Although some are genuinely local, most are effectively branches of national parties, the same army of canvassers fighting both local and parliamentary elections. This has three compelling centralizing implications:

- ◆ close ideological identification between national and local politics;
- ◆ local politicians often look to the national party for inspiration and guidance;
- ◆ national leaders expect to dominate local parties, even suspending the membership of councillors of whom they disapprove.

However, local parties can sometimes be ideologically more extreme. In the 1980s, a tough breed of New Right councillors seemed intent on outdoing their central counterparts in neo-liberalism, while local socialism moved further to the left than the Westminster party. Local Liberal Democrat parties tend to be less ideologically focused and more pragmatic, varying from area to area according to local conditions. New Labour kept a watchful eye on its local parties and was fully prepared to suspend those seriously 'off message'.

Party animals The impact of parties on local politics can be examined at two levels. Within the community they can act as catalysts, mobilizing electorates, educating the public, stimulating interest in issues, improving accountability, aggregating and articulating interests, recruiting members and promoting citizen participation. Within the town hall the language is of party control and discipline. Such domination, particularly in urban areas, increased considerably after the 1974 reorganization. It is manifest in a number of ways.

- ◆ *Party groups*. The local government equivalents of parliamentary parties, groups can meet behind closed doors to plan strategy.
- ◆ *Council committees*. These generally reflect the balance in the council chamber.
- ◆ *Committee chairs*. The majority party can monopolize these influential positions.
- ◆ *Local 'Cabinets'*. Senior councillors from the majority party can form a Cabinet.
- ◆ *Council leaders*. The majority party leader can become a council leader, a kind of local prime minister.
- ◆ *Elected mayors*. Although candidates may stand as independents, there is a strong likelihood that they will be party figures. (Of eight elected mayors in post after May 2002, three were independents and five party representatives.)
- ◆ *Political appointments*. Officers and advisers can be chosen with sympathetic views.

The establishment of the Widdicombe Committee on the Conduct of Local Authority Business was prompted by concern over what was seen as excessive party politicization. It reported in 1986 with legislation following in 1989. This limited party dominance in certain ways by extending the rights of minority parties and limiting the use of political advisers.

No overall control Recent years have seen an increase in the number of 'hung councils', largely resulting from the Liberal Democrat surge at the expense of the Conservatives. Here the parties must work together. Sometimes a formal coalition between two or more parties will see committee chairs shared and even cross-party agreement on policy. However, in most cases the largest party takes the lead, holding the chairs but making policy concessions to other parties. In a minority of cases no effective power-sharing arrangement is found and the result is prolonged wrangling (Leach and Stewart 1992).

Local interest groups

In several respects local interest group behaviour resembles that at national level. Although only a small proportion may be active at any time, the potential is enormous; Newton identified over 4,000 organizations in Birmingham alone (1976: 38). The rise of single-issue politics from the 1980s has added to the number. Local groups seek channels of access to officers, leading councillors, backbench councillors and local opinion. As with groups operating in the central government arena, there are insiders and outsiders and evidence of pluralism, corporatism and elitism.

Insiders This category includes chambers of commerce, companies, professional bodies and sometimes trade unions. Saunders (1980) showed councillors of the London borough of Croydon hand in glove with private business interests in facilitating the commercial development of the town centre, confirming Dearlove's findings in Kensington and Chelsea (1973). Here we find local corporatism of the 'gin-and-tonic' kind. However, councils are not always captured exclusively by capitalist interests. In Sheffield, for example, the local trade unions, through the Trades and Labour Council, for long enjoyed a close relationship with councillors (Hampton 1970). But councils cannot ignore the structural imperatives of locally based capitalism, particularly if they are concerned about employment. By the late 1990s, Labour councils were offering incentives to manufacturers and retailers to set up camp in their business parks and development sites. New Labour's policy of contracting out to the private sector (Best Value) and the encouraging of PPPs increased the links with business interests.

Outsiders Movements representing squatters, ethnic minorities, one-parent families and other dispossessed sections of society can all be on the outside when the municipal banquets are held. Radical groups concerned with, say, environmental issues may also encounter the cold face of officialdom. Even citizens' groups can be excluded in favour of establishment interests in areas such as housing (Dunleavy 1981). Although great efforts were made by left-wing councils to work with the underprivileged during the 1980s, they were often branded the 'loony left', suffering at the hands of the media and the modernizing wing of their own party.

The extent to which local groups play a part in policy-making is conditioned by the central–local government relationship. Sometimes it is better for a group to turn its attention to Westminster or even Brussels. As Cockburn's study of Lambeth noted: 'Deals that matter most to [local capitalist interests] over taxation and employment policy, grants and control, are deals done at Westminster and Whitehall' (1977: 45).

'Yes Councillor': municipal mandarins

Local government has traditionally worked through large permanent bureaucracies, raising the Weberian problem of the dictatorship of the official. Formally, councillors make policies that officers implement, but in practice matters are more complex. Councillors are essentially laypeople while officers are bureaucrats, with all the tricks of a poor man's Sir Humphrey Appleby. Indeed, the bureaucratic threat can be greater than that in Whitehall. Ministers are full-time politicians while most councillors are part-timers. Moreover, unlike many civil servants, the top administrators are not *generalists* but professionally qualified *specialists*, their authority reinforced by professional associations. Local bureaucrats can also gain authority through formal and informal networks with Whitehall and even with Brussels. A constant flow of official circulars landing on their desks to explain legislation, set standards and impose obligations can lend weight to their arguments.

> The view of the expert can become too narrow. Professional enthusiasm can carry the expert beyond the bounds of good judgement, and 'Bumbledom' can be a real danger... The control of the expert by the amateur representing his fellow citizens is the key to the whole of our system of government.
>
> *Report of the Royal Commission on Local Government in Greater London, 1957–60,*
> Cmnd 1194 (1960)

There is often an underlying class dimension. Officials are generally middle class and much of their work entails informal consultation with local elites, where they 'believe that they are behaving quite properly and [do]...not see that they are consulting a minority opinion' (Hill 1974: 87). Some local bureaucrats resent working-class councillors, whom they see as managers *manqué*, with delusions of grandeur (Henney 1984: 321–41). As in other parts of the state, the culture is male-dominated, although women's particular managerial skills are increasingly recognized in some authorities (Maddock 1993).

Management and Leadership: the Dilemma of Local Democracy

> In general we suffer from too much government – especially local government.
>
> Norman Tebbit, *Unfinished Business* (1993)

How is a local authority to be organized? It is expected to be a vehicle for political participation of ordinary citizens but it controls an enterprise dwarfing many commercial undertakings. The quest to marry the two antagonistic objectives has formed a key area of post-war debate. The traditional organization of a local authority entailed departments responsible for different services headed by chief officers and responsible to committees of elected councillors. Critics alleged this to be cumbersome and lacking central direction. The reports of the Maud (1967) and Bains (1972) committees recommended concentrating decision-making power in a small board or policy committee of senior councillors. However, while authorities tried various experiments, councillors in general resisted the loss of power this kind of **corporate management** model implied.

In the changed climate of the 1980s 'New Public Management' became a recognizable international movement (Lowndes 1997), which suggested that mere tinkering with the age-old machinery would not suffice (Hambleton 1996: 94). The rise of CCT and the concept of the enabling authority changed the municipal culture, calling more for lawyers and accountants than councillors. Indeed, Conservative minister Nicholas Ridley (1988) envisaged them meeting only a few times a year.

We can't go on meeting like this: cabinets and elected mayors

In September 1990 the Audit Commission published *We Can't Go On Meeting Like This*, its punning title condemning labyrinthine committee structures that

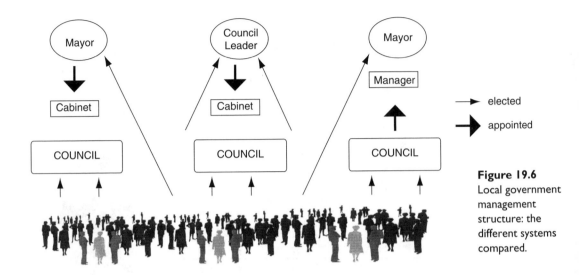

Figure 19.6
Local government management structure: the different systems compared.

were ill-equipped for speedy decision-making. Environment Secretary Michael Heseltine continued the debate, advocating local cabinets and appointed council managers or directly elected US-style mayors, with high profiles and thrusting leadership styles (see Elcock 1995). New Labour maintained the momentum, their 1998 white paper (DETR 1998a) foreshadowing the 2000 Local Government Act. This required all 494 councils to separate councillors' decision-making and democratic representational roles. They were given three options (figure 19.6):

◆   a directly elected executive mayor who appoints a cabinet from among councillors;
◆   a leader, elected by the council, who then appoints a cabinet;
◆   a directly elected mayor working in tandem with a full-time manager appointed by the council.

Councils choosing **elected mayors** would need public support through referendums, and local people could themselves demand such a referendum.

Turn again Livingstone, Lord Mayor of London The Greater London area, without an elected authority since the GLC's abolition, was seen as a particularly suitable launch-pad for the mayoral system. After much speculation, the model emerged. Elected by the supplementary vote system (see pp. 266–7), the mayor would work with three or four deputies and a bureaucracy of around 250 (much smaller than the 25,000 serving the old GLC). With an annual budget of some £3.3 billion, he/she would set policy objectives to be approved by a 25-member Greater London Assembly (GLA). This would be elected by the additional member system (see p. 267), with fourteen chosen by FPTP and eleven from London-wide party lists. The mayor's responsibilities would include public transport, the fire service, strategic planning, trunk roads, traffic

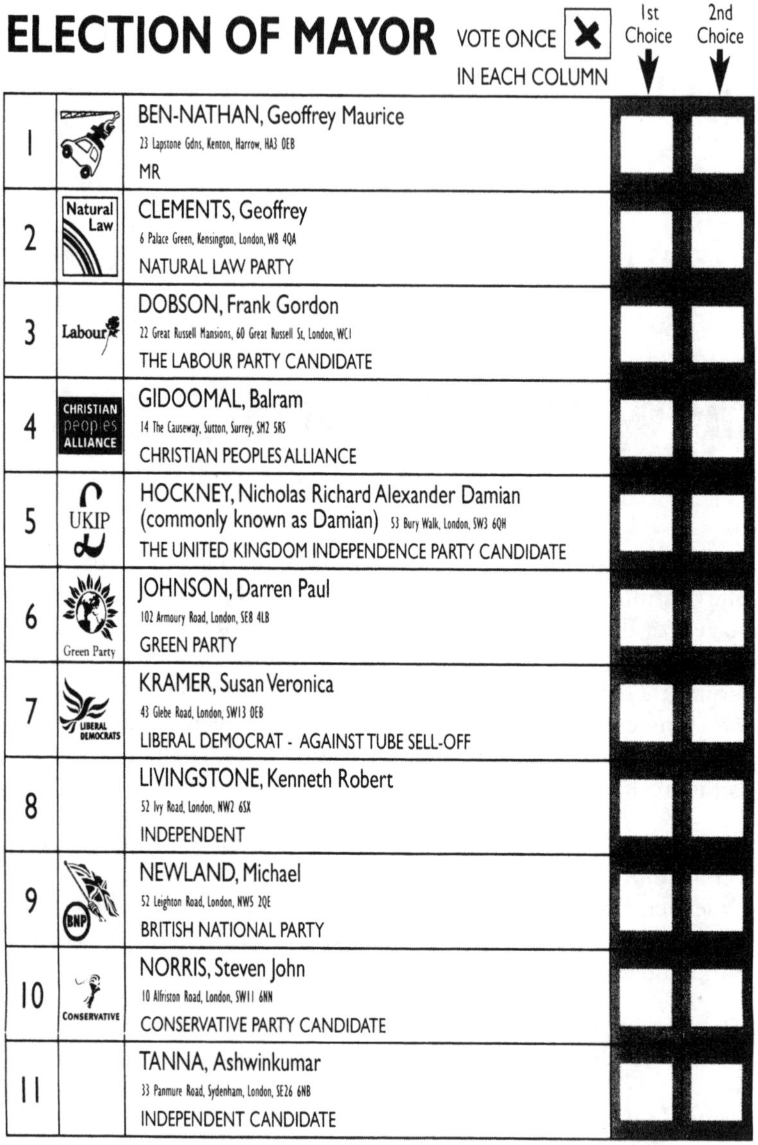

Figure 19.7
Ballot paper for the first London mayoral election, 1999.

			1st Choice ▼	2nd Choice ▼
1		BEN-NATHAN, Geoffrey Maurice 23 Lapstone Gdns, Kenton, Harrow, HA3 0EB MR		
2	Natural Law	CLEMENTS, Geoffrey 6 Palace Green, Kensington, London, W8 4QA NATURAL LAW PARTY		
3	Labour	DOBSON, Frank Gordon 22 Great Russell Mansions, 60 Great Russell St, London, WC1 THE LABOUR PARTY CANDIDATE		
4	CHRISTIAN peoples ALLIANCE	GIDOOMAL, Balram 14 The Causeway, Sutton, Surrey, SM2 5RS CHRISTIAN PEOPLES ALLIANCE		
5	UKIP	HOCKNEY, Nicholas Richard Alexander Damian (commonly known as Damian) 53 Bury Walk, London, SW3 6QH THE UNITED KINGDOM INDEPENDENCE PARTY CANDIDATE		
6	Green Party	JOHNSON, Darren Paul 102 Armoury Road, London, SE8 4LB GREEN PARTY		
7	LIBERAL DEMOCRATS	KRAMER, Susan Veronica 43 Glebe Road, London, SW13 0EB LIBERAL DEMOCRAT - AGAINST TUBE SELL-OFF		
8		LIVINGSTONE, Kenneth Robert 52 Ivy Road, London, NW2 6SX INDEPENDENT		
9	BNP	NEWLAND, Michael 52 Leighton Road, London, NW5 2QE BRITISH NATIONAL PARTY		
10	CONSERVATIVE	NORRIS, Steven John 10 Alfriston Road, London, SW11 6NN CONSERVATIVE PARTY CANDIDATE		
11		TANNA, Ashwinkumar 33 Panmure Road, Sydenham, London, SE26 6NB INDEPENDENT CANDIDATE		

ELECTION OF MAYOR VOTE ONCE ☒ IN EACH COLUMN

management, the ambulance service and possibly the arts. In addition, responsibility for the Metropolitan Police Force would be inherited from the home secretary. With a salary in excess of £100,000 per annum, the expectation was that formidable personalities would be attracted to the new position. In the event, no fewer than eleven candidates featured on the ballot paper (figure 19.7), with all the main parties represented.

However, political skulduggery of the lowest kind accompanied the nomination process. The Conservative front runner was Lord (Jeffrey) Archer, who

> **One member, one (0.0009 per cent of a) vote? Labour's mayoral electoral college**
>
> Three sections, each worth one-third:
>
> 1   London MPs, MEPs and GLA candidates (75)
> 2   Labour members in London (35,604)
> 3   Unions and affiliated societies
>
> A vote from each MP, MEP or candidate was worth 0.44 per cent, while that of a party member counted for only 0.0009 per cent.

was discredited during his campaign (eventually finding himself imprisoned for a different matter), but the final choice of Stephen Norris offered voters a scarcely less colourful candidate. In the Labour Party a battle of extraordinary bitterness erupted, which cast doubt on the intention to allow elected mayors any real power independent of the Westminster machines. Brent MP Ken Livingstone announced an early intention to stand but, as ex-leader of the GLC, he was Blair's candidate from hell. The Prime Minister went to extreme lengths to prevent Livingstone's selection, including creating a stacked electoral college.

Buoyed by his high standing in the polls, Livingstone declared the system corrupt and promptly stood as an independent. Blair gained media support, with both the *Mirror* and the *Sun* on side, the former telling readers to vote Conservative as Norris had a better chance of defeating Livingstone than

Ken Livingstone wins the London mayoral election, 2000

Photo: Times Newspapers Ltd

Table 19.2 Choosing London's Mayor by supplementary vote, June 2000

Candidate	First vote	First & second vote
Ken Livingstone (Ind)	667,877	776,427
Steven Norris (Con)	464,434	564,137
Frank Dobson (Lab)	223,884	
Susan Kramer (Lib Dem)	203,452	

Labour's Frank Dobson. However, the assault from the central machine had angered party workers and made a martyr of Livingstone. In May 2000 he savoured success (table 19.2), sweetened even more by the humiliation of Dobson, seen by commentators as the unfortunate fall guy in a sordid farrago of machine politics.

At the same time, the new Greater London Assembly was elected, using yellow ballot papers to distinguish them from the white ones for the Mayor. Labour and Conservatives gained nine seats each, the Liberal Democrats four, with three going to the Greens. In the case of the latter two parties, all seats were gained as 'additional members', demonstrating the advantage of PR to small parties.

Beyond London However, although the elected mayor system was the one favoured by the government it was not to prove widely popular. While a few authorities, including Lewisham and Newham, had adopted it by 2002, far more were rejecting the idea. In Southwark, where the government used special powers to impose a referendum, only 11 per cent turned out, and of those only 31 per cent were in favour. In the May 2002 local elections seven authorities held mayoral contests but turnouts were not dramatically increased (highest 42 per cent, lowest 24.75). In Middlesborough, controversial ex-police chief Ray Mallon (aka Robocop) won, demonstrating the possibility of individuals defeating the party machines. The dignity of the new office was not enhanced in Hartlepool, where the winning candidate, by an overwhelming majority, was a monkey, also standing as an independent (i.e. a man in a monkey suit – the mascot of the local football club). The government, perhaps chastened, announced its intention to relinquish its power to force authorities to hold mayoral referendums.

Cabinets Given that all authorities were obliged to adopt one of the options by June 2002, the vast majority favoured that of a leader elected by the council, who would then appoint a cabinet. These are usually from the majority party. The other councillors form committees, their composition reflecting party balance in the full council. Unlike the committees of old, their role is scrutiny of the cabinet rather than decision-making. There is provision to co-opt non-council members onto committees.

There are various criticisms of the new leadership models, a principal fear being that the role and status of 'backbench' councillors is downgraded.

Indeed, the February 1998 white paper had noted that 'being a "backbench" councillor...could be less time-consuming' (DETR 1998b: para. 5.21). Others see the divide between the policy and constituency roles as being artificial (Wilson and Game 1994: 318). Moreover, there seemed little argument to show why speedy decisions would be better decisions. There was also a feeling that the cabinets would be more easily prey to Westminster influence.

Finance

The world of local government finance is mysterious and arcane. However, its study provides an important key to understanding local government's relationship with the centre. Local expenditure (figure 19.8b) is by definition public expenditure (comprising around 25 per cent of the total) and any central government will take great interest. The scale (some £81 billion in 2001/2) is huge, for the services traditionally provided tend to be labour-intensive, with no easy routes to savings.

Gross expenditure falls into two categories.

◆ *Capital expenditure* covers items of lasting value.
◆ *Revenue expenditure* covers current expenditure incurred in the running of services (e.g. payments to contractors, wages) and non-current expenditure (e.g. loan charges).

Local authority income comes from three principal sources: fees and charges, local taxation and grants from central government (figure 19.8a). In addition, money can be borrowed and paid back from future current income. Each source has been made subject to increasing central control.

Fees and charges

Local authorities have always provided many services where charging is possible. In the nineteenth century, they were able to raise large amounts from water, electricity, gas, roads and public transport, but nationalization reduced

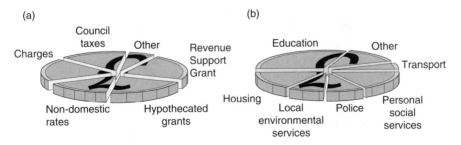

(a)

Council taxes   Other   Revenue Support Grant

Charges

Non-domestic rates   Hypothecated grants

(b)

Education   Other

Transport

Housing   Local environmental services   Police   Personal social services

Figure 19.8
Local authority income (a) and expenditure (b), 1999/2000.

Source: Annual Abstract of Statistics, 2002.

these opportunities. Labour Party ideology was also opposed to charging, seeing local government as a vehicle for socialism.

The hand of the centre At first sight it might appear that central government has little interest in local charges. However, if a service is offered below cost a subsidy is required from some other source – ultimately taxpayers. The Thatcher government introduced **deregulation** and commercial pricing; public transport fares and housing rents were raised and the 1989 Local Government and Housing Act gave the centre the right to designate further areas for charges.

Borrowing

Like individuals and organizations, local authorities have the right to borrow and they do so for the same kinds of reasons. If we cannot afford a holiday in Disneyland we do not go, but when we purchase a car or a house, we borrow because there is a tangible asset to act as collateral. Thus, local authorities generally only borrow for *capital expenditure* (schools, houses, machines and the like). Borrowing has the additional advantage of spreading costs over the successive generations. An alternative to borrowing is the PFI (see p. 579), whereby private contractors build and maintain a facility and 'rent' it to the authority, a method much favoured by New Labour.

The hand of the centre However, authorities do not have complete freedom. Before 1981 they required central loan sanction. Originally this was to ensure prudence but in the post-war era it became an instrument of demand management. The Thatcher government's 1980 Local Government Planning and Land Act introduced a general power for the centre to set ceilings on capital expenditure, and although Labour's June 2002 Draft Local Government Bill increased freedom to borrow where an authority could afford the repayments, it retained central power to set limits.

Local taxation

In both political and constitutional terms local taxation has been by far the most significant element of local government income, the essential guarantee of local autonomy. The original instrument was through rates – a tax with liability based on the occupation of domestic and non-domestic property. Broadly speaking, the more desirable a property, the higher the tax. The system came increasingly under criticism, accused of being:

◆ regressive (see p. 507);
◆ outdated (introduced in 1601 to finance the poor law);
◆ a disincentive to property improvement;

"We're in Band C!"

- ◆ lacking buoyancy (not rising automatically with inflation);
- ◆ insufficient in yield.

In addition, the non-domestic rate appeared unfair to commerce and industry; although contributing around 50 per cent of income, businesses had no corporate vote. Moreover, the system seemed fiendishly designed to penalize the middle classes, with over 50 per cent of adults in lower income groups benefiting from rebate schemes.

The hand of the centre Central interference in local taxation was to provide one of the greatest policy dramas of the post-war era. In 1984 the Conservative government introduced rate limitation, to be known as rate-capping. The move was of great constitutional significance because it denied a community the right to spend its own money.

After their 1987 election victory the Conservatives went further, replacing the rates with a 'community charge'. This fell equally on all individuals and was quickly dubbed a **poll tax**. The goal was to make councils accountable to more people for their spending. The previous poll tax had led to the Peasants Revolt of 1381 but in 1990 it was the middle classes revolting, with stormy and sometimes violent scenes outside council chambers (Butler et al. 1994). The poll tax helped to bring down Thatcher and on April Fool's Day 1993 it followed her off the stage. Its successor, the council tax, returned to property values and slipped into place relatively quietly (Keen and Travers 1994).

The non-domestic rate had also been reformed as a National Business Rate (about £15 million in 2001). Instead of being paid to councils it was collected nationally and redistributed, making it more like a central grant. This survived the poll tax, as did the capping regime, despite Labour's opposition promise to end it.

Central grants

Central government commands the heights of the taxation system with an unparalleled fundraising capability through income and sales taxes, as well as other forms of duty. Local government has been obliged to rely upon some of this revenue being passed back in the form of grants. Central grants can also help to redistribute the nation's wealth in favour of the poorer areas, through a process of equalization. There are in principle two types of grants:

- *specific*: for particular services (housing, education, police, etc.), usually with the centre contributing a given percentage of expenditure incurred;
- *general*: currently known as the Revenue Support Grant (RSG), this supplements a local authority's general income and allows local discretion in spending.

In 2000/1 the RSG (at £19 billion) accounted for over half of all 'aggregate external finance' (AEF), the remainder comprising non-domestic rates (25 per cent) and specific and special grants (19 per cent).

The hand of the centre The complex system entails two basic operations: determining the overall size of the cake and sharing it between authorities. In the first task the secretary of state works with an advisory body, the Consultative Committee on Local Government Finance (CCLGF), bringing together ministers, civil servants and local government representatives. However, the final decision is a political one taken by the Treasury and Cabinet. The second operation is no matter of simple division; like a just parent with different-sized children, central government is supposed to ensure that the slice on each authority's plate reflects its own resources and responsibilities.

Beginning with the 1980 Local Government Planning and Land Act, a series of reforms toughened the regime with increasingly severe 'holdback' penalties for 'overspending'. By the 1990s, in harness with the capping regime, it had become a razor-sharp tool of central control, its complexity bewildering to officers and councillors alike. The system was castigated by the Audit Commission (1993a) for its lack of accountability and failings in terms of economy, efficiency and effectiveness. In 1998 Labour promised greater stability by setting the AEF distribution formula for a three-year period.

By the mid-1990s, capping and the centralization of the non-domestic rate meant that local tax covered only some 10 per cent of local government spending in England (figure 19.8b) and only about 7 per cent in Wales. This could be compared with some 53 per cent in 1989/90 (Wilson and Game 1994: 161). Producing a 'gearing effect', whereby a 1 per cent rise in an authority's spending required a council tax rise of some 10 per cent, it meant that local discretion was considerably curtailed. Local taxes in Britain, as a percentage of local authority revenue, were just one-fifth of those in France and Germany and less than half the level in Italy. The degree of detailed central control would, in the view of Tony Travers (1996), have impressed Stalin.

Auditing the books

Sleaze is not confined to the Palace of Westminster. Revelations of the Poulson affair in the 1970s exposed the corrupt awarding of contracts and *Private Eye* has for long logged a catalogue of 'rotten boroughs'. A number of characteristics leave local government open to corruption. Single-party rule produces local oligarchs who may make the authority their fiefdom, doing favours to themselves and their friends. The appointment of senior officers and policy advisers is a patronage power that can be abused, council 'newspapers' can promote party propaganda, attendance allowances can be claimed for token appearances, the awarding of contracts offers temptations of bribery, and 'fact-finding' can become junketing in sunny climes or even the fleshpots of the world (Doig 1995: 104).

Hence, like other organizations, local authorities must submit their accounts for annual audit. Originally this aimed to ensure good accounting practice, prevent corruption, and identify *ultra vires* expenditure. In 1983 the system was toughened up with the creation of the Audit Commission, a centralized watchdog quango. This was to add special 'value-for-money' audits to the function. It soon claimed some notable scalps. In 1993 Lambeth Council was accused of fraud and malpractice, including over £20 million of unauthorized highways expenditure. In 1994 a damning report came from District Auditor John Magill concerning Westminster Council under Dame Shirley Porter. Officers and members were accused of 'wilful misconduct' and gerrymandering through the sale of council houses; surcharges were put at some £31 million (*Guardian*, 26 March 1997). In 2002, the 'Donnygate' scandal saw Peter Birks, formerly chair of Doncaster Council's planning committee, jailed for four years after receiving a £160,000 farmhouse for pushing through a housing development application for a property developer. Ray Stockhill, former deputy council leader and mayor, received a two-year suspended sentence for accepting payments of over £30,00 from the same source.

Following the Widdicombe report and recommendations from the Nolan Committee, the 2000 Local Government Act made provision for a code of ethics to be drawn up in consultation with the LGA. This would be adopted by all authorities, with alleged breaches investigated by a Standards Agency and councillors and officers facing suspension if found in breach.

Local Government in a Centralist State

Although a steady erosion of local autonomy by central government has been a persistent post-war trend, it was to be accelerated in the 1980s. New Right policies, centring upon public expenditure cuts and rolling back the social democratic state, had severe implications for local government, the major arm of the welfare state. The outcome was fierce central–local battle as many left-wing authorities began to resist central cuts.

> The fundamental idea of Centralisation is, *distrust*. It puts no Faith in Man; believes not in Hope, nor in the everlastingness of truth; and treats charity as an idle word. Its synonyms are, irresponsible control; meddling interference; and arbitrary taxation.
>
> J. Toulmin Smith, *Local Self-Government and Centralization* (1851)

The intergovernmental relationship was even dragged into the courts as, for example, when Lord Denning ruled against the GLC's 'Fares Fair' policy. The Widdicombe Committee reminded councillors that the fact that a local authority is elected

> may lend political authority to its actions within the law, . . . but does not provide a mandate to act outside or above the law. Its continued existence . . . depends on the contribution it can make to good government. (Widdicombe 1986a: ch. 3, para. 49)

However, the 'law' is anything the central government wishes to drive through Parliament, and 'good government' is whatever the Cabinet or prime minister approve of.

The things they said

Local government can be a tool for achieving socialist change. This has been submerged in parliamentary, centralist views of progress.

David Blunkett (as leader of Sheffield City Council), interviewed in M. Boddy and C. Fudge, *Local Socialism: The Way Ahead* (1984)

Conceptualizing central–local intergovernmental relations

The decline in the autonomy of local government has given rise to a number of theoretical models explaining the **central–local relationship**.

Agency The idea that local government should be an agency of the centre, with little will of its own, is essentially the Benthamite position, justified on grounds of efficiency rather than democracy. From the 1930s, W. A. Robson (1966) lamented the loss of the latter. Writing in the 1990s, King (1993: 196) could still employ the agency terminology, likening the central–local relationship to that between government and its Next Steps agencies. Chandler (2001) suggests the idea of the steward, rather than the agent, with some discretion but no real independent power.

Partnership In the early 1970s, scholars refuted the agency model by noting that differences in per capita spending on particular services (education, housing, social services) between authorities demonstrated local autonomy (Boaden 1971; Davies 1972). It was argued that central and local government existed together in a largely harmonious social democratic partnership.

Power-dependence Rhodes (1981) offered a power-dependence model, stressing that local authorities, like other organizations, were engaged in a pluralistic bargaining process with the centre. In this they had a number of resources (expertise, organization, information) and there was no reason to believe that the wishes of the centre must always prevail. This was underlined throughout the 1980s as the centre was repeatedly forced to pass new legislation following successive failures to impose its will.

However, certain less novel policies, such as selling council houses, worked well, leading John (1994a) to argue that the power-dependence model ignored central government's capacity to learn and ultimately dominate. More generally, Hogwood (1997: 715) noted that a party's duration in office is a key factor in explaining radical change. Thus the Major years, following so long a period of Conservative rule, saw a more effective marginalizing of local government.

Dual state The neo-Marxist 'dual-state thesis' (Saunders 1984: 24) depicts central government as a closed system of corporate decision-making (concerned with **collective investment**) and local government as relatively open (concerned with **collective consumption**). In a capitalist society the logic in each case favours central domination, because the interests of capital come first.

Marxist A Marxist view portrays local authorities as the mandataries of a greater power – not central government but the forces of wealth and capital (Cockburn 1977). The history of local government can indeed be read as a series of responses to the needs of the capitalist economy (Castells 1977). Paradoxically, from the 1980s, as communist systems collapsed throughout the world, the Marxist analysis of power in capitalist society became more compelling. Under conditions of fiscal crisis (O'Connor 1973), the business voice was amplified at the expense of elected representatives in the ways described above.

The wider network

The model of a single central–local relationship is simplistic. The real world of local governance is messy and bewilderingly complex, with relationships varying from one authority to another and arising around different policy areas and issues within networks of interested parties (Rhodes 1988). Thus, for example, the poll tax issue would engage one network, local management of schools another. Voluntary societies, environmentalists, private-sector providers and large business interests move on and off the stage in an ever-changing policy drama. Moreover, the relationship is not static over time. In the immediate post-war years the vocabulary of partnership seemed appropriate, while the 1980s were characterized by antagonism and mistrust.

EU membership introduces further complexity. Authorities can lobby at Brussels, arguing the case for *subsidiarity* to reclaim responsibilities (thereby hoisting the British government – the leading advocate of the principle – with its own petard). Indeed, the European Commission successfully brought an enforcement action against the UK government for failing to implement a directive protecting workers in conditions of CCT (preventing them being rehired at a cheaper rate) (Woodhouse 1995: 413). Authorities have not themselves responded uniformly to European opportunities; some have created special EU units, some have even established a lobbying presence in Brussels, sometimes in consortia, while others have remained minimalist (John 1994b). With devolution for Scotland and Wales and a greater regional focus in other EU countries, EU membership could set the cat amongst the central–local pigeons, strengthening calls for English regionalism (see pp. 155–6).

Local Democracy in Crisis

> It is but a small proportion of the public business of a country which can be well done, or safely attempted, by the central authorities; ... the legislative portion at least of the governing body busies itself far too much with local affairs.
>
> J. S. Mill (utilitarian philosopher), *On Representative Government* (1861)

There is in British politics what Andrew Marr (1995: 65) has called a 'malign dynamic' – the more unpopular a Westminster government becomes, the more the people vote for its opponents locally, giving the centre ever more reason to reduce the power of local government. Throughout the 1980s and 1990s there was a feeling that local democracy in Britain was in crisis, perhaps near extinction. Indeed, according to Major's former adviser, Baroness Hogg, in 1990 ministers had seriously considered abolishing it altogether (*Observer*, 14 July 1996).

Concern led the public service union UNISON and the local authority associations in 1993 to establish a Commission for Local Democracy, including representatives from the major parties, local officials and academics. Chaired by Simon Jenkins, former editor of *The Times*, it reported in 1995 with over forty proposals, including elected mayors, directly elected health and police authorities, proportional representation, more councillors, citizen rights to call for referendums, the end of capping and a new settlement for the central–local financial relationship (Commission for Local Democracy 1995). By the opening years of the twenty-first century several of these had been implemented yet much remained to be done.

In June 1997, the UK government signed the EU *Charter of Local Self-Government*, and a series of consultation papers spoke the language of democratic renewal, ethics and finance. Yet there was tension between the commitment to decentralization and the emphasis on standards and inspection (Stewart 2000: 289). Despite the rhetoric, critics saw continuing cuts in grants, contracting out, increased use of PFI, control over schools, social services further threatened and spending caps screwed down. Quangocracy continued to flourish and managerialism squeezed out democratic accountability (see Wilson 2001). Centralism was underlined in a March 1998 pamphlet published by the Institute for Public Policy Research, in which Tony Blair warned local government:

> If you are unwilling or unable to work the modern agenda then government will have to look to other partners to take on your role.

With fast-food chains operating in Education Action Zones there could be little doubt who the new partners would be.

In June 2002, the Commission on Local Governance, a body established by the Local Government Information Unit, responded to the December 2001 white paper (DTLGR 2001). It outlined an extensive reform agenda, including reducing the voting age to sixteen, PR, the ability to end elected mayoral systems where they are not wanted, referendums on matters of community interest, raising the majority of revenue through local taxation and fewer ring-fenced grants. The argument was that only with a genuine transfer of resources, functions and power to local authorities could local democracy be revived.

When you have provided the proper constitution of local authority you must provide that the local authority must have sufficient powers; and that it gets these powers by diminishing the excessive and exaggerated powers that have been heaped on the central authorities in London.

Lord Salisbury (Conservative prime minister) speaking on his government's creation of the LCC (1888), quoted in K. Young and P. L. Garside, *Metropolitan London* (1982)

In conclusion, we may ask whether local government has any legitimate claim to autonomy. Has it any defence against central government and the constitutional doctrine of the supremacy of parliament? The answer to this is very clearly 'Yes', providing we go beyond the lawyer's wig and gown and address the spirit of democracy. Throughout history communities have had a spontaneous desire to provide services collectively. The idea that local government is nothing more than a creation of Westminster can be seen as a myth established by nineteenth-century legislation and perpetuated by centralist politicians of all shades. Localism can be said to be embedded in the evolution of the constitution. Aristotle declared that one who lives without politics is either a god or a beast. Local democracy, by permitting ordinary people to shape their communal lives, enriches democracy and the quality of life.

Key points

- Local government is the self-government of territorial units of the state.
- Local governance refers to the more complex set of processes and institutions that shape communal life.
- Britain has a long history of local government, combining both localist and centralist forces.
- Industrialization promoted urbanization and marked a traumatic break with the past. The new bourgeoisie advanced the municipal institutions.
- The significance of local government lies in the services for which it is responsible.
- Modern local government is essentially political and cannot be understood without reference to political parties and interest groups.
- The 1980s and 1990s saw some dramatic revamping of local government in terms of areal pattern, management and functions.
- Today a number of local services are provided by unelected bodies – a 'new magistracy'.
- Local government operates in the shadow of central government, not least because of the latter's financial control.
- Despite the legislative supremacy of Westminster, local government retains a moral justification derived from the ancient traditions and conventions of communal life.

Review your understanding of the following terms and concepts

body corporate
borough
CCT
central–local relations
centralism
collective consumption
collective investment
community charge (poll tax)
corporate management
council
council officer

council leader
council tax
county
county borough
elected mayor
enabling authority
local authority
local bureaucracy
local governance
localist tradition
metropolitan county

parish
rate-capping
rates
Revenue Support Grant
shire county
single-tier system
specific grant
ultra vires
unitary system

Assignment

Study the extract from *The Times* and answer the following questions.

Mark (%)

1   'There's a reason why people all over the world put an X in a box: it's simple and it works.' Discuss.   30

Touch-screen voting rubs out the old pencil

By Helen Rumbelow

THE cold wind of change blew through largely deserted polling stations last night [2 May 2002] as an array of hi-tech voting options piloted in local elections failed to connect.

In East London the stubby pencil's role in democracy died a lonely little death, mourned only by the dwindling minority who bothered to turn up.

People seemed underwhelmed by the schemes – including voting by mobile phones, Internet or in shopping centres – introduced by many of the 174 English councils to lure them into becoming active citizens. Turnout appeared to have fallen below the 29.6 per cent who voted in 2000 – the last local polls not held on general election day.

Newham council in East London conducted the biggest experiment by abolishing the ballot paper, pencil and box in favour of computers. Instead of retreating to a booth to cross "X" in a box with a pencil on a string, they were supposed to register their vote by touching a screen – but some simply scuttled home....

Thomas Teighe, 80, had expected to vote as he had done for his entire adult life, but when he walked into his local primary school to be confronted with the machine, futuristically called "The Edge" he turned tail and fled.

"I haven't got time to muck about. I'm an old man," he said. "There's a reason why people all over the world put an X in a box: it's simple and it works. This is crackpot."

Mr Teighe was not alone. Dozens violated their right to privacy by calling for assistance....

John Muraszczuk, 52, could not imagine going back to paper. "It's just like at work. When you get a laptop you can't imagine how you worked with typewriters," he said.

....

© Times Newspapers Ltd (3 May 2002)

---

2 'Low turnout at local elections is a consequence of the marginalization of local government by the centre rather than lack of interest in democracy.' Discuss. 40

3 Discover whether your own local authority has experimented with new voting methods. If it has, ascertain the effect on turnout. 30

Questions for discussion

1 What were the implications of the industrial revolution for the development of English local government?

2 Suggest and evaluate some ways of increasing the turnout at local elections.

3   'It is impossible to understand the internal workings of local government without reference to parties and interest groups.' Discuss.

4   'The professional expertise of senior local government officers means that they must inevitably dominate councillors.' Discuss.

5   Examine the problems faced by the Banham Commission.

6   What constitutional problems are posed by the concept of the enabling authority?

7   'A system of popularly elected mayors would revitalize local government in Britain.' Discuss.

8   'Central government dominates local government, not because of the constitutional supremacy of Parliament, but because it stands for the interests of capital while local government stands only for the community.' Discuss.

9   Why can local government be said to be in crisis?

10 Present the case against central-government capping of local taxation.

Topic for debate

This house believes that a system of elected mayors will further reduce the role of ordinary people in local politics.

Further reading

Local libraries contain much information on local government in the area. This can furnish material for local projects.

Chandler, J. A. (2001) *Local Government Today*, 3rd edn.
Up-to-date view of the rapidly changing structure and processes of local government.

Checkland, S. G. and E. O. A. (eds) (1974) *The Poor Law Report of 1834*.
Unique insight into the utilitarian and moralistic outlook that was central to industrialization.

Commission for Local Democracy (1995) *Taking Charge: The Rebirth of Local Democracy, Final Report*.
Details an extensive and thought-provoking reform agenda covering local government and quangocracy.

Dunleavy, P. J. (1980) *Urban Political Analysis*.
Lively and provocative, though introducing some highly sophisticated analysis. Not for beginners.

Elcock, H. (1994) *Local Government*, 3rd edn.
Insight into policy-making and administration under the Thatcher reforms.

Rhodes, R. (1988) *Beyond Westminster and Whitehall: The Sub-central Government of Britain*.
Clear exposition of the power-dependence analysis and much else.

Stewart, J. (2000) *The Nature of British Local Government*.
A stimulating mix of anecdotal evidence and systematic research, illuminated by history and contemporary developments.

Stoker, G. (ed.) (2000) *The New Politics of Local Governance*.
Authoritative essays edited by a scholar with a keen interest in reform.

Wilson, D. and Game, C. (1997) *Local Government in the United Kingdom*.
Well-set-out and readable analysis providing good introduction to theory.

For light relief

Roy Hattersley, *A Yorkshire Boyhood*.
Labour ex-politician recounts his local government years.

Winifred Holtby, *South Riding*.
Few novels take county government as their background, but here by-laws and drainage are entwined with the passions of ordinary people.

On the net

http://www.local-regions.odpm.gov.uk
Local government now comes within the ambit of the Office of the Deputy Prime Minister.

http://www.lgiu.gov.uk
The Local Government Information Unit is a good starting point for independent information and analysis and links to local authority sites. Check your own local authority's website to find out what your elected representatives have been doing; you may even be able to read the minutes of council meetings.

http://www.info4local.gov.uk
This website is one way local government learns about central government initiatives, but it's useful for students too.

http://www.lcga.gov.uk
Much of the Local Government Association's website is open to the public as well as to its members (councillors and officers). In addition to a wide range of news and up-to-date statistics, it covers local government relations with central government and other organizations.

20

Justice and Politics: Trials and Errors

In this chapter we turn to the institutions applying the laws that emerge from the political process. We begin by mapping the institutional stage upon which legal dramas are enacted: the system of courts. Next we examine the *dramatis personae* – the lawyers and judges – and place a critical lens upon the constitutional principle of judicial impartiality. Section four examines the role of judges in the political process and the final section considers certain special institutions concerned with administrative justice, the protection of citizens from the state itself. In each section we shall find that the dignified world of wig and gown is not so far removed from the undignified world of politics that decides who gets what when how.

Many books on politics say little, if anything, about judges, courts and the administration of justice. This is because the law is supposed to be above politics and the judges, like high priests, to be outside party, class and faction. They are expected to dispense justice to weak and powerful, rich and poor, without fear or favour. However, we shall find that the judicial process and those working within it are by no means insulated from the controversies and vicissitudes of political life.

Of all our constitutional institutions, none is as august and dignified as those associated with the administration of justice. Judges deck themselves in the regalia of another age as necessarily as plumbers wear boiler-suits, and the most venerable members of the judiciary sit in the House of Lords. In court, judges expect impeccable courtesy and deference (indeed, failure to display this can be punished as *contempt*), enshrined in archaic forms of language. When Lord Chief Justice Taylor tried to abolish wigs in 1996, he met with obdurate opposition from barristers addicted to 'pantomime flummery' (Robertson

Hogarth's 'The Bench'

Source: Mary Evans Picture Library

1997). Yet the pageantry and splendour has a purpose: it is intended to bestow upon the system an aura of power, wisdom and integrity. Through these legal custodians the principle of the rule of law is manifested. This is the orthodox view; in this chapter we put it to the test.

The Legal System

The administration of justice is shared by the Lord Chancellor's Department, responsible for administering the courts and appointing judges, and part of the Home Office. Under John Smith the Labour Party was committed to amalgamating these into a single Ministry of Justice and, although this was dropped from the 1997 manifesto, the new Lord Chancellor, Derry Irvine, was credited with this as a long-term ambition (*Sunday Times*, 8 Feb. 1998). Home Office responsibilities for examining suspected miscarriages of justice were transferred in March 1997 to a new quango, the Criminal Cases Review Commission.

> Judgement must always be passed with complete solemnity – because it's such rot. Suppose a judge throws a woman into clink for having stolen a corncake for her child. And he isn't wearing his robes. Or he's scratching himself while passing sentence ... then the sentence he passes is a disgrace and the law is violated. It would be easier for a judge's robe and a judge's hat to pass sentence than for a man without all that paraphernalia.
>
> Azdak in Bertolt Brecht's *The Caucasian Chalk Circle* (1948)

The courts

The structure of the courts in England and Wales is hierarchical (figure 20.1); superior courts check the actions of those below through a process of appeal. The organization reflects a fundamental dichotomy between **civil jurisdiction** (citizen versus citizen using such laws as tort and contract) and **criminal jurisdiction** (state versus citizen as in crimes such as burglary or murder).

Civil jurisdiction Minor cases begin in county courts, presided over by itinerant circuit judges, while more serious ones are heard in the High Court. Appeals go on to a Court of Appeal (Civil Division) and thence, upon further appeal, to the House of Lords, the highest court in the land.

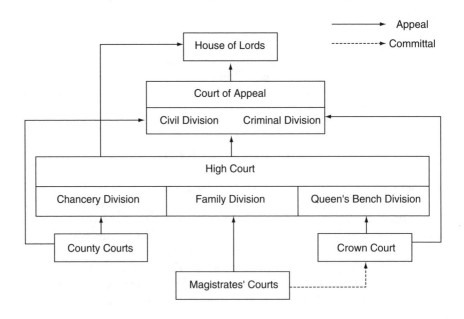

Figure 20.1
The courts in
England and Wales.

Criminal jurisdiction Minor criminal cases are tried summarily (without a jury) in a magistrate's court. For serious criminal cases the magistrate's court conducts committal proceedings, which merely decide whether there is a case to answer. If there is, it will go to a Crown Court to be tried before a jury and presided over by a High Court judge or circuit judge. Appeals from the Crown Court may be taken to the High Court (on a point of law) or the Court of Appeal (Criminal Division), and thence to the House of Lords.

'Re-inventing' the system In the 1990s came a taste of the 're-inventing' that had been visited on other parts of the state; the courts were given performance targets and citizen's charters, and managerialism came to the Lord Chancellor's Department. Critics began to imagine the courts peopled by consultants with clipboards rather than bewigged lawyers. There was concern that justice and accountancy did not mix, that judicial considerations were giving way to politically motivated cost savings. In April 1995 the Courts Service Agency took over the administration of justice, with the usual constitutional problems of agencification (Woodhouse 1995: 404). In 1996 Lord Woolf's report, *Access to Justice*, proposed a radical overhaul of civil justice to reduce delay. However, the government refused to make the necessary resources available, announcing that the system should be made to pay for itself through increased court fees. In addition, the discretion of the courts to waive or reduce fees in cases of financial hardship was withdrawn. Angered judges argued that this would restrict access to justice and in *R. v. Lord Chancellor ex parte Witham*, in 1997, the High Court ruled it illegal.

In response to continuing criticism of the criminal justice system (including uneven sentencing, the conduct of jury trials and the treatment of young offenders), senior Appeal Court judge Sir Robin Auld was asked to make further recommendations for reform. His report (published in October 2001; see p. 640) recommended a unified criminal court in England and Wales with three divisions. In the newly created intermediate-level of district criminal courts, professional judges aided by two lay magistrates would deal with cases more serious than those currently tried by magistrates alone, while the most serious would be tried by judge and jury in the Crown division. A National Criminal Justice Board, working through local criminal justice boards, would replace a collection of existing bodies to provide overall direction of the criminal justice system.

The European dimension

To the domestic system must be added two European courts.

The European Court of Human Rights The European Convention on Human Rights (ECHR) was signed by a number of European countries in 1950. Alleged breaches are investigated by the European Commission on Human Rights and cases appear before the Court. Although ratified by the UK the Convention was not incorporated into domestic law until the 1998 Human Rights Act, so judges were unable to apply it in domestic courts. However, since 1966 UK citizens had been enabled to petition the Commission and a number of cases against the British government were upheld (see Lester 1994). Particularly controversial was the 1994 judgement that the shooting by the SAS of three IRA suspects in Gibraltar was unlawful. Incorporation of the Convention can be expected to increase the area for controversy by making the courts more political (p. 649).

The European Court of Justice (ECJ) As the importance of the EU increases in the lives of states and citizens so does its court. All UK courts must take notice of its decisions and lower courts may seek definitive rulings on the meaning of European law and treaties (see p. 66).

Access to the law

In England,
Justice is open
to all, like the
Ritz hotel.

Attributed to
James Matthew
(1830–1908;
British judge)

A prerequisite of a just legal system is that all have equal access. Yet in practice this is by no means the case; the lawyers' clientele remain predominantly middle class (Zander 1969). There are various reasons for this.

♦ *Cost*. Lawyers' fees, protected by the monopolistic practices of the Law Society, mean that the law does not come cheap. For many it is better to suffer a wrong than risk an expensive lawsuit.

♦ *Legal expertise*. It is in the nature of the legal profession to take a greater interest in the problems of the wealthy than the poor. The intricacies of business and commerce tend to preoccupy the legal mind, to the exclusion of problems with landlords, local authorities and social security agencies.

♦ *The nature of the law*. The law places its greatest emphasis on the management and protection of property.

♦ *Class*. The upper-middle-class image of the profession is itself a deterrent. A yawning gulf exists between working-class people and the typical smooth-talking, self-confident lawyer. Fear of embarrassment, of appearing foolish, tends to keep the ordinary person away from the intimidating consulting room.

Attempts have been made to improve access. First, there is a system of *legal aid*, whereby the state gives financial assistance to litigants. Introduced in the Legal Aid and Advice Act (1949) it represented a significant development, both for the law and for democracy. Generally aid depends upon income and the merits of the case. However, it is subject to abuse both by wealthy individuals finding a technical means to qualify and by 'fat cat' barristers claiming huge fees; earnings for the year 1995/6 totalled £286 million (*Independent*, 18 June 1998).

With unemployment driving more people into debt and mortgage difficulties, the 1980s saw a great rise in the number of claimants and the government attempted to ease the cost by reducing eligibility. The Legal Aid Act (1988) transferred administration from the Law Society to a new quango, the Legal Aid Board. In 1995 the system was cash limited and solicitors and advice agencies were to compete for contracts to hold legal aid budgets; regional boards, rather than the courts, were to decide who qualified. The government continued the quest for cuts in the £1.5 billion bill by excluding personal injury cases, extending the 'no win, no fee' principle throughout civil proceedings and involving the private insurance market. To critics this compromised the government's professed commitment to human rights.

The *Dramatis Personae*

> I dined at my Lord Chancellor's, where three Sergeants at law told their stories, how long they had detained their clients in tedious processes by tricks, as if so many highway thieves should have met and discovered the purses they had taken.
>
> John Evelyn (1620–1706), *Diary* (26 Nov. 1686)

The courts are rather like churches – nothing without the people inside them. Control is jealously guarded by a veritable priesthood of curates, vicars, bishops and even an archbishop in the form of the Lord Chancellor. The law, perhaps the oldest and most venerable of the professions, saw its heyday under the Victorians. The capitalist bourgeoisie based their claim to wealth, prestige and power on property and needed lawyers to secure these. The reform of the law along Benthamite lines, through Acts of Parliament, was the basis for establishing the new order, and the huge increase in private and public legislation made Parliament an earthly paradise for the great Victorian lawyers. The natural partners of the capitalists, like them the lawyers were hard working, generally became immensely wealthy and registered this with a profound sense of their own dignity and importance. Respect for the law became, in practice, a veneration of lawyers that endures to this day.

> The Law is the true embodiment
> Of everything that's excellent.
> It has no kind of fault or flaw,
> And I, my lords, embody the law.
>
> The Lord Chancellor in Gilbert and Sullivan's *Iolanthe*

In the administration of justice lawyers fall into three categories: solicitors, barristers and the judiciary. Although bound together with dense legal bindweed, they have long practised a strict division of labour. While not entirely unique to Britain, the system is relatively unusual and not much admired by lawyers from other countries.

> The Lawyer is exclusively occupied with the details of predatory fraud either in achieving or in checking chicanery, and success in the profession is therefore accepted as marking a large endowment of that barbarian astuteness which has always commanded men's respect and fear.
>
> Thorstein Veblen (1857–1929; American social scientist),
> *The Theory of the Leisure Class* (1899)

Solicitors

Solicitors can be employed in various contexts, including national and local government, but they mainly practise privately, usually in partnerships, dealing directly with the public. They are collectively represented by their 'trade union', the Law Society, which has enjoyed considerable influence as an 'insider' pressure group *par excellence*. Although they may work very closely with clients, perhaps understanding every nuance of their cases, they were by convention prohibited from appearing in a superior court, having to instruct a barrister, their superior in the legal pecking order.

In January 1989 the Lord Chancellor, Lord Mackay of Clashfern, unveiled three green papers proposing reforms of the profession which placed some very lively cats among the legal pigeons. The goal was to introduce free-market disciplines into the cloistered world of wig and gown: breaking the barristers' advocacy monopoly, allowing lawyers to take cases on a US-style 'no win, no fee' basis, to advertise their services and to publish fees. The profession was enraged, even Lord Hailsham, recently retired Lord Chancellor and once staunch member of the Thatcher Cabinet, expressed hostility. After much lobbying a white paper appeared (Lord Chancellor's Department 1989), with the original proposal modified in certain important respects. The most innovative feature of the resulting Courts and Legal Services Act (1990) was the right of audience for lawyers provided they had gained a certificate of advocacy. However, barristers could expect to maintain their hegemony in the rarefied atmosphere of the upper courts.

Barristers

Known collectively as 'the Bar', barristers are far less numerous than solicitors and, despite their superior status, dependent on the latter for business. They may advance to a higher grade by 'taking silk', when they are formally appointed a Queen's Counsel (QC) by the Lord Chancellor. At the apex stand two political appointees: the *Attorney General* (the government's attorney) and the *Solicitor General* (the government's solicitor). A number of barristers become MPs, their allegiance going predominantly to the Conservative Party or Labour's right (such as Clement Attlee, John Smith and Tony Blair).

As a group barristers remain socially insulated, over half operating in the hothouse of London in one of the four great Inns of Court, marked by much tradition, ritual and perhaps snobbery. They are richly remunerated. Lord Falconer QC had to be persuaded to leave a £500,000-a-year commercial practice to become Blair's Solicitor General in 1997 (*The Times*, 27 June 1997). A report in *The Lawyer* revealed the thirty leading barristers' chambers to have received a total annual income of £406 million in 2000–1 (*The Times*, 3 Sept. 2001). Controlling the profession through the General Council of the Bar and a Bar Secretariat, the Inns of Court have an ancient lineage, being well established by the fifteenth century. They were originally concerned with training barristers through lectures and 'arguments', and successful students would duly be 'called to the Bar'. This training gradually declined until, by the early nineteenth century, the call was a formality, the student being merely required to pay an appropriate fee and symbolize attendance for twelve terms by consuming a prescribed number of dinners. Nineteenth-century reforms added to wealth and gastronomic capacity a requirement to pass examinations.

The organization continues to reflect that of the ancient Oxbridge colleges (Jackson 1960: 217). Traditionally, the Bar has been no place for a woman. In 1995, they accounted for 16 per cent of the pool of suitable candidates for silk, 8.5 per cent of applicants and only 5.8 per cent of QCs appointed (*Independent*, 27 June 1996). Five years later there had been some improvement (11 per cent of applicants and 15 per cent of the appointments) but the Bar remained male-dominated, with only 26 per cent of barristers being women (Lord Chancellor's Department 2000).

A client is fain to hire a lawyer to keep from the injury of other lawyers – as Christians that travel in Turkey are forced to hire Janissaries, to protect them from the insolencies of other Turks.

Samuel Butler (1835–1902; English satirist), *Prose Observations*

The judiciary

For historical reasons it is mainly from the Bar that judges have been chosen. This has an important implication for the legal system because judicial office is seen as legal business rather than as an aspect of public service. It helps to legitimate the law by reinforcing the impression of independence. In the sense that appointment is seen as promotion (although one which the richest barristers will spurn), the judiciary may be regarded as the top of the legal hierarchy (figure 20.2).

Appointments, made by the Lord Chancellor, have long been based on secret 'soundings' or 'consultations' among existing judges and senior lawyers. The system was given a resounding vote of confidence by the Commons Home Affairs Select Committee in 1996, which agreed that practical difficulties prevented using advertisements, competition and interviews to fill the vacancies on the High Court bench and above. Reformers have long argued for an independent Judicial Appointments Commission, staffed with lay people as well as representatives from both sides of the legal profession. Such a reform was under consideration soon after Labour came to power in 1997, but after stern judicial opposition it was rejected. However, for the first time, High Court vacancies were to be advertised within the profession.

> The English judge ensures in a quiet but effective manner that his pay accords with his status.
>
> D. Pannick, *Judges* (1987: 12–13)

Magistrates

At the bottom of the hierarchy are the unpaid magistrates sitting in the local courts as Justices of the Peace (JPs), most of whom are not lawyers (they are advised by clerks who are qualified lawyers). In large cities there are also stipendiary (professionally qualified and paid) magistrates. JPs were key figures in local government until the municipal reforms following industrialization swept them from centre stage. They retained a legal role, which was increased with responsibility for juvenile cases after 1908. Despite the reforming hand of the Attlee government the system remains elitist. Formal appointment is by the Lord Chancellor acting on the advice of local committees. Technically anyone can become a magistrate, but the process is often in the hands of secretive local oligarchies within political parties, chambers of commerce and the Freemasons.

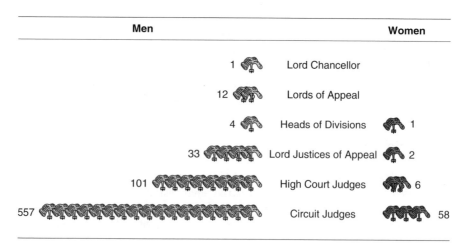

Figure 20.2
The judicial hierarchy, 2001.

Men		Women
1	Lord Chancellor	
12	Lords of Appeal	
4	Heads of Divisions	1
33	Lord Justices of Appeal	2
101	High Court Judges	6
557	Circuit Judges	58

Source: Data from *Judicial Statistics* (2001).

"The jury will ignore that last remark..."

Reproduced by permission of *Punch*

Twelve men good and true: the jury

Although we have introduced the highest and most mighty we have not encompassed the full judicial *dramatis personae* until we consider the twelve ordinary people forming the **jury**. These are mainly used in serious criminal cases and their job is to decide innocence or guilt. They are advised by the judge, who will also pass sentence. Selected randomly from the population, juries are without doubt the most democratic aspect of the legal system – perhaps the most democratic aspect of the whole political system. In the eighteenth century Lord Camden stated: 'trial by jury is indeed the foundation of our free constitution; take that away and the whole fabric will soon moulder into dust' (Jackson 1960). Here ordinary citizens are allowed to speak so authoritatively that the most lofty in the land must heed their words. It was a jury that acquitted Clive Ponting of charges of treason, against the direction of the judge.

However, juries live under threat. The police in particular find them tiresome, conducting an unceasing campaign for their abolition or limitation. In 1965, Robert Mark (as Chief Constable of Leicester) called for majority verdicts (rather than unanimity) and in the 1967 Criminal Justice Act the Labour government duly obliged. In December 2000, the New Labour government attempted to curb the right to trial by jury by reintroducing the Criminal Justice (Mode of Trial) Bill, despite two previous attempts having been defeated by the Lords. Some 18,000 defendants a year in 'either-way' cases (around seven hundred middle-ranking offences such as assault, theft and some drug crimes) would lose the right to choose how their cases would be heard. Instead, magistrates would decide whether to try cases themselves or send them to the Crown Court to be heard before a judge and jury.

In opposition, Jack Straw had attacked the Conservatives' proposals for such reforms as 'shortsighted', but as home secretary he now found the case for change 'overwhelming'. However, yet again there was vehement opposition in the Lords, including from Labour peers such as Helena Kennedy QC, who argued strongly against removing this long-established and fundamental right. The proposal was to surface yet again in the Auld Report. However, in January 2002, after a prolonged barrage of criticism from lawyers, Labour peers and civil liberties groups, Home Secretary David Blunkett jettisoned the plan. Less controversially, Auld also proposed that serious cases against young offenders should no longer be tried in the Crown Court but by a youth court comprising a judge and at least two experienced magistrates.

Juries are, in any case, only used in a minority of cases, no longer being used in Crown Courts where the accused pleads guilty – which most do. Yet the demise of the system would constitute a grave threat to democracy. In Northern Ireland fears of intimidation led, in 1973, to juries being dispensed with in certain terrorism cases. In these 'Diplock courts' convictions were often based on confessions obtained during long hours of police interrogation, where allegations of ill-treatment were subsequently proved.

Radical lawyer Michael Mansfield (1997) argues that far from being contracted, the system should be extended, with all crimes eligible for jury trial. The Auld Report made some recommendations for improving the system, with juries being provided at the start of a trial with written summaries of cases and lists of issues that needed to be decided. It also recommended making it more difficult to evade jury service. The tendency of professional people to escape service on the grounds of work commitments can lead to a preponderance of the working-class or unemployed. Tabloid horror stories report jurors celebrating 'over a pint' with the defendants after their acquittal (Gibb 1988). The 2002 Criminal Justice Bill sought to reduce grounds for exemption but introduced three new circumstances under which a trial could dispense with a jury.

Questions of Impartiality

The iconic statue above the Central Criminal Court (the Old Bailey) shows Justice blindfolded, not knowing who sits on the balance she holds. Judges favour neither rich nor poor, neither right nor left. This picture of **judicial impartiality** is essential to the legitimation of liberal-democratic government. Judges must appear to stand above the confused mêlée of classes, parties and interests. But do they?

Who are the judges? Social characteristics

The British judiciary has for long been tied by silken threads of class to the Establishment, one important condition until recently having been success as a barrister. The career path ensures that judges will be relatively old and predominantly male, and the likelihood that their faces will be white is almost as certain as that their wigs will be so. In 2000, there were still no black or

Asian judges on the High Court bench. However, with the relatively reformist Derry Irvine in the office of Lord Chancellor, there was a slow but steady increase in both ethnic minorities and women; between 1998 and 2001, the proportion of women in the judiciary as a whole had increased from 10 to 14 per cent (Lord Chancellor's Department 2001b). Of particular significance was the elevation of Lady Justice Butler-Sloss to Head the Family Division. However, there was still a long way to go, particularly at the highest levels; there were still only 6 women among the 107 High Court judges, and only 2 per cent of judges at lower levels were from ethnic minorities.

This soil does not nourish radical saplings; the hand of patronage will not be laid upon any suspect characters. From the beginning, selection is by their seniors, who fashion the clay in their own image before administering the breath of life. When those from less propitious backgrounds receive the call – and there is evidence of a widening entry to the Inns of Court School of Law (Bar Council 1989: 51), they are unlikely to make any impression on the impassive face of tradition. Characteristically motivated by social aspiration, with little desire to challenge the status quo, they will already have been subject to a battery of socializing pressures and will make sure they join the right clubs and say the right things with the right accents. One club has appeared particularly attractive: the Freemasons, a shadowy organization involving strange rites, secret handshakes and rolled-up trouser-legs. Even the chair of the new Criminal Cases Review Commission was reported to be a member. Rumours regularly circulate that membership interferes with judicial impartiality and in 1997 Home Secretary Jack Straw announced that all new recruits to the criminal justice system should declare their membership, existing members being invited to sign a voluntary register. Judicial hostility was palpable, with even the Lord Chancellor in full cry.

In 1994 a less secretive process was introduced for appointments below High Court level, with open advertisements in newspapers. Yet despite protestations from Lord Chancellor Lord Mackay that the 'old boy network' no longer operated, figures released by his department in 1995 revealed that 80 per cent of Lords of Appeal, Heads of Division, Lords Justices of Appeal and High Court judges had Oxbridge backgrounds, as had over 50 per cent of middle-ranking circuit judges. Only amongst the lower-ranking district judges was social composition more mixed. Yet even here 12 per cent had travelled by the Oxbridge route. As for sex equality, by the end of the decade there was no evidence of a dramatic change; overall, women comprised only 24 per cent of applicants and 27 per cent of appointments, and of the 15 applying to become circuit judges, only 3 were appointed (Lord Chancellor's Department 2000).

In May 1995 Sir Thomas Legg, Permanent Secretary in the Lord Chancellor's Department, told the Commons Home Affairs Committee: 'it is not the function of the professional judiciary to be representative of the community'. However, reformers argue that they should reflect the heterogeneity of the society they judge in order to bring some sympathy with the unemployed, unqualified, discriminated against and dispossessed. The judiciary are the high and the mighty and, if the Sermon on the Mount is to be believed, such worries that they may have concern the next world rather than this. Although some judges are more liberal than others, critics argue that in general their social background leads to a tendency to act in a certain way with respect to issues such as the following.

Class Generally judges are more lenient towards members of the professions than they are towards the working class or the unemployed (Box 1971). Prudent solicitors recognize this when advising clients to wear a conventional middle-class uniform in court. This is not to deny that there are liberal judges (Lord Justice Woolf, for example, has expressed publicly his desire for reform), but they tend to stand out as the exception. Radical lawyers such as Helena Kennedy, Lord Lestor and Michael Mansfield point to inequity, campaigning for the rights of the disadvantaged and wrongly imprisoned. In large cities, law centres financed by charities and local authorities have been established to combat the bias, by directing legal attention away from business and property matters to concerns affecting ordinary people, such as welfare legislation, consumer affairs and employment problems.

Framing Eve The male domination of the legal profession and judiciary is manifest in the way women are treated. Sexism is institutionalized into the law itself as well as its practice. Until the late nineteenth century, marriage meant that a woman surrendered all separate legal and property rights and until very recently wives could not be raped by their husbands, who had contractual rights to sex upon demand.

Helena Kennedy, one of the few women QCs, found herself in a world of sexist innuendo and jokes about prostitutes and rape cases. To her, journalist Andrew Neil's libel action against a newspaper that had suggested he had consorted with a prostitute resembled a 'stag party', with amusing definitions of terms such as 'bimbo' (Kennedy 1992: 141–2). Judges regularly display excessive leniency in rape cases, the women said to have been 'asking for it'.

Although far fewer women commit crimes than men, it is often said that, like Eve, they lie behind them. They can receive harsher sentences than men because, as mothers, community service is less suitable. Indeed, 53 per cent of women in prison have fewer than two convictions compared with 22 per cent of men (Kennedy 1992: 22–3). Women also have problems in obtaining realistic damages for personal injuries because the economic value of housework is not acknowledged.

Compensation for rape is particularly difficult. For example, a man who had suffered brain damage in a road accident became more sexually violent. In two cases he subjected women to brutal assaults, forcing one to strip, trussing her up 'like a chicken', raping and stabbing her. The women received £1,000 and £3,600 from the Criminal Injuries Compensation Board. After suing in the High Court they received £7,080 and £10,480. Although sentenced to life imprisonment, the man later received £45,750 in compensation for the car accident (Kennedy 1992: 28).

> *Prosecuting Counsel*: And you say she consented?
> *Defendant*: I didn't say she consented.
> *PC*: Did she agree?
> *D*: She didn't agree.
> *PC*: Having said no at first, she just gave in?
> *D*: She enjoyed it.
> *Judge*: The enjoyment wiped out her initial resistance – is that what you are saying?
> *D*: Yes.
>
> From a trial at the Old Bailey, reported by Sue Lees in *New Statesman* (December 1989)

Black justice Judges will hotly deny that decisions are influenced by racial factors. However, Home Office statistics reveal that while black people constitute less than 6 per cent of the population they constitute 22 per cent of the prison population. Although social deprivation must account for some of this there are other factors. Kennedy (1992: 162) reports research by probation services showing that black defendants are more likely to receive immediate custodial or suspended sentences. Average sentence length for a West Indian male is some eight months longer than for his white counterpart (*House of Commons Debates*, 11 Nov. 1991). Various forms of racial stereotyping emerge in court; Asians are more likely to get bail than those of Afro-Caribbean descent because they are thought to be more hard working. West Indians are assumed to be more violent and sexually insatiable. Black women are held to be inherently promiscuous, making it doubly difficult for them to bring rape cases (Kennedy 1992: 161–89). In the area of race relations, judges have proceeded 'on the basis that legislation is primarily an interference with the rights of individuals to discriminate and that the public interest is best served by restricting the impact of that legislation as far as possible' (Griffith 1981: 225).

Party *Prima facie* the evidence suggests a natural bias of the judiciary towards the right. It has appeared that Labour governments have been more likely 'to act in ways which offend the judicial sense of rightness, the judicial sense of where the public interest lies' (Griffith 1981: 236–7). However, as we will see, from the mid-1980s reforms to the legal profession and policies towards crime, sentencing and punishment soured relations with the Conservative Party and contributed to increased judicial political activism.

Moral issues Members of sexual minorities, prostitutes, holders of unorthodox views, squatters, student protesters and so on can all expect rough justice. In 1976, for example, the House of Lords opined, in dispensing with his right to refuse the adoption of his child, that a homosexual had nothing to offer his son. According to gay rights campaigner Peter Tatchell, men having consensual sex with males over sixteen are five times more likely to be prosecuted than those having sex with girls under sixteen and three times less likely to get off with a caution.

Police actions The judiciary has generally supported the police in areas such as questioning, seizure, obtaining 'confessions', conduct of identification parades, and telephone tapping, when legal powers have been exceeded. It is generally recognized by the Director of Public Prosecutions, in deciding whether or not to proceed against the police, that it is exceedingly difficult to secure a conviction. Even the five-year inquiry under retired High Court Judge Sir John May into the wrongful imprisonment of the Guildford Four on the basis of false confessions was only mildly critical of the police. Helena Kennedy (1992: 6) reports that criminal lawyers will present cases on the assumption that 'the judges will always prefer the police account unless the defence case is overwhelming'.

Security In matters of national security the judiciary is willing to set most other considerations aside in siding with the state. In the *Hosenball* case (1977), an American journalist was ordered to be deported by Merlyn Rees, the Labour Home Secretary, for obtaining for publication material said to be harmful to UK security. Lord Denning, in dismissing an appeal, said, 'when the state is in danger...even the rules of natural justice had to take second place' (*The Times*, 30 March 1977). In the case of Sarah Tisdall, a severe sentence was imposed for leaking a memo, while in the Ponting case the judge equated the interests of the state with those of the government (p. 474). In IRA cases, judicial enthusiasm to convict has resulted in serious miscarriages of justice, such as the cases of the Guildford Four, the Maguire family and the Birmingham Six.

Property rights versus civil rights The rise of the bourgeoisie was dependent upon property rights. These are legally vested in individuals through contracts and leases, their protection being one of the primary purposes of the law. Without a Bill of Rights or a written constitution, human rights are not vested, so that judges have been asked not to *protect* a right but to *assert* it, often against a powerful private interest (Griffith 1981: 222). However, incorporation of the ECHR (see p. 73) changed this.

Trade unions Trade unions have since their inception been opposed by judges. In the nineteenth century, when a series of Combination Acts sought to restrict their growth, the judiciary assisted the process through statutory interpretation and common-law decisions. Indeed, towards the end of the century, when Parliament began to doubt the value of legal penalties, it was necessary to curb judicial anti-unionism with legislation. Hence the 1875 Conspiracy and Protection of Property Act effectively legalized strikes and the 1906 Trade Disputes Act reversed the notorious Taff Vale Judgment (p. 282). In 1913, further judicial zeal was curbed with the Trade Union Act to reverse the 1910 Osborne Judgment, which prevented the fledgling Labour Party from using union funds. Conservative legislation during the 1980s was designed to push more industrial relations issues into the courts, which were not slow to respond, interpreting it in a way that cut union protection to a minimum (Marsh 1992: 109). The miners', printers' and seamen's unions all suffered from large-scale sequestration of funds under court orders.

Source: Mary Evans Picture Library

Central–local relations In this political minefield the courts have frequently been friendly to the right, as a number of *causes célèbres* show. In the 1976 *Tameside* case a newly elected Conservative council cancelled a plan for comprehensive education prepared by its Labour predecessor. The Labour Secretary of State intervened under powers in the 1944 Education Act but the House of Lords supported the council on the grounds of a local mandate for its actions. However, in the 'Fares Fair' case, although the High Court upheld the Labour-controlled GLC's right to reduce London Transport fares, the Appeal Court and House of Lords ruled that the statutory duty to provide 'economic' transport ruled out the policy. This time the local mandate was rejected (Griffith 1991: 301–7).

Judges are constantly asked to decide what is in the *public interest*. However, they see this from a narrow perspective, consistently exercising a conservative bias and led ineluctably to the view that 'stability above all is necessary for the health of the people and is the supreme law' (Griffith 1981: 235). Beyond this, judges also operate more overtly in the political world.

Judges and Politics

The principle of the separation of powers would exclude judges from the political process. However, in the real world the judiciary dips more than a toe in the murky swamp. This is institutionalized in the constitutionally anomalous position of its head, the Lord Chancellor. Appointed through prime ministerial patronage rather than elected, he is also a key member of the executive and of the legislature (pp. 69–70). Lord Hailsham was a controversial politician before his appointment and Lord Mackay became increasingly political as he backed the New Right reforms. The position became even more political under Blair's appointee, Lord Irvine. Noted for an overbearing style, he was soon chairing three key cabinet committees driving through constitutional reforms. Informed critics increasingly question so anomalous an office (Steyn 1997).

The Attorney General and Solicitor General are also political appointees; Lord Falconer QC was a long-standing personal friend of Tony Blair. Also appointed through the secretive machinery of political patronage are the Law Lords, able to pronounce on issues of the day from the upper House. Beyond this formal proximity to power there are other ways in which judges enter the world of politics.

Judges making law

Parliamentary sovereignty decrees that judges should discover and apply the law rather than make it. However, in reality they play an exceedingly important law-making role.

Evolving the common law Much British law is no more than a body of past judgements, a great coral reef of wisdom from successive ages. In trials lawyers will delve into the records to find *precedents* to guide current decisions. This body of **case law** is continually evolving. Where two or more cases appear to have been resolved differently, or where social conditions have changed, the judge will exercise discretion and so create a further precedent.

Interpreting statute law Statute law is made by politicians in Parliament, and takes precedence over the common law. However, this does not rule out the creative role of the judiciary. No Act of Parliament can take into account all the circumstances of any particular case and invariably some interpretation, or *statutory construction*, is required. Although judges try to reflect the legislators' intentions, they do not always succeed. For example, the Law Lords decided that the race relations legislation (intended to outlaw discrimination generally) did not apply to private clubs. Again, much legislation invokes the concept of 'reasonableness' in determining standards of acceptable behaviour, which in practice means what *judges* regard as reasonable. Moreover, where loopholes exist in legislation (which they often do), judges can show great ingenuity in inserting their own policy judgements.

> The Common Law of England has been laboriously built about a mythical figure – the figure of the 'reasonable man'.
>
> A. P. Herbert (1890–1971; British writer and politician), *Uncommon Law* (1935)

The Law Commission This quango, composed entirely of lawyers, is responsible for revising the law. Its role is defined formally as technical and non-political, concerned with clarifying obscure language, repealing obsolete statutes, and consolidating and codifying masses of complicated statute or common law. However, it can make major recommendations with more than a cosmetic impact. For example, the controversial 1986 Public Order Act (replacing that of 1936 and consolidating various other pieces of relevant law) incorporated most of the recommendations of a report made by the Commission three years earlier.

Judicial activism

In the great debates of the day, judges are by no means shrinking violets. When delivering judgements their exegesis will often pass comment on various matters of social concern, such as the role of the family, discipline in schools, moral standards, and so on. They can even take off their wigs and gowns and enter the political fray directly.

Lunchtime sandwiches Restrictions on judicial pronouncements came in the form of the Kilmuir guidelines laid down in 1955, though observance of these has varied with Lord Chancellors and they were relaxed by Lord Mackay in 1988. Judges even began to discuss issues over lunchtime sandwiches with journalists (Dyer 1995). Lord Chief Justice Taylor gave regular press conferences and speeches, including the Dimbleby Lecture, in which he attacked the Conservative government's handling of the criminal justice system.

Flattering invitations Governments can invite judges into the political realm in various ways. Legislation can be drawn up that asks them to adjudicate in controversial social matters, as in Heath's Industrial Relations Court. Restrictive union legislation during the 1980s also brought judges into some bitter political struggles. In addition, leading members of the judiciary are frequently asked to head inquiries into controversial questions. Reports such as Scarman (race relations), Nolan (sleaze) and Taylor (the Hillsborough disaster) make their authors' names household words. This places them in the front line of controversy and open to political attack as, for example, when Lord Howe publicly denounced Sir Richard Scott's inquiry into the Matrix Churchill affair.

Judicial review of legislation In many countries (including the USA and France) judges are responsible for reviewing legislation in the light of the constitution and basic civil rights. The doctrine of parliamentary supremacy has rendered this abhorrent to the British constitution. However, the incorporation of the ECHR (see p. 72) modified this position. A minister introducing a bill must produce a certificate of compatibility showing whether it complies with the Convention, and provisions in breach must be debated. Parliament has established a Human Rights Committee of both houses to consider such issues. Moreover, if the courts consider that an Act is in conflict with the Convention, they may refer it to this committee.

Judicial review of executive actions While unable to strike down legislation, judges have had the power to quash executive actions under it when challenged in the courts. This can produce a serious check since, in reality, it may be dissatisfaction with the legislation itself that produces the action.

Traditionally, judges had been content to confine such review to the principle of *ultra vires*. Where they brought in other considerations (reasonableness, fairness), they did so only on the basis of legislative intent, thereby respecting parliamentary sovereignty. However, calls for judicial review were to rise sharply from the mid-1980s (figure 20.3) as lawyers, individuals and pressure groups became more aware and judges, concerned about a growth in executive power since 1979, became more willing to consider the spirit as well as the letter of the law. This power came to public attention in 2000 when the High Court ruled that the Lottery Commission had acted unfairly in excluding Camelot's bid to run the lottery, forcing it to reconsider. The case for judicial activism has been put by Mr Justice Laws in asserting that political controversy should not be grounds for believing a decision to be outside the courts' jurisdiction (Woodhouse 1995: 405–6). Some claimed that development had gone so far as to create a new system of accountability in the UK (Stone 1995). The more robust approach caused such early alarm in official circles that a highway code was produced in 1987 entitled *The Judge Over Your Shoulder*, darkly warning bureaucrats to beware of judicial policemen.

Moreover, even before its incorporation, a greater willingness had emerged to use the ECHR. In finding against a health authority wishing to discontinue treatment of a ten-year-old girl with leukaemia, Mr Justice Laws ruled that the ECHR could be taken as 'persuasive legal authority' (Woodhouse 1995: 412–13). However, cases of conflict had obliged judges to uphold domestic law so that incorporation, through the 1998 Human Rights Act (coming into force in October 2000), opened up new vistas of judicial activism. The Act first took effect in Scotland (being tied to devolution) and resulted in a deluge of challenges (Woodhouse 2001a: 226). Within a year of being introduced in England and Wales over 600 cases had come to the High Court and above, many with far-reaching implications (Woodhouse 2002: 254).

EU membership The EU increased the scope for judicial activism, judges acquiring the powers held by constitutional courts in other countries in a process of 'constitution creep' (Thompson 1997: 186). Indeed, they appeared ahead of politicians in recognizing their responsibility to review domestic legislation in the light of EU law. The courts' powers to suspend an Act of Parliament breaching EU law was revealed in the *Factortame* case (see p. 72). EU law can also be a basis for judicial review. The Equal Opportunities Commission (EOC) claimed that, in denying certain rights to those working less than eight hours a week, the 1978 Employment Protection Act conflicted with EU law. In finding for the EOC the House of Lords demonstrated its unequivocal acceptance of the supremacy of EU law.

Perhaps more importantly, EU membership liberalized judicial attitudes towards statutory interpretation. The courts now refer to *Hansard* in determining the intention behind legislation. Originally prohibited, this first became necessary to establish whether national law was intended to comply with EU law, and it has since been extended to all cases of ambiguity.

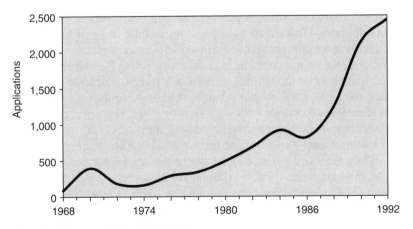

Figure 20.3
The increase in the number of applications to apply for judicial review of administrative action.

Source: Data from Butler and Butler (1994: 318).

Open conflict with government

In 1990, crime rates reached the highest levels since records began in 1851 (*Criminal Statistics*, 1993). In September 1991 Archbishop of Canterbury George Carey declared that 'human wrongdoing is inextricably linked to social deprivation, poverty, poor housing and illiteracy'. The government was unwilling to accept that its policies were implicated and blame was placed on judicial liberalism. There were even attacks from the podium at the 1995 Conservative conference, party chairman Brian Mawhinney urging members to write to judges to complain about light sentences.

Tabloid justice
If you can't do the time, don't do the crime.

Home Secretary Michael Howard's 'prison works' soundbite

The government began to meddle with judicial discretion. The 1994 Criminal Justice and Public Order Act contained several controversial measures, including an end to the traditional right of silence. A suspect's refusal to speak could now be cited in court as a suggestion of guilt. Lord Chief Justice Taylor expressed open opposition, arguing that this undermined a cornerstone of British justice: the presumption of innocence. The 1997 Crime (Sentences) Bill aimed to deal with 'soft' judges through mandatory prison sentences for certain offenders (see p. 674), the judiciary complaining that the government was taking more notice of the tabloids than the judges.

In the Lords, former Master of the Rolls Lord Donaldson condemned the lack of trust in the judiciary, while Lord Williams, former chairman of the Bar Council, spoke of 'a perversion of justice'. Lord Chief Justice Taylor took the unprecedented step of issuing a public condemnation. Perhaps the only succour for the government was Her Majesty's Opposition, determined to show it too could be as tough as the tabloids demanded. To some extent the House of Lords began to appear as a liberal court and 'soft judges', concerned about harsh sentencing, human rights and the welfare of asylum-seekers, appeared more in tune with radical pressure groups. Yet much of the judicial opposition was constitutional rather than ideological. Judges may well have felt that so long a period of single-party rule was itself unconstitutional, producing 'arrogance...with regard to the law and judicial decisions' (Woodhouse 1996: 424). The battle was for judicial independence. Again, in some cases, as when adjudging Howard to have acted unlawfully in April 1994, by introducing a scheme for compensating victims of violent crimes without parliamentary approval, the courts could be said to be protecting Parliament's rights in a way the House was no longer able to. Labour's return to office did not promise to reduce the executive–judicial tension. Although promising constitutional reforms there was resonance with the tough-on-crime rhetoric, 'zero tolerance' and a commitment to the neoliberal economic agenda.

The Human Rights Act promised further conflict, giving more power to the judges. While the Lord Chancellor spoke of the need for a dialogue with the executive, the judges demurred, Lord Bingham commenting: 'I do not myself see it as the role of judges to engage in a dialogue' (Woodhouse 2002: 254). New Labour Home Secretaries Jack Straw and David Blunkett both found themselves in conflict with the judiciary over issues such as freedom of speech, sentencing, juries and treatment of asylum-seekers. There were also controversial security issues following the attack of 11 September 2001. Where national security is involved, there is a right to opt out of ECHR provisions, but judging what constitutes such a threat remains problematic. In July 2001, the Human Rights Act was invoked in the High Court to lift a long-standing Home Office ban on the entry into Britain of Louis Farrakhan, inflammatory leader of a body termed the Nation of Islam. However, in April 2002, the government won an appeal against this on the grounds of public order.

In June 2002 Home Office Minister Lord Falconer publicly accused lawyers of cynically manipulating the system to allow offenders to escape conviction. A white paper proposed making conviction easier, Blair claiming that the 'biggest miscarriage of justice is when the guilty walk away unpunished'. Lawyers feared a tabloid-driven agenda and David Bean and Bruce Houlder, chairmen of the Bar Council and Criminal Bar Association respectively, declared the conviction of the innocent the greater injustice. They accused government of evading responsibility for police under-resourcing (Ahmed 2002). The November 2002 Criminal Justice Bill allowed previous convictions of an accused to be heared (i.e. mentioned) in certain cases, restricted trial by jury and permitted exceptions to the double-jeopardy rule. The government infuriated lawyers with its tabloidspeak of 'victim justice' rather than criminal justice.

Interest affiliation

Judges may be associated with interest groups and political movements. Indeed, many move in the shadowy world of the freemasons (see p. 641). Judicial affiliations were brought to public attention in 2000 in the case of General Pinochet. Lord Hoffmann, one of the Law Lords hearing his appeal against extradition, was found to be closely linked with Amnesty International. The House of Lords was forced to hear the case again, thus opening the door to a surge of challenges on similar grounds (Woodhouse 2001a: 223). The media began taking an interest in judicial affiliations, highlighting, for example, the religious backgrounds of judges involved in a case concerning the separation of Siamese twins against their parents' wishes in 2000.

Administrative Justice

We have seen how judges are drawn into politics through judicial review of executive actions, often where citizens seek **redress of grievance** not from a fellow citizen but from the state itself. This became increasingly likely during the twentieth century, with a burgeoning of the welfare state, an extensive road-building programme, intensified activity by coercive forces such as police and immigration control, and increased regulation of social life in areas ranging from rent control and race relations to gender equality. The process of expansion was further accelerated from the 1980s as reforms associated with the new public management movement (see p. 488) reduced ministerial responsibility to Parliament (Flinders 2001). It can be said that Britain has become a 'contracting state', inviting more and more legal remedies in areas previously seen as the province of politics. The opportunities for judges to consider grievances against the state were further enhanced by the 1998 Human Rights Act.

Some countries deal with this through separate systems of courts and a body of **administrative law** such as the French *droit administratif*. However, in Britain most of the relevant law is in the form of general statutes and a haphazard body of common law. This is supplemented by a system of administrative tribunals and public enquiries and the office of ombudsman.

Administrative tribunals

Although taking multifarious forms, **administrative tribunals** (table 20.1) are generally bodies adjudicating in various categories of cases where a citizen feels aggrieved by some action of a government official or fellow citizen (employer or landlord). They offer the advantages of speed, informality and expertise. Most are standing bodies, concerned with areas such as rents, social security, pensions, benefits, immigration, housing and the NHS, though others arise on an ad hoc basis for particular cases. They hardly constitute a system, more a motley counterpane, defying precise enumeration. Some are so closely woven into the state fabric that it is difficult to discover whether they are tribunals or merely committees. The Leggatt Report (see below) found seventy different tribunal systems in England and Wales, employing 3,500 people and hearing around a million cases a year.

Dissatisfaction following the Crichel Down affair led to the establishment in 1954 of the Franks Committee on Administrative Tribunals and Inquiries. Its 1957 report contained a number of indictments.

Table 20.1 Cases received by various administrative tribunals, 2001

Tribunal	No. of cases	Tribunal	No. of cases
Immigration Adjudicators	62,650	Pension Appeal Tribunals	2,728
Immigration Appeal Tribunals	22,463	Employment Appeal Tribunals	1,489
Social Security and Child Support Commissioners	7,167	Lands Tribunals	515
VAT Tribunals	3,104	Special Commissioner on Income Tax	195

Source: Data from Judicial Statistics, 2001.

The Crichel Down affair

This famous 1954 case highlighted the question of minister–civil servant relationships. It concerned the restoration of land previously requisitioned by the government for military purposes. Although the former owners wished to regain possession, Ministry of Agriculture officials thwarted them with underhand tactics. The owners, well-connected members of the upper-middle class, were able to fight for their rights and after a public inquiry the officials were severely censured and Minister Sir Thomas Dugdale resigned.

◆ The minister whose department was subject to the complaint appointed the tribunal, making it judge in its own cause.
◆ Members were not legally qualified and in many cases legal representation was denied.
◆ The methods of hearing evidence were not strictly controlled.
◆ Decisions were often given without reasons.
◆ Justice was not *seen* to be done, hearings often being conducted like masonic rituals.
◆ There was no appeals machinery.

Franks wanted chairpersons appointed by the Lord Chancellor and an independent body to create tribunals and keep them under constant review. He also argued for greater openness, legal representation, reasoned decisions and a right of appeal to the courts. Some reform followed: proceedings became public unless personal privacy was involved, limited appeals machinery was introduced (appellate tribunals and the courts) and some legal representation permitted.

In 1958 a Council on Tribunals of ten to fifteen members was created as a watchdog appointed by the Lord Chancellor. However, with less power than Franks envisaged, it could not appoint tribunals, award compensation, hear appeals, or overturn decisions. Its pleas for more powers have been unheeded by bureaucrats keen to cocoon themselves against the winds of justice. The Council has also complained at the lack of government consultation when relevant legislation is being drafted. Although some tribunal chairpersons are now legally qualified, appointment still remains within the patronage of the minister, selecting from a list approved by the Lord Chancellor. Members are also appointed by ministers, which means in practice by officials of the interested department.

In May 2000, acknowledging the haphazard nature of the system, the Lord Chancellor set up a review under retired appeal court judge Sir Andrew Leggatt. Reporting in August 2001, Leggatt identified the flaws in the existing system, seeing the main problem as lack of independence from government departments. He proposed a single system covering a wide range of tribunals (including employment, tax, social security and immigration) under the Lord

Chancellor. He also argued for better trained chairpersons and less use of solicitors and barristers, allowing users to represent themselves. The proposals were criticized by lawyers, who saw them as a Canute-like attempt to hold back the tide, particularly in employment law.

Apologists have made much of the informality of tribunals but this has been reduced, the Council on Tribunals publishing *Model Rules of Procedure* in 1991. The virtue of expertise is also questionable; in practice this can mean the opportunity for officials to obfuscate with fog, which a skilled judge would dispel. To citizens tribunals can appear as a Kafkaesque part of the Establishment, often more anxious to protect bureaucrats than pursue justice.

Public inquiries

Government and officials have another alternative to the courts in the **public inquiry**, particularly in cases of collective grievance in areas such as planning and state acquisition of land. Hearings, sometimes dragging on for years, are conducted before interested parties and voluminous reports issued. The Franks Report led to more stringency in their operation; the reports are now published and reasons given for recommendations. Increasingly, major inquiries are chaired by eminent lawyers (p. 648). However, they remain heavily dominated by officials. Although not bound, ministers tend to follow their recommendations, which is not surprising, since the inspectors are from the heavenly list of the great and the good, chosen as a 'safe pair of hands'.

As with tribunals, bureaucrats like to see these exercises as administrative operations (Wraith and Lamb 1971: 13) but the siting of airports, nuclear power stations and motorways affects the quality of people's lives and incites intense feeling. Large-scale public hearings, such as that considering Heathrow Airport's fifth terminal, attract considerable media attention and involve pressure groups, local authorities and private companies. However, the general feeling of those who attend is often one of impotence before a bland wall of polite bureaucratic intransigence. Where protesters give vent to their feelings they may be removed by the inspector's ever-present henchmen in blue. As a result there is an increased tendency for protesters to ignore this avenue and resort to direct action (see chapter 17).

The ombudsmen

A limitation of the tribunal system is its uneven spread. Some departments, such as Work and Pensions, are heavily tribunalized, while others, such as the DfES, have few. In addition, they are limited to certain categories of complaint and cannot cover the full scope of administrative discretion. A 1961 report by the British section of Justice, the legal reform group, recommended introducing an **ombudsman system** based on the Scandinavian model – a trouble-shooter to investigate citizens' complaints about **maladministration** (Whyatt 1961). The idea was received frostily by both officials and government.

A very British ombudsman The Labour government proved more sympathetic but the British version created in 1967 was so locked into existing institutions that it was but a pale shadow of the Nordic prototype. Even the term 'ombudsman' (people's friend) was translated through Whitehallspeak into 'Parliamentary Commissioner for Administration' (PCA), who was to be a servant not of the people but of Parliament. The principle was guardedly extended to the NHS, local government and the devolved assemblies. The local ombudsman receives the lion's share of complaints – around 14,000 a year, compared with the PCA's 2000.

In 1977 Justice assessed the impact of the new institution. The report's title, *Our Fettered Ombudsman*, betrayed its conclusion (Widdicombe 1977). Britain's PCA is shackled by heavy chains forged by the unharmonious blacksmiths of Whitehall.

- *Access.* People cannot address their ombudsman directly; they must go through their MP or MSP. This protects the traditional role of MPs in the redress of grievances. A number of critics, including the PCA himself, have argued for direct access, but this has only been permitted for complaints concerning the NHS, the Welsh Assembly and local government.
- *Maladministration.* Meaning no more than bad administration, the term has proved restrictive. Richard Crossman, when introducing the bill, provided a catalogue of bureaucratic natural shocks to lengthen Hamlet's soliloquy, including 'bias, neglect, inattention, delay, incompetence, ineptitude, perversity, turpitude, arbitrariness, and so on'. Generally the PCA is permitted to consider only the *procedure* of decision-making, not the actual decision. However, it is often the latter that causes the suffering. Widdicombe recommended that 'unreasonable, unjust, or oppressive decisions' should be investigated, as in other countries. With the support of their select committee, successive ombudsmen have managed to widen their scope.
- *Limited jurisdiction.* Complaints that may be pursued through the courts or tribunals are excluded, as is sensitive public-sector territory such as the armed forces, police and government contracting. The result is that little more than half the complaints are investigated.
- *Limited autonomy.* Although formally independent, the ombudsman's real autonomy is questionable. While the executive cannot sack him, it appoints him in the first place, along with his staff. (In November 2002 Ann Abraham became the first woman PCA.) Moreover, legal advice comes from the Treasury Solicitor rather than from the courts (although, since Widdicombe, sources of advice have broadened). Until the appointment of the ex-judge Cecil Clothier in 1979, the first three incumbents were ex-civil servants; justified on the grounds that, as ex-poachers, they would be best able to stalk their prey along the

> I remain concerned at the length of time that it takes departments and agencies both to respond to the statement of complaint which is the precursor of an investigation and to agree to redress when investigation by my office has disclosed injustice resulting from maladministration.
>
> *Report of the Parliamentary Commissioner for Administration, 2001–2002*

burrows of Whitehall. However, they were never particularly zealous gamekeepers, acting more like civil servants, sidling shyly out of the media limelight, denying any political role and delivering pious apologias for their position.

◆ *Enforcement.* Following an investigation, the PCA submits a report, not to the citizen but to the MP and department concerned. Although this may contain recommendations, there is no power of enforcement. However, departments have generally tried to comply to avoid adverse publicity. In his first major case, in 1968, the PCA scored an impressive goal by securing compensation for four ex-prisoners of war, held at a concentration camp at Sachsenhausen in Germany, after their having been refused by three Foreign Office ministers. Another high-profile case was Barlow Clowes in 1989, where compensation was secured for thousands of investors brought to financial ruin by the collapse of a financial investment company to which the Department of Trade and Industry had given a licence. In 1993, under the 'Open Government' initiative, the ombudsman was finally given a power of enforcement.

Ombudsmen or ombudsmice? Designed for a deferential and secretive polity, these are very British ombudsmen. They remain on the sidelines of political life; few know of the system and few use it. Little confidence could be gained when New Labour's Jack Straw became the first minister to refuse a demand by the Ombudsman Sir Michael Buckley for the release of information under the 'Open Government' code. And in May 2002, the Home Office and Cabinet Office were accused of obstructive behaviour in response to his request for papers relating to the Hinduja case (see p. 302). To critics, the value of the ombudsmen lies perhaps more in protecting bureaucracy than citizens.

The Citizen's Charter: freedom, equality and fraternity – or your money back

Citizens' rights were supposed to be further augmented with the issue by the Cabinet Office (1991) of *The Citizen's Charter*. It was soon followed by numerous glossy progeny covering specific services (patients, passengers, parents), setting performance targets and telling people how to complain.

Hailed as John Major's 'big idea', this laid down standards for various services, allowing the public to complain, and in some cases receive compensation, much as they might in a department store.

As with a number of Conservative initiatives, this was relaunched by New Labour under a new name. *Service First* came into operation in June 1998 with what the government claimed were tougher standards set in consultation with 'customers'. However, critics have seen the charters as fig leaves to conceal falling standards. Certainly they were not charters in the sense normally understood: people's demands for rights (Kingdom 1996). Neither could they be seen as substitutes for the redress offered through Parliament or the courts. In 1993 a 'Charterline' established to hear complaints was scrapped for lack of calls.

Judicial review

As explained above (p. 648), actions of the executive can be examined by judges if they are brought before the courts; recourse to this avenue increased from the end of the 1970s. All departments are vulnerable. The Foreign Secretary was declared at fault in the Pergau Dam affair and the Transport Secretary was found to have abused his powers over night-flying restrictions at Heathrow, Gatwick and Stansted. The Department of Health was in trouble over availability of beds and the Ministry of Defence was found to have acted unlawfully in requiring women to leave the armed forces on becoming pregnant. The December 1992 decision to close thirty-one pits, with 30,000 job losses (to make the industry more attractive for privatization), was outlawed. There were also calls for greater openness. The Matrix Churchill case, in particular, made the courts sceptical of ministerial use of public interest immunity certificates (p. 475).

However, the department proving most susceptible has been the Home Office, with a long-running series of clashes over asylum, prisoners' rights, sentencing policy (including Michael Howard's intervention in the James Bulger case, where the convicted were children), the handling of miscarriages of justice (the Guildford Four, the Birmingham Six, the Broadwater Three, Judith Ward, Stefan Kisko, the Taylor sisters) and victims' compensation. In finding Home Secretary Kenneth Baker in contempt (in July 1993) for deciding to deport a Zairian asylum seeker in defiance of a court order, the courts were challenging ministers' claims to the protection of Crown immunity.

However, despite a number of high-profile cases, judicial review remains discretionary, striking intermittently and unpredictably and leading some to doubt whether it can be regarded as meaningful control over government (Rawlings 1986). Despite the burgeoning number of cases, only a minority concern central government. Moreover, being expensive it is unavailable to many individuals and groups.

Towards an administrative court

In 1971 Justice suggested creating a special division of the High Court to provide an avenue to appeal from tribunals on points of law. This would have resembled the prestigious French *Conseil d'Etat*, a supreme administrative tribunal through which ordinary citizens can, at small cost, obtain a wide range of remedies against officialdom. The suggestion met bureaucratic opposition on the grounds that such a court would lack expertise. However, increasing use has been made of the Queen's Bench Division of the High Court in public law cases with specialist judges. This was renamed the Administrative Court, the change coinciding with the coming into force of the Human Rights Act, which was expected to increase the need for it. A leading judge, Mr Justice Walker Scott, was appointed with overall responsibility and the arcane names of its orders were made more user-friendly (thus *mandamus*, compelling an authority to act, became a mandatory order, and *certiorari*, preventing action, became a quashing order).

Law and Politics

If the law
suppose
that...the law is
a ass.

Mr Bumble in
Charles Dickens's
Oliver Twist
(1837–8)

Writing in 1998 Nevil Johnson noted how 'during the past 20 years or more the decisions of judges and of other office holders and institutions with adjudicatory functions have begun to impinge more often and more insistently on the spheres of political and administrative discretion in Britain' (1998: 148). This chapter bears this out. While the confrontational style of the post-1979 governments may well have stimulated judicial activism, there are other contributory factors: a political culture that, perhaps because of sleaze scandals, is less willing to trust its leaders; more judicial review; the enlarging presence of the EU in daily life; a growth in tribunals, and the regular use of judges in inquiries. Significantly, the Blair government, by incorporating the ECHR, accepting the EU Social Chapter, setting devolution in motion and promising freedom of information legislation is increasing this tendency. Should Britain take the final step to a written constitution, the involvement of judges would increase even more.

However, while many of these developments proceed in the name of freedom and rights, the greater involvement of judges at the expense of the discretionary power of ministers narrows the area under democratic control and accountability; the people do not appoint judges and they cannot remove them. Judicial involvement may be supported by the argument that the law protects the 'public interest'. However, when judges consider the public interest, the public they have in mind is perhaps more that in the public school than in the public convenience. When the state agencies claim to be enforcing a neutral law, through neutral machinery, they are walking a perilous psychological tightrope. That they have been able to defy political gravity with such conspicuous success is testimony to the forces of socialization that shape popular attitudes.

Key points

- Within the British state the legal institutions are the most august and venerated.
- The organization of the courts is hierarchical and reflects a fundamental dichotomy between civil and criminal jurisdiction.
- The European Court of Human Rights and the European Court of Justice are playing an increasing part in British justice.
- The jury system is the only democratic chink in the legal system.
- High costs mean that for many people access to the law is restricted.
- The legal profession assumed particular importance during the eighteenth and nineteenth centuries as the industrial bourgeoisie sought to safeguard property and wealth.
- Lawyers and judges are generally from the upper-middle classes, predominantly male and white. These factors call into question their impartiality.
- Although the role of judges is formally seen as interpreting and applying the law, they are in reality able to shape it in a number of ways.
- The New Right reforms were to create considerable and uncharacteristic tension between the Conservatives and judiciary.
- Britain does not have a special set of administrative law and courts. The vacuum is filled with administrative tribunals, ombudsmen and citizen's charters.
- Law and the legal system cannot be regarded as above politics and lawyers are increasingly entering the political sphere.

Review your understanding of the following terms and concepts

administrative law	JP	ombudsman
administrative tribunal	judicial activism	Parliamentary
barrister	judicial impartiality	Commissioner for
case law	judicial review	Administration (PCA)
citizen's charter	judiciary	public inquiry
civil jurisdiction	jury	redress of grievance
common law	legal aid	rule of law
criminal jurisdiction	Lord Chancellor	solicitor
European Court of Human	magistrate	statute law
Rights	maladministration	

Assignment

Study the extract from *The Times* on p. 660 and answer the following questions.

Mark (%)

1 Why do you think senior members of the judiciary strongly
   oppose the idea of a judicial appointments commission?   20

Irvine drops plan for lay people to help pick judges

By Frances Gibb, LEGAL CORRESPONDENT

The Lord Chancellor has ditched controversial plans for a judicial appointments commission, in which lay people would have helped in the selection of judges.

Lord Irvine of Lairg said yesterday that he had decided not to consult on the idea of setting up a commission because of the 'very heavy workload' facing his department.

Instead, he announced other reforming measures aimed at modernising the judiciary in the run-up to the millennium and improving "openness, flexibility and effectiveness" of the system.

Vacancies for High Court judgeships will be advertised for the first time within the legal profession, ending the system of appointment to the senior judiciary by invitation only. There are currently 93 High Court judges on a salary of £108,192. Under the previous Lord Chancellor, advertising of vacancies of lower judicial ranks such as circuit and district judges was introduced.

Lord Irvine is also to consider setting up a judges' ombudsman to handle complaints from aggrieved candidates for judicial posts. The proposal for a judicial appointments commission, Labour policy for some years although omitted from the election manifesto, is strongly opposed by the senior judiciary.

But Lord Irvine is understood to have changed his mind about a commission without the need for lobbying by senior judges. A Lord Chancellor's Department spokesman said: "It is his decision entirely. Obviously he talks to senior judges, but he feels that a commission is really not necessary at the moment. One can never say 'never', but it is really on the back-burner. He would rather get on with the changes he thinks should be made."

2   Are there any grounds for suspicion that Lord Irvine's change of mind resulted from judicial opposition?   20
3   What would you see as the advantages and disadvantages of involving lay people in the selection of judges?   30
4   How might open advertising of senior posts within the legal profession alter the nature of the judiciary?   30

Questions for discussion

1   Why did the nineteenth century see important developments in the legal profession?
2   Evaluate the principle of trial by jury. Why do you think bodies such as the police are unhappy with it?
3   Assess the role of British judges in shaping the law.
4   'The way judges are appointed means that they must nurse conservative leanings and have little sympathy with working people or left-wing movements.' Discuss.
5   What likely problems face women bringing rape charges in our courts?
6   'The British ombudsmen do little more than legitimate bureaucratic power.' Discuss.
7   How might the incorporation of the ECHR change the role of British judges?
8   How far is Britain's system of administrative tribunals an adequate substitute for a full-scale system of administrative law?
9   Discuss whether judges should be Freemasons.
10 'The political involvement of judges has increased, is increasing and should be curtailed.' Discuss.

Topic for debate

This house gives a black mark to white justice.

Further reading

Griffith, J. A. G. (1997) *The Politics of the Judiciary*, 5th edn.
First published 1977. Lively critique of the judiciary and its alleged political neutrality. Continues to irritate in establishment circles.

Harris, P. (1997) *An Introduction to the Law*, 5th edn.
Introductory text portraying the law and the legal system as living institutions.

Kairys, P. (ed.) (1982) *The Politics of Law: A Progressive Critique*.
Readings on law in society.

Kennedy, H. (1992) *Eve was Framed*.
Searching, semi-autobiographical polemic by woman barrister criticizing the legal profession, with special emphasis on its sexism.

Lee, S. (1988) *Judging Judges*.
Defends judges against critics of the left.

Rosenberg, J. (1997) *Trial of Strength*.
Details the battle between ministers and judges over who makes the law.

Thompson, E. P. (1975) *Whigs and Hunters*.
Explores the relationship between the law and economic power.

For light relief

Charles Dickens, *Bleak House*.
Satire on the Court of Chancery. Tells of *Jarndyce and Jarndyce*, a case which continues interminably for the profit of the lawyers and the ruin of others.

Franz Kafka, *The Trial*.
A nightmare vision of a judicial system. Begins: 'Someone must have slandered Joseph K., because one morning, without his having done anything wrong, he was arrested'.

John Mortimer, *Rumpole of the Bailey*.
Humorous tales by famous playwright /barrister. Also available as videos.

David Pannick, *Advocates*.
Thought-provoking and amusing account of the practices and morality of the Bar.

Twelve Angry Men.
Classic film in a jury room, starring Henry Fonda.

On the net

http://www.ombudsman.org
This site includes the PCA's annual reports and extensive statistics.

http://www.lcd.gov.uk
The Lord Chancellor's Department is at the heart of the criminal justice system. A vast amount of information is available here, plus links to related sites.

http://www.ccrc.gov.uk
Find out about miscarriages of justice investigated by the Criminal Cases Review Commission.

http://www.lawcomm.gov.uk
If you are interested in the Law Commission's role in law reform, take heed of the warning that some of the documents available here may be very large.

21

The Coercive State: the Politics of Law and Order

One of the defining characteristics of the state is the right to use violence. Although a necessary power, it is one fraught with danger, evoking fears of a 'police state' or military dictatorship. The world is full of examples of how real this threat is. Clearly debates around issues of law and order must be central to politics. This chapter begins with the evolution of the police service, and its organization and culture. We then focus on its twin functions of fighting crime and maintaining public order. This leads to a consideration of four trends in modern policing – centralization, militarization, politicization and the increasing involvement of the private sector. This is followed by an examination of the crucial function of monitoring – the police complaints procedure. We also go beyond the police to consider the more shadowy world of the military and the security services. We conclude by asking whether the coercive policing of modern times should or could revert to a more consensal style.

There are grounds for believing that policing in the UK is a model for the world. Certainly many men and women in all ranks serve with dedication, tact, and often great bravery. Yet the position they are in is necessarily one of acute political sensitivity. Policing can only enjoy legitimacy in a society that constantly debates its role and evaluates its operation. It is a measure of the success of British policing that a number of associated issues feature openly in modern political debate. We turn to these after briefly reviewing the evolution of the police service.

Evolution

Although the history of policing may be traced back before the Norman Conquest, lying in the principle that a community accepted a joint responsibility for maintaining the peace, like most of the apparatus of the modern state, the police service was largely a nineteenth-century creation of the bourgeoisie. In the dense unholy urban communities, lawlessness could thrive and an ever-present threat of civil unrest was made more terrifying to the propertied by the spectre of the French Revolution and its terrible aftermath. An early move to strengthen law and order was made in the eighteenth century by Henry Fielding (author of the classic *Tom Jones*), a justice at London's Bow Street Court, who gathered together a group of upper-class vigilantes – the celebrated Bow Street Runners.

Radical agitation in the 1815–19 period saw magistrates bringing in the cavalry to break up a large but peaceful working-class demonstration in Manchester in August 1819. Known as the Peterloo Massacre, it created a scandal and was clearly no way to legitimate the political order. As Home Secretary, Sir Robert Peel secured a number of important penal reforms, introducing the concept of modern policing in the Metropolitan Police Act (1829). This was a paid, uniformed, full-time, disciplined and specially trained corps. It became the model for other municipalities, consolidated under the 1856 County and Borough Police Act.

Structure, accountability and control

There are forty-three police services in England and Wales; by 2002, they were employing nearly 130,000 police officers (18 per cent of them women) as well as over 50,000 civilians (table 21.1). Although nominally under local government this image has always been misleading and recent reforms have left it even more removed from community control. The key figures in the chain of command and accountability are the local police authority, the chief constable and the home secretary. Parliament also has a part to play, though a smaller one than might be expected.

Table 21.1 Size of the police force in England and Wales, 1971–2001

Year	Men	Women	Year	Men	Women
1971	93,500	3,800	1991	112,100	15,000
1981	108,800	10,700	1996	108,500	18,800
1986	109,900	11,700	2001	102,100	21,200

Source: Data from *Social Trends* (1988: table 12.27; 2002: table 9.24) and *Annual Abstract of Statistics* (1998: table 4.2).

The police authority Supposed to represent their communities, police author-ities cover single counties or joint areas formed by adjacent unitary authorities. Their forebears, the nineteenth-century watch committees, exercised consider-able control and could dismiss officers and demand weekly reports (Baldwin and Kinsey 1982: 106). However, their role has been gradually reduced so that today it is mainly limited to consulting the local community about their concerns and priorities, identifying local objectives and setting targets within objectives set by the home secretary.

Membership has also changed to reduce the role of local councillors who, before April 1995, comprised two-thirds of the police committee, with one-third being JPs. Under the 1994 Police and Magistrates Court Act police authorities became independent precepting bodies (effectively quangos). Their seventeen members comprise nine councillors, three JPs, and five appointed by the home secretary. Thanks to concessions forced by the House of Lords, authorities retained the freedom to appoint their own chairs.

London's Metropolitan Police (the 'Met') was the direct responsibility of the home secretary until the 1999 reforms of London government, when it came under a new twenty-three member Metropolitan Police Authority and the mayor. The authority comprises eleven members one from the GLA represen-tative of the district councils outside London that had come under the Met, and eleven magistrates and independents, with one appointed by the home secretary to reflect the authority's national functions.

The chief constable In day-to-day policing the key figure is the chief constable who, as a servant of the Crown, is not under the direction of the police authority. Although an annual report is usually presented to the police author-ity, this is not obligatory. One element of control the authority does have is over funding, although this is limited (see below).

> Not only can the chief constable do what he likes, but he can spend all our money doing it.
>
> Gabrielle Cox (Manchester Police Committee chairperson), quoted in the *Guardian* (11 Aug. 1984)

The home secretary The home secretary is in a sense the minister for the police. Although having considerable formal powers, incumbents have generally been timid. In the 1980s Douglas Hurd was admired for the way he was able to cultivate 'an appearance of almost deliberate powerlessness when it comes to police operation' (Evans 1986a). When power has been used it has more often been to direct police authorities rather than chief constables. During 1984, when the South Yorkshire authority tried to withhold funds for policing the miners' strike, the Chief Constable sought the support of both Home Secretary and Attorney General, the latter applying to the High Court for powers to coerce the authority (Oliver 1987: 215–21). However, from the 1990s, both Conservative and Labour home secretaries began to take a stronger line.

Parliament Since, as officers of the Crown, the police escape local account-ability, it might be thought that they are accountable to Parliament through the home secretary. However, a 'catch 22' situation obtains: the Speaker has ruled that, because the police administration lies with police authorities, the home secretary is *not* answerable (*House of Commons Debates* 1958: col. 1259).

Who controls? The lack of accountability can be defended on the grounds that it insulates the police from politicians and prevents the rise of a **police state**. However, it can be argued that evils are more likely in the absence of democratic accountability. We explore this later in the chapter.

> Had the Metropolitan Police been influenced over the past ten years by elected representatives...many of the mistakes would have been avoided and its reputation would stand far higher.
>
> Roy Hattersley (Shadow Home Secretary), quoted in J. Benyon (ed.),
> *Scarman and After* (1984: 108)

Culture and the Policing Function

Policing entails two broad functions – fighting crime and maintaining public order. Both require considerable discretion and the way this is exercised shapes society, making policing an essentially political role. Hence it is important to study the ideas and attitudes informing actions – the **police culture**.

Police culture

> Reading isn't an occupation we encourage among police officers. We try to keep the paperwork down to a minimum.
>
> Joe Orton
> (1933–67; British dramatist),
> *Loot* (1965)

Policing is an all-consuming occupation and can create an incestuous professional community. Socializing in the community being policed is obviously difficult, officers often spending their leisure hours with each other, reinforcing attitudes and creating strong pressure to conform. This culture is secretive, as is shown in a tendency to join the Freemasons. In 1988 the *Sunday Times* acquired a list of no fewer than a hundred senior Scotland Yard officers who were active members. There were believed to be some 5,000 Masons in the Metropolitan force alone and allegations circulated that membership enhanced promotion prospects, influenced investigations and led to cover-ups (Chittenden 1988). Although the Home Affairs Select Committee concluded in March 1997 that the problem was exaggerated, serious public concern led Home Secretary Jack Straw to follow their recommendation that new recruits to the police, probation and prison services, as well as judges, should register Freemason membership.

Characteristically, the police are associated with certain attitudes towards race, gender, class and ideology.

Race A traditional reluctance to employ black people, and their disinclination to apply, reinforces white police culture. Attracting increasing attention since the 1970s it is one of the major problems of policing today. Research by the Policy Studies Institute in the 1980s found the casual manner in which racist language was used its most telling feature. West Indians were regularly referred to as 'nigger', 'sooty', 'coon', 'spade', 'monkey' and 'spook', while Asians were

"Look, this is damn silly if we're both masons."

invariably 'Pakis', regardless of origins. These norms led officers who did not think of themselves as racists to use the terms (Smith and Gray 1985: 390–3). The Police Complaints Authority's 1993 annual report recorded 172 complaints of racism, but in only a single case were charges recommended.

Such attitudes have helped to precipitate racial disturbances. The 1986 Broadwater Farm riots in Tottenham, during which a policeman was brutally murdered, illustrated the intensity of feeling. Subsequent research revealed that 75 per cent of young blacks perceived the police as being unjust towards them; as many as 67 per cent of young whites agreed (Lea et al. 1986). Confidence was not restored in the 1997 Stephen Lawrence case, in which five white youths were accused of murdering a black student. The Met failed to convict and displayed a profound lack of sympathy towards the Lawrence family. During the public inquiry under Sir William Macpherson, Home Office expert Paul Pugh declared police racial awareness training to have been a waste of money. While apologizing for the way the case had been handled, Metropolitan Commissioner Paul Condon resisted calls for resignation, and no officer faced disciplinary charges, all leaving with pension rights fully intact.

With its suggestion of institutional racism, the 1999 Macpherson Report was probably the most trenchant recognition of the problem ever published. The same year, a report from H. M. Inspector of Constabulary declared racism to be endemic throughout Britain's police forces and noted a failure to recruit and retain black officers (see also p. 697). Despite the inclusion of specific

I freely admit that I hate, loath and despise niggers...I don't let it affect my job though.

Police officer quoted in D. Smith and J. Gray, *Police and People in London* (1985: 403)

> We've got a young lad in there, he's dead, we don't know who he is and we'd like to clarify that point. If he's not your son, all well and good, but we need to know and I'm sure you'd like to know too.
>
> Inspector Ian Little, senior police officer, to Stephen Lawrence's parents at the hospital after their son had been pronounced dead, quoted in the *Independent* (8 April 1998)

provisions relating to the police in the 2000 Race Relations (Amendment) Act, the Police Complaints Authority noted a threefold increase in racial complaints between 1998/9 and 2000/1.

Gender The police ethos is overtly masculine, similar to that found in other predominantly male preserves like the army or rugger clubs (the police field formidable teams, sometimes including internationals). Women often experience great difficulty in developing a career, constituting only a small proportion of the service (see table 21.1). The conversation and jokes mock women colleagues ('plonks'). Smith and Gray (1985: 373), choosing a deliberately mild example, report an older constable enthusing over the practice whereby new WPCs were always 'stamped on the bare bum' with the official rubber stamp. The absence of women is a question not merely of unequal opportunity, it has deep operational and political implications. The non-consensual pattern of policing (see below), which can actually incite violence, is a product of the macho culture.

In February 1993 the Home Office released a report by academic researchers on sex discrimination in the police service, disclosing that nearly all policewomen experience sexual harassment ranging from 'groping' to rape. Women were also twice as likely as men to take sick leave because of frustration over career development (*Guardian*, 12 Feb. 1993). Alison Halford, who rose to become one of Britain's seniormost policewomen, brought a celebrated case to the Equal Opportunities Commission after being rejected for promotion to deputy chief constable nine times while less qualified men advanced. The service responded by bringing disciplinary charges against her. Both cases were dropped and a financial settlement accepted by Halford; her subsequent book title summed up her career – *No Way up the Greasy Pole* (1993). However, 1995 saw Britain's first woman chief constable when Pauline Clare was appointed to head the Lancashire force. By 2002, there were four women at this level, all graduates. Clearly changes were taking place, but for reformers the pace remained slow.

Attitudes towards women in general are similarly sexist. A particular problem arises with rape. In the first place, victims are loath to report, and those that do so (about one in four) have been subject to humiliating scepticism (Benn et al. 1983). The Greenham Common demonstrations, where women stepped outside traditional structures of protest to express a particularly female view of the arms race, widened awareness of the problem with a huge number of arrests for trivial offences, intimidating dawn raids, many injuries, sexual harassment, strip searching and photographing. Similarly, wives who became involved in the miners' strikes experienced humiliation and abuse: mocked for their poverty, locked in vans for up to two hours and 'refused access to a toilet...offered a milk bottle instead' (Benn 1985: 132).

Class The police stand in a curious position socially; approved of by the middle classes, whose privileges they work to protect, they have traditionally recruited from the working class (Reiner 1982). Yet paradoxically they appear to oppress the working class. In the Met, officers divided the citizenry into two broad categories – 'slag' or 'rubbish' and 'respectable people' – defined largely in terms of social class (Smith and Gray 1985: 434). The class basis is not surprising, because the job can be variously onerous, boring and dangerous; between 1981 and 1987, 111 police officers in England and Wales were killed on duty (Lambert 1988). Hence the police are among the most oppressed of the working class, suffering from an alarming rise in stress-related illnesses (Evans 1986a); in Greater Manchester in 2000, 56 per cent of all retirements from the force were on medical grounds (*BBC News*, 19 June 2002).

Political complexion Although officially neutral, the police service is clearly right wing, as many as 80 per cent designating themselves Conservative (Kettle 1980: 31; Reiner 1993). Indeed, the National Front experienced little difficulty in seducing 'chief constables and even the Home Office into providing the movement with the necessary facilities for its public campaigns' (Walvin 1984: 142).

Police culture exerts a constant socializing effect. As recruits work their way up, the pressure is to conform, to become more macho, more racist and more right wing. Indeed, higher-class recruits may even affect lower-class accents (Smith and Gray 1985: 435). The successful officer will not usually be one who stands out against prevailing norms, and those in positions of authority will tend to promote in their own image. However, the culture affects the pattern of policing in both fighting crime and maintaining public order.

Fighting crime

The image of the police treating all equally belongs largely to a fantasy world of cops and robbers. Police culture tends to favour the white and the wealthy and offences relating to property dominate crime statistics (table 21.2). The weight of police suspicion bears most heavily on the lower sections of the working class (unskilled workers, the unemployed and the young), who are more likely to receive contempt and abuse. Researchers listened to an officer, not considered unusual, addressing a boy in the absence of his parents:

> 'You're a fucking little cunt aren't you? You've been at it again haven't you, you little bastard?...I'm going to nail your fucking hide to the wall'. (Smith and Gray 1985: 420)

Table 21.2 Fighting crime: recorded crime and detection rates, 2001

Crime	No. of crimes reported (thousands)	Detection rate (%)[a]
Theft and handling stolen goods	2145.4	17
Criminal damage	960.1	14
Burglary	836.0	12
Violence against the person	600.9	62
Fraud and forgery	319.3	29
Drug offences	113.5	95
Robbery	95.2	18
Sexual offences	37.3	53
Other	63.2	73
Total	5170.8	24

[a]Only 59% of all crimes detected actually resulted in a charge or summons.
Source: *Social Trends* (2002: table 9.17) and *Annual Abstract of Statistics* (2001: table 11.1)

It is unlikely that a stockbroker would be addressed in such terms. The evidence is that black people, particularly West Indians, are far more likely than others to be stopped and even arrested on the grounds of intuition. Yet the popular view that blacks are more prone to commit violent crime is not borne out by the statistics.

Various areas have caused concern, including brutality, false confessions and the decision to prosecute.

Police brutality The macho style has resulted in a harrowing catalogue of atrocities. For example, in 1969 in Leeds, David Oluwale, a Nigerian, was singled out for 'special treatment' in which he was urinated on, beaten severely and his body abandoned in the countryside; in an ensuing cover-up notebooks were doctored. In 1976, Liddle Towers was set upon by police outside a Gateshead club, subsequently dying from injuries received; although his doctor described his body as 'pulped', a Labour home secretary refused to set up an official enquiry. In June 1979, Jimmy Kelly was set upon by police as he walked home from a pub in Huyton, Liverpool, subsequently dying in police custody. Further journalistic investigations into this force disclosed a long trail of beatings and sadism.

Deaths in police custody continued to hit the headlines in the 1990s. In July 1990 Oliver Price died after being held in a necklock by police. In August 1993 Joy Gardner died of suffocation after police taped over her mouth when attempting to deport her. The three police officers charged with her manslaughter were subsequently acquitted. In January 1999 Roger Sylvester died after being restrained by eight police officers. While not all deaths in custody are specifically related to police treatment, the trend during the 1990s was disturbing, numbers peaking at sixty-five in 1998/9 (though by 2000/1 they had almost halved to thirty-two).

False confessions and miscarriages of justice Formal protection for suspects was based on the famous though ill-understood Judges' Rules, permitting the right to silence and access to a solicitor or friend. These did not carry statutory force, were applied capriciously and subject to abuse. In addition, 'confessions' extracted by police officers appeared to reflect the talents of Agatha Christie rather than Sherlock Holmes. A major *cause célèbre* was the *Confait* case: three boys convicted of murder and arson on the basis of false confessions after a male homosexual had been found dead in his blazing home in April 1972. This led in 1977 to a Royal Commission on Criminal Procedure, set up against police wishes, which reported in 1981. Sir David McNee, Metropolitan Police Commissioner, argued that the things the police did were necessary and should therefore be legalized (Koffman 1985: 15).

The resultant Police and Criminal Evidence Act (1984) (PACE) made provision for restricting police power: all interviews were to be taped, suspects given the right to have a solicitor present and confessions were to be unforced and only used as evidence if taped. Yet in reality little changed; indeed suspects were arrested more often, detention was authorized as a matter of routine, the law on interrogation remained unclear, the right to legal advice proved difficult to enforce and the taping of interviews was easily evaded. Police could also pressurize suspects (Sanders and Young 1995). The Act actually *increased* police powers.

Public concern about miscarriages of justice continued to hit the headlines. In 1989, the West Midlands serious crime squad was suspended, pending an inquiry, after a series of trials collapsed amidst allegations of fabricated evidence. Officers from the squad had been involved in the controversial conviction of the 'Birmingham Six', imprisoned for the pub bombings of 21 November 1974. In January 1990 the 'Guildford Four', convicted on the basis of false confessions for the pub bombings of 5 October 1974, walked free. In 1997, the 'Bridgewater Three' were released after being imprisoned for the murder of newspaper boy Carl Bridgewater on the basis of improper methods by Staffordshire police.

In 1991 a Royal Commission on Criminal Justice was established 'to examine the effectiveness of the criminal justice system in England and Wales in securing the conviction of those guilty of criminal offences *and the acquittal of those who are innocent*' (emphasis added). However, it simply recommended fine tuning, suggesting no fundamental reforms and offering 'little comfort to those now languishing in jails for crimes they did not commit, convicted on the basis of confessions they did not want to make' (Sanders and Young 1995: 140). Concern led to the Criminal Appeal Act (1995) establishing the Criminal Cases Review Commission. However, with its chair a Freemason and its membership heavily weighted towards the prosecuting authorities, its independence appeared questionable (Mansfield 1997).

The decision to prosecute Arrest does not in itself mean that a criminal prosecution will follow and traditionally the police enjoyed discretion over this decision. This unsatisfactory state eventually led in 1986 to the creation for England and Wales of a Crown Prosecution Service (CPS), under a Director of Public Prosecutions. Many problems dogged the new service, including inadequate funding, police scepticism, some very expensive trials ending in acquittals, such as those of three footballers accused of taking bribes (two trials and the police investigation costing £12 million) and a failure to prosecute police accused of offences. Of the eight most serious cases of deaths in police custody between 1990 and 1995, only two resulted in prosecution. The relatives' support group, Inquest, argued that 'the perception is that the police are above the law and that those deaths are not taken seriously' (*Guardian*, 5 Oct. 1996). The same New Right managerialism that had affected much of the state was also apparent in the CPS. In 1998 its director, Dame Barbara Mills, abruptly retired, having 'become synonymous with the worst aspects of the service; its overblown bureaucracy, its poor morale and its civil service mentality' (*The Times*, 21 May 1998).

Her poisoned chalice was taken up by David Calvert-Smith QC. So uncomfortable was the position that he was even to feature in a BBC Radio 4 programme, *On the Ropes*! There were numerous cases of failure to convict and the CPS was accused variously of delaying, failing to provide prosecuting lawyers with the right documents and failing to disclose evidence. By 2002 the rate of acquittals, which had stood at around 32 per cent in the 1980s, had reached 68 per cent (O'Reilly and Robbins 2002). Outrage followed the case of Damilola Taylor, a ten-year-old boy murdered on his way home from Peckham library. With suggestions of pressure from politicians after the fiasco of the Stephen Lawrence trial, the police and DPP brought a case against four boys with very little evidence to convict. They were acquitted in April 2002 and, amidst mounting concern, the DPP was asked by Attorney General Lord Goldsmith to review the CPS.

Reform and resistance to reform

By 2002, crime rates were increasing, detection rates were down to 24 per cent (see table 21.2) and convictions were as low as 9 per cent. In addition, the fear of crime, particularly street crime, had risen markedly. A variety of measures to improve crime-fighting were unveiled in a 2001 white paper, *Policing in a New Century*, including a non-emergency telephone number (rather like NHS Direct), attempts to increase recruitment levels by lifting a ban on foreigners, and recruiting thousands of uniformed community support officers to patrol the streets and deal with low-level anti-social behaviour.

Maintaining public order

Despite the increase in powers (under the 1984 Act), the police record in crime-fighting is questionable. The prolonged failure to catch the 'Yorkshire Ripper' in the 1980s provided bizarre evidence of ineptitude. However, in the second of their functions they can appear more effective. Maintaining **public order** is a

Bobbies on the beat: policing the social justice march, April 1997

Photo: *The Socialist*

more overtly political function. Indeed the police can sometimes be cast as instruments of government policy; they often act as if they are protecting not public order but the state itself, working through the Special Branch and in liaison with MI6. It is here that some of the worst police violence has been seen.

In making public order decisions police culture leads officers to have little empathy with the people who march in support of causes such as anti-fascism, gay rights, CND, Irish republicanism or Greenpeace. They can see such people as unpatriotic enemies, expressing views such as: 'It's the scum of the earth. Why should we protect that?' (Smith and Gray 1985: 436). Legislation tends to support police action. In the early 1980s powers rested mainly on the 1936 Public Order Act. This was replaced by a designer Public Order Act (1986) intended to legitimize many of the powers they had already been assuming without authorization. The 1994 Criminal Justice and Public Order Act contained a number of new measures roundly criticized by civil liberties groups. Powers to stop and search were increased and police were enabled to restrict travellers, squatters, protesters and those attending raves. A new offence of 'aggravated trespass' made trespass a criminal rather than a civil offence, giving the police the right to act against those demonstrating against, say, new roads, airport runways or foxhunting. It was easy to find grounds to act against protesters offending the government and critics feared a police state. Only days before Easter 1996 the Home Secretary gave the police new stop-and-search powers under the Prevention of Terrorism Act.

The change of government in 1997 did little to stop the momentum. In 1998 Jack Straw unveiled his Crime and Disorder Bill, which promised night-time curfews for children and special parenting classes. Straw's rhetoric

> Criminality and thuggery masquerading as political protest.
>
> Home Secretary Jack Straw on the anti-capitalism May Day protests (House of Commons, 2 May 2000)

proclaimed: 'This is about implementing a zero-tolerance strategy'. It was certainly the strategy adopted at the state visit of Chinese premier Jiang Zemin in October 1999, when peaceful demonstrators had flags and banners ripped from their hands and Chinese secret police mingled with the Met. Following widespread condemnation and a High Court challenge by the Free Tibet Campaign, the Met conceded that its officers had acted unlawfully. However, strong-arm tactics continued to be in evidence at demonstrations.

Making the punishment fit the crime: penal policy

> My object all sublime,
> I shall achieve in time,
> To let the punishment fit the crime,
> The punishment fit the crime.
>
> W. S. Gilbert, *The Mikado*

The treatment of the convicted is a major cause for debate, with two polar extremes: a tough retributive approach that can even include death (capital punishment), or punishment as a means of rehabilitation. Those arguing the latter case characterize prisons as 'universities of crime', with some 60 per cent of their 'graduates' reoffending within two years.

For most of the twentieth century, home secretaries aimed to limit or reduce the prison population. However, Conservative Michael Howard reversed the thinking with his 'prison works' mantra. An October 1993 promise to expand the prison building programme was followed in September 1995 with plans for Britain's first 'boot camp' for young offenders. The 1997 Crime (Sentences) Act established mandatory prison terms, including 'life' for anyone aged eighteen or over convicted for a second time of a serious violent or sexual crime.

New Labour, keen to refute any accusations of being 'soft on crime', generally supported these policies, and its own Crime and Disorder Act (1998) toughened up the treatment of young offenders. They would be forced to make reparations to their victims and the principle of *doli incapax* (presuming that children under fourteen cannot distinguish between right and wrong) was abolished. However, it also included plans for the early release of minor offenders and the extension of electronic tagging and community-service orders as alternatives to prison. The public appeared to approve of the tough line, British Social Attitudes Surveys indicating considerable support for greater police powers and stiffer sentencing, as well as firmer discipline in home and school (Tarling and Dowds 1998).

Whether or not prison works, Britain's rate of imprisonment is almost the highest in Europe. Between 1980 and 2000 the average prison population increased by around a third (figure 21.1); it continued its inexorable rise, reaching 75,000 in 2002 and leaving Home Office statisticians struggling

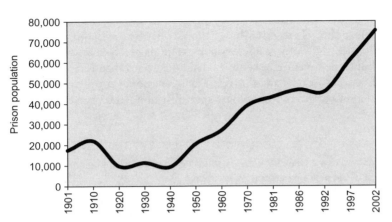

Figure 21.1
A punitive society?
Prison population,
1901–2002

Source: Data from Butler and Butler (1994: 320) and Home Office Research and Statistics Directorate.

to adapt their predictive models to the reality. A series of damming reports from Her Majesty's Chief Inspector of Prisons, Judge Stephen Tumim, detailed grim and insanitary conditions in Britain's overcrowded prisons. The 1995 Learmont Report on the Parkhurst Prison breakout chronicled 'mind-numbing bureaucratic incompetence' (*The Times*, 18 Oct. 1995). The following year, forty-six prisons were classed as overcrowded and a record number of prisoners (sixty-four) committed suicide.

Tough penal measures provoke opposition from the judiciary and prison reform groups. Research evidence suggests that the likelihood of being caught is the more serious deterrent (Downs 1997), though of course this requires more police resources.

Trends in Modern Policing

Traditionally the British police service was decentralized, non-militaristic and apolitical. This remains the official picture but, like so much of the constitution, the formal principles mask reality.

Centralization: a national police service?

> The combination of a centralised police system and an unwritten constitution is the stuff that dictators dream about.
>
> John Alderson (retired chief constable and academic), *A New Cromwell: The Centralization of the Police* (1994)

Local policing and a plurality of forces were justified in terms of local democracy and responsiveness to local conditions. Moreover, the absence of a single national service is a crucial bulwark against the growth of a monolithic police state. The police themselves have consistently resisted the idea of a single service under the home secretary and responsible to Parliament. However, throughout the twentieth century insidious **centralization** has taken place beneath a pluralistic facade through amalgamation, centralized staff organizations, communications technology, specialist units and the strategy of central government.

> I am inclined to the view that we are witnessing a move, perhaps unintended, for national control of the police by central government.
>
> Sir John Smith (ACPO President), speech (4 Feb. 1994)

Amalgamation From the outset, central government was concerned to enlarge police areas. An 1882 Act forbade new boroughs with populations less than 20,000 from establishing their own forces and the 1888 Local Government Act insisted that those with populations below 10,000 merge their forces with those of the parent county under joint committees. Amalgamation was further advanced under the emergency conditions of the second world war.

A royal commission reviewing the constitutional position of the police argued in 1962 that a single force would be more efficient and offer a clear line of accountability. Although the 1964 Police Act stopped short of unification, it increased the home secretary's power to effect amalgamations and strengthened the system of central inspection. Governments did promote amalgamations and the Local Government Act (1972) created some joint forces (such as Thames Valley and West Mercia). A 1993 white paper questioned whether forty-three separate organizations made 'the most effective use of resources available for policing' (Home Office 1993: 41–2) and Home Secretary Kenneth Clarke favoured massive reductions down to twenty-two authorities (Loveday 1996).

Centralized staff associations De facto centralization of the police service has occurred through the development of national associations. Important among these is the Police Federation, a kind of union representing all officers up to the rank of chief inspector (officially the police cannot join a union). It speaks for members in negotiations with government and through public pronouncements as if for a single force.

Of even greater significance is the Association of Chief Police Officers (ACPO) representing senior officers, including chief constables. ACPO does more than speak for its members, it organizes policing nationally, particularly through the National Reporting Centre (NRC), which coordinates policing throughout the country and liaises with the Home Office and MI5 (Boateng 1985: 240). It was established at Scotland Yard in response to fears for public order in the early 1970s. ACPO also operates the Mutual Aid Coordination Centre set up by the 1964 Police Act, whereby police may be deployed anywhere in the country like a national force. The system was particularly visible during the 1984/5 miners' strike, when convoys of blue minibuses became a familiar sight on the M1.

Advanced communications technology Forces now operate sophisticated computer and electronic communications systems. These assist in the collection and collation of vast quantities of data for national records, offering 'precise and rapid central control' (Campbell 1980: 65). In 1959 the Home Office, the Metropolitan force and the Prison Commission set up a Joint Automatic Data Processing Unit, which led in 1969 to the establishment of the Police National Computer Unit at Hendon to supervise a complex communications network of almost a thousand terminals located throughout the country. Liberty estimated that in 1991 at least 70,000 individuals were under surveillance in the national computer (*Independent*, 18 Dec. 1991). The 11 September terrorist attack in 2001 led to increased surveillance, with particular attention to electronic communication (see p. 693).

Specialist units Further centralization comes from the development of specialist CID squads, including regional crime squads, the National Drugs Intelligence Unit, the National Identification Bureau and the Serious Fraud Office. In addition, there are the specialist squads of the Metropolitan force such as the Special Branch, concerned with national security and working with MI5, and the Royalty and Diplomatic Protection Service. Even the Crown Prosecution Service can be seen as part of the centralizing tendency.

Central government strategy Finally, there is the role of central government. Whitehall's ability to influence policing is by no means new; it has been part of the hidden constitution since the early twentieth century, particularly in class disputes (Morgan 1987). The policing of the miners' strike gave a number of important insights into this. Strategy was coordinated by a high-powered cabinet committee (Misc. 101) chaired by Thatcher and including leading ministers and a representative of the armed forces. It received regular reports from the NRC. The Cabinet Office also played a part, by word of mouth to mask a link between the Coal Board and police (Boateng 1985: 239).

The Police and Magistrates Court Act (1994) aimed to increase Home Office control over policing (Jones and Newburn 1995). Ex-chief constable-turned-academic, John Alderson (1994), saw the legislation creating Britain's first 'Minister of Police'. Senior officers were placed on fixed-term contracts renewed by the home secretary, putting them under pressure to act in a manner likely to gain ministerial approval. Ian Oliver, chief constable of Grampian, who voiced objections, was effectively sacked in 1998 by Scottish Secretary Donald Dewar. Moreover, police authorities began to complain of excessive interference with the shortlists for their independent members (*Police Review*, 18 Nov. 1994).

Central government also sidelined local government in crime prevention. Programmes such as Safer Cities, Crime Concern, Inner City Task Forces,

Neighbourhood Watch and schemes for Citizen Patrols were developed by the Home Office and other central departments. Where they looked for local involvement, the preference was again for the business community (Loveday 1994). Home Secretary David Blunkett's 2002 white paper, *Policing in a New Century*, envisaged further centralization, with provision for home secretaries to overrule chief constables and send in 'hit squads' to run 'failing' forces.

Towards a British 'FBI' In July 1989, Metropolitan Police Commissioner Peter Imbert, in a lecture to the Police Foundation, called for an even tighter degree of central control with the creation of a single, national detective force along the lines of the US Federal Bureau of Investigation (FBI). Comprising police, customs officers, lawyers, accountants, computer experts and immigration officers, the new body would be centrally funded, responsible to Parliament through the home secretary and with access to a national computerized intelligence system. Local forces would exist alongside but be required to yield some of their sovereignty. A move in this direction was seen in the 1997 Police Act, which made provision for a National Crime Squad for England and Wales (launched in April 1998 with 1,450 detectives seconded for three- to five-year terms) and put the National Criminal Intelligence Service on a UK-wide statutory basis.

With such centralizing forces at work, why does government resist the formation of a single police service? Official arguments are couched in terms of democracy and local control and accountability, yet the reality of these is highly questionable. Moreover, British democracy has never depended upon such a principle. Hence critics argue that the formal fragmentation of the service serves as a convenient fiction to permit a *de facto* centralization which can evade inconvenient accountability to Parliament.

Militarization

The economic problems of the 1970s saw waves of unrest, with much 'goodwill' between the police and people breaking down. Demonstrations and strikes saw new styles of **militarization**, with marching in troops, charges, visors, CS gas, and intimidatory tactics such as the rhythmic beating of riot shield (see p. 673). Forces now have arsenals of rubber bullets, riot shields, water cannon and armoured vehicles. In the year ending April 2000, gun use averaged over 200 operations a week and firearms were issued on 10,915 occasions (Robbins and Clark 2001). Once officers are armed, mistakes can be fatal. In January 1998, a naked man, James Ashby, was shot dead at point-blank range in front of his girlfriend by police raiding his flat in East Sussex. In September 1999, Harry Stanley, a painter and decorator, was shot dead while carrying a wooden chair leg in a plastic bag (mistaken for a sawn-off shotgun). Between 1995 and 2001, twelve people were killed by the police (Ahmed and Thompson 2002).

A third force? In some countries there exists within the coercive apparatus of the state a third force, poised between the police and the military. This avoids using the military to quell civil disturbance, while protecting police relationships with citizens. However, the hallmark of such forces is savagery. In France, for example, the Compagnie Républicaine de Sécurité is dreaded; in the Paris riots of 1968 it injured 1,500 in a single night. Britain traditionally eschewed such a force but today we are witnessing the appearance of **paramilitary** units.

In the early 1970s, establishment fears of left-wing movements led to the creation of a National Security Committee, with representatives of the military, intelligence services, Home Office, Department of Trade and police, to prepare for nothing less than an internal attack on the state (Bunyan 1977: 293). It recommended better training in riot control, the use of firearms and regular joint police–military exercises. Additionally, a Special Patrol Group (SPG), established in London by the Labour government some years earlier to combat crime, was given a paramilitary remit while remaining formally within the police service. A key mover was Metropolitan Commissioner Sir Robert Mark, who had made detailed studies of the methods of the RUC and B-Specials in Northern Ireland. The new elite corps was to have an independent command structure based on Scotland Yard. Members, selected from young volunteers from the London police divisions, distinguished by the letters CO on their shoulders, served for two-year terms.

The SPG's existence remained largely unknown until the India House incident in 1973 when, in a religious protest, two Pakistanis from Bradford invaded the Indian High Commission with toy guns. Within four minutes, and without being asked to drop the guns, they were shot dead by SPG guards who became overnight heroes. Another celebrated operation was the Grunwick industrial dispute of 1977, where an employer sought to deprive his employees (Asian women) of trade union rights. When mass picketing took place, the SPG moved in and their brutality astonished prominent figures present. However, the Labour government ignored TUC demands for a Home Office enquiry and Home Secretary Merlyn Rees supported the SPG.

The Blair Peach affair in April 1979 brought home the extent to which the SPG operated in a realm above the law. Peach, one of the objectors to a National Front demonstration (held with extreme provocation in the largely black area of Southall), was struck on the head with a rubber cosh filled with lead (an unauthorized weapon) by an SPG officer. Before long he was dead. The events following this had all the characteristics of a cover-up and no prosecutions were made (Rollo 1980: 165).

His tongue was stuck to his upper jaw, and the upper part of his head was all red as if he was bleeding inside.

Local resident who attempted to administer aid to Blair Peach, quoted in J. Rollo, 'The Special Patrol Group', in P. Hain (ed.), *Policing the Police* (1980: 158)

Militarism quickly spread; today most forces have some kind of SPG clone under an independent chain of command. Known variously as Mobile Support Units, Special Operations Units and Tactical Aid Groups, some have themselves been involved in *causes célèbres*. Firearms units, sometimes known as Trojan patrols, resemble the US 'Swat Squads', with black fireproof overalls, body armour and military-style helmets. In 2001 it was reported that some had quietly armed themselves with the Heckler & Koch G36K, a high-velocity military assault rifle used by German special forces and capable of piercing body armour (Robbins and Clark 2001). In addition they can use stun guns (tasers), which deliver an electric shock, causing uncontrollable muscle contractions.

Politicization

Although formally outside politics, it has already been shown that policing has political consequences. Where there is inequality, the police must constantly seek to restrain the 'have nots' from threatening the 'haves' and it is not surprising that they feel an affinity with the political right. However, involvement in politics goes beyond this to an overt presence as a political pressure group.

Publicity campaigning Although the Police Federation and ACPO are statutorily restricted, they have broken out of this straitjacket to become mouthpieces of collective police views. Unlike the civil service, the police do not subscribe to the Trappist monk school of public relations; they have argued against light sentences, juries, community policing and a suspect's right to silence. They have also made strong moral judgements about schools, drugs, parents, the church, industrial relations and homosexuality.

The politicizing of the police was never better illustrated than when the Police Federation actually launched a Law and Order Campaign in 1975. The movement arose over frustration that 'soft' groups were having a liberalizing effect on the law, policing and penal policy. Their campaign copied the methods of other pressure groups with public speaking engagements, feeding the media and lobbying. After some confrontation with the government, the Federation announced in February 1978 its intention to make law and order an issue in the forthcoming general election, even sponsoring large newspaper advertisements. The Conservatives became enthusiastic, pledging 'unstinting backing' for the police. However, this relationship was to sour under Home Secretaries Clarke and Howard in the 1990s, with their managerial reforms (see below).

Police superstars Leading police figures have sought to project themselves as national celebrities. In particular, Metropolitan commissioners have found a unique platform. Notable was Sir Robert Mark, brought in by the libertarian Home Secretary Roy Jenkins, in 1967, to clear up internal corruption. He soon revealed a fiercely anti-libertarian stance on many social issues (Kettle 1980: 13). In 1973 he delivered the BBC Dimbleby Lecture, giving him the largest audience any policeman had ever had. This has been seen as the coming of age of politically assertive policing in Britain.

Following this a number of senior officers have enjoyed celebrity. James Anderton, Chief Constable of Greater Manchester, was particularly prominent during the 1980s, proclaiming that AIDS sufferers and drug addicts dwelt in 'a cess-pit of their own making'. He charmed the Establishment on television and radio current affairs programmes and chat-shows, though was eventually restrained after proclaiming that he heard 'voices'.

Rising crime rates have helped keep chief constables in the political limelight with statements upon the state of society. Paul Condon caused an outcry in July 1995 by suggesting that most London muggings were committed by young black males. West Yorkshire's Chief Constable, Keith Halliwell, made contributions to the drugs debate and in 1998 became the government's 'Drugs Tsar', though in July 2002 he was to make a high-profile resignation to register his disapproval of the reclassification of cannabis.

A climate of corporatism Senior officers have enjoyed direct links with Whitehall. When Michael Foot put forward proposals to amend the law on picketing, Sir Robert Mark told 'Jimmy Waddell [Sir James Waddell, high-ranking Home Office civil servant] in no uncertain terms' that he would conduct a vigorous public campaign against such laws. 'Happily they were abandoned and no harm was done' (Mark 1978: 151–2). The police service has been seen unequivocally as a pressure group, enjoying close insider status. Whenever there is a proposal for a change in the law relating to criminal or judicial procedure, or whenever there is a *cause célèbre* involving the police, a well-maintained network springs into life.

The politics of confrontation However, when differences become irreconcilable corporatism is replaced with confrontation. This was increasingly the case from the early 1980s, as both main parties tried to introduce the kind of radical reforms that were being implemented in other parts of the public sector. The key issue was crime rates; despite substantial increases in expenditure, these rose by 91 per cent between 1981 and 1995 (figure 21.2) (Mirrlees-Black et al. 1996). Abandoning the 'adulation towards the police demonstrated by Mrs Thatcher' (Loveday 1996: 23), the Major government alleged inefficiency and sought to 'destabilise established police interests'. A critical report on management compiled by businessman Sir Patrick Sheehy (1993) (see below) produced outspoken condemnation of the government from the police associations and on 30 July 1993, 20,000 officers congregated in an unprecedented protest rally.

> The time is ripe for taking on the boys and girls in blue.
>
> The Sheehy report (1993)

The hostile atmosphere continued under New Labour. As Home Secretary, Jack Straw endured booing and jeering at Police Federation conferences, and his successor, David Blunkett, was soon reminded of the negotiating weight of both the Federation and ACPO. The Police Federation condemned Blunkett's reform

Figure 21.2
Crime rates and
expenditure on
police and prison
services,
1989–2002.

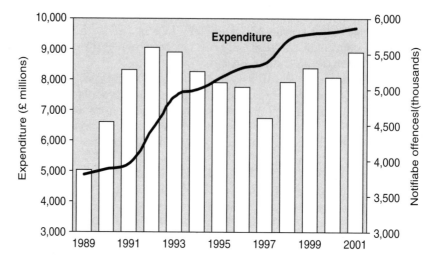

Source: Data from *Social Trends, Annual Abstract of Statistics* and *House of Commons Library Research Papers* (various years).

package on pay and conditions, voting 10:1 to reject it. The Metropolitan Police Federation even began to consider using the Human Rights Act to overturn a 1919 ban on strike action. In April 2002 Blunkett announced a surprise climbdown in the face of ACPO opposition. In forces alleged to be failing, chief constables would be allowed a period to put things right before the 'hit squad' would move in. In May 2002, after being forced to sit through a fiercely critical speech from the Federation president, he was obliged to apologize for the way he had handled demands for change.

> This man is a bully. Police officers deal with bullies on a daily basis; they don't scare us, we take them on.
>
> Glen Smyth, chair of Metropolitan Police Federation, speaking of David Blunkett
> (BBC news, 24 Feb. 2002)

Helping the police with inquiries: suspicious customers

While the police service itself has not been privatized and suspects are not yet seriously referred to as 'customers', the New Right reforms did not pass them by. Private-sector involvement was stimulated and attempts made to import managerial practice.

DIY crime fighting The rise (and perceived rise) in crime rates led, during the 1980s and 1990s, to calls for citizens to become more active in crime prevention and even detection. They were encouraged by 'crime-busting' television programmes, often relaying footage from a steady accretion of CCTV cameras on urban buildings. Domestic alarms became almost as ubiquitous as television aerials and the Neighbourhood Watch movement saw thousands of suburban community groups coming together to keep a watchful eye over their cars, houses and garden gnomes. To critics this is not far removed from vigilantism – individuals taking the law into their own hands, making citizen's arrests and even using violence. Jack Straw's curfews and parenting classes even suggested a policing role for families. The danger of DIY policing is of a lynch-mob mentality, seen in the hounding of paedophiles. However, the courts often find against over-zealous amateur law enforcers.

Privatization The 1980s saw considerable expansion of the private security industry, with militaristically uniformed guards patrolling shopping malls, car parks and even residential areas. Sometimes private security firms work in conjunction with the police. By 1997 the £2-billion-a-year industry of some 8,000 firms with 170,000 employees was dwarfing the state police service (*Observer*, 14 Feb. 1993). When firms such as Group Four took over the transport of prisoners, embarrassing escapes led wags to comment on Thatcher's desire to set the people free! However, the industry remains largely unregulated (Loveday 1994). Its employees (some of them convicted criminals) are themselves responsible for an estimated 2,000 crimes a year (*Evening Standard*, 15 July 1997). Yet David Blunkett's 2002 reforms proposed that the police use private security firms and civilian investigators (such as accountants for fraud cases).

From 1993 major privatizations were also seen in the prison service, with contracts awarded to build and run new prisons. Jack Straw, to boos and cries of 'rubbish' at the 1998 Prison Officers' Association conference, declared himself, despite his earlier opposition, a 'convert' to the idea (*Independent*, 20 May 1998). The Adam Smith Institute has envisaged a future in which the state police operate in competition with private-sector agencies.

Managerialism The 1993 Sheehy Report was highly critical of 'cosy relationships'; recruits could expect a job for life, there was little performance appraisal and the service was top heavy with senior grades. Its proposals included performance-related pay, fixed-term contracts, the abolition of certain senior ranks, limitations on pension rights, compulsory redundancies, the removal of certain allowances and a ban on overtime. There was also to be a cut in starting salaries. The proposals incurred the bitter wrath of the police and lower starting salaries were rejected outright. Home Secretary Michael Howard also agreed to drop other key recommendations, including performance-related pay, short fixed-term contracts and a higher age for full retirement pension entitlements. However, the management culture of the service was changed, with increased paperwork at all levels.

Quis Custodiet ipsos Custodes?
Who Guards the Guards?

Being subject to only weak democratic control, modern policing raises the age-old question: 'Who guards the guards?'

The complaints procedure

One safeguard against improper policing is a mechanism whereby members of the public can have complaints investigated. The Police Act (1964) placed an obligation on chief constables to investigate all complaints, bringing in officers from other forces if they so wished. If the chief constable believed that a criminal offence might have occurred, a report was sent to the Director of Public Prosecutions. The system left many unhappy. In the 1970s, investigations into allegations of police brutality and deaths in police custody seemed unsatisfactory to victims' families. The police response complained of agitation by left-wing extremists. However, the 1976 Police Act established a quango, the Police Complaints Board (PCB), a lay body with a limited supervisory role over the process. The system had many weaknesses, the greatest being that the investigation remained in police hands, justified on the grounds that only they could do the job. However, calls for independent investigation continued from many quarters, including Liberty, Justice, the Law Society, the Runnymede Trust, the local ombudsman and the Labour Party. In 1980, the PCB itself recommended investigation by an independent team of seconded police officers.

Following serious race and anti-police riots in Brixton, Lord Scarman's report (1981: para. 4.2) cited the absence of an independent **police complaints procedure** as one of five crucial factors contributing to the breakdown of police–community relations. Cynicism meant that people did not even bother to lodge complaints. The Police and Criminal Evidence Act (1984) established a three-tiered approach, adding to the existing system a conciliation mechanism for non-serious complaints and independent supervision of police investigation into serious ones by a Police Complaints Authority (PCA), which replaced the PCB.

Although the first chairman, Sir Cecil Clothier, had formerly been the ombudsman, the reform fell short of truly independent investigation. Initially the chief constable (or police authority if senior officers were involved) would decide whether the matter could be solved by informal conciliation. If not, an officer would be appointed to conduct an enquiry under PCA supervision. However, the PCA's 1987 report castigated the Metropolitan force (which received a quarter of all complaints) for making it difficult to achieve 'a dialogue at senior level'. In November 1988 the Commons Home Affairs Committee, following a suggestion from Sir Cecil himself, recommended regular parliamentary scrutiny of the procedure. It also advocated strengthening the PCA's ability to acquire evidence. The response of the Police Federation in its

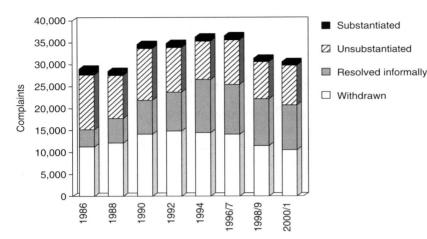

Figure 21.3
The outcome of complaints received by the police, 1986–2001.

Note: The number of complaints is greater than the number of cases received since each case may represent several complaints.

Source: Data from *Social Trends* (2002: table 9.16).

1989 annual conference was a vote of no confidence in the PCA, which was accused of siding with complainants.

Despite a steady increase in complaints, peaking in the mid-1990s at over 35,000 a year, the number substantiated remains very low (figure 21.3), falling from around 4–5 per cent in the mid-1980s to only 2–3 per cent in the late 1990s. However, an increasing proportion are resolved informally. Although dismissals may result, this can be avoided by retirement or resignation before proceedings have been completed. For example, in 1996/7 charges proved against 377 officers resulted in 77 dismissals and a further 65 retirements. The PCA's annual reports are often critical and note where forces have failed to implement its recommendations. In 2000/1 it highlighted concern about deaths associated with pursuits by police vehicles (increasing from nine to twenty-five in only four years).

The PCA regularly complains of underfunding. Indeed, in 1998, Jack Straw used inadequate resources as grounds for rejecting the Home Affairs Select Committee's recommendation that the PCA be allowed to commission independent investigations. However, funding for 2000/1 was increased by over a third to £4.4 million, with plans to establish an Independent Police Complaints Commission in 2003. Would this new body be able to deal with the police

> If one of the boys working for me got himself into trouble, I would get all of us together and I would literally script him out of it. I would write all the parts out and if we followed them closely we couldn't be defeated.
>
> Metropolitan Police sergeant interviewed by D. J. Smith and J. Gray,
> *Police and People in London* (1985: 355)

tradition of sticking together when under attack – the tradition that had prevented the identification of Blair Peach's killer?

Beyond the Blue Horizon

It is not only through the police service that the state exerts its coercive power. Although less overt than they have been in Northern Ireland, there are other fingers on the iron hand which can operate on the home front, including the military and the security services.

The military

Ostensibly states have a military arm to defend themselves from invasion or to subjugate other states. During the imperialist era Britain's military was a feared world power. In two hellish world wars it became even more central but with the post-war dismantling of empire it was anticipated that the men on horseback would retire to their barracks. However, they were to seek a role rather nearer home to confront the 'enemy within'.

Policy-making for the military Control of the military is vested formally in government ministers responsible to Parliament, which grants its funds. The modern history of political control dates from the creation of the Committee of Imperial Defence in 1902 after the Boer war. During the second world war this was replaced by the War Cabinet and a Ministry of Defence established. In 1964 the three service departments were amalgamated under the Secretary of State for Defence and a Defence Council.

The service chiefs are, like civil servants, heavily involved in decision-making. Sometimes appearing as the more arrogant of the British upper class, they take it hard if politicians resist their 'advice'. Here is another corporatist enclave where the select influence the destiny of the nation away from the prying eyes of democracy. Few outsider groups were as 'outside' as the CND. Parliament and the full Cabinet have very little hold on the reins; thus defence spending reached astronomical heights (figure 21.4) and the arms industry grew fat. Talk of a post-cold-war peace dividend proved over-optimistic as new flashpoints were identified the world over.

Class and the military The majority of those marching to venues like the Somme were from the working class but the people who matter in the military, the top brass, follow very much in the traditions of British elitism. Today members of the royal family continue to hold high military rank. Before the rise of the industrial bourgeoisie, commissions in the army and navy were reserved for the sons of the aristocracy and wealth was needed for their purchase and subsequent promotion. However, the worldwide policing necessary to protect free trade made the bourgeoisie more than a little concerned and

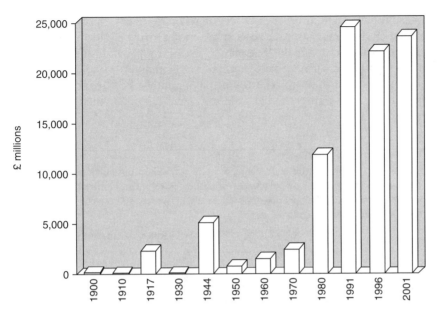

Figure 21.4
Defence
expenditure,
1900–2001.

Source: Data from Butler and Butler (1994: 393–5) and *Annual Abstract of Statistics* (2001: table 4.2).

a modernization programme placed the military in the hands of the new elite. The social prestige is such that, unlike privates or sergeants, retired officers retain their titles like honours, even having them engraved on their tombstones to proclaim their stature long after the worms have digested their entrails. However, to admit the existence of elitism in the service is tantamount to taking voluntary redundancy – after writing a Fabian Society pamphlet accusing the army of sexism, racism and elitism, in January 1999 Major Eric Joyce was asked to resign or face compulsory discharge. In 2001 he became a Labour MP.

Race and the military The British army probably has a worse record of racism than any other state institution, remaining largely untouched by the post-1970s anti-discriminatory laws. In 1997 only 1 per cent of military personnel came from ethnic minorities, compared with more than 5 per cent of the civil service (*Financial Times*, 14 Oct. 1997). Prince Charles himself expressed concern at the milk-white complexions of his royal guards. Given the role of the army in subduing foreign enemies, a racist culture is not entirely surprising. This was confirmed in March 1996 by a highly critical report from the Commission for Racial Equality. A 1997 review of ethnic minority initiatives commissioned by the Ministry of Defence revealed racial insults, harassment and physical injury, leading most black recruits to an early return to civvy street.

The military on the home front The military in any state contains a fearsome potential for violence. Most *coups d'état* are military-backed and it is not unusual for a state to direct such power on its own citizens. In Britain, the 1714 Riot Act enabled magistrates to call in the military to quell disturbances, while today governments can make 'reasonable' use of troops in riotous situations. In the confrontation with the miners there were rumours of soldiers in police uniforms, distinguishable by the absence of a number. Perhaps the most telling post-war use of the army in civil situations has been in Northern Ireland from 1969 (see chapter 6).

> There is no horror, no cruelty, sacrilege, or perjury, no imposture, no infamous transaction, no cynical robbery, no bold plunder or shabby betrayal that has not been ... perpetrated ... under no other pretext than those elastic words, so convenient and yet so terrible: 'for reasons of state'.
>
> Mikhail Bakunin (1814–76; Russian anarchist)

Overt military involvement in civil affairs can be conducted by a special elite corps – the Special Air Service (SAS) – which first caught the public imagination in 1980 when, under the eyes of television cameras, it daringly ended a siege of the Iranian Embassy. It also operated under cover in Northern Ireland, where codes permitted extra military freedoms, buttressed by special emergency powers granted by Parliament.

Although conventions restrict the use of troops in mainland Britain, there is nothing to prevent these changing. The royal prerogative means that in a state of emergency troops can be used in any way at all. An army–police anti-terrorist operation at Heathrow airport in 1974 greatly alarmed Prime Minister Wilson, who realized how easily troops could be turned against the government (James 1987). It was chillingly explained afterwards that the purpose of the exercise was 'to accustom the public to the reality of troops deploying through the high street' (*Guardian*, 8 Jan. 1974).

The security services: the 'cloak and dagger' of the state

Courses on British government often ignore the **security services**, not because such matters should not be discussed in front of children but because they are things that nobody is supposed to talk about. Here we meet agencies operating below the level of public accountability and consciousness. People have some vague notion from the novels of John Le Carré and Ian Fleming that they exist, but these are chauvinistic fantasies about superhuman figures like James Bond.

The services are not new. The Home Office, with an historic responsibility for state security, has maintained an ad hoc network of spies and informers, partnering the industrial capitalism rising in the eighteenth century (Bunyan 1977: 153). They comprise a number of agencies.

- The *Special Branch* of the Met was created in 1883 to be concerned mainly with criminal offences against the state and subversive organizations. It has always been heavily involved with Irish affairs. The emphasis is on intelligence gathering and 'watching', with 'political policing' (Bunyan 1977: ch. 3).
- *MI5* was established in 1909 to root out subversive activity at home. Today it works closely with the Special Branch, calling on police powers (of arrest and so on) when required.
- *MI6*, the *Secret Intelligence Service*, is concerned with organizing espionage overseas. In 1919 it 'poured in agents and several million pounds in a vain effort to subvert the [Russian] revolution' (Bunyan 1977: 155).
- The *Government Communications Headquarters* (GCHQ) at Cheltenham is concerned with worldwide electronic surveillance.
- The *Defence Intelligence Staff* of the Ministry of Defence oversees the work of the intelligence staffs of the armed services.
- The ordinary *police service* (liberally interpreting its public order function) is increasingly concerned with matters of security.

Although separate organizations, they work together at various levels, coordinated by Scotland Yard (Campbell 1980: 116). The paranoid secrecy of the state is never more tight-lipped than here, serving not merely to safeguard Britain's secrets from potential enemies, but to conceal the fact that the agencies can sail

"None of you knows each other, I trust."

extremely close to the wind. When joining MI5, Peter Wright (1987: 31) was told that it could not be part of Whitehall because its work 'very often involved transgressing propriety or the law'.

The British government long fostered the idea that the security services did not actually exist: the Head of MI6 in 1956 (and former head of MI5), Sir Dick Goldsmith White, was officially listed as Deputy Under Secretary at the Foreign Office and Superintending Under Secretary of the Library and Records Department (Bunyan 1977: 189–90). However, a surprising break with tradition came in 1991 with the appointment of Stella Rimington as MI5 head; not only was she a woman but she was named. In July 1993 MI5 published a booklet on the security service, revealing some 2,000 people operating in its secretive world. However, when Rimington decided to publish her own memoirs she fell from grace and described the vetting process as 'Kafkaesque' (see p. 477).

The class factor Unlike the police service, the security services remain very much a bastion of the lordly amateur male establishment world of John Buchan, even to the extent, according to Peter Wright (1987: 36), of closing down MI5 once a year for the Lord's test match, where they have an unofficially reserved patch in the Lord's Tavern. The girls managing the files are debutantes recruited from the aristocracy, perhaps the best vetting of all. Despite some attempts to advertise in the late 1990s, recruitment is traditionally conducted on an informal basis and most members (including the spies) have come from the public school–Oxbridge hothouse.

What are the buggers up to? The security services protect the state from subversion and espionage. Their activities are potentially infinite in their variety. After the first world war, fear of communism saw working-class activists harassed and even imprisoned. The National Unemployed Workers' Movement was kept under constant surveillance by the Special Branch, its leaders eventually arrested and its documents confiscated. One notorious act concerned the Zinoviev letter.

In the soft-focus days of the 1960s, when the Beatles, Mary Quant and student uprisings seemed to symbolize a new era, and Harold Wilson appeared to be making Labour a natural party of government, members of the Establishment talked long into the nights of *coups* to prevent the drift. In 1965, the

---

The Zinoviev letter

This letter was reputedly uncovered during the 1924 general election campaign. Apparently sent by Gregory Zinoviev, president of the Communist International, to a prominent member of the British Communist Party, it urged armed revolution. The resulting paranoia effectively ruined Labour's election chances. A middle-man named Thurn, who received £7,500 from the Conservative Party, touted the letter around and ensured its publication in the *Daily Mail*. Its authenticity was never proved and it appears to have been the product of a dirty tricks operation involving 'members of MI6 and MI5, the top personnel at the Foreign Office, and the Tory party' (Bunyan 1977: 159).

Lord Chancellor was reduced to driving around Green Park when holding discussions with the Attorney General, believing it 'more likely than not that MI5 were bugging the telephones in my office'. In this Orwellian scenario he could hardly complain to the Prime Minister, who believed he too was under surveillance (Knightly 1986).

Clearly the definition of **subversion** must have a considerable bearing on whom the security services fix their attentions upon and it was a Labour home secretary who threw the gates open. The definition given by Lord Denning in his 1963 report on the Profumo scandal was contemplating 'the overthrow of the government by unlawful means'. However, in 1978, Merlyn Rees dispensed with 'unlawful', redefining subversives as those who 'threaten the safety or well being of the state, and are intended to undermine or overthrow parliamentary democracy by political, industrial, or violent means'. This gave the green light to the security services (Kettle 1980: 52–3), allowing them to turn inward on the body politic like a virus, investigating left-wing politicians, trade unionists and anyone expressing an unorthodox political opinion, despite their innocence of any crime. In 1990, Colin Wallace claimed that, as an army public relations officer in the 1970s, he had been involved in MI5 operations ('Clockwork Orange') to smear British politicians (*Observer*, 4 Feb. 1990).

'There are also certain matters of personal conduct which could quite possibly leave you open to blackmail.'

Shit!! . . .

I thought about it for a little while. They must have been bugging my phone. There was no other explanation. And for ages.

Alan Clark on meeting with Cabinet Secretary Sir Robert Armstrong,
shortly after becoming a minister, *Diaries* (24 June 1983)

The advance of technology lifts the capability to gather, collect and collate information to truly Kafkaesque levels. An unprecedented bank of computer data was built up, focusing on leaders of groups like CND, Greenpeace, the trade unions, schools and universities, hospitals, the theatre and the media. In 2001, a private security firm with close links to MI5 was reported to be spying on environmental and green organizations, and Anita Roddick's Body Shop group, to collect information for oil companies including Shell and BP (Chittenden and Rufford 2001). Phones are tapped, people photographed and mail opened. During the miners' strike, a complex operation involved informers, spies and *agents provocateurs*. From the early 1970s the security services found an increased role in Northern Ireland, where they saw the IRA as part of a communist threat (Pilger 1998: 516–17).

The ending of the cold war left MI5 casting around for a *raison d'être* but by 1993 some 70 per cent of its resources were devoted to 'counter-terrorism'. Stella Rimington was well-equipped for tackling the 'enemy within', having been active during the battle with the miners in 1984 and monitoring trade

> Diana, to her dying day, thought it was MI5 on behalf of the establishment at the height of the 'wars of the Wales' who bugged her and were responsible for the Squidgy tapes.
>
> Anthony Holden, 'Royal Blues', in *Red Pepper* (Oct. 1997)

unions under the brief to target 'domestic subversion'. This thinking had led to the ban on union membership at GCHQ. Ironically, civil liberties groups have alleged that GCHQ bugged trade unionists and there were even suspicions that it was responsible for the 'Squidgygate' and 'Camillagate' tapes.

In August 1997, former MI5 officer David Shayler disclosed in a newspaper article that Home Secretary Jack Straw's file was still held, and that files existed on ministers Peter Mandelson and Harriet Harman. In July 1998 Straw opened a window of light, but did little to allay fears, by revealing that MI5 currently held nearly half a million files (*The Times*, 30 July 1998).

Even objectors to road and airport development have been targeted. In February 1993 Channel 4's *Dispatches* showed extraordinary levels of surveillance of those protesting against a motorway through Twyford Down, with police, private security firms and even a detective agency, and names faxed to the Department of Transport. John Alderson saw MI5 involvement in policing as the acorn of a police state (*Red Pepper*, April 1996).

> The tragedy of the Police State is that it always regards all opposition as a crime, and there are no degrees.
>
> Lord Vansittart (1881–1957; British diplomat), House of Lords speech (June 1947)

Although the attack of 11 September 2001 enabled the state to move to heightened levels of surveillance and detention, there had already been significant changes in response to the fear of terrorism. The 2000 Terrorism Act replaced the Prevention of Terrorism Act and the Northern Ireland Emergency Provisions Act (both of which required annual renewal) with a permanent UK-wide measure. This included a new definition of terrorism. Previously the use of violence for political ends, it became

> the use or threat, for the purpose of advancing a political, religious or ideological cause, of action that involves serious violence against any person or property, endangers the life of any person or creates a serious risk to the health or safety of the public or a section of the public.

In addition to promoting renewed vigilance and calls for increased funding for MI6, the new definition opened the door to a draconian catalogue of measures on the home front. The security services and police could arrest, detain and request samples from anyone. In addition, emails could be monitored, courts could admit as evidence transcripts of phone conversations bugged by MI5, banks could be compelled to release customers' details and suspects' assets could be seized. In 2002, Home Secretary Blunkett attempted to extend the powers of electronic surveillance to almost any public body, from the Food Standards Agency to local government. Although widespread criticism forced a climbdown, the government's Performance and Innovations Unit quietly brought out a report on the inter-departmental sharing of information as a necessary move to enable the introduction of ID cards, suggesting only a tactical retreat.

Who watches the watchers?

Dissatisfaction with the current state of affairs led in 1989 to a Security Services Act; for the first time, official recognition was given to the existence of MI5 (though not of MI6) and a tribunal was created to hear complaints. In addition, a commissioner (a Law Lord) would oversee warrants for bugging and entering and make an annual report to Parliament, though this could be edited by the prime minister. Critics such as the Campaign for Freedom of Information regarded this as rather little rather late and well short of full parliamentary oversight.

A report from the House of Commons Home Affairs Committee (1993) noted that, while all the country's closest allies had independent oversight of their security services, Britain's operated beyond the realm of parliamentary scrutiny. Among elected politicians, only the prime minister is formally in the know, but even this is doubtful. The British tradition of the neutral civil service has created a situation in which 'Ministers, and Prime Ministers, increasingly become putty, on questions of "security", in their senior adviser's hands' (Thompson 1980: 157). The Blunt case in particular called into question the relationship of the security services to their elected masters. In 1964 this aristocratic self-confessed spy, a former member of MI5, struck a secret deal with the security agencies, guaranteeing immunity from prosecution (and allowing him to retain his prestigious royal appointment as Surveyor of the Queen's Pictures) in exchange for information. Despite promises, Labour governments have never conducted a scourge of the security services. David Shayler, after blowing the whistle on what he saw as MI5 inefficiency and bungling, came under investigation for suspected breach of the Official Secrets Act, which led to his prosecution (see p. 474).

> The club of ex-Home Secretaries is, in my view, one of the worst features of British public life: they all compliment each other... but nobody believes [they] are really kept informed by the security services.
>
> Tony Benn, *Diaries* (1991: 587)

The spies Although the security services have an impressive record of probing and harassing the left, they have enjoyed rather less success in catching real spies. The result has been some embarrassing post-war scandals, including those of Blake, Burgess, Maclean, Philby, Vassall and Blunt. Of course, the spies have come from upper-class backgrounds because of the security services' recruitment practices. The Establishment cannot tolerate such behaviour from within its ranks; they are not merely traitors, they are class traitors.

> If you ask me to strike a balance in my own life, I'd say that the right I've done is greater than the wrong I've done.
>
> Kim Philby (civil servant who spied for the Russians), interview in Moscow
> in the *Sunday Times* (27 March 1988)

The Coercive State and the Community

It would of course be absurd to expect policing and other forms of state coercion to operate without force and violence; this is why they are created. While it is not the only cause of disharmony, capitalism, with its tendency towards inequality, needs a strong state (Gamble 1988). Hence the emergence of the modern police service was tied to the industrial revolution. Yet the service managed to develop an ethos of community spirit linked with the gradual assimilation of the working class into the system, reaching a peak in the post-war corporatist decades. Dixon of Dock Green, a caring 'bobby' featuring in a long-running television series, did not seem grossly at variance with reality.

> PC Attilla Rees, ox broad, barge booted, stamping out of Handcuff House in a heavy beef-red huff, blackbrowed under his damp helmet ... limbering down to the strand to see that the sea is still there.
>
> Dylan Thomas (1914–53), *Under Milk Wood* (1954)

Yet the neoliberal right was never entirely at ease with the idea of **consensus policing** and from the late 1970s it was explicitly rejected with the 'enemy within' rhetoric. Thatcher recognized the key role that would be given to the police, promising in the 1979 Conservative manifesto to 'spend more on fighting crime even while we economize elsewhere'. In the bitter events of the miners' strike, while criticism of police tactics reached a crescendo, the government refused to encourage a negotiated settlement. Since then society has continued to be darkened by the spectre of violence.

The alternative to the strong arm

Against the trend came the Scarman Report, which saw the roots of crime, riots and public disorder in the social environment (1981: para. 2.38). It aroused considerable public and official interest, with recommendations favouring **community policing** including:

◆   new recruitment procedures to screen out racism and sexism and en-
    courage more black people and women to apply;
◆   outlawing of discriminatory practices;
◆   increased community consultation;
◆   reduction in police discretionary powers;
◆   increased accountability by means of lay visitors to police stations.

One of the most prominent advocates of community policing has been John Alderson (a former barrister) who, as Chief Constable of Devon and Cornwall, sought to concern *every* officer with community relations. However, in the neoliberal environment the approach could not flourish. He was consistently opposed by the Police Federation, which sent deputations to question his use of resources and he finally left to take up an academic post. However, with four women chief constables in post by 2002, there was the possibility of a further change in attitudes. Maria Wallis, appointed to Devon and Cornwall in July 2002, had studied social administration at Bristol University with a view to becoming a social worker. Referring to herself as a 'people person', she had come to see policing as being 'about helping and supporting people' (Ford 2002) and became a police constable.

> I never saw any of them again – except the cops. No way has yet been invented to say goodbye to them.
>
> Philip Marlowe, in Raymond Chandler's *The Long Goodbye* (1954)

Reports regularly reveal a majority preferring the friendly 'bobby on the beat' to the 'Sweeny' image of fast cars and tough policing. With surveys showing fear of crime higher than justified by the reality, and many afraid to go out at night or travel by public transport, the case for community policing is strong.

Policing at arm's length

Yet hurdles stand in the way of a return to a community approach. Reports such as those from Scarman and Macpherson do not recognize all the problems. They ignore fundamental contradictions between the community approach and the features of modern policing, including increased centralization, militarization and the incorporation of the security forces. They also fail to emphasize democratic control through elected councils as the way to local accountability. Without this, community policing can become community control (Gordon 1984: 56). Since the 1995 reforms to police authorities, the 'long arm of the law' is at a longer 'arm's length' from the democratic state than ever before.

Key points

- Every state requires a right to use physical force and coercion. The liberal-democratic state is no exception; indeed the market freedom requires a strong state.
- The modern police service in Britain was a creature of the industrial revolution. Previously policing was undertaken on a voluntary basis by local communities.
- Britain formally has a number of separate police authorities upon which local government is represented. However, forces are under the firm control of their chief constables.
- It is sometimes said that policing is outside politics, but this is untenable.
- There are acute problems in policing associated with sexism and racism.
- Since the 1970s British policing has become increasingly centralized, militarized and politicized.
- Through ACPO the police can enjoy most of the advantages of a national force without responsibility to Parliament.
- The police complaints process is controversial because the police themselves conduct any inquiries.
- Britain imprisons a higher proportion of its population than any comparable country.
- The military and security services play a policing role, though they do so covertly and with less accountability than the police themselves.
- There is an alternative to coercive policing in community policing.

Review your understanding of the following terms and concepts

Association of Chief Police Officers (ACPO)
centralization
chief constable
community policing
consensus policing
crime-fighting
Crown Prosecution Service
Judges' Rules
'Met'

MI5 and MI6
militarization
paramilitary unit
penal policy
police authority
police committee
Police Complaints Authority
police complaints procedure
police culture
Police Federation

police state
politicization
public order
security services
Special Patrol Group
subversion

Assignment

Study the extract from the *Independent* on p. 697 and answer the following questions.

Mark (%)

1   Explain the meaning of the term 'institutional racism'.   10

Police chief admits to racism in ranks

By Kathy Marks

IN AN unprecedented admission by a senior officer, the Chief Constable of Greater Manchester acknowledged yesterday that his force was infected by institutional racism.

David Wilmot, head of the second-largest force in England and Wales, made the declaration at a hearing of the Stephen Lawrence inquiry in Manchester. His attitude was in stark contrast to that of Sir Paul Condon, the Metropolitan Police Commissioner, who steadfastly refused to recognise institutional racism within the Met when he appeared before the inquiry two weeks ago.

Mr Wilmot told the public inquiry: "We live in a society that has institutional racism, and Greater Manchester Police is no exception. We accept that we have a problem with some overt racism, and certainly that we have a problem with internalised racism."

Sir William Macpherson of Cluny, the inquiry chairman, responded with an oblique but unmistakable criticism of Sir Paul. "There is a reluctance to accept that it is there, which means that it will probably never be cured," he said.

Manchester was the inquiry's first stop on a regional tour aimed at taking the temperature in racially sensitive cities outside London and identifying lessons to be learnt from the Met's abortive investigation of the racist murder of Stephen Lawrence, an 18-year-old student, in 1993.

Manchester's large Afro-Caribbean and Asian Communities suffer a high level of racial crime and harassment – an estimated 21,000 become victims each year – and have a history of chequered relations with the police.

Mr Wilmot is the first chief constable to have acknowledged institutional racism within his own force.

Independent, 14 Oct. 1998

Questions for discussion

1   Why did the industrial revolution threaten a breakdown in traditional methods of policing?
2   Evaluate the role of the local police authority.
3   How could the rise of the private security industry threaten liberal democracy?
4   'Allegations of police brutality and false confessions only undermine the morale of police officers and reduce their effectiveness.' Discuss.
5   'The security services stand outside the political system.' Discuss.
6   Examine the proposition that Britain has a national police service in all but name.
7   Identify the weaknesses in the police complaints procedures. How could they be improved?
8   What is meant by 'community policing'? What factors inhibit it?
9   Is it true that 'prison works'?
10   How do the police influence government policy? Is this desirable?

Topic for debate

This house believes that policing is no job for a woman.

Further reading

Baxter, J. and Koffman, L. (eds) (1985) *Police, the Constitution and the Community.*
Book of readings. See especially M. Benn, 'Policing women' and P. Boateng, 'Crisis in account-ability'.

Benn, M. et al. (1983) *The Rape Controversy.*
Looks at the area where the macho police culture is at its most destructive.

Hain, P. et al. (eds) (1980) *Policing the Police.*
Critical book of readings. See especially the chapters by M. Kettle and D. Campbell.

Halford, A. (1993) *No Way up the Greasy Pole.*
Inside account of sexism in the police service by its most celebrated victim.

Knightly, P. (1986) *The Second Oldest Profession: The Spy as Bureaucrat, Fantasist and Whore.*
Specialist journalist's account of a field too boggy for most academics.

Newburn, T. (1995) *Crime and Criminal Justice Policy.*
All aspects clearly presented in historical context.

Reiner R. (1993) *The Politics of the Police,* 2nd edn.
Clear treatment of the central points of analysis.

Reiner R. (ed.) (1996) *Policing.*
Collection of significant articles.

Smith, D. J. and Gray, J. (1985) *Police and People in London*.
A powerful study of the Metropolitan Police Force at work.

Urban, M. (1997) *UK Eyes Alpha: The Inside Story of British Intelligence*.
BBC journalist reports wide range of interviews with those involved. Title is the security term for highly sensitive intelligence.

For light relief

Bertolt Brecht, *The Threepenny Opera*.
Satirical musical play on the relationship between capitalism and law and order.

Robert Harris, *Enigma*.
Tense novel of code-breaking and spying based on second-world-war events.

Stephen Knight, *The Brotherhood*.
An exposé of freemasonry in Britain in the higher reaches of the Establishment, including MI5, judiciary and police.

G. F. Newman, *Law and Order*.
A powerful and realistic novel exploring police–Establishment relations.

Prime Suspect.
TV series available on video. Shows in dramatic form some of the problems facing women in the police service.

On the net

http://www.homeoffice.gov.uk
http://www.mod.gov.uk
The Home Office and MoD websites are good starting points for many of the issues dealt with in this chapter.

http://mi5.gov.uk
Once so secretive that its very existence was denied, the security service now has its own website.

22

Thinking Synoptically

An important theme of this book has been the interconnected nature of the subject matter. Governments are deeply enmeshed in a dense biomass of political life, and politics is a process involving not merely the institutions of state but also those of the economy and civil society, and subject to a range of influences emanating from the global context. Political energy issues from multifarious sources, including differences in ideology, wealth, education, employment status, class, gender, race, geographical location, and so on. Moreover, the process embraces institutions well beyond the formal Westminster–Whitehall terrain, encompassing the judiciary, the police, the military, the secret services, trade unions, private firms, thousands of pressure groups espousing an infinity of causes, and giant peak organizations like the TUC and CBI. Yet despite this seamless cohesion the previous chapters have been characterized by distinct focuses. There are two principal reasons for this.

- ◆ *Verisimilitude.* The world of government and politics really is to some extent formally compartmentalized through the organizational structures of the state. Thus, for example, the judiciary is distinct from the civil service, Parliament is distinct from local government, and so on. We saw in chapter 3 that this division is actually part of the constitution: the division of authority is seen as a protection from overpowerful government.
- ◆ *Pedagogical necessity.* It is a natural characteristic of the human intellect to split up, compartmentalize and classify any subject matter under study; this helps us to make sense of the complexity of the world surrounding us. This is partly what we mean by 'analysis'. Thus, for example, actors will split up a play into its scenes, acts and dialogues in the process of mastering it.

However, ultimately the actors will want to rebuild the play in its entirety to reveal its dramatic intent. When we take a **holistic** or **synoptic** perspective we view our subject as a whole **system,** rather than in terms of its parts, and it may be argued that it is only from such a perspective that the political drama can be fully understood. To take another analogy, a football team is something qualitatively different from the eleven individuals who comprise it. To assess its likely success we need to understand how these individuals relate together. The potential energy of the team as a goal-scoring machine may be greater than the sum of that of each individual; this increase gained from working together is termed 'synergy'.

There are various ways of conceiving politics in holistic terms. Here we introduce two closely related perspectives that underlie much political study and debate: the organic and the systemic.

Organic theories of the state

A long-prevailing view of the state has pictured it as a living organism (usually the human body), with its various organs fulfilling particular functions but bound together in mutual dependence. This goes back to the Ancient Greeks, but a particular version flourished in the nineteenth century amongst a school of biological political theorists. The notion of the organism was not merely metaphor; the state was believed to be a life form, capable of birth, life, disease and death. They also spoke of the state's adaptation to its environment through a slow process of evolution in which some organs became more important and others (like the human appendix) withered away.

> States, like men, have their growth, their manhood, their decrepitude, their decay.
>
> Walter Savage Landor (1775–1864; English writer), *Imaginary Conversations* (1824–9)

Functionalism

The organic view was to underlie an approach to the study of society and the state termed **functionalism.** This argued that state structures and institutions must, like the organs of the body, perform certain necessary functions (respiration, reproduction, digestion, and so on) for it to survive. The approach was applied by influential anthropologists like A. R. Radcliffe-Brown (1881–1955) and Bronislaw Malinowski (1884–1942) to explain and compare primitive societies in which formal institutions did not exist. Thus while a society might not have a parliament in the sense understood by western culture, it would necessarily require the function of making rules.

A function only has meaning in terms of the *whole* and, by the same reasoning, if an institution acts in a way that is harmful to the whole, then it is, like a disease in an organism, dysfunctional. The sociologists Talcott Parsons (1902–79) and Robert Merton (b. 1910) adapted the anthropologists' ideas more specifically to industrialized societies, revealing that even here it is possible to ask questions based on functional analysis. Thus we may enquire whether an institution really fulfils 'the function' it is supposed to (does Parliament really make laws?), or whether those functions are fulfilled elsewhere (the civil service, the Cabinet, and so on). It can be seen that questions such as these, which seek to look behind the institutional facade, arise throughout this book.

However, organic and functionalist thinking has ideological implications. It leads to a Burkean form of conservatism that institutions should be allowed to grow naturally and not be tampered with – a veneration of the status quo. On the other hand, the organic view can also entail the idea of *death* followed by *rebirth* – in other words, *revolution*.

Systems theory and the political system

The organic view demanded a degree of metaphysical faith and fell out of favour. However, it was replaced with the idea of the **political system** (figure 22.1). Although the term is often used loosely to denote little more than 'where politics takes place', the concept is essentially holistic. Systems theory was pioneered by the biologist Ludwig von Bertallanfy, who stressed that 'Each part depends not only on conditions within itself, but also . . . on conditions within the *whole* of which it is part' (1952: xix). The concept was introduced into political science by the American scholar David Easton, who entitled a seminal work *The Political System*, on the holistic premise that 'the phenomena of politics tend to cohere and to be mutually related' (1953: 97).

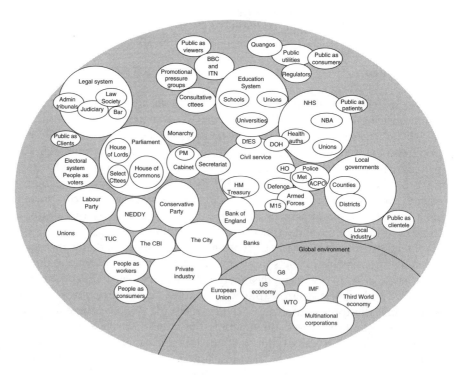

Figure 22.1
Politics as a system.

The systems approach advanced thinking by adding to the organic view a mechanical one. The system differs fundamentally from the organism in that it does not evolve under some internal dynamic of its own; it is conceived as a machine *designed* to fulfil a particular purpose. Thus a car is designed to transport us; it will never seek to place its own interest before its rider as might a horse (an organic system). Perceived in this way the state becomes something that can be *changed* on the basis of *reason* – an enlightenment belief. Bentham and the Philosophical Radicals saw the state as a constitutional Meccano set to be constructed at will. We have seen throughout this book how the rising bourgeoisie made prolific use of the idea of deliberate change, to the extent of sculpting the modern British liberal-democratic state.

Policy networks

The network image is yet another way of seeing politics in holistic or synoptic terms (Smith 1993: 74). The essence of this approach is an appreciation of the way a large range of actors are linked together in relationships of power and dependence. They are sometimes said to constitute policy communities – shifting combinations of levels of governance, private interests, key individuals and bureaucracies, where there is no single centre of power (see Richardson and Jordan 1979; Rhodes and Marsh 1992; Grant and MacNamara 1995).

The governance perspective

Chapter 1 considered how the 'Westminster model' of the governmental process is outmoded and misleading. The governance perspective that is increasingly used by scholars again focuses on the broader picture of what really happens in the politics of the state (Pierre and Stoker 2000). It emphasizes the concept of multi-level governance (Smith 1997) – the relations between bodies such as NATO, the World Bank and the EU, the transnational corporations, NGOs operating above the level of nation-states and the further layers of government and quasi-government at provincial, regional and local levels. Governance entails subtle processes of negotiation, bargaining, exchange and compromise across an unlimited political space.

A synoptic study strategy

If politics is perceived synoptically, one is drawn to conceptualize the parts of the political system in terms of their relationships to the whole and to each other (figure 22.1). This can open the door to a level of understanding far deeper than that gained from compartmentalized knowledge. We realize that the behaviour of some element (say a pressure group) cannot be fully explained without understanding its relationship with other elements (other pressure groups, the mass media, Parliament, public opinion, the civil service, international organizations, its own rank and file, society at large, and so on).

There is no limit to the level at which the synoptic perspective may be focused. Systems may be conceived as consisting of *subsystems* (for example, the select committee system may be seen as a subsystem of the House of Commons and the latter as a subsystem of Parliament) and may themselves be seen as part of larger systems (for example, the political system itself can be seen as a subsystem of the British social system, or of the national economy or of the world economy) *ad infinitum*.

Some lessons on synoptic thinking come from science in general and particularly from meteorology, where it is crucially necessary to take a global perspective. The range of influences that shape our weather are so complex that, even with computers capable of performing hundreds of millions of calculations a second (the present state of the art), it will always be impossible to include every causal factor; hence we will never be able to predict weather with complete accuracy. Scientists speak of the 'butterfly effect' wherein a butterfly flapping its wings may set in motion a chain of events that will alter the course of a tornado on the other side of the globe. Politics is full of such causal chains. Clinton's election in the USA may have contributed to the election of Blair in Britain, a currency speculator in one part of the world may precipitate something like Black Wednesday in Britain. To think in a consciously synoptic way is constantly to pose a battery of relevant questions about any particular part of the political system. When you think about any political question try to conceptualize the overall system in the way depicted in figure 22.1, and try to think how the particular part of the system you are concerned with relates to all other aspects. Never imagine that you can fully understand one part without appreciating its place in the whole system.

In developing a synoptic perspective it can also be helpful to focus not on particular institutions or structures, but on some of the broad themes underlying the discipline of political science. Themes which have run through this book include power, continuity and change, participation and representation, and political culture. By understanding the way these are manifest throughout the political system we are naturally led to a synoptic view.

Power Power was specifically examined in chapter 1 but, as probably the most pervasive concept in politics, it surfaces throughout. Power can be defined variously. It is the ability to make others act in accordance with one's wishes, despite any desire on their part not to do so. Ultimately it is the ability to get what one wants and much of politics is about who gets what. The focus directs attention both at, and beyond, the institutions of the state: Parliament, the Cabinet, the civil service, the mass media, multinational corporations, and so on. The starting point for study must be questions such as 'What is power?', 'Who has it?', 'How does power differ from authority?' There are few questions to be asked in politics that do not entail some discussion of who has, and who does not have, power.

Participation and representation Politics in a democracy is about people participating in the formation of public policy. The most obvious way in which ordinary people do this is through the electoral system, although this is limited to choosing representatives. Chapter 9 examined elections and electoral behaviour, but again there is more to it than this. People can participate in numerous ways, some more democratic than others. They may become MPs, stand for a local council, join a party, donate a large sum to a party, join a pressure group, demonstrate in the high street, lobby an MP, take direct action, raise money for a cause, write to a newspaper, make a speech at Hyde Park Corner or argue in the pub. Even the Welsh farmer throwing an egg at John Prescott in the 2001 election campaign was participating in politics. Once again it can be seen that this theme takes us into most corners of our political system.

Political culture This encapsulates the spirit of the polity: its institutions, history, popular attitudes and prevailing ideology. It introduces some of the big socio-political questions of the day, many linked to class, gender and race. Can we speak of a ruling class? Is there such a thing as a political elite? Is there corruption in high places? What are the implications of xenophobia within society? Why are there so few women in political life? The way our politicians act, the policies they make and the power they are allowed are all conditioned by the invisible, but very tangible, phenomenon of political culture. If we have some understanding of this we will have something to say on most of the political issues of our time.

Continuity and change This theme has a particular resonance in a polity that venerates its unbroken link with the past. It is clear from the previous chapters, many of which open with an historical perspective, that continuity marks the development of virtually all Britain's political institutions: Westminster, Whitehall, local government, the judiciary, and of course the unwritten constitution itself. Yet, as Walter Bagehot observed, change is forever taking place beneath the surface. An understanding of the twin forces of continuity and change produces a synoptic view that embraces not only the breadth of the political landscape but also the all-important historical dimension.

Review your understanding of the following terms and concepts

functionalism	holistic view	synoptic view
governance	political system	

Questions for discussion

1 'Power corrupts'. Discuss in the light of modern government and politics.
2 'It is through political culture that the attitudes of ordinary people can set the parameters in which the powerful operate.' Discuss.
3 'British politics and government remain largely a male preserve.' Discuss.
4 'Representative government is an effective means of giving power to ordinary people.' Discuss.
5 'An obsession with the value of continuity with the past has prevented the modernization of British government.' Discuss.
6 'Government for the people, but not by the people.' How fair is this as a description of representative government in Britain?
7 'A young man wearing the clothes of his great grandfather.' How far can the British constitution be so characterized?
8 'It's the Sun wot won it' (1992), 'It's the Sun wot swung it' (1997). So does the Sun have power?

Further reading

Dunleavy, P., Gamble, A., Holliday, I. and Peele, G. (2000) Developments in British Politics 6.
Latest in regular series in which eminent scholars concentrate on contemporary development.

Harrison, B. (1996) The Transformation of British Politics 1860–1995.
Charts the history of British politics from the time of Bagehot, noting the significance of social and economic change.

Hazell, R. (ed.) (1999) Constitutional Futures: A History of the Next Ten Years.
A number of scholars gaze into their crystal balls to assess possible effects of political reforms in Britain. Widens the scope with comparative material.

Seldon, A. (ed.) (2001) The Blair Effect: The Blair Government, 1997–2001.
A synoptic tour de force by leading academics and journalists covers virtually all aspects of a key contemporary period.

Marr, A. (1995) Ruling Britannia.
Thought-provoking 'constitutional audit' of the past two decades.

For light relief

Anthony Burgess, Clockwork Orange.
An alarming vision of a future dominated by technology, violence and authoritarian government. Made into a film by Stanley Kubrick in 1971.

Nick Cohen (1999) *Cruel Britannia: Reports on the Sinister and Preposterous*.
Collected writings of crusading journalist, pricking PR bubbles and mocking the pretensions and hypocrisy of some members of the political class.

Aldous Huxley, *Brave New World*.
A fable set in the seventh century AF (after Ford), where life is subjugated by science, all under World Controller Mustapha Mond. In *Brave New World Revisited*, Huxley believes his prophecies are already (1958) coming frighteningly true.

William Morris, *News from Nowhere*.
A utopian socialist fantasy.

George Orwell, *Nineteen Eighty-Four*.
A nightmare of totalitarianism with 'newspeak' and 'doublethink', where war is peace, freedom is slavery and ignorance is strength.

Alvin Toffler, *Future Shock*.
The effects of the communications technology revolution.

Chronology of Events

427BC Birth of Plato.
384BC Birth of Aristotle.
1066 Norman Conquest.
1086 Domesday Book.
1154 Henry II first Plantagenet English king.
1170 Thomas Becket murdered.
1215 Magna Carta.
1258 Simon de Montfort forces reforms on Henry III.
1265 De Montfort's Parliament; defeat and death of de Montfort.
1284 Edward I completes conquest of Wales.
1290 Edward I begins conquest of Scotland.
1295 Edward I's 'Model Parliament'.
1314 Robert the Bruce secures Scottish independence.
1327 Edward II deposed and murdered.
1338 Hundred Years War begins.
1362 English becomes official language in Parliament and courts.
1381 Peasants' Revolt.
1399 Richard II deposed by Henry IV.
1400 Welsh revolt under Owen Glendower.
1415 Battle of Agincourt.
1450 Jack Cade's rebellion against Henry VI.

1453 Final English defeat and end of Hundred Years War.
1455 Wars of the Roses begin.
1476 Caxton sets up printing press.
1485 Battle of Bosworth Field; Tudor dynasty begins.
1493 Vasco da Gama finds sea route to India.
1515 Thomas Wolsey becomes Lord Chancellor and Cardinal.
1517 Martin Luther begins Reformation.
1534 Act of Supremacy; Henry VIII takes control of Church in England.
1535 Thomas More executed.
1536 Ann Boleyn executed.
1558 Elizabeth I becomes Queen.
1577 Drake begins circumnavigation.
1588 Spanish Armada defeated.
1600 English East India Company founded.
1601 Elizabethan Poor Law; rates introduced.
1603 Irish revolts suppressed. Death of Elizabeth I; accession of James VI of Scotland as James I of England.
1605 Gunpowder plot.
1611 English and Scottish Protestants settle in Ulster.

1620   Pilgrim Fathers settle in New England.
1628   Petition of Right to Charles I by Commons.
1629   Charles I tries to rule without Parliament.
1635   John Hampden refuses to pay ship money.
1642   Charles I attempts to arrest five members of Parliament. Outbreak of civil war.
1644   Battle of Marston Moor. North lost to Charles I. Royalist campaign in Scotland.
1645   New Model Army formed. Royalist army crushed at Naseby.
1646   Charles I surrenders to Scots.
1647   Charles I handed over to Parliament, seized by army, flees to Carisbrooke Castle.
1648   Second civil war; New Model Army defeats Scots and Royalists.
1649   Charles I executed; England governed as republic under Cromwell. England suppresses Ireland.
1651   Cromwell becomes supreme in all Britain after the Battle of Worcester. First English Navigation Acts. Thomas Hobbes publishes *Leviathan*.
1655   English take Jamaica.
1658   Cromwell dissolves Rump Parliament, becomes Lord Protector.
1660   Restoration of monarchy; Charles II returns from exile.
1665   Great Plague of London.
1666   Great Fire of London.
1681   Charles II tries to rule without Parliament; establishes Oxford Parliament.
1685   Monmouth's rebellion crushed by James II at Sedgemoor.
1688   William of Orange lands with army in England; flight of James II. The 'Glorious Revolution'.
1689   Bill of Rights limits monarchy.

1690   Locke's *Two Treatises on Government*. Battle of the Boyne; William crushes Irish.
1693   National Debt begun.
1694   Bank of England founded.
1701   Act of Settlement establishes Hanoverian succession.
1707   Act of Union of English and Scottish Parliaments.
1714   Death of Queen Anne; accession of Elector of Hanover as George I. Riot Act enables magistrates to call in military to quell civil disorder.
1715   Septennial Act; Parliament prolongs its life from three to seven years.
1720   'South Sea' bubble.
1721   Robert Walpole seen as first prime minister.
1733   John Kay invents flying shuttle. Jethro Tull advocates new agricultural technology.
1742   Walpole falls.
1748   Montesquieu publishes *L'Esprit des Lois*.
1757   Pitt as Secretary of State is main force in British government. Clive conquers Bengal.
1759   Canal age begins.
1760   Beginning of 100-year period termed industrial revolution.
1763   First British empire at its height.
1764   John Wilkes expelled from Commons.
1769   Richard Arkwright invents water frame for spinning.
1770   James Cook discovers New South Wales.
1774   Warren Hastings appointed first Governor General of India.
1776   American Declaration of Independence. Adam Smith's *Wealth of Nations*.
1783   Treaty of Versailles; American independence recognized. Pitt the Younger becomes PM.
1784   Last appearance of monarch in Cabinet.
1785   Cartwright invents power loom.

1787   American Constitution drafted. Consolidated Fund established. Creation of Royal Ulster Constabulary.

1789   Washington first US President. French Revolution begins with storming of the Bastille (14 July). Bentham's *Introduction to the Principles of Morals and Legislation*.

1792   Denmark first country to prohibit slave trade. France becomes republic.

1798   Battle of Vinegar Hill.

1800   Parliamentary union of Great Britain and Ireland.

1804   Napoleon Bonaparte becomes French Emperor.

1805   Battle of Trafalgar; victory and death of Nelson.

1807   Slave trade abolished in British empire. Napoleon in control of all Europe. Britain blockaded by continent.

1811   Luddite riots against new machinery.

1812   Napoleon retreats from Moscow.

1814   Napoleon abdicates; Louis XVIII King of France.

1815   Napoleon escapes from Elba. Battle of Waterloo. Corn Law protects British agricultural interests at expense of commerce.

1819   'Peterloo Massacre'.

1823   USA announces 'Monroe Doctrine'.

1824   Repeal of Combination Acts legalizes trade unions.

1829   Metropolitan Police formed.

1832   First Reform Bill.

1833   First British Factory Act. First government grant for education.

1834   Poor Law Amendment Act. 'Tolpuddle Martyrs' transported to discourage working-class association.

1835   Municipal Corporations Act. Peel's 'Tamworth Manifesto'.

1836   Chartist movement formed.

1837   Queen Victoria's accession.

1839   Anti-Corn-Law League formed.

1842   Chartists present second Charter.

1845   Irish potato famine.

1846   Corn Laws repealed; Peel resigns; Conservatives split; Disraeli becomes leader.

1848   Revolutionary movement throughout Europe. French Republic proclaimed. Marx and Engels produce *Communist Manifesto*.

1851   Great Exhibition.

1854   Crimean war; France and England declare war against Russia. Much British bureaucratic incompetence exposed; Northcote–Trevelyan Report.

1855   Crimean war ends.

1856   Bessemer process invented.

1858   British Crown assumes sovereignty over India.

1859   Darwin's *Origin of the Species*. J. S. Mill's *On Liberty*.

1861   American civil war begins. J. S. Mill's *Considerations on Representative Government*. Public Accounts Committee established.

1864   First Socialist International.

1865   American civil war ends.

1866   Office of Comptroller and Auditor General established.

1867   Second Great Reform Bill. Bagehot's *The English Constitution*. Volume I of Marx's *Capital*.

1868   Disraeli succeeds Lord Derby as PM; later defeated by Gladstone in general election.

1870   Forster's Education Act sets up school boards.

1872   Secret ballot introduced.

1874   General election; Disraeli succeeds Gladstone as PM.

1880   Gladstone returned as PM.

1883   National insurance introduced in Germany. Special Branch of the Met. established.

1884   Third Parliamentary Reform Bill. Fabian Society founded.

1885   Dicey's *Law and the Constitution*.

1886   First Irish Home Rule Bill defeated in Commons. Unionist defectors from Liberals join Conservatives.

1888   County Councils Act.

1889   Second Socialist International. Great strike at London Docks. First Official Secrets Act.

1890   Parnell ruined by divorce case.

1893   Second Irish Home Rule Bill rejected in Lords. Independent Labour Party formed.

1894   Manchester Ship Canal opens. Gladstone resigns.

1899   Boer war starts.

1900   Labour Party formed. 'Khaki Election'.

1901   Queen Victoria dies. Taff Vale Judgment.

1902   Boer war ends. Committee of Imperial Defence established.

1903   First flight of heavier-than-air machine at Kitty Hawk, USA. Emmeline Pankhurst forms Women's Social and Political Union.

1905   Liberal landslide; first Labour MPs.

1906   Suffragette activism. Trades Disputes Act reverses Taff Vale Judgment.

1908   Asquith becomes PM.

1909   Old-age state pension scheme introduced. Lords reject 'People's Budget'. Henry Ford begins manufacturing cheap motor cars. MI5 established.

1910   Edward VII's death; accession of George V. Labour exchanges established. Liberals battle with House of Lords, win two general elections, but become dependent upon Irish MPs. Osborne Judgment.

1911   Parliament Act reduces Lords' power. MPs to be paid. National Insurance introduced. Second Official Secrets Act passed with notorious Section 2.

1912   Third Irish Home Rule Bill. *Titanic* disaster.

1913   'Cat and Mouse Act'.

1914   Archduke Ferdinand assassinated; war in Europe. Britain declares war on Germany. Coalition government formed. Irish Bill passed but put in cold storage.

1916   Lloyd George becomes PM. New coalition reduces role of Liberals. Easter uprising in Ireland. Battle of the Somme; 420,000 British soldiers killed ('lions led by donkeys').

1917   USA declares war on Germany. Russia proclaimed a republic; Bolshevik revolution. Balfour Declaration.

1918   Armistice signed. Women given vote. 'Coupon Election'. Sinn Féin MPs win majority of Irish seats but set up own Parliament (Dáil). Michael Collins forms IRA. New Labour Party constitution.

1919   Versailles Treaty. League of Nations established (Germany excluded).

1920   Black and Tans sent into Ireland.

1921   Irish settlement; Irish Free State set up; Ulster to remain in UK.

1922   1922 Committee formed. Conservatives win general election. First woman takes seat in Commons.

1923   Baldwin dissolves Parliament over tariff reform. General election makes Labour second-largest party; they rule for 10 months with Liberal support.

1924   Liberals withdraw support over Campbell case. Zinoviev letter affair. Conservatives return triumphantly to office.

1925   Winston Churchill puts Britain back on gold standard. Drastic cuts in wages and industrial unrest.

1926   General strike.

1928   Equal Franchise Act; voting age for women lowered to 21.

1929   Labour wins election as largest single party for the first time. Second Labour government under MacDonald. Liberal decline becomes inevitable. Wall Street crash. BBC established.

1931   Economic depression; Cabinet split over public expenditure cuts. MacDonald resigns. Surprise coalition under MacDonald overwhelmingly endorsed by electorate. Henderson becomes Labour leader.

1932   Lansbury becomes Labour leader.

1933   Hitler appointed Chancellor by Hindenburg and begins to gain iron control in Germany.

1934   Hitler becomes dictator. Foundation of NCCL.

1935   Baldwin succeeds MacDonald as PM. Attlee becomes Labour leader. Conservatives win election.

1936   Spanish civil war breaks out. Public Order Act. Keynes's *General Theory of Employment, Interest and Money*. BBC TV begins.

1937   Chamberlain forms coalition.

1938   Germany annexes Austria. British navy mobilized. Chamberlain signs Munich Agreement with Hitler.

1939   Britain recognizes Franco government in Spain; civil war ends. Conscription introduced. Germany invades Poland. Britain declares war on Germany. Third Official Secrets Act.

1940   Labour joins coalition; Churchill forms National Government. Army evacuated from Dunkirk. Italy declares war on Britain and France. Germans capture Paris. Battle of Britain. Attlee recognized as deputy PM.

1941   Japanese attack Pearl Harbor.

1942   Beveridge Report.

1943   Mussolini overthrown. Italian Fascist Party dissolved.

1944   D-Day invasion of Europe. Paris liberated. Bretton Woods Agreement; IMF and World Bank established. Great Education Act.

1945   Mussolini and mistress shot by Italian partisans. Suicide of Hitler and mistress. End of second world war against Germany (2 May). UN Charter signed. Landslide Labour victory; Attlee becomes PM. Britain begins to create modern welfare state; accepts Keynesian principles. Atomic bomb against Japan. Russia declares war against Japan. Japan surrenders. Lend–Lease terminated. Nuremberg Trials of major war criminals. UN formed. Attlee takes decision that Britain will manufacture atomic bombs.

1946   US eventually approves loan to Britain.

1947   Nationalization begins (coal). Marshall Aid plan begins. India and Pakistan become dominions. Marriage of Princess Elizabeth.

1948   End of British mandate for Palestine; partition into Jewish and Arab states. NHS established. Electricity nationalized. Republic of Ireland Bill signed.

1949   Parliament Act reduces Lords' power. NATO formed after Russians blockade Berlin. Gas nationalized.

1950   Rebuilt House of Commons opened. Labour secures narrow election victory.

1951   Resignation of Bevan over NHS charges. Attlee dissolves Parliament. Labour defeated in election, despite receiving most votes; Churchill becomes PM.

1952   George VI's death.

1953   Elizabeth II's coronation; ceremony televised. Steel de-nationalized.

1954   Crichel Down case. Food rationing ends.

1955   Churchill resigns as PM; succeeded by Eden. Conservative general election victory. Independent TV begins. Gaitskell succeeds Attlee as Labour leader.

1956   Britain's first atomic power station starts working at Calder Hall. Suez crisis. Anthony Crosland publishes *The Future of Socialism*.

1957   Eden resigns as PM; replaced by Macmillan. Franks Report on tribunals and inquiries.

1958   EEC treaty comes into force; Britain stays out. CND launched under Bertrand Russell; first London–Aldermaston protest march. Life Peerage Act. First women peers in House of Lords.

1959   Conservatives' third successive election victory.

1960   Macmillan's 'wind of change' speech; Conservatives form Monday Club. Plowden Report on public expenditure; PES system begins. Kennedy elected US president. Herbert Report on Greater London. Momentous Labour conference; Gaitskell makes 'fight, fight, and fight again' vow.

1961   Justice Report, *The Citizen and the Administration*. Neddy established.

1962   Cuban missile crisis. 'Beeching axe' reduces British Rail network. 'Night of the Long Knives'. First post-war Immigration Act; limits entry to those with jobs. Vassall spy scandal. Royal commission on police reports.

1963   British application to join EEC rejected. Harold Wilson becomes Labour leader after Gaitskell's death. Profumo scandal. Peerage Act enables peers to renounce hereditary titles. Macmillan resigns as PM; succeeded by Sir Alec Douglas-Home. Kennedy assassinated.

1964   First elections for new GLC; Labour victory. Nelson Mandela sentenced to life imprisonment. Labour gains narrow general election victory; Wilson PM. DEA created. Import surcharge and export tax introduced to improve balance of payments. Government, TUC and employers agree policy on productivity, prices and income. Police Act limits local control of police forces.

1965   Douglas-Home resigns; Heath elected Conservative leader under new procedure. BP strike North Sea oil. Death penalty abolished. Prices and Incomes Board created.

1966   Election increases Labour majority to almost 100. Frank Cousins resigns from government over incomes policy. Industrial Reorganization Corporation created. Prices and incomes freeze. Post Office becomes public corporation. Sir Edmund Compton becomes first ombudsman.

1967   Jo Grimond resigns as Liberal leader; replaced by Jeremy Thorpe. Britain makes another application to join EEC. Criminal Justice Act allows majority verdicts from juries. *Rookes v. Barnard* judgement attacks right to strike.

1968   NHS prescription charges re-introduced. France vetoes British entry into EEC. Northern Ireland disturbances begin. Enoch Powell's 'Rivers of Blood' speech. Fulton Report on civil service.

1969   British army units to be deployed in N. Ireland. Voting age lowered to 18. Government seeks TUC voluntary agreement to curb unofficial strikes. Redcliffe-Maud Report on local government.

1970   Heath gains surprise election victory. Third application to join EEC. Army uses rubber bullets in

N. Ireland. Heath's economic policy a 'dash for growth'.

1971   Currency decimalized. Immigration Act reduces status of Commonwealth immigrants to that of aliens. Both Houses of Parliament vote to join EEC. Compton Report on interrogation of IRA suspects finds evidence of ill-treatment. US balance of trade slides into deficit with major consequences for world capitalism.

1972   'Bloody Sunday' in Londonderry; 13 civilians killed. Power crisis; state of emergency and power cuts. Increased IRA bombing. Direct Westminster rule over N. Ireland introduced. Decision taken to float pound. Local Government Act to reorganize system.

1973   Britain, Ireland and Denmark join EEC. Heath U-turns on economic policy; nationalization of lame ducks. N. Ireland referendum strongly supports retaining link with Britain. VAT introduced. First sitting of new Ulster Assembly collapses in chaos. Diplock Courts introduced in terrorist cases. Arab–Israeli war; oil prices quadruple. Fuel conservation measures include three-day week. Collapse of long boom becomes apparent. 'Snake in the Tunnel' agreement in Europe. India House incident brings existence of Special Patrol Group to public attention. Sir Robert Mark delivers BBC Dimbleby Lecture.

1974   End of direct rule in N. Ireland. Parliament debates energy crisis. Miners' strike. Reorganized local government and NHS systems come into operation. Heath calls election to decide 'who governs'; no clear result; Labour becomes minority government. Miners return to work. Ulster assembly collapses; direct rule resumed. Red

Lion Square disorders. End of statutory incomes policy. Guildford pub bombing kills five. Second election in October returns Labour (majority 3). Birmingham pub bombing (21 killed). Anti-terrorist bill rushed through Parliament proscribes IRA. IRA bombs in London.

1975   Margaret Thatcher defeats Heath to become Conservative leader. Referendum on remaining in EEC; 2 to 1 majority 'Yes'. First live broadcast of Commons. Unemployment exceeds 1 million. Balcombe Street siege; two Londoners held in flat by IRA. National Enterprise Board established. Anti-sex discrimination and equal pay legislation come into force. Ombudsman system extended to NHS.

1976   Wilson's unexpected resignation; Callaghan becomes PM. Britain begins exporting North Sea oil. David Steel elected Liberal leader. Britain found guilty by European Commission on Human Rights of torturing detainees in Ulster. Lord Hailsham expounds 'elective dictatorship' thesis. Blunt spy scandal. Police Complaints Board established; Sir Robert Mark resigns. PM announces death of Keynesianism: 'we cannot . . . spend our way out of a recession'.

1977   Government loses absolute majority; Lib–Lab pact. Grunwick dispute. Violent racist clashes in Lewisham. *Hosenball* case.

1978   Special Liberal assembly votes to continue Lib–Lab pact until July. Regular broadcasting of parliamentary proceedings begins. Publication of *The Times* suspended in year-long dispute over new technology. IRA bombing in British cities. IMF

Articles redrawn to mark end of Bretton Woods Agreement. Public-sector strikes bring 'Winter of Discontent'.

1979   Scottish and Welsh referendums reject devolution proposals. Government defeated on no-confidence motion; PM announces general election. Blair Peach dies in clash with police. Thatcher wins election, becoming first woman PM. Conservatives also dominate in European elections. Earl Mountbatten and others killed by bomb on boat in Sligo. Lancaster House talks to settle Rhodesia's (Zimbabwe's) future. All foreign exchange controls removed. New system of Commons select committees introduced.

1980   Bristol race riots. Zimbabwe becomes independent with Robert Mugabe as PM. National Front and Anti-Nazi League clashes at Lewisham. Iranian Embassy seized; later stormed by SAS. Bombings and violence in Ulster mark 10 years of internment. Callaghan retires as Labour leader; replaced by Foot. Reagan becomes US president. Local Government Planning and Land Act reforms block grant system, giving more central control.

1981   Labour leadership election method changed to give unions and constituencies a say. 'Gang of Four' establish Council for Social Democracy; SDP formed. Rupert Murdoch buys *The Times*. Engagement of Prince Charles and Lady Diana Spencer. Racial anti-police violence at Brixton. IRA hunger strikes; death of Bobby Sands. SDP alliance with Liberals. Extensive public expenditure cuts. Inner-city riots and savage confrontations with police. Lonrho take over the *Observer*.

Prince Charles marries Lady Diana. Benn unsuccessfully challenges Healey for Labour deputy leadership. Privatization of state North Sea oil assets announced. OPEC unify oil price structure. Anglo-Irish summit agrees on Intergovernmental Council; uproar in Commons; Ian Paisley promises to make province ungovernable. Benn elected off Shadow Cabinet. Scarman Report on Brixton riots. Arthur Scargill elected NUM leader. Labour NEC investigates Militant Tendency. Law Lords rule against GLC's 'Fares Fair' policy. British Nationality Act closes door to non-whites.

1982   Unemployment reaches 3 million; Thatcher's popularity at all-time low. Falklands war; Carrington resigns as Foreign Secretary. Thatcher's popularity soars. Roy Jenkins becomes SDP leader. IRA bombs in Hyde Park and Regent's Park; 11 killed. Greenham Common anti-nuclear protest begins.

1983   Labour NEC expels 5 members of Militant. Ian MacGregor appointed NCB chairman. 'Falklands election' gives Conservatives 144 majority. Bernard Weatherill elected Speaker against Thatcher's wishes. Jenkins resigns as SDP leader; succeeded by Owen. Public expenditure cuts of £500 million. 38 IRA prisoners escape from Maze prison; governor resigns. Kinnock replaces Foot as Labour leader. First US Cruise missiles arrive at Greenham Common. Massive bomb outside Harrods. US invades Grenada. Audit Commission established.

1984   Trade union membership banned at GCHQ. NCB announces 20,000 job losses and 21 pit closures; miners' strike begins. Sarah Tisdall jailed for leaking documents about Cruise missiles. Labour gains in European Parliament elections; Conservatives retain majority. Immigration rules further toughened. Robert Maxwell buys Mirror Group. 18 councils rate-capped. Clive Ponting charged under Official Secrets Act. Police and Criminal Evidence Act. Police Complaints Authority replaces Police Complaints Board. IRA bomb in Brighton hotel housing Conservative leaders for party conference. NUM assets sequestred; talks with NCB repeatedly break down. BT privatized; massive profits on first day's trading.

1985   House of Lords televised live. Oxford refuses Thatcher honorary degree. Clive Ponting acquitted. Miners drift back to work after repeated failures of talks. Fourth government defeat in Lords over GLC abolition. European Court of Human Rights holds that British immigration rules discriminate against women. Violent rioting in Brixton after police accidentally shoot Mrs Cherry Groce. Broadwater Farm riots (Tottenham). Miners in Notts and South Derbyshire join Union of Democratic Mineworkers. Anglo-Irish Agreement; mass resignation of Ulster Unionist MPs. Control of *Daily Telegraph* passes to Canadian, Conrad Black. Westland affair begins. Church of England *Faith in the City* report.

1986   Heseltine resigns criticizing Thatcher style. Brittan resigns over Westland affair. Murdoch prints *Sunday Times* and *News of the World* at Wapping; violent demonstrations by print unions. GLC and metropolitan counties

abolished. Labour NEC begins disciplinary action against 16 Militants at Liverpool. John Stalker suspended and taken off N. Ireland inquiry into RUC 'Shoot to Kill' policy. Gifford Report on Broadwater Farm riots. Appeal Court bans *Spycatcher* by former MI5 officer, Peter Wright. Stalker reinstated by Greater Manchester police force. Marmaduke Hussey appointed as BBC Chairman. The *Independent* launched. 'Big Bang' in City as computers are introduced. *Spycatcher* case. British Gas privatized. US air attack on Libya from British bases. Crown Prosecution Service comes into operation. New Public Order Act increases police powers.

1987   BA privatization. 'Birmingham Six' case (pub bombing) referred to Court of Appeal after much campaigning; they will not be acquitted. SAS shoot 8 IRA men and a civilian in County Tyrone. European Court of Human Rights dismisses case of GCHQ workers. Injunction prevents showing on BBC of Zircon spy satellite. Relaunch of formal Liberal–SDP Alliance. Enforced resignation of BBC Director General Alasdair Milne. Peter Imbert replaces Sir Kenneth Newman as head of Metropolitan Police. President Reagan admits 'arms for hostages' deal with Iran ('Irangate' scandal). Three men convicted of murder of PC Blakelock on Broadwater Farm estate. Moscow talks between Thatcher and Gorbachev. Thawing of cold war. Thatcher's third successive general election triumph but support concentrated in south.

1988   Thatcher becomes longest-serving PM of century. Budget reduces top rate tax to 40 per cent (lowest in Europe); £2,000 million of tax cuts go to wealthiest. Imports rising faster than exports; fuelled by consumer credit boom. Ibbs Report on civil service. SAS gun down suspected IRA members in Gibraltar. Trade deficit rises to record £2,150 million. Inflation begins upward spiral. Poll tax bill receives royal assent after stormy passage. Church continues to attack Thatcherite policies. SDP and Liberals form Social and Liberal Democratic Party; Paddy Ashdown emerges as leader. Benn and Heffer challenge Kinnock/ Hattersley leadership but easily defeated. Scargill loses place on TUC's General Council.

European Commission President Jacques Delors declares that 1992 single market will mean workers' rights and social reform. Thatcher resists French and German call for Britain to join EMS; Bruges speech encapsulates her Euroscepticism. Last act of *Spycatcher* drama; High Court rules newspapers free to comment and publish extracts. Legislation replaces Section 2 of Official Secrets Act. Broadcasting Standards Authority set up. British Steel privatized. Police Federation passes vote of no confidence in Police Complaints Authority. Media interviews with Sinn Féin banned. Formation of Charter88. BerlinWall comes down.

1989   White papers on NHS and legal reforms. Ayatollah Khomeini's *fatwa* on Salman Rushdie. Conservative losses in European elections; Greens gain 15 per cent of votes but no seats. Televising of Commons begins. Investigation into police corruption in West Midlands. Water privatization. Lawson's dramatic resignation; John Major replaces him as Chancellor.

1990   Nelson Mandela released from prison. 'Guildford Four' released. Cold war ends; dramatic changes in Eastern Europe. Anti-poll-tax demonstrations. Labour's popularity over Conservatives higher than ever before (24 per cent). Iraq invades Kuwait; condemned by UN; US and British troops sent. Interest rates rise in attempt to control inflation; many council house buyers suffer. Conservatives lose safe seats to Labour and SLD in by-elections and local elections. Geoffrey Howe's devastating resignation speech. Conservative leadership contest; John Major emerges as party leader and PM.

1991   Gulf war. IRA bombs in London. Woolf Report into prison riots. Electricity privatization. 'Birmingham Six' freed by Court of Appeal. Major NHS reforms. N. Ireland talks begin. Citizen's Charter launched. Robert Maxwell drowns.

1992   Maastricht Treaty signed. Unexpected Conservative general election victory (majority 21). Intensification of IRA bombing campaign on British mainland, especially London. Betty Boothroyd first woman Speaker of Commons. Kinnock resigns; John Smith elected Labour leader. 3000th death in N. Ireland since 1969. UK leaves ERM on 'Black Wednesday'. Labour conference reduces union power in party. Criminal Justice Act comes into force. Matrix Churchill trial collapses. Uncomfortable disclosures on the private lives of Conservative politicians. Separation of Prince and Princess of Wales. Queen's '*annus horribilis*'.

1993   Single European Market comes into force. Inflation lowest for 25 years; unemployment 3 million. James Bulger murder. Maastricht Bill defeated in Commons. Sheehy Report on police. Care in the Community programme instigated. IRA bomb in City of London. Scott Inquiry into arms-to-Iraq begins. Council tax replaces poll tax. Extensive Lib Dem and Labour gains in local elections. Further defence cuts announced. Decisive Lords vote against referendum on Maastricht. Government defeated on Social Chapter opt-out but wins subsequent no-confidence vote. ERM effectively suspended. Britain ratifies Maastricht Treaty. BNP wins council seat in Isle of Dogs. Labour agrees to OMOV for candidate selection. Major calls for 'back to basics'. Anglo-Irish 'Downing Street Declaration'.

1994   District auditor alleges gerrymandering by Conservative Westminster Council. Sleaze allegations and government resignations. Free vote reduces homosexual age of consent to 18. Ordination of women priests approved. UK reluctantly accepts modified rules on QMV in an enlarged EU. Rail privatization begins. Further Conservative losses in local elections. Channel tunnel opens. John Smith dies. Conservative setbacks in Euro elections; Lib Dems gain first two seats. Prince of Wales admits adultery. *Sunday Times'* allegations of cash for questions. Jacques Santer succeeds Delors as EC president. Pergau Dam affair. Blair elected Labour leader; Prescott deputy. Kinnock appointed European Commissioner. IRA ceasefire. Nolan Committee established. Criminal Justice Act comes into

force. National Lottery launched. Gerry Adams visits mainland. Whip withdrawn from eight Conservative rebels; Government becomes dependent on Ulster Unionists. Government defeated on VAT increases on domestic fuel.

1995   Austria, Finland and Sweden join EU. Resignations of ministers, PPSs, etc. continue due to sleaze etc. Joint framework document on N. Ireland. Baring Bank collapse. 'Cash-for-questions' MPs suspended; 'whipless Tories' reinstated. Labour approves new Clause Four. Further Conservative losses in local elections. First direct talks between British government and Sinn Féin for 23 years. First report of Nolan Committee. Harold Wilson dies. New parliamentary boundaries approved. Shell UK abandons plan to dump Brent Spar oil rig at sea.

Major throws down gauntlet over party leadership; John Redwood stands but defeated. Labour reduces union conference vote to 50 per cent. David Trimble elected Official Unionist leader. European Court of Human Rights rules 1988 Gibraltar killings unlawful. Prison Service director Derek Lewis sacked after Learmont report. Referendum Party launched. MPs agree to reveal outside earnings. Princess of Wales gives frank TV interview. N. Ireland talks and weapons decommissioning. Eurosceptics cause government defeat on EU fishing quotas. Conservative majority falls to 3 as Emma Nicholson defects to Lib Dems.

1996   Labour's all-women shortlists ruled illegal. Gerry Adams meets Bill Clinton. Privatized rail services begin. Canary Wharf bomb ends IRA ceasefire. Scott

Report on Arms-for-Iraq affair. N. Ireland peace talks boycotted by most participants. Dunblane shooting. Link between BSE and CJD admitted. EU ban on British beef exports. After by-election Conservative majority down to one. Arthur Scargill launches Socialist Labour Party. Further substantial Labour and Lib Dem gains in local elections. Revised register of MPs' interests published. Westminster councillors surcharged for gerrymandering.

Former US Senator George Mitchell to chair N. Ireland peace talks; Sinn Féin excluded in absence of IRA ceasefire. Manchester bomb injures nearly 200. Violence following Orange Order marches. Multi-party talks re-open at Stormont. Prince and Princess of Wales divorce. Standards and Privileges Committee launches cash-for-questions inquiry. Labour and Lib Dems announce joint talks on constitutional reform. By-election eliminates government's majority.

1997 Major government becomes increasingly fragile; secures Ulster Unionist support by promising a N. Ireland Grand Committee. N. Ireland situation deteriorates. MoD admits failures over Gulf war syndrome. Stephen Lawrence inquest returns verdict of unlawful killing; public criticism of police failure to achieve convictions. Worldwide ban on UK beef exports.

Major calls general election for 1 May, heralding longest-ever campaign. Multi-party N. Ireland talks adjourned. Rail and road transport disrupted by bombs and bomb threats. Labour election landslide; overall swing 10.6 per

cent but lowest turnout since 1935. Conservatives wiped out in Scotland and Wales and lose many seats in south-east. Major resigns. Number of women MPs and Lib Dems doubled. Blair youngest PM since 1812; five women in first Cabinet. Mandelson given powerful role as Minister without Portfolio.

Bank of England given power to set interest rates. UK signs up to EU Social Chapter. William Hague elected Conservative leader. Blair announces renewed contacts with Sinn Féin, providing ceasefire maintained. Amsterdam Summit fails to resolve key issues prior to EU expansion. Brown's first Budget maintains overall Conservative spending plans. Windfall tax on privatized utilities to subsidize welfare-to-work programme. Senior Lib Dems on joint cabinet committee. Downey Report on cash-for-questions affair.

NATO invites Poland, Czech Republic and Hungary to join. Former agent David Shayler questions MI5 accountability. N. Ireland Secretary Mo Mowlam invites Sinn Féin to multi-party talks. Death of Princess of Wales provokes unprecedented public grief and debate on monarchy. Scottish and Welsh referendums approve devolution proposals. Chancellor announces commitment to single currency, but not in first phase. Keith Halliwell appointed 'drugs tsar'. Blair holds historic meetings with Gerry Adams, despite setbacks, including bombs. Formula One tobacco sponsorship controversy. Kyoto climate summit. 47 Labour MPs defy three-line whip over lone-parent benefit cuts. High Court supports surcharges on

Westminster City Council. BSE enquiry begins.

1998   Blair announces new inquiry into Bloody Sunday. Sinn Féin temporarily expelled from peace talks after IRA blamed for two murders. Countryside March against foxhunting ban. European Commission rules 11 countries eligible to join single currency. EU begins entry negotiations with five former East European countries. France and Britain ratify nuclear test ban treaty.

Good Friday Agreement. Row continues over arms shipments to Sierra Leone. Birmingham G8 summit calls for further trade liberalization. Referendums back Good Friday Agreement. Lords defeat legislation to lower homosexual age of consent to 16. N. Ireland Assembly inaugural meeting; David Trimble chosen as 'first minister'. Extra 800 British troops sent to N. Ireland. Violence continues; Omagh bomb kills 29.

Conservative party conference reveals deep divisions over Europe. Lords defeat Euro-elections bill five times. Welsh Secretary Ron Davies resigns after Clapham Common incident. Mandelson 'outed' as homosexual; BBC criticized for attempting to censor reporting of the disclosure. Neill Report proposes reforming rules governing party financing and campaigns. Jenkins Report on electoral reform recommends PR. Bank of England makes first interest rate cut after six increases since gaining the power.

Met Commissioner Sir Paul Condon apologizes to Lawrence inquiry but denies institutional racism. BSE inquiry reveals serious government and civil service shortcomings. Queen's Speech attended by slightly less ceremony.

Spain calls for extradition of former Chilean dictator Pinochet undergoing medical treatment in London. EU lifts ban on British beef exports.

Conservative leader in Lords sacked over secret deal with Labour over Lords reform. Paris court refuses request for extradition of former MI5 officer Derek Shayler. Prince Charles's 50th birthday party hosted by Camilla Parker-Bowles. Royal assent for Human Rights Act. Joint Lab–Lib Dem cabinet committee has remit broadened. Mandelson resigns from Cabinet after revelations of undeclared loan from colleague Geoffrey Robinson (who also resigns).

1999   Euro introduced in 11 EU countries. NHS crisis following winter flu epidemic. Paddy Ashdown announces retirement. Bill to remove hereditary peers from Lords. Free vote in Commons reduces age of homosexual consent to 16. Damning Foreign Affairs Select Committee report on arms-to-Sierra Leone affair; scandal over select committee leaks to ministers. In line with ECHR, death penalty abolished for any offence. Welfare Reform and Pensions Bill; Blair proclaims end of 'something for nothing' welfare state. Alun Michael narrowly defeats Rhodri Morgan for Welsh Labour leadership. Macpherson Report on Stephen Lawrence inquiry alleges institutional racism in Met. Budget cuts basic rate of income tax. European Commission resign *en bloc* following corruption report. After failure of negotiations, NATO begins bombing Yugoslavia on humanitarian grounds, its first-ever attack on a sovereign state.

Prominent human rights lawyer Rosemary Nelson murdered by Loyalist Red Hand Defenders. National minimum wage (£3.60 per hour) comes into force. Four members of IRA's Balcombe Street gang released from prison as a confidence-building measure for Sinn Féin. First elections to Scottish and Welsh assemblies. Lords support government-backed amendment allowing 92 hereditary peers to remain for interim period. David Steel and Lord Elis Thomas elected presiding officers for Scottish and Welsh assemblies respectively. Biggest revolt of Labour MPs since taking power sees 67 opposing welfare reforms. Labour losses in European Parliament elections (using PR).

Long-awaited Freedom of Information Bill disappoints critics. Hilary Benn, son of Tony Benn, wins Leeds Central by-election; Benn senior announces retirement as MP. Death of Screaming Lord Such, leader of Monster Raving Loony Party. Trimble calls for Mo Mowlam's resignation because of loss of Unionist confidence. Scottish Parliament formally opened by Queen. 18 parades held in N. Ireland amidst tight security. Crime statistics suggest police reluctance to combat suspected black criminality following Macpherson Report. Charles Kennedy elected Lib Dem leader. John Stevens to take over as Met Commissioner. Greenham Common Peace Group announces disbanding after 18 years. Patton Report on RUC. Lord Archer secures nomination as Conservative candidate for London Mayor. Paddington train crash (31 dead; 244 injured)

prompts criticism of rail privatization.

Cabinet reshuffle brings back Mandelson to replace Mo Mowlam as N. Ireland Secretary. Home Office announces asylum applications likely to reach a record 700,000. House of Lords gives third reading to Lords reform bill; 90 (of 92) hereditaries elected for interim period. Australian referendum rejects republicanism. N. Ireland talks reconvened at Stormont; IRA to begin decommissioning weapons. Archer steps down as a candidate for London mayoralty over false alibi in libel case; loses party whip. RUC awarded George Medal for gallantry. Portillo wins by-election in Kensington and Chelsea (following Alan Clark's death).

N. Ireland Assembly confirms appointment of a ten-member executive to work under Trimble. In line with an ECHR ruling, ban on homosexuals in armed forces lifted. European Court of Human Rights rules that Bulger killers had not received fair trials. Inaugural meeting of Council of the Isles. Shaun Woodward defects to Labour following sacking from shadow cabinet. Kenneth Clarke and John Major attack Hague's move to right. New Year's honours list contains record number of 1998 names; government plans to mark millennium with 2000 names thwarted by two refusals.

2000 Millennium celebrations throughout world. Neill Committee recommends new methods for dealing with corruption amongst MPs. Wakeham Report on Lords reform. Lord Archer expelled from Conservatives. First Secretary of Welsh Assembly resigns in face of a confidence vote; replaced by

Rhodri Morgan. John Major announces retirement as MP. Ken Livingstone stands as independent in London mayoral election; suspended from Labour Party but elected Mayor. New Greater London Assembly meets.

Budget marks transition from three years of restraint to increased public spending. Civil list to be frozen until 2011. Private security firm to run Brixton prison. Cherie Blair gives birth to son, Leo; Blair takes 14 days' paternity leave. His elder son, Euan, arrested in Leicester Square for drunkenness. Betty Boothroyd announces resignation as Speaker. Blair attends G8 summit to discuss scrapping third world debt. House of Lords again defy Commons over repeal of Section 28.

Blair complains of 'mindless thuggery' by May Day anti-capitalist demonstrators. 45 Labour backbenchers vote against plan to sell off 51 per cent of NATS. Walkout by prison officers over government privatization plans. Direct rule imposed on N. Ireland for 108 days, delegated powers restored on 30 May. Scottish Parliament repeals Section 28 despite popular opposition. Queen Mother celebrates 100th birthday.

Militant hauliers and farmers bring country to a virtual standstill by blocking oil refineries in protest against fuel prices. Two fatal stabbings and 69 serious injuries at Notting Hill Carnival when police try lighter touch. House of Lords reject government bill restricting right to trial by jury. Long-awaited BSE report criticizes MAFF and 25 individuals for their handling of crisis. Hatfield train crash (4 killed) heightens public concern about railways. Michael

Martin controversially elected new Speaker. Edward Heath announces retirement as MP. Formal coalition in Welsh assembly between ruling Labour Party and Lib Dems.

Human Rights Act comes into force. Ken Livingstone appoints Bob Kiley as London's transport commissioner. Compensation payment of £320,000 to parents of Stephen Lawrence from Met. November 'mini budget' offers £1.75 billion in what looks like concession to prevent fuel price protests. Damning NAO report on failing Millennium Dome. Nigerian schoolboy Damilola Taylor murdered. Communications white paper proposes umbrella regulatory authority (OFCOM) to replace existing range of regulatory bodies. President Clinton visits N. Ireland to revive faltering peace process.

2001   Mandelson resigns (again) over Hinduja passport affair; Keith Vaz also implicated. Commons vote for outright ban on hunting with hounds. New Criminal Justice and Police Bill giving power to store DNA samples even when suspects are not charged, or found innocent. Scottish executive agrees to free care for elderly after Lib Dem pressure in coalition.

Blair steps up efforts to advance N. Ireland peace process through meetings with all sides. Ban on livestock movements following foot-and-mouth outbreak. New Terrorism Act (2000) supersedes N. Ireland (Emergency Provisions) Act and other legislation. Police raid various London addresses and nine Algerians linked with al-Qaeda network detained.

Electoral Commission created by 2000 Political Parties, Elections and Referendums Act comes into being. Blair's first meeting with US President Bush at Camp David. Foot-and-mouth crisis causes postponement of local elections, effectively postponing general election. Pre-election Budget announces tax cuts and more spending on NHS and education. National minimum wage increased to £4.10 per hour. Hammond report on Hinduja affair exonerates Mandelson.

Blair and Charles Kennedy reach agreement on promise of a review and possible referendum on PR. Commons agrees Speaker will be elected by secret ballot. House of Lords reject ban on hunting with hounds. Government announces sell-off of 49 per cent stake in NATS to a consortium of seven airlines. *News of the World* obtains tapes of Countess of Wessex and reporter posing as an Arab sheikh. Deputy PM John Prescott unveils plans for PPP for London Underground; opposed by London Mayor Ken Livingstone. David Shayler prosecuted under Official Secrets legislation; denied defence under ECHR.

Decennial UK census on 29 April. Dissolution of Parliament for general election means that seven bills, including the one on foxhunting, are lost. Labour landslide victory, as expected; concern over 59.4 per cent turnout, lowest since universal franchise in 1918. Conservative gains in local elections. Queen's Speech demonstrates government commitment to substantial private-sector role in state services. William Hague resigns; battle for Conservative succession sees Iain Duncan Smith emerge as victor.

Tense race relations in Oldham with three nights of rioting by Asian youths, Britain's worst violence since 1985; NF and BNP involved. In London anti-capitalist demonstrations see damage to property and 65 arrests. Perjury trial of Jeffrey Archer results in 4-year jail sentence. Race riots in several northern towns. Report on Paddington train disaster censures Railtrack. Amidst some public outrage Parole Board directs release of Bulger killers. Serious rioting in Belfast injures 40 police officers. Government suffers first Commons defeat since taking power over proposed select committee composition. Dame Stella Rimington, former MI5 head, allowed to publish memoirs after threat to invoke 1998 Human Rights Act. David Trimble formally resigns as First Minister of N. Ireland Assembly after IRA failure to decommission.

Terrorist attacks on Pentagon and World Trade Center on 11 September. Government promises new anti-terrorist measures in emergency Commons debate. Labour Party member and millionaire Gavyn Davies appointed as BBC chairman. Scottish Parliament bans foxhunting. Blair sets up a war cabinet to supervise UK involvement in US action in Afghanistan. Furore over email message by 'spin doctor' Jo Moore after 9/11 attack.

Home Secretary David Blunkett effectively promises to decriminalize cannabis for personal use. Death of Lord Hailsham. Elizabeth Filkin denied automatic re-appointment as Parliamentary Commissioner for Standards after MPs' fear that she had been too zealous. City and railway industry stunned when Transport Secretary Stephen Byers takes Railtrack into administration on grounds of insolvency. Anti-terrorism Bill rushed through Commons encounters opposition in Lords.

Long-awaited white paper on Lords reform; large proportion of appointees prompts opposition. Fury when Lord Chancellor announces that FOI Act will not come into force until 2005. Baroness Williams becomes Lords Lib Dem leader. Trimble re-elected as N. Ireland First Minister despite rebellion in own party. RUC renamed Police Service of Northern Ireland. Anti-terrorism Bill enacted with modification by Lords. Labour MP Paul Marsden defects to Lib Dems, alleging bullying by whips.

2002   Enron scandal in USA spreads to UK; revelations that both main parties had accepted financial aid from the company. Suspected Islamic activists detained in police swoops in various parts of country. Strategic Rail Authority publishes ten-year plan envisaging investment of £67.5 billion through PPPs.

Simultaneous 'resignations' of Jo Moore and Martin Sixsmith reveal bitter internal battles; minister Stephen Byers gives 'misleading impression' to Commons. Philip Mawer to replace Elizabeth Filkin (see above). Keith Vaz suspended from Commons following Filkin investigation. White paper on immigration toughens up rules and introduces citizenship pledge. Government gives go-ahead to PPP for London Underground despite backbench opposition.

Death of Princess Margaret. Death of Queen Mother; thousands watch funeral. Labour vacates Millbank headquarters

owing to expense; telephone canvassing staff move to Tyneside. Budget announces dramatic spending increase, particularly on health and education; National Insurance contributions raised. Synagogue in North London desecrated indicating a rise of anti-Semitism. Sir Andrew Turnbull appointed as Cabinet Secretary and Head of Civil Service. Suspects in Damilola Taylor case acquitted; CPS heavily criticized. Stephen Byers resigns after further media pressure. Paul Boateng becomes first black cabinet member in reshuffle.

Local elections see advances for BNP in northern towns. First mayoral elections held in seven authorities. Government plans for Lords reform effectively abandoned after fierce opposition and a joint Lords–Commons committee established to reconsider issue. Communications Bill proposes one of world's most liberal regulatory regimes. Resignation of Deputy PM John Prescott from RMT union highlights growing union disaffection with government.

Home Secretary David Blunkett withdraws controversial draft order (snooper's charter) giving public bodies access to telephone and internet records. Queen's Golden Jubilee celebrations judged a success with huge public participation, but bizarre intervention of Queen to halt trial of Princess Diana's butler later throws monarchy into fresh controversy. Disappointing outcome from UN Johannesburg summit on sustainable development. Surprising revelation by Edwina Currie of former affair with John Major. Police raid Stormont offices of

Sinn Féin on suspicion of espionage. Stormont suspended for fourth time since devolution. Iain Duncan Smith troubled by rivals within his party. Some modernization of Commons ends unsocial hours and allows bills to 'roll over'. Criminal Justice Bill reduces grounds for jury exemption but curtails right to trial by jury.

After a tense year marked by US threats (backed by Britain) to attack Iraq, UN weapons inspectors eventually allowed in. President Bush remains sceptical. Firefighters' strike over a 40 per cent pay claim precipitates confrontation with government and reveals growing hostility from some unions towards New Labour. Cherie Blair hounded by media over dealings with an Australian con man.

Glossary

Words in **bold** type within entries refer to terms or concepts found elsewhere in the Glossary. Remember to consult the Index to locate more information and for terms (especially institutions and organizations) not included here.

absolute majority A majority greater than 50 per cent.

abstention Deliberate non-voting.

accountability Answerability to a higher authority (the people, in a **democracy**).

Act of Parliament Law passed by Parliament.

administrative law Concerned with cases between the citizen and the state.

administrative tribunal Deals with citizens' grievances against the state.

advanced capitalism Modern, hi-tech, multinational **capitalist** economy. Distinguished from late capitalism (capitalism in crisis and decay). Technology makes workers less important, increasing opportunities for the few to amass wealth.

adversary politics Description of British **two-party system**, seeing it based on argument rather than compromise between parties.

advisory body Set up by government to conduct an inquiry and come up with recommendations.

agency capture Control of an agency by the enterprise it is supposed to be regulating.

anarchy Society without government.

anthropocentrism Seeing human life as the principle criterion of value.

aristocracy Government by an enlightened elite.

arm's length administration Quasi-autonomous agencies running various state services with little government interference.

art of the possible Classic aphorism used to define politics, drawing attention to compromising and wheeling and dealing evident in real world.

authoritative allocation of values Definition of politics. May be contrasted with **market** allocation in that allocation is on the basis of political authority, rather than ability to pay.

authority Form of **power** distinguished by the fact that it is accepted by those over whom it is held.

autonomy   Self-determination; usually of a state.

behaviouralism   Approach to social sciences, including political science, taking only observable phenomena as its data.

bill   The form in which legislation is introduced into Parliament (when passed it becomes an **Act**).

Bill of Rights   Constitutional document guaranteeing citizens' rights.

bipartisan   Consisting of two parties.

block vote   Large number of votes tied together and cast at one go; a controversial feature of the Labour Party conference.

body corporate   Organization with a persona in law (e.g. local authority).

borough   Historic **local government** area based on a town which had gained a royal charter entitling it to certain freedoms.

bourgeoisie   French term for town-dweller appropriated by Marx to denote a capital-owning social **class** spawned by the industrial revolution; to Marx, the ruling class.

broadsheet   Quality newspaper.

budgetary process   Method whereby government determines its annual expenditure and sources of income.

bureaucracy   Strictly speaking, rule by officials. Weber argued that the growth of **socialism** would result in such rule. Used without pejorative connotations to denote a large hierarchical organization.

by-election   Election held following death or retirement of sitting member.

Cabinet   Group of leading ministers heading the government.

cabinet government   Government by a team rather than a single ruler; *see also* **collective responsibility**.

Cabinet Secretariat   Special part of **civil service** responsible for servicing the Cabinet and its committees; can be influential in policy.

Cabinet Secretary   Head of **Cabinet Secretariat** (and of civil service).

cadre party   Party in Parliament consisting of MPs; may or may not have a mass membership outside Parliament.

capitalism   Mode of production in which private individuals, rather than the state, own materials necessary to produce what society needs for its survival.

case law   Law resulting from previous judicial decisions (precedent).

central–local relations   Relationship between central government and its territorially based agencies; most often in connection with **local government**.

centralization   Central government's dominance over other state agencies.

ceremonial   Ostentatious aspects of government usually with little importance for decision-making, but often crucial for **legitimation**.

Chartism   Working-class organization founded in 1836 demanding universal male suffrage without property qualification.

citizen   Member of a **state**, with rights and obligations.

city-state   Political unit about which most Ancient Greek political thought was written; very small and not comparable with complex modern **nation-states**.

civic culture   Political culture in which people have confidence in, and will cooperate with, government.

civil jurisdiction   Pertaining to that part of the legal system concerned with cases involving one citizen against another.

civil rights   Rights accruing to individuals as **citizens** which may not be infringed by other citizens or by the state.

civil service   The central government **bureaucracy**.

civil society   That part of social life outside the control of the state.

class   Section of population sharing a common social status; almost invariably associated with socioeconomic factors. Usually divided into upper, middle and lower. In

Marxist terms, seen as a dichotomy arising from the position of individuals in the productive process; *see also* **bourgeoisie** and **proletariat**.

coalition   Parties working together as a government.

cold war   State of East–West tension beginning after the second world war.

collective consumption   Services consumed collectively by the population (e.g. education).

collective investment   State role in investing in the economy (e.g. road building).

collective responsibility   Constitutional convention reflecting the idea of **cabinet government**; entails various things including the idea that ministers participate in collective **policy-making**.

collectivism   Sees the collectivity, rather than the individual, as the essential human unit.

colonialism   Form of domination of one state over another associated with **imperialism**; may be established after military conquest or economic penetration of a weak economy (**neocolonialism**).

common law   Law formed on the basis of precedents set in previous cases; reflects the accumulated wisdom of the past rather than legislation.

communism   Ideology of equality and the common ownership of property.

community policing   Form of policing in which the force becomes deeply involved in community affairs to establish mutual trust.

comparative advantage   Economic theory underpinning the philosophy of **free trade** associated with Adam Smith, arguing that if each nation produces that which it does most efficiently, the world will maximize its wealth.

consensus   Harmony between possibly opposed factions. The era of consensus politics in Britain (late 1940s– mid-1970s) saw Labour and Conservatives in agreement over a wide range of policies.

consensus policing   Policing based on gaining the consent and cooperation of those policed rather than force.

conservatism   View of politics, society and the constitution which believes in the wisdom of the past and is suspicious of radical change. Has deep intellectual antecedents; associated particularly with Edmund Burke and the ideology of the Conservative Party.

consociationalism   Two or more communities living harmoniously in the same state (as in Belgium).

constituency   Territorial electoral division (e.g. Glasgow Hillhead). Can also denote the nature of a politician's support (e.g. 'small businessmen are the natural constituency of the Conservative Party').

constitution   Set of rules, customs and conventions defining the composition and powers of state institutions and regulating their relationships to each other and to private **citizens**; unwritten constitutions do not exist as a single document but in the form of custom and practice and various laws.

constitutional amendment   Formal change to the **constitution**.

constitutional convention   Regularly observed practices regarded as part of the **constitution**.

constitutional government   Government constrained by rules and procedures laid down in the **constitution**; contrasted with arbitrary government.

constitutional monarchy   Political system in which a **monarchy** is so constrained by the **constitution** that it plays no part in decision-making.

consultative body   Set up by government to bring together interested parties for policy discussions.

consumer voting model   Voting behaviour model seeing voters as shoppers in a political market-place, choosing parties on the basis of their shop windows (**manifestos**, etc.).

contracting-out   Privatization of work previously done by the state, often enforced, as in CCT (compulsory competitive tendering in local government) and market-testing (civil service).

core executive   The complex network of people, relationships, structures and procedures around the **Cabinet**.

corporate management   Form of management urged upon **local government** which seeks to unify control of its services under a single chief executive.

corporatism   Theory of **pressure group** activity in which the government incorporates certain groups into the **policy-making** process.

county   Top-tier **local authority** with ancient lineage.

criminal jurisdiction   Pertaining to the criminal law in which the crimes are against the state rather than against a particular person.

cross-bencher   Member of House of Lords disdaining allegiance to any party.

cross-border body   Body set up to consider certain policy areas across national boundaries (e.g. N. Ireland and Eire).

cross-class voting   Phenomenon whereby individuals belonging to one social class vote for a party ostensibly supporting the interests of another.

D-notice system   Voluntary code whereby the press restrains itself from publishing material on defence which officials want kept secret.

de facto   In actuality.

de jure   According to law.

deference   Belief amongst citizens that they should not play much part in government; they are happy to leave things to those whom they believe to be superior.

delegated legislation   Laws made by **bureaucrats** with power delegated by Parliament.

demand management   Keynesian principle whereby government uses its financial influence in the economy to

manipulate the level of aggregate demand to maintain full employment.

democracy   Rule by all **citizens** in a community.

demos   Greek word for the people as a collectivity (hence **democracy**).

deregulation   Removal by the state of controls tending to protect state services from competition (e.g. local authority transport services).

détente   Reduction of tension between states; used particularly of East–West relations during the **cold war**.

determinism   Doctrine that everything that happens does so because of other forces; downgrades human free choice (**voluntarism**) as a factor explaining events.

devolution   State authority passed down from a higher level of government to sub-national areas; *see also* **federalism**.

dignified and **efficient elements** Distinction between those elements of a **constitution** which have no direct impact on **policy-making** and those which do; does *not* mean that the dignified elements are unimportant.

direct democracy   Form of **democracy** in which **citizens** actually take part in making decisions; almost impossible in the real world.

ecocentrism   Placing nature in general before human life as a criterion of value.

economic and monetary union (**EMU**)   The linking of economies and currencies of a number of states; a major project of the EU.

economic planning   Government intervention in the economy to achieve certain future goals, such as full employment, economic growth, balance of payments; opposed by **monetarists**.

elected mayor   Politician elected by all citizens in a local government area to lead the authority.

election campaign   Efforts made by **political parties** in the run-up to an election to win voters' support.

electoral quota   Number of votes a candidate requires to be elected under certain systems of **proportional representation**.

electoral swing   Calculation measuring the percentage shift of party support across the country; may or may not be uniform.

electoral volatility   Condition in which the electorate cannot be relied upon to vote regularly for the same party.

elitism   Body of thought on **power** in society which sees as inevitable the formation of elites which will consolidate their positions, collude with each other and control government in their own interests.

embourgeoisement   Process whereby members of the working class acquire middle-class habits and characteristics.

endogenous explanation   Explaining national political events solely in terms of factors internal to the country.

Enlightenment   Seventeenth-century European intellectual movement which saw a flowering of science and faith in rational thought and progress in social and political life.

entrenchment   Often used of **constitutions** to denote provisions that cannot be changed by the normal process of law-making; absent in the UK.

environmentalism   **Ideology** derived from ecology aiming to prevent human despoilation of life forms.

Establishment   Imprecise term used for a narrow, upper-middle-class elite with much power in society.

Eurosceptic   Those opposed to European **federalism**.

exchange rate   Value of one currency in terms of that of another country.

Exchange Rate Mechanism (ERM)   A system of fixing currencies against each other on the way to complete **economic and monetary union**.

executive   That part of an organization responsible for policy-making; in politics usually with reference to the

government, or more narrowly, the **Cabinet**; *see also* **core executive**.

executive agency   Civil service body created to administer functions hived off from the main body of the civil service (often referred to in the UK as Next Steps agencies).

executive body   Quango responsible for actually administering some state function (e.g. Arts Council).

exogenous explanation   Explanation of internal political events based on external factors.

Fabianism   Approach to social and political reform advocated by the Fabian Society, stressing small incremental advances rather than revolution.

faction   Segment within a party; usually considered more hard-edged than a **tendency**.

false consciousness   Errors of perception concerning one's self-interest; may explain why working-class people support the Conservatives.

fascism   **Ideology** espousing nationalism, militarism and demagoguery.

federalism   Process whereby states voluntarily pool their **sovereignty**, thereby creating a higher level of government.

feminism   **Ideology** supporting equal rights for women.

fiscal policy   Taxation policy; may be used in pursuit of various objectives (e.g. full employment or pollution control).

floating voter   Member of electorate who easily changes party allegiance.

franchise   The right to vote in elections.

free press   Doctrine that newspapers should be free to print what they like without government direction or censorship.

free trade   Free flow of goods in international trade, unimpeded by tariff barriers; has fuelled much political controversy.

Freedom of Information Act   Legislation giving citizens a legal 'right to know' much of what happens in government.

functionalism Body of theory looking primarily at the way institutions and practices contribute to the working of a social or political system; may be contrasted with an institutional approach.

Gemeinschaft **and** *Gesellschaft* German terms meaning community (based on bonds of affection, kinship, etc.) and association (based on contract), respectively.

General Will A shared feeling/view amongst people, beyond self-interest, of their common good; central to thinking of Rousseau.

generalist Civil servant with no special or professional skill; often holding a high position within the British service.

globalization Growing interdependence of individuals, countries and regions of the world.

'Golden Age' of Parliament Period approximately between the 1832 and 1867 Reform Acts when Parliament appeared to have the power to bring down governments; ended by the rise of party discipline.

golden share State-owned share in a privatized company enabling it to have control over certain key decisions.

governance The act of governing, whether by a formal **government** of elected ministers and officials or by other holders of power such as the IMF. With inter-state groupings, such as the EU, we can speak of multi-level governance.

government (1) The process of ruling a community; (2) An elite group formally recognized as being in control of the community.

green paper Government document to stimulate public debate; *see also* **white paper**.

Hansard Official record of parliamentary proceedings.

hegemony Rule or domination often of one state over others; used by neo-Marxists of a **class** dominating society by holding leading positions in various walks of life.

hereditary peer Member of House of Lords by right of inheritance of title.

hidden hand Used by Adam Smith and neoliberal economists to account for the order which comes out of an unregulated **market**.

historical materialism Marx's 'scientific' theory of history, which sees it shaped by the means of production.

hiving off Chopping off pieces of public **bureaucracy** to form semi-autonomous **executive agencies** responsible for some clearly defined block of work.

holism Theory stressing the *whole* of the object of study rather than the parts.

ideology Political doctrine claiming to give a universally applicable theory of people and society from which may be derived a programme of political action.

imperialism Extension of the **hegemony** of one country by conquest (military or economic) and imposed rule over others.

incrementalism Theory of government decision-making holding that radical steps are impossible or undesirable.

individualism Doctrine seeing the individual as the prime unit in morality and politics; underlies the theories of classical economists in which individuals pursue their own self-interest.

industrial revolution Period between 1760 and 1860 (approximately) based on multiple innovations in production methods and technologies; revolutionary in the social transformation it induced.

inflation General rise in prices throughout the economy; often measured by the Retail Price Index (RPI).

inner cabinet Unofficial **Cabinet** consisting of the PM and a few chosen members of the government.

insider group **Pressure group** with a close, secretive relationship with government.

institutional racism   Entrenched practices reflecting **racist** attitudes, such as discrimination in job appointments or immigration procedures.

instrumental explanation   An interpretation of politics seeing the state as an instrument of some greater power behind the throne; in **Marxism**, this is the **bourgeoisie**.

interest aggregation   Bringing interests together to construct a body sufficiently large (party or group) to have political clout.

interest group   Association of people with some common concern; *see also* **pressure group**.

intergovernmental organization   Association of governments in which each retains its **sovereignty**; *see also* **supragovernmental**.

international associations   Associations formed across nations such as NATO and the United Nations Organization.

Iron Curtain   Powerful image employed by the West to describe the separation between the communist East European bloc and the capitalist West.

iron law of oligarchy   Sociological 'law' postulated by Michels stating that in any **political party** a small elite would eventually gain control.

jingoism   Chauvinistic militarism (from an anti-Russian music-hall song of 1878).

judicial impartiality   Constitutional principle that judges are impartial with regard to the interests within society.

judicial review   Part of the principle of the **separation of powers**. The **judiciary** is able to review legislation and actions of the **executive** in terms of their constitutionality. In Britain this is restricted to actions of the executive.

judiciary   The body of judges.

jury   Part of judicial system; highly democratic in that the jury is selected at random, so does not include power-seekers in the way electoral politics does. Used by the Greeks not only for legal decisions.

Keynesianism   Economic theory arguing that the free **market**, left to itself, will not automatically work for the benefit of all. Consequently the state must intervene to achieve desirable social ends, particularly full employment.

laissez-faire   Slogan adopted by classical economists; the state should keep out of the private **capitalist** economy.

legislative process   Series of stages by which a **bill** becomes an **Act**; entails passage through Parliament.

legislature   Institution formally charged with making laws – Parliament.

legitimacy   Quality of being popularly accepted as rightful and just.

legitimation   Actions and processes designed to secure **legitimacy**; may entail deception.

Leviathan   Huge sea monster – Hobbes's term for the all-powerful ruler.

liberal democracy   Form of **democracy** based upon elections and representative institutions which places great stress upon the idea of individual freedom defined in terms of a *limited* role for government and the state; linked with idea of **market** economy.

liberalism   **Ideology** seeing minimum government and individual freedom as its prime virtues; attractive to **capitalism** by permitting the operation of the free **market**.

life peer   Member of House of Lords, ennobled for life but not able to pass the title down.

limited government   Government restrained from arbitrary rule; accomplished variously by **rule of law**, **separation of powers**, or a **constitution**.

lobby   (verb) To seek the ear of a member of government; (noun) (cap.) The 'club' of parliamentary correspondents who receive unattributable briefings from government.

lobbyist One practised in the art and craft of dealing with MPs and ministers on behalf of **pressure groups**.

local authority Body responsible for delivering local government services; comprises a work force, a **bureaucracy** and an elected council.

local governance Broadly, the function of various locally based public bodies, elected *and* unelected.

local government Self-government by the people of some subnational territorial unit within the state through an elected council.

local politics Party and pressure-group activity, demonstrating, bargaining, and lobbying taking place within a unit of **local government**.

long boom Period from the end of the second world war to the beginning of the 1970s when the developed **capitalist** countries enjoyed rising standards of living and a great rise in material wealth.

machinery of government Institutions through which **government** works; **civil service** departments, **local authorities**, etc.

macroeconomic policy Policy concerning the aggregate performance of the national economy.

maladministration Bad administration causing inconvenience or suffering.

managerialism Approach to government in which the public sector tries to ape private-sector methods; tends to reduce elected politicians' authority.

mandarin Term used to describe members of the upper echelons of the **civil service**. Originally used of officials in imperial China.

mandate Approval for a set of policies gained by a party elected to office on the basis of a **manifesto**.

manifesto Set of policy promises made by the parties to entice electors.

market Key mechanism (based on price) in classical economic theory; it is said to work as if controlled by a **hidden hand** to achieve optimum allocation of the resources in society.

market-testing Examination of public-sector functions to see if they can be **contracted out** to the private sector.

Marxism Body of thought with many strands deriving from the ideas of Marx; sees the private ownership of materials needed for production as the key explaining society and politics.

mass party **Political party** organized throughout the country with thousands of members.

media mogul Owner of newspaper and broadcasting empires; often global in scope.

MEP Member of the European Parliament.

mercantilism Economic doctrine favoured in the sixteenth and seventeenth centuries. Argued that a country should seek to export as much as possible, while restricting imports. Did not suit the **capitalists** of the **industrial revolution**, who favoured **free trade**.

meritocracy Literally, rule by the most able; more colloquially, refers to a system (educational or social) where promotion is based on merit, usually measured by examination performance.

militarization Used of police to refer to greater use of defensive and offensive weapons and militaristic tactics.

mind politics Term used in this book to denote an arena of political activity concerned with influencing what people think, rather than allocating values.

ministerial adviser Expert from outside the **civil service** who advises ministers on policy; may adopt openly partisan stance and is not welcomed by the **bureaucrats**.

ministerial responsibility Doctrine declaring that the minister in a government department is the only one who should be questioned, praised and blamed. May be expected to resign where extreme shortcomings are revealed (e.g. Lord Carrington over the Falklands war).

minority government   Government by a party without an **absolute majority**, relying on support from other parties.

mixed economy   One in which **capitalism** is modified so that some of the productive capital in society is owned by the people (e.g. Britain before the **privatization** programme).

mob rule   The down side of **democracy**; term used by opponents of democracy.

monarchy   Rule by a single person; usually hereditary.

monetarism   Economic doctrine holding that governments should do little in the economy, being content to control the rate at which the quantity of money in circulation rises. Everything else is then said to take care of itself through the **market**.

money supply   Quantity of money in the economy, believed to be causally linked with **inflation**.

monopoly   An industry in which a single firm exists with no competition to keep its prices in control.

multi-member constituency   Electoral district returning more than one candidate; a prerequisite of **proportional representation**.

multi-party system   **Political system** in which three or more parties contest elections and gain seats in the assembly. Often associated with coalition government.

multipolarity   Describes the fragmented world after the breakdown of the bipolar East–West stand-off known as the **cold war**.

nation-state   The state as understood today; to be contrasted with the **city-states** of Ancient Greece.

nationalism   Ideological attachment to the nation and its interests.

nationalization   State acquisition of private property or a business within its territory.

natural law   System of law deriving from human nature, rather than invented by reason; an idea present in political thought from the time of the Ancient Greeks. The great Roman statesman Cicero (106–43 BC) spoke of 'right reason – which is in accordance with nature, and is unchangeable and eternal' (*Republic*, III, 22).

natural monopoly   An industry where the technical problems of competition are so great that it is better for society if **monopoly** is permitted (e.g. telecommunications, railways).

natural rights   Rights (say to life or property) that some philosophers believe to come from nature rather than from government.

neocolonialism   Form of domination characteristic of the post-war era in which **capitalists** from the developed world effectively dominate the less-developed economies through **multinational corporations**.

neocorporatism   Used to distinguish the practice of post-war **corporatism** from the pre-war fascist variant.

neoliberalism   **Ideology** aiming to replace **social democracy** by returning to *laissez-faire* principles; *see also* **New Right** and **Thatcherism**.

neopluralism   A theoretical approach that gives a critical acceptance to traditional **pluralism** and also recognizes overarching forms of power such as that of capital.

New Right   Term for a resurgence of anti-social-democratic thought; in many ways restating the free-market ideas of the nineteenth-century economists.

New World Order   Term used by President Bush (senior) to denote the post-cold-war world based on **capitalism**.

news management   The practice of politicians and their press secretaries attempting to influence the reporting of politics; *see also* **spin doctor**.

non-aligned world   Group of nations professing neutrality during the **cold war**.

north–south divide   Political gulf between the north and south of Britain emerging from the late 1970s.

official censorship   Government restriction on what people can see, hear or read.

official secrecy   The keeping of state secrets; justified on the grounds of national security.

oligarchy   Oppressive rule by a small group.

ombudsman   Common term for **citizens'** trouble-shooter (e.g. the Parliamentary Commissioner for Administration) who investigates complaints of **maladministration**.

opinion poll   Survey of public opinion on some issue by use of sampling techniques.

organic system   System which has grown naturally rather than having been designed by people.

outsider group   **Pressure group** that government is unwilling to listen to.

paramilitary   Militaristic methods and equipment used by non-military organizations (e.g. Special Patrol Group).

parish   One of the oldest units of **local government**; very small and based on the area around the church.

parliamentary privilege   Set of privileges accorded to MPs; supposed to enable them to perform better as representatives, without fear of, say, libel.

parliamentary questions   (PQs) Questions from MPs to members of the government on a rota system.

parliamentary sovereignty   Belief that Parliament is the supreme source of **sovereignty** in the **constitution**. Dicey believed this to be the only morally defensible version of sovereignty in a **democracy**.

partisan dealignment   Tendency of voters to break away from stable (especially class-based) identification with a **political party**.

partisanship   Political bias, as in newspaper reporting and editorial comment.

partition   Political division of a country; as in Ireland.

party conference   Usually the highly publicized annual meeting of all elements of the mass party organization.

party discipline   MPs' obedience to their party leadership.

party identification   Used by psephologists to describe voters who always vote for the same party regardless.

party list   Feature in **proportional representation** electoral systems; displays the candidates of a party, sometimes in order of preference.

party system   Usually defined in terms of the number of parties taking part in the political fray.

patriarchy   Society in which men dominate women.

patronage   Making appointments on the basis of favour rather than electoral choice or expertise.

peak organization   Umbrella organization formed by the association of a number of **pressure groups** (e.g. the TUC).

peer group   Body of individuals equal in some significant respect (age, rank, status etc.).

pluralism   Theory of politics seeing **pressure groups** as central to the political process; generally holds their effect to be benign and democratic.

pluralist stagnation   Right-wing explanation for Britain's post-war economic failure claiming that too many **pressure groups** were being permitted to voice their demands.

police complaints procedure   System for handling complaints against the police.

police culture   Characteristic set of attitudes held by the police.

police state Totalitarian state where police are under control of the government.

Policy Cabinet A small **Cabinet** of about five, the members of which are concerned with the whole area of government policy, rather than being responsible for specific departments. Has never really been tried.

policy implementation Carrying out government policy; formally the task of the **bureaucracy**.

policy-making Essential act of **government** in the modern state. The extent to which government is free to make policy is a matter of debate.

policy networks Loosely knit and changing complexes of interest groups, politicians and officials brought together, sometimes in harmony sometimes in conflict, over policy issues.

polis Ancient Greek term for city.

political culture Set of ideas and attitudes held towards the **political system**.

political party Group formed for the purpose of gaining political office, usually through winning elections.

political philosophy Generalized answers to fundamental questions such as the nature of justice.

political science May loosely be used to denote the study of politics generally, or more rigorously to indicate the application of scientific method.

political socialization Social process through which individuals develop an awareness of political values, norms and processes; continues throughout life.

political system A whole consisting of institutions of **government** and the society they serve, a concept stressing the **holistic** nature of politics; no part can be properly understood without reference to its place in the whole.

political theory Theories about political institutions, law, **constitutions, democracy**, etc.

political thought Corpus of theories whereby people have sought to explain political behaviour, values, and mechanisms and institutions of **political systems**.

politicization Process whereby an institution may become actively involved in politics (e.g. the **civil service** and police).

politics–administration dichotomy Long-standing distinction between making policy and carrying it out; underlies **separation of powers** between **executive** and **legislature**.

polity The political organization of a state.

poll tax Tax placed on all citizens equally regardless of ability to pay; imposed in 1381 (causing Peasants' Revolt) and as community charge in late 1980s.

polyarchy Robert Dahl's term for a form of **pluralism** seeing in groups a more effective balance of power than in the **constitution**.

populism Form of **government** supposed to enshrine the will of the people. Some political leaders have an instinctively populist appeal. Presidents, where directly elected, may claim populist mandate.

positive law Law believed to have been made by applying human reason rather than by some metaphysical power such as God; *see also* **natural law**.

postmodernism A vaguely defined stage beyond the modernism of the **Enlightenment**.

power Key concept in the study and practice of politics; the ability to achieve some desired effect regardless of opposition. May take many forms.

power-sharing executive An **executive** formed to reflect both majority and minority interests.

preferential voting System that permits voters to indicate alternative preferences.

presidential government   System of **government** by one person, usually elected directly by the people.

press baron   **Capitalist** owner of large-circulation newspapers; today empires extend into the media and entertainments industry, hence **media mogul**.

pressure group   Association wishing to influence government policy.

primary elections   Elections held before the real elections to choose the candidates.

private finance initiative (PFI)   Means of financing state capital projects (eg. school buildings) by 'renting' them from private-sector providers; used as an alternative to borrowing.

private members' bills   **Bills** introduced into Parliament by MPs in their personal capacity rather than by the government; rarely get onto the statute book.

privatization   Transfer of state-owned assets into private hands.

proletariat   Marx's term for the working class.

promotional group   **Pressure group** concerned with promoting an ideal rather than the self-interest of its members (e.g. RSPCA).

proportional representation   Electoral system intended to create an assembly that accurately reflects the level of support for the parties in the country.

psephology   Study of elections and electoral behaviour.

public choice theory   Theory seeking to explain and analyse politics on the basis of the **individualist** premises of classical economics.

public corporation   Body created by government in the image of a private company but owned by the state, rather than private shareholders.

public expenditure   State expenditure by the state, including redistribution through transfer payments.

public inquiry   Official inquiry into some matter of public concern.

public interest   Vague term meaning the collective interest of society. What is, or is not, in the public interest is often a matter of judgement. In the Ponting case, the judge denied the right of a citizen to make up his own mind on the matter, declaring that only the government could decide.

public order   Well-regulated civic life.

public–private partnership (PPP)   Means of providing a public service through involvement of the private sector.

public sector borrowing requirement (PSBR)   Amount of money government wishes to borrow in any year.

qualified majority voting   Voting in which more than a simple majority is required for success.

quango   Quasi-Autonomous Non-Government Organization.

Queen's Speech   Great day in the ceremonial calendar of British politics, marking the annual opening of Parliament and outlining the government's proposed programme for the year.

Question Time   One-hour period in the Parliamentary timetable when MPs address questions to ministers.

racism   Attribution of characteristics of superiority and inferiority to members of particular races.

rational decision-making   Making a decision on the basis of reason rather than self-interest, political advantage or prejudice.

rationalism   Faith in reason, as opposed to religion or superstition.

redress of grievance   Means taken to right a wrong (often inflicted by the state on a citizen).

referendum   Popular vote on a particular issue rather than to choose a representative; being used increasingly in Britain.

regionalism   Giving political power to geographical regions of the state; *see also* **devolution**.

regulation   A major government role; instead of providing a service, exerts control over those that do (often through agencies).

representative government   Form of **government** in which a minority acts on behalf of the rest of the population.

republic   State in which supreme power rests with the people; contrasted with **monarchy**.

royal prerogative   Set of special privileges enjoyed exclusively by the monarch since medieval times; today many of the most important are effectively held by the PM.

rule of law   Constitutional doctrine that the ultimate source of **authority** in the state is the law; kings and governments are themselves subject to it.

sectional group   **Pressure group** composed of members of society from some sectional interest.

sectoral cleavage   An alternative to class as an explanation of voting behaviour.

security services   State agencies concerned with espionage (MI5 and MI6).

select committee   Committee of MPs established to undertake some particular task on behalf of Parliament and scrutinize the **executive**.

selective incentive   Inducement made by a **pressure group** or **political party** to recruit and retain members.

separation of powers   Constitutional doctrine in which the various functions of **government** (rule-making, rule execution and judging) are placed with separate institutions in order to check each other and prevent despotism.

separatism   Desire to be governed as a separate state; *see also* **devolution**.

sexism   Attitudes falsely ascribing certain attributes to one sex, usually to justify inequality.

Shadow Cabinet   Opposition frontbench team.

single currency   The result of a joining together of currencies of different states as in the creation of the euro.

single-party system   **Political system** in which one party dominates; under totalitarian regimes may actually eliminate its rivals by force.

sleaze   Term increasingly used to describe corrupt or dubious behaviour by politician.

social class   *See* **class**.

social democracy   Ideology of moderate **socialism**, mixed economy, welfare state, etc.

socialism   Egalitarian **ideology** under which the state actively cares for citizens. Reformist socialism aims to achieve this by reform of liberal institutions rather than violent confrontation (*see also* **Fabianism**); revolutionary socialism aims to overthrow capitalism by force.

sovereignty   Concept of the ultimate source of **power** within the state.

'special relationship'   Britain's view of its relationship with the US.

spin doctor   Politician's aide concerned with **news management**.

spoils system   System of **patronage** in which election victors distribute offices to those who have assisted them.

sponsorship   Relationship of MPs to various non-party organizations (e.g. some Labour MPs are sponsored by trade unions).

standing committees of Parliament   Committees of MPs considering **bills** during their process through Parliament (the committee stage).

state   In simple terms, a sovereign community, within a defined territory.

state of nature   A condition imagined by some philosophers (Hobbes, Locke, Rousseau) as a basis for determining what the role of **government** should be.

statute   Laws made by Parliament.

structural explanation   Explanation of political behaviour seeing it as determined by the structure in which it takes place (e.g. the **capitalist** economy).

subgovernment Community formed by those concerned with policy in a certain area (**insider pressure groups, civil service**, the specialist press, ministers, etc.); sometimes termed a policy community.

subsidiarity Principle that the powers of different levels of government should always be placed as low (that is as close to the people) as is compatible with efficiency.

subversion Attempt to overthrow the government by unlawful means.

suffragette Woman active in the cause of women's voting rights.

supragovernmental organizations International authorities standing above national governments.

synopticity Taking an analytical perspective that sees all aspects of politics as belonging to a larger whole.

system Set of elements interacting together to constitute a larger whole.

tabloid Popular newspapers; also called 'redtops' or 'the gutter press'.

tactical voting Behaviour designed to keep out a disliked candidate by supporting the rival most likely to defeat him or her.

tendency Used in politics to designate sections within parties (e.g. Militant Tendency).

territorial management Government role in balancing the **devolutionary** claims of different regions.

Thatcherism Neoliberalism as espoused by Margaret Thatcher.

think-tank Body of intellectuals set up privately or by government to consider public policy alternatives.

'third way' Ideological position espoused by New Labour (and others) claiming to be between **social democracy** and **neoliberalism**.

transnational corporation Private company operating in the global economy and not located within any particular country.

tripartism Form of **corporatism** developed in Britain in the immediate post-war decades involving government, employers and unions.

two-party system **Political system** in which two equal parties monopolize in terms of votes and parliamentary seats.

tyranny Oppressive rule.

ultra vires Legal principle restraining public bodies within a framework of powers prescribed by the **sovereign** body.

underclass Disadvantaged class developing during the 1980s (unemployed, ethnic minorities, etc.).

unitary system **Local government** areal structure without subdivisions.

utilitarianism Moral philosophy preached by Bentham, J. S. Mill and others; sees the maximization of utility (happiness) as the basis for all law, morality, political institutions and right behaviour.

variable geometry Term used to describe a process whereby groups of members move towards integration at differing speeds (applied to EU).

violence, state Legitimate use of force against citizens (e.g. police).

voluntarism View that humans control their own actions, rather than acting as the system forces them to do.

welfare statism A social democratic kind of ideology.

West Lothian question Term used to describe the problem of Scottish MPs being able to vote on certain English matters at Westminster while English MPs cannot vote on issues coming before the Scottish Parliament.

whip MP charged with maintaining **party discipline** in Parliament.

white paper Document published by government to outline and explain its policy; *see also* **green paper**.

world economy The idea that all countries are interlocked through trade.

xenophobia Fear (and often hatred) of foreigners.

Bibliography

Abrahams, M. (1958) 'Class distinctions in Britain', in *The Future of the Welfare State*, London, Conservative Political Centre.

Adonis, A. (1993) *Parliament Today*, Manchester, Manchester University Press.

Adonis, A. and Pollard, S. (1997) *A Class Act: The Myth of Britain's Classless Society*, London, Hamish Hamilton.

Ahmed, K. (2002) 'Top lawyers attack legal reform plans', *Observer* (23 June).

Ahmed, K. and Thompson, T. (2001) 'Police to be armed with sleep darts', *Observer* (15 July).

Alderman, K. (1998) 'The Conservative Party leadership election of 1997', *Parliamentary Affairs* 51(1), 1–16.

Alderman, K. and Carter, N. (1994) 'The Labour Party and the trade unions: loosening the ties', *Parliamentary Affairs*, 47(4), 321–37.

Alderson, J. (1994) *A New Cromwell: The Centralisation of the Police*, London, Charter88.

Almond, G. A. and Verba, S. (1963) *The Civic Culture*, Princeton, NJ, Princeton University Press.

Almond, G. A. and Verba, S. (eds) (1980) *The Civic Culture Revisited*, Boston, MA, Little Brown

Althusser, L. (1969) *For Marx* (transl. B. Brewster), Harmondsworth, Penguin.

Amery, L. S. (1947) *Thoughts on the Constitution*, London, Oxford University Press.

Arblaster, A. (1984) *The Rise and Decline of Western Liberalism*, Oxford, Blackwell.

Armstrong, P., Glyn, A. and Harrison, J. (1991) *Capitalism Since 1945*, Oxford, Blackwell.

Atkinson, A. B. and Harrison, A. J. (1978) *The Distribution of Personal Wealth in Britain*, Cambridge, Cambridge University Press.

Audit Commission (1990) *We Can't Go On Meeting Like This*, Abingdon, Audit Commission Publications.

Audit Commission (1993a) *Passing the Buck: The Impact of Standard Spending Assessments on Economy, Efficiency and Effectiveness*, London, HMSO.

Audit Commission (1993b) *Realising the Benefits of Competition: The Client Role for Contracted Services*, London, HMSO.

Auerback, M. M. (1959) *The Conservatism Illusion*, New York, Colombia University Press.

Aughey, A. (2001) *Nationalism, Devolution and the Challenge to the United Kingdom State*, London, Pluto.

Auld, R. (chair) (2001) *Review of the Criminal Courts of England and Wales*, London, Stationery Office.

Bagehot, W. (1963) *The English Constitution*, London, Fontana (first published 1867).

Baggott, R. (1995a) 'From confrontation to consultation: pressure groups from Thatcher to Major', *Parliamentary Affairs*, 48(3), 484–502.

Baggott, R. (1995b) *Pressure Groups Today*, Manchester, Manchester University Press.

Bains, M. A. (chairman) (1972) *The New Local Authorities: Management and Structure*, London, HMSO.

Baird, V. (1998) 'Money, markets and madness', *New Internationalist*, no. 306 (Oct.), 7–8.

Baker, D. and Fountain, I. (1996) 'Eton gent or Essex man? The Conservative parliamentary elite', in Ludlam and Smith (eds), pp. 86–97.

Baldwin, R. and Kinsey, R. (1982) *Police Powers and Politics*, London, Quartet.

Balogh, T. (1968) 'The apotheosis of the dilettante: the establishment of mandarins', in Thomas, H. (ed.), *Crisis in the Civil Service*, London, Anthony Blond.

Bannister, N. (1993) 'Clean water challenge', *Guardian* (14 July).

Banton, M. (1985) *Promoting Racial Harmony*, Cambridge, Cambridge University Press.

Bar Council (1989) *Quality of Justice: The Bar's Response*, London, Bar Council.

Barberis, P. (ed.) (1996) *The Whitehall Reader*, Buckingham, Open University Press.

Barker, R. (1994) *Politics, Peoples and Government*, Basingstoke, Macmillan.

Barnett, A. (1982) *Iron Britannia*, London, Allison and Busby.

Barnett, S. and Gaber, I. (2001) *Westminster Tales: The Twentieth Century Crisis in Political Journalism*, London, Continuum.

Barrett Brown, M. (2001) *The Captive Party: How Labour was Taken Over by Capital*, Nottingham, Socialist Renewal.

Barron, J., Crawley, G. and Wood, T. (1991) *Councillors in Crisis*, Basingstoke, Macmillan.

Bartle, J. and Griffiths, D. (eds) (2001) *Political Communications Transformed: From Morrison to Mandelson*, Basingstoke, Palgrave.

Bauman, Z. (2000) *Community: Seeking Security in an Insecure World*, Cambridge, Polity.

Baxter, J. and Koffman, L. (eds) (1985) *Police, the Constitution and the Community*, Abingdon, Professional Books.

Beer, S. H. (1956) 'Pressure groups and parties in Britain', *American Political Science Review*, 50(1), 1–23.

Beer, S. H. (1965) *Modern British Politics*, London, Faber.

Beer, S. H. (1982) *Britain Against Itself*, London, Faber.

Bell, Daniel (1960) *The End of Ideology*, Glencoe, IL, Free Press.

Bellamy, R. and Castiglione, D. (1996) 'Introduction: constitutions and politics', *Political Studies*, 44, 413–16.

Benn, M. (1985) 'Policing women', in Baxter and Koffman (eds).

Benn, M. et al. (1983) *The Rape Controversy*, London, National Council for Civil Liberties.

Benn, T. (1979) *Arguments for Socialism*, Harmondsworth, Penguin.

Bentley, A. F. (1967) *The Process of Government*, Cambridge, MA, Harvard University Press (first published 1908).

Bentley, M. (1984) *Politics Without Democracy, 1815–1914*, London, Fontana.

Berlin, I. (1970) 'Two concepts of liberty', in Berlin, I., *Four Essays on Liberty*, Oxford, Oxford University Press.

Beveridge, W. (chairman) (1942) *Social Insurance and Allied Services*, Cmd 6404, London, HMSO.

Bhavnani, K. K. and R. (1985) 'Racism and resistance in Britain', in Coates et al. (eds), pp. 147–59.

Birch, A. H. (1959) *Small Town Politics*, Oxford, Oxford University Press.

Birkinshaw, P. (1988) *Freedom of Information: The Law, The Practice and the Ideal*, London, Weidenfeld and Nicolson.

Birkinshaw, P. (1991) *Reforming the Secret State*, Buckingham, Open University Press.

Birkinshaw, P. (1997) 'Freedom of information', *Parliamentary Affairs*, 50(1), 164–81.

Bishop, M., Kay, J. and Mayer, C. (eds) (1995) *The Regulatory Challenge*, Oxford, Oxford University Press.

Black, E. (2000) 'MPs rebel over paper votes', *Sunday Times* (24 Dec.).

Black, I. (2002) 'Blair allied with European right in summit labour talks', *Guardian* (16 March).

Blake, R. (1985) *The Conservative Party from Peel to Thatcher*, London, Fontana.

Boaden, N. (1971) *Urban Policy Making*, Cambridge, Cambridge University Press.

Boateng, P. (1985) 'Crisis in accountability', in Baxter and Koffman (eds), pp. 237–45.

Bogdanor, V. (1981) *The People and the Party System*, Cambridge, Cambridge University Press.

Bogdanor, V. (1996a) 'The monarchy and the constitution', *Parliamentary Affairs*, 49(3), 407–22.

Bogdanor, V. (1996b) *Politics and the Constitution: Essays on British Government*, Aldershot, Dartmouth.

Bogdanor, V. (1997a) 'Let the people come to the aid of the parties', *Observer* (13 April).

Bogdanor, V. (1997b) *The Monarchy and the Constitution*, Oxford, Oxford University Press.

Bogdanor, V. (2000) 'The Guardian has got it wrong', *Guardian* (6 Dec.).

Bogdanor, V. (2001) 'Civil Service reform: a critique', in *Civil Service Reform: A PMPA Report*, London, Public Management and Policy Association, pp. 3–17.

Bottomore, T. (1964) *Elites in Society*, Harmondsworth, Penguin.

Bower, T. (1988) *Maxwell: The Outsider*, London, Aurum Press.

Box, S. (1971) *Deviance, Reality and Society*, London, Holt, Rinehart and Winston.

Bradbury, J. and Mitchell, J. (2001) 'Devolution: new policies for old?', *Parliamentary Affairs*, 54, 257–75.

Brand, J. (1992) *British Parliamentary Parties: Policy and Power*, Oxford, Oxford University Press.

Brazier, C. (1997) 'State of the world report', *New Internationalist*, no. 287 (Jan./Feb.), 4–9.

Brett, E. A. (1985) *The World Economy Since the War: The Politics of Uneven Development*, Basingstoke, Macmillan.

Brittan, L. (1993) 'Time to retune to Emu harmony', *Financial Times* (27 Oct.).

Brittan, S. (1983) 'Privatisation: a new approach', *Financial Times* (17 Nov.).

Brown, J. A. (1992) 'The Major effect: changes in party leadership and party popularity', *Parliamentary Affairs*, 45(4), 545–64.

Bruce-Gardyne, J. (1984) *Mrs Thatcher's First Administration*, London, Macmillan.

Bull, H. (1977) *The Anarchical Society*, London, Macmillan.

Bunyan, A. (1977) *The History and Practice of the Political Police in Britain*, London, Quartet.

Burch, M. and Holliday, I. (1996) *The British Cabinet System*, Hemel Hempstead, Prentice Hall/Harvester Wheatsheaf.

Burch, M. and Moran, M. (1984) 'Who are the new Tories?', *New Society* (11 Oct.).

Burke, E. (1782) *Reform of Representation in the House of Commons*, in *Works* (1861, vol. VI), London, Bohn.

Burke, J. (2001) 'No more cool Britannia for Europe's leper', *Observer* (11 March).

Burley, A, and Mattli, W. (1993) 'Europe before the Court: a political theory of legal integration', *International Organization*, 47 (Winter), 41–76.

Burnham, J. (1942) *The Managerial Revolution*, London, Putnam.

Burnham, J., Jones, G. W. and Elgie, R. (1995) 'The parliamentary activity of John Major, 1990–94', *British Journal of Political Science*, 25(4), 551–63.

Butler, D. (1960) 'The paradox of party difference', *American Behavioral Scientist*, 4(3).

Butler, D. (1995) *British General Elections Since 1945*, Oxford, Blackwell.

Butler, D. and Butler, G. (1994) *British Political Facts, 1900–1994*, Basingstoke, Macmillan.

Butler, D. and Kavanagh, D. (eds) (1987) *The British General Election of 1987*, Basingstoke, Macmillan.

Butler, D. and Kavanagh, D. (eds) (1992) *The British General Election of 1992*, Basingstoke, Macmillan.

Butler, D. and Kavanagh, D. (eds) (1997) *The British General Election of 1997*, Basingstoke, Macmillan.

Butler, D. and Kavanagh, D (2002) *The British General Election of 2001*, Basingstoke, Palgrave.

Butler, D. and Rose, R. (1960) *The British General Election of 1959*, London, Macmillan.

Butler, D. and Stokes, D. (1969) *Political Change in Britain*, London, Macmillan.

Butler, D. E., Adonis, A. and Travers, T. (1994) *Failure in British Government: The Politics of the Poll Tax*, Oxford, Oxford University Press.

Butler, M. (1986) *Europe: More than a Continent*, London, Heinemann.

Cabinet Office (1991) *The Citizen's Charter: Raising the Standard*, Cm 1599, London, HMSO.

Cabinet Office (1993) *Open Government*, Cm 2290, London, HMSO.

Cabinet Office (1994a) *The Civil Service: Continuity and Change*, Cm 2627, London, HMSO.

Cabinet Office (1994b) *Review of Fast Stream Recruitment*, London, HMSO.

Cabinet Office (1996) *Development and Training for Civil Servants: A Framework for Action*, Cm 3321, London, Stationery Office.

Cabinet Office (1999a) *Bringing in and Bringing on Talent*, London, Stationery Office.

Cabinet Office (1999b) *Modernising Government*, Cm 4310, London, Stationery Office.

Cabinet Office (2000) *Raising Standards and Upholding Integrity: The Prevention of Corruption: The Government's Proposals for the Reform of the Criminal Law of Corruption in England and Wales*, Cm 4759, London, Stationery Office.

Cahanum, S. (1997) 'Finishing school: Asian girls in the British educational system', in Giddens (1997b), pp. 344–7.

Cahill, K. (2001) *Who Owns Britain? The Hidden Facts Behind Landownership in the UK and Ireland*, Edinburgh, Canongate Books.

Callaghan, J. (1987) *Time and Chance*, London, Collins.

Callaghan, J. (1997) *Great Power Complex*, London, Pluto.

Camilleri, J. A. and Falk, J. (1992) *The End of Sovereignty?* Aldershot, Edward Elgar.

Campaign for Freedom of Information (2001) *Double Blow to Freedom of Information*, press release (13 Nov.).

Campbell, D. (1980) 'Society under surveillance', in Hain et al. (eds), pp. 65–150.

Cannadine, D. (1992) *The Decline and Fall of the British Aristocracy*, London, Picador.

Carr-Brown, J. (2001) 'No. 10 spins its own news on Pravda.com', *Sunday Times* (18 Feb.).

Castells, M. (1977) *The Urban Question*, London, Edward Arnold.

Cawson, A. (1986) *Corporatism and Political Theory*, Oxford, Basil Blackwell.

Cecil, H. (1912) *Conservatism*, London, Thornton Butterworth.

Chandler, J. A. (2001) *Local Government Today*, 3rd edn, Manchester, Manchester University Press.

Chapman, R. A. (1996) 'Tragedy and farce: the decision to privatise the RAS agency', *Public Policy and Administration*, 11(1), 1–7.

Chapman, R. A. (2000) 'Recruitment to the Fast Stream Development Programme', *Public Policy and Administration*, 15(1), 3–14.

Chapman, R. A. and O'Toole, B. J. (1995) 'The role of the civil service: a traditional view in a period of change', *Public Policy and Administration*, 10(2), 3–20.

Charmley, J. (1998) 'The Conservative defeat: an historical perspective', *Political Quarterly*, 69(2), 118–25.

Checkland, S. G. and E. O. A. (eds) (1974) *The Poor Law Report of 1834*, Harmondsworth, Penguin.

Chittenden, M. (1988) 'Freemasonry "rife" among top police', *Sunday Times* (10 April).

Chittenden, M. and Rufford, N. (2001) 'MI6 "firm" spied on green groups', *Sunday Times* (17 June).

Chomsky, N. (1997) *World Orders, Old and New*, London, Pluto.

Chrimes, S. B. (1967) *English Constitutional History*, 4th edn, London, Oxford University Press.

Clarke, H. D. and Stewart, M. C. (1995) 'Economic evaluations, prime ministerial approval and governing party support: rival models reconsidered', *British Journal of Political Science*, 25(2), 145–70.

Clifford, P. and Heath, A. (1994) 'The election campaign', in Heath et al. (eds), pp. 7–23.

Coates, D., Johnson, G. and Bush, R. (1985) *A Socialist Anatomy of Britain*, Cambridge, Polity.

Cockburn, C. (1977) *The Local State*, London, Pluto Press.

Cockerell, M., Hennessy, P. and Walker, P. (1984) *Sources Close to the Prime Minister: Inside the Hidden World of the News Manipulators*, London, Macmillan.

Cohen, B. J. (1995) 'Towards a mosaic economy: economic relations in the post-cold-war era', in Freiden, J. A. and Lake, D. A. (eds), *International Political Economy: Perspectives on Global Power and Wealth*, London, Routledge, pp. 519–31.

Cohen, N. (1999) 'How Britain mortgaged the future', *New Statesman* (18 Oct.), 25–7.

Coleman, S. (2001) 'Online campaigning', *Parliamentary Affairs*, 54, 679–88.

Collings, D. and Seldon, A. (2001) 'Conservatives in opposition', *Parliamentary Affairs*, 54, 624–37.

Commission for Local Democracy (1995) *Taking Charge: The Rebirth of Local Democracy, Final Report*, London, Municipal Journal.

Conservative and Unionist Party (1997) *Our Party: Blueprint for Change*, London, Conservative and Unionist Party.

Cornford, F. M. (editor and translator) (1941) *The Republic of Plato*, Oxford, Clarendon Press.

Cosgrave, P. (1978) *Margaret Thatcher: A Tory and Her Party*, London, Hutchinson.

Cowley, P. (2001) 'The Commons: Mr Blair's lapdog?' *Parliamentary Affairs*, 54, 815–28.

Cowley, P. and Stuart, M. (2001) 'Parliament: a few headaches and a dose of modernisation', *Parliamentary Affairs*, 54(2), 238–56.

Cracknell, D. (2001) 'United they're damned', *Sunday Times* (23 Dec.).

Crewe, I. (1983) 'Representation and ethnic minorities in Britain', in Glazer, N. and Young, K. (eds), *Ethnic Pluralism and Public Policy: Achieving Equality in the United States and Britain*, London, Heinemann.

Crewe, I. (1986) 'On the death and resurrection of class voting: some comments on *How Britain Votes*', *Political Studies*, 34(4), 620–38.

Crewe, I. (1988) 'Has the electorate become Thatcherite?', in Skidelsky, R. (ed.) *Thatcherism*, London, Chatto and Windus.

Crewe, I. (1992) 'A nation of liars? Opinion polls and the 1992 election', *Parliamentary Affairs*, 45(4), 475–95.

Crewe, I. (1993) 'Voting and the electorate', in Dunleavy et al. (eds), pp. 92–122.

Crewe, I. (1997) 'The opinion polls: confidence restored?' *Parliamentary Affairs*, 50(4), 569–85.

Crewe, I. (2001) 'The opinion polls: still biased to Labour', *Parliamentary Affairs*, 54, 650–65.

Crewe, I. and King, A. (1997) *SDP: The Birth, Life and Death of the Social Democratic Party*, Oxford, Oxford University Press.

Crick, B. (1964) *In Defence of Politics*, Harmondsworth, Penguin (5th edn, London, Continuum, 2000).

Crick, B. (1987) *Socialism*, Buckingham, Open University Press.

Crick, B. (ed.) (1991) *National Identities: The Constitution of the United Kingdom*, Oxford, Blackwell.

Criddle, B. (1997) 'MPs and candidates', in Butler and Kavanagh (eds), pp. 186–209.

Criddle, B. (2001) 'MPs and candidates', in Butler and Kavanagh (eds), pp. 182–207.

Crosland, A. (1956) *The Future of Socialism*, London, Jonathan Cape.

Cross, C. (1963) *The Liberals in Power 1905–1914*, London, Pall Mall Press.

Crossman, R. H. S. (1963) 'Introduction', in Bagehot, W., *The English Constitution*, London, Fontana.

Crossman, R. H. S. (1975–7) *Diaries of a Cabinet Minister*, 3 vols, London, Jonathan Cape.

Crouch, C. (1979) *State and Economy in Contemporary Capitalism*, London, Croom Helm.

Curran, J. and Seaton, J. (1998) *Power Without Responsibility: The Press and Broadcasting in Britain*, 5th edn, London, Routledge.

Curtice, J. (1996) 'What future for the opinion polls?', in Rallings, C. et al. (eds), *British Elections and Parties Yearbook 1995*, London, Frank Cass, pp. 139–56.

Curtice, J. (2001) 'So much command of the Commons, so little over the electorate', *Independent* (9 June).

Curtice, J. and Semetko, H. (1994) 'Does it matter what the papers say?', in Heath et al. (eds), pp. 43–63.

Curtice, J. and Steed, M. (1987) 'Analysis', in Butler and Kavanagh (eds), pp. 316–62.

Curtice, J. and Steed, M. (1992) 'Appendix: the results analysed', in Butler and Kavanagh (eds), pp. 322–62.

Daalder, H. (1964) *Cabinet Reform in Britain, 1914–63*, Stanford, CA, Stanford University Press.

Dahl, R. (1956) *A Preface to Democratic Theory*, Chicago, IL, University of Chicago Press.

Dahl, R. (1985) *A Preface to Economic Democracy*, Cambridge, Polity.

Dahl, R. and Lindblom, C. E. (1976) *Politics, Economics and Welfare*, New York, Harper.

Dangerfield, G. (1936) *The Strange Death of Liberal England*, London, Constable.

Davies, B. (1972) *Variations in Children's Services among British Urban Authorities*, London, Bell.

de Jonquieres, G. (1983) 'The BT sale: why are the stakes so high?', *Financial Times* (3 May).

Deacon, D., Goldin, P. and Billig, M. (2001) 'Press and broadcasting: "real issues" and real coverage', *Parliamentary Affairs*, 54, 666–78.

Deakin, N. and Parry, R. (2000) *The Treasury and Social Policy: The Contest for Control of Welfare Policy*, Basingstoke, Macmillan.

Deane, P. (1963) *The First Industrial Revolution*, Cambridge, Cambridge University Press.

Dearlove, J. (1973) *The Politics of Policy in Local Government*, London, Cambridge University Press.

Denemark, D. (1996) 'Thinking ahead to mixed-member proportional representation', *Party Politics*, 2(3), 409–20.

Denny, C. (2002) 'British economy defies world downturn', *Guardian* (26 Jan.).

Denver, D. (1994) *Elections and Voting Behaviour in Britain*, 2nd edn, Hemel Hempstead, Philip Allan.

Denver, D. (1998) 'The British electorate in the 1990s', *West European Politics*, 21(1), 197–217.

Denver, D., Norris, P., Broughton, D. and Rallings, C. (eds) (1993) *British Elections and Parties Yearbook, 1993*, Hemel Hempstead, Harvester Wheatsheaf.

Department of the Environment (1983) *Streamlining the Cities*, Cmnd 9063, London, HMSO.

Department of the Environment, Transport and the Regions (1998a) *Modern Local Government: In Touch With the People*, London, Stationery Office.

Department of the Environment, Transport and the Regions (1998b) *Modernising Local Government: Local Democracy and Community Leadership*, London, Stationery Office.

Department for Transport, Local Government and the Regions (2001) *Strong Local Leadership: Quality Public Services*, Cm 5327, London, Stationery Office.

Department for Transport, Local Government and the Regions (2002) *Your Region, Your Choice: Revitalising the English Regions*, Cm 5511, London, Stationery Office.

Devine, F. (1997) *Social Class in America and Britain*, Edinburgh, Edinburgh University Press.

Dicey, A. V. (1959) *An Introduction to the Study of the Law of the Constitution*, 10th edn, London, Macmillan (first published 1885).

Diplock, S. (ed.) (2001) *None of the Above: Non-voters and the 2001 Election*, London, Hansard Society.

Doig, A. (1984) 'Public service and private gain', *Public Money*, 4(3).

Doig, A. (1995) 'Continuing cause for concern? Probity in local government', *Local Government Studies*, 21(1), 99–114.

Doig, A. (2001) 'Picking up the threads or "back to basics" scandals?', *Parliamentary Affairs*, 54(1), 36–75.

Done, K. (2000) 'Prescott defends air traffic control part privatisation', *Financial Times* (20 April).

Dorey, P. (1995) *British Politics Since 1945*, Oxford, Blackwell.

Dowding, K. (1995) *The Civil Service*, London, Routledge.

Downs, A. (1957) *An Economic Theory of Democracy*, New York, Harper and Row.

Downs, D. (1997) 'What should the next government do about crime?' *Howard Journal of Criminal Justice*, 36(1), 1–13.

Draper, D. (1997) *Blair's 100 Days*, London, Faber.

Driver, S. and Martell, L (1988) *New Labour: Politics after Thatcherism*, Cambridge, Polity.

Drucker, H. et al. (eds) (1986) *Developments in British Politics 2*, London, Macmillan.

Duff, A. (1997) *The Treaty of Amsterdam*, London, The Federal Trust.

Dunleavy, P. (1980) *Urban Political Analysis*, London, Macmillan.

Dunleavy, P. (1981) *The Politics of Mass Housing in Britain: Corporate Power and Professional Influence in the Welfare State*, Oxford, Clarendon Press.

Dunleavy, P. (1991) *Democracy, Bureaucracy and Public Choice*, Hemel Hempstead, Harvester Wheatsheaf.

Dunleavy, P. (1993) 'The political parties', in Dunleavy et al., pp. 123–53.

Dunleavy, P. and Husbands, C. T. (1985) *British Democracy at the Crossroads: Voting and Party Competition in the 1980s*, London, George Allen & Unwin.

Dunleavy, P. and Jones, G. W., with Burnham, J., Elgie, R. and Fysh, P. (1993) 'Leaders, politics and institutional change: the decline of prime ministerial accountability to the House of Commons, 1868–1990', *British Journal of Political Science*, 23(2), 267–98.

Dunleavy, P. and Rhodes, R. A. W. (1990) 'Core executive studies in Britain', *Public Administration*, 68(1), 3–28.

Dunleavy, P., Gamble, A., Holliday, I. and Peele, G. (1993) *Developments in British Politics 4*, Basingstoke, Macmillan.

Dunleavy, P., Gamble, A., Holliday, I. and Peele, G. (2000) *Developments in British Politics 6*, Basingstoke, Macmillan.

Dunleavy, P., Margetts, H., O'Duffy, B. and Weir, S. (1997) *Making Votes Count*, Democratic Audit Paper 11, Colchester, University of Essex, Democratic Audit.

Dunleavy, P., Margetts, H., Smith, T. and Weir, S. (2001a) 'Constitutional reform, New Labour and public trust in government', *Parliamentary Affairs*, 54, 405–24.

Dunleavy, P., Margetts, H., Smith, T. and Weir, S. (2001b) *Voices of the People: Popular Attitudes to Democratic Renewal in Britain*, London, Politico's.

Durham University (2000) *Who Runs the North East Now?* Durham, Durham University.

Dutt, M. (1995) 'God's guerillas', *New Internationalist*, no. 270 (Aug.), 7–10.

Duverger, M. (1966) *The Idea of Politics*, London, Methuen.

Dyer, C. (1995) 'And the verdict m'lud?', *Guardian* (7 April).

Easton, D. (1953) *The Political System*, New York, Knopf.

Eckstein, H. (1960) *Pressure Group Politics*, London, George Allen & Unwin.

Ecologist (1992) 'Whose common future?' special issue of *The Ecologist*, 22(4).

Efficiency Unit (1988) *Improving Management in Government: The Next Steps* (the Ibbs Report), London, HMSO.

Elcock, H. (1991) *Change and Decay: Public Administration in the 1990s*, Harlow, Longman.

Elcock, H. (1994) *Local Government*, 2nd edn, London, Routledge.

Elcock, H. (1995) 'Leading people: some issues of local government leadership in Britain and America', *Local Government Studies*, 21(4), 546–67.

Elcock, H. (1997) 'The north of England and a Europe of the regions, or, when is a region not a region?' in Keating and Loughlin (eds), pp. 422–35.

Eldridge, J. (ed.) (1993) *Getting the Message: News, Truth and Power*, London, Routledge.

Electoral Commission (2001) *Election 2001: The Official Results*, London, Politico's.

Elkington, J. and Burke, T. (1989) *The Green Capitalists*, London, Gollancz.

Elliot, L. (2001) 'IMF warns of global recession', *Guardian* (29 Sept.).

Elshtain, J. B. (1981) *Public Man, Private Woman*, Princeton, NJ, Princeton University Press.

Evans, G. (1993) 'Class conflict and inequality', in Jowell, R. et al., *International Social Attitudes: The 10th British Social Attitudes Report*, Aldershot, Dartmouth, pp. 123–41.

Evans, M. (1995) *Charter88: A Successful Challenge to the British Tradition?* Aldershot, Dartmouth.

Evans, P. (1986a) 'Police are all too often a target of those frustrated by society', *The Times* (10 Nov.).

Evans, P. (1986b) 'The low profile policy', *The Times* (11 Nov.).

Ewing, K. D. and Gearty, C. A. (1990) *Freedom under Thatcher: Civil Liberties in Modern Britain*, Oxford, Clarendon Press.

Eysenck, H. J. (1951) 'Primary social attitudes', *British Journal of Sociology*, 2, 198–209.

Farnham, D. (1996) 'New Labour, the new unions and the new labour market', *Parliamentary Affairs*, 49(4), 584–98.

Farrell, D. (1997) *Comparing Electoral Systems*, London, Prentice Hall.

Filkin, G. et al. (2000) *Towards a New Localism*, New Local Government Network and Institute for Public Policy.

Finer, S. E. (1956) 'The individual responsibility of ministers', *Public Administration*, 34, 377–96.

Finer, S. E. (ed.) (1975) *Adversarial Politics and Electoral Reform*, London, Anthony Wigram.

Fisher, J. (1994) 'Political donations to the Conservative Party', *Parliamentary Affairs*, 47(1), 61–72.

Fisher, J. (1997) 'Donations to political parties', *Parliamentary Affairs*, 50(2), 235–45.

Flinders, M. (2001) 'Mechanisms of judicial accountability on British Central Government', *Parliamentary Affairs*, 54, 54–71.

Foley, M. (2000) *The British Presidency*, Manchester, Manchester University Press.

Forbes, I. (1996) 'The privatisation of sex equality policy', *Parliamentary Affairs*, 49(1), 143–60.

Ford, R. (2002) 'New police chief boosts ranks of women at the top', *The Times* (3 May).

Fox, J. (1975) 'The brains behind the throne', in Herman and Alt (eds), pp. 277–92.

Franks, O. (1957) *Report of the Committee on Administrative Tribunals and Inquiries*, Cmnd 218, London, HMSO.

Franks, Lord O. (1972) *Departmental Committee on Section 2 of the Official Secrets Act 1911*, Cmnd 5104, London, HMSO.

Friedman, M. and R. (1985) *The Tyranny of the Status Quo*, Harmondsworth, Penguin.

Fry, G. K. (1986) 'Inside Whitehall', in Drucker et al. (eds).

Fry, G. K. (1995) *Policy and Management in the British Civil Service*, Hemel Hempstead, Prentice Hall/Harvester Wheatsheaf.

Fryer, P. (1988) *Black People in the British Empire*, London, Pluto.

Fukuyama, F. (1992) *The End of History and the Last Man*, London, Hamish Hamilton.

Fulton, Lord (1968) *The Civil Service, Vol. 1: Report of the Committee*, Cmnd 3638, London, HMSO.

Galbraith, J. K. (1993) *The Culture of Contentment*, London, Penguin.

Gallup (1976) 'Voting behaviour in Britain, 1945–1974', in Rose, R. (ed.), *Studies in British Politics*, 3rd edn, Basingstoke, Macmillan.

Gamble, A. (1981) *An Introduction to Modern Social and Political Thought*, Basingstoke, Macmillan.

Gamble, A. (1988) *The Free Economy and the Strong State*, Basingstoke, Macmillan.

Gamble, A. (1990) *Britain in Decline*, 3rd edn, Basingstoke, Macmillan.

Gamble, A. and Wright, T. (1997) 'New Labour and old left', *Political Quarterly*, 68(2), 125–7.

Game, C. (1997) 'How many, where and how? Taking stock of local government reorganisation', *Local Government Policy Making*, 23(4), 3–23.

Garnsey, E. (1982) 'Women's work and theories of class stratification', in Held, D. and Giddens, A. (eds), *Classes, Power and Conflict*, London, Macmillan.

Gavin, N. T. (1996) 'Class voting and the Labour Party in Britain', *Electoral Studies*, 15(3), 311–26.

George, Stephen (1991) *Politics and Policy in the European Community*, Oxford, Oxford University Press.

George, Stephen (1994) *An Awkward Partner: Britain in the European Community*, 2nd edn, Oxford, Oxford University Press.

George, Susan (1991) *The Debt Boomerang*, London, Pluto.

Gibb, F. (1988) 'Justice by lottery?', *The Times* (25 Oct.).

Gibb, F. (1994) 'Judicious adverts set new benchmark', *The Times* (27 Sept.).

Gibson, R. and Ward, S. (eds) (2000) *Reinvigorating Democracy? British Politics and the Internet*, Ashgate.

Giddens, A. (1973) *The Class Structure of the Advanced Societies*, London, Hutchinson.

Giddens, A. (1979) *The Class Structure of the Advanced Societies*, 2nd edn, London, Hutchinson.

Giddens, A. (1990) *The Consequences of Modernity*, Cambridge, Polity.

Giddens, A. (1997) *Sociology: Introductory Readings*, Cambridge, Polity.

Giddens, A. (1998) *The Third Way: The Renewal of Social Democracy*, Cambridge, Polity.

Giddens, A. (1999) 'Better than warmed-over porridge', *New Statesman* (12 Feb.).

Giddens, A. (2001) *Sociology*, 4th edn, Cambridge, Polity.

Giddings, P. and Drewry, G. (1996) *Westminster and Europe: The Impact of the European Union on the Westminster Parliament*, Basingstoke, Macmillan.

Gladden, E. N. (1967) *Civil Services of the United Kingdom*, London, Frank Cass.

Glasgow University Media Group (1976) *Bad News*, (1980) *More Bad News*, (1982) *Really Bad News*, London, Routledge and Kegan Paul.

Goldsmith, E. (1972) *A Blueprint for Survival*, Harmondsworth, Penguin.

Goldthorpe, J. (1982) 'On the service class: its formation and future', in Giddens, A. and MacKenzie, G. (eds), *Social Class and the Division of Labour: Essays in Honour of Ilya Neustadt*, Cambridge, Cambridge University Press.

Goldthorpe, J. (1987) *Social Mobility and Class Structure in Modern Britain*, 2nd edn, Oxford, Clarendon Press.

Goodin, R. (1986) 'The principle of voluntary agreement', *Public Administration*, 64(4), 435–44.

Goodin, R. (1992) *Green Political Theory*, Cambridge, Polity.

Goodman, A., Johnson, P. and Webb, S. (1997) *Income Inequality in the UK*, Oxford, Oxford University Press.

Gordon, D. and Townsend, P. (eds) (2001) *Breadline Europe: The Measurement of Poverty*, London, Policy Press.

Gordon, P. (1984) 'Community policing: towards the local police state', *Critical Social Policy*, 4(1), 39–58.

Gordon, P. and Klug, F. (1986) *New Right, New Racism*, London, Searchlight Publications.

Gough, I. (1979) *The Political Economy of the Welfare State*, London, Macmillan.

Graham, C. (2000) *Regulating Public Utilities: A Constitutional Approach*, Oxford, Hart.

Grahl, J. and Teague, P. (1990) *1992: The Big Market*, London, Lawrence and Wishart.

Gramsci, A. (1971) *Selections from Prison Notebooks*, London, Lawrence and Wishart.

Grant, W. (1984) 'The role and power of pressure groups', in Borthwick, R. L. and Spence, J. E. (1984) *British Politics in Perspective*, Leicester, Leicester University Press, pp. 123–44.

Grant, W. (1987) *Business and Politics*, London, Macmillan.

Grant, W. (1993) *The Politics of Economic Policy*, Hemel Hempstead, Harvester Wheatsheaf.

Grant, W. (1995) *Pressure Groups, Politics and Democracy*, 2nd edn, Hemel Hempstead, Harvester Wheatsheaf.

Grant, W. (2001) 'Pressure politics: from "insider" politics to direct action', *Parliamentary Affairs*, 54, 337–48.

Grant, W. and MacNamara, A. (1995) 'When policy communities intersect: the case of agriculture and banking', *Political Studies*, 43(3), 509–15.

Grant, W. and Marsh, D. (1977) *The CBI*, London, Hodder and Stoughton.

Gray, J. (1995) *Enlightenment's Wake: Politics and Culture at the Close of the Modern Age*, London, Routledge.

Gray, J. (1998) *False Dawn: The Utopia of the Global Free Market*, London, Granta (revised edn 1999 entitled *False Dawn: The Delusions of Global Capitalism*).

Greenwood, J., Pyper, R. and Wilson, D. (2002) *New Public Administration in Britain*, London, Routledge.

Greer, G. (1970) *The Female Eunuch*, London, MacGibbon & Kee.

Grice, A. (1997) 'Don't mention the party', *Sunday Times* (23 March).

Griffith, J. A. G. (1981) *The Politics of the Judiciary*, London, Fontana.

Griffith, J. A. G. (1991) *The Politics of the Judiciary*, 4th edn, London, Fontana (5th edn 1994).

Groom, I. (1997) 'If at first you don't succeed', *Financial Times* (11 Sept.).

Gunn, S. (1988) 'Reining in the peers', *Marxism Today*, 32 (June), 3.

Guttsman, W. S. (1963) *The British Political Elite*, London, MacGibbon & Kee.

Hailsham, Lord (1978) *The Dilemma of Democracy*, London, Collins.

Hain, P. et al. (eds) (1980) *Policing the Police*, London, Calder.

Halford, A. (1993) *No Way up the Greasy Pole*, London, Constable.

Hall, W. and Weir, S. (1996) *The Untouchables: Power and Accountability in the Quango State*, Colchester, University of Essex, Democratic Audit and London, Charter88.

Hambleton, R. (1996) 'Reinventing local government: lessons from the USA', *Local Government Studies*, 22(1), 93–112.

Hampsher-Monk, I. (1987) *The Political Philosophy of Edmund Burke*, Harlow, Longman.

Hampton, W. (1970) *Democracy and Community*, London, Oxford University Press.

Hansard Society (1993) *Making the Law: Report of the Commission on the Legislative Process*, London, Hansard Society.

Harden, I. and Lewis, N. (1986) *The Noble Lie*, London, Hutchinson.

Harris, P. (1997) *An Introduction to the Law*, 5th edn, London, Weidenfeld and Nicolson.

Harrison, B. (1996) *The Transformation of British Politics 1860–1995*, Oxford, Oxford University Press.

Harrison, D. (1993) 'Who pays for the party?' *Observer* (20 June).

Harrison, M. (1985) *TV News: Whose Bias?*, Hermitage, Policy Journals.

Harrison, M. (1987) 'Broadcasting', in Butler and Kavanagh (eds), pp. 139–62.

Harrison, M. (1992) 'Politics on the air', in Butler and Kavanagh (eds), pp. 155–79.

Harrop, M. and Scammell, M. (1992) 'The tabloid war', in Butler and Kavanagh (eds), pp. 180–210.

Harvey, D. (1989) *The Condition of Postmodernity*, Oxford, Blackwell.

Harvie, C. (1991) 'English regionalism: the dog that never barked', in Crick (ed), pp. 105–18.

Hattersley, R. (1996) *Who Goes Home? Scenes from Political Life*, London, Little, Brown.

Hawley, J. S. (ed.) (1984) *Fundamentalism and Gender*, Oxford, Oxford University Press.

Hayek, F. von (1976) *The Road to Serfdom*, London, Routledge (first published 1944).

Hazell, R. (ed.) (1999) *Constitutional Futures: A History of the Next Ten Years*, Oxford, Oxford University Press.

Heath, A. and Park, A. (1998) 'Thatcher's children?' in Jowell et al., pp. 1–22.

Heath, A., Jowell, R. and Curtice, J. (1987) 'Trendless fluctuation: a reply to Crewe', *Political Studies*, 35(2), 256–77.

Heath, A., Jowell, R. and Curtice, J. (with Taylor, B.) (1994) *Labour's Last Chance? The 1992 Election and Beyond*, Aldershot, Dartmouth.

Heath, E. (1972) *My Style of Government*, London, Evening Standard Publications.

Heathcoat Amory, E. (2001)'Sleaze and a lunch too far for "Sir Humphrey"', *Daily Mail* (13 Feb).

Heclo, H. and Wildavsky, A. (1974) *The Private Government of Public Money*, London, Macmillan.

Heffer, S. (1988) 'Labour brings the House down on its own head', *Daily Telegraph* (8 April).

Heffernan, R. and Marqusee, M. (1992) *Defeat from the Jaws of Victory: Inside Kinnock's Labour Party*, Oxford, Blackwell.

Held, D. (1987) *Models of Democracy*, Cambridge, Polity.

Held, D. (1989) 'The decline of the nation state', in Hall, S. and Jacques, M. (eds), *New Times*, London, Lawrence and Wishart, pp. 191–204.

Held, D. and McGrew, A. (1993) 'Globalisation and the liberal democratic state', *Government and Opposition*, 28(2), 261–88.

Held, D., McGrew, A., Goldblatt, D. and Perraton, J. (1999) *Global Transformations*, Cambridge, Polity.

Hencke, D. (1992) 'More Whitehall staff face market test for jobs', *Guardian* (21 July).

Hennessy, P. (1985) 'The megaphone theory of "Yes Minister"', *Listener* (19 and 26 Dec.).

Hennessy, P. (1986) *Cabinet*, Oxford, Basil Blackwell.

Hennessy, P. (1990) *Whitehall*, London, Fontana (2nd edn, London, Pimlico, 2001).

Hennessy, P. (1992) *Never Again: Britain 1945–1951*, London, Jonathan Cape.

Hennessy, P. (1994) 'The throne behind the power', *The Economist* (24 Dec.).

Hennessy, P. (1995) *The Hidden Wiring: Unearthing the British Constitution*, London, Cassell.

Hennessy, P. (1998) 'The Blair style of government', *Government and Opposition*, 33(1) 3–20.

Hennessy, P. (2000) *The Prime Minister: The Office and its Holders Since 1945*, London, Allen Lane.

Hennessy, T. (1997) *A History of Northern Ireland 1920–1996*, Basingstoke, Macmillan.

Henney, A. (1984) *Inside Local Government: A Case for Radical Reform*, London, Sinclair Browne.

Herman, V. and Alt, J. E. (eds) (1975) *Cabinet Studies*, Basingstoke, Macmillan.

Heseltine, M. (1986) 'Deliberate attempt made to avoid discussion of issues', *The Times* (10 Jan.).

Hewart, Lord (1929) *The New Despotism*, London, Ernest Benn.

Heywood, A. (1994) *Political Ideas and Concepts*, Basingstoke, Macmillan.

Hill, D. (1974) *Democratic Theory and Local Government*, London, George Allen & Unwin.

Hills, J. (1981) 'Britain', in Lovenduski, J. and Hills, J. (eds), *The Politics of the Second Electorate: Women and Public Participation*, London, Routledge and Kegan Paul, pp. 8–32.

Himmelweit, H., Humphreys, P. and Jaeger, M. (1985) *How Voters Decide*, Milton Keynes, Open University Press.

Hirst, P. (1995) 'Quangos and democratic government', *Parliamentary Affairs*, 48(2), 341–59.

Hirst, P. and Thompson, G. (1966) *Globalization in Question*, Cambridge, Polity.

Hobbes, T. (1985) *Leviathan* (ed. C. B. Macpherson), Harmondsworth, Penguin (first published 1651).

Hobsbawm, E. (1990) *Nations and Nationalism Since 1780*, Cambridge, Cambridge University Press.

Hobsbawm, E. (1995) *Age of Extremes*, London, Abacus.

Hobson, D. (1999) *The National Wealth: Who Gets What in Britain*, London, HarperCollins.

Hoggart, R. (1958) *The Uses of Literacy*, Harmondsworth, Penguin.

Hogwood, B. W. (1997) 'The machinery of government, 1979–97', *Political Studies*, 45(4), 704–15.

Holden, A. (1997) 'Royal blues', *Red Pepper* (Oct.).

Holland, P. (1978) *The Quango Explosion*, London, Conservative Political Centre.

Holland, P. (1981a) *The Governance of Quangos*, London, Adam Smith Institute.

Holland, P. (1981b) *Quango, Quango, Quango*, London, Adam Smith Institute.

Hollingsworth, M. (1986) *The Press and Discontent: A Question of Censorship*, London, Pluto.

Hollingsworth, M. (1997) 'Get out of this one, Mr Spin', *Observer Review* (16 Feb.).

Holme, R. and Elliot, M. (eds) (1988) *1688–1988: Time for a New Constitution*, London, Macmillan.

Holt, R. (2001) *Second Amongst Equals: Chancellors of the Exchequer and the British Economy*, Imprint Academic.

Home, Lord (1976) *The Way the Wind Blows*, London, Collins.

Home Office (1993) *Police Reform: A Police Service for the Twenty-first Century*, Cm 2281, London, HMSO.

Home Office (2000) *Raising Standards and Upholding Integrity: The Prevention of Corruption*, Cm 4759, London, Stationery Office.

Hood, C. (1979) 'Keeping the centre small: explanations of agency type', *Political Studies*, 26(1), 30–46.

Hood Phillips, O. (1987) *Constitutional and Administrative Law*, 7th edn, London, Sweet and Maxwell.

Hoogvelt, A. (1997) *Globalisation and the Postcolonial World*, Basingstoke, Macmillan.

Horsman, M. and Marshall, A. (1994) *After the Nation State*, London, HarperCollins.

Hoskyns, Sir J. (1984) 'Conservatism is not enough', *Political Quarterly*, 55(1), 3–16.

Hoskyns, J. (2000) *Just in Time: Inside the Thatcher Revolution*, Aurum Press,

House of Commons Expenditure Committee (1977) *The Civil Service: Eleventh Report and Volumes of Evidence, 1976/7, Vols. I–III*, HC 535, London, HMSO.

House of Commons Foreign Affairs Committee (1996) *The Future Role of the Commonwealth*, Cm 3303, London, Stationery Office.

House of Commons Home Affairs Committee (1993) *Accountability of the Security Service*, HC 270, Session 1992/3, London, HMSO.

House of Commons Public Service Committee (1996) *Ministerial Accountability and Responsibility*, HC 313-I, Session 1995/6, London, Stationery Office.

House of Commons Treasury and Civil Service Committee (1994) *The Role of* the Civil Service, HC 27-I, Session 1993/4, London, HMSO.

Howe, G. (1994) Conflict of Loyalty, Basingstoke, Macmillan.

Hume, D. (1882) 'That politics may be reduced to a science', reprinted in Dahl, R. and Neubauer, D. E. (1968) Readings in Modern Political Analysis, Englewood Cliffs, NJ, Prentice Hall.

Humphrys, J. (2001) 'Don't blame me, minister, if the voters are losing faith', Sunday Times (24 Dec.).

Hunt, D. (1995) 'Accountability in the NHS', Parliamentary Affairs, 48(2), 297–305.

Hunter, F. (1953) Community Power Structure, Chapel Hill, NC, University of North Carolina Press.

Hutton, W. (1986) The Revolution that Never Was, London, Longman.

Hutton, W. (1996) The State We're In, London, Vintage.

Hutton, W. (1998) 'What is Power?', Observer (1 Nov.).

Hutton, W. (2002) The World We're In, London, Little Brown.

Illich, I. (1975) Medical Nemesis, London, Calder and Boyars.

Ingham, B. (1991) Kill the Messenger, London, Fontana.

Jackson, R. M. (1960) The Machinery of Justice in England, Cambridge, Cambridge University Press.

Jacobs, M. (1996) The Politics of the Real World, London, Earthscan.

Jaggar, A. (1983) Feminist Politics and Human Nature, Brighton, Harvester.

James, B. (1987) 'The coup that never was . . .', The Times (7 Aug.).

Jenkins, S. (1995) Accountable to None: The Tory Nationalisation of Britain, Harmondsworth, Penguin.

Jennings, I. (1959) Cabinet Government, 3rd edn, Cambridge, Cambridge University Press.

Jennings, I. (1966) The British Constitution, 5th edn, Cambridge, Cambridge University Press.

John, P. (1994a) 'Central–local government relations in the 1980s and 1990s: towards a policy learning approach', Local Government Studies, 20(3), 412–36.

John, P. (1994b) The Europeanisation of British Local Government: New Management Strategies, York, Joseph Rowntree Foundation.

Johnson, N. (1998) 'The judicial dimension of British politics', West European Politics, 21(1), 148–66.

Johnson, R. W. (1985) The Politics of Recession, London, Macmillan.

Johnston, R. J. and Pattie, C. J. (1996) 'The strength of party identification among the British electorate', Electoral Studies, 15(3), 295–309.

Johnston, R. J. and Pattie, C. J. (1997) 'Towards an understanding of turnout in British general elections', Parliamentary Affairs, 50(2), 280–91.

Johnston, R. J., Pattie, C. J. and Allsopp, J. G. (1988) A Nation Dividing? The Electoral Map of Great Britain 1979–87, Harlow, Longman.

Johnston, R. J., Pattie, C. J., Rossiter, D., Dorling, D., Tunstall, H. and McAllister, I. (1998) 'Anatomy of a Labour landslide: the constituency system and the 1997 general election', Parliamentary Affairs, 50(2), 131–48.

Johnston, R., Pattie, C. J., Dorling, D. and Rossiter, D. (2001) From Votes to Seats: The Operation of the British Electoral System Since 1945, Manchester, Manchester University Press.

Jones, B. (1997) 'Wales: a developing political economy', in Keating and Loughlin (eds).

Jones, G. (2002) 'Labour chief denies move to ease out the Speaker', Daily Telegraph (12 Feb.).

Jones, G. and Stewart, J. (1995) 'Key questions, open debate', Local Government Chronicle (17 March).

Jones, G. W. (1983) 'Prime ministers' departments really do create problems: a rejoinder to Patrick Weller', Public Administration, 61(1), 79–84.

Jones, J. B. (2000) 'Post referendum politics' and 'Labour pain' in J. B. Jones and D. Balsom (eds), *The Road to the National Assembly for Wales*, Cardiff, Wales University Press.

Jones, R. A. (2001) *The Politics and Economics of the European Union*, 2nd edn, Cheltenham, Edward Elgar.

Jones, T. and Newburn, T. (1995) 'Local government and policing: arresting the decline of local influence', *Local Government Studies*, 21(3), 448–60.

Jordan, G. (1991) *The Commercial Lobbyists: Politics for Profit in Britain*, Aberdeen, Aberdeen University Press.

Jowell, R., Curtice, J., Park, A., Brook, L., Thompson, K. and Bryan, C. (1998) *British Social Attitudes: The 14th Report. The End of Conservative Values?* Aldershot, Ashgate.

Judge, D. (ed.) (1983) *The Politics of Parliamentary Reform*, London, Heinemann.

Kairys, P. (ed.) (1982) *The Politics of Law: A Progressive Critique*, London, Pantheon.

Kavanagh, D. (1980) 'Political culture in Britain: the decline of the civic culture', in Almond and Verba (eds).

Kavanagh, D. (1995) *Election Campaigning: The New Marketing of Politics*, Oxford, Blackwell.

Kavanagh, D. (1996) 'British party conferences and the political rhetoric of the 1990s', *Government and Opposition*, 31(1), 27–44.

Kavanagh, D. (1997a) 'The Labour campaign', *Parliamentary Affairs*, 50(4), 533–41.

Kavanagh, D. (1997b) *The Reordering of British Politics: Politics After Thatcher*, Oxford, Oxford University Press.

Kavanagh, D. (1998) 'Power in the parties: R. T. McKenzie and after', *West European Politics*, 21(1), 28–43.

Kay, J. (1993) *The Foundations of Corporate Success*, Oxford, Oxford University Press.

Kearney, H. (1990) *The British Isles: A History of Four Nations*, Cambridge, Cambridge University Press.

Keating, M. and Loughlin, J. (eds) (1997) *The Political Economy of Regionalism*, London, Frank Cass.

Keegan, W. (1984) *Mrs Thatcher's Economic Experiment*, Harmondsworth, Penguin.

Keen, P. and Travers, T. (1994) *Implementing the Council Tax*, York, Joseph Rowntree Foundation.

Kellas, J. (1975) *The Scottish Political System*, Cambridge, Cambridge University Press.

Kellner, P. (1998) 'What Blair must do next', *Evening Standard* (27 July).

Kellner, P. and Crowther-Hunt, Lord (1980) *The Civil Servants: An Enquiry into Britain's Ruling Class*, London, Macdonald.

Kennedy, H. (1992) *Eve was Framed*, London, Chatto and Windus.

Kenny, M. and Smith, M. J. (1997) '(Mis)understanding Blair', *Political Quarterly*, 68(3), 220–30.

Kettle, M. (1980) 'The politics of policing and the policing of politics', in Hain et al. (eds), pp. 9–64.

King, A. (2001) *Does the United Kingdom Still Have a Constitution?* London, Sweet and Maxwell.

King, A. (ed.) (1985) *The British Prime Minister*, 2nd edn, Basingstoke, Macmillan.

King, A. et al. (1993) *Britain at the Polls 1992*, Chatham, NJ, Chatham House.

King, D. (1993) 'Government beyond Whitehall', in Dunleavy et al. (eds), pp. 194–218.

Kingdom, J. (1991) *Local Government and Politics in Britain*, Hemel Hempstead, Philip Allan.

Kingdom, J. (1992) *No Such Thing as Society*, Buckingham, Open University Press.

Kingdom, J. (1996) 'Citizen or state consumer: a fistful of charters', in Chandler, J. A. (ed.), *The Citizen's*

Charter, Aldershot, Dartmouth, pp. 7–23.

Kirchheimer, O. (1966) 'The transformation of West European Party Systems', in LaPalombara, J. and Weiner, M. (eds), *Political Parties and Political Development*, Princeton, NJ, Princeton University Press, pp. 177–200.

Klare, M. T. (1992) 'US military policy in the post-cold-war era', in Miliband and Panitch (eds), pp. 131–42.

Klein, R. (1989) *The Politics of the NHS*, 2nd edn, Harlow, Longman.

Klug, F. (1997) 'Can human rights fill Britain's morality gap?' *Political Quarterly*, 68(2), 143–52.

Klug, F. (2000) *Values for a Godless Age: The Story of the United Kingdom's New Bill of Rights*, London, Penguin.

Klug, F., Starmer, K. and Weir, S. (1996) 'Civil liberties and the parliamentary watchdog: the passage of the Criminal Justice and Public Order Act 1994', *Parliamentary Affairs*, 49(4), 536–49.

Knightly, P. (1986) *The Second Oldest Profession: The Spy as Bureaucrat, Fantasist and Whore*, London, André Deutsch.

Koffman, L. (1985) 'Safeguarding the rights of the citizen', in Baxter and Koffman (eds), pp. 11–37.

Lacey, R. (1997) 'Ministry of Agriculture: Ministry of Truth', *Political Quarterly*, 68(3), 245–54.

Lambert, A. (1988) 'Who should police the police?', *Independent* (10 Sept.).

Lansdale, J. (2001) 'Blair refuses to justify record before top MPs', *The Times* (15 March).

Laski, H. J. (1938) *Parliamentary Government in England*, London, George Allen & Unwin.

Lasswell, H. D. (1936) *Politics: Who Gets What, When, How?*, New York, McGraw Hill (reprinted 1958).

Lasswell, H. D. and Kaplan, A. (1950) *Power and Society*, New Haven, CT, Yale University Press.

Lawrence, D. H. (1950) 'Nottingham and the mining country', in *Selected Essays*, Harmondsworth, Penguin.

Lawson, N. (1993) *The View from Number 11: Memoirs of a Tory Radical*, London, Corgi.

Lea, J. et al. (1986) 'The fear and loathing at Broadwater Farm', *Guardian* (4 June).

Leach, R. (1998) 'Local government reorganisation RIP?', *Political Quarterly*, 69(1), 31–40.

Leach, S. and Stewart, J. (1992) *The Politics of Hung Authorities*, Basingstoke, Macmillan.

Lee, S. (1988) *Judging Judges*, London, Faber and Faber.

Leftwich, A. (1984) *What is Politics? The Activity and its Study*, Oxford, Blackwell.

Leggatt, A. (2001) *Tribunals for Users: One System, One Service*, London, Stationery Office.

Lehmbruch, G. and Schmitter, P. (eds) (1982) *Patterns of Corporatist Policy-Making*, London, Sage.

Lent, A. and Sowemimo, M. (1996) 'Remaking the opposition?', in Ludlam and Smith (eds), pp. 121–42.

Lester, Lord (1994) 'European rights and the British constitution', in Jowell, J. and Oliver, D. (eds), *The Changing Constitution*, 3rd edn, Oxford, Oxford University Press.

Leys, C. (1998) 'Controlling the waves', *Red Pepper* (April).

Lijphart, A. (1994) *Electoral Systems and Party Systems: A Study of Twenty-Seven Democracies 1945–1990*, Oxford, Oxford University Press.

Lijphart, A. (1996) 'The Framework proposal for Northern Ireland and the theory of power sharing', *Government and Opposition*, 31(3), 267–74.

Lindblom, C. E. (1959) 'The science of muddling through', *Public Administration Review*, 19, 79–88.

Lister, I. (1987) 'Global and international approaches to political education', in C. Harber (ed.), *Political Education in Britain*, Lewes, Falmer Press.

Lively, J. (1978) 'Pluralism and consensus', in Birnbaum, P., Lively, J. and Parry, G. (eds), *Democracy, Consensus and Social Contract*, London, Sage.

Lockwood, D. (1966) 'Sources of variation in working class images of society', *Sociological Review*, 14, 249–67.

Lodge, J. (ed.) (1993) *The European Community and the Challenge of the Future*, London, Pinter.

Lord Chancellor's Department (1989) *Legal Services: A Framework for the Future*, Cm 740, London, HMSO.

Lord Chancellor's Department (2000) *Judicial Appointments 1999–2000*, London, Stationery Office.

Lord Chancellor's Department (2001a) *The House of Lords: Completing the Reform*, Cm 5291, London, Stationery Office.

Lord Chancellor's Department (2001b) *Judicial Appointments in England and Wales: The Appointment of Lawyers to the Professional Judiciary*, London, Stationery Office.

Louis, W. R. and Bull, H. (eds) (1986) *The Special Relationship: Anglo-American Relations Since 1945*, Oxford, Oxford University Press.

Loveday, B. (1994) 'The competing role of central and local agencies in crime prevention strategies', *Local Government Studies*, 20(3), 361–73.

Loveday, B. (1996) 'Business as usual? The new police authorities and the Police and Magistrates' Courts Act', *Local Government Studies*, 22(2), 22–39.

Lovelock, J. E. (1987) *Gaia: A New Look at Life on Earth*, Oxford, Oxford University Press.

Lovenduski, J. (1996) 'Sex, gender and British politics', *Parliamentary Affairs*, 49(1), 1–16.

Lovenduski, J. (1997) 'Gender politics: a breakthrough for women', *Parliamentary Affairs*, 50(4), 708–19.

Lovenduski, J. (2001) 'Women and politics: minority representation or critical mass?' *Parliamentary Affairs*, 54, 743–58.

Lovenduski, J. and Norris, P. (1994) 'Labour and the unions: after the Brighton conference', *Government and Opposition*, 29(3), 201–17.

Lovenduski, J. and Norris, P. (eds) (1996) *Women in Politics*, Oxford, Oxford University Press.

Lowe, P. and Goyder, J. (eds) (1983) *Environmental Groups in Politics*, London, Allen and Unwin.

Lowndes, V. (1997) 'Change in public service management: new institutions and new managerial regimes', *Local Government Studies*, 23(2), 42–66.

Ludlam, S. (1996) 'The spectre haunting Conservatism: Europe and backbench rebellion', in Ludlam and Smith (eds), pp. 98–120.

Ludlum, S. and Smith. M. (eds) (2001) *New Labour in Government*, Basingstoke, Palgrave.

McAllister, I. (1998) 'The Welsh devolution referendum', *Parliamentary Affairs*, 51(2), 149–65.

McAlpine, A. (1997) *Once a Jolly Bagman*, London, Weidenfeld and Nicolson.

MacDonald, M. (1986) *Children of Wrath: Political Violence in Northern Ireland*, Cambridge, Polity.

McGarry, J. and O'Leary, B. (1997) *Explaining Northern Ireland: Broken Images*, Oxford, Blackwell.

MacIver, D. (ed.) (1996) *The Liberal Democrats*, Hemel Hempstead, Prentice Hall Harvester.

McKenzie, R. (1967) *British Political Parties*, 2nd rev. edn, London, Heinemann.

McKenzie, R. and Silver, A. (1968) *Angels in Marble*, London, Heinemann.

Mackenzie, W. J. M. (1969) *Politics and Social Science*, Harmondsworth, Penguin.

McKie, D. (1994) 'Uncivil servants sign off', *Guardian* (23 April).

McNair, B. (2000) *Journalism and Democracy*, London, Routledge.

Maddock, S. (1993) 'Barriers to women are barriers to local government', *Local Government Studies*, 19(3), 341–50.

Magdoff, H. (1992) 'Globalisation: to what end?' in Miliband and Panitch (eds), pp. 44–75.

Magnus, P. (1963) *Gladstone*, London, Murray.

Mahl (pseud.) (1995) 'Women on the edge of time', *New Internationalist*, no. 270 (Aug.), 7–10.

Mair, L. (1970) *Primitive Government*, Harmondsworth, Penguin.

Mallalieu, J. P. W. (1941) *Passed to You Please*, London, Victor Gollancz.

Mandel, E. (1983) 'Economics', in McLellan, D., *Marx: The First Hundred Years*, London, Fontana, pp. 189–238.

Mandelson, P. and Liddle, R. (1996) *The Blair Phenomenon: Can New Labour Deliver?* London, Faber.

Mansfield, M. (1997) 'Justice for all', *Red Pepper* (April).

Mark, R. (1978) *In the Office of Constable*, London, Collins.

Marquand, D. (1988) *The Unprincipled Society*, London, Fontana.

Marr, A. (1992) *The Battle for Scotland*, Harmondsworth, Penguin.

Marr, A. (1995) *Ruling Britannia*, Harmondsworth, Penguin.

Marr, A. (1998) 'New Labour is no different here. With so much dodgy cash sloshing around, how long until there's a real stink?' *Guardian Unlimited* website (accessed 4 Oct. 1998).

Marsh, A. (1978) *Protest and Political Consciousness*, London, Sage.

Marsh, D. (1992) *The New Politics of British Trade Unionism*, Basingstoke, Macmillan.

Marsh, D. (1993) 'The media and politics', in Dunleavy et. al. (eds), pp. 332–49.

Marsh, D. and Locksley, G. (1987) 'The influence of business', in *British Politics: A Reader*, Manchester, Manchester University Press, pp. 215–26.

Marsh, D. and Rhodes, R. A. W. (1992) (eds) *Implementing Thatcherite Policies: Audit of an Era*, Buckingham, Open University Press.

Marshall, G. (1997) 'The referendum: what, when, how?', *Parliamentary Affairs*, 50(2), 307–13.

Martin, S. and Pearce, G. (1994) 'The demise of the lone ranger: prospects for unitary authorities in the "New Europe"', *Local Government Policy Making*, 20(5), 14–20.

Marwick, A. (1982) *British Society Since 1945*, Harmondsworth, Penguin.

Maud, Sir J. (chairman) (1967) *Management of Local Government*, London, HMSO.

Mazey, S. and Richardson, J. (1993) *Lobbying in the European Community*, Oxford, Oxford University Press.

Meadows, D. H., Meadows, D. L., Randers, J. and Behrens, W. III (1972) *The Limits to Growth*, London, Earth Island.

Mercer, P. (1994) *The Directory of British Political Organisations*, Harlow, Longman.

Michels, R. (1962) *Political Parties*, New York, Collier (first published 1920).

Middlemass, K. (1979) *Politics in Industrial Society*, London, André Deutsch.

Miles, R. (1996) 'Small investors who made big killings', *Guardian* (23 Nov.).

Miliband, R. (1961) *Parliamentary Socialism*, London, Merlin.

Miliband, R. (1984) *Capitalist Democracy in Britain*, Oxford, Oxford University Press.

Miliband, R. and Panitch, L. (eds) (1992) *New World Order: Socialist Register 1992*, London, Merlin.

Miller, J. B. D. (1962) *The Nature of Politics*, Harmondsworth, Penguin.

Miller, W. (1991) *Media and Voters*, Oxford, Clarendon Press.

Mills, C. W. (1959) *The Power Elite*, New York, Oxford University Press.

Milne, A. (1988) *DG: Memoirs of a British Broadcaster*, London, Hodder and Stoughton.

Minkin, L. (1980) *The Labour Party Conference*, Manchester, Manchester University Press.

Mirrlees-Black, C., Mayhew P. and Percy, A. (1996) *The 1996 British Crime Survey*, London, Home Office Statistical Bulletin 19/96.

Mitchell, A. (1994) 'Backbench influence: a personal view', *Parliamentary Affairs*, 47(4), 687–704.

Mitchell, D. (1982) 'Intervention, control and accountability: the National Enterprise Board', *Public Administration Bulletin*, 38, 40–65.

Monbiot, G. (2002) 'Global democracy: a parliament for the planet', *New Internationalist*, no. 342 (Jan./Feb.), 12–14.

Moran, M. (2001) 'The rise of the regulatory state in Britain', *Parliamentary Affairs*, 54, 19–31.

Morgan, J. (1987) *Conflict and Order: The Police and Labour Disputes in England and Wales 1900–1939*, Oxford, Clarendon Press.

Morgan, K. and Roberts, E. (1993) *The Democratic Deficit: A Guide to Quangoland*, Papers in Planning Research, University of Wales.

Morgan, R. (2000) *Variable Geometry UK*, Institute of Welsh Affairs, Discussion Paper 13.

Morley, J. (1903) *Life of William Ewart Gladstone, Vol. I*, London, Macmillan.

Morrison, H. (1933) *Socialism and Transport*, London, Constable.

Mountfield, R. (1997) 'The new senior civil service: managing the paradox', *Public Administration*, 75(2), 307–12.

Mugham, A. (1993) 'Party leaders and presidentialism in the 1992 election: a post war perspective', in Denver et al. (eds), pp. 193–204.

Mugham, A. (2002) *Media and the Presidentialisation of Parliamentary Elections*, Basingstoke, Palgrave.

Mullard, M. (1993) *The Politics of Public Expenditure*, London, Routledge.

Mullard, M. (1997) 'The politics of public expenditure control: a problem of politics or language games', *Political Quarterly*, 68(3), 266–75.

Muller, W. D. (1977) *The Kept Men*, Hassocks, Harvester.

Murray, C. (1990) *The Emerging British Underclass*, London, Institute of Economic Affairs.

National Audit Office (1996) *The Work of the Directors General of Telecommunications, Gas Supply, Water Services and Electricity Supply*, HC 645, Session 1995/6, London, HMSO.

Navarro, V. (1976) *Medicine Under Capitalism*, London, Croom Helm.

Newburn, T. (1995) *Crime and Criminal Justice Policy*, Harlow, Longman.

Newton, K. (1976) *Second City Politics*, Oxford, Clarendon Press.

Newton, K. (1986) 'Mass media', in Drucker et al. (eds), pp. 313–28.

Newton, K. (1993) 'Economic voting in the 1992 general election', in Denver et al. (eds), pp. 158–76.

Newton, K. (1998) 'Politics and the news media: mobilisation or political malaise?' in Jowell et al., pp. 151–68.

Nicholson, E. (1996) *Secret Society*, London, Indigo.

Nicholson, M. (2001) 'Labour MSPs forced to cave in on free care', *Financial Times* (26 Jan.).

Niskanen, W. A. (1973) *Bureaucracy: Servant or Master?*, London, Institute of Economic Affairs.

Nolan, Lord (chair) (1995) *First Report of the Committee on Standards in Public Life*, Cm 2850–I, London, HMSO.

Norris, P. (1993) 'The gender-generation gap', in Denver et al., pp. 129–42.

Norris, P. (1996a) *Electoral Change Since 1945*, Oxford, Blackwell.

Norris, P. (1996b) 'The Nolan Committee: financial interests and constituency service', *Government and Opposition*, 31(4), 441–8.

Norris, P. (1996c) 'Women politicians: transforming Westminster', *Parliamentary Affairs*, 49(1), 89–102.

Norris, P. (ed.) (2001) *Britain Votes 2001*, Oxford, Oxford University Press.

Norris, P. and Lovenduski, J. (1994) *Political Recruitment: Gender, Race and Class in the British Parliament*, Cambridge, Cambridge University Press.

Norton, P. (1978) *Conservative Dissidents: Dissent Within the Conservative Party 1970–74*, London, Maurice Temple Smith.

Norton, P. (1993a) 'The Conservative Party from Thatcher to Major', in King et al., pp. 29–69.

Norton, P. (1993b) *Does Parliament Matter?* Hemel Hempstead, Harvester Wheatsheaf.

Norton, P. (1994) 'The growth of the constituency role of the MP', *Parliamentary Affairs*, 47(4), 705–20.

Norton, P. (ed.) (1996) *The Conservative Party*, Hemel Hempstead, Prentice Hall/ Harvester.

Norton, P. (1997) 'The United Kingdom: restoring confidence', *Parliamentary Affairs*, 50(3), 357–72.

Norton, P. and Aughey, A. (1981) *Conservatives and Conservatism*, London, Temple Smith.

Norton-Taylor, R., Lloyd, M. and Cook, S. (1996) *Knee Deep in Dishonour: The Scott Report and its Aftermath*, London, Gollancz.

Nugent, N. (1994) *The Government and Politics of the European Community*, 3rd edn, Basingstoke, Macmillan.

Oakeshott, M. (1962) *Rationalism in Politics and Other Essays*, London, Methuen.

Oborne, P. (2001) 'The eunuchs of the Cabinet', *Spectator* (15 Dec.).

O'Connor, J. (1973) *The Fiscal Crisis of the State*, New York, St Martin's Press.

O'Leary, B. (1989) 'The limits to coercive consociationalism in Northern Ireland', *Political Studies*, 37, 562–88.

Oliver, I. (1987) *Police, Government and Accountability*, London, Macmillan.

Olson, M. (1968) *The Logic of Collective Action*, New York, Schocken.

Olson, M. (1982) *The Rise and Decline of Nations*, New Haven, CT, Yale University Press.

O'Reilly, J. and Robbins, T. (2002) 'Bandit country UK: why criminals win', *Observer* (10 March).

Osborne, D. and Gaebler, T. (1992) *Reinventing Government*, Reading, MA, Addison-Wesley.

Ostrogorski, M. (1902) *Democracy and the Organisation of Political Parties*, London, Macmillan.

Oxfam (1998) *Small Arms, Wrong Hands*, Oxford, Oxfam.

Page, E. (2001) *Governing by Numbers, Delegated Legislation and Everyday Policy Making*, Oxford, Hart.

Painter, C. (1994) 'Public service reform: reinventing or abandoning government', *Political Quarterly*, 95(2), 242–62.

Paley, W. (1842) *Works*, London, Bohn (first published 1785).

Panitch, L. and Miliband, R. (1992) 'The new world order and the socialist agenda', in Miliband and Panitch (eds), pp. 1–25.

Parkin, S. (1988) 'Green strategy', in F. Dodds (ed.), *Into the 21st Century: An Agenda for Political Realignment*, Basingstoke, Green Print.

Parris, M. (1996) *Scorn*, Harmondsworth, Penguin.

Pateman, C. (1983) 'Feminism and democracy', in Duncan, G. (ed.), *Democratic Theory and Practice*, Cambridge, Cambridge University Press.

Pattie, C. J. and Johnston, R. J. (1996) 'Paying their way: local associations, the constituency quota scheme and Conservative Party finance', *Political Studies*, 44, 921–35.

Pattie, C. J., Johnston, R. and Fieldhouse, E. (1993) '*Plus ça change?* The changing electoral geography of

Britain, 1979–1992', in Denver et al. (eds), pp. 85–99.

Pattie, C. J., Fieldhouse, E. and Johnston, R. J. (1994) 'The price of conscience', *British Journal of Political Science*, 24, 359–80.

Paxman, J. (1991) *Friends in High Places*, London, Penguin.

Peele, G. (1986) 'The state and civil liberties', in Drucker et al. (eds), pp. 144–74.

Peele, G. (1991) *British Party Politics: Competing for Power in the 1990s*, Hemel Hempstead, Philip Allan.

Peele, G. (1998) 'Towards "New Conservatives"? Organisational reform and the Conservative Party', *Political Quarterly*, 69(2), 141–7.

Pelling, H. (1968) *A Short History of the Labour Party*, 3rd edn, London, Macmillan.

Pelling, H. and Reid, A. J. (1997) *A Short History of the Labour Party*, 11th edn, Basingstoke, Macmillan.

Perkins, A. (2001) 'Blair: first among equals?' *Guardian* (6 Oct.).

Perrigo, S. (1996) 'Women and change in the Labour Party 1979–1995', *Parliamentary Affairs*, 49(1), 116–29.

Pienaar, J. (1987) 'Contemptible smear by Livingstone', *Independent* (10 July).

Pienaar, J. (1988) 'A cabinet exile reflects on the cravings of power', *Independent* (15 Sept.).

Pierre, J. and Stoker, G. (2000) 'Towards multi-level governance', in Dunleavy et al. (eds), pp. 29–46.

Pilger, J. (1998) *Hidden Agendas*, London, Vintage.

Pilger, J. (2002) *The New Rulers of the World*, London, Verso.

Pimlott, B. (1992) *Harold Wilson*, London, HarperCollins.

Pimlott, B. (1996) *The Queen: A Biography of Elizabeth II*, London, HarperCollins.

Pinto-Duschinsky, M. (1972) 'Central Office and power in the Conservative Party', *Political Studies*, 20(1), 1–16.

Pinto-Duschinsky, M. (1997) 'Tory troops are in worse state than feared', *The Times* (6 June).

Pliatzky, L. (1980) *Report on Non-Departmental Public Bodies*, Cmnd 7797, London, HMSO.

Plowden, W. (1994) *Ministers and Mandarins*, London, IPPR.

Ponting, C. (1986) *Whitehall: Tragedy and Farce*, London, Hamish Hamilton.

Porritt, J. and Winner, D. (1988) *The Coming of the Greens*, London, Fontana.

Poulantzas, N. (1973) *Political Power and Social Classes*, London, New Left Books.

Preston, P. (1997) 'Party free or parti pris?' *Observer* (2 March).

Prosser, T. (1996) 'Understanding the British constitution', *Political Studies*, 44(3), 473–87.

Punnett, R. M. (1975) 'Her Majesty's shadow government', in Herman and Alt (eds), pp. 140–56.

Pyke, N. (2001) 'Windfall pay-offs for Blair's advisers', *Independent on Sunday* (11 March).

Raab, C. D. (1994) 'Open government: policy information and information policy', *Political Quarterly*, 65(3), 340–7.

Rallings, C. and Thrasher, M. (1994) *Explaining Electoral Turnout: A Secondary Analysis of Local Election Statistics*, London, HMSO.

Rallings, C. and Thrasher, M. (1996) *Enhancing Local Electoral Turnout: A Guide to Current Practice and Future Reform*, York, Joseph Rowntree Foundation.

Ramphal, S. (1997) 'The Commonwealth in the global neighbourhood', *The Round Table*, no. 342, 175–85.

Randall, V. (1982) *Women and Politics*, Basingstoke, Macmillan.

Rau, C. B. (1996) 'United Nations at 50: retrospect and prospect', *Round Table*, no. 337, 25–62.

Rawlings, H. F. (1986) 'Judicial review and the "control of government"', *Public Administration*, 64(2), 142–3.

Rawnsley, A. (2000) *Servants of the People: The Inside Story of New Labour*, London, Hamish Hamilton.

Rawnsley, A. (2001) 'Good, bad and ugly', *Observer* (11 March).

Redcliffe-Maud, Lord (chairman) (1969) *Royal Commission on Local Government in England 1966–69, Vol. I*, Cmnd 4040, London, HMSO.

Redlich, J. and Hirst, F. W. (1970) *Local Government in England, Vol. II* (ed. Keith-Lucas, B.), London, Macmillan (first published 1903).

Reiner, R. (1982) 'Who are the police?', *Political Quarterly*, 53(2), 469–71.

Reiner, R. (1993) *The Politics of the Police*, 2nd edn, Hemel Hempstead, Harvester Wheatsheaf.

Reiner, R. (ed.) (1996) *Policing*, Aldershot, Dartmouth.

Rhodes, R. A. W. (1981) *Control and Power in Central–Local Government Relations*, Farnborough, Gower.

Rhodes, R. A. W. (1988) *Beyond Westminster and Whitehall: The Sub-central Government of Britain*, London, George Allen & Unwin.

Rhodes, R. A. W. (1994) 'The hollowing out of the state: the changing nature of the public service in Britain', *Political Quarterly*, 65(2), 138–51.

Rhodes, R. A. W. (ed.) (2000) *Transforming British Government, Volume 1: Changing Institutions, Volume 2: Changing Roles and Relationships*, Basingstoke, Macmillan.

Rhodes, R. A. W. and Dunleavy, P. (1995) *Prime Minister, Cabinet and Core Executive*, Basingstoke, Macmillan.

Rhodes, R. A. W. and Marsh, D. (1992) *Policy Networks in British Government*, Oxford, Oxford University Press.

Rhodes, R. A. W. and Weller, P. (eds) (2001) *The Changing World of Top Officials: Mandarins or Valets*, Buckingham, Open University Press.

Richards, D. (1996) 'Recruitment to the highest grades in the civil service: drawing the curtains open', *Public Administration*, 74(4), 657–77.

Richards, P. G. (1970) *Parliament and Conscience*, London, George Allen & Unwin.

Richardson, J. J. and Jordan, A. G. (1979) *Government Under Pressure*, Oxford, Martin Robertson.

Riddell, P. (1985) *The Thatcher Government*, Oxford, Basil Blackwell.

Riddell, P. (1993) *Honest Opportunism: The Rise of the Career Politician*, London, Hamish Hamilton.

Riddell, P. (1997) 'Cracks in the Cabinet cement', *The Times* (10 Nov.).

Riddell, P. (2000) *Parliament under Blair*, London, Politico's.

Riddell, P. (2001) 'New look behind the revolving doors of power', *The Times* (13 June).

Ridley, F. F. and Wilson, D. (1995) *The Quango Debate*, Oxford, Oxford University Press.

Ridley, N. (1988) *The Local Right*, London, Centre for Policy Studies.

Rimington, S. (2001) *Open Secret*, London, Hutchinson.

Robbins, T. and Clark, J. (2001) 'Police buy top assault rifle to tame gunmen', *Sunday Times* (17 June).

Robertson, G. (1997) 'Justice in all fairness', *Guardian* (30 April).

Robson, W. A. (1966) *Local Government in Crisis*, London, George Allen & Unwin.

Rogaly, J. (1997) 'If television rescues Major it will be a miracle', *Financial Times* (18 March).

Rogers, A. (1997) *Secrecy and Power in the British State*, London, Pluto.

Rollo, J. (1980) 'The Special Patrol Group', in Hain (ed.), pp. 153–208.

Rose, R. (1964) 'Parties, factions and tendencies in British politics', *Political Studies*, 12(1), 33–46.

Rose, R. (2001) *The Prime Minister in a Shrinking World*, Cambridge, Polity.

Rose, R. and McAllister, I. (1986) *Voters Begin to Choose: From Closed Class to Open Elections*, Beverly Hills, CA, Sage.

Rosenberg, J. (1997) *Trial of Strength*, London, Richard Cohen.

Roth, A. (1981) *The Business Backgrounds of MPs*, London, Parliamentary Profiles.

Rousseau, J. J. (1913) *The Social Contract*, London, Dent (first published 1762).

Rowan, D. (1998) 'Meet the new world government', *Guardian* (22 Feb.).

Rowbotham, S. (1973) *Woman's Consciousness, Man's World*, Harmondsworth, Penguin.

Royal Commission on the Distribution of Income and Wealth (1976) *Report No. 3: Higher Incomes from Employment*, London, HMSO.

Ruddat, K. and Rennie, R. (2000) 2020: *Public Visions for Local Governance*, New Local Government Network.

Rush, M. (2001) *The Role of the Member of Parliament Since 1868*, Oxford, Oxford University Press.

Russell, M. (2000) *Reforming the House of Lords: Lessons from Overseas*, Oxford, Oxford University Press.

Russell, M. (2001) 'What are second chambers for?' *Parliamentary Affairs*, 54, 442–58.

Ryle, M. (1988) *Ecology and Socialism*, London, Radius.

Saggar, S. (1992) *Race and Politics in Britain*, Hemel Hempstead, Harvester Wheatsheaf.

Saggar, S. (2001) 'The race card, again', *Parliamentary Affairs*, 54, 759–74.

Salisbury, R. H. (1969) 'An exchange theory of interest groups', *Midwest Journal of Political Science*, 13, 1–32.

Sampson, A. (1992) *The Essential Anatomy of Britain: Democracy in Crisis*, London, Hodder and Stoughton.

Sanders, A. and Young, R. (1995) 'The PACE regime for suspects detained by the police', *Political Quarterly*, 66(2), 126–40.

Sanders, D., Clarke, H., Stewart, M. and Whiteley, P. (2001) 'The economy and voting', *Parliamentary Affairs*, 54, 789–802.

Saunders, P. (1980) *Urban Politics: A Sociological Interpretation*, Harmondsworth, Penguin.

Saunders, P. (1984) 'Rethinking local politics', in Boddy, M. and Fudge, C. (eds), *Local Socialism: The Way Ahead*, London, Macmillan, pp. 22–48.

Saunders, P. (1995) 'Privatization, share ownership and voting', *British Journal of Political Science*, 25(1), 131–7.

Scammell, M. (1995) *Designer Politics: How Elections are Won*, Basingstoke, Macmillan.

Scammell, M. (2000) 'New media, new politics', in Dunleavy et al. (eds), pp. 169–84.

Scarman, Lord (1981) *The Brixton Disorders, 10–12 April 1981: Report of an Inquiry*, Cmnd 8427, London, HMSO (reprinted by Penguin 1982).

Scattschneider, E. E. (1960) *The Semi-Sovereign People*, New York, Holt, Rinehart and Winston.

Scharpf, F. (1988) 'The joint decision trap: lessons from German federalism and European integration', *Public Administration*, 66, 239–78.

Schmitter, P. (1974) 'Still the century of corporatism', *Review of Politics*, 36, 85–131.

Scott, J. (1985) 'The British upper class', in Coates et al. (eds), pp. 29–54.

Scott, J. (1991) *Who Rules Britain?* Cambridge, Polity.

Scruton, R. (1980) *The Meaning of Conservatism*, Harmondsworth, Penguin.

Sedgemore, B. (1980) *The Secret Constitution*, London, Hodder and Stoughton.

Seldon, A. (ed.) (2001) *The Blair Effect: The Blair Government, 1997–2001*, London, Little Brown.

Select Committee on Defence (1982) *The Handling of Press and Public Information During the Falklands Conflict: First Report*, HC 17-1, London, HMSO.

Self, P. and Storing, H. (1962) *The State and the Farmer*, London, George Allen & Unwin.

Seltman, C. (1956) *Women in Antiquity*, London, Pan.

Semetko, H., Scammell, M. and Goddard, P. (1997) 'Television', *Parliamentary Affairs*, 50(4), 609–15.

Seyd, P. and Whiteley, P. (1992) *Labour's Grass Roots*, Oxford, Clarendon Press.

Seymour-Ure, C. (1997) 'Editorial opinion and the national press', *Parliamentary Affairs*, 50(4), 586–608.

Shaw, E. (1996) *The Labour Party Since 1945: Old Labour, New Labour*, Oxford, Blackwell.

Shell, D. (1992) *The House of Lords*, Hemel Hempstead, Harvester Wheatsheaf.

Shell, D. (1994) 'The House of Lords: time for a change?', *Parliamentary Affairs*, 47(4), 721–37.

Sherman, J. (2001) 'MPs want new sleaze watchdog with real bite', *The Times* (14 Feb.).

Sherman, J. (2002a) 'Mapping the rise of a new No 10 powerbase', *The Times* (31 Jan.).

Sherman, J. (2002b) 'Ministers to break rules on leaks', *The Times* (8 Feb.).

Sieghart, M. (2001) 'The magnificent seven', *The Times* (15 Oct.).

Simhony, A. (1991) 'On forcing individuals to be free: T. H. Green's liberal theory of positive freedom', *Political Studies*, 39(2), 303–20.

Simon, H. A. (1947) *Administrative Behaviour*, London, Macmillan.

Sivanandan, V. (1981) 'From resistance to rebellion', *Race and Class*, 23 (Autumn).

Skelcher, C. (1995) 'Reforming the quangos', *Political Quarterly*, 69(1), 41–7.

Skelcher, C. and Davies, H. (1996) 'Understanding the new magistracy: a study of characteristics and attitudes', *Local Government Studies*, 22(2), 8–21.

Smith, A. (1982) *Wealth of Nations*, Harmondsworth, Penguin (first published 1776).

Smith, A. (1997) 'Studying multi-level governance: examples from French translations of the structural funds', *Public Administration*, 75, 711–29.

Smith, D. J. and Gray, J. (1985) *Police and People in London*, Aldershot, Gower.

Smith, M. (1993) *Pressure Power and Policy: State Autonomy and Policy Networks in Britain and the United States*, Hemel Hempstead, Harvester Wheatsheaf.

Smith, M. (1995) 'Utilities row as profits hit £7.7 billion', *Observer* (2 April).

Smith, M. (1999) *The Core Executive in Britain*, Basingstoke, Macmillan.

Sperling, L. (1997) 'Quangos: political representation and women consumers of public services', *Policy and Politics*, 25(2), 119–28.

Spretnack, C. and Capra, F. (1986) *Green Politics: The Global Promise*, London, Collins.

Squires, J. and Wickham-Jones, M. (2002) 'Mainstreaming in Westminster and Whitehall: from Labour's Ministry for Women to the Women and Equality Unit', *Parliamentary Affairs*, 55, 57–70.

Stanworth, P. and Giddens, A. (eds) (1974) *Elites and Power in British Society*, Cambridge, Cambridge University Press.

Stanyer, J. (2001a) *The Creation of Political News: Television and British Party Political Conferences*, Falmer, Brighton, Sussex Academic Press.

Stanyer, J. (2001b) 'The new media and the old: the press, broadcasting and the Internet', *Parliamentary Affairs*, 54, 249–59.

Stenton, F. M. (1941) *Anglo-Saxon England*, Oxford, Clarendon Press.

Stevenson, J. (1993) *Third Party Politics Since 1945*, Oxford, Blackwell.

Stewart, J. (1992) 'The rebuilding of public accountability', paper presented at European Policy Forum, December.

Stewart, J. (1995) 'Appointed boards and local government', *Parliamentary Affairs*, 48(2), 226–41.

Stewart, J. (2000) *The Nature of British Local Government*, Basingstoke, Macmillan.

Steyn, Lord (1997) 'The weakest and least dangerous department of government', *Public Law*, Spring, 84–5.

Stiglitz, J. (2002) *Globalization and its Discontents*, New York, Norton.

Stoker, G. (1993) 'Introduction: local government reorganisation as a garbage can process', *Local Government Policy Making*, 19(4), 3–5.

Stoker, G. (ed.) (2000) *The New Politics of Local Governance*, Basingstoke, Macmillan.

Stone, B. (1995) 'Administrative accountability in the Westminster democracies: towards a new conceptual framework', *Governance*.

Strange, S. (1992) 'States, firms and diplomacy', *International Affairs*, 8, 505–26, 68(1), 1–15.

Stuart, C. (ed.) (1975) *The Reith Diaries*, London, Collins.

Studlar, D. T. (1983) 'The ethnic vote 1983: problems of analysis and interpretation', *New Community*, 9 (1–2), 92–100.

Summerskill, B. (2000) 'Tories' corporate gifts fall to record low', *Guardian* (31 Dec.).

Suresh, K. T. (2001) 'Tourism in India: GATS in action', *WDM in Action* (Autumn), 11.

Tarling, R. and Dowds, L. (1998) 'Crime and punishment', in Jowell et al., pp. 197–214.

Taylor, A. J. P. (1965) *English History 1914–1945*, London, Oxford University Press.

Tempest, M. (2002) 'Lords reform architect condemns concessions', *Guardian* (9 Jan.).

Thain, C. and Wright, M. (1995) *The Treasury and Whitehall: The Planning and Control of Public Expenditure 1976–1993*, Oxford, Clarendon.

Thatcher, M. (1998) 'Regulating the regulators: the regulatory regime for the British privatised utilities', *Parliamentary Affairs*, 51(2), 209–22.

Theakston, K. (1995) *The Civil Service Since 1945*, Oxford, Blackwell.

Theakston, K. (1999) *Leadership in Whitehall*, Basingstoke, Macmillan.

Theakston, K. and Fry, G. K. (1989) 'Britain's administrative elite: permanent secretaries 1900–1986', *Public Administration*, 67(2), 129–48.

Thomas, H. (ed.) (1959) *The Establishment*, London, Anthony Blond.

Thompson, B. (1997) 'Conclusion: judges as trouble-shooters', *Parliamentary Affairs*, 50(1), 182–9.

Thompson, E. P. (1975) *Whigs and Hunters*, London, Allen Lane.

Thompson, E. P. (1980) 'The logic of exterminism', *New Left Review*, no. 121 (May–June), 3–32.

Thompson, E. P. (1982) 'The heavy dancers of the air', *New Society* (11 Nov.), 244.

Thompson, J. B. (1995) *The Media and Modernity: A Social Theory of the Media*, Cambridge, Polity.

Thranhardt, D. (1995) 'The political uses of xenophobia in England, France and Germany', *Party Politics*, 1(9), 323–45.

Tickle, A. and Welsh, I. (eds) (1998) *Environment and Society in Eastern Europe*, Harlow, Addison Wesley Longman.

Timmins, N. and Kampfner, J. (1997) 'New tricks for old dogs', *Financial Times* (18 March).

Toynbee, P. and Walker, D. (2001) *Did Things Get Better? An Audit of Labour's Successes and Failures*, Harmondsworth, Penguin.

Travers, T. (1996) 'Town hall turns red', *Guardian* (11 Dec.).

Travis, T. (1996) 'Carey attacks "prison works" policies', *Guardian* (10 May).

Treasury (1991) *Competing for Quality: Buying Better Public Services*, Cm 1730, London, HMSO.

Treasury (1997) *Public Expenditure: Statistical Analysis 1997–98*, Cm 3601, London, Stationery Office.

Trench, A. (ed.) (2001) *The State of the Nation: The Second Year of Devolution in the United Kingdom*, London, Imprint Academic.

Tunstall, J. (1970) *The Westminster Lobby Correspondents*, London, Routledge and Kegan Paul.

Turner, D. R. (1969) *The Shadow Cabinet in British Politics*, London, Routledge and Kegan Paul.

Unseem, M. (1984) *The Inner Circle: Large Corporations and the Rise of Business Political Activity in the US and the UK*, Oxford, Oxford University Press.

Urban, M. (1997) *UK Eyes Alpha: The Inside Story of British Intelligence*, London, Faber.

Urry, J. (1985) 'The class structure', in Coates et al. (eds).

Urwin, D. (1989) *Western Europe Since 1945*, 4th edn, Harlow, Longman.

Urwin, D. (1997) *A Political History of Western Europe Since 1945*, Harlow, Addison Wesley Longman.

Van der Gaag, N. (1995) 'Women: still something to shout about', *New Internationalist*, no. 270 (Aug.), 7–10.

Vidal, J. (1997) *McLibel: Burger Culture on Trial*, Basingstoke, Macmillan.

Vincent, A. (1992) *Modern Political Ideologies*, Oxford, Blackwell.

Von Bertallanfy, L. (1952) *General Systems Theory*, New York, Harper.

Wagstyl, S. (1996) 'Nice work if you can get it', *Financial Times* (18 Dec.).

Walker, P. G. (1972) *The Cabinet*, London, Fontana.

Wall, A. and Owen, B. (2002) *Health Policy*, 2nd edn, London, Routledge.

Wallas, G. (1948) *Human Nature in Politics*, London, Constable.

Waller, R. and Criddle, B. (1997) *Almanac of British Politics*, London, Routledge.

Wallerstein, I. (1979) *The Capitalist World Economy*, Cambridge, Cambridge University Press.

Walvin, J. (1984) *Passage to Britain*, Harmondsworth, Penguin.

Ward, G. (1993) 'Reforming the public sector: privatisation and the role of advisers', *Political Quarterly*, 94, 298–305.

Wass, Sir D. (1984) *Government and the Governed* (BBC Reith Lectures), London, Routledge and Kegan Paul.

Watt, N. and Ward, L. (2002) 'Tory peers scorn leader's plan', *Guardian* (24 Jan.).

Watts, D. (1997) *Political Communication Today*, Manchester, Manchester University Press.

Wayne, M. (1998) *Dissident Voices: The Politics of Television and Cultural Change*, London, Pluto.

Weber, M. (1978) *Economy and Society, Vol. II*, Berkeley, CA, University of California Press (first published 1922).

Webster, P. and Bowditch, G. (1997) 'White Paper becomes a best seller', *The Times* (25 July).

Weir, S. (1995) 'Quangos: questions of democratic accountability', *Parliamentary Affairs*, 48(2), 307–22.

Weir, S. and Boyle, K. (1997) 'Human rights in the UK: introduction to the special issue', *Political Quarterly*, 68(2), 128–34.

Weir, S. and Hall, W. (eds) (1994) *Ego Trip: Extra-Governmental Organisations in the United Kingdom and their Accountability*, London, Charter88 Trust.

White, M. (2001) 'Why Labour MPs are the new opposition', *Guardian* (7 June).

White, S. (ed.) (2001) *New Labour: The Progressive Future?* Basingstoke, Palgrave.

Whiteley, P. (1997) 'The Conservative campaign', *Parliamentary Affairs*, 50(4), 542–54.

Whiteley, P. and Winyard, S. (1984) 'The origins of the "New Poverty Lobby"', *Public Administration*, 61(1), 32–54.

Whiteley, P., Seyd, P. and Richardson, J. (1994) *True Blues: The Politics of Conservative Party Membership*, Oxford, Clarendon Press.

Whyatt, J. (1961) *The Citizen and the Administration*, London, Justice.

Widdicombe, D. (1977) *Our Fettered Ombudsman*, London, Justice.

Widdicombe, D. (1986a) *The Conduct of Local Authority Business*, Cmnd 9797, London, HMSO.

Widdicombe, D. (1986b) *Research Volume 1: The Political Organisation of Local Authorities*, Cmnd 9798, London, HMSO.

Wilkenson, H. (1995) *No Turning Back: Generations and the Genderquake*, London, Demos.

Willetts, D. (1996) *Blair's Gurus*, London, Centre for Policy Studies.

Willetts, D. (1998) 'Conservative renewal', *Political Quarterly*, 69(2), 110–17.

Williams, F. (1969) 'A prime minister remembers: the war and post-war memories of the Rt. Hon. Earl Attlee', in King, A. (ed.), *The British Prime Minister*, Basingstoke, Macmillan.

Williamson, N. (1995) 'Civil service ready for Blair, says Sir Robin', *The Times* (20 Nov.).

Wilson, D. (2001) 'Local government: balancing diversity and uniformity', *Parliamentary Affairs*, 54(2), 289–307.

Wilson, D. and Game, C., with Leach, S. and Stoker, G. (1994) *Local Government in the United Kingdom*, Basingstoke, Macmillan.

Wilson, D. and Game, C. (1997) *Local Government in the United Kingdom*, Basingstoke, Macmillan.

Wilson, H. (1974) *The Labour Government 1964–70*, Harmondsworth, Penguin.

Wilson, H. H. (1961) *Pressure Group: The Campaign for Commercial Television*, Harmondsworth, Penguin.

Wilson, R. (1999) *Report to the Prime Minister from Sir Richard Wilson, Head of the Home Civil Service*, London, Cabinet Office.

Wilson, T. (1966) *The Downfall of the Liberal Party 1914–1935*, London, Collins.

Winter, M. (1996) 'Intersecting departmental responsibilities, administrative confusion and the role of science in government: the case of BSE', *Parliamentary Affairs*, 49(4), 550–65.

Wintour, P. and Pallister, D. (1995) 'Revelations that led to sleaze inquiry', *Guardian* (12 May).

Woodhouse, D. (1995) 'Politicians and the judiciary: a changing relationship', *Parliamentary Affairs*, 48(3), 401–18.

Woodhouse, D. (1996) 'Politicians and the judges: a conflict of interest', *Parliamentary Affairs*, 49(3), 423–40.

Woodhouse, D. (1998) 'The Parliamentary Commissioner for Standards: lessons from the "Cash for Questions" inquiry', *Parliamentary Affairs*, 51(1), 51–61.

Woodhouse, D. (2001a) 'The law and politics: more power to the judges – and to the people?' *Parliamentary Affairs*, 54, 223–37.

Woodhouse, D. (2001b) *The Office of the Lord Chancellor*, Hart Publishing.

Woodhouse, D. (2002) 'The law and politics: in the shadow of the Human Rights Act', *Parliamentary Affairs*, 55, 254–70.

Woodroffe, J. (1999) 'Who's the boss around here?', *WDM in Action* (Autumn), pp. 8–10.

World Trade Organization (1998) *Trade, Income Disparity and Poverty*, Geneva, WTO.

Wraith, R. E. and Lamb, G. B. (1971) *Public Inquiries as Instruments of Government*, London, George Allen & Unwin.

Wright, E. O. (1985) *Classes*, London, Verso.

Wright, P. (1987) *Spycatcher*, New York, Viking.

Wyatt, W. (1973) 'Parliament the waste land', *Sunday Times* (4 Nov.).

Young, A. (2001) *The Politics of Regulation*, Basingstoke, Palgrave.

Young, H. (1989) *One of Us*, London, Macmillan.

Young, H. (1998) *This Blessed Plot: Britain and Europe from Churchill to Blair*, Basingstoke, Macmillan.

Zander, M. (1969) 'Who goes to solicitors?', *Law Society's Gazette*, no. 66.

Index

Using the index The index draws together references to the myriad people, events and institutions discussed in the text, and also to the concepts underlying the study of politics. You should begin searching by looking up the most specific term possible. Analytical subheadings and cross-references will guide you to the various aspects of a topic, highlighting interrelationships and reinforcing a synoptic study strategy. Use the **Glossary** for brief definitions and the **Contents** for an overview of the whole book. Note that material in the Glossary and Chronology is not indexed. The index is arranged in word-by-word order, ignoring 'and', 'in', etc.; page numbers in *italics* refer to illustrations.

Index compiled by Ann Kingdom